JUN 1 9 2000
RECEIVED

JUN 1 4 2006

Date Due

THE REAL WORLDS OF

CANADIAN POLITICS

CASES IN PROCESS AND POLICY

Robert M. Campbell
and
Leslie A. Pal

broadview press

Cataloguing in Publication Data

Campbell, Robert Malcolm
 The real worlds of Canadian politics: Cases in process and policy

2nd ed.
Includes bibliographical references and index.
ISBN 0-921149-78-6

1. Canada — Politics and government — 1984 – .*
2. Canada — Politics and government — 1984 – .
Case studies.* I. Pal, Leslie Alexander, 1954 – .
II. Title.

FC630.C34 1991   971.064'7   C91-093826-1
F1034.2.C34 1991

broadview press
P.O. Box 1243
Peterborough, Ontario
K9J 7H5   Canada

in the US, broadview press
269 Portage Rd.
Lewiston, NY
14092   USA

printed in Canada

CONTENTS

PREFACE TO THE SECOND EDITION

We were encouraged to write a second edition of *The Real Worlds of Canadian Politics* for two reasons: the first edition was well received, but as a collection of case studies of contemporary policy issues, was rapidly outstripped by events. Several of the original cases, such as the CF-18 affair, pharmaceutical patents, and pornography legislation, while of historical interest for the sharp light they cast on some of the forces that drive Canadian politics, were more or less resolved two years ago and so were dropped. Issues such as abortion, free trade, and the Meech Lake accord, however, continued to evolve dramatically, and so we decided to thoroughly revise and update them. They were complemented by two new cases: the Goods and Services Tax (GST) and the confrontation at Oka/Kanesatake. We jointly bear full responsibility for the results, but Campbell was the principal author of the chapters on the Meech Lake accord and the GST, and Pal wrote the chapters on abortion, free trade, and Oka.

Many of the reviews of *Real Worlds* suggested that we try to incorporate more explicit theory into the book, either in the cases themselves or in a concluding chapter. Since we have not taken up this suggestion, we owe our critics an explanation. The absence of explicit theory does not mean that the book is not *theoretically informed*. The selection of cases, the highlighting of points and key forces, and the discussion sections in each chapter are all guided by theory. It is our view, however, that a heavy-handed emphasis on theory sometimes threatens to squeeze out the colour and life of politics as most people experience it. We made a choice, therefore, that this book would try to do something different: it would blend a more journalistic, narrative style with unobtrusive analysis and observation. Students therefore may not come away from this book with a refined theoretical apparatus explaining, for instance, federalism, but they should have a richer appreciation of the variety of forces that influence intergovernmental relations, not least of which are the capricious elements of character and circumstance. If the cases succeed in piquing appreciation of the rich variety of political phenomenon, they should also succeed in illuminating theoretical questions.

Rob Beamish, Ted Morton, and J. Rick Ponting shared their expertise and advice as we shaped the book, and we were fortunate to have several exemplary research assistants: Joelle Favreau, Scott Powell, Marc Vincent, and Laureen Whyte. The University of Trent Committee on Research and the Frost Centre for Canadian Heritage and Development Studies provided generous research support. Don Lepan, the president of Broadview Press, was once again a model of patient if firm encouragement as we laboured over the manuscript. Terry Teskey copyedited this edition with the same aplomb and grace that she demonstrated with the first.

Colleagues, publishers, and editors all suffer as a manuscript progresses, but the greatest price is paid by an author's spouse and family. Miraculously, Mary Pal and Christl Verduyn gave their blessings once more to this endeavour, and just as importantly, their counsel and support. Our children's benediction was perhaps less willing, but ultimately given with cheerful ease to fathers who, in their eyes, must seem to inhabit some very unreal worlds indeed. We dedicate this book to them.

INTRODUCTION

Most undergraduate courses in Canadian politics rely on traditional texts to cast light on the particular subject at hand: federalism, political leadership, parties, and so on. These courses, for which this book has been designed, have at their disposal several large and learned tomes that embrace virtually every detail of the political process in this country. In talking to colleagues (some, the authors of these tomes) and in our own teaching, we have noticed that the virtues of large and exhaustive texts can simultaneously become liabilities. It is difficult, for one thing, to write with passion and style when the purpose of the enterprise is analytical. And yet most students *take* introductory courses in politics because they are excited or agitated about what they perceive to be "real politics": fire and blood, strife and conflict, the quest for peace and the chilling disciplines of power. Even the best introductory texts on Canadian politics sometimes have the character of an autopsy. The system is stretched out on the unyielding slab, and readers are given a catalogue of limbs and organs, skeletal features, sinews and nerves, and even blemishes and congenital deformations. As useful as pathology is, however, no student of medicine would ever concentrate exclusively on cadavers. In politics, this means some exposure to the political process, to institutions and forces as they combine in complex and marvelous ways to produce odd or exciting results.

Most of the main texts presently being used across the country recognize this, of course, and have incorporated a case study to illustrate the ways in which the various parts of the system combine and clash in real life. This book is nothing more than an extended version of this stratagem; instead of a single, short case study, we provide six extensive ones. This book tries to open a small window into the real world of Canadian politics; not a world of clean charts and straight arrows that tidily delineate the flows of power, but a complex and shifting world of issues, personalities, forces, and institutions as they combine in process.

The use of the plural *Worlds* in our title is deliberate. We want to show that beneath the canopy of a single political system there can be tremendous variety in political processes and public policy. Not all elements or ingredients of the system carry the same weight in each and every case. Sometimes the fact that

Canada is a federal system is critical and determining, sometimes it is not. The executive does not always dominate the legislature. The judiciary plays bit parts in some political dramas, leading roles in others. The cases chosen for this book not only illustrate how the different components of the political system interact, but also why certain features are operative in certain circumstances and not in others. The key political institutions and players vary enormously from case to case in the many worlds of Canadian politics. It is useful to consider politics in terms of "issue networks" or "sub-governments": processes, actors, institutions, and even political discourse will vary across these networks. In economic policy, for example, producer groups (e.g., manufacturers, labour unions, agriculture) are clear players, and the terms of debate are, for better or worse, set within the limits of modern economic theory. The politics of abortion or native issues are entirely different: the actors change, the issues mutate, and the language shifts. Business organizations, for example, have little to do with abortion, and none of the main players in the abortion policy arena rely on economic concepts to make their claims.

Cases have their limits, of course, chief among which is their limited representativeness if they are not carefully selected. They have a prime virtue, however, in that they can delineate the complex elements of a process in narrative rather than analytical form. This is the other contribution that we hope to make with this volume. To take *process* and *policy outcomes* seriously means taking a unique sequence of events and understanding it from the perspective of the actors. Why did they do what they did, what structural constraints did they face, and how did these combine to produce (or not produce) policy? Indeed, most people, when they think of politics, think in terms of "stories" and issues and personalities, of "what happened." It is easy to dismiss this as uninformed and superficial, but it captures something that academic analyses often miss: politics as the engagement of living wills, of real persons with interests and passions, visions and mad dreams. Politics at this level—perhaps the primordial level—demands a narrative voice rather than an exclusively analytical one. That is why, in the cases that follow, we have tried to blend the analysis of larger forces with an appreciation of the situation as seen by political actors themselves. We have tried to tell "the story", weaving in as best we can the elements of personality and circumstance, irony and comedy.

For this edition, we chose five cases: the Supreme Court's 1988 decision to strike down Canada's 1969 abortion legislation in the Morgentaler case, and the subsequent struggle to draft acceptable legislation in the form of Bill C-43; the Meech Lake accord and its tortuous progress to the final debacle in the summer of 1990; the free trade agreement with the United States, signed in January 1988;

the confrontation between Mohawk Warriors and the armed forces at Oka/Kanesatake from July to September 1990; and the design and passage of the Goods and Services Tax. All five are recent, and two of them (abortion and free trade) began in the Mulroney government's first term (1984-88). Together they cast an interesting light on the federal Conservative government in this period, but each case study takes pains to develop the background specific to the issue. The chapter on abortion, for example, examines the legacy of nineteenth-century British law for Canada's treatment of abortion and contraception in the 1969 legislative changes. The chapter on the GST shows how the tax that it replaced— the Manufacturers Sales Tax—has been almost universally reviled for over a generation.

The cases were not selected randomly. The Meech Lake accord was clearly the federal government's key initiative on the intergovernmental front, reflecting its view of the proper relation of Quebec to the rest of Canada, and its willingness to decentralize certain powers. The accord's failure has set in train political forces in Quebec and the rest of Canada that threaten to dramatically alter the terms of Confederation. The Free Trade Agreement and the GST are two of Ottawa's most important economic intiatives, and together reflect not merely the government's policy position but neo-conservative precepts that have gradually gained ascendancy throughout the industrialized world. The abortion case illustrates the growing importance of the Charter of Rights and Freedoms, the mechanisms of judicial politics, and the legislative challenge of regulating morality in the modern age. The Oka crisis at first blush seems an aberration in a country that prides itself on the peaceful resolution of political conflict, but was nothing more than the latest eruption in a policy field where tensions verge on the volcanic. In each of these areas, profound changes have created new political issues, which in turn transform the Canadian political process and its capacity to deal with these issues. Free trade raises questions about national sovereignty; Meech Lake may transform the nature of the Canadian political system; an evolving political role for the courts in the context of the Charter makes politics far less predictable; women's issues and aboriginal nationalism literally change the conceptualization of politics itself.

Looking for contrasts is not in itself a method. Each of the five cases contained in this book, while emphasizing one or two key themes, also touches on several others that we consider important to anyone trying to grasp the realities of Canadian politics. These themes include the ones outlined above concerning the new politics of the 1980s and 1990s, as well as more enduring ones about the nature of political institutions and policy processes. Synoptic Table I summarizes the thematic orientations of each of the cases, explained in somewhat greater detail below. Synoptic Table II, which accompanies the final section of this introduction, reverses the axes and shows how the cases bear on different dimensions of the political process.

Synoptic Table I

CHAPTER	PRINCIPAL THEMES	SUB-THEMES
Abortion	– role of the courts – the Charter	– feminist politics – reproductive rights – drafting legislation
Meech Lake	– intergovernmental bargaining – constitution-making	– interest groups – unpredictability of politics
Free Trade	– international trade politics – political symbols	– party competition – role of Senate
Oka/Kanesatake	– native claims – political symbols – administrative rules	– role of courts – federalism – nationalism
GST	– federalism – role of Senate – technical vs. political	– drafting legislation – economic policy

---

THE CASES: AN OVERVIEW

Abortion

Despite, or perhaps because of, a Supreme Court decision in January 1988, abortion remains one of the most divisive and explosive issues in Canadian public life. The January decision struck down the law that had prohibited abortion in Canada (except under certain narrow conditions) since 1969. Parliament wrestled with the issue through the summer of 1988, and in an extraordinary Commons debate, completely failed to reach consensus on even a direction in which a new law should go.

This case study delves into the contested zone between politics and morality. Its main theme is the role of the courts, especially after the Charter of Rights and Freedoms, in the modern political process. In 1969, after a debate the terms of which have not changed that much in recent years, Parliament passed amendments to the Criminal Code that prohibited abortion except when the mother's life and health were in danger and the procedure was approved by a hospital committee. In one of those jests of fate that confound virtually every political theory based on "grand forces" and "structural constraints," a single man, Henry Morgentaler, decided to fight the law through the courts and have it changed. The story of Morgentaler's battle is virtually synonymous with the story of Canada's abortion policy, since it was through Morgentaler's efforts that the law was finally struck down by the Supreme Court in January 1988. It is both a fascinating and a disturbing saga of deliberate disobedience that forced authorities to raid illegal clinics, lay charges, and go through court arguments on the law's validity. The role of courts was critical in this case, since Morgentaler and the pro-abortion lobby decided quite early that getting legislative change through Parliament was virtually impossible: abortion was *so* contested that politicians wished to avoid dealing with it at all costs. Moreover, while the forces on both sides of the issue were committed and well organized, it was difficult to generate widespread popular support for either of the extreme options (complete, unfettered choice vs. complete prohibition of abortion).

This strategy of litigation was enhanced after 1982 with the adoption of the Charter of Rights and Freedoms. Section 7 of the Charter protects the liberty of the person, and the Charter as a whole has precedence over legislation passed by federal and provincial governments. Interpretation of the Charter is up to the courts, particularly the Supreme Court, and this has changed the relationship of the legislature to the courts in the Canadian political system. Legislation may now be struck down by the courts if they deem it to be inconsistent with the Charter. Henry Morgentaler began his crusade well before the Charter, but his last assault, which led finally to the Supreme Court, incorporated the argument that Canada's 1969 abortion law was inconsistent with the Charter because it interfered with the liberty of the (female) person. It is expensive and difficult to use the courts as an avenue of political protest, but with the Charter now in play, many interest groups will at least consider the litigation route because it favours rights-based, minoritarian claims over the majoritarian logic of legislatures.

The abortion case also bears on several other themes of contemporary Canadian politics. It provides a perspective on feminist politics in Canada since the contemporary Canadian feminist movement has been bound up with the fight for abortion choice. Indeed, the early feminist movement in Canada was drawn into the the fight for "free abortion on demand" (as the slogan then was), as many radical women drifted out of the student and peace movements into feminist organizing. Other, primarily economic, issues eventually eclipsed abortion as the central focus of the women's movement, but ironically, as the decade of the 1980s closed, abortion rights began once again to demand defence. The first edition of this book predicted in early 1989 that abortion politics would not go away simply because the Supreme Court had struck down the old law, and that anti-abortion forces were in the ascendancy and could be expected to mount a new assault for tougher laws. This is precisely what happened. The chapter traces out the street and court battles over 1989 that culminated in the sensational Dodd and Daigle cases, and the resulting national pressure on the federal government to introduce some legislative framework to govern abortions. The Conservative answer was the carefully worded Bill C-43, which could be read as both restricting and liberalizing abortion, within a federal framework that actually passed the buck to the provinces. Predictably, the only thing anyone could agree on was that the legislation would almost immediately be challenged in the courts. As it turned out, Bill C-43 will never be challenged anywhere: on 31 January 1991 the Senate defeated it by a tie vote. The government refuses to try its hand at abortion legislation again.

The Meech Lake Accord

The chapter on the Meech Lake accord focuses carefully on the dynamics of intergovernmental bargaining and constitution-making in Canada. It also explores what turned out to be a central priority on the Conservative government agenda in the latter half of its mandate.

Prime Minister Trudeau's legacy to the country was his patriation of the constitution and the entrenchment of a Charter of Rights and Freedoms. The legacy was soured, however, by Quebec's refusal to sign the agreement in 1981. Premier Levesque, though the leader of a separatist government, broadly reflected Quebec's sentiments that the province had been betrayed. Flags flew at half mast throughout the province. Clearly this was an intolerable situation. Even while the Charter and the new constitution had the effect of law in Quebec, the province was not a willing participant, and so almost one-third of the country's population could be viewed as reluctant partners in Confederation.

Brian Mulroney vowed to change this, and to initiate a new round of constitutional talks to bring Quebec back in. These talks culminated in two extraordinary sessions in 1987, one at a government retreat at Meech Lake and another in the Langevin block of Parliament in Ottawa. The result was the Meech Lake accord, a short statement that gave Quebec the designation of "distinct society" in the constitution, and extended some powers and prerogatives for the other provinces. Premier Bourassa proclaimed himself well satisfied with the accord, and immediately had it passed in the Quebec National Assembly. All but two provinces (Manitoba and New Brunswick) followed suit over the next year, and for a while it seemed as though the accord would pass within the three-year limit imposed by the constitution. It did not, and the twisted and acrimonious path of its demise has led the country much closer to dissolution than unity.

There could be no more perfect illustration than this case of the dynamics of modern Canadian intergovernmental negotiations. The Meech Lake process was, for instance, closed. The Prime Minister and ten premiers sat together in a stuffy room through the small hours of the night, trading and arguing, playing their cards and seeking their advantages. Public participation in the process came afterwards, and even then it was largely a charade. In 1988 the Prime Minister stated that the accord could not be re-opened; in June 1990 he did precisely that in order to entice Newfoundland and Manitoba to support it. In a bizarre hybrid of elite policy and democratic policy-making, the first ministers met behind closed doors for a week, and the entire event was covered exhaustively but uncomprehendingly by the media. Meech collapsed in confused acrimony as the Newfoundland legislature simply suspended its vote and Elijah Harper, a native MLA in the Manitoba legislature, held up a feather and said "no" often enough to make ratification impossible.

The case also demonstrates the bargaining strategies and tactics of the players. Despite the accord's collapse, Premier Bourassa emerges from this vignette as a master of the intergovernmental poker game. The complex interplay of provincial legislative politics (e.g., the minority government situation in Manitoba, and election of a Liberal government under Clyde Wells in Newfoundland) had dramatic effects on the intergovernmental bargaining process. In this world of Canadian politics, the stakes are about governmental power and jurisdiction. The winners are those who can claim that they have enhanced their powers; the losers let power slither from their grasp. Of course, part of the game is never to admit losing, and so the comedy of Meech Lake was played out in the immediate aftermath of the agreement, as groups and individuals tried to envision the ultimate effects of the accord on the balance of federal and provincial powers. A strong sentiment arose that Mulroney had sold out the national government in what Pierre Trudeau called a "gutless" manoeuvre. The attempt to salvage the accord only reinforced this perception, as the Prime Minister appeared to be willing tro accept anything in order to let Meech live.

The reactions to Meech Lake form a sub-theme of the case study. Few political issues manage to stimulate such a broad response from the political community (free trade is another example), and the committee rooms of Parliament echoed with the impassioned pleas of groups both favouring and condemning the agreement. Interestingly, the sides were fairly balanced, with no clear group or interest tending to dominate. This reflects the ambiguity of the accord, and its open texture. The issue came down to the meaning of the words in the text, over which there was ample disagreement. The chapter documents the different interpretations and the various alternatives that were offered, ones so subtle that they clearly illustrate the constipating legalism of constitutional politics.

Another sub-theme is the role of accident and personality in real politics. The Meech Lake accord was propelled, it is true, by certain broad forces. The absence of Quebec from the national constitutional framework would have compelled action no matter which government had been in power or who might have been at its helm. Nonetheless, the case shows how the Meech Lake accord is the result of a specific political and personal chemistry. Brian Mulroney shaped the negotiations by his style and approach, learned as a labour negotiator. David Peterson of Ontario was a reluctant participant at first, and then emerged in the last days of Meech as its key defender; Don Getty of Alberta wanted to discuss Senate reform; and Robert Bourassa of Quebec came in with a minimal package that skilfully capitalized on the feeling of most provinces, whatever their reluctance to give up powers, that Quebec had to come into the constitutional fold. Clyde Wells appeared on the scene after the accord was first signed, and became its most visible and truculent opponent. The fortunes of Meech Lake also show that affairs of state are just as often the creatures of fate as of men. Mulroney's initiative depended on Bourassa's support in Quebec. Howard Pawley of Manitoba had signed the agreement and then shortly afterwards was forced into a provincial election through the disgruntlement of one backbencher. The Liberals held the balance of power, and did not support the Meech Lake accord. Without their support, the provincial Conservatives could not pass the necessary legislation. Richard Hatfield of New Brunswick was defeated by Frank McKenna's Liberals. McKenna won every seat in the provincial legislature, and opposed the accord as well. Clyde Wells won power in Newfoundland *after* the accord was passed there, but he simply proposed to rescind that approval. The real world of politics is unpredictable and mercurial.

The Free Trade Deal

At one level the Free Trade Agreement (FTA) was merely a component of Canada's international trading policy, an aspect of economic strategy. In the end it was much more than that; it quickly swelled to almost impossible proportions. It was an economic policy, a cultural policy, a daring gambit, a drastic error, a key to Canada's future in the global economy, the tight coffin of our national aspirations. It became virtually the only issue of the 21 November 1988 federal election. The Prime Minister had launched the initiative in 1985 with the promise that an FTA would stimulate industry and jobs across the country, provide guaranteed access to American markets, and immunize Canada evermore from capricious and irrational spasms of US trade protection laws. Opponents claimed that everything from crime to dangerously flawed blood tests would result from the FTA with the United States.

Free trade is to Canadian public policy what Ithaca was to Ulysses: a dream to pursue through all trials, a goal, however unrealistic, to strain for. Almost every generation since Confederation has tried its hand at free trade with the United States, and even Pierre Trudeau's Liberal government in 1983 thought that some limited version of it might be worth negotiating. Ironically, Brian Mulroney, the man who finally signed a deal more comprehensive than anything ever contemplated by a Canadian prime minister, indeed the most comprehensive trade deal in history, rejected the idea in 1983. The rise of protectionism in the United States, the lack of American interest in sectoral trade, and ultimately the possibility that a good deal would be the crowning glory of Tory economic promises to produce more jobs everywhere and especially in the regions, finally pushed an uncertain cabinet and government into the talks. The case shows how, far from being clear about their goals, federal politicians were confused, evasive, and even fainthearted. After two years of negotiations, weeks before the deadline, the deal looked dead. Frantic eleventh-hour interventions at the highest political levels yielded an agreement bare minutes before the legal time limit ran out. The following year saw an extraordinarily wide-ranging debate on the FTA as the government produced legislation to implement the deal and, in November 1988, fought an election campaign around it. Ironically, the issue that swept up such storm and passion virtually sank from public view once implementation began in 1989. The media carry occasional stories of plant closings, economic reports supporting or damning the agreement, and news of some dispute resolutions, but the FTA has simply disappeared as an object of sustained public attention. The chapter argues that this is because its effects are so diffuse and disaggregated.

The FTA case shows another world of Canadian politics, the world of international and bilateral negotiations. Not all negotiations are like the one that produced the FTA, but most contain at least some of the features that made the FTA talks especially difficult. In talks like these, position is everything, and Canada walked into the talks in a position of weakness. The Americans neither needed nor especially wanted a deal with Canada; this was evident from the initial reluctance in Congress to permit the talks at all, and the trade sanctions Canada suffered in softwood lumber and shakes and shingles while the talks were underway. As well, there has to be clarity of purpose if negotiations are to succeed. The cabinet was not at all clear about what it wanted, and was even more confused about what it might have to concede in order to attain its vaporous aspirations. This indecision might not have been an impediment had the Canadian position been consistent from the beginning, but it was not. It was hopelessly inconsistent. Canada wanted a free trade deal with the United States, but simultaneously wanted to exempt certain things (culture, the Auto Pact, social programmes) from the discussions. In this the American position was at least logical: if there were to be talks at all, they had to start by putting everything on the table. This structural weakness on the Canadian side created some of the difficulties in the final days of the negotiations.

The FTA carried a heavy burden of political symbolism. It had few ardent supporters, but those who opposed it were adamant about what it could and would do to the country. The FTA, as important as it was substantively, came to be seen as an attack on the fundamental nature of the country. Canada, it was said in various quarters, was unique because of its more collectivist traditions compared to the US, because of its social programs that showed a commitment to community caring, because of its spirit of public and not just private enterprise, because of its cultural forms in theatre and prose and painting and broadcasting. The FTA would threaten all of that, by insidiously injecting foreign microbes into the Canadian body politic. Indeed, one critic did compare the FTA to AIDS: the effects of the virus would take decades to become visible, but when they did, that would be the end of Canada.

The supplementary themes of this case are numerous. It illustrates the power of party competition, for example, in the way that the Liberals and the NDP decided to stake out their opposition to the deal. It provides a bit part to the Senate, which in a dramatic move in August 1988, agreed to John Turner's request not to pass the enabling legislation until a federal election had permitted the people to vote on free trade. It even touches on intergovernmental bargaining, since in the early stages of the talks, the provinces insisted that they be consulted, and everyone thought that any trade deal would have to include provincial jurisdiction. The ultimate deal did not, perhaps because Ottawa knew it would have difficulty in enforcing provincial compliance. Finally, it exposes some of the drama and the strategies of election campaigns: the FTA was forced onto the election agenda through deliberate Liberal tactics, and almost succeeded in burying the Conservatives.

Canada's fortunes under the FTA are ambiguous at best. The deal was introduced at the worst possible time, during a time of rising interest rates and a high dollar. Export prospects were dim, and for the first few months of 1989, every plant closing was ascribed to the FTA. The economic statistics are much more difficult to decipher, and the best guesses are that the FTA had little net impact *either way* on economic performance. Its impact on trade-dispute resolution has been modestly positive, through the chapter shows some instances in which Canadian interests were sacrificed because of the agreement's stipulations. Like abortion, the FTA is not over: it is still in its implementation phase and will be for another five years. In the midst of this the subsidies issue will once more be addressed, and may perhaps re-open wounds and revive the debate of 1988.

Confrontation at Oka/Kanesatake

Canadians are not used to war or domestic insurrection: the country clings to the notion that it is a peaceable kingdom wherein disputes are resolved democratically at the ballot box. This appears to be true of the debate over free trade, but is somewhat questionable in the abortion case, where street demonstrations and civil disobedience are increasingly popular political tools. The confrontation at Oka, a small town outside of Montreal, in the summer of 1990 shattered the myth and exposed a depth of discontent and grievance among aboriginal peoples that few Canadians realized existed. The issue began innocuously enough, though typically, around a land dispute. The Mohawks at Kanesatake are an Indian community that never signed a treaty with the federal government; indeed, they have occupied the area for only about two hundred years. Their lands are the results of purchases and transfers from Ottawa, but large sections were owned by religious orders, which in turn sold them to private interests. The Kanesatake Mohawks have been engaged in land appeals since 1868, and took their appeals as far as the Judicial Committee of the Privy Council in the early twentieth century. Their legal appeals were denied then, as they were by Ottawa later in the 1970s.

The immediate conflict started when the town council of Oka decided to expand the existing golf course on what the Mohawks claimed was their land. Several members of a militant splinter in the Mohawk community, the Warriors

Society, decided in March 1990 to erect barricades near the proposed expansion to prevent construction. While peaceful, the barricade succeeded in its purpose of stopping development, and in July the town council asked police to remove it. A police officer was shot in the head and killed in a dawn raid on 11 July, and Oka became an instant national issue. Mohawk Warriors at the nearby reserve of Kahnawake erected a sympathy barrier blocking the Mercier Bridge, a vital link over the St. Lawrence River for sixty thousand daily commuters from the community of Châteauguay. The resulting turmoil was unique in modern Canadian history: mobs gathered nightly at the bridge, burning Indians and politicians in effigy and hurling Molotov cocktails, obscenities, and rocks at police. Negotiations went nowhere over the following weeks, and on 8 August the Quebec cabinet met and decided to ask the Canadian armed forces to intervene. Thousands of soldiers arrived and turned the Montreal south shore into an armed camp. The threat of violence hung in the air for weeks as the army slowly tightened the noose around the handful of Mohawks pinned down in Kanesatake. The seige ended on 26 September when the Warriors surrendered.

Oka, far from being an aberration in Canadian politics, resonated with themes and tensions that have been part of Canadian history for over two hundred years. The events at Kanesatake and Kahnawake cannot be understood without a grasp of the evolution of Canadian-aboriginal relations since the pre-Confederation period. The conflict was initially over land, and a fairly trivial amount at that. After the July police raid, Mohawks and natives across the country began to demand recognition of their sovereignty and right to self-determination. The federal and Quebec governments tried to keep talks focused on removal of the barriers and transfers of the land originally in question, but within a few days native negotiators were insisting on something much more fundamental and challenging: they wanted to be treated as a nation. Aboriginal leaders across Canada debated whether the Mohawk Warriors were right to use violence, and there were severe internal disagreements in Kanesatake and Kahnawake over tactics and the very presence of the Warriors Society, but on the question of aboriginal rights and the essential justice of the Mohawk claim there was extraordinary solidarity. That solidarity was expressed in concrete form: all across Canada native bands erected barricades to block railroads, highways, and logging companies. Some pulled down hydro towers, and the Peigans in Alberta tried to re-route a river.

For many Canadians these were inexplicable and provocative acts. Oka is a prism through which some of the roots of these issues may be explored. One problem, for example, is the patchwork of agreements and treaties that govern relations between natives and governments in Canada. Early pre-Confederation treaties were military alliances, without transfers of land, and aboriginals were treated as independent peoples and allies. After Confederation, as interest shifted towards encouragement of settlement, treaties were struck across western Canada with various tribes and bands to transfer lands and extinguish aboriginal title. These numbered treaties (eleven in all) are the bedrock upon which some key native claims have been erected. The treaties are ambiguous, however, and do not include all aboriginal peoples (e.g, the Inuit, the Métis, most bands in British Columbia and Quebec). Ottawa's broader responsibilities for natives are therefore contained in the Indian Act, the first consolidated version of which was passed in 1876. The Indian Act has become over time a lightening rod for aboriginal discontent: it is paternalistic and invasive, and historically was the instrument whereby white society imposed its demands and perceptions on native life. Much of contemporary native politics may be seen as an effort to retain what is good in the Indian Act (not much, but at minimum the admission of special rights for aboriginal peoples) and supersede it with some new relationship that recognizes the aboriginal right to self-government.

The events in Oka/Kanesatake also demand some reflection on recent policy developments. Since the mid-1970s, the federal government and native organizations have been groping towards a policy framework of "self-government" and "aboriginal rights," and in fact succeeded in entrenching aboriginal rights in the Charter of Rights and Freedoms in 1982. The problem is that opinions as to what "aboriginal rights" means vary drastically, and disputes over the definition of self-government are just as sharp. Three consecutive first ministers' conferences grappled with the question, but failed to achieve consensus. Some provincial premiers insisted on knowing what self-government meant before they entrenched it in a constitutional amendment; native leaders demanded entrenchment as a recognition of their status as "First Nations." Since 1987, Ottawa has tried to implement self-government on a case-by-case basis, but has committed so few resources to the initiative that it has had virtually no results. Meanwhile, native frustration over the imperceptible pace of resolution of claims and grievances continues to mount.

The events at Oka, given the historical legacies of native-white relations in Canada, may have been the first of a long series of confrontations that lie ahead. The symbolic importance of the barricades for Mohawks and other natives cannot be underestimated: for many it was a moment of glory for natives, who stood their ground in the face of the overwhelming military power of the majority society.

The Goods and Services Tax

The last half of 1990 was perhaps the most bizarre political year Canadians had ever witnessed. In June they were glued to the tragi-comedy of Meech Lake, with Elijah Harper and Clyde Wells playing Brutus to Brian Mulroney's Caesar. With the collapse of the accord, Canadians barely had time to stoke up their summer barbecues before Oka exploded into barricades and military occupation. The year was then crowned by a political battle equally marked by farce and drama: the Goods and Services Tax (GST). The farce came in the form of the Liberal-dominated Senate's decision to hold up and conceivably even defeat the tax bill, which the government wished to implement on 1 January 1991. The chamber of "sober second thought" became anything but sober, as senators blew kazoos and shouted epithets at each other in a complete breakdown of parliamentary decorum. The drama came from the importance of the tax to the government's fiscal programme, the constitutional principle involved in a dispute between an elected and appointed chamber, and finally in the Prime Minister's use of an obscure constitutional provision to "stack" the Senate with supporters who would neutralize the Liberal's predominance.

The GST replaced the Manufacturers Sales Tax, introduced in 1924. The old tax was attacked almost immediately, and criticism never abated. Despite some alterations to its rate and incidence, the Manufacturers Sales Tax was blamed for a whole host of economic irrationalities. Every government, every commission of inquiry, and virtually every economist and policy analyst in the post-war period has argued that the tax needed to be replaced by something broader in scope, that would tax services as well as manufactured goods, and not discriminate against domestic producers. The problem for governments, however, was that taxes are universally disliked by the populace, and any change to the old regime, short of simple abolition, would generate strong political opposition. The Mulroney Conservatives, however, decided to embark as early as 1984 on a major overhaul of the Canadian tax system, and the GST soon emerged as the key component of its national strategy. Tax reform proceeded in two phases. The first consisted of personal and corporate income tax changes, which were passed in 1988. The second phase was soon dominated by the GST issue. The federal government would have preferred to develop a national sales tax in cooperation with the provinces, but federal-provincial negotiations failed to reach an agreement in 1989, and Ottawa decided to go it alone. It introduced background and technical papers that year, and Bill C-62 was formally introduced in Parliament in January 1990. The GST bill unleashed a paroxysm of national discontent and opposition throughout the year, with the Senate fight only the legislative expression of a furious tax revolt.

Bill C-62 passed the House of Commons in April and was then sent to face the Liberal majority in the Senate. The Tories had had their problems with the Senate before (e.g., the Meech Lake accord and free trade), but this time it appeared that the Liberals were determined to "axe the tax." Millions of dollars had been spent on government advertising and private-sector preparations to implement the tax on 1 January 1991, and so the stakes were high. Relying on a moribund section of the BNA Act, the Prime Minister appointed eight "extra" senators to pull up the Tory side in the upper chamber. In typical Canadian fashion, federal political parties and provincial governments launched court actions claiming that this manoeuvre was illegal and that the GST itself was unconstitutional. Opinion polls taken in October showed that fully 75 per cent of Canadians opposed the tax, and Liberal senators perversely claimed that they— never elected, only appointed—were the true trumpets of democracy in trying to defeat the bill. Filibusters peppered the October agenda, kicked off in fine fashion by a 4 October mêlée in which senators leaped on tables and chairs, shouted out "Hitler" to the Speaker, thumped desks, blew whistles and kazoos, and read from the Bible and petitions against the bill. Bill C-62 eventually passed, but not before it severely undermined any sense Canadians might have retained of the dignity of parliamentary institutions.

Passage of the GST, from concept to law, took four hard years. It was acrimonious and poisonous, and in many ways was emblematic of federal politics in the second Mulroney mandate. The case illustrates the difficulties of tax legislation, difficulties that were compounded by the unusual truculence that marked the country in the last half of 1990. It also casts light on the complexities of intergovernmental bargaining, since the preferred Tory strategy was to coordinate its tax with those of the provinces. This initiative failed, and its failure uncoupled the first and second phases of tax reform, putting the Tories in an exposed position. From another perspective, the GST underscores the tension between the Senate and the House of Commons. The swamp of the Senate with eight additional Tory members may nullify this as an important factor in federal politics for several years, but even with the extra strength, the Conservatives do not have a majority in the Senate. Finally, the GST, like all of the other cases in this second edition, reveals the potency of symbols in the real worlds of politics. Public policies are too often thought of in terms of the stated goals, their direct impact. Consideration of the five cases collected in this volume shows that policies also have a symbolic dimension, they are assessed both for what they will do and, less precisely, for what they *mean*. These two dimensions co-exist, of course, and cannot be untangled completely, but they are distinct. At Oka, for example, Mohawks were in their minds fighting for issues much broader than a simple land claim over a golf course, and without an appreciation of the *meaning* of their struggle, the entire sad episode makes little sense. The GST is a fine example of a similar phenomenon. In purely technical terms, a tax like the GST makes overwhelming economic sense. In political terms, the GST become the symbol of the Mulroney government itself, a metaphor for all of its unpopular policies. It was despised less for what it would do than for what it represented.

CASES AND THE STUDY OF CANADIAN POLITICS

These five cases illustrate a few of the real worlds of Canadian politics. Other cases might have dealt more directly, for example, with things like the media's effect on politics, or provincial and municipal politics. Any volume, even with different cases, would eventually arrive at the same portrait of our political life: not the tepid perfection of a cubist drawing, but the raw, riotous colour and power of passions and principle, structure and symbol.

This book may be used in several ways. It should provide some enjoyment, and its narrative structure should permit a more vigorous and engaged reading than is typical of texts in the field. We have given each essay, inconspicuously we hope, an analytical framework, so that the reader will be introduced to the necessary background on native land claims, trade negotiations, or sales taxes, as needed. Each essay also ends with several discussion questions. These questions can be used in several ways. One way is to read the questions before plunging into the case, thereby using them as signposts for what is important in the story. Another way is to use the list of questions as a basis for group discussion of the case. This introduction and the synoptic tables provide a guide to some of the themes expressed in each of the cases, but readers should also take note of other aspects of politics that are revealed, even if only briefly, in the narrative. The essay on the FTA, for example, mentions in passing several characteristics of the American political system that pose a sharp contrast to the Canadian practice; the Oka issue outlines some of the practical questions of aboriginal self-government and national sovereignty. Finally, the cases should not be treated separately. One of our purposes in writing them was to develop sharp contrasts in the different styles of politics that develop around different types of political issues. Readers should think about how the politics of moral regulation (e.g., abortion) are different from and similar to the politics of economic policy (e.g., the GST). How does capitalism affect policy-making, and how do governments respond to different interests? What is the balance of power between different institutions

Synoptic Table II

ASPECT OF SYSTEM	PRINCIPAL CHAPTERS	COGNATE CHAPTERS
Institutions		
Cabinet	1, 2	4
Legislature	1, 3, 5	2
Senate	3, 5	2
Judiciary	1, 4	5
Bureaucracy	4, 5	3
Actors		
Parties	3, 4	5
Interest Groups	1, 2, 3	5
Experts	3, 5	2
Processes		
Political Symbols	1, 4	2, 3
Intergovernmentalism	2, 3, 5	1, 4
Regionalism	2	3

of Canadian government, such as the legislature, the Senate, the judiciary, and the executive? How do party politics affect this institutional balance?

Synoptic Table II may be used as a guide to exploring some of the broader aspects of the Canadian political system. The cases show how similar elements of the system get combined in different ways around different policy issues. The student interested in regionalism, for example, will find that theme developed principally in the chapters on the GST and Meech Lake. Other, cognate chapters also may treat the same theme, though in more muted tones. In the case of regionalism, Chapter 3 on the Free Trade Agreement addresses, as part of its story, the tensions between the provincial governments and Ottawa during the negotiations.

A key point to bear in mind is that the cases allow the examination of different aspects of the same processes or institutions in different political worlds. Parties, for instance, may be examined from the perspective of the differing policy proposals they put forward (e.g., in the case of the FTA or Meech Lake), the tensions generated between national and provincial wings (e.g., the Liberals and Meech Lake), or their strategies and tactics during election campaigns (e.g., the November 1988 election over free trade). The same might be said of political symbols and political language: these arise most powerfully in the abortion, Oka, and Meech Lake cases. Comparison of the role of the courts in the aboriginal rights and abortion cases can also help provide fruitful perspectives on how these institutions operate in the contemporary Canadian state.

If read creatively, both for the contrasts they provide and the generalizations they might stimulate, these cases should help develop an analytical appreciation of the policy process as well as a sharp sense of politics as it is lived and felt.

COURTS, POLITICS, AND MORALITY:

CANADA'S ABORTION SAGA

After almost twenty years of struggle, Henry Morgentaler finally won in January 1988. The Supreme Court of Canada upheld Morgentaler's appeal and declared Canada's abortion law unconstitutional, striking down abortion legislation that had been on the books since 1969. The dry legal decision of 1988 raised the curtain on two years of melodrama and farce: provincial governments trying to regulate abortion as a health matter, boyfriends seeking injunctions against their partners, marches, more court cases, and bumbling federal attempts to design compromise legislation. Bill C-43 was barely passed by the House of Commons in 1990, but in a dramatic reversal was rejected by the Senate in January 1991. The story of Canada's abortion law illuminates several issues. It shows the difficulty of forging public policy for sensitive moral issues, and the growing prominence of a "rights-based" mentality in Canadian political discourse, especially since the Charter. It highlights the increasing importance of feminism as a political force, and uncovers the pivotal role and special dynamics of courts in the policy process: Canadian pro-abortion rights activists, realizing that politicians were unwilling to tackle reforms in the 1970s, decided to aim at judicial victory instead. Finally, the abortion issue challenges our ability to reconcile rights with obligations, technology with humanity, and public laws with personal morality. The Supreme Court's 1988 abortion decision did not resolve these or any other issues. The failure to pass Bill C-43 ensures that abortion will be contested in the courts, the provincial legislatures, and the streets.

Rarely are an issue and an institution so starkly contrasted as are abortion and the Supreme Court. No matter what one feels about abortion, it is clearly an issue defined by feelings: feelings about life, motherhood, and the rights of women. Abortion forces a consideration of the archetypal human experiences: birth, life, and death. No one who has thought seriously about it can resist its tremendous emotional undertow. In contrast, the Supreme Court, which in

January 1988 declared Canada's abortion law unconstitutional, is deliberately designed to suppress passion and extinguish feeling. Issues are addressed and resolved in the cold, clean language of legal reasoning. Nine judges (seven in the abortion case) sit surrounded by dark oak and frozen marble, betraying passion only when their reason has been offended. And so the abortion issue as it is seen on the streets—with all of its confusion and passion—is rendered calm and precise in the serenity of the judicial chamber.

Most Canadians, of course, have only a dim sense of the Supreme Court as an institution. The role of this court and others in the Canadian judicial system has increased substantially with the adoption in 1982 of the Charter of Rights and Freedoms. Since the Charter guarantees constitutional rights, and since only the courts (and ultimately the Supreme Court) can determine precisely what the Charter means, these decisions will assume increasing significance, both for elaborating what the Charter says and for guiding legislatures as to what is legally permissible. In this new game, interest groups and other policy actors will increasingly see the courts as a means whereby they can win their political battles through constitutional interpretation. This is what happened in Canada's abortion saga. Pro-abortion rights activists, symbolized by Henry Morgentaler, deliberately broke the law in the hope of forcing the issue into the courts. Joe Borowski, Canada's best known anti-abortion crusader, went before the Supreme Court in October 1988 to press his case that the fetus is a person and thus protected by law.[1]

Canada's abortion saga has passed through several stages. The first was the period of agitation for reform in the 1960s that eventually led to Criminal Code amendments in 1969. Before those amendments, abortion was illegal and anyone convicted of "procuring a miscarriage" was liable to life imprisonment. From the perspective of the 1980s this agitation assumed a curious form: it was not led by women or feminists convinced of the right to abortion, but by physicians and lawyers who wanted to minimize criminal liability for performing abortions. The second period comprises the first of Henry Morgentaler's judicial assaults on the law. Only a year after the new abortion law was passed, Morgentaler was arrested in Montreal for performing abortions at a clinic he had established exclusively for that purpose. Between 1970 and 1976 Morgentaler faced two separate arrests, three jury trials, and an eighteen-month jail sentence (he served ten months). In 1976 he retreated from the field.

The third stage begins with Morgentaler's re-entry to the fray. Convinced that abortions were becoming harder to get because of agitation by anti-abortion rights forces, and incensed that Joe Borowski was preparing a court case to argue that the fetus is a person under Canadian law, Morgentaler decided in 1982 to open abortion clinics in Winnipeg and Toronto. Both opened in 1983 amid demonstrations of support and protest, and a few incidents of violence. Morgentaler was once again arrested, and his Toronto case eventually made its way to the Supreme Court in October 1986. On 28 January 1988 the Court upheld Morgentaler's appeal and struck down the law that he had been fighting for almost twenty years.

The fourth stage is the aftermath of the Court's decision and the federal government's attempt to devise and pass new legislation. The initial reaction to the Court's decision among pro-abortion rights partisans was euphoria. That soon changed as it became clear that provincial governments would squeeze into the legislative vacuum left by the 1988 decision. British Columbia was first in announcing that it would refuse to pay for abortions unless they conformed to procedures under the old federal law. After Henry Morgentaler re-opened his Winnipeg clinic in June 1988, the Manitoba government announced that it would not pay for abortions performed there. Predictably, court cases ensued in British Columbia, and later in New Brunswick, as pro-abortion rights activists and sympathizers tried to ensure that abortion would be treated like any other medical service. The Mulroney government introduced a "resolution" on abortion that showed anything but resolve: it was so amorphous that it was defeated in a free vote in the House of Commons. In 1989 it tried again, against the backdrop of a bizarre summer during which Chantal Daigle was first denied an abortion by the courts and then later, in a rare emergency hearing, was granted leave to an abortion by the Supreme Court—in the midst of which the Court was told that she had defied the original order and procured an abortion in the United States. Legislative hearings dragged on into 1990, and Bill C-43 was finally passed by the House of Commons (140–131) on 29 May 1990. From there it went to the Senate, where the same arguments were heard on both sides of the issue. In a free vote on 31 January 1991, the Senate exercised its rarely used power to defeat government legislation, and killed Bill C-43. The government said that it would not try again. There would be no abortion law in Canada.

While this complex story highlights the role of the courts and the Charter in modern Canadian politics, it also illustrates several other aspects of the real worlds of politics. First, it demonstrates the importance of political symbols and language in struggles over public policy. Real politics in a pluralistic, democratic state is about argument and debate, about winning hearts and minds. It is not simply a matter of raw numbers or brute force. This was clear in the abortion saga, which pitted one man, Henry Morgentaler, and a minority political movement against a law that elected politicians would have preferred to leave alone. They made their case in the courts by argument, and they took that argument and others into the public square. This chapter will give glimpses of how those arguments were shaped, the assumptions they took for granted, and the ways that they evolved in light of new circumstances. The vital core of the arguments on both sides, however, was symbolic. It was not so much (though this was important) a matter of rational claims for or against abortion, but what abortion meant. Did it mean the decline of the family and a de-valuation of life, or did it mean the new dawn of women's rights and the primary basis of their liberation from a patriarchal power structure? This dimension of meaning was deliberately tapped on both sides to evoke responses from people, responses that would open them to the competing rational arguments. In the early 1970s the Abortion Caravan dragged a coffin, filled with knives and coathangers, from one end of the country to the other. Years later, Joe Borowski would paint the outside wall of his health food store with the picture of a graveyard and a sign reading "Pro-Choicers Have a Place for Unwanted Babies."

This chapter will also throw some light on the difficulties governments sometimes face in making and passing laws. In some areas, such as free trade, Meech Lake, and the GST, government seem prepared to take the initiative. Both free trade and the GST are enormously controversial, but in both cases government seemed to take the bit in its teeth and forge ahead despite opposition. In cases like abortion, governments seem paralysed. Nothing is done, agreement seems impossible, legislation languishes, and people agitate fruitlessly for decades. So, as these contrasting issues show, governments are not by any means always incapacitated, vacillating, or undetermined. The question, then, is: why resolve and backbone in some cases but not others? The abortion question provides some clues. It deals with the body and sexuality, and is entwined with what has perhaps been the most fundamental challenge to traditional post-war politics in western states—feminism. It touches on issues of religious belief and invites debates about rights, particularly reproductive rights. Opposition to free trade, the Meech Lake Accord, or the GST is not organized as a sexual protest, a gender protest, or a religious protest. These forces have been evident, but were never the principal axes of debate. Abortion is burdened with so many of society's most volatile convictions that it is enormously difficult to find a middle ground. Issues like these have a centrifugal force that flings people to the extremes, where the stakes of victory or defeat are highest.

Finally, the abortion case throws some light on the practical politics of Canadian feminism since the 1960s. The complex tapestry of Canada's abortion saga shows how a movement, an issue, and a man came to be interwoven. They remained distinct, as patterns on a tapestry always must be, but they needed each other to have full effect. This chapter will show how Canadian feminism, with its early roots in the radical student movement of the late 1960s, gradually came to focus on abortion as a central issue in the struggle for women's rights. The "pro-choice" slogan emerged in the mid-1970s and continued to dominate the feminist agenda, even as other issues like Charter rights and equity employment were added to the list. Early on, the movement decided on a strategy of court challenges, but it needed to find a doctor who would be prepared to break the law, face life imprisonment and the loss of his or her medical licence and reputation, as well as bear some of the enormous legal costs involved in going to the courts. Henry Morgentaler entered the picture, not because he was a feminist, but because of a personal agenda to prove the power of his will. And so they helped each other: Morgentaler by steadfastly refusing to obey the law and being prepared to risk everything in his court challenges, local feminist, pro-abortion rights networks by providing volunteers to staff clinics and raising funds to pay the lawyers. Immediately after the 1988 Supreme Court decision, Morgentaler went quietly back to his Toronto clinic. Within a year he was back in the courts, but the centre of gravity of the abortion issue had shifted. The multiple battlegrounds in 1988–89—provincial, federal, judicial—made the movement more important than the man, particularly as anti-abortion rights activists gained in strength and organization.

CONTRACEPTION AND ABORTION, 1892–1969

Canada's first abortion law[2] simply copied an 1803 British law that first made abortion a statutory offence. Before 1803 Britain relied on the common law understanding that abortion was an offence after "quickening"—the sensation a woman has of fetal movement sometime between the thirteenth and sixteenth week after conception. The 1803 legislation made abortion a punishable offence both before and after quickening, and those provisions were included in the 1861 Offenses Against the Person Act.[3] The relevant provisions of the British legislative tradition were incorporated in Canada's first Criminal Code of 1892 as sections 271–274[4] with two changes from the original British legislation. The first reduced the maximum penalty for self-induced abortions from life imprisonment to seven years (by 1969 it had been reduced further to two years). The second added an explicit "saving" provision, which absolved those who in good faith did something considered necessary for the preservation of the mother's life, and as a consequence killed the fetus. This latter provision was introduced to protect physicians in those cases where, in trying to save the mother's life, they caused an abortion. These provisions, with some small changes in numbering and wording, remained as Canada's abortion law until 1969.[5]

Abortion was not a significant political issue in Canada until the late 1950s. The absence of agitation did not mean that abortions were not being performed.

They were done in practically every major Canadian city, and the Abortion Squad of the Metropolitan Toronto Police Force estimated that before the 1969 legislation, thousands of criminal abortions were procured annually in that area alone.[6] At that time there were several ways to get an abortion, most of them expensive or dangerous. A woman could try to self-induce, she could go to a back-street abortionist, or she could approach a physician. Since the only exception allowed under the law was an abortion done to save the mother, most physicians were reluctant to perform a procedure that could land them in jail for life.[7] While there are no conclusive figures, anecdotal evidence suggests that illegal abortions were a fact of Canadian life in back streets, motel rooms, and even hospitals, where records would be discreetly fudged (e.g., abortions entered as "routine D & C's" [dilatation and curettage] for menstrual complications). Women with money or access to a sympathetic physician were consequently the most likely to get safe abortions.

The first public call for a change in Canada's abortion law came not from an organized movement or political party, but from the media, particularly a 1959 article in *Chatelaine*.[8] Arguing that Canada had the "stiffest abortion law in the world,"[9] it suggested broadening the permissible grounds for abortion to include rape, eugenic considerations, or threat of serious mental or physical breakdown. The article faithfully reflected the key pro-abortion rights arguments of the next decades: (1) abortion needs to be an option in cases such as rape, incest, fetuses with potentially severe deformities, or the burdens of additional children; (2) abortions will always be performed, legally or illegally; (3) competently performed abortions are safe and untraumatic, and can be psychologically beneficial; (4) unwanted children carry the scars of neglect into adulthood; (5) abortion is a matter of individual choice; (6) the fetus is neither a person nor a human being; and (7) the quality of life ultimately matters more than the simple fact of living.

The article is just as interesting for what it omitted, however. For example, abortion was not framed as a "women's issue." While it mentioned women, of course, it never directly identified abortion as a women's issue in the sense that the absence of legalized abortion services reflected societal oppression of women. Moreover, the only passage that invoked the concept of "rights" compared the opposing "right to life" of the mother and fetus. By the 1970s and certainly after the adoption of the Charter of Rights and Freedoms, it was inconceivable that any pro-abortion rights spokesperson would neglect to claim that abortion was every woman's right. The article also overlooked the notion of equity among different categories of women—poor vs. rich, rural vs. urban, educated vs. uneducated. A major pro-abortion rights theme after the 1969 legislative changes was that the law worked inequitably, and hence unjustly, with regard to women in different parts of the country or in different social classes. The silence on these issues simply confirms that there was no feminist (in the modern sense of the term) pro-abortion lobby until the early 1970s.[10]

If there was no organized feminist pressure to liberalize the abortion law, where was the impetus for change? Canadian pro-abortion rights agitation went through two distinct phases before entering the political arena in the 1960s.[11] The first was a preparatory phase in which the issue was championed almost solely in the press. After *Chatelaine's* 1959 article, the abortion question was ignored for two years until the *Globe and Mail* carried a series of editorials, op-ed pieces, and letters to the editor between 1961 and 1963.[12] The *Globe's* key argument was that "thousands of illegal abortions are performed in Canada every year, generally by unqualified persons, and they leave behind them a wake of death and physical and mental wreckage." A law so widely disobeyed "brings all law into contempt."[13]

The second phase began in 1963 and consisted of a review of the abortion question by several professional associations, principally the Canadian Bar Association (CBA) and the Canadian Medical Association (CMA), both of which had an interest in the issue because of its criminal law and medical aspects. The CBA wrestled unsuccessfully with a liberalizing resolution from 1963 to 1965; in 1966 the tide turned and, despite a vocal dissenting minority, the association voted in favour of legalized abortion on grounds of danger to the mother's life or health, unwanted pregnancy due to rape, or danger of a defective child.[14] The CMA took its lead from a proposal developed by the Ontario Medical Association between 1963 and 1965. The resolution called for legalized abortion in cases requiring the preservation of the "life or physical or mental health" of the mother.[15] The first long stage of abortion reform in Canada was not the work of charismatic individuals or broad coalitions. It was the result of uncoordinated actions, coincidental events, and the new sexual consciousness of the 1960s. There was then no organized feminist movement, though women's voices were heard at key points in the debate. As noted earlier, there was no call for abortion as a woman's right; the arguments were entirely pragmatic. A nineteenth-century law was forcing women to seek the services of quacks and butchers, and since no law would ever stop women from needing abortions, the legislation had to be relaxed in order to eradicate the back-alley carnage and exploitation, which at the height of the debate in 1967 was sometimes estimated to involve 100,000 Canadian women a year. The leaders of the 1960s fight were the CBA and the CMA, supported by stinging editorials in the press, principally in the *Globe and Mail*.[16] Since 1892 Canadian physicians had had the option of performing an abortion if that was the only way to save the mother's life. By the 1960s, however, most of the physical

risks of pregnancy had either disappeared or been substantially reduced, and thus
the purely medical grounds for abortions were practically non-existent. All legal
therapeutic abortions were performed in hospitals, which were legally responsible
for every surgical procedure undertaken by medical staff. The therapeutic abortion committees (TACs) that had been informally established by Canadian hospitals were protective devices to shield both doctors and hospitals from legal
liability. The CMA and CBA lobbies in the 1960s wanted the law clarified not in
order to allow more abortions, but to clarify the legal status of physicians who
performed them. Added to the considerable prestige and pressure of the CBA
and CMA were the yearly calls between 1963 and 1966 by the National Council
of Women of Canada for a review of the abortion law.

These pressures for review of abortion might have been fruitless had the
federal government not already been in the midst of a review of other issues
regarding the family and sexuality—legalization of contraceptives and widening
of the grounds for divorce.[17] These legislative initiatives reflected the sexual
revolution of the 1960s. The birth control pill seemed so reliable that unwanted
pregnancies could be considered, for perhaps the first time, as pure accidents.
Cultural concepts of sex, pregnancy, and abortion were radically redefined. Sex
went from being procreational to being recreational; a contracepting woman with
an unwanted pregnancy was an almost entirely innocent third party, and abortion
was a way to rectify the error. Added to this were the tragic thalidomide cases,
which focused world attention on quality-of-life issues, for both newborns and
parents. This was the new social landscape upon which abortion would be situated
in the 1960s.

Another important factor was the disorganized nature of the anti-abortion
rights activists. While many were Catholic, the Canadian Roman Catholic
Church—which might have been expected to lead the resistance—"did not play
a leading role in the formation of the right-to-life movement in Canada."[18] The
second Vatican Council (1962–65) absorbed so much energy from the Canadian
bishops, and generated so much turmoil on the issue of contraception, that the
Canadian Catholic hierarchy did not react to the abortion controversy until 1967.[19]
At that point the Church's arguments against liberalized abortion were over-
whelmed by pragmatic arguments in favour of change coming from the CBA, the
CMA, and other scattered associations. Other Christian denominations, such as
the United and Anglican churches, either vacillated on the issue or cautiously
endorsed a relaxed law. The fractured Christian consensus on abortion made the
Catholic Church seem isolated as well as backward.[20]

Inset I

CRIMINAL CODE, 1970
CHAPTER C-34, SECTION 251

(1) Everyone who, with intent to procure the miscarriage of a female person, whether or not she is pregnant, uses any means for the purpose of carrying out his intention is guilty of an indictable offence and is liable to imprisonment for life.

(2) Every female person who, being pregnant, with intent to procure her own miscarriage, uses any means for the purpose of carrying out her intention is guilty of an indictable offence and is liable to imprisonment for two years.

(3) In this section "means" includes

  (a) the administration of a drug or other noxious thing;

  (b) the use of an instrument; and

  (c) manipulation of any kind.

(4) Subsections (1) and (2) do not apply to

  (a) a qualified medical practitioner, other than a member of a therapeutic abortion committee for any hospital, who in good faith uses in an accredited or approved hospital any means for the purpose of carrying out his intention to procure the miscarriage of a female person, or

  (b) a female person who, being pregnant, permits a qualified medical practitioner to use in an accredited or approved hospital any means for the purpose of carrying out her intention to procure her own miscarriage, if, before the use of those means, the therapeutic abortion committee for that accredited or approved hospital, by a majority of the members of the committee and at a meeting of the committee at which the case of the female person has been reviewed,

  (c) has by certificate in writing stated that in its opinion the continuation of the pregnancy of the female person would or would be likely to endanger her life or health, and

  (d) has caused a copy of such certificate to be given to the qualified medical practitioner.

NOTE: Sect. 251 contained three other subsections not reproduced here. Subsection 5 gave the provincial ministers of health the power to demand copies of abortion certificates, while subsections 6 and 7 defined the terms in the other sections.

Finally, the appointment of Pierre Trudeau as justice minister in April 1967 brightened the outlook for liberalized abortion (along with birth control, divorce, and homosexuality), since Trudeau was a known supporter of relaxed legislation.

As a result of these forces and pressures, the abortion issue finally reached the parliamentary arena in October 1967. On 3 October 1967 the House of Commons Standing Committee on Health and Welfare began hearings on three private member's bills (two NDP and one Liberal) on abortion. The Liberal bill would simply have legislated the prevailing practice in many Canadian hospitals of having applications to perform abortions reviewed by physicians on a TAC. The two NDP bills would have liberalized access to abortions. The Committee heard from several organizations in its October–December meetings.[21] Henry Morgentaler, as past president of the Humanist Fellowship of Montreal, was asked to present its brief on 19 October 1967. He recommended that "any woman should have the right to have termination of pregnancy on request up to three months of pregnancy."[22] He was suggesting a standard of viability: when the fetus is capable of living, with assistance, outside the mother (roughly at six months after conception) it becomes a "baby" and should not be aborted. Committee exchanges with Morgentaler and other witnesses were often sharp, emotional, and sarcastic. The MPs were as divided in their opinions as their witnesses were.

It was surprising, therefore, when on 19 December 1967 the Committee handed down an interim report. With a bare quorum of thirteen members, it voted 11–2 in favour of a relaxed abortion law. Noting that "opinion on abortion varies widely throughout Canada," the Committee proposed that therapeutic abortions be permitted where "pregnancy will seriously endanger the life or the health of the mother."[23] Something was up, and two days later, in a move that caught almost everyone by surprise, the government tabled an omnibus bill to amend various sections of the Criminal Code, including abortion. It was clearly a masterstroke designed to minimize controversy over the morality provisions of the bill: on the same day that the bill was introduced, it was read for the first time, and Parliament immediately adjourned for the Christmas holiday. Abortion was to be legal if a woman's continued pregnancy "would or would be likely to endanger her life or health." The omnibus bill had to be re-introduced after the 1968 election, and full debate (for four acrimonious months) only began in January 1969. The closest that the House of Commons came to a specific vote on abortion was on 9 May 1969, when the government allowed a motion to delete the abortion clause from the omnibus bill. Interestingly, 143 of 264 MPs were present (54 per cent), with 107 of them voting against deletion (i.e., in favour of the abortion clause), and 36 for.[24] The omnibus bill, including all revisions to the Criminal Code, was passed by the Commons on 14 May and became law on 27 June 1969. With its passage Canada had a new abortion law in the form of section 251 of the Criminal Code (see Inset I).

Section 251 can be broken down conceptually into two key parts. The first (subsections 1 and 2) stated that anyone who attempted to perform an abortion on a pregnant woman was liable to life imprisonment (self-induced abortions were liable to two years' imprisonment). The second (subsection 4) listed the exceptions against the first part. Abortion was legal only if (1) it was performed by a qualified physician in (2) an accredited or approved hospital whose (3) TAC had a certified majority opinion that the "continuation of the pregnancy of such a female person would or would be likely to endanger her life or health." The TAC had to have at least three members, each of whom was a qualified physician at that hospital.[25] Thus, in terms of its strict legal language, the new abortion section of the Criminal Code was at best only a modest liberalization of the pre-1969 practice that absolved doctors of criminal liability if they performed an abortion to save the mother's life. The problem with that "saving provision" had been that it was somewhat narrow; that was why hospitals had set up TACs in the first place, to ensure that abortions were within the law.

Section 251 had several weaknesses. From a feminist perspective, it still left the real control over abortions in the hands of doctors, not women. Moreover, that control was exercised through a time-consuming, bureaucratic process involving TACs and certificates. While the legislation did not compel hospitals to establish TACs, no abortion was legal in Canada unless approved by a TAC.[26] The justificatory language was so vague ("would be likely to endanger her life or health") that it could conceivably include anything from the simple mental stress of having a child to a real physical threat to life. The same legislation could be read as either too slack or too narrow. The incentives to disobey remained strong, and it was difficult to enforce the law—police officers could scarcely patrol every hospital and back alley.

It should not be surprising, in light of all of these factors, that the 1969 abortion law generated dissatisfaction on both sides of the issue. From the pro-abortion rights perspective, the law simply recapitulated the prevailing practice and tidied up the legal language. Abortion in Canada would be mired in red tape and humiliating bureaucratic delays, and women would continue to suffer. Those opposed to abortion saw disaster of another sort: the law's ambiguous phrasing on endangerment would encourage routine abortion for almost any reason. Both sides felt that the government had outwitted and outmanoeuvred them. Both were determined to win next time.

FEMINISM, HENRY MORGENTALER, AND THE QUEBEC TRIALS, 1969–76

For two weeks they carried the coffin across Canada, down the streets of Kamloops, Edmonton, Regina, Winnipeg, the Lakehead, Sudbury, and Toronto. In every place they stopped, they gathered petitions for abortion reform. The trek had started in Vancouver on 27 April 1970 and culminated in a two-day demonstration in Ottawa. On 9 May about 500 women rallied on Parliament Hill and then made their way to 24 Sussex Drive, brandishing coat hangers, lilies, and the coffin for the women who had died at abortionists' hands. Two days later, a small group chained themselves to the Commons Visitor's Gallery and shouted "Free Abortion on Demand" and "Every Child a Wanted Child" at the gaping MPs below. This was the Abortion Caravan, the first organized fusion of feminism and the abortion issue in Canada.[27]

The Canadian feminist movement was submerged in the New Left politics of the middle and late 1960s, a politics that hinged on student radicalism and anti-war protests. A key group in this early phase was the Student Union for Peace Action (SUPA), formed in Regina in 1964 to coordinate political action aimed at abolishing war, racism, and poverty.[28] SUPA, for all its rhetoric of liberation, was organized along classic sexist lines: the "girls" made sandwiches and placards while the "guys" made speeches and revolution. When SUPA dissolved in 1967, many female radicals had begun to re-conceptualize their experience in feminist terms. This migration of activists from the New Left to feminism showed up in the Abortion Caravan, which was conceived by the Vancouver Women's Caucus, many of whose members had been SUPA activists at Simon Fraser University.[29] As one sympathetic observer put it at the time, "Abortion law reform is one of many concerns of women's liberation, but it has served as no other issue to link university and working women, the economically comfortable and the poor, young and middle-aged in an urgent personal struggle to achieve a definable goal."[30] The Abortion Caravan was the "glue that stuck the first feminist network in Canada together."[31] Not all feminists were convinced that free abortion on demand should be the movement's highest priority, but the left wing (especially the Young Socialists, a Trotskyist group) kept up the pro-abortion rights momentum in the early years.[32]

Whereas in the 1960s the critique of the abortion law had been based on almost purely pragmatic considerations, the new feminist movement introduced the idea of rights into the debate. The 1970 Report of the Royal Commission on the Status of Women reflected the shift by making both arguments simultaneously in favour of liberalization. The Commission pointed out that the 1969 law would have no effect on the number of illegal abortions and consequent maternal deaths and injuries, and moreover that it discriminated against women who could not afford an abortion outside Canada. But the Commission then shifted ground to the rights argument: "We have come to the conclusion that each woman should have the right to decide if she will terminate pregnancy."[33] The Commission recommended abortion on demand for women pregnant for twelve weeks or less; women pregnant longer than that would have to be endangered physically or mentally by the pregnancy, or face a "substantial risk" that the child would be greatly handicapped if born.[34]

The Abortion Caravan and the Royal Commission report were symptomatic of rising dissatisfaction with the new abortion law. As a physician in general family practice and as someone who was a known supporter of liberalized abortion, Henry Morgentaler experienced the law's limitations directly in the supplications of the desperate women who visited his Montreal office. After Morgentaler presented the Humanist Fellowship brief on abortion in 1967 to the Standing Committee on Health and Welfare, the subsequent publicity attracted numerous calls from women seeking abortions. For a year he refused to do abortions, referring the women instead to doctors who would. The personal risks were just too great—a possible life sentence, the ruination of his career, and the financial collapse of his family. But Morgentaler knew that he was living a lie: how could he attack the abortion law as unjust and yet refuse to help women victimized by that injustice? In 1968 he made a decision that changed the course of Canada's abortion politics, a decision that almost twenty years later would grow into one of the country's most important constitutional decisions under the new Charter of Rights and Freedoms. He decided to do abortions, without fanfare at first, but openly and even proudly. In what became his trademark tactic, he simply declared the law to be unjust, openly broke it, defied the authorities to arrest and prosecute him, and then fought his case implacably in the courts. Henry Morgentaler was different, even extraordinary, not because of his convictions, since these were shared by many, but because of his complete refusal to surrender. No sanction, no fine, no jail term, no law would stop him. What events shaped this man and placed him on Canada's historical stage?

Henry Morgentaler was born and grew up in the Polish textile city of Lodz. His parents were Jews who had rejected their religion in favour of socialism, and the young Morgentaler felt triply ostracized and unwanted: as a Jew, as a socialist, and by his own mother, who he was convinced did not love him.[35] Morgentaler's anti-Catholicism sprang from these experiences, since the Polish Catholic churches were notoriously anti-Semitic.[36] Morgentaler and his family spent 1939–44 in the Lodz ghetto under German occupation. His father, sister, and girlfriend were taken away and disappeared, and in 1944 Morgentaler, his younger brother,

and his mother were transported to Auschwitz. His mother was removed and he
never saw her again. Morgentaler was also separated from his brother for a time,
but the two were re-united after the war. The ghetto, Auschwitz, and the horror
he witnessed there left Henry Morgentaler an atheist.[37]

Re-united with his childhood sweetheart after the war, Morgentaler pursued
medical studies in Germany, and then the two of them sailed to Canada in 1950.
It took Morgentaler five years to get his medical diploma, his citizenship, and
finally a licence to practise medicine, but he soon established himself as a general
practitioner in an east-end working-class district of Montreal. In 1961, despite
financial and professional success, a family and a home, Morgentaler was unhappy.
He underwent psychoanalysis to deal with his discontent and the feeling that
"something deep down was unfulfilled."[38] His marriage dissolved and he began
to look outside himself for a larger public role. In 1964 he became the president
of the Montreal Humanist Fellowship and gradually began to feel that being active
"as a sort of mover of history" was important. His psychoanalysis had shown him
that his Holocaust experiences had crushed him into a sense of impotence. He
realized, as he put it,

> that I could do something—not merely survive, but use my personality, my
> talents, and my abilities in a very active way. Later, I came to the conclusion
> that, under some circumstances, it is imperative to defy authority—necessary
> for my self-esteem, to prove my manhood in direct conflict.[39]

In 1968 Morgentaler decided to mesh his political convictions with his medical
work, and concentrated on family practice (i.e., fitting IUDs, prescribing oral contraceptives, and performing vasectomies and abortions). At that time there were
two principal abortion techniques. The one used most commonly by illegal abortionists was the insertion of some long, sharp object to puncture the amniotic sac.
The procedure could introduce infections, and left the woman alone to cope with
the miscarriage and its aftermath. The other technique was dilatation and curettage (D&C), a somewhat tricky surgical procedure that required full anaesthetic.[40]
It was safer, but required a skilled surgeon, as well as the full array of hospital
services to deal with the anaesthetic and recovery. Morgentaler's research led him
to a technique developed in 1958 in China and just beginning to be used in
Europe, though still unknown in Canada—vacuum aspiration or vacuum suction.
He ordered a vacuum aspirator from England, managed to get it past dozing
Customs officials, and began to train himself in the technique. As its name implies,
vacuum aspiration involves insertion into the uterus of a hollow plastic rod (called
a cannula), which is connected to a vacuum aspirator with clear plastic tubing.
The cannula is run around the uterus, and the machine sucks out the fetus. The

only anaesthetic is the para-cervical block to allow dilatation: the patient is awake for the entire procedure. The transparent tubing allows the abortionist to gauge whether the fetal matter has been completely extracted, though Morgentaler added a modified supplementary curettage to ensure that nothing would remain to cause bleeding or infection. The entire procedure lasts from about five to fifteen minutes, and is virtually painless except for some mild uterine cramps.[41] Morgentaler charged from $250 to $300 per abortion, though he always claimed to reduce his fees for indigent women.

By introducing vacuum aspiration techniques to Canada, Morgentaler dramatically changed the assumptions that had underpinned previous legislation. A Morgentaler abortion did not require a hospital, an anaesthetist, or even a particularly skilled physician; no complicated medical histories were needed, and patients were done in thirty minutes; the investment in medical equipment was minuscule (about $5,000 in 1970), and not much more than a general practice office was needed, with only a few staff.[42] Abortion clinics no longer had to be housed in major hospitals—they could now be established in local neighbour-hoods. That is precisely what Morgentaler did in 1969 with his first abortion clinic at an unassuming Montreal bungalow at 2990 Rue Honoré-Beaugrand. He kept a low profile, but word spread and clients increased. It was only a matter of time before provincial authorities came after him (in Canada, criminal law is enforced by provincial authorities): without hospital accreditation, a TAC, or certification of mother's health, he was clearly breaking the law. On 1 June 1970 his clinic was raided by Montreal police, and three days later Morgentaler was charged with conspiracy to commit abortion and procuring abortion.

Morgentaler had clearly violated section 251 of the Criminal Code. Police, in conducting their rather heavy-handed raid, had accumulated sufficient evidence to show (indeed, Morgentaler never denied it) that he had performed abortions outside the law. The issue was not that clear, however, because the justice system assumes that charges must be proved and gives the accused an opportunity to defend him/herself. Morgentaler's Montreal lawyer was the flamboyant and shrewd Claude Armand-Sheppard, who knew that with a jury trial, his client's only chance was to have public opinion behind him. Armand-Sheppard recog-nized, as did Morgentaler's subsequent lawyers in the Winnipeg and Toronto cases, that the trials were in fact political manoeuvres in the guise of courtroom tactics. The court cases were condensations of vast forces swirling around a single issue—the whole weight of the pro- and anti-abortion rights arguments, the entire edifice of Canada's abortion laws, rested on the thin shoulders of a Montreal doctor who could be perceived as either a saintly guardian of women's rights or a criminal making money from human misery. Morgentaler's Jewishness made him an easy target for latent anti-Semitism. Armand-Sheppard decided that Quebec public opinion was not yet ready to support Henry Morgentaler, and he released a battery of writs, motions, and appeals that threw the charges into legal limbo for over three years.[43]

Morgentaler was out on bail during this time, and regularly attracted attention by criticizing the abortion law as well as what he considered the stupid and hypocritical legal system that upheld it. He was emboldened to take stronger action when, on 22 January 1973, the United States Supreme Court handed down its decision in *Roe vs. Wade* and legalized abortion throughout America.[44] The pro-abortion rights movement was encouraged by the decision, and decided that it could push harder for legislative change in Canada.[45] On 16 March 1973 Morgentaler announced to a Toronto rally that he had personally aborted over five thousand women: the meeting erupted in applause and cheers, and the crowd of feminists and civil libertarians went wild, giving Morgentaler a standing ovation.[46] Morgentaler made the same announcement several times in the next week, but while his clinic remained under surveillance, there were no raids and no new charges. His challenge to the federal and provincial authorities was stunning: from the perspective of the Criminal Code and the criminal justice system, that is, from the point of view of what is law, it was as though he had publicly admitted committing five thousand murders or five thousand rapes. Still nothing happened. The last straw was a CTV broadcast of a W5 documentary showing Morgentaler performing an abortion at his clinic. The show aired on 13 May 1973—Mother's Day.

The system finally lashed back at Henry Morgentaler on 15 August 1973. Seventeen policemen stormed into his clinic while he was doing an abortion. They arrested Morgentaler, eleven patients, three nurses, and a receptionist. Morgentaler finally went before a jury of eleven men and one woman on 18 October 1973, three years after the first charges against him had been laid. Armand-Sheppard's defence was based on section 45 of the Criminal Code, which absolved anyone of criminal liability in performing a surgical procedure as long as the procedure was done with reasonable care and it was reasonable to do the operation. This was supplemented and eventually overshadowed by the "defence of necessity" granted in common law.[47] The defence of necessity, like all common law principles, is general and must be applied case by case, but implied an immunity from criminal liability for performing an abortion if it was necessary to save the life of the mother.

The trial took a month. In the end, the jury deliberated for almost ten hours, reappearing periodically for advice on the meaning of section 45, and finally acquitted Morgentaler on 13 November 1973. The Crown immediately appealed to the Quebec Court of Appeal, but in the meantime the Quebec Revenue department came after Morgentaler for $354,799 it claimed he owed in back taxes on revenues from his self-confessed five thousand to seven thousand abortions.[48] Provincial tax assessors seized Morgentaler's professional and private documents, diaries and tapes, and closed his bank account. At this point it became clear that the law and the government intended to make an example of this Montreal abortionist who had goaded and insulted them into action. This impression must have been confirmed for Morgentaler on 25 April 1974, when the Quebec Court of Appeal upheld the Crown's appeal of Morgentaler's jury acquittal. It ruled that the necessity defence could not properly be invoked in this case since abortion was legally available—there had, in short, been choices and opportunities, not "necessity."[49] More astonishing than this, however, was that the Court of Appeal then proceeded to overturn the jury acquittal and substitute a conviction. It instructed the judge who had presided over the jury trial to sentence Morgentaler, but since Morgentaler had immediately appealed to the Supreme Court, the trial judge declined. On 14 May the Court of Appeal directly ordered sentencing, and Morgentaler was placed in the Parthenais maximum-security prison to await the decision. On 25 July 1974 he was sentenced to eighteen months in prison and three years' probation. His only hope was that the Supreme Court would strike down the Court of Appeal's power to substitute a conviction for a jury acquittal. His hopes were dashed when eight months later, on 26 March 1975, the Supreme Court rejected his appeal.[50] The next day Morgentaler was taken to the Bordeaux jail. Without his clinic, his bank account, or his freedom, he seemed finished.

The Quebec trials and their implications were far from over. The Supreme Court decision to uphold the power of a Court of Appeal to substitute conviction for jury acquittal seemed such a gross affront to the role of juries in a democratic system that the federal government in late 1975 passed the "Morgentaler amendment" to the Criminal Code, allowing Courts of Appeal to set aside jury acquittals and order new trials, but not to reverse those acquittals. Other developments were not so benign. On 5 May 1975, when Morgentaler had been in jail for only about a month, Quebec Attorney General Jerome Choquette once again signed preferred indictments against him on new abortion charges. It seems that Quebec officials hoped to get Morgentaler to plead guilty in exchange for being allowed to serve concurrent sentences.[51] Morgentaler refused to plead guilty to anything, went before another jury (seven men and five women), used the defence of necessity (which the judge explicitly told the jury it could not consider), and on 9 June 1975 was acquitted. The Crown predictably appealed, but on 20 January 1976 the Quebec Court of Appeal upheld the acquittal. The Crown appealed this too. In a somewhat bizarre gesture of redress, Ron Basford, the new federal minister of justice, set aside Morgentaler's conviction on the first trial and ordered a re-trial before a jury. (There had been some pressure in cabinet to pardon Morgentaler, but this was as far as Basford was prepared to go.) On 18 September 1976 a jury acquitted Morgentaler on the first set of charges on which he had been tried twice before, once before a jury and once before the Quebec Court of Appeal. That same day, the Crown announced that it would press fresh charges against Morgentaler in early November. Morgentaler's salvation came from a fitting enough source: public opinion. On 15 November 1976 the people of Quebec turned against the ruling Liberals and elected a *Parti québécois* government. The new justice minister, Marc Andre-Bedard, announced that there would be no further attempts to prosecute Morgentaler or any other doctor performing abortions in Quebec. The federal abortion law was clearly unenforceable.

By deliberately breaking the law and goading the authorities, Morgentaler turned himself into a martyr, and like all martyrs he suffered. He had to close his abortion clinic, his medical licence was revoked, and the Revenue department pursued him for a settlement on back taxes. He had had a heart attack while in prison. The woman he had lived with for years left him; his first wife demanded a divorce. It took him several years to re-establish himself. But, also like most martyrs, he had some victories. Even though his attack on the federal law had failed, he could get some satisfaction that abortions for almost one-third of the Canadian population—all of Quebec—were available and would eventually be supported by public funds. His trials had forced the Morgentaler amendment, undeniably an important buttress for civil liberties in Canada. In September 1975 Ottawa appointed a Committee on the Operation of the Abortion Law (the Badgley Committee), and while its 1977 report eschewed any recommendations, it provided credible evidence of the law's shortcomings.

Morgentaler's travails had little discernible effect, however, on public opinion. In 1976, at the height of his notoriety, a national survey commissioned by the Badgley Committee showed that "there was no strong mandate either to 'tighten' or to 'reform' the existing legislation...most persons implicitly endorsed the status quo."[52] There was no broad, national demand for a new law. In the long run, Morgentaler's most important victory was in becoming a symbol. Paradoxically, this *man* came to represent one of the most critical issues of *women's* rights. The balance between Morgentaler and feminism in the abortion battles of the mid-1970s was an interesting illustration of the concatenation of individual struggles and broad political movements. Feminism as a movement nurtured most of the pro-abortion thinking after 1970, but movements do not go to court, individuals do. As well, in the case of a challenge to the abortion law, a renegade physician like Morgentaler was needed because of the medical nature of the procedure.

Morgentaler was not a feminist, but his personal agenda coincided nicely with that of the women's movement in the period. But he could not pursue his crusade on his own. Later, in the Winnipeg and Toronto battles, his potent symbolic force and adamancy were wedded much more intimately to a support network both to staff the clinics and to help raise funds for his legal bills. Until then, however, Morgentaler nursed his wounds and steeled his will for the next, ultimate, confrontation.

WINNIPEG, TORONTO, AND THE SUPREME COURT, 1982–88

Throughout the 1970s, Henry Morgentaler and his supporters claimed that in their actions they were only exercising the right and responsibility of civil disobedience. From the anti-abortion rights perspective, of course, they were simply breaking the law. Morgentaler's deliberate disobedience incensed his opponents almost as much as the idea that he was, from their viewpoint, a cold-blooded baby killer. One man who had watched Morgentaler from afar became convinced that two could play the courtroom game. Joe Borowski, a former trade unionist, a former Manitoba NDP cabinet minister, and an oddball character with a strange mix of unflinching integrity and single-minded determination, became in the early 1970s a leading and outspoken opponent of abortion. His reasons were an amalgam of legal principles (respect for the rule of law) and religious conviction (he is Catholic).[53] He resigned his cabinet post in 1971 and left the NDP to fight abortion, and in particular to fight Henry Morgentaler.

Morgentaler's 1975 Supreme Court appeal had been the first attempt to claim a "right to abortion" under the Canadian Bill of Rights (the 1961 predecessor of the Charter of Rights and Freedoms). While the Court had dismissed the argument, Borowski realized that it might cut both ways: if medical evidence could be adduced to show that the fetus was a human life from the moment of conception, then it might gain the status of a "person" under law and receive all the protections available thereby. Borowski engaged Morris Shumiatcher, one of Canada's most distinguished jurists and a former president of the Canadian Civil Liberties Union, to argue the case. To cut travel costs, the case was launched in 1977 in Shumiatcher's home town of Regina rather than in Winnipeg. Federal lawyers immediately challenged Borowski on two points: whether he had any right to bring such a case to trial (whether he had standing) and whether the case should be heard in provincial rather than federal court. It took four years simply to resolve these procedural issues. They went all the way to the Supreme Court, which in December 1981 decided, on the first question, that Borowski did have standing and that he could challenge the 1969 abortion law on behalf of the unborn. It took another nine months for the Court to decide that the challenge should be launched in provincial rather than federal court. So, as of August 1982, Joe Borowski and Morris Shumiatcher began preparations for their case before the Saskatchewan Court of Queen's Bench in Regina.

Morgentaler was enraged when he heard that Borowski had been granted standing.[54] Morgentaler had lain low since 1976, rebuilding his life and relatively happy with the abortion situation in Quebec. He was less happy with developments outside Quebec. On the face of it, the pro-abortion rights movement had become institutionalized in various committees and coalitions for the establishment of abortion clinics, and had succeeded at the ground level in creating "women's health centres" that provided reproductive counselling and abortion referrals. And in a brilliant strategic move, the mainstream of the movement had re-designated itself as "pro-choice." The slogan of "free abortion on demand" had little appeal for the broad Canadian public. "Choice," on the other hand, had the cachet of individual liberty and acceptance of different lifestyles. Who could oppose "choice"? But while the number of abortions had increased steadily from 1970 (in 1980 there were 65,855 abortions as opposed to 368,030 live births, or 17.8 abortions for every 100 births), there were signs that anti-abortion rights forces were beginning to rally. Morgentaler claimed that one-third of the 2,000 abortions his Quebec clinic performed annually were for out-of-province women.[55] Throughout the country, anti-abortion rights groups had succeeded in closing several hospital TACs—in Newfoundland, for example, there was only one hospital left in 1982 that performed abortions.

Morgentaler decided to once again enter the fray. On 4 April 1982 he sent federal Justice Minister Jean Chrétien a telegram demanding reform to the abortion law. He said that he was considering establishing private abortion clinics in other provinces because "no jury in any major city in Canada would find me guilty for such a humanitarian action."[56] Within a week the League for Life of Manitoba sent telegrams to Chrétien and Roland Penner, the NDP attorney general for Manitoba, vowing to fight Morgentaler if he tried to establish a Winnipeg clinic.[57] The Manitoba College of Physicians and Surgeons followed some months later by stating that it would not license a Morgentaler abortion clinic, and Roland Penner said that he would not stay prosecution if Morgentaler broke the law.[58] By this time Morgentaler had made it clear that his key targets were Winnipeg and Toronto, the former because its NDP provincial government was on record as supporting liberalized abortion, and the latter in large part because he had been invited by a coalition of pro-abortion rights groups.[59] The strategy in both cases was the same: deliberately break the law, force the authorities to prosecute, get a jury acquittal, and expose the abortion law as insupportable and unenforceable. Morgentaler was playing his Quebec card. He made this clear in a Winnipeg press conference on 30 November 1982. Roland Penner, in a meeting with Morgentaler that day, had reiterated his position that while he was personally "pro-choice," as the provincial attorney general he was bound to uphold the law. Morgentaler said that he would go ahead and establish a clinic anyway, and as in Quebec, would use the defence of necessity if he went to trial.[60] A week later Roy McMurtry, the attorney general for Ontario, also warned that he would have no choice but to prosecute if Morgentaler performed illegal abortions.[61]

The following year was exceedingly busy and confusing. It saw three separate court actions, the establishment of two clinics (one each in Winnipeg and Toronto), several raids and arrests, and many marches and demonstrations. Morgentaler himself was threatened by a Toronto man brandishing clipping shears, and someone else tried to burn down his Toronto clinic.

Borowski's trial was colourful, but the case remained under appeal by year's end. Several groups saw the significance of Borowski's legal gambit and sought standing in the case. On 23 January 1983 Mr. Justice Matheson of the Saskatchewan Court of Queen's Bench denied such standing to the Canadian Abortion Rights Action League, the Canadian Civil Liberties Union, and Campaign Life. He scheduled the case for 9 May. In 1982, however, the Canadian Charter of Rights and Freedoms had been adopted as part of Canada's constitution, and so when the case opened in Regina, Shumiatcher changed his argument (from the old Canadian Bill of Rights) to claim that the abortion law was unconstitutional because it violated the unborn child's "right to life" under section 7 of the Charter. Shumiatcher set out over the next weeks to show that TACs were merely a rubber-stamp for abortions and that leading international medical experts believed that life begins at or around conception. Federal lawyers simply rejected the relevance of these arguments; they set out to show that the abortion law was a valid law, however it might be interpreted by TACs, and that the fetus, whether alive or not, was not a legal person until born.[62] The case ended on 27 May 1983, and Justice Matheson reserved his decision until 13 October. He decided against Borowski, ruling that section 251 of the Criminal Code was a valid law and that the fetus was not a legal person. The case had cost Borowski $350,000 (most of it raised through donations), but he freely admitted that this was only the "first round in a three-round bout," the next steps being the Saskatchewan Court of Appeal and finally the Supreme Court of Canada.[63] A month later Borowski filed a formal notice of appeal.[64] The Saskatchewan Court of Appeal hearing did not begin until 15 December 1985.

Opponents rallied the moment that Morgentaler announced he would open a Winnipeg abortion clinic in March 1983.[65] They tried to have his municipal permits revoked, 1,800 local residents signed a petition opposing the clinic, another 35,000-name petition was published in the *Winnipeg Free Press*, and demonstrators picketed the opening on 7 May. Morgentaler had written to the provincial health minister asking to have his clinic declared an "approved hospital" and therefore a legal abortion facility under section 251. The application was denied, but Morgentaler opened anyway.[66] Since he was openly flouting the law, it was merely a matter of time before charges were laid. Police raided the clinic on the morning of 3 June 1983, arriving in six squad cars and striding through the ranks of surprised anti-abortion pickets. Borowski rushed to the clinic minutes after the raid began to express his jubilation that the clinic was closed. Eleven people were taken away, but Morgentaler was not among them. He was in Montreal.[67] He had enlisted the services of Dr. Robert Scott, an Ontario physician, to do abortions at the Winnipeg clinic. On 10 June police laid charges of conspiracy to procure abortions against Morgentaler, Scott, and six staff members.[68]

Morgentaler was far from chastened by the raid and the charges. He reopened the Winnipeg clinic on 6 June, and two days later, at a press conference in Toronto, he announced that he would open a Toronto clinic on Harbord Street in one week, despite promises by Roy McMurtry to lay charges if he did.[69] The clinic would be staffed by Dr. Leslie Smoling, and Morgentaler and his supporters showed that they were preparing for a long and expensive legal battle—they announced a Pro-Choice Defence Fund with a target of $500,000. At this point, Morgentaler began to fight a two-front war. On 14 June he appeared in Winnipeg to face conspiracy charges, and the following day he was in Toronto to open his new clinic. The Harbord clinic opening was a macabre circus: pro- and anti-abortion rights pickets marched before the clinic, and within an hour of opening a man attacked Morgentaler with garden shears.[70] On 25 June Winnipeg police raided the clinic for the second time, once again arresting Scott and the clinic staff, and laying more charges. They also seized the abortion equipment and files as evidence. Predictably, Morgentaler vowed to re-open.[71] On 5 July Toronto police raided the Harbord Street clinic, seized equipment and files, arrested Smoling, and issued a warrant for Morgentaler's arrest. Minutes later, clinic staff defiantly re-opened the clinic. Morgentaler surrendered himself on 7 July.[72]

In 1982 it seemed that abortion was "the forgotten issue of the women's movement in Canada."[73] Henry Morgentaler and Joe Borowski changed all that. And yet the political process proved remarkably resilient after Morgentaler's first conviction. Politicians obviously had no taste to tackle Canada's most divisive public issue. They could find support for inaction from polls that showed that the broad centre of the population could live with section 251. Pro- and anti-abortion rights forces, of course, could not live with the law, and had decided ultimately to pursue the judicial route. But before the Charter of Rights and Freedoms this had not been notably successful either, since without a constitutional standard of rights (which is what the Charter provides) against which to measure laws, the courts cannot "strike down" legislation. The judicial route had to be supplemented with a strategy to win over public opinion. Thus the struggle moved inevitably back to the streets: indeed, the demonstrations were meant to send signals to politicians and conceivably even judges. Pro-choice rallies occurred through the summer in both Winnipeg and Toronto, and small knots of anti-abortion picketers kept vigils at the clinics. The war of street numbers eventually culminated in the 1 October National Day of Action for Choice. While pro- and anti-abortion rights groups turned out in small numbers across Canada, Toronto saw about twenty thousand anti-abortion protesters march silently by Morgentaler's clinic (some estimates were as high as forty thousand).[74] Simultaneously, a small group of one thousand to two thousand pro-abortion rights supporters rallied at Toronto City Hall. This was a setback to the prestige of the pro-abortion rights movement, and suggested that the political momentum might have shifted against it.[75] But in a fundamental sense, street politics mattered less now than did legal manoeuvres. The courts and the lawyers had seized the issue, and they would relentlessly pursue it to the finish.

Morgentaler faced two sets of charges and two court appearances in Winnipeg and Toronto. The Toronto trial of Morgentaler, Scott, and Smoling began on 21 November (the Ontario Attorney General had decided to skip the preliminary hearing and go directly to trial) before Mr. Justice W.D. Parker of the Supreme Court of Ontario. Morris Manning, Morgentaler's lawyer, immediately launched a challenge to the abortion law's constitutionality based on its violation of several rights listed in the Charter of Rights and Freedoms.[76] Thus before the court could proceed to the charges against the three doctors, it had to decide whether the law upon which the charges were based was constitutionally valid. With the beginning of the Ontario trial, the Winnipeg case fell into limbo and never revived. The Manitoba government and the courts agreed to postpone the Winnipeg trial until the Toronto one was completed, but the Toronto case eventually led to the Supreme Court. This was not the end of other battles with Manitoban authorities, however. Morgentaler re-opened the Winnipeg clinic on 23 March 1985; it was raided the same day and new charges were laid. Six days later the Manitoba College of Physicians and Surgeons suspended his medical licence for his "apparent willful and deliberate resort" to breaking the law. Morgentaler vowed both to re-open the clinic and to continue to perform abortions, even without a licence. Police raided the clinic again on 30 March, and Morgentaler entered a court battle to regain his medical licence that involved appeals up to the Manitoba Court of Appeal in 1986. But these were mere skirmishes. The real action had shifted to Toronto.

The 250-seat Toronto courtroom was crammed with pro- and anti-abortion rights supporters as Morris Manning began his assault on the abortion law's constitutionality. Mr. Justice Parker heard Manning argue that the abortion law violated rights to life, liberty, and security of the person; the right to freedom of thought, belief, opinion, and expression; and the right not to be subjected to cruel and unusual treatment. For good measure, Manning added that the federal abortion law, since it dealt with hospital procedures, violated provincial jurisdiction over health.[77] In support of these arguments, Manning called witnesses and tried to adduce evidence that current abortion procedures actually threatened the mental and physical health of women, were ensnared in bureaucratic red tape, and were accessible only to women who could afford to travel. Manning went on for four weeks, but when the moment came for federal and Ontario government lawyers Arthur Pennington and Alan Cooper to rebut, they refused, simply asserting that it was not Judge Parker's job to decide how laws are to be applied. They argued that the law was valid in the strict legal sense, and that its administration was not a constitutional matter for courts to decide.[78]

Manning summed up his arguments on 19 and 20 January 1984. Pennington and Cooper summed up in March, making three arguments. The first was that the fetus is a human life, and that aborting it is not akin to removing a wart. No one has to decide—indeed, no one can—whether the fetus is a person, but it has value, and the law's purpose is not simply to regard the rights of the mother, but to balance those rights against the rights of the fetus. The second argument was less impassioned but equally important: the simple fact that not all Canadians had equal access to abortion facilities did not invalidate the law, since many federal programmes were "marred" in this way. Finally, they warned Judge Parker against usurping the role of Parliament and "Americanizing" the Canadian Charter of Rights and Freedoms by imposing the views of an unelected judge on the people. Parliamentary transcripts clearly showed that during the constitutional debates, both government and official opposition did not want section 7 of the Charter to apply to abortion.[79] And so was raised a new and puzzling question: are the courts to judge disputes in law, or are they, armed now with the Charter, to make laws? The Charter, as part of the constitution, is the standard against which all Canadian laws must be judged. That judgment, of course, comes from the courts. But how far can the courts go in using the Charter to strike down laws, however imperfect, that have been made by a democratically elected legislature? In this case, the evidence was clear that the politicians had thought they were preventing the application of section 7 of the Charter to abortion. Yet Henry Morgentaler had no doubts that he and his supporters, in seeking legislative change, "may succeed in the judicial sphere where we have not succeeded in the political sphere."[80]

Judge Parker took the spring to make up his mind, no doubt aware that the stakes were high enough that almost any ruling he made would ultimately be appealed to the Supreme Court of Canada. On 20 July 1984 he decided against Morgentaler and Manning. He rejected all of Manning's arguments on the grounds that the Charter only protects freedoms so deeply rooted in the country's traditions that they may be deemed fundamental. "No unfettered legal right to an abortion can be found in our law, nor can it be said that a right to an abortion is deeply rooted in the traditions or conscience of this country."[81] Manning was disappointed that the court had not seized this opportunity to "develop the law" through the Charter, while Morgentaler mused that he might re-open his Toronto abortion clinic, closed since the raid a year earlier.[82] As could be expected, Manning appealed Parker's decision to the Ontario Court of Appeal, but the appeal was denied. Morgentaler, Smoling, and Scott were then scheduled to a jury trial on 15 October.

After jury selection, the trial began on 19 October.[83] The prosecution's case was straightforward: it had only to show that Morgentaler, Smoling, and Scott conspired to perform abortions outside of section 251. It could show that Morgentaler had anticipated arrest and trial and had taken the precaution of circulating a "guidebook" to clinic staff so that the proper evidence of a defence of necessity would be available.[84] Manning's defence was essentially the defence of necessity, since he could no longer argue the constitutional validity of the law. Witness after witness, question after question, Manning strove to show that clinical abortions were safe, that access to abortion was miserably inadequate, and that women were driven to go to the United States or elsewhere to get abortions. In his formal summation to the jury, Manning urged it not simply to apply the law, but to decide whether the law was good or bad and to "send a message to the government." Judge Parker admonished him for suggesting that the jury was not bound by the law, and also pointed out that the defence of necessity applied only when imminent peril would result from obedience to the law, or when there was no reasonable alternative, or when the good results of disobedience outweighed the bad.[85] On 8 November 1984, after six hours of deliberation, the jury unanimously acquitted the three doctors. It was an extraordinary verdict, since the accused had admitted to breaking the law and the judge had in essence disallowed his defence. In the technical, legal sense, the defence of necessity should not have been accepted, and yet the jury trained its attention on the inadequacies of the law.[86] Morgentaler's supporters sprang into jubilant action to raise donations to cover legal fees,[87] while opponents wondered openly if now they might not also break laws to further their cause.[88] The day after his acquittal, Morgentaler promised to re-open the Harbord Street clinic and demanded that the authorities leave him alone.[89]

The weary cycle started again. On 4 December 1984 Roy McMurtry announced that the Crown would appeal the jury acquittal, Manning promised a cross-appeal against the Attorney General, and Morgentaler defiantly said that he would open his clinic. The clinic opened quietly on 10 December, and Morgentaler ignored McMurtry's plea to keep it closed until the legal issues were resolved. On 19 December the police arrested Scott outside the clinic, and Morgentaler surrendered himself the next day. The charges were never pursued because of the outstanding appeals, and on 7 January Morgentaler opened the Harbord clinic again. For good measure, he performed some abortions there himself. By now the abortion issue had become a parody of itself: protesters from both sides marched through the winter; Morgentaler announced plans to open clinics in Calgary, Nova Scotia, and New Brunswick; and the Winnipeg raids continued. Anti-abortion rights activists were clearly frustrated by events and Morgentaler's apparent ability to flout the law, and began to intensify their protests. Toronto Catholics were urged by Emmett Cardinal Carter to picket Morgentaler's clinic.[90] Large anti-abortion rights demonstrations continued through February 1985, and pro-abortion rights activists began to feel a shift in public mood against Morgentaler.[91]

In April several anti-abortion groups (the Catholic Women's League of Canada, the Hamilton Right To Life Association, the Alliance for Life, and the Coalition for the Protection of Human Life) sought to intervene in the Crown's appeal of Morgentaler's latest jury acquittal. They were denied and the appeal began on 19 April 1985. The Crown's main arguments to the Ontario Court of Appeal were that the defence of necessity was inapplicable and that Manning should not have enjoined the jury to ignore the law.[92] Manning had a rough ride before the court. His counter-arguments to the appeal went back to the constitutional invalidity of the abortion law, but the judges were decidedly unsympathetic, grilling him with interjections and eventually declining to take seriously his key constitutional claims.[93] The court's scepticism flowered into a decision on 1 October 1985 to overturn the jury acquittal because of fundamental errors in law regarding the defence of necessity and the jury's role in upholding the law.[94] Morgentaler immediately announced his intention to appeal to the Supreme Court of Canada. Another dreary year went by as pro- and anti-abortionists continued to slug and slash at each other, like numbed and bloodied boxers in the final desperate rounds of a fight. There were sit-ins at the Toronto clinic and legal skirmishing in Winnipeg over Morgentaler's medical licence; Robert Scott opened a second abortion clinic in Toronto in May 1986 and was arrested and charged in late September; anti-abortionists talked about forming their own political party, and managed to capture TACs in Newfoundland and PEI and thereby halt all abortions in those two provinces.

Finally, on 7 October 1986, the case came before the Supreme Court of Canada. This was the apex of Henry Morgentaler's long history of legal and political challenges to Canada's abortion law. Twenty years after deciding that he needed to "prove his manhood" by defying authority, he faced the highest court in the country, winner take all. In addition to the formidable talents of his lawyer, Morris Manning, he had a weapon he could never have imagined twenty years earlier: a constitutionally entrenched Charter of Rights and Freedoms that invited appointed judges to weigh laws against rights. It was a momentous event in Canadian legal and political history, but curiously flattened by the Court's own dry and sombre procedures. Henry Morgentaler's twenty-year challenge, all the raids and arrests and jail terms, came down to four days of lawyerly discourse in a room that muffles both passion and pain, placing them between the precise calipers of the law. When it was over, the issue dropped into the dark cold sea of judicial rumination, and a decision did not surface until 28 January 1988—fifteen months later. The only event of note in the intervening period was Joe Borowski's defeat in the Saskatchewan Court of Appeal on 30 April 1987. Unruffled, Borowski did what he always expected he would have to do: he appealed to the Supreme Court. Ironically, Borowski was claiming rights for the fetus under the same section of the Charter that Morgentaler had used to argue the constitutional invalidity of section 251 of the Criminal Code.

Seven Supreme Court judges heard the case of *R. vs. Morgentaler*. Five ruled that the law was invalid, two ruled that it was not. But judicial conclusions can be arrived at by different forms of judicial reasoning, so that even though five judges struck down the law, they did so by different means. Inset II summarizes the opinions of the seven judges on five key questions. Manning originally proposed thirteen separate grounds of appeal, but the primary focus of the oral presentations was section 7 of the Charter.[95] Chief Justice Brian Dickson wrote on behalf of himself and Justice Lamer that section 7 "does impose upon courts the duty to review the substance of legislation once it has been determined that the legislation infringes an individual's right to "life, liberty and security of the person."[96] Dickson went on to say that "state interference with bodily integrity and serious state-imposed psychological stress" constituted a breach of the security of the person. Commenting on section 251, he said,

Inset II

R. vs. MORGENTALER (1988)
JUDICIAL OPINIONS

Issue	Dickson/ Lamer	Beetz/ Estey	Wilson	McIntyre/ LaForest
1. Does section 7 of the charter allow Court review of substance of legislation?	yes	no comment	yes	no comment
2. Did section 251 affect security of the person?	yes	yes	yes	no
3. Are the section 251 proceedures fair?	no	no	no	not unfair
4. Is there a "right to abortion" for women?	no	no	yes	no
5. Does the state have an interest in protecting the fetus?	yes	yes	yes	no comment

At the most basic, physical and emotional level, every pregnant woman is told by the section that she cannot submit to a generally safe medical procedure that might be of clear benefit to her unless she meets criteria entirely unrelated to her own priorities and aspirations. Not only does the removal of decision making power threaten women in a physical sense; the indecision of knowing whether an abortion will be granted inflicts emotional stress. Section 251 clearly interferes with a woman's bodily integrity in both a physical and emotional sense. Forcing a woman, by threat of criminal sanction, to carry a foetus to term unless she meets certain criteria unrelated to her own priorities and aspirations, is a profound interference with a woman's body and thus a violation of security of the person.[97]

Section 251 created delays and induced psychological stress and thus violated section 7 of the Charter, and its implementation was fundamentally unfair. While Dickson recognized that state protection of fetal interests "may well be deserving of constitutional recognition" under section 1 of the Charter, he concluded that the abortion law did this in an unfair and arbitrary fashion.

Justice Beetz, writing for himself and Justice Estey, also concluded that the abortion law was unconstitutional in terms of section 7 and that its violation of the security of the person was not saved by section 1 of the Charter.[98] He arrived at this conclusion by a different process of reasoning, however. Dickson had reasoned that the abortion law violated "security of the person," and that this violation did not accord with the principles of fundamental justice. Beetz reasoned that section 7 did not create a new right, but a right to "security of the person" in the sense of access to medical services to save one's life, and that the procedures under the abortion law prevented that. Thus security of the person under section 7 must include "a right of access to medical treatment for a condition representing a danger to life or health without fear of criminal sanction."[99] The procedural complexity of section 251, by unnecessarily delaying access to medical help, threatened pregnant women's health in arbitrary and unfair ways.

Justice Bertha Wilson, while also striking down the abortion law, reasoned that the law's procedures were irrelevant to the primary question of whether a woman could be forced to carry a fetus against her will. If she could not, even the best procedures in the world could not save the law. Wilson argued that section 7 of the Charter must be read as guaranteeing "life, liberty and security of the person," not just physical and emotional security as Dickson had presumed. The concept of liberty in particular was critical: "Thus, the rights guaranteed in the Charter erect around each individual, metaphorically speaking, an invisible fence over which the state will not be allowed to trespass. The role of the courts is to map out, piece by piece, the perimeters of the fence."[100] Liberty is inextricably entwined with dignity, or the ability to choose one's life and way of living. The decision to abort, in Wilson's view, was fundamental to personal autonomy, and moreover it fell into the category of reproductive rights, which are an integral part of the recent struggle for women's rights.[101] The abortion law had clearly violated this right, and so contravened section 7 with respect to liberty. It also affected security of the person.

Wilson's final considerations were about whether the abortion law had deprived women of their rights in accordance with "principles of fundamental justice." Her approach was different from Dickson's and Beetz's; she did not identify "fundamental justice" with fair procedures, but with the freedom of conscience and religion cited in the Charter. Once again, the abortion law failed. Section 1 of the Charter did not save the abortion law either, because while the objective of protecting the fetus was valid, the law had taken inappropriate means to do it. Wilson then echoed the *Roe vs. Wade* idea of "compelling interest" and basically suggested a permissive approach to abortion for the early stages of pregnancy and a restrictive approach in the later stages.

Justice McIntyre wrote the dissent on behalf of himself and Justice La Forest. He made it immediately clear that the core of his dissent concerned the role of courts in the policy process: "But the courts must not, in the guise of interpretation, postulate rights and freedoms which do not have a firm and a reasonably identifiable base in the Charter."[102] The courts had to refrain from "imposing or creating other values." McIntrye's approach was somewhat more prosaic than Dickson's and certainly more so than Wilson's. He noted that nowhere did the Charter guarantee a "right to abortion." To conclude that Canadian women had such a right required reading it into section 7. Legislators had deliberately worded section 7 to preclude court review of abortion law.[103] A wider historical review of Canadian abortion legislation showed that abortion on demand has never been generally accepted. McIntyre closed by arguing that the evidence for the procedural unfairness of the abortion law was questionable and sometimes weak, since tens of thousands of abortions were performed each year in Toronto and there was no testimony from any woman who had ever been denied an abortion.

This review of the Supreme Court "decision" shows that it was in fact, as most court decisions are, an amalgam of sometimes significantly different arguments, some with similar conclusions and others not. The 1969 abortion law was unconstitutional, that much was certain. But did Canadian women now have a "right to abortion"? Only Justice Wilson went that far. Did it mean that the government could still regulate first-trimester abortions if it found more procedurally fair mechanisms? Yes, since both Dickson and Beetz had focused on the procedural unfairness of section 251, hinting that cleaner rules might escape judicial sanction. Could there be an abortion law that controlled access in the later stages of pregnancy? Absolutely, since all five in the majority acknowledged the state's interest in protecting the fetus.

The Court decision, in short, did not decide very much. It struck down the old law, but ambiguously, and gave no guidance whatsoever for what might replace it. In the first days of its release, the decision was predictably hailed and reviled, but, just as predictably, for all the wrong reasons. Pro-abortion rights activists claimed a "great victory for women's rights" while their opponents lamented the "disaster". Only for Henry Morgentaler, standing outside on the court steps in the cold Ottawa wind, was the result an unequivocal victory: "I still cannot believe it is possible after waiting for 20 years.... It is beyond my wildest dreams."[104]

AFTERMATH AND NEW LEGISLATION

For Morgentaler it was a dream; for most Canadians, and certainly the federal and provincial governments, the politics of abortion have been a nightmare. A few days after the decision, the Conservative government in Ottawa promised to "provide leadership and act quickly" to develop a new abortion policy.[105] The issue split the party caucus so severely, however, that nothing happened for four months. In May the Prime Minister announced that the abortion question would be put to a free vote in the Commons.[106] No guidance was given to provincial governments on how to deal with the abortion question, and so some jurisdictions, such as British Columbia, Alberta, and Saskatchewan, took steps to either limit the availability of abortion services or ensure that abortions would not be paid for through provincial medicare schemes. Henry Morgentaler quietly worked at his Toronto clinic and re-opened the Winnipeg one on 27 June.

The Tory government, in the face of its severely split caucus, spent the spring and summer trying to come up with the least divisive policy options. It had to show leadership, but also allow a free vote. Finally, the government scheduled a vote in mid-July for a three-part "resolution" that set out different general approaches to drafting abortion legislation. MPs would be free to vote by conscience; the government hoped to get some sense of Parliament's sentiments on the issue by the distribution of votes for the three options. The opposition parties criticized the government's abdication of leadership and the procedural peculiarity of prohibiting amendments to the motion. After protracted negotiations, the government withdrew its original motion, submitted a revised version on 26 July 1988, and allowed MPs to make amendments. Rather than three options, the resolution offered a single set of principles for the drafting of future abortion legislation. MPs were to vote in favour of or against the resolution or amendments made to it. The resolution said that any abortion legislation presented to Parliament should "prohibit the performance of an abortion" except

- When, during the earlier stages of pregnancy: a qualified medical practitioner is of the opinion that the continuation of the pregnancy of a woman would, or would be likely to, threaten her physical or mental well-being; when the woman in consultation with a qualified medical practitioner decides to terminate her pregnancy; and when the termination is performed by a qualified medical practitioner; and
- When, during the subsequent stages of pregnancy: the termination of the pregnancy satisfies further conditions, including a condition that after a certain point in time, the termination would only be permitted where, in the opinion of two qualified medical practitioners, the continuation of

the pregnancy would, or would be likely to, endanger the woman's life or seriously endanger her health.

With MPs released from the normal shackles of party discipline, amendments came from every corner of the House, some trying to reduce the number of conditions contained in the resolution, others trying to narrow them. The core support for restrictions came from the Tory benches, while NDP members favoured liberalization. Friday, 28 July 1988, was a lesson in both parliamentary chaos and the *immobilisme* of contemporary abortion politics. Every proposal was defeated. The government's main resolution was defeated 147 votes to 76. An amendment that would have left the choice of abortion to the woman in the early stages and demanded only one doctor's opinion in the later stages was defeated 191 to 29. An amendment that would have left the decision entirely up to a woman and her doctor was defeated 198 to 20. An amendment that would have restricted abortions to the first twelve weeks of pregnancy was defeated 202 to 17. The one amendment that came closest to victory (introduced by Gus Mitges), by virtue of having been defeated by the least number of votes, would have prohibited abortions except on the evidence of two doctors that the continuation of the pregnancy would endanger the woman's life.[107] This was an almost pure "pro-life" amendment, and interestingly, not one of the twenty-nine female MPs voted for it. The votes broke down almost perfectly along gender lines, with female MPs from all parties voting for the more permissive amendments. A group of about seventy male Conservatives formed the core of the anti-abortion votes, but in themselves would never have been able to defeat the government's resolution. The parliamentary outcome showed how pro- and anti-abortion rights forces are entangled in an unwilling and crippling embrace. The government's resolution, its hope for policy guidance, was defeated because both sides disliked it for different reasons and voted it down. Despite parliamentary defeat, abortion did not fall completely off the agenda in 1988. It surfaced in several ways, for example, in the federal election campaign. At least seventy-four anti-abortion rights candidates were elected on 21 November 1988. These seventy-four had either voted in favour of protecting the fetus from the moment of conception or had promised in writing to do so. Also, several nomination races were fought out between pro- and anti-abortion rights candidates, and anti-abortion rights activists targeted thirty ridings in which to mount direct mail campaigns.[108]

The first year after the Supreme Court's decision on *Morgentaler* was therefore inconclusive and confusing. The pro-abortion rights lobby was initially happy with the situation, arguing that the absence of an abortion law was in itself not a difficulty. It merely meant that abortion was now a medical procedure to be decided by a woman and her physician. The anti-abortion rights movement called the situation a "legal vacuum" and demanded new legislation. While the chaos over the 1988 abortion resolution suggested that the two sides were mutually paralysed, deeper forces were gathering that would explode in the next year to force the governments once more to attempt a legislative solution. One unanticipated effect of the Supreme Court's decision to strike down section 251 was to invite a wider debate on the proper scope of a new law. Before *Morgentaler*, public discussion had focused on the specifics of section 251 and the Charter. The Court's reluctance to give guidance on the question of fetal rights, as well as the different rationales offered by the various judges, encouraged a wide variety of interpretations. The Law Reform Commission of Canada, for example, in November 1988 issued a report entitled *Crimes Against the Foetus* that tried to sketch out new federal legislation on abortion.[109] The Commission's majority report would have allowed abortions on consent of the mother by qualified medical personnel where the mother's physical or psychological health was threatened or where the fetus suffered from a lethal defect.[110]

The other effect of the Court's decision, as mentioned earlier, was a federal legislative void that was rapidly filled by provincial regulations. Abortion under section 251 had been regulated by criminal law, but as a medical procedure could also be regulated by provincial powers over health. While no province could ban abortion outright, all of them could regulate it through two instruments. One was public payment for the procedure under provincial medicare schemes. The other was regulating where abortions could be performed (i.e., in accredited hospitals rather than clinics) and under what administrative conditions (e.g., committees of approval similar to TACs). Several provinces in 1988 used some or all of these tactics to restrict access. The first was British Columbia, which within two days of the Supreme Court decision in *Morgentaler*, announced that it would pay only for those abortions performed in accredited hospitals and approved by a TAC, and in cases where the life of the mother was threatened by the pregnancy. Premier Vander Zalm, an outspoken opponent of abortion, and his provincial cabinet issued an order in February to amend the Medical Services Act. The British Columbia Civil Liberties Association took the order to court, and the BC Supreme Court ruled against the government on 7 March 1988. The ruling struck down the government's action on technical grounds, but implied that even more procedurally correct attempts to do the same thing would run into legal trouble. The government decided not to appeal, and instead launched a $20 million "pro-life" campaign. The New Brunswick government passed similar regulations, stipulating that abortions could be performed only in accredited hospitals and with the statement of two physicians that the procedure was medically required. Neither New Brunswick nor Nova Scotia would tolerate private abortion clinics, whereas Manitoba allowed them but would not pay for abortions performed in them. Ontario and Quebec had the least restrictive regimes, allowing clinics and paying for most or all of the costs of their abortions.[111] Ironically, in light of the prominence of the "equality of access" issue in the Supreme Court's *Morgentaler* decision, the combined result of the court decision and the federal government's inaction in 1988 was *less* uniformity across the country, as provinces made their own rules to regulate abortion.

Pro-abortion rights activists and civil libertarians successfully fought these attempted restrictions in the courts. The mood among their opponents, however, was increasingly bellicose. From the anti-abortion rights perspective, the federal government had abdicated its responsibility to deal with a legal vacuum, and provincial attempts to regulate abortion were being quashed in the courts. Mounting frustration led some within the movement to conclude that perhaps the only way to fight Henry Morgentaler's cause was to use Henry Morgentaler's methods: ignore the law and do what you think is right. By the end of 1988 and into 1989, anti-abortion rights tactics became more militant and uncompromising. The first major confrontations occurred in British Columbia in early 1989. On 21 January about 150 protesters blockaded and shut down the Everywoman's Health Clinic in east Vancouver. The court issued an injunction to stop the blockade, but it was ignored by the protesters, and so police were called in to enforce the injunction. Thirteen people were arrested (ten men and three women), and on 9 February the BC Supreme Court sentenced four of them to twenty-four days in jail and the other nine to fifteen days in jail. Several of the defendants told the court that they had had to obey a higher law. One said that he was caught between the "Supreme Court of Heaven and Earth," while another said that she had had no choice but to protest: "Since Parliament and the courts have not acted, I, like many other normally law-abiding citizens...placed our bodies between the killers and the unborn."[112] On the same day, forty-five other protesters remained in jail because they refused to promise that they would stay at least one block away from the clinic. They had been arrested with over fifty others in front of the clinic for disobeying the injunction. The entire group of protesters was charged with criminal offenses for deliberately ignoring the injunction and obstructing access to the clinic. Mr. Justice Josiah Wood of the BC Supreme Court described their conduct as defiance of the rule of law.[113] The trial invoked all the emotional rituals of courtroom abortion arguments: miniature replicas of fetuses, disquisitions on church law and Nazi Germany, readings from the Bible, and prosecution claims that the fetus in law was no more a human being than a seal pup, a tree, or a timber wolf is.[114]

Mr. Justice Wood found the BC protestors guilty of contempt of court, but delayed sentencing so that all the accused could address the court. One German-born protester expressed his feelings of guilt for Nazi genocide programs, another said that his mother might have aborted him had the procedure been available at the time, others worked with handicapped children, most were religious. Some were teenagers and a few were World War II veterans. Few had ever broken any laws. As a group, they were a microcosm of the Canadian anti-abortion rights movement. The court was lenient: the protesters were given suspended sentences of three months in jail, on the grounds that they had been induced to violate the injunction by unnamed leaders and had not really understood the seriousness of their actions.[115] Leniency notwithstanding, the protesters were forbidden to come within a block of the clinic for a year. The next day three of the protesters disobeyed the order, and were jailed. All citizens, said Mr. Justice Wood, "must obey the law."[116]

A day later the Supreme Court of Canada issued its 7–0 judgment in the Borowski case. The court ruled that since there presently was no abortion law in Canada, the question of fetal rights was moot. Its judgment was, in short, a non-judgment on the central issue in the case. The court argued that a decision in this case, an abstract one since no practical dispute was at issue, would only have confused the public and brought the court into a policy arena reserved for the legislature.[117] This last rationale was particularly flimsy in light of the politics of the Morgentaler appeal and decision, as well as the new reality of Canadian judicial decisions under the Charter. Courts were deeply implicated in policy-making because their judgments would now, under the Charter, set the outer limits for federal and provincial legislation. Moreover, any new abortion law would probably be taken to the courts anyway, as the judges themselves admitted.[118] Joe Borowski's ten-year battle thus ended in defeat where his adversary's had ended in legal victory. With characteristic pugnacity, Borowski commented that had he been in Ottawa for the decision he "probably would have gone into the court and punched the judges in the nose."[119] "Enough is enough; we are going to fill the jails with our bodies. We are going to do what the negroes did in the United States. They filled up the jails. They clogged the justice system. We consider abortion far worse than apartheid and racial discrimination."[120] Henry Morgentaler was predictably pleased with the decision, but criticized anti-abortion rights activists for resorting to illegal tactics. These tactics included the ones used in BC at Everywoman's Health Clinic and pioneered in the United States by a group called Operation Rescue: going limp, linking arms and blocking clinics with a human wall of protesters. In April, demonstrators went further and chained them-

selves to the clinic's door. As Borowski suggested, the tactics borrowed both the
language and manoeuvres of the American civil rights protests of the 1960s.

It had been a tense winter. The summer of 1989 was worse, blighted with
events so melodramatic that movie rights were sold to some of them. Courts,
naturally, were at the centre of things, but in the end looked somewhat pathetic
and powerless as citizens took matters into their own hands. The federal government had been paralysed for a year, but the Barbara Dodd and Chantal Daigle
cases of July and August finally compelled it to act. Few pieces of Canadian
legislation have had more colourful or compelling backdrops.

Like a play that opens with a minor character pronouncing its larger themes,
the "abortion summer" of 1989 opened not with Canadian events but American
ones. On 3 July the United States Supreme Court released its decision upholding
the constitutionality of some components of Missouri's abortion law, most significantly those banning public hospitals and public employees from performing
abortions. The decision, while it did not reverse the 1973 *Roe vs. Wade* judgement,
clearly restricted the right to abortion and empowered states to implement those
restrictions. Legislators in Florida, Louisiana, Mississippi, and Minnesota, among
others, immediately promised to introduce legislation similar to Missouri's. In
Canada the decision was greeted with predictable jubilation and dismay, but
anyone pausing to consider the decision that day would have concluded that the
apparently inexorable movement over the last two decades to liberalize abortion
had been stalled, at least momentarily. Canadian abortion rights supporters, while
despondent over provincial developments, could at least take comfort in the absence of federal legislation. What was not illegal was by definition permitted, and
so Canadian women, in principle at least, enjoyed access to abortion services that
might soon be denied to American women.

Within days the flaw in this logic would become glaringly evident. The absence
of written law does not mean the complete absence of legal constraint, since in
Canada there are common law traditions that may, upon judicial reflection, still
apply to a given behaviour. But the nature of common law is that it is expressed
in particular cases and decisions on those cases, and so cannot be determined in
detail in advance of concrete disputes. Determined litigants, in short, could bring
all sorts of arguments to court, and the court, in the absence of a clear, written
legal guideline, would have to treat those arguments seriously in light of existing
legal principles. This is what happened in July and August 1989: two men tried
to stop their girlfriends' abortions through legal injunctions.[121] Gregory Murphy
won an Ontario Supreme Court injunction against Barbara Dodd on 4 July 1989.
The injunction, granted by Mr. Justice John O'Driscoll, prohibited Dodd from
having an abortion on her fifteen-week old fetus anywhere in Ontario, including

private clinics like Henry Morgentaler's. Murphy's claim argued that an abortion would violate the fetus's right to equality and life, liberty and security as guaranteed under the Charter (the section 7 argument that had been left moot in the Borowski case). Both Murphy and Dodd were hearing impaired, and Murphy claimed that although they had agreed to have a child, Dodd's parents had pressured her into having the abortion. Murphy's submission to the court was accompanied by an ultrasound picture of the fetus, and a statement that he wanted the child and would support it and its mother if she agreed.[122] Several days later a Manitoba court, facing the same arguments from a Winnipeg man who wanted to prevent his former girlfriend's abortion, decided that the woman had absolute control over her body.[123] Two courts, same arguments: two diametrically opposed decisions.

The Dodd-Murphy case made instant national headlines, and the litigants' personal lives became public knowledge. Murphy had received the injunction in part because Dodd had not appeared before Justice O'Driscoll to oppose it. In the ensuing days it was argued by Dodd's lawyer Clayton Ruby, women's groups like the National Action Committee on the Status of Women, and disabled persons' groups that Dodd's rights had been violated by the judicial process. She had not understood the documents that she had been served, and had had difficulty finding a lawyer. Ruby filed affidavits with the court on 7 July stating that Dodd had been having sexual relations with Murphy and another man, Christen Mucciato, around the time of conception, and did not know which one was the father. "When I told Greg of these test results he said, 'Okay, let's have the baby.'" At that moment I couldn't bring myself to tell Greg that I was still seeing Christen behind his back."[124] Dodd said that Murphy had encouraged her to work as an exotic dancer and had made extravagant claims about his personal power and connections. He had intimidated her and insisted that she work while he stayed home as a house-husband.

Murphy's success at winning an injunction encouraged Jean-Guy Tremblay of Pointe-aux-Trembles on 7 July to file for an injunction against Chantal Daigle, his former girlfriend. Within a week, the Daigle-Tremblay case would dominate the headlines, but the Dodd-Murphy denouement dragged out over several more days. In hearings before the Ontario Supreme Court, Dodd's lawyer repeated claims from her earlier affidavits, arguing that Murphy had lied to and misled the court in order to get his injunction. Murphy's lawyer tried to rebut claims that Dodd had not understood the legal process by producing evidence that she had argued her own case over the custody of her two previous children and knew the system very well. The court was unpersuaded, and on 11 July set aside the injunction on the grounds that Dodd had received insufficient notice of the initial hearing and that there were elements of fraud in the original depositions.[125] The presiding judge refused to stay his ruling for a day to give Murphy's lawyer time to appeal, and Barbara Dodd had her abortion that night at Henry Morgentaler's clinic. While the Canadian Abortion Rights Action League was gratified by the decision, anti-abortion rights groups were not entirely dismayed. The initial success of the injunction had, from their point of view, breached the notion that abortion was entirely up to the woman. Moreover, the Ontario Supreme Court's decision was based entirely on procedural irregularities, not on the issue of abortion rights or indeed on the right to seek injunctions.

This might have been the end of the Dodd-Murphy melodrama, but a few days after her abortion, Dodd held a sensational news conference saying that she had changed her mind about the pro-choice position. Greg Murphy was at her side. Dodd claimed that she had felt manipulated by pro-abortion rights activists through the whirlwind of judicial hearings, and felt abandoned by them after her abortion.[126] The next day she held an interview at the Toronto headquarters of Campaign Life wearing an anti-abortion T-shirt, saying that she was now an anti-abortion advocate. While Dodd described Murphy as a "rare man" who loved her enough to fight for their child and still forgive her after the abortion, Dodd's family held a news conference to claim that Murphy had manipulated her into changing her mind.[127] Both pro- and anti-abortion rights groups were skeptical of Dodd's sudden change of heart, but her conversion obviously strengthened the anti-abortion side, and Campaign Life arranged several interviews and press conferences so that she could state her case. Dodd and Murphy's final pirouettes before the public were, like some of Henry Morgentaler's performances in earlier years, perhaps less important for their substance than their form. Once again, individuals, movements, court challenges, and public policy were inextricably tangled.

The political thicket surrounding abortion got even denser with the Tremblay-Daigle case. Tremblay's injunction was inspired by Murphy's, and he also had initial success. Tremblay and Daigle had met in November 1988 at a Montreal shopping mall, and were living together within three months. Daigle became pregnant and the couple planned to marry, but on 3 July 1989 Daigle moved out of the apartment and decided to abort her twenty-week old fetus. She said that Tremblay had become physically abusive and possessive, and that they quarrelled frequently. Tremblay and his lawyer successfully sought a temporary injunction on 7 July, with a hearing scheduled for the 17th. As pro- and anti-abortion rights supporters milled outside the Val d'Or courtroom, Mr. Justice Jacques Viens of the Quebec Superior Court listened to opposing arguments. The temporary injunction was to expire at 5 p.m., but it was extended for a few hours as the judge deliberated. Following so closely on the Dodd decision, his ruling stunned the country. He upheld the injunction, citing the Quebec Charter of Rights and Freedoms. While the Canadian Charter of Rights and Freedoms did not give the fetus the right to life, Viens concluded that because articles 1 and 2 of the Quebec Charter referred to "etre humain" (human being), although the remainder referred to "personne" (person), the fetus as a human being was guaranteed the right to life as well as the right to assistance.[128] Viens considered the balance of Daigle's rights against the fetus's, and found in favour of the fetus. The province in which Henry Morgentaler had started his long fight against section 251 had now rendered the first unambiguous victory for the anti-abortion side since 1988: the fetus and its father were given rights against the mother.[129]

Pro- and anti-abortion groups, seasoned and scarred in the Dodd-Murphy battles, mobilized quickly. Chantal Daigle immediately appealed the ruling to the Quebec Court of Appeal, which heard the case but on 20 July decided that the issues were too complex to resolve quickly and so delayed its ruling. The delay made it impossible for Daigle to get an abortion in Quebec, where clinics and hospitals refuse to do them after the fetus is twenty weeks old. She could get one in the United States, however, where some facilities perform them up to twenty-six weeks. The delay illustrated how unsuited the courts were to this type of decision-making. Pressure for new legislation increased, and on 20 July the Prime Minister finally announced that an abortion bill would come before Parliament in the fall. His announcement was all but drowned out in the intense media scrutiny of the private lives of Daigle and Tremblay. Tremblay, confident of victory, publicly admitted that though he wanted to have the baby, he could not care for it. He rejected claims that he had abused Daigle, noting that he had never hit her "hard enough to leave marks."[130] This was hardly an endorsement for the anti-abortion rights side, and women marched and demonstrated through Quebec to support Daigle. She needed it: on 26 July the Quebec Court of Appeal in a 3-2 decision upheld the injunction. Chantal Daigle could not get an abortion in Quebec.

The Quebec Court of Appeal decision is reminiscent of the 1988 Supreme Court ruling in *Morgentaler*, not because of its conclusions (which were opposite), but because the majority was so diverse in its reasoning. Once again, while it appeared that there was a single ruling, in fact the judges were deeply divided. Three justices (Bernier, Nichols, and Lebel) upheld the injunction. Bernier did so not because of the Canadian or Quebec Charters, or because of the Civil Code, but because he concluded that the fetus has a natural right to life. Bernier also found that there was some basis to the idea of father's rights. Justice Nichols, on the other hand, found no basis for fetal rights in either the Canadian or Quebec

Charters, or natural law. Canadian common law and custom, however, revealed that by tradition the fetus enjoys legal status. Justice Lebel, the third member of the majority, agreed with the Viens decision and found a basis for fetal rights in the Quebec Charter and Civil Code. Lebel also recognized father's rights. All three judges, in addition to recognizing fetal rights, concluded that these rights outweighed those of the mother. The dissenting justices (Chouinard and Tourigny) found no fetal rights hidden in the Quebec Charter or Civil Code, took exception with the use of injunctions in such personal matters, and argued that the entire question of fetal rights had to be governed by precedents under the Canadian Charter, none of which had recognized such rights. Justice Tourigny, the only woman on the court, wrote the main dissent and argued that Daigle's testimony of psychological trauma and stress due to the pregnancy was in itself sufficient ground to justify the abortion.[131]

Chantal Daigle appealed to the Supreme Court, but her advanced stage of pregnancy made every moment count. On 1 August a panel of five Supreme Court judges took fifteen minutes to grant Daigle leave to appeal and state her arguments one week later. Over that week, however, the tangled logic of Canadian abortion politics projected itself once more into the issue. Daigle and Tremblay became almost bit players in their own drama as governments and interest groups sought intervenor status. Nine of them got it: the Attorney General of Canada, the Attorney General of Quebec, the Canadian Abortion Rights Action League, the Women's Legal Education Action Fund, the Canadian Civil Liberties Association, the Campaign Life Coalition, Canadian Physicians for Life, L'association des medicins du Québec pour le respect de la vie, and REAL (Real, Equal, and Active for Life) Women of Canada. The federal government's intervention was almost grotesque: in an inflamed personal conflict that had raised the most painful ethical dilemmas, on an issue that it had evaded for over a year, Ottawa was supporting neither side, only appearing "to defend our right to legislate at the federal level."[132]

The court heard the appeal on 8 August, but in mid-afternoon was told that Chantal Daigle had already had her abortion. In an interview given after the hearing, Daigle said that she was "very, very angry and nobody was going to stop me getting my way."[133] Defying the injunction, she travelled to Boston and had her twenty-two-week-old fetus aborted. The announcement in the midst of the judicial proceedings upstaged the Court's decision, which was to unanimously quash the injunction. At the time it simply issued its decision; the reasons for that decision were not issued until 16 November 1989. In this instance the Court acted decisively with a single, unanimous decision. It was careful to narrow the scope of its considerations by pointing out that it could judge only the legal dimension of existence of fetal "personhood" and rights, but then proceeded to refute Tremblay's case point by point. Reading fetal rights into the Quebec Charter or Civil Code was simply "linguistic analysis" that did not in fact yield any clear substantive conclusions about fetal rights. Neither did the Court find any common law precedents establishing fetal rights. It also dismissed the idea of "father's rights" to veto a decision to abort. Interestingly, the Court deliberately did not comment on whether section 7 of the Canadian Charter of Rights and Freedoms conferred any legal rights on the fetus.[134]

The abortion issue in 1989 had gone into the streets and from there back to the courts, culminating once more in a Supreme Court decision. In two years, nothing had been resolved, perhaps not even the question of fetal rights, while bitterness and despondency had grown on both sides of the issue. A measure of how little had changed was Henry Morgentaler's attempt to perform abortions in Nova Scotia. In an eerie echo of his fight in Winnipeg, Morgentaler defied a law forbidding abortions outside of accredited hospitals by openly performing seven of them in his Halifax clinic, and was simultaneously served with an injunction barring him from performing any more in the province.[135] This tired rehearsal of old arguments and tactics, along with the more sensational Dodd and Daigle cases, formed the backdrop for Ottawa's introduction of a new abortion law in the form of Bill C-43. The Tories had tried to evade the issue for over a year. Their first fumbled attempt at legislation in 1988 had exposed the divisions within and between the political parties; their second attempt was more cautious. A caucus committee was established to review alternatives, and the government's final legislative proposals were thoroughly vetted in the party. Unlike 1988, when it had allowed a completely free vote, this time the cabinet (forty members) was to support the bill, while the remaining 128 Tory MPs could vote as they wished. Given full attendance in the 295-seat House of Commons, the government needed 148 votes to pass the bill. On third reading, with some absences in the House, Bill C-43 was passed by only nine votes, 140 to 131.

Bill C-43 was introduced for reading to the House of Commons by Doug Lewis, minister of justice and attorney general of Canada, on 3 November 1989. Second-reading debate extended over seven days and ended with a vote to refer the Bill to committee on November 28. The legislative committee on Bill C-43 heard witnesses for over three months and reported the bill back to the House unamended in May 1990. Thirty separate amendments were proposed at that stage, but all were defeated. On 29 May, shepherded by the new minister of justice, Kim Campbell, the bill was finally passed by the House of Commons. Despite months of debate, expert commentary, and dozens of submissions to the legislative committee, opinion on the legislation continued to be deeply divided over not only its principles, but its likely effects as well. Government spokespersons cited this as evidence of the bill's careful balance of considerations, pleasing no one entirely but serving the larger national interest. For some, the legislation meant abortion on demand; others described it as an attack on women's rights that would severely restrict access to abortion services. The text of the bill in Inset III shows how this could be. Like section 251,[136] Bill C-43 placed abortion once again in the Criminal Code. In an echo of the old law, abortion would be a crime unless performed under specific conditions. Section 251's restrictions had been considered by the Supreme Court in *Morgentaler* as too strict. Bill C-43 proposed the following: abortions were legal if done by or under the direction of a physician who believed that the pregnancy threatened the health or life of the mother. The bill did away with TACs, making the decision to abort essentially one between a woman and her physician. The explanatory notes that accompanied the bill said that while eugenics, rape, incest, or socio-economic welfare were not specifically mentioned, "these factors could be included in the determination of health if their effect was to threaten a woman's health."[137] The differences between the old and the new law were ably summarized by Justice Minister Lewis:

> Under the old law there was a requirement for a therapeutic abortion committee; under the new bill it is one qualified medical practitioner. Under the old law there was no definition of "health"; under the new one we have defined "health." Under the old section 251 it required an accredited or approved hospital; under the new law there is no hospital requirement. That is left to the provinces to regulate. Under the old law the doctor who performed an abortion could not be on the abortion committee; under the new law the doctor who gives the opinion can be the same doctor who performs the abortion. Under the old law it was an expressed liability for women who intentionally seek an abortion; under the new law it is a liability for a woman only if she knowingly and intentionally seeks or has an abortion outside the exemption. Under the old law there was a requirement for a certificate from the doctor; under the new law there is no certificate.[138]

The Commons debate over Bill C-43 may not have been Parliament's finest hour, but it raised the institution momentarily from its customary mire of partisan petulance and bombast. Of the ninety-seven MPs who spoke on second reading, most stated their misgivings with a measure of grace not usually found in contemporary politics. The pro-abortion rights side, for example, argued that the bill was contradictory since it apparently prohibited all abortions at any stage of pregnancy, and then created a loophole to allow them. As Mary Clancy (Liberal) put it, "Women do not want their rights surreptitiously through the back door."[139] The *Morgentaler* decision was interpreted as having given women the right to

---

Inset III

BILL C-43
AN ACT RESPECTING ABORTION

*H*er *Majesty, by and with the advice and consent of the Senate and House of Commons of Canada, enacts as follows:*

1. Sections 287 and 288 of the *Criminal Code* are repealed and the following substituted therefor:

287

(1) Every person who induces an abortion on a female person is guilty of an indictable offence and liable to imprisonment for a term not exceeding two years, unless the abortion is induced by or under the direction of a medical practioner who is of the opinion that, if the abortion were not induced, the health or life of the female person would be likely to be threatened.

(2) For the purposes of this section,

"health" includes, for greater certainty, physical, mental and psychological health;

"medical practioner", in respect of an abortion induced in a province, means a person who is entitled to practise medicine under the laws of that province;

"opinion" means an opinion formed using generally accepted standards of the medical profession.

(3) For the purposes of this section and section 288, inducing an abortion does not include using a drug, device or other means on a female person that is likely to prevent implantation of a fertilized ovum.

288

Every one who unlawfully supplies or procures a drug or other noxious thing or an instrument or thing, knowing that it is intended to be used or employed to induce an abortion on a female person, is guilty of an indictable offence and liable to imprisonment for a term not exceeding two years.

2. This Act shall come into force on a day to be fixed by order of the Governor in Council.

---

security of the person, and no purpose would be served by dragging women through the courts. NDP speakers in particular emphasized the responsibility of women in facing the difficult choice of abortion. From this perspective, the real problem in abortion was access, and the last two years had shown what recalcitrant

CANADA'S ABORTION SAGA

provincial governments and anti-abortion rights activists could accomplish. The bill, it was argued, did nothing to improve access. In fact, it would do precisely the opposite: doctors, fearing third-party prosecutions, would restrict abortion to narrow grounds, and moreover might even refuse, for personal reasons, to support a women's decision to abort. Dawn Black (NDP) attacked Lewis on this score: "The Minister of Justice has been using the language of choice when discussing this bill. There is no choice for women involved in this bill. The minister is being hypocritical when he uses the language of choice in relation to this bill which makes abortion the doctor's decision based on health criteria, not the woman's choice based on her own personal criteria."[140]

These criticisms were echoed in pro-abortion rights submissions to the legislative committee on Bill C-43. The Canadian Abortion Rights Action League (CARAL) cited five major objections to the bill.[141] First, just as "safe, legal abortion services are basic to women's reproductive health and overall well-being, reproductive choice is fundamental to women's social equality." Without control over their bodies, women could not be autonomous human beings. Bill C-43 gave the abortion decision to the doctor. Second, the use of the criminal law, a blunt and invasive instrument, to regulate abortion was both unnecessary and unjustified. Abortion was a private matter, was already regulated by health and other legislation, and should be a medical, not legal, matter between woman and physician. Third, the bill would restrict access to abortion. The existence of a criminal law on abortion would provide anti-abortion activists avenues to charge women and doctors. The bill would do nothing to improve real access to services for rural and poor women, and would still allow provinces to control access through health legislation. Fourth, the narrowing of permissible grounds for abortion under the bill, in addition to the anticipated delays and uncertainty, would increase risks to health suffered by women seeking abortions. Finally, CARAL cited commissioned public opinion research to the effect that the silent majority of Canadians favoured a pro-choice position.

The bill was also criticized from the anti-abortion rights perspective as being too lax. All the key arguments were contained in the Alliance for Life (AL) submission to the legislative committee. Whereas the CARAL submission had begun, as did almost all the pro-abortion rights arguments, with the rights of women, the AL brief opened with the statement that "abortion is the only medical procedure which involves the deliberate destruction of human life."[142] Therefore, AL agreed that abortion should be retained in the Criminal Code to ensure adequate protection of the "child's inherent right to life." As a human being, the fetus had rights, the right to life being the most basic of all; these rights should not be subject to discrimination. And yet, for AL, the exemptions provided in

Bill C-43 were "so broad as to allow virtually all abortions to be conducted with impunity." By exempting abortions induced by "or under the direction" of a medical practitioner, the bill would allow non-physicians who qualify under medical-standards legislation (e.g., nurses) to perform abortions under a physician's direction. Large-scale, clinic-based abortion facilities would therefore be possible, run by only one physician. The bill's definition of health—which might include socio-economic and lifestyle considerations—was so vague that it would simultaneously ensure abortion on demand from sympathetic physicians and encourage women to lie about the true state of their health. And whereas CARAL had argued that evidence showed that abortions (if performed in the first fifteen weeks) had fewer risks than pregnancy, AL marshalled statistics to highlight the health problems attendant to abortions (e.g., post-abortion syndrome, inability to conceive, increased risk of perinatal death). Bill C-43 therefore provided no real protection for "pre-born human beings."[143]

After hundreds of pages of testimony before the legislative committee, the bill was reported out without amendment. Amendments proposed at the report stage were either disallowed by the Speaker or defeated on division, and the bill went on to third reading, where it was finally passed by a bare margin of 140–131, once more without amendment. From there it went to the Senate, where it languished until January 1991 because of the fall battle over the GST. The same groups appeared before committee, and the same arguments were heard. In a free vote on 31 January 1991, the Senate split 43–43. Under Senate rules that constitutes a defeat, and so Bill C-43 died in the upper chamber.

How did Bill C-43 manage to pass in the Commons but not in the Senate, in the face of such adamant opposition on both sides of the issue? One reason for the Commons passage was that the federal government clearly stated that this would be its last attempt to legislate in the abortion field. If this bill failed, there would be no other. As well, the support of the cabinet gave the bill an assured forty votes, or almost one-third of what it eventually received. The bill's successful passage must also be credited to its creative ambiguity. It was indeed compromise legislation whose text, if read literally, appealed in some measure to both sides. The real crux was not the text, but the way in which women, doctors, provincial governments, and anti-abortion rights activists would be likely to behave with reference to that text. Nobody could be certain, and the bill gained some momentum from its ambiguous consequences. Finally, it was clear to at least the MPs who eventually voted for the bill that some sort of legislation, however imperfect it might be from their point of view, was better than no legislation. Several MPs who identified themselves as pro-choice eventually voted for Bill C-43 because they were persuaded that it would provide a national framework for abortion and establish, at least in a minimal sense, an entitlement to the procedure.

These last reasons hinge on the government's rationale for the provisions of Bill C-43.[144] The government had decided to use the criminal law to deal with abortion because jurisdiction over health resides with the provinces. While some experts had argued that the federal government could enforce access to abortion through the Canada Health Act, the government's own view was that in order to ensure a national framework it would have to rely on powers within its own jurisdiction. Bill C-43, in the government's view, provided an entitlement, but it was up to the provinces to ensure appropriate access. The bill's reliance on one doctor as opposed to a TAC, and its broad definition of health, were consistent with the opinions in the *Morgentaler* case. Finally, while private prosecutions were certainly possible under the new law, the government noted that the attorney general of any province could enter a stay of proceedings in cases where the prosecution was frivolous or malicious. Whatever one may think of the specific provisions of Bill C-43, they revealed some political adroitness. The federal government could claim that it had shown leadership and legislated in a delicate and difficult area. It could state with conviction that it had provided both an entitlement for women and a protection for the fetus. However, all the crucial decisions about access and entitlement would have been thrown back onto the provinces. Provinces would have to decide whether abortions could be performed in clinics or hospitals and whether public funds would pay for them, and provinces would have to deal with third-party prosecutions. Provinces, in short, would have paid the political price of Bill C-43.

Bill C-43's defeat in the Senate was by no means predictable, though it was clear that, whatever the outcome, it would be close. The reasons for its defeat in the upper chamber are similar to the reasons for its close passage in the House: it was a compromise that pleased no one entirely, and so the pro- and anti- sides could be expected to be fairly balanced. The crucial difference in the Senate was that while it was a free vote, there was no guaranteed cabinet support (which in the Commons had amounted to almost 30 per cent of its support). Another twist was that under Senate rules, a tie is counted as a defeat. Only 86 out of 112 senators voted, and they split evenly (the Speaker of the Senate has the option to cast a vote *before* the main vote is taken, but he declined). So, as with free trade and the GST, the unelected upper chamber once again flexed its muscles, this time to the point of defeating a central piece of government legislation. The justice minister and Prime Minister Mulroney immediately stated that the government would not try again before the next election, and perhaps never. The irony of this outcome is that its political effect is likely to be not much different from what might have happened had Bill C-43 passed. The "chill factor" will be removed, in that physicians will not have to worry about potentially violating criminal law when performing abortions, but most of the key issues (e.g., on financing and clinics) will still be up to the provinces. Anti-abortion forces will not disappear, and the possibility of injunctions still exists, though governments may move to restrict it.

DISCUSSION

The politics of abortion in Canada will move to a new but familiar phase with the defeat of Bill C-43. It will be one of local and provincial battles, court cases and prosecutions to test and limit the law. This phase, and the ones that preceded it, illustrate several important points about contemporary Canadian politics.

It is clear that since the Charter, the courts are more entangled in the policy process than ever before. During the debate over Bill C-43, opposition members called for an immediate reference to the Supreme Court to test the bill's constitutionality. The government refused, stating that this would abdicate Parliament's responsibility to legislate. That the idea of a reference could be seriously entertained at all, however, shows how thin the line between legislature and courts has become. As institutions, furthermore, the courts may be ill-equipped to deal with some policy issues. The simple fact that the Charter now gives the Supreme Court wide latitude in reviewing legislation does not necessarily make the judges either infallible or any better equipped to solve public policy problems than elected politicians or ordinary citizens. Unelected and largely unaccountable, judges are removed from the daily context of politics. Moreover, they reason about policy problems through the application of legal principles. This is often essential, of course, but it sometimes ignores the more prosaic considerations that must be the foundation of good public policy. Consider the way that the courts have dealt with the question of access, for example. Most people choose where to live, and where they live makes a difference in the level of public services they enjoy. Rural residents (and as a practical matter this includes most people outside of the major centres) have "unequal" access to medical services, including abortion, and will continue to have "unequal" access. The courts declared that access under section 251 was inadequate, but they never defined what level of access would be acceptable. Another example of the limits of courts in the policy-making process was the legal circus surrounding the Dodd and Daigle cases.

The politics of abortion in Canada also casts some light on the "New Right" and contemporary feminism. Abortion is obviously contentious, but it holds a special place in the new politics of morality that have swept the western democracies in the last ten years. These new politics are partly a reflection of the new political agendas of neo-conservative governments in Britain and the United States. Ronald Reagan and Margaret Thatcher, and to some extent Brian Mulroney and Bill Vander Zalm, pursued policies that call for the maximum of freedom in the economic sphere (hence deregulation, privatization, tax reform, and free trade) and a heightened restraint in the moral sphere. This restraint has led to a reassertion of family values, and attacks on pornography, prostitution, drugs, and homosexuality. The anti-abortion movement, while it antedates these new politics, has been affected by them. Leading members of Campaign Life, for example, are also affiliated with REAL Women, a conservative, pro-family, anti-feminist women's organization.[145] Abortion holds a special place in this galaxy of causes because it condenses all of them within itself. Abortion is about women's rights, and hence about family, sexuality, promiscuity, and reproduction. It is also about the nature of human life, when it occurs, and how it should be respected.

The anti-abortion rights movement thus is part of a broader agenda that has seen some successes in the last few years. This may give it additional momentum, but there are several other reasons why it will probably continue to gain visibility and strength over the next few years. The first is simply the dynamics of action and reaction that were evident in the Morgentaler saga: the more abortion clinics around, the greater the affront and the more likely people are to picket and demonstrate. The defeat of Bill C-43 may lead to easier access to abortion and to more clinics, and anti-abortion rights protests and interventions can be expected to increase. The second reason is that it would seem that while Morgentaler was winning in the courts, the anti-abortion rights forces were winning in the streets. Their demonstrations and rallies were larger and represented a broader cross-section of Canadian society than anything pro-abortionists could muster since 1980. This may be in part because the anti-abortion rights movement can rely on a pre-existing network of religious and community organizations, whereas the pro-abortion rights movement has been largely confined to feminist and civil liberties groups that have sprung up only in the last decade. The third reason is that anti-abortion rights groups are getting smarter by appropriating the rhetoric of their enemies. Alliance for Life, for example, circulates an anti-abortion pamphlet entitled *Personhood and Discrimination* that draws analogies between the struggle for women's rights and the struggle for fetal rights. The whole conceptual apparatus of "rights" is increasingly being used to argue against abortion.

Those who oppose abortion may get help from an unexpected and unwilling source: modern feminism. We saw that the right to an abortion became the focus for the Canadian feminist movement in the early 1970s. While Canadian feminism certainly expanded beyond abortion by the 1980s to include economic demands such as equity employment, abortion was always near the heart of the movement. Not all feminists, of course, supported abortion, but these so-called "maternal feminists" were a minority. More recently, some feminists in the mainstream of the women's movement have begun to have second thoughts about abortion. Feminism itself had attacked the idea that pregnancy was some sort of illness that required technological medicine administered by (usually) male doctors. Pregnancy was entirely normal, and to regard it otherwise was to perpetuate sexist stereotypes of the "delicacy" of women.[146] But this undermined the notion of pregnancy as a "threat to the mother's health," outside of a few rare occurrences. Feminism's view of pregnancy inevitably led to the conclusion that abortion was a right, and not a health necessity as had been argued up to the 1960s.[147]

Advances in medical technology have forced a reconsideration of the choices people make. Medical technology now makes it possible to discern exceedingly small fetal abnormalities quite early. The possibility of choosing abortion for eugenic reasons has been attacked by groups representing the disabled. The new technology has also provided new knowledge about the fetus and its development in the first trimester, knowledge that makes it increasingly difficult to treat the fetus as mere "tissue."[148] Some feminists are also beginning to re-evaluate women's experiences of abortion as being much less benign than previously assumed. A particularly heretical thought is that easy abortion may in fact be more in men's interest than in women's: by providing an easy way out of "accidents," it makes women more sexually available.[149]

Modern feminist discourse no longer focuses on abortion, in part no doubt because it seems as though that issue has now been won. Instead, recent thinking has turned to the broader question of reproductive rights, of which abortion is only a part. The issue of reproductive rights stems from recently available medical technologies that can (1) operate on the fetus while in utero, and thus treat it in practice as a person with rights separate from the mother's, (2) determine the fetus's genetic make-up, and thus provide information that might be used to abort for what most people would see as eugenic reasons, (3) allow a woman to "rent" her uterus for surrogate motherhood, or (4) use fetal tissue for medical treatments.[150] Some feminists also worry that these new technologies are male in spirit, since they are invasive and controlling, as well as in practice, since they are usually dominated by male physicians and researchers. These considerations are leading some radical feminists to think about "lay abortions," because the techniques are relatively simple, and women aborting women would express their power and control over their own bodies.[151] For other feminists, it raises urgent and troubling questions about an easy embrace of abortion "rights." The pro-abortion rights movement is not synonymous with feminism, and the internal debates over reproductive technologies may simply show the openness and vitality of the contemporary women's movement. But insofar as contemporary feminism engages in a wider debate on reproduction and abortion, it may present a less united front and so give its opponents an edge.

Abortion will continue to be controversial in Canada. The Supreme Court's 1988 decision in the Morgentaler case led to two years of street demonstrations, court battles, and divergent provincial regulations on access. The defeat of Bill C-43 is not likely to change that very much. The provinces still have control over health, and so can determine whether abortions must be performed in hospitals or clinics. This is crucial, since Henry Morgentaler's entire crusade may be seen as a struggle for free-standing abortion clinics. If abortions must be performed in accredited hospitals, the doctors who perform them will be regulated by hospital board policies and procedures. Clinics, on the other hand, will be open targets for anti-abortion protesters, who seem increasingly prepared to use forceful tactics to prevent abortions. While injunctions like the ones in the Dodd and Daigle cases are now unlikely in light of the Supreme Court's strong ruling, virtually every aspect of law that affects abortion is open to legal challenge *from both sides*. On balance, the defeat of Bill C-43 served the interests of the pro-abortion rights lobby, as have most recent court decisions dealing with abortion. The anti-abortion rights movement should not be discounted, however, for several reasons.

First, even a few well-publicized actions against physicians performing abortions may be enough to dissuade other doctors. Second, as noted above, there has been a gradual shift in anti-abortion arguments from religious to medical and rights-related grounds. The adoption of "mainstream" forms of discourse may provide new rhetorical muscle to moral arguments that have little resonance in a secular society. Third, the pro-abortion rights movement, having won the argument of rights, now must struggle for access. But access is more of an administrative matter than one of rights. While the movement will argue strenuously that a right is a right, and that all women must have access regardless of income or geographical location, in practice it will be pressing claims for medical resources and personnel. Claims of this sort are less compelling than claims for rights. Moreover, the anti-abortion rights movement at minimum need only maintain the status quo. Statistics Canada data show that in 1988 there were 360,000 live births, and 65,000 legal abortions, that half of abortions are performed on women under the age of twenty-five, and that over 99 per cent of abortions occur before the twentieth week of pregnancy. From the anti-abortion perspective, these are not happy statistics, but they will be used to argue that abortion rates are already high in Canada and that there is more than enough access.

There have been no clear winners and losers in this story. Twenty years after he began, Henry Morgentaler was fighting virtually the same battles, though with different antagonists. The relatively small circle of lawyers, doctors, and legislators that had decided abortion policy in the 1960s is now crowded with religious organizations, pro- and anti-abortion lobbies, women's organizations, constitutional experts, and provincial governments. Beyond that circle is a new one, however, or at least one whose lines were more sharply drawn. The courts in the 1970s emerged as the strategic vantage point from which to launch assaults on the law. The Charter accentuates this further, forcing judges to be the sometimes unwilling partners of legislators in designing the scope and ambit of law and policy.

Discussion Questions

1 How does the Charter affect the role of the courts in Canadian democracy? Discuss in relation to the different court decisions regarding abortion.

2 Both pro- and anti-abortion groups are intensely devoted to their respective causes. Anti-abortion groups in particular are likely to organize all their politics around this single issue, voting, for example, only on that criterion. What might the effects of "single-issue" politics be on the political system?

3 How are "moral" policy issues different, if at all, from economic policy issues such as the Free Trade Agreement? How are they debated and what are their dynamics?

4 Canadian federal politicians were often criticized for their inaction on the abortion question, though this inaction might also be seen as a measure of prudence in trying not to incite further divisions over an already divisive issue. Discuss.

5 Discuss the issue of "reproductive rights". In what ways does this issue affect the question of abortion?

6 Prostaglandins (drugs that induce miscarriage) are available in Canada in forms such as the "morning-after pill," and section 287 of the Criminal Code explicitly exempts the use of a drug, device, or other means to prevent implantation of a fertilized ovum. Does this make the whole attempt to regulate abortion pointless?

7   From an interest-group perspective, what are the advantages and disadvantages of using the courts to effect policy change?

8   Discuss the nature of judicial Charter interpretation. How do courts go about reasoning in respect of "rights" enumerated in the Charter, and what are the advantages and disadvantages of such reasoning for public policy making?

9   One of the most telling critiques of the abortion law was that its application varied across the country. Since it was a federal law with national application, this seemed objectionable. But other policy fields (e.g., health and education) are within the provincial field, and variations are expected. Discuss the notion of uniformity and national standards with respect both to national policies and to ones under provincial jurisdiction.

10 Compare the provisions of Bill C-43 with the majority's reasoning in *Morgentaler*. Do you think that the bill successfully responded to the legal criticisms of section 251?

Chronology

3 October 1967	— House of Commons Standing Committee on Health and Welfare begins hearings on three private member's abortion bills
19 December 1967	— House of Commons Standing Committee on Health and Welfare tables interim report on abortion law
21 December 1967	— Government tables omnibus bill to amend the Criminal Code, including abortion sections
13 March 1968	— House of Commons Standing Committee on Health and Welfare tables final report on abortion law
19 December 1968	— omnibus bill to amend Criminal Code re-introduced into Commons
27 June 1969	— new section 251 of the Criminal Code becomes law
4 June 1970	— Morgentaler arrested for operating Montreal clinic; charged with conspiracy to commit abortion and procuring abortion; arraigned and released on bail two days later

12 June 1970	– preliminary inquiry begins before Justice Fauteux; defence request for postponement denied
16 June 1970	– defence application to Quebec Court of Queen's Bench for writs of prohibition against Justice Fauteux
20 July 1970	– Justice Desaulniers orders Justice Fauteux to suspend further proceedings
25 September 1970	– application made by Morgentaler before the Quebec Court of Queen's Bench that all further proceedings against him be stopped
30 October 1970	– Quebec Court of Queen's Bench dismisses application to prohibit charges, but finds procedural unfairness in the way that Morgentaler's clinic was raided and the preliminary inquiry handled
25 October 1971	– Quebec government appeal to Quebec Court of Appeal against dismissal and discharge dismissed
25 November 1971	– papers filed with Supreme Court of Canada for leave to appeal decision by Quebec Court of Appeal
25 January 1972	– Supreme Court refuses leave to appeal
22 January 1973	– United States Supreme Court hands down decision in *Roe vs. Wade*
16 March 1973	– Morgentaler makes public announcement in Toronto that he has personally aborted over 5,000 women
13 May 1973	– *W5* documentary on abortion broadcast on Mother's Day, with segment showing Morgentaler aborting a woman at his clinic
15 August 1973	– police raid Morgentaler's Montreal clinic, make arrests, and seize equipment; Morgentaler arraigned the next day and returned to jail pending bail hearing
29 August 1973	– Quebec Attorney General Jerome Choquette takes unusual step of preferring indictment regarding Morgentaler's twelve charges of performing illegal abortions; Morgentaler's defence counsel applies to Quebec Court of Appeal to quash the indictment; application rejected 21 September
18 October 1973	– jury trial begins; jury consists of 11 men and 1 woman
13 November 1973	– after almost 10 hours of deliberation, jury acquits Morgentaler; Crown files notice of appeal

13 February 1974	— Quebec Superior Court upholds order that Morgentaler pay the provincial government $354,799 in back taxes for 1969–72. Provincial tax inspectors seize Morgentaler's papers, diaries, and tapes and close his bank account
25 April 1974	— Quebec Court of Appeal upholds Crown appeal of jury acquittal and directs trial judge to pass sentence; Morgentaler appeals to Supreme Court
2 May 1974	— trial judge (Justice Hugessen) refuses to pass sentence as directed because of Morgentaler's appeal to Supreme Court
14 May 1974	— Quebec Court of Appeal once again orders the trial judge to pass sentence and directs that Morgentaler be put in jail; Morgentaler seeks to appeal this ruling as well to Supreme Court; appeal denied, and Morgentaler put in Parthenais prison 2 days later
3 June 1974	— Supreme Court rejects Morgentaler's second appeal and orders him to return to trial judge for sentencing
25 July 1974	— Morgentaler sentenced to 18 months' imprisonment and 3 years' probation following release precluding his performing abortions except in an accredited hospital
26 March 1975	— Supreme Court, in 6–3 decision, dismisses Morgentaler's appeal of the 25 April 1974 ruling of the Quebec Court of Appeal overturning the jury acquittal
27 March 1975	— Morgentaler taken to Bordeaux Jail; 6 weeks later is moved, at his request, to the Waterloo Rehabilitation Centre
5 May 1975	— Choquette signs order for preferred indictment against Morgentaler for new abortion charges
29 May 1975	— Morgentaler arraigned before Quebec Court of Queen's Bench on charge that he performed an illegal abortion on 15 August 1973; jury consists of 7 men and 5 women
9 June 1975	— jury acquits Morgentaler after fifty-five minutes' deliberation, despite instruction by presiding judge (Justice Bisson) that the defence of necessity is not available to the accused; Crown appeals to Quebec

	Court of Appeal and lays ten more charges against Morgentaler
29 September 1975	— Badgley Committee (Committee on the Operation of the Abortion Law) appointed
20 January 1976	— Quebec Court of Appeal dismisses Crown appeal and upholds jury acquittal
22 January 1976	— Ronald Basford, federal minister of justice, sets aside the conviction on the original indictment and orders a retrial
9 February 1976	— Crown announces that it will appeal to Supreme Court against Quebec Court of Appeal upholding of jury acquittal; leave to appeal is denied by Supreme Court on 15 March 1976
17 July 1976	— Otto Lang, federal minister of justice, introduces Bill C-71, which includes the "Morgentaler amendment," preventing a court of appeal from reversing jury acquittals
18 September 1976	— jury acquits Morgentaler on retrial of original indictment; on the same day, Morgentaler ordered to appear in court in November on 8 new charges of performing illegal abortions
5 April 1982	— Morgentaler sends telegram to Jean Chrétien (minister of justice) urging amendment of abortion law; says he is considering establishment of clinics in other provinces
15 April 1982	— League for Life (Manitoba group) sends telegram to Roland Penner (attorney general, Manitoba) saying it will fight Morgentaler's attempt to establish a clinic in Manitoba; telegram to Chrétien as well
24 April 1982	— in address to the Canadian Abortion Rights Action League (CARAL), Morgentaler announces that he is ready to establish clinics across the country, especially in Toronto
9 August 1982	— Supreme Court rules that Borowski should go before the Saskatchewan Court of Queen's Bench to argue case that Bill of Rights protects fetus
23 November 1982	— Manitoba College of Physicians and Surgeons says it will not license a Morgentaler abortion clinic; Roland

	Penner says that he will not stay prosecution should Morgentaler try to establish one
30 November 1982	— Penner and Morgentaler hold joint press conference in Winnipeg; Penner says he has no choice but to prosecute; Morgentaler vows to open Winnipeg clinic
9 December 1982	— Roy McMurtry (attorney general, Ontario) says he too will have no choice but to prosecute should Morgentaler try to establish a clinic in Ontario
5 January 1983	— CARAL announces that it will seek standing in Borowski's Regina court case
28 January 1983	— Mr. Justice Matheson schedules Borowski case for 9 May 1983; denies standing to CARAL, Canadian Civil Liberties Union, and Campaign Life
9 February 1983	— community group starts fight to revoke Morgentaler's occupancy permit for Winnipeg clinic; while Morgentaler has development permit, his occupancy permit will be delayed
2 March 1983	— Morgentaler receives licence from Manitoba College of Physicians and Surgeons, empowering him to perform legal therapeutic abortions; Penner warns Morgentaler that he must use a therapeutic abortion committee
29 March 1983	— Morgentaler announces opening of clinic delayed to April 18; Winnipeg Catholic diocese denounces clinic and *Winnipeg Free Press* publishes petition with 35,000 names against abortion
2 May 1983	— Morgentaler's request to have Winnipeg clinic declared a hospital denied by province
May 1983	— after several delays and attempts by anti-abortion rights groups to quash occupancy permit, Morgentaler's Winnipeg abortion clinic opens; Borowski sets up pickets for May 6 opening
9 May 1983	— Borowski case begins in Regina
28 May 1983	— Regina case finishes; Mr. Justice Matheson reserves decision; Borowski returns to Winnipeg for a sit-in at Penner's office
3 June 1983	— Winnipeg clinic raided by police

CANADA'S ABORTION SAGA

14 June 1983	— Morgentaler in Winnipeg to face charges; first time he has been in court since Quebec trials in 1970s
15 June 1983	— Morgentaler opens Toronto clinic amid demonstrations
20 June 1983	— Morris Manning (Morgentaler's Toronto lawyer) asks Supreme Court of Ontario for an injunction against police interference with clinic since abortion law is unconstitutional
25 June 1983	— police raid Winnipeg clinic for second time; Morgentaler vows to stay open
5 July 1983	— police raid Morgentaler's Toronto clinic; Supreme Court of Ontario dismisses application for injunction
5 October 1983	— preliminary hearings begin before Provincial Court Judge Kris Stefanson on Winnipeg charges
13 October 1983	— Mr. Justice Matheson of Saskatchewan Court of Queen's Bench decides against Borowksi in Regina case
20 October 1983	— preliminary hearings end in Winnipeg; Judge Stefanson decides that Morgentaler should go forward to trial in January or February 1984
14 November 1983	— Borowski files appeal of Regina decision with the Saskatchewan Court of Appeal
21 November 1983	— Toronto trial opens in the Supreme Court of Ontario before Associate Chief Justice William Parker; before the charges themselves can be addressed, Manning launches a challenge to the constitutionality of the abortion law; this issue must be resolved before the substance of the charges themselves may be addressed
8 December 1983	— Penner drops conspiracy charges against Morgentaler and staff; replaces them with charges against Morgentaler, Scott, and nurse Lynn Crocker of performing illegal abortions
25 January 1984	— Mr. Justice Peter Morse of Manitoba Court of Queen's Bench agrees to 3-month delay in Winnipeg trial so that Ontario trial may proceed first

20 July 1984   – after several months of argument, delay, and judicial reflection, Mr. Justice Parker decides against Morgentaler and rejects Manning's constitutional challenge of the abortion law; Parker sets September 17 as date for criminal trial

10 August 1984   – Morgentaler and Manning launch appeal of Parker's decision to Ontario Court of Appeal

15 October 1984   – appeal denied and trial begins before Mr. Justice Parker with selection of jury

19 October 1984   – jury selected and Toronto trial against Morgentaler, Smoling, and Scott begins

8 November 1984   – jury acquits the defendants in Toronto trial; next day Morgentaler promises to re-open Toronto clinic and demands that McMurtry not interfere

10 November 1984   – Greg Brodsky (Morgentaler's Winnipeg lawyer) announces that the Winnipeg clinic will remain closed until appeals from Toronto trial are completed; Winnipeg trial postponed indefinitely, until the Ontario case is resolved

4 December 1984   – McMurtry announces that Crown will appeal jury verdict to Ontario Court of Appeal; Morgentaler says he will open clinic anyway, and Manning launches cross-appeal against McMurtry

11 December 1984   – McMurtry asks Morgentaler to stop performing abortions at Toronto clinic until Crown appeal is resolved; Morgentaler refuses

19 December 1984   – Toronto police issue warrant for Morgentaler's arrest; Scott arrested outside clinic that evening; Morgentaler surrenders himself the next day

4 January 1985   – Morgentaler and Scott appear before Ontario Provincial Court Judge Walter Hryciuk on whether a trial should proceed on new charges, or be delayed until the resolution of Crown appeal

8 March 1985   – Manitoba College of Physicians and Surgeons renews Morgentaler's medical licence; the president of the College resigns in protest three days later

23 March 1985   – police raid Winnipeg clinic as it re-opens and arrest Morgentaler; new charges laid

29 March 1985	— Manitoba College of Physicians and Surgeons suspends Morgentaler's medical licence for 7 days for his "apparent willful and deliberate resort" to performing abortions in an unapproved facility; Morgentaler promises to do abortions anyway
30 March 1985	— police raid Winnipeg clinic again on Saturday for the second time in 8 days and arrest Morgentaler; he vows to re-open on Monday
4 April 1985	— Manitoba College of Physicians and Surgeons wins interim injunction from Chief Justice Archibald Dewar of the Manitoba Court of Queen's Bench prohibiting Morgentaler from practising medicine in province until licence suspension can come to trail; Morgentaler agrees to abide by the injunction because of severe penalties attached; on the same day, Morgentaler is charged with 3 more abortion offenses as result of March 30 raid on clinic
9 April 1985	— Brodsky files a motion with the Manitoba Court of Queen's Bench to quash Morgentaler's licence suspension
15 April 1985	— Crown and defence lawyers agree to delay any further court action regarding Winnipeg abortion charges until Ontario trial is resolved
19 April 1985	— Crown appeal of Ontario Supreme Court jury acquittal begins before the Ontario Court of Appeal
7 May 1985	— appeal hearing ends; Ontario Court of Appeal reserves judgment
9 September 1985	— Mr. Justice James Wilson of Manitoba Court of Queen's Bench upholds temporary injunction by Manitoba College of Physicians and Surgeons against Morgentaler until College's civil suit seeking permanent injunction comes to trial; Morgentaler appeals
October 1985	— Ontario Court of Appeal overturns Morgentaler's 1984 jury acquittal and orders new trial; Morgentaler appeals
21 October 1985	— Manitoba College of Physicians and Surgeons refuses to license Morgentaler's Winnipeg clinic for abortions

CANADA'S ABORTION SAGA

15 December 1985	— Saskatchewan Court of Appeal begins hearings of Borowski's appeal of 1983 Regina decision; hearings last three days; court reserves judgment
15 May 1986	— Manitoba College of Physicians and Surgeons refuses for a second time to license Morgentaler's Winnipeg clinic for abortions
27 May 1986	— Robert Scott opens Toronto's second free-standing illegal abortion clinic
12 June 1986	— Manitoba Court of Appeal upholds College of Physicians and Surgeons' injunction against Morgentaler
24 September 1986	— Morgentaler, Scott, and Nikki Colodny arrested and charged, but charges stayed at Crown's request; the trio are released without bail and back at their clinics the same day
7 October 1986	— Supreme Court begins hearing Morgentaler appeal of Ontario Court of Appeal's overturning of 1983 jury acquittal; Manning focuses on Charter of Rights and Freedoms and the unconstitutionality of the abortion law; hearings end on October 10; court reserves judgment
30 April 1987	— Saskatchewan Court of Appeal rules against Borowski's claim that the Charter of Rights and Freedoms protects the fetus; Borowski appeals to Supreme Court
29 July 1987	— Supreme Court gives Borowski leave to appeal
23 September 1987	— Ontario drops 1986 charges against Morgentaler, Scott and Colodny pending judgment by Supreme Court on Morgentaler appeal; Manitoba government decides not to drop its charges
28 January 1988	— Supreme Court issues its 5–2 decision striking down the abortion law; next day the federal government pledges speedy action on new law
30 January 1988	— British Columbia announces that its health plan will only pay for abortions performed in hospitals after approval by a TAC
18 February 1988	— British Columbia Civil Liberties Association launches court challenge against provincial policy on abortion

7 March 1988	– British Columbia Supreme Court strikes down provincial regulations on abortion funding
12 May 1988	– Prime Minister Mulroney announces a free vote on abortion in Commons
June 1988	– Supreme Court postpones Borowski hearings to October
28 July 1988	– Commons free vote defeats government's abortion resolution as well as five amendments allowed by the Speaker; both pro- and anti-abortion rights forces declare a victory
2 September 1988	– federal government announces that it will not introduce new abortion legislation until after the national election
3 October 1988	– Borowski case begins before Supreme Court
22 November 1988	– Law Reform Commission releases its report *Crimes Against the Foetus* with proposals for a new abortion law
12 December 1988	– Morgentaler launches court action against New Brunswick's policy of not paying for abortions performed outside of approved hospitals
January-March 1989	– highly publicized anti-abortion protests in British Columbia lead to charges and injunctions against the protesters
10 March 1989	– Supreme Court rules that the issues raised in the Borowski case were moot since there was no abortion law; the Court states no position on the question of fetal rights
3 July 1989	– US Supreme Court upholds parts of Missouri's abortion law, which prohibited public hospitals and public employees from performing abortions
4 July 1989	– Gregory Murphy obtains an injunction from the Ontario Supreme Court preventing Barbara Dodd from having an abortion
7 July 1989	– Jean-Guy Tremblay obtains an injunction from the Quebec Superior Court preventing Chantal Daigle from having an abortion

11 July 1989	— Supreme Court of Ontario sets aside the Dodd injunction, citing procedural irregularities
17 July 1989	— Quebec Superior Court upholds the Daigle injunction on the grounds that the Quebec Charter of Rights and Freedoms protects the fetus
26 July 1989	— Quebec Court of Appeal upholds the Superior Court ruling in the Daigle case
1 August 1989	— Supreme Court gives Chantal Daigle leave to appeal
8 August 1989	— in midst of deciding on the Daigle injunction, the Supreme Court is informed that Ms. Daigle has already had the abortion; the judges continue to consider the case and rule to lift the injunction
27 October 1989	— Morgentaler charged with performing illegal abortions (i.e., outside of approved hospital) in Nova Scotia
3 November 1989	— Federal government introduces Bill C-43
22 May 1990	— Bill C-43 returned without amendments from committee to House for third reading
29 May 1990	— Bill C-43 passes third reading in the House of Commons 140–131 votes
31 January 1991	— Senate defeats Bill C-43 in a free vote, 43–43 (under Senate rules, a tie is a defeat)

Notes

1   Anyone who writes about abortion policy must address the question of language. The sides of the debate are so clearly drawn and unalterably opposed that they concede nothing in terminology. "Pro-choice" is ideologically loaded, and moreover inaccurate since most people in that camp want taxpayers to be forced to pay for abortions, even if they disapprove of them. "Pro-life" is also loaded, in that it implies that the other side is not, and since surveys show that many who consider themselves "pro-life" also tend to favour capital punishment. Thus "abortion clinics" become "abortuaries" (a clever play on abattoir and mortuary), and the "fetus" or "fetal matter" becomes "the baby." Choices are unavoidable, and we have tried

to make ours as dispassionately as possible. We will use the terms "pro-abortion rights" and "anti-abortion rights" because they seem better to capture the real agendas of people in the respective camps.

2   Canada's statutory provisions regarding abortion have, since 1892, been part of the Criminal Code, but for ease of reference we shall refer to the "abortion law."

3   Lord Ellenborough's Act, 1803 (U.K.), 43 Geo. III, c. 58, s. 3. The 1861 Offenses Against the Person Act attached a maximum penalty of life imprisonment for performing abortions. In practice, women attempting self-induced abortions were rarely prosecuted: the law was aimed at the back-street abortionist; see Daniel Callahan, *Abortion: Law, Choice and Morality* (London: Macmillan, 1970), 142.

4   Diana Dimmer and Loreta Zubas, *Update on the Abortion Law in Canada* (Ottawa: National Association of Women and the Law, 1985), 2.

5   Interestingly, another section of the Criminal Code lumped abortion and contraception together, making it an indictable offence to "offer to sell, advertise, publish an advertisement of or have for sale or disposal any medicine, drug or article intended or represented as a means of preventing conception or causing abortion." Criminal Code of Canada, 1892, s. 179(c).

6   Committee on the Operation of the Abortion Law, *Report* (Ottawa: 1977), 67–68. Hereinafter referred to as Badgley Committee, *Report*.

7   Arrest and conviction remained rare, however: between 1900 and 1972, a total of 1,793 individuals were charged with procuring or attempting to procure an abortion; 64 per cent of these (1,155) were convicted. See Badgley Committee, *Report*, 68.

8   Joan Finnigan, "Should Canada Change its Abortion Law?" *Chatelaine* (August 1959), 103–105.

9   Ibid., 103.

10   Anne Collins, *The Big Evasion: Abortion, The Issue That Won't Go Away* (Toronto: Lester and Orpen Dennys, 1985), 16.

11   Alphonse de Valk, *Morality and Law in Canadian Politics: The Abortion Controversy* (Montreal: Palm Publishers, 1974).

12   *Globe and Mail*, 1 September 1961; op-ed articles appeared in *Globe and Mail*, 2–10 October 1961; 2 January 1963.

13   *Globe and Mail*, 2 January 1963.

14   de Valk, *Morality and Law in Canadian Politics*, 14–16; 23–26.

15   Ibid., 18. In June 1967 the CMA accepted deformity and sexual offenses as legal grounds also.

16   Collins, *The Big Evasion*, 17.

17   de Valk, *Morality and Law in Canadian Politics*, 27.

18   Collins, *The Big Evasion*, 41.

19   De Valk, *Morality and Law in Canadian Politics*, chap. 8.

20   Despite its ineffectiveness, the Catholic Church has long been the principal opponent of abortion rights, and its adversaries use this to their advantage (see, for example, the description of the quite deliberate selection of the Catholic Church as the "enemy" for political purposes, in Bernard Nathanson, *Aborting America* [New York: Doubleday, 1979, 50–51]). The Church's theological position on abortion is therefore of some interest. It is sometimes

thought that until 1869 the Church permitted abortions to the time of quickening. In fact, the Church has always held abortion to be morally reprehensible. The pre-1869 distinction was with regard to penital practice, in that punishment for aborting the "unformed" fetus was less severe. By 1869 the distinction between "formed" and "unformed" fetuses was medically unacceptable, and so the punishment of excommunication was extended to all abortions in the *Apostolicae Sedis* of Pius IX. Another error is that the Church opposes abortion because it believes that the soul is infused at birth. The Roman Catholic Church has never officially taken a position on "ensoulment"; its opposition to abortion is based rather on the more general principles that God, not man, creates life, and the prohibition of harm to innocents. This is a practical, not a theological, argument. See John Connory, S.J., *Abortion: The Development of the Roman Catholic Perspective* (Chicago: Loyola University Press, 1977) and John Noonan, Jr., *Contraception* (Cambridge: Harvard University Press, 1965). For a cogent critique of the Catholic position see Callahan, *Abortion*, chap. 12.

21   Canadian Bar Association; Humanist Fellowship of Montreal, Inc.; Canadian Medical Association; Association for the Modernization of Canadian Abortion Laws; Emergency Organization for the Defence of Unborn Children; Catholic Physicians Guild of Manitoba; Presbyterian Church of Canada; National Council of Women; Canadian Abortion Law Reform Association; Women's Liberation Group, Anglican Church of Canada.

22   House of Commons, Standing Committee on Health and Welfare, *Minutes of Proceedings and Evidence*, no. 3, 19 October 1967, 66.

23   House of Commons, Standing Committee on Health and Welfare, *First Report*, 19 December 1967.

24   House of Commons, *Journals of the House of Commons of Canada*, vol. 115, 9 May 1969, 1016–1017.

25   Section 251 was the "abortion law," but several other Criminal Code provisions, still in effect after the 1988 Morgentaler decision, govern aspects of abortion. Section 159(2)(c) prohibits the sale or advertising of things that will cause abortion; section 221(1) makes it unlawful to kill the fetus during the birth process; section 252 prohibits the procurement of things that will cause abortion. Sections 159(2)(c) and 252 are weakened by their respective reliance on the terms "without lawful justification" and "unlawfully."

26   One estimate held that in 1976 only 20.1 per cent of civilian hospitals in Canada had a TAC. This was in part because only 41 per cent of Canadian hospitals had the obstetrical and gynecological staff and facilities needed to perform abortions and hence even be eligible to establish a TAC. Of the eligible hospitals, only 48 per cent had TACs. Hospitals failed to establish TACs for two types of reasons: religious and professional/ethical. Fully one-quarter of eligible hospitals without TACs were owned by or affiliated with religious denominations. See Badgley Committee, *Report*, 27–31.

27   Myrna Kostash, *Long Way from Home: The Story of the Sixties Generation in Canada* (Toronto: James Lorimer, 1980), 176–178.

28   Krista Maeots, "Abortion Caravan," *The Canadian Forum* (July–August 1970), 157.

29   Kostash, *Long Way from Home*, 176.

30   Maeots, "Abortion Caravan," 157. See also Eleanor Wright Pelrine, *Abortion in Canada* (Toronto: New Press, 1971), 14: "And the right to "abortion on demand" has become the rallying cry of the women's liberation movement...their slogan "This uterus is not government property" symbolizes the feelings of many Canadian women."

31 Collins, *The Big Evasion*, 25.

32 Kostash, *Long Way from Home*, 178.

33 Royal Commission on the Status of Women, *Report* (Ottawa: Information Canada, 1970), 286.

34 Ibid., 286–287.

35 Eleanor Wright Pelrine, *Morgentaler: The Doctor Who Couldn't Turn Away* (Toronto: James Lorimer, 1983), 5–6.

36 Ibid., 6.

37 Ibid., 15.

38 Ibid., 22.

39 Ibid., 25.

40 Another popular technique, developed in 1960 and perfected in Sweden, was saline injection, or "insillation." This was devised to deal with aborting pregnancies after the fourteenth week. A small amount of amniotic fluid is removed and replaced with either a salt or glucose solution that usually kills the fetus and induces labour within thirty-six hours. Other, less widely used techniques are hysterotomy (a mini-caesarean section—fourteen to eighteen weeks) and D & E (dilatation and evacuation that combines vacuum aspiration with use of forceps to remove the larger bits of fetal matter—thirteen to twenty-two weeks). See Henry Morgentaler, *Abortion and Contraception* (Don Mills: General, 1982), chap. 4.

41 Pelrine, *Morgentaler*, 35–45. These pages reproduce an article Morgentaler published on the technique in the *Canadian Medical Journal*.

42 A side issue, though one of some importance in light of the legal bills Morgentaler later faced, was whether he made any money. Even at a conservative estimate, Morgentaler likely grossed between $600,000 and $800,000 a year in 1970 dollars. See Pelrine, *Morgentaler*, 48–49.

43 Pelrine, *Morgentaler*, 75-76; see also Bernard M. Dickens, "The Morgentaler Case: Criminal Process and Abortion Law," *Osgoode Hall Law Journal, 14* (October 1976): 230–232.

44 *Roe et al. v. Wade*, District Attorney of Dallas County, 410 U.S. 113 (1973). The majority opinion in the 7–2 decision was written by Mr. Justice Blackmun. An unmarried pregnant woman (Jane Roe) brought action against the constitutionality of several articles of the Penal Code of the State of Texas that prohibited abortions except to save the life of the mother. Roe argued that women have a right to terminate pregnancy, and this right is grounded in the right to personal liberty and privacy. Blackmun noted that while the American Constitution did not "explicitly mention any right of privacy," the Supreme Court itself, in a long series of decisions, had recognized such a right or "zones of privacy" as residing in the Constitution, and that right was broad enough to encompass a woman's decision to abort. The right was absolute, however, only in the first trimester before the fetus became viable; after that point the state had an interest in protecting fetal life and could regulate abortion even to the point of proscribing it, except when the mother's life or health had to be preserved.

45 Morgentaler, *Abortion and Contraception*, x; Pelrine, *Morgentaler*, 82.

46 Pelrine, *Morgentaler*, 83.

47 Common law defenses against criminal acts are supported by section 7(3) of the Criminal Code.

48 Collins, *The Big Evasion*, 141.

49 Dickens, "The Morgentaler Case," 235.

50   For this appeal, Armand-Sheppard had for the first time prepared several Canadian Bill of
      Rights arguments to claim that women had the right to abortion; see Dickens, "The Mor-
      gentaler Case," 237.

51   Pelrine, *Morgentaler*, 190.

52   Badgley Committee, *Report*, 135.

53   Collins, *The Big Evasion*, 1–13. Borowski quit the cabinet of NDP Premier Ed Schreyer in
      1971 after he discovered that provincial medicare was paying for abortions performed on
      Manitoba women outside of Canada. He considered this illegal. He later started a health
      food store in Winnipeg and devoted himself full-time to battling abortion.

54   Collins, *The Big Evasion*, 34–35.

55   *Globe and Mail*, 20 November 1982.

56   *Winnipeg Free Press*, 5 April 1982.

57   *Winnipeg Free Press*, 15 April 1982.

58   *Winnipeg Free Press*, 23 November 1982.

59   Collins, *The Big Evasion*.

60   *Winnipeg Free Press*, 1 December 1982.

61   *Globe and Mail*, 10 December 1982.

62   *Globe and Mail*, 10 May 1983.

63   *Winnipeg Free Press*, 14 October 1983.

64   *Globe and Mail*, 15 November 1983.

65   He made the announcement on 27 January at a University of Manitoba debate with Borowski;
      Winnipeg Free Press, 28 January 1983.

66   *Winnipeg Free Press*, 3 May 1983. Morgentaler had tried this ploy during the Quebec trials,
      and while on the surface it appeared a reasonable way out of the impasse, it was in fact
      unworkable. Section 251 referred to "accredited" or "approved" hospitals. Accreditation is
      done by the Canadian Council on Hospital Accreditation, and its minimum standards for the
      range of diagnostic, surgical, and obstetrical services far exceeded those available in
      Morgentaler's clinic. While standards for provincial approval vary widely, most demand a
      minimum physician/bed ratio. As it happened, Manitoba did not have such a ratio require-
      ment, but it was simply absurd to label his little operation a hospital—it was analogous to a
      dentist demanding that his or her office be declared a "hospital." For a fuller discussion, see
      Badgley Committee, *Report*, chap. 5.

67   *Globe and Mail*, 4 June 1983.

68   *Winnipeg Free Press*, 11 June 1983.

69   *Globe and Mail*, 8 June 1983.

70   *Globe and Mail*, 16 June 1983.

71   *Winnipeg Free Press*, 27 June 1983.

72   *Globe and Mail*, 6 July 1983. Morris Manning, Morgentaler's Toronto lawyer, had earlier tried
      to get an injunction against police interference with the clinic, and the court's denial of in-
      junction was delivered virtually in the midst of the raid; see Kirk Makin, "Clinic's Bid Rejected
      But Right of Courts Affirmed by Judge," *Globe and Mail*, 6 July 1983.

73 Kathleen McDonnell, "Claim No Easy Victories: The Fight for Reproductive Rights," in *Still Ain't Satisfied: Canadian Feminism Today*, ed. Maureen Fitzgerald, Connie Guberman, and Margie Wolfe (Toronto: The Women's Press, 1982), 33.

74 *Globe and Mail*, 30 October 1983.

75 A little over a year later, Morgentaler's clinic staff and other supporters worried openly about this shift; see *Globe and Mail*, 21 February 1985.

76 *Globe and Mail*, 22 November 1983.

77 *Globe and Mail*, 22 November 1983.

78 *Globe and Mail*, 17 December 1983. Pennington and Cooper cross-examined Manning's witnesses in an effort to undermine the claims of capricious administration of the abortion law by TACs. They also developed an initial defence that the fetus was human and therefore had rights too.

79 *Globe and Mail*, 21 March 1984; *Winnipeg Free Press*, 22 March 1984; *Globe and Mail*, 6 April 1984. Pennington, the federal lawyer, made the arguments about the fetus and the law's application, while Cooper, the Ontario government lawyer, made the Charter argument.

80 *Globe and Mail*, 7 May 1984.

81 *Globe and Mail*, 21 July 1984.

82 *Globe and Mail*, 21 July 1984.

83 Manning secured the services of two American professional jury selection consultants. In the end, it took a review of 132 people before 12 could be selected for the jury: 6 men and 6 women, 6 married with children and 6 single. Alan Cooper remarked that the selection "was probably the most important thing we will do here."

84 *Globe and Mail*, 24, 25 October 1984.

85 *Winnipeg Free Press*, 6 November 1984.

86 Jury deliberations are secret, but it is plausible that this jury took a common-sense approach to assessing the doctors' guilt. Abortions were performed in hospitals everyday for largely non-medical reasons, and these three physicians were doing exactly the same thing but without bureaucratic permission. Alternatively, though this is speculative, the jury may have been swayed by Bora Laskin's dissent on the defence-of-necessity decision by the Supreme Court in 1975. Laskin had allowed for a greater degree of jury latitude than had his brothers on the Court. The jury, in the midst of its deliberations, asked to see the text of this earlier decision.

87 *Globe and Mail*, 9 November 1984.

88 *Globe and Mail*, 9 November 1984. Several years later anti-abortion activists were to copy Morgentaler's tactics, openly breaking laws and disobeying injunctions in attempts to stop abortions.

89 *Globe and Mail*, 10 November 1984.

90 *Globe and Mail*, 12 February 1985.

91 *Globe and Mail*, 21, 22 February 1985.

92 *Globe and Mail*, 30 April 1985.

93 *Globe and Mail*, 1, 4 May 1985.

94 *Globe and Mail*, 2 October 1985.

95   Section 7 reads: "Everyone has the right to life, liberty and security of the person and the right not to be deprived thereof except in accordance with the principles of fundamental justice."

96   *R. v. Morgentaler*, Reasons for Judgment by the Rt. Hon. Brian Dickson, 11.

97   Ibid., 16.

98   Section 1 reads: "The Canadian Charter of Rights and Freedoms guarantees the rights and freedoms set out in it subject only to such reasonable limits prescribed by law as can be demonstrably justified in a free and democratic society."

99   *R. v. Morgentaler*, Reasons...Beetz, 3.

100   *R. v. Morgentaler*, Reasons...Wilson, 5.

101   Ibid., 14-15.

102   *R. v. Morgentaler*, Reasons...McIntyre, 6.

103   Ibid., 12-13.

104   *Globe and Mail*, 29 January 1988.

105   *Globe and Mail*, 30 January 1988.

106   *Globe and Mail*, 13 May 1988.

107   *Globe and Mail*, 29 July 1988.

108   *Globe and Mail*, 23 November 1988.

109   Canada, Law Reform Commission, *Crimes Against the Foetus*, Working Paper 58 (Ottawa: Law Reform Commission, 1988). This monograph was the result of research on the wider issue of protection of human life that started in 1986.

110   Ibid., 64. In cases where the fetus was capable of independent survival, medical authorization would have to be given by two physicians. The proposal was therefore a combination of gestational, health, and eugenic rationales.

111   *Globe and Mail*, 28 January 1989. For a discussion of attempts to regulate abortion through health legislation, see Sheilah L. Martin, *Women's Reproductive Health, the Charter of Rights and Freedoms, and the Canada Health Act* (Ottawa: Canadian Advisory Council on the Status of Women, 1989).

112   *Globe and Mail*, 10 February 1989.

113   *Globe and Mail*, 24 February 1989.

114   *Globe and Mail*, 3 March 1989.

115   *Globe and Mail*, 7 March 1989.

116   *Globe and Mail*, 8 March 1989.

117   *Globe and Mail*, 10 March 1989.

118   This led to speculation that the government might pass a new abortion law and immediately refer it to the courts for a judgement. Under such a procedure, the courts would be virtual partners in the legislative process.

119   *Globe and Mail*, 10 March 1989.

120   *Toronto Star*, 10 March 1989.

121   This tactic had been tried without success as far back as 1984. The father got an initial injunction, which was then overturned by the Ontario Supreme Court. The tactic also failed in 1988 in Alberta. Private prosecutions had always been possible under section 251.

122 *Globe and Mail*, 5 July 1989. Dodd had two previous children, aged five and four, from another relationship. Those children were living with their father.

123 *Diamond v. Hirsch*, Man. Q. B., 6 July 1989.

124 *Globe and Mail*, 8 July 1989.

125 *Globe and Mail*, 12 July 1989.

126 *Globe and Mail*, 19 July 1989.

127 *Maclean's*, 31 July 1989.

128 *Daigle v. Tremblay*, (1989) S.C.R. cites the English translation of the two sections:

   • Every human being has a right to life, and to personal security, inviolability and freedom.

   • Every human being whose life is in peril has a right to assistance.

   Viens also found some basis for fetal rights in the Civil Code.

129 An interesting twist in the ruling, however, was that the injunction was contingent on the status of the fetus, not the father. In theory, the Viens ruling meant that anyone could apply for an injunction to stop an abortion.

130 *Globe and Mail*, 26 July 1989.

131 *Tremblay v. Daigle*, (1989) R.J.Q. 1735, 59 D.L.R. (4th), 609–642.

132 Doug Lewis, minister of justice, as quoted in the *Globe and Mail*, 2 August 1989.

133 *Globe and Mail*, 14 August 1989. The interview was given to Radio-Canada. Daigle also gave an interview to the British tabloid *The Mail*, for which she received $8,000.

134 *Tremblay v. Daigle*, (1989) S.C.R.

135 *Chronicle-Herald*, 27 October 1989; 31 October 1989. The provincial legislation was already before the courts in a case initiated by the Canadian Abortion Rights Action League. The injunction was granted by the Supreme Court of Nova Scotia on 6 November 1989. The Nova Scotia Court of Appeal refused to overturn the injunction in February 1990, and so Morgentaler appealed once more to the Supreme Court. Morgentaler went to trial in June 1990 on the first set of charges of performing illegal abortions in the province.

136 For convenience of reference, this chapter has referred to the old abortion law as section 251 of the Criminal Code as numbered under the 1970 *Revised Statutes*. The *Revised Statutes* of Canada, 1985, however, renumbered the Code so that the old section 251 became section 287, and that is what Bill C-43 proposed to replace.

137 Canada, Minister of Justice and Attorney General of Canada, "New Abortion Legislation: Background Information," 3 November 1989, 6.

138 Canada, Parliament, House of Commons, Legislative Committee on Bill C-43, *Minutes and Proceedings of Evidence*, no. 1, 5 December 1989, 40.

139 Canada, Parliament, House of Commons, *Debates*, 7 November 1989, 5680. Hereafter referred to as *Debates*.

140 *Debates*, 7 November 1989, 5668.

141 Brief by Canadian Abortion Rights Action League, Canada, Parliament, House of Commons, Legislative Committee on Bill C-43, *Minutes and Proceedings of Evidence*, Appendix C-43/3.

142 Brief by Alliance for Life, Canada, Parliament, House of Commons, Legislative Committee on Bill C-43, *Minutes and Proceedings of Evidence*, Appendix C-43/41.

143   It might seem surprising that neither Alliance for Life nor any of the other anti-abortion rights
      groups objected to the bill's potential to permit abortions at *any* stage of pregnancy, even
      after twenty weeks. A gestational approach, however, implies that the fetus becomes "more
      human" at the later stages of pregnancy, a view that is rejected by anti-abortion activists.

144   The following is summarized from testimony by Doug Lewis, minister of justice and attorney
      general of Canada, Canada, Parliament, House of Commons, Legislative Committee on Bill
      C-43, *Minutes and Proceedings of Evidence*, no. 1, 5 December 1989.

145   Karen Dubinsky, *Lament for a "Patriarchy Lost"?: Anti-Feminism, Anti-Abortion and R.E.A.L.
      Women in Canada* (Ottawa: Canadian Research Institute for the Advancement of Women,
      1985).

146   Several passages from *Our Bodies, Ourselves*, a feminist health guide, demonstrate these points:
      "Pregnancy, labour and birth are normal bodily processes, uncomplicated most of the time
      when healthy, self-confident women receive skilled and caring support for the entire childbear-
      ing year." In fact, feminism comes to argue that pregnancy is potency, since it is the quin-
      tessential female experience. For example, consider this description of positive symptoms
      during the first trimester: "You may feel an increased sensuality, a kind of sexual opening
      out toward the world, heightened perceptions, a feeling of being in love. A lot of new energy.
      A feeling of being really special, fertile, potent, creative. Expectation. Great excitement. Im-
      patience. Harmony. Peace." See The Boston Women's Health Book Collective, *The New Our
      Bodies, Ourselves* (New York: Simon and Schuster, 1984), passages at 327 and 344, respec-
      tively.

147   Note, however, that CARAL claimed that the risks of abortions performed before fifteen weeks
      were lower than those of carrying to term. Henry Morgentaler has also emphasized his safety
      record.

148   One of the ironies of Canada's abortion saga is that Henry Morgentaler constantly argued that
      his position was "rational" and "scientific", when medical science appeared to be steadily
      undermining the validity of his view that the fetus is just a lump of tissue. Dr. Bernard
      Nathanson, who was the Henry Morgentaler of the United States, was persuaded by this
      medical evidence, not moral or religious conviction, to change his views. See Nathanson,
      Aborting America, 160–161.

149   Kathleen McDonnell, *Not An Easy Choice: A Feminist Re-Examines Abortion* (Toronto: The
      Women's Press, 1984). McDonnell points out that one of the leading American funders of
      abortion reform has been the Playboy Foundation. In any case, this thought may not be as
      heretical as it first appears, since it echoes the feminist re-evaluation of the social effects of
      the birth control pill. Before the pill, fear of pregnancy was a useful defence against sexual
      advances. The pill removed that defence, and fear of pregnancy was replaced by fear of
      prudishness. The pill thus has come under feminist attack both for its worrisome physical
      effects and for its false promise of sexual liberation. For example, see Germaine Greer, *Sex
      and Destiny: The Politics of Human Fertility* (Toronto: Stoddart, 1984), esp. chaps. 6 and 8.

150   The Royal Commission on New Reproductive Technologies was appointed on 25 October 1989
      to consider these and other issues.

151   McDonnell, *Not An Easy Choice*, 128–129.

The Rise and Fall of the Meech Lake Accord

In the spring of 1987 the federal and provincial governments struck an accord that promised to end Quebec's five years in the constitutional wilderness. The accord encouraged Canadian federalism's evolution away from former prime minister Trudeau's goal of a strong and dominant central government to one of equal partnership between Ottawa and the provinces.

The success of the 1987 constitutional process was unanticipated, as was its breathtaking pace. In contrast to previous protracted constitutional experiences, the 1987 agreement was first broached and then agreed to by the eleven first ministers within a five-week period. This "miracle" agreement was the procedural result of a controlled, secret process pursued by the Mulroney government—a closed and elitist approach that generated as much controversy as the accord's most crucial feature, the "distinct society" clause. Ironically, the accord's ratification process did not have this elitist quality and extended over three years, during which time the federal government lost control of the process and the agreement unravelled.

Constitutional change has had a permanent place on the Canadian policy agenda for decades, and is a political "world" unto itself, which best illustrates the real character of Canadian politics and the roles of its major players.[1]

At 5:30 on the morning of 3 June 1987, Prime Minister Mulroney and the ten premiers emerged from the fourth-floor boardroom of the Langevin Building across from Parliament Hill. Their suits were rumpled and they looked tired and drawn. For the previous twenty hours, these eleven men had been locked up together in one of the biggest card games in Canadian history. It was an invitation-only affair: no press, bureaucrats, citizens, cabinet ministers, or MPs were there. Only the first ministers had been invited to play. The stakes were high: power, money, and status. It was a game of constitution-making. The eleven men emerged to face an equally dishevelled media throng awaiting news of the winner. The extraordinary announcement was that all players had won—there were no losers. Canada had a "new" constitution.

This all-night session in the Langevin building formalized the "miracle" accord that the eleven men had struck in a nine-hour meeting at Meech Lake a month earlier. The centerpiece of the deal was Quebec's agreement to sign the constitution, after five years of refusing to sign. The key ingredient was the constitutional recognition of Quebec as a "distinct society." The 10 other governments agreed to this clause in return for a series of quid pro quo's.

For the next three years the accord was hurtled helter-skelter through an extended and divisive ratification process, which required the approval of all eleven legislatures. Along the way, public hearings and reports abounded; compromises came and went; governments fell; threats were uttered; Quebec and western separatism loomed; the ghosts of prime ministers past appeared; aboriginal, multicultural, minority, and women's groups protested; political personalities clashed; courts decided; racist language policies appeared; pro- and anti-Meech Lake interest groups proliferated; hopes were raised and dashed. The country seemed on the verge of tearing itself apart as the clock ticked toward the 23 June 1990 ratification deadline. Finally, on 22 June 1990, Elijah Harper—an Ojibway-Cree Indian and member of the Manitoba legislature—said "No, Mr. Speaker" for the ninth time, effectively blocking Manitoba's ratification of the accord. Meech Lake was dead. Quebec's future in the Canadian federation looked uncertain.

The rise and fall of Meech Lake was as cranky and divisive an affair as it was long and complicated. How the deal was made and came undone tells us much about one of the key worlds of Canadian politics, federal-provincial relations, and one of its key activities, amending the constitution. Indeed, federalism is probably the dominant world of Canadian politics. One of the foremost activities in this world has been the attempt to amend the constitution, mainly because it has been so difficult to do so. An extraordinary amount of time, energy, and creativity has been expended, first, in attempting to patriate the constitution, second, in ensuring that constitutional arrangements and practice reflect changing social and economic realities and, third, in accommodating the specific needs of the provinces, particularly Quebec, and others, such as aboriginal groups. This has resulted in a variety of federal provincial institutional mechanisms and processes—such as the first ministers' conference—whose importance rivals the parliamentary process itself. It has also created one of the most decentralized federal systems in the world, in which the premiers command a substantial amount of political authority.

THE RISE AND FALL OF THE MEECH LAKE ACCORD

The intense days of 30 April 1987 at Meech Lake, 2–3 June 1987 in the Langevin building, and 3–9 June 1990 in the Ottawa conference centre illustrate the closed character of relations among first ministers, and the relatively secret processes of federal-provincial relations and of amending the constitution. These events also demonstrated the political dominance of the executive branch of government and the immense political power of the prime minister and the premiers. The 1987 constitutional deal-making and the strategic position of the first ministers in the ratification process illustrated what has aptly been called the system of *executive federalism* in Canada.

Executive federalism is not the only world of Canadian politics, even in the realm of amending the constitution. The ratification process was far more leisurely—up to three *years*—and relatively open—it had to be passed by all eleven legislatures. This was in stark contrast to the hectic, indeed frenetic, pace set at the closed first ministers conferences, and the secret negotiations leading up to them. The ratification process allowed the other worlds of Canadian politics to deal themselves into the constitution-making game, albeit with limited success. After June 1987 the ratification process was directly affected by elections, interest groups, the territories, the courts, political parties, aboriginal groups, and legislatures. The process surrounding constitutional amendment became an issue unto itself. For many, it became *the* issue, as important as the core issue in the accord: Quebec's place in the federation. The ratification process demonstrated the uneasy relationship between the federal–provincial world (a world of government-to-government relationships) and the other worlds (of government-to-people relations). For a time, the former seemed to have neutralized the latter, but this dominance ended a few months after the Langevin meeting, as the result of a series of key political events (including elections in New Brunswick, Manitoba, and Newfoundland, which produced new governments not party to the arrangements struck in June 1987). Over time, non-governmental interests rallied with increasing effect against Meech Lake (women, the territories, native groups, minority language groups, Charter supporters) and doubts were articulated about the deal whenever open public hearings were allowed (House of Commons, Senate; some provinces, particularly New Brunswick and Manitoba). Symbolic of the conflict between these two worlds was the fact that it was ultimately a non-governmental player—Elijah Harper, as a representative of aboriginal groups—who pulled the plug on Meech Lake.

The events surrounding the Meech Lake story offer a microcosm of Canadian political life, albeit an elaborate one. Its many twists and turns can be followed in a chronology appended to this chapter.

THE RISE AND FALL OF THE MEECH LAKE ACCORD

SETTING THE STAGE

The amendment process in a constitution must balance the requirement of stability with the need for change. Constitutions comprise political systems' basic rules of the game: they establish who has political power, how it is to be used, and what the rights of citizens are. One wants a constitution to be altered only with difficulty, precisely to ensure that power is not easily seized, say, by one level of government at the expense of another, or by the government to the detriment of citizens. On the other hand, times change and constitutions must reflect these changes when necessary. The framers of constitutions cannot anticipate all possible national conditions or needs, and an overly rigid constitution may very well constrain effective governance.

There are two "ideal types" of constitutions, rigid and flexible ones. Most countries, including Canada, have a rigid constitution (see Appendix I). Canada is a federal state, which allows the sub-national governments to be involved in the process of constitutional change, with the provision of some sort of "minority veto." Amending the constitution has been a complicated and often cumbersome business. On the other hand, the process has been simplified by the absence of popular involvement. Canada has little to no tradition of using the referendum mechanism.[2] It has been the *governments* of Canada that have changed the constitution, and the public has been involved only indirectly via electing these governments.

Up to 1982, Canada's constitution was the British North America Act, 1867, changes to which required a statute of the Parliament of the United Kingdom[3]. The federal government managed to carry out some constitutional changes in this arrangement, both with and without provincial compliance.[4] The most important was in 1949; amendment [section 91 (1)] specified that Ottawa could change the constitution in areas of exclusive federal jurisdiction. This had the unintended effect of limiting the federal government's amending authority to a severely restricted area. The constitution had become exceedingly rigid: a federal initiative to amend it could be effected only with provincial unanimity. The 1960s and 1970s saw an extended but unsuccessful public debate on developing a home-grown amending formula.[5] This debate developed increased momentum as a result of the election of the Parti québécois and the holding of a Quebec referendum on independence in 1980. During the course of the referendum, Prime Minister Trudeau promised a "new deal" for Quebec if the province rejected independence. This set the stage for the patriation of the constitution in 1982, and the adoption of an indigenous amending formula.

THE RISE AND FALL OF THE MEECH LAKE ACCORD

The constitutional process of the early 1980s was complicated and eventful; four points can be highlighted. First and most dramatic was the fact that the province of Quebec did not sign the new constitution. The Quebec government felt betrayed by the other provinces, which, in its eyes, had ganged up and acted behind its back. The substance of the constitutional settlement did not address the fundamental question of Quebec's role in Confederation. It did not acknowledge Quebec's "collective" or "distinct" identity, nor did it assign to Quebec powers to protect this identity. It did not address the issue of guarantees for the French language in Quebec, particularly given the adoption of the Charter of Rights and Freedoms. And Quebec appeared to have lost its constitutional veto. It felt that Trudeau had betrayed it by not delivering on the promise of a "renewed federalism." Hence, the constitutional accomplishment of 1981–82 was seriously flawed, and was considered by most Quebeckers to have been illegitimately imposed on it.[6]

Second, a new four-part amending formula was set (section 38[1]). The basic formula was to be parliamentary approval plus approval by two-thirds of the provinces (comprising more than 50 percent of the population).[7] But unanimity would be required in certain "national" areas, like the creation of new provinces or the altering of national institutions.

The creation of a new amending formula was a hollow accomplishment, given Quebec's attitude to the new constitution. Unanimity was now required for constitutional alterations of a national sort (e.g., Senate reform), and it was hardly likely that the Quebec government would be willing to take part in these sorts of discussions until its own grievances had been dealt with. After 1982 Quebec participated in constitutional conferences in only a limited way.

Third, the constitutional events of 1981–82 had a popular dimension to them that was unusual for Canada, whose constitutional experiences had been of an exclusively governmental character. There were two reasons for this break with tradition. While participation in the formal constitutional process remained restricted to governments, political confrontations between the federal and provincial governments saw each side jockeying for political position and looking for popular support to back up and legitimate its position. Second, the constitutional package's including the Charter of Rights and Freedoms encouraged popular participation, with various groups and interests rallying around the so-called people's package. There was thus an unusually high degree of participation in this constitutional round, particularly by native, multicultural, and women's groups. Many Canadians came to feel that the new constitution—or at least specific parts of it—was "theirs." This created expectations about public involvement in future constitutional exercises.[8] And these expectations in turn were in

THE RISE AND FALL OF THE MEECH LAKE ACCORD

tension with the 1982 amending formula itself, which reproduced the principle of government, as opposed to popular, control of amending the constitution.

Fourth, the effective domain of the Charter of Rights and Freedoms was limited by section 33, the so-called notwithstanding or *non obstante* clause. This entitled Parliament or provincial governments to assert that a particular law could operate without being subject to the rights guaranteed by the Charter. This balancing of legislative and judicial authority was requested by the provinces,[9] but future events would demonstrate that it was an unstable balance. In the period before Meech Lake, the province of Quebec used the notwithstanding clause to limit the Charter's impact on its existing and newly passed statutes.

The Road to Meech Lake, 1984-1987

Five years after the patriation of the constitution, on 30 April 1987, the federal government and all ten provinces reached a new constitutional agreement at Meech Lake. This was a surprising, even miraculous, development, as constitutional concerns had fallen off the policy agenda as a priority matter after 1982. Moreover, an ongoing constitutional stalemate had seemed inevitable, given the rigidity of the unanimity requirement of the new amending formula and the political reality that any attempt to bring Quebec into the constitution would look like "favouritism."

Two critical elections changed this constitutional situation. On 4 September 1984 the Progressive Conservatives won a landslide victory in the national election, which included an electoral breakthrough in Quebec, where it won fifty-eight of seventy-five seats. And in the Quebec election of 2 December 1985 the Liberals defeated the Parti québécois in a solid victory. Instead of a federal Liberal party confronting the Parti québécois, a federal Conservative government faced a provincial Liberal party. Gone were the towering, indeed mythic, figures of Pierre Trudeau and Rene Levesque—the "mind" vs. the "heart" of Quebec—whose philosophical and political differences over the nature of Canada and Quebec's role in it were matched only by their personal antagonisms. History had replaced them with less imposing but pragmatic players—Brian Mulroney and Robert Bourassa—who also happened to be close friends.

Although a bilingual Quebecker like Trudeau, Mulroney was a "process" and not an "ideas" person. His political skills were honed in the backrooms of politics, and he developed superb negotiating skills in his managerial capacity in the private sector. While Trudeau's rigorous intellectual vision of a pan-Canadian federalism with a strong central government had acted as a constraint on constitutional negotiations, Mulroney's gut feel for an equal partnership between the federal and provincial governments was less formal and fixed and would allow him to be more flexible in negotiations. The successful completion of a constitutional deal would be as important for him as the substance of any deal. During his leadership campaign in the spring of 1983 and during the 1984 federal election, he promised to bring Quebec into the constitutional family. He proposed to "breathe a new spirit into federalism," but he did not offer any specifics on constitutional approaches. Indeed, he declared that this issue would not be a top priority for his government. More urgent, he argued, was the creation of a mood of "national reconciliation," which could best be accomplished by placing his "new federalism" at the service of economic recovery. Once relations with the provinces and Quebec had improved, constitutional negotiations could take place "at the opportune moment."[10] This approach to constitutional change continued after the election.[11] Mulroney continued to offer no details or plans for constitutional negotiations; he was biding his time waiting for the results of the Quebec election.

Robert Bourassa had previously served as premier of Quebec in the early 1970s. A committed federalist, he was a technocrat by training and temperament, and an extremely experienced and able one. In contrast to the federal Conservatives, the Quebec Liberals were open and specific in setting out the conditions of Quebec's signing the constitution. In early February 1985, the party released the policy paper *Maîtriser l'avenir* ("Mastering Our Future"), which became the basis for the constitutional process that led up to Meech Lake. The five conditions were:

- explicit recognition of Quebec as a "distinct society" in the preamble to the constitution;
- extension of Quebec's authority in the recruitment and selection of immigrants into Quebec;
- granting to Quebec the key role in the appointment of the three Supreme Court justices with expertise in civil law;
- limitation of the federal government's spending power in areas of provincial jurisdiction;
- granting to Quebec a full veto on all constitutional questions, with the veto entrenched in the amending formula.[12]

Compared to previous considerations presented by Quebec governments, this was not an especially ambitious list (which in fact reflected Quebec's weak bargaining position in the post-referendum, post-patriation period[13]). There was little public reaction to the document and the conditions.

During the run-up to the December 1985 election, Bourassa sent out a variety of encouraging political signals. To the question "Is [constitutional] negotiation a priority?", he replied, "Certainly otherwise we risk compromising the constitutional negotiations if we do not succeed with the present federal government which has shown its interest in having Quebec accept the constitutional accord."[14] In late October 1985 it was announced that Gil Rémillard, a professor of constitutional law, would run as a Liberal candidate in the provincial election. The ties between the federal Conservatives and the Quebec Liberals appeared set: Rémillard had been, up to this time, a special adviser to Brian Mulroney.

The foundation for the constitutional deal was laid in the sixteen months preceding the Meech Lake meeting. This groundwork was characterized by two features: caution and secrecy. On the one hand, the lead players in the process— Quebec and Ottawa—took extraordinary care to allay the various regions' concerns and doubts about the conditions of Quebec's re-entry into Canada. The Mulroney government did not want to start a constitutional process that could not be successfully completed. On the other hand, Mulroney played out this process as an exercise in executive federalism, behind closed doors and with first minsters and bureaucratic aides alone, in order to increase the likelihood of getting a deal. The process was so closed that few in Canada, including the media, knew what was taking place. Only the eleven governments were involved.

In March the new Quebec government pressed for a constitutional conference to deal with its newly adopted five points.[15] Ottawa reacted cautiously[16]; the Prime Minister was non-committal on the five points.[17] Ottawa did not reply positively to the Quebec overture until four months later when, emerging from a meeting of the Priorities and Planning Committee (a kind of "inner cabinet"), Mulroney announced that "I think it's timely" to review the constitutional process.[18]

Before the 27th Annual Premiers' Conference in August, both Bourassa and Mulroney tried to convince the other premiers to adopt the constitutional changes, to get Quebec to sign.[19] The premiers were wary of the veto and the distinct society clause[20] and, at the conference, many premiers wanted to focus on economic and agricultural issues. Bourassa then played his trump card: Quebec would not participate in any constitutional discussions that did not first address its grievances. This was unsettling to the western premiers in particular, who were anxious to pursue Senate reform. The premiers then committed themselves to a "Quebec Round" of constitutional talks. What came to be called the "Edmonton Declaration" stated,

> The premiers unanimously agreed that their top constitutional priority is to embark immediately upon a federal-provincial process, using Quebec's five proposals as a basis for discussion, to bring about Quebec's full and active participation in the Canadian federation.

THE RISE AND FALL OF THE MEECH LAKE ACCORD

> There was a consensus among the premiers that then they will pursue further constitutional discussions on matters raised by some provinces which will include, amongst other items, Senate reform, fisheries, property rights, etc.

No timetable for negotiations was set and nothing specific was said about what might be included in a new constitutional agreement.[21]

The federal government continued to be cautious. Senator Lowell Murray—minister of state for federal-provincial relations—urged restraint and ruled out constitutional talks at the November First Ministers' Conference.[22] Over the next few weeks, Murray and Norman Spector (secretary to the cabinet for federal-provincial relations) went on a tour of the provinces, as did Quebec's Rémillard.[23] Prime Minister Mulroney himself was mum.[24] He declared that, "unless we feel there is a reasonable chance for all parties to carry out the negotiations to a successful conclusion, we will not reopen the constitutional debate."[25]

The opposition parties were less reticent about endorsing the Quebec conditions. In an interview with *Le Devoir* on 13 June 1986, Liberal leader John Turner supported each of the distinct society, immigration, Supreme Court, opting out, and veto proposals.[26] The Quebec wing of the Liberal party endorsed the distinct society proposal at a convention in early November and rallied around John Turner and his support for Quebec's five conditions. This involved a substantial break from the recent Liberal constitutional position of Pierre Trudeau and Jean Chrétien, the latter not attending the convention.[27] At its national congress in March, the NDP accepted the idea of including the distinct society clause in the preamble to the constitution and recognized that Quebec should have the right to veto or opt out with financial compensation.[28]

A year after Rémillard had first offered to re-open the constitutional debate, Bourassa sensed that Ottawa was dragging its feet. He played his trump card again, announcing that he would not attend the First Ministers' Conference on native self-government later that month.[29] This brought the intended result; five days later Mulroney announced that "the time is ripe for the premiers of the provinces and the Prime Minister of Canada to give this matter further consideration." A First Ministers' Conference would be held at Meech Lake on 30 April to discuss Quebec's place in the constitution.[30]

Mulroney refused to offer details of the federal government's constitutional position.[31] The Prime Minister had Senator Murray write to each of the provincial governments, outlining Ottawa's response to Quebec's five conditions. In the ten days before the Meech Lake meeting, Mulroney telephoned each of the premiers.[32] In the House of Commons, the Prime Minister declined the request to table the federal correspondence with the provinces.[33]

THE RISE AND FALL OF THE MEECH LAKE ACCORD

As the Prime Minister and the premiers arrived at Meech Lake, Canadians could hardly anticipate that Canada was on the verge of a constitutional breakthrough. Indeed, Canadians barely realized that the meeting was taking place. Coverage on the eve of the meeting was insubstantial, the media having been caught napping.[34] Only the Quebec and Alberta governments had declared their constitutional positions. What little was reported suggested that the meeting would be fraught with difficulties. Most provinces appeared to be opposed to one or two of Quebec's demands, and Quebec's Bourassa himself was under enormous nationalist pressure not to be co-opted.[35] On the other hand, the federal government had been cautiously tilling the constitutional grounds for over a year behind closed doors, to build up inter-governmental consensus while containing public expectations and pressures. That the public was unaware of what was going on was a strategic success that suggested nothing about what might have been accomplished before the first ministers arrived at Meech Lake. Governments had portrayed the event in low-key terms, as a "tentative" or "preliminary" meeting in which views and feelings would be canvassed. As Newfoundland premier Peckford put it, "Going in, I thought our chances for a deal were limited."[36]

FROM THE MEECH LAKE MIRACLE TO THE LANGEVIN CONFIRMATION

The Prime Minister and the premiers gathered on a cold, early spring day at Meech Lake in the Gatineau Hills. The meeting started at noon in an ordinary second-storey meeting room in Wilson House, a building frequently used for cabinet meetings. Other than a few bureaucrats, only the first ministers attended this closed-door session, which lasted for nine hours.

The meeting was organized around discussion of each of Quebec's five conditions. For each item, Prime Minister Mulroney would hand out the federal government's proposal, which reflected the discussions and negotiations that had taken place over the last year. The first ministers would then discuss the proposal until a working agreement was reached, and the meeting would move on to the next federal proposal. The least controversial items—such as immigration and judicial appointments—were discussed first, in order to create momentum, although there was a longer discussion of the latter than had been anticipated. The discussion of shared-cost programmes was divisive, as many provinces were committed in principle to a continued federal presence or predominance in some social and economic areas. This issue was finally settled by supper. The distinct society issue was also troublesome, since many provinces were not keen on assigning special status to Quebec. Discussion then shifted to Senate reform. Once that was settled, the final compromise was made on the distinct society issue. By 9:45pm, it was all done: agreement had been reached.[37]

The Meech Lake constitutional accord was an "agreement in principle" amongst the first ministers. It contained six ingredients, phrased in rather broad and general terms (which made it easier for the first ministers to come to an agreement). The accord, reflecting the strategy enunciated in the Edmonton Declaration, dealt with Quebec's five proposals and a plan for the next round of constitutional discussions (see Inset I for the text of the accord). These loosely written "principles" would have to be translated into more precise legal language by government officials for a constitutional conference planned to be held "within weeks."

The accord first asserted that Quebec's existence as a *distinct society* should be explicitly acknowledged. The constitution would recognize the existence of both French-speaking and English-speaking Canada, the former centred in but not limited to Quebec and the latter centred outside but also existing within Quebec. All governments were assigned the responsibility of preserving this "fundamental characteristic", and the Quebec government would have the added responsibility of preserving and promoting Quebec's distinct identity.

Second, the accord assigned to all of the provinces the right to negotiate an immigration agreement with the federal government "appropriate to [its] needs and conditions," which agreement could then be entrenched in the constitution. The federal government reached such an agreement with Quebec at Meech Lake. The accord also established certain safeguards concerning Quebec's cultural security, by guaranteeing the province a level of immigration proportional to its share of the population. For demographic reasons, Quebec was also given the right to exceed that figure by 5 per cent in a given year.[38]

Third, Quebec had requested a role in appointing the three judges on the *Supreme Court* that had to have expertise in the civil law (i.e., the law practiced in Quebec, in distinction from the common law). The accord agreed to this request and went a step further, in determining that *all* federal appointments to the Supreme Court would be made from lists of candidates provided by the provinces.[39]

Fourth, *all* provinces were given the right to opt out of any future national *shared-cost* programme in an area of provincial jurisdiction. Moreover, a province would be given "reasonable" compensation if it opted out, as long as (1) it developed a similar programme that was (2) compatible with "national objectives." This proposal would not affect existing shared-cost programmes.

Fifth, Quebec had requested a full veto on constitutional matters, to be entrenched in the *amending formula*. The Meech Lake agreement established the

Inset I

THE MEECH LAKE ACCORD

(First Ministers' Meeting on the Constitution: Draft Statement of Principle)

At their meeting today at Meech Lake, the Prime Minister and the ten Premiers agreed to ask to transform into a constitutional text the agreement in principle found in the attached document.

First Ministers also agreed to hold a constitutional conference within weeks to approve a formal text intended to allow Quebec to resume its place as a full participant in Canada's constitutional development.

QUEBEC'S DISTINCT SOCIETY

(1) The Constitution of Canada shall be interpreted in a manner consistent with
   a) the recognition that the existence of French-speaking Canada, centered in but not limited to Quebec, and English-speaking Canada, concentrated outside Quebec but also present in Quebec, constitutes a fundamental characteristic of Canada; and
   b) the recognition that Quebec constitutes within Canada a distinct society.
(2) Parliament and the provincial legislatures, in the exercise of their respective powers, are committed to preserving the fundamental characteristic of Canada referred to in paragraph (1)(a).
(3) The role of the legislature and Government of Quebec to preserve and promote the distinct identity of Quebec referred to in paragraph (1)(b) is affirmed.

IMMIGRATION

- Provide under the Constitution that the Government of Canada shall negotiate an immigration agreement appropriate to the needs and circumstances of a province that so requests and that, once concluded, the agreement may be entrenched at the request of the province;
- such agreements must recognize the federal government's power to set national standards and objectives relating to immigration, such as the ability to determine the general categories of immigrants, to establish overall levels of immigration, and prescribe categories of inadmissible persons;
- under the foregoing provisions, conclude in the first instance an agreement with Quebec that would:
  - incorporate the principles of the Cullen-Couture agreement on the selection abroad and in Canada of independent immigrants, visitors for medical treatment, students and temporary workers, and on the selection of refugees abroad and economic criteria for family reunification and assisted relatives;

THE RISE AND FALL OF THE MEECH LAKE ACCORD

- guarantee the at Quebec will receive a number of immigrants, including refugees, within the annual total established by the federal government for all of Canada proportionate to its share of the population of Canada, with the right to exceed that figure by 5% for demographic reasons; and
- provide an undertaking by Canada to withdraw services (except citizenship services) for the reception and integration (including linguistic and cultural) of all foreign nationals wishing to settle in Quebec where services are to be provided by Quebec, with such withdrawal to be accompanied by reasonable compensation;

- nothing in the foregoing should be construed as preventing the negotiation of similar agreements with other provinces.

SUPREME COURT OF CANADA

- Entrench the Supreme Court and the requirement that at least three of the nine justices appointed be from the civil bar;
- provide that, where there is a vacancy on the Supreme Court, the federal government shall appoint a person from a list of candidates proposed by the provinces and who is acceptable to the federal government.

SPENDING POWER

- Stipulate that Canada must provide reasonable compensation to any province that does not participate in a future national shared-cost program in an area of exclusive provincial jurisdiction if that province undertakes its own initiative of programs comparable with national objectives.

AMENDING FORMULA

- Maintain the current amending formula set out in section 38, which requires the consent of Parliament and at least two thirds of the provinces representing at least fifty percent of the population;
- guarantee reasonable compensation in all cases where a province opts out of an amendment transferring provincial jurisdiction to Parliament;
- because opting out of constitutional amendments set out in section 42 of the *Constitution Act, 1982* is not possible, require the consent of Parliament and all the provinces for such amendments.

SECOND ROUND

- Require that a First Ministers' Conference on the Constitution be held not less than once per year and that the first be held within twelve months of proclamation of this amendment but not later than the end of 1988;
- entrench in the Constitution the following items on the agenda:

1) Senate reform including:
  — the functions and role of the Senate;
  — the powers of the Senate;
  — the method of selection of Senators;
  — the distribution of Senate seats;
2) fisheries roles and responsibilities; and
3) other agreed upon matters;
- entrench in the Constitution the annual First Ministers' Conference on the Economy now held under the terms of the February 1985 Memorandum of Agreement;
- until constitutional amendments regarding the Senate are accomplished the federal government shall appoint persons from lists of candidates provided by provinces where vacancies occur and who are acceptable to the federal government.

principle of unanimity for constitutional amendments relating to proposed changes in Canada's national institutions (section 42). *Each* province was to be given a veto in this area, regarding such matters as the powers of the Senate and the Supreme Court, the method of selection of members of the Senate and the Supreme Court, the creation of new provinces, and so on.[40]

The political logic of these five ingredients was clear. Quebec had proposed that it be given increased powers in the area of immigration, selection of Supreme Court justices, shared-cost programmes, and the amending formula. The Meech Lake constitutional accord granted Quebec its requests—but at the same time the accord assigned to the other provinces precisely what Quebec received. Quebec won the distinct society clause—the necessary condition for any deal. At the same time, the rest of Canada was assigned the responsibility of preserving the "fundamental characteristic of Canada." In short, the Meech Lake consensus was reached by assigning to all provinces the incredible power that Quebec had presented as its condition for signing the constitution.

The consensus was also forged by the promise of constitutional developments to come. The sixth and last ingredient of the Meech Lake deal was titled the "Second Round," reflecting the second half of the Edmonton Declaration. Following this "Quebec Round," the accord proposed to institutionalize first ministers' conferences on a permanent basis. The first ministers agreed to hold a constitutional conference before the end of 1988—and every year thereafter. The annual first ministers' conference on the economy would also be entrenched in the constitution. The short-term agenda for constitutional conferences was set

THE RISE AND FALL OF THE MEECH LAKE ACCORD

and entrenched, and would include Senate reform and fisheries (inducements for Alberta and Newfoundland, respectively). Senate reform had been a major discussion item—and potential stumbling block—at Meech Lake. Over and above the guarantee of constitutional discussions in perpetuity until the Senate was reformed, the first ministers agreed to an interim arrangement: federal Senate appointments were to be made from lists of candidates provided by the provincial governments. In sum, the Meech Lake accord was a classic inter-governmental affair, with governments shuffling powers amongst themselves. Quebec's constitutional future was the centerpiece of the accord, which dealt exclusively with *governmental* issues.

Inset II

MEECH LAKE: A REPORTER'S PERSPECTIVE

"We got to Meech Lake on April 30th, on a very cold night. It was very difficult physically—we were segregated by about a mile from the main building. We were allowed to stand outside it, if we wanted to endure the walk and the rain. We could walk around the building, signalling to people through the window to come and talk to us. Officials who weren't allowed in the actual room where the negotiations were taking place, came out and told us that they didn't know anything.... They signed their deal, the flashbulbs started going off on the third floor, and they all had champagne glasses in their hands when they called the media in. We all trooped in.... They grouped us into a set piece, all the first ministers standing in a semi-circle around the Prime Minister...with glasses of champagne in their hands. The Prime Minister carefully walked around that semi-circle, shook hands and they all patted him on the back. He made a statement. Bourassa and Peterson made statements. There were a variety of interviews. But unfortunately, they said, we have no detailed document for you; it's not ready. We'll tell you tomorrow what's in the deal. They tried to reduce us that night to reporting the hand-shaking, the historic achievement of re-introducing Quebec to the Constitution, on the basis of giving us only the broadest outlines. This was deliberate; the document was ready, the paper existed. After all, it was hard to do a deal when you're not working with drafts. Word processors and xerox machines were all up there in Wilson House. The decision to manage this process without a paper trail is an astonishing public policy decision. It is manipulative and cynical, and it began that night...."

Elly Alboim, "Inside the News Story: Meech Lake as Viewed by an Ottawa Bureau Chief," in R. Gibbins (ed.), *Meech Lake and Canada: Perspectives from the West* (Edmonton: Academic Publishing, 1988), p. 239.

THE RISE AND FALL OF THE MEECH LAKE ACCORD

Upon completion of the agreement, reporters were let in to the meeting room (see Inset II), and the first ministers toasted each other as Prime Minister Mulroney declared, "Now, gentlemen, we can go out there and tell Canadians their federation works. Canada is whole again. Quebec has joined the constitutional family."[41]

The next morning, Mulroney reported in the House of Commons that a constitutional agreement had been reached, one that "is good for Canada, and good for Canadians." There was immediate non-partisan support given to the Meech Lake deal. Opposition leader Turner congratulated Mulroney, Bourassa, and the premiers "for their constructive work and the result achieved.... It is a happy day for Canada and for Quebec...[to] bring Quebec...fully into the Canadian family." NDP leader Broadbent echoed these comments: "The coming together of the Canadian family is desired by us all." Both leaders expressed certain reservations, which they did not pursue, awaiting the opportunity to read the agreement as well as a more appropriate moment. Foreshadowing a crucial feature of the discussion of the accord, Turner made a self-congratulatory comment:

> We refrained from politicizing this question in the House of Commons. I as much as Members of the Official Opposition and the New Democrats purposely avoided embarrassing the government about this issue. We knew that...it was desirable that the interests of the country take precedence over partisan considerations.[42]

Public reaction to the events of 30 April 1987 was relatively quiet. There were some dissenting notes from, for example, Acadian groups (concern about the future of francophone minorities outside Quebec) and the territories (chary of the provincial veto over the creation of new provinces).[43] The event had not been especially widely advertised, and so little anticipation had built up about what was going on at Meech Lake. For example, in the West, the agreement was marked by a mixture of "yawns and praise." A few days after the meeting, there was little media coverage of the event.[44] In Quebec, though, reaction was akin to spontaneous combustion. Parti québécois leader Johnson characterized the agreement as "the monster of Meech Lake...a leap backwards for Quebec." Nationalist critics claimed that the distinct society clause was ambiguous and that Quebec had not acquired a constitutional veto. Columnist Lysiane Gagnon concluded that "Quebec didn't even achieve a shadow of special status. The other provinces...will have everything Quebec asked for."[45]

Political reaction started to heat up as the accord began to divide the Liberal party. Turner had been advised by several Liberal advisers to temper his enthusiasm for the deal. He inquired whether Meech Lake would kill the possibility of a future national day-care programme, and mused that "Mr. Mulroney gave away too much...who was speaking for the federal interest? Who was speaking for Canada?" He concluded that the provincial veto had effectively killed the possibility of Senate reform, which NDP leader Broadbent also stated was now "dead as a dodo."[46] Former cabinet minister Donald Johnston resigned from the Liberal shadow cabinet to speak out against Meech Lake, which he claimed eroded the powers of the central government and undermined the possibility of a bilingual Canada.[47] His resignation symbolized the emerging split in the federal Liberal caucus between francophones and anglophones, and overshadowed the substance of the constitutional deal.[48]

On 11 May 1987 all three federal party leaders endorsed the agreement when it was tabled in the House of Commons, extending the unusually strong non-partisan support surrounding the accord. Prime Minister Mulroney presented the agreement in a compelling manner, characterizing the accord as Canada saying "yes" to Quebec. He tried to assuage a number of concerns: medicare could have been established under the new spending power provisions, Parliament would continue to be able to protect minority linguistic rights, and unfinished constitutional business—like aboriginal self-government—would be pursued. He asked that "we put aside party politics at this great moment in our history."[49]

The opposition leaders obliged the Prime Minister. Turner endorsed Meech Lake, despite having substantial reservations: the absence of constitutional recognition of Canada's multicultural reality and the aboriginal peoples; the potential weakening of the federal government's spending power and its capacity to initiate national programs; the impossibility of Senate reform generated by the unanimity principle of the amending formula.[50]

NDP leader Broadbent took a similar tack, maintaining that "an extreme effort should be made for a non-partisan approach." He endorsed the accord despite having a lengthy list of reservations: the ambiguity of the phrase "distinct society," the ambiguity of the word "compatible" with regard to the national objectives of shared-cost programmes, the absence of the aboriginal issue on the constitutional agenda, the provincial veto of the creation of new provinces, and the rigidity of the amending formula ("almost irretrievably bad").[51]

By characterizing the Meech Lake agreement as a nation-building exercise designed to make Quebec a member of the constitutional family, Prime Minister Mulroney made it all but impossible for the parties to oppose the accord—lest they appear to be anti-Quebec. This would doom their political future in that key province. The resulting all-party support gave Meech Lake considerable political momentum, imposed party discipline on individual MPs, and seriously limited the extent to which the agreement could be scrutinized and criticized in the House of Commons. This extended and strengthened the closed character of the Meech Lake process.

As the national political leaders were endorsing Meech Lake, the province of Quebec began parliamentary hearings, the only province to offer hearings on the Meech Lake principles before the constitutional conference in June.[52]

The opposition Parti québécois claimed that the distinct society clause constituted only a "symbol," amounting to little, particularly if the Canadian Charter prevailed over it. The spending power clause was seen to be a major and unacceptable shift of authority to the federal government. Many organized interests opposed the accord. There was criticism of the government for the undemocratic processes surrounding Meech Lake and for holding a constitutional discussion in the absence of a final, legal text.[53] However, an editorial in *Le Devoir* suggested that Meech Lake "arouses a superb lack of interest within the great majority of Québécois."[54]

Two provinces became identified as potential opponents of the accord. Manitoba's Premier Pawley was perhaps least happy with Meech Lake. He was especially concerned that the wording of the shared-cost principle not undermine federal spending power. He planned to seek more precision in the phrase "national standards" at the constitutional conference. He also raised what would become the most prominent anti-Meech Lake issue: the question of process. "This is a very deplorable situation, if we have a constitutional draft being circulated and then we are being advised by anyone that we create problems if we ask questions."[55] Ontario Premier Peterson—head of a minority government—concurred; he sensed a growing feeling that the agreement was "cooked up in a locked room somewhere."[56]

In the run-up to the June First Ministers' Conference, various groups outside the "governments' world" criticized the agreement. These included women's groups (who worried about the impact of the distinct society clause on women's rights), native peoples' organizations (who felt left out of the process and criticized the absence of aboriginal rights on the agenda of future constitutional conferences), and a loose coalition of historians and constitutional experts. Government leaders in the Yukon and Northwest Territories stated that they would seek court action against the agreement. A multitude of social groups expressed concern that the development of national social programmes would be constrained by the spending power changes.[57]

A few days before the First Ministers' Conference on the constitution, there was an electrifying development. Former prime minister Pierre Trudeau broke a three-year period of political silence by launching an unexpected[58] vitriolic attack on the Meech Lake agreement and its designers. In an article published simultaneously in the *Toronto Star* and *La Presse*, Trudeau criticized the distinct society clause, claiming that Quebec did not need special powers. "Those who fought for a single Canada, bilingual and multicultural, can say goodbye to that dream. We are henceforth to have two Canadas, each defined in terms of its language." He described Quebec's politicians as "snivellers and losers" while Prime Minister Mulroney was characterized as a "weakling" who "with the complicity of ten provincial premiers...will render the Canadian state totally impotent."[59]

The Trudeau intervention created further headaches for an already divided Liberal party. The ethnic community, anglophone Quebeckers, and grassroots Liberal supporters spoke openly against the accord and Turner's handling of Meech Lake.[60] On the other hand, Quebec francophone Liberals continued to support Meech Lake. And John Turner refused to allow party misgivings about the agreement to be articulated, pressing instead for the government to commit itself to open hearings on Meech Lake before the principles became law.[61] While dividing the Liberals, Trudeau's intervention strengthened the resolve of the premiers on the eve of the constitutional conference.[62]

On 2 June 1987, the first ministers arrived in Ottawa for a constitutional conference that would attempt to formalize in precise legal terms the broad principles agreed upon a month earlier. During this month, certain political tendencies had become clear. First, there were two visions of Canada being played out, the Trudeau vision of a strong federal government protecting the national interest, versus a decentralist vision of strong provinces with augmented authority in an equal partnership with the federal government. As Ottawa's and the premiers' reaction to Trudeau's intervention indicated, the latter vision was in the ascendancy. Second, the political process surrounding the constitutional developments had become simple and asymmetrical. On the one hand, an all-party consensus had developed at the federal level that was well insulated from criticism. At the provincial level, certain premiers felt political pressure (Bourassa, Pawley, and Peterson) and were targets for interest group pressure. There was an array of interests against the accord—natives, women, the territories, social policy groups, minority groups—but they lacked an avenue of effective political intervention.

The eleven first ministers met in the fourth-floor boardroom of the Langevin Building, home of the Prime Minister's Office and the Privy Council Office, across Wellington Street from Parliament Hill. Once again, they were isolated behind closed doors in one room, with only a few bureaucrats present, and the process was tightly controlled. The meeting began at 10am and was not expected to last long: a signing ceremony had been organized for 2pm. Instead, the meeting became a marathon, and did not conclude until 5:30 the following morning.

THE RISE AND FALL OF THE MEECH LAKE ACCORD

The first ministers would discuss a particular clause, which would then be drafted and typed; the leader would bring it back to his delegation, located in small rooms down the hall. There it would be discussed, a response prepared, and the leader would return to the private meeting. This process happened fifteen to twenty times.[63]

Of the six ingredients of the Meech Lake agreement, two items produced the most difficulties and caused the meeting to be so extended: shared-cost programmes and the distinct society clause. The former was addressed by Ontario's Peterson and, particularly, Manitoba's Pawley. Concerned that national social programmes could no longer be developed, they argued that provinces should not be given financial compensation unless they met national objectives and criteria set by the federal government. Alberta's Getty, British Columbia's Vander Zalm, and Quebec's Bourassa were not as sympathetic to this position. Peterson wanted the distinct society clause spelled out in detail, as he was concerned about the impact that it might have on aboriginal, multicultural, and women's rights. Ironically, Premiers Peterson and Pawley played, in effect, the central government's role, articulating and defending the national interest. The federal government chose to limit itself to a negotiator's role. Peterson and Pawley held out tenaciously for changes in these two areas. They reluctantly joined the consensus with the other nine first ministers, but only after a torturous and agonizing meeting wore them down by dawn.[64]

There were a number of changes to the principles agreed upon at Meech Lake, two of which could be described as major (see Appendix II for the draft constitutional resolution). The biggest change was with regard to the *distinct society* clause (see section 2 of the Constitution Act, 1867 in Appendix II). In the first instance, the section was to be placed within the 1867 constitution itself; Quebec had originally asked only that this be placed in the preamble to the constitution, so this was—from its perspective—a significant development. There were two further changes. First, the description of the "major characteristics" of Canada underwent a subtle but substantial change. In the Meech Lake agreement, Canada had been described as consisting of "French-speaking *Canada*...and English-speaking *Canada*." The Langevin proposals changed this to "French-speaking *Canadians*...and English-speaking *Canadians*." The former had seemed to imply the existence of "two Canadas", while the latter suggested the existence of one Canada composed of different individuals. Second, a new section 2(4) was added, specifying that the existing rights of Parliament and the provincial legislatures were not affected by the agreement, either by the distinct society clause or by other features. This was designed to guarantee that the existing constitutional

THE RISE AND FALL OF THE MEECH LAKE ACCORD

division of powers was not affected, particularly with regard to control over language policy.

The second major change centred on the *spending power* clause (see Constitution Act, 1867, section 106A(1), (2)). In a key political compromise, Quebec's Bourassa agreed to a change in the language of the clause and Manitoba's Pawley swallowed his anxiety about the issue.[65] The Meech Lake document stated that financial compensation would be granted to opting-out provinces who initiated programs "compatible with national objectives." This was changed by adding the word "the", to make section 106A(1) read "compatible with *the* national objectives." To those with apprehensions, this appeared to be far more forceful and forthright about actual, concrete objectives, set nationally. Moreover, the clause referred to a program "that is established by the national government," whereas the Meech Lake agreement made no reference to anything actually established by the federal government. At the same time, to alleviate Bourassa's concern, a new clause 106A(2) was added stating that this section did not extend the jurisdiction of either level of government, thus assuring Quebec that the federal spending power would be limited.

Another substantial change dealt with concerns about how the distinct society might affect *Charter rights*. A new section was added (Constitution Act, 1982, section 16) "protecting" aboriginal and multicultural guarantees from the distinct society clause. A less important change—in response to a request by Alberta's Getty—had the preamble to the 1987 Constitutional Accord and the motion to amend the constitution include the statement that the constitution "would recognize the principle of equality of all of the provinces."

These were major changes[66] to have been accomplished under the given conditions (and would belie the claim made later that changes would "unravel" the agreement). This had been a tense and exhausting meeting, almost twenty hours long, which ended at 5:30 in the morning. An official signing ceremony took place at noon on 3 June 1987. Exhausting as this meeting had been, no one could have been prepared for the torturous and futile journey that this constitutional agreement was about to take.

THE RATIFICATION PROCESS

"Today we welcome Quebec back to the Canadian constitutional family," declared Prime Minister Mulroney at the signing ceremony on 3 June 1987; "today we close one chapter in Canadian history and begin another."[67]

The signing ceremony also closed one chapter in the constitutional process—the executive federalism stage—and started another potentially more complicated chapter—the legislative stage. This was a legacy of the 1982 patriation of the constitution, the ratification process. Any constitutional change proposed by first ministers would have to be *unanimously* endorsed by all eleven legislatures and within a rather odd time frame—three years from the date when the proposed change was first endorsed by one of the legislatures. If even one of the legislatures declined the proposal or was unable to pass the constitutional legislation within the three-year time limit, then the proposed changes would die. This is an extreme form of the minority veto discussed earlier, which had made the Canadian constitution quite rigid (see Appendix I).

In the halcyon days of June 1987, ratification was not anticipated to be an overwhelming challenge. After all, each of the first ministers had made a political commitment to have his legislature pass the package. Given party discipline and the command of majorities in the legislatures,[68] the ratification process promised to be smooth. And, as Premier Bourassa noted, it would be difficult to act against the first ministers' unanimous will to accept Quebec's adherence to the constitution.[69] However, the ratification process turned out to be a bloody, bruising, and losing battle.

Ratification Gets Rolling: The First Eighteen Months (1987–88)

Quebec's Bourassa acted quickly to make it difficult for governments to reject or amend the agreement. A fortnight after the Langevin meeting, the National Assembly began a marathon emergency debate on the proposal. Governments'—including Quebec's—ratification strategy was simple and clear: amendments would not be considered. Women's issues, aboriginal rights, the future of the North: these and other issues would have to wait until the next round of constitutional discussions. On the eve of St. Jean Baptiste day—23 June 1987, after no public hearings—the National Assembly passed the legislation. This set the clock ticking: the three-year deadline would end on 23 June 1990. The move also gave the Meech Lake ratification process considerable political momentum, for once Quebec had ratified the agreement, opposition to Meech Lake would be equated to opposition to Quebec.[70] Later that summer the Saskatchewan legislature debated and endorsed Meech Lake, with no public hearings.[71] Early indications, then, were that governments would have no difficulty using their majorities to pass the accord, with no opportunities for amendments, and little public debate.

The federal ratification process began with political skirmishes over how to proceed. Mulroney responded to opposition pressures for public hearings, announcing on 5 June 1987 that a special joint committee of the Senate and House of Commons would be created and would hold hearings. (Much to the annoyance of the government, the Liberal-dominated Senate decided to create its own committee and would hold hearings in the North in August.[72]) The seventeen-member joint committee comprised twelve MPs and five Senators.[73] The character of the federal public hearings was made controversial by three decisions. First was the decision to hold all hearings in Ottawa, and not travel around the country to hear public reactions. Second, the hearings were held in August, a time when Canadians tend not to be politically active or attentive in what is a holiday month. These two decisions extended the government's strategy of limiting public input and scrutiny of the accord. Third, and most critical, was the government decision that no changes could be made to the constitutional document agreed to by the first ministers: it was to be an all-or-nothing deal.[74] In a phrase to be repeated endlessly over the next years, Senator Murray described the constitutional package as "a seamless web" and "an integrated whole":

> Some critics of the accord assume the first ministers undertook to negotiate more than they did...suggestions to improve the accord and broaden its scope often are mis-placed, no matter how well-intentioned they are. If any egregious errors in the amendment are identified, they can, as First Ministers agree, be amended immediately.[75]

The federal government's position, then, was that there were no flaws in the agreement, that it had to be accepted or rejected in total, and that the committee should consider changes only to blatant or outrageous errors. Even these would have to be approved by eleven governments. Anything more would risk unravelling the seamless web. The position was a politically compelling one, as it suggested that this particular package of constitutional proposals was the only package that could generate consensus amongst the eleven governments. This rather muted the potential value and impact of the federal hearings process. It also created an asymmetrical debate between the Meech Lake package—which existed in real terms and had been agreed to by the eleven governments—and a vast array of alternative packages of proposals—none of which existed and no one of which could be guaranteed to receive the support of all eleven governments.

In the weeks before the federal hearings began, criticism of the accord came from a wide array of quarters and became increasingly vociferous. The Meech Lake process was described by critics as having been closed and hasty. "Eleven men met in the middle of the night while their limousines waited outside, with the engines running," claimed activist Rosemary McCarney. The Women's Legal Education and Action Fund complained that "the equality rights of women and minorities have been forgotten in the accord." The Canadian Ethnographic Council asked that multiculturalism be given equal status to bilingualism. The Yukon

Supreme Court heard the Yukon government's lawsuit against the accord, and the NDP's Audrey McLaughlin won a federal by-election in the Yukon on an anti-Meech campaign. On the election trail, Ontario Premier Peterson's sympathetic responses to critics suggested that he might consider re-opening discussions. At a Liberal Party conference in Port Hope, a beleaguered John Turner was directed to seek improvements to the accord.[76]

The special joint committee hearings began on 4 August 1987. Testimony was heard from 131 groups and individuals and 301 written submissions were made. The hearings had two "tracks." On one track were academics and constitutional experts, evenly divided in their views on whether Meech Lake was good or bad for Canada. On the other track were organized interests, more or less unanimous in criticizing the accord, albeit for different reasons.[77] (Of course, the most important interests who favoured the accord did not appear: the eleven governments.) Criticism of the accord focused on eight issues, which were rehearsed endlessly:

- the impact of the distinct society clause on Charter rights, a concern articulated particularly by linguistic minority and women's groups;
- the lack of precision in the distinct society clause, which some saw as either symbolic and empty leading to disillusionment in Quebec) or real and substantial (creating a "two-Canadas" situation);
- the exclusiveness of the distinct society clause, which critics believed should also include the multicultural and aboriginal realities of Canada;
- discrimination against the territories, which were excluded from the constitutional process, not given an opportunity to make nominations to the Supreme Court and the Senate, and were unlikely to become provinces given the amending formula's unanimity provision;
- the weakening of the federal government in various ways: by assigning authority to the provinces in Supreme Court and Senate appointments and in immigration policy; by guaranteeing compensation for opting out of shared-cost programmes; and thereby ensuring provincial predominance by entrenching and making permanent first ministers' conferences;
- the constraining of Senate reform, which critics saw as impossible given the unanimity provision of the amending formula;
- the neglect of aboriginal issues, which critics insisted should—at a minimum—have a guaranteed place on the constitutional agenda;
- the constitutional process, which critics claimed was closed, rushed, and undemocratic.

As the hearings proceeded, it was transparently clear that the committee was not going to entertain any amendments, despite this substantial array of serious concerns and complaints. Government officials and supporters of the accord carried the day by playing the political trump card—Quebec's future in Canada. Regardless of problems or lacunae—which supporters claimed were debatable—the political reality was that this was the Quebec Round of constitutional negotiations, a round that had been triumphant, as Quebec had agreed to sign the constitution. Any problems, complaints, oversights, or improvements unrelated to Quebec could wait until the next round of constitutional talks.

A symbolic example of how trade-offs on non-Quebec matters would not be entertained was how the concern of women's groups was deflected off the agenda. After Meech Lake, the Langevin meeting had added a clause 16 to the 1982 Constitution Act (see Appendix II) that stated that nothing in section 2 of the Constitution Act, 1867—dealing with the distinct society clause—affected the Charter, including multicultural and aboriginal rights. Women's groups were concerned that clause 16 did not include any reference to women's equality rights, won in a hard battle in 1981–82.[78] There was some sympathy for this position, even amongst Conservative members of the joint committee such as David Daubney and Leo Duguay. On 18 August the Prime Minister intervened to derail the claims of the women's groups. He cited an article in *La Presse* by columnist Lysiane Gagnon: "A lot of people are using that as a Trojan horse," wrote Gagnon, "not because they're trying to protect women's rights, but because they don't want a distinct society and the Meech Lake Accord." Mulroney observed, "It's a thoughtful piece, some of whose judgments I share." Women's groups were outraged and described these comments as wicked, but the damage was done. The Prime Minister had transformed a rights issue into an issue of English-Canada-versus-French-Canada.[79] The Prime Minister took MPs Daubney and Duguay for a no nonsense lunch, and the issue was no longer raised.[80]

The essence of the Meech Lake constitutional accord was Quebec's place in Canada. Nothing better symbolized the division on this issue than the conflicting testimony before the joint committee of Pierre Trudeau and Solange Chaput-Rolland. According to Trudeau, Quebec did not need the special powers implied by the distinct society clause to protect itself. The other provinces had gone along with the deal only because they would be given more powers themselves. In the future, Trudeau reckoned, the national government would be run by "a kind of remote control by the provinces." "Of course, finally peace has been restored to federal-provincial relations. Yes, peace! But at what price?"[81] The previous day, Chaput-Rolland had made an emotional and telling case in favour of the agreement. Working from a different vision of federalism, she maintained that

Quebeckers were desperately looking for a signal that Canadians wanted Quebec to remain in Canada. Meech Lake was seen as finally making concrete the "renewed federalism" promised to Quebeckers for having rejected separatism in the 1980 referendum.[82]

The joint committee hearings ended on 2 September, and less than three weeks later the committee issued its predictable report. It opened with the clinching argument: "The question before us...is not whether a different solution might have been reached or whether other constitutional issues might also have been added. It is quite simply whether or not the accord agreed upon should be adopted." Its conclusion: the accord "represents a reasonable and workable package of constitutional reforms."[83]

The Constitutional Amendment, 1987 was introduced for debate in the House of Commons on 29 September 1987. It was an odd, drawn-out, shapeless, and anti-climatic affair. For peculiar scheduling reasons, it was impossible to arrange for all three party leaders to speak on the opening day of debate—or even on the same day—and this undermined whatever drama the debate might have had. Only John Turner spoke on 29 September, Mulroney and Broadbent to follow four weeks later on 26 October. Seventy-seven MPs participated in the month-long debate. Opposition leader Turner continued to juggle the demands of Quebec MPs with those of parliamentary and extra-parliamentary critics. He continued to follow the non-partisan high road, but he submitted an extensive series of amendments dealing with aboriginal and multicultural rights, linguistic minorities, the precedence of the Charter, more constrained opting-out provisions, elimination of the unanimity formula, and a constitutional conference on aboriginal rights.[84] NDP leader Broadbent characterized the constitutional process as a "remarkably creative and productive non-partisan approach" but continued to express concern about aboriginal rights, the North, women's rights, multiculturalism, and visible minorities.[85] The final vote on 26 October 1987 was 242–16, with the House of Commons almost full (258 of 282 MPs voted).[86] The constitutional agreement would now proceed to the Senate, which had 180 days to deal with it. As a harbinger of things to come, the Senate took 178 days to respond.

The ratification process then split into two parallel tracks. One was the seemingly inexorable journey to ratification, in which governments (eg. Quebec, Saskatchewan, Ottawa) used their majorities to contain scrutiny and criticism and guarantee the passage of Meech Lake. The other track, though, offered a far less certain journey. Executive federalism and the closed Meech Lake strategy were given a resounding jolt by their political antithesis: elections. In New Brunswick and Manitoba, voters elected new governments that had not been signatories to the Meech Lake agreement.

On 13 October 1987 Liberal Frank McKenna won an astonishing electoral mandate, capturing every seat in the legislature. McKenna had been an early critic of the accord in his testimony before the special joint committee. During the election campaign, he declared that a Liberal victory would be a vote for changing the Meech Lake deal,[87] a position he maintained after the election. He articulated traditional Liberal concerns about the accord's impact on Charter and minority language rights and the federal government's capacity to carry out regionally sensitive social and economic programmes. He also wanted the fisheries removed as a topic for future constitutional conferences.[88]

The other first ministers exerted considerable political and moral pressure on McKenna to avoid breaking the deal that would bring Quebec back into the constitution. There was some talk of a "political" agreement—a foreshadowing of what was to become the idea of a "parallel accord"—that would allay McKenna's concerns by offering assurances of future constitutional change.[89] The federal government was anxious to get the agreement ratified by all eleven legislatures as quickly as possible—before other elections could foment further dissent. Senator Murray thus insisted that the "political reality" was that McKenna had six months to sign. McKenna was unmoved: "I'm still operating on a three-year timetable."[90] In May 1988 he announced that public hearings in New Brunswick would not take place until the fall, but the federal election would delay the start of public hearings until late January 1989 and their completion until late spring or early summer. So, it could not be anticipated that the report on the constitutional agreement would reach the New Brunswick legislature for debate until the autumn of 1989—almost two and a half years after the Langevin meeting, and eight months before the ratification deadline. Standing one against ten, Premier McKenna was in an extremely exposed and isolated position for a time.[91] McKenna was not alone for long, however, for support for Meech Lake in Manitoba disintegrated quickly.

Manitoba Premier Pawley had faced considerable anti-accord sentiments within the provincial NDP through the fall of 1987 . Pawley himself announced that he was reconsidering his support, prompted by Ottawa's decision to push ahead with the Free Trade Agreement in the absence of provincial unanimity.[92] The NDP government fell unexpectedly in March 1988, precipitating an election on April 26, as well as Pawley's resignation as NDP leader. An anti-Meech Lake movement had grown through the winter, and dozens of (mainly rural) municipalities had passed motions condemning the accord for giving Quebec special privileges and for undermining the process of Senate reform.[93] By the time the government fell, fifteen NDP provincial riding associations had passed resolutions asking the government to reject the agreement, and the NDP had to devise a face-saving compromise at its convention in March.[94] The pro-accord Conservatives led by Gary Filmon had a lead going into the election, but managed to win only twenty-five of the province's fifty-seven seats. The Liberal party won twenty seats, led by Sharon Carstairs, a long-time ally of Jean Chrétien and critic of Meech Lake. After the election she declared that "Meech Lake is dead." NDP was support was unlikely, as a disproportionate number of its seats were in northern Manitoba, where there was strong native sentiment against the accord. When the Filmon government presented its Throne Speech in July 1988, the constitutional agreement was given a low priority; public hearings would not be held until the fall.[95] The situation in Manitoba, then, looked no more promising than in New Brunswick.

The accord-threatening developments in New Brunswick and Manitoba were exacerbated by other events. A fierce, two-week Meech Lake debate in Nova Scotia in March was suspended until the end of the session. Its non-completion was ominous, given the provincial election looming on the horizon.[96] The ratification process was also decelerating at the national level. The Senate committee had held public hearings in Whitehorse, Yellowknife, and Iqaluit in the fall of 1987, focusing on issues of particular concern to northerners. On 1 March 1988 it recommended a number of amendments:

- the territories should be allowed to nominate senators and Supreme Court justices;
- the territories should be allowed to participate in constitutional conferences;
- the creation of new provinces should be a matter between only the territories and the federal government;
- aboriginal issues should be placed as a continuing item on the constitutional agenda;
- aboriginal people should be characterized in the constitution as a distinct society.[97]

These were passed on to the Liberal-dominated Senate, whose highly partisan constitutional hearings had been held on and off again from October 1987 through March 1988. On 18 April the Senate sent the constitutional bill back to the House of Commons with nine amendments (similar to those proposed by Liberal leader Turner in the House of Commons the previous October). These were described by Senator Murray as "killer amendments," that could scuttle the constitutional deal. The House of Commons would have to consider these amendments and the Meech Lake agreement again.[98]

THE RISE AND FALL OF THE MEECH LAKE ACCORD

Outside of immediate government circles, there was substantial anti-Meech Lake momentum. Labour opposition surfaced during the winter. The Canadian Union of Public Employees (CUPE) passed a resolution at its January meeting describing the agreement as "flawed, inadequate and unacceptable." The National Union of Provincial Government Employees (Canada's second-largest union) passed a resolution condemning the agreement for the vagueness of its language, the absence of public debate, and the threat to social programmes created by the opting-out provision.[99] In April 1988 Saskatchewan introduced its new language law, which declared that there would be no French Hansard and only some bills would be translated into French at some future time. For many observers—New Brunswick Premier McKenna among them—this action seemed to underscore the weak protection given to minority language rights by the Meech Lake agreement.[100] In March, La fédération des francophones hors Québec—which spoke for one million francophones outside Quebec—wrote Prime Minister Mulroney and stated that the Meech Lake constitutional agreement was "incomplete and unacceptable" and a threat to minority rights.[101] Leadership heir-apparent Jean Chrétien criticized the deal for weakening the federal government ("Who will speak for Canada?") and for threatening Charter rights ("I know that some lawyers argue that the Charter will not be overridden, but I also know that some lawyers can be wrong.")[102] In Ontario, the Liberals' annual meeting only narrowly defeated a motion proposing three amendments to the Meech Lake deal. During an interview in May, Premier Peterson stated that "I'm not saying there can't be an amendment somewhere.... We're reasonable." This set alarm bells ringing in first ministers' offices across the country, and the next day Peterson asserted that no amendments would be made at this time.[103] Prime Minister Mulroney tried to characterize extra-governmental criticism of Meech Lake as "anti-Quebec": "Let those who oppose Meech Lake say so squarely.... Those who want to send a message to Quebec and Canada that they are against the accord, let them stand up and stop hiding behind other people. We'll see what Canadians and Quebeckers have to say about that."[104] Chrétien criticized the logic of this claim and the accord's backers for saying that "anybody who speaks out is anti-Quebec.... Nobody would be able to say I'm anti-Quebec."[105]

The ratification process appeared to have lost steam—outside of government circles. Opinion polls in early April indicated that only one in four Canadians supported the accord, down from 50 per cent support the previous year. Public support for the accord never bounced back from this dismal level. The Saskatchewan language controversy, the criticism by francophone groups outside of Quebec, the New Brunswick and Manitoba elections and their ensuing Meech Lake doubts, the Senate amendments, court challenges by the territories, the

THE RISE AND FALL OF THE MEECH LAKE ACCORD

divisions within the Liberal party, and the agreement's rough treatment in the Nova Scotia legislature amounted to a huge political weight against the ratification process. On top of all this, three of Canada's cleverest lawyers were taking the agreement to court, claiming that it was unconstitutional.[106]

Events and opinion outside of the narrow confines of the legislatures swung clearly against Meech Lake. But public support and extra-parliamentary happenings were not as important as votes in the legislatures. The ratification process was controlled by governments. And governments' ratification of the accord speeded up throughout the remainder of 1988.

Because the Senate had passed amendments to the constitutional legislation, the House of Commons had to pass the original constitutional act again. The legislation was reintroduced on 19 May 1988, and the debate was lethargic and without surprises. Ray Hnatyshyn, a future governor-general, led off for the government, and urged that the opposition parties not introduce amendments, as "such proposals could only encourage their provincial cousins." The Liberals' Kaplan asserted that "the government has made a terrible tactical mistake in insisting that the agreement is a seamless web." Prime Minister Mulroney admitted that "the Meech Lake Accord is not perfect" but insisted that the 1981–82 constitutional deal had "deprive[d] the federal government of the flexibility inherent in a comprehensive negotiation." With less than half his caucus present, beleaguered Liberal leader Turner reintroduced the amendments he had proposed last fall. NDP leader Broadbent remained a strong supporter, echoing Pauline Jewett's comments that "Meech is stronger than we ever dreamed, and better, and more effective."[107] The House of Commons voted 200–7 to override the Senate amendments on 23 June 1987—exactly one year after Quebec had ratified Meech Lake and two years before the ratification deadline.[108]

Alberta became the third province to ratify. The process in this province was quintessentially Meech. The Conservative government turned down the opposition request for legislative hearings, so the NDP sponsored its own public hearings across the province. A total of 150 submissions were made, all but one negative towards Meech Lake. By and large, the media ignored the hearings. On 7 December 1987 a snap vote was called, surprising opposition members who were in another part of the legislative buildings. Despite its unpopularity within the province, the constitutional agreement was passed unanimously.[109]

Five more provinces ratified the constitutional agreement through the spring and summer of 1988. Prince Edward Island became the fourth province, and the first Atlantic province, to approve the accord. PEI was also only the second province to hold public hearings, which were held over five days in April and May. The constitutional committee recommended that the agreement be ac-

THE RISE AND FALL OF THE MEECH LAKE ACCORD

cepted, with outstanding concerns and issues to be pursued in the next constitutional round.[110] Nova Scotia was the fifth province to ratify Meech Lake. After two fierce weeks in March, the government waited until two days before the session ended to conclude the debate, without public hearings. Premier Buchanan was absent for almost all of the debate. The agreement passed 35–7 in May. During the summer election, Liberal leader MacLean promised, if elected, to try to convince the premiers to change the agreement. In the event, Buchanan's Conservatives were returned to office.[111]

Ontario was one of only two provinces to this point to hold hearings, but Premier Peterson had made it clear that amendments would not be considered. The committee gave unanimous but "reluctant" support to the agreement, its reservations assuaged by the prospect of Quebec's re-entry into the constitutional family. The committee issued two "companion resolutions," requesting that a broader conceptualization of Canada's fundamental character be developed and that aboriginal rights be placed on the constitutional agenda. On 29 June 1988 Ontario became the sixth province to ratify the agreement, by a vote of 112–8.[112] Later that day British Columbia became the seventh province to pass the constitutional agreement. Of all the provinces, BC's ratification of Meech Lake produced the least amount of fanfare. A motion was presented on 28 June 1988, the day the Attorney General resigned, which stole its thunder. A quick debate gave the motion perfunctory treatment, and it passed 42–5.[113] Newfoundland was the eighth province to ratify the accord. A motion was introduced in mid-March, and an opposition filibuster was attempted. Opposition leader Liberal Clyde Wells criticized the accord for weakening federal spending power and Charter rights, as well as for creating a rigid amending formula. In July the ratification motion passed 28–10, with fourteen members absent, including Premier Peckford.[114]

Two judicial decisions knocked away some constraints on the ratification process. During the summer, the Supreme Court rejected the territories' appeal that the Meech Lake agreement was unconstitutional. In September 1988 the Canadian Coalition on the Constitution's challenge of the constitutionality of the Meech Lake accord was thrown out of the Federal Court of Canada, on the grounds that the accord was only a "tentative agreement" that could not be disputed in the courts.[115]

At the halfway point in the three-year ratification period, the process was still unfolding. Ratification had gone relatively smoothly at the federal level, where all-party agreement insulated an already tightly controlled process. The process had been similar in all provinces save for New Brunswick and Manitoba, where elections had created openings for opponents of the accord. These provincial governments awaited the result of the November 1988 federal election, to see whether this would affect the process.

There was little discussion of Meech Lake in the 1988 election, which was dominated by the free trade issue. This would likely have been the case even in the absence of the free trade issue, as the three major parties had made Meech Lake a non-partisan matter. Each party eyed Quebec as an electoral prize that required its fidelity to Meech Lake. The Conservatives emerged as the big electoral winner nationally, but also and particularly in Quebec, where they won sixty of seventy-five seats. This was a disheartening result for the Liberals and the NDP, given the trials each endured in supporting Meech Lake, and the anticipation of electoral success in Quebec. Prime Minister Mulroney interpreted this electoral victory and dominance within Quebec as signifying popular approval of Meech Lake, which "obliged" Manitoba and New Brunswick to pass the constitutional agreement. Neither provincial government found this argument compelling.[116]

Ratification Stalls in 1989

As 1988 drew to a close, the fate of the Meech Lake constitutional accord was by no means settled, but it could be envisioned that it would eventually be ratified by the two remaining governments. Then an unanticipated development unleashed a series of events that threatened to halt the ratification process.

On 15 December 1988 the Supreme Court struck down certain sections of Bill 101, Quebec's language law, those sections dealing with the language used in signs. Bill 101 had insisted that signs in Quebec be exclusively in French, in order to protect the French language. The Court ruled that "it has not been demonstrated that the prohibition of the use of any language other than French...is necessary to the defence and enhancement of the status of the French language in Quebec, or that it is proportionate to that legislative purpose." Its unanimous decision endorsed earlier verdicts by the Quebec Superior Court in 1984 and the Quebec Court of Appeal in 1986. In an agonizing decision, Quebec premier Bourassa then introduced Bill 178. This was a compromise law, which proposed to allow bilingual signs inside buildings but insisted on unilingual French sides outside buildings. In the process, Bourassa invoked section 33 of the Charter, the notwithstanding clause, to overturn the Supreme Court decision and to protect the Quebec government from legal attack on this bill for the next five years. This action provoked the resignation of three (of four) of Bourassa's English cabinet ministers as well as the wrath of Quebec nationalists who supported Bill 101 and the language status quo.[117]

There was widespread criticism of Bourassa's action outside of Quebec. While Prime Minister Mulroney appeared prepared to accept the idea of French-only signs in Quebec, he pleaded with Bourassa not to use the notwithstanding clause. Mulroney feared that an anti-Quebec backlash would hurt the chances of ratifying the Meech Lake agreement. But, as Quebec House leader Michel Gratton explained, "every lawyer we consulted told us that unless we used the notwithstanding clause we would be back in court in January."[118] While the federal government condemned Bill 178 for undermining minority language rights in Quebec, it blamed the previous Liberal government for constructing a constitution in 1981–82 that contained the notwithstanding clause.[119]

The Prime Minister's fears of an anti-Meech Lake backlash were confirmed within days in Manitoba. Premier Filmon had introduced the Meech Lake legislation in the Manitoba legislature on 16 December, the day after the Supreme Court ruling and two days before the introduction of Bill 178. At the time, he characterized the accord as "too narrow a foundation upon which to build," but concluded that it was "a necessary first step." He proposed to devise a companion resolution (as Ontario had done) to register Manitoba's concerns. But Filmon suspended the legislative debate on Meech Lake as a result of Quebec's Bill 178. Quebec's action, he claimed, was a "national tragedy to which we had no option but to respond.... We could not sit by idly and let our principles of justice and fair play be compromised." Bill 178 was seen to "violate the spirit of Meech Lake," and further debate on the accord "may invite a very negative anti-Quebec backlash." He worried about Premier Bourassa's claim that, had the Meech Lake accord been ratified, the distinct society clause would have been used to justify Bill 178.[120] New Brunswick Premier McKenna concurred and said that "the government of Canada has a role to play in promoting and protecting the role of minorities. This is one of the additions we wanted to see to Meech Lake."[121]

The Supreme Court's decision and the subsequent Bill 178 seriously weakened the momentum towards ratifying Meech Lake. It strengthened Manitoba's and New Brunswick's resolve to hang tough and seek constitutional changes. It focused increased scrutiny on what Quebec had attained at Meech Lake and weakened the already low degree of support for the accord in English Canada. Later, in the Throne Speech debate in the spring, Opposition leader Turner criticized Quebec's attack on minority language rights and its use of the notwithstanding clause to neutralize the Charter, and he castigated Prime Minister Mulroney for not criticizing Quebec's action. Mulroney retorted that former prime minister Trudeau had paid too high a price for patriation in 1981–82 in accepting the notwithstanding clause, which, he claimed, made the constitution "not worth the paper it was printed on."[122]

THE RISE AND FALL OF THE MEECH LAKE ACCORD

The ratification process slowed to a crawl over the first nine months of 1989. New Brunswick's long-promised public hearings began on 25 January and continued until mid-February. Social and political groups came from all across Canada, as the New Brunswick hearings offered Meech Lake opponents access to the ratification process. On the first day aboriginal and women's groups demanded the rejection of the accord, and the hearings continued in a decidedly anti-Meech spirit.[123] On 13 March the Manitoba government announced an all-party task force on the Meech Lake deal, and hearings were held between 6 April and 2 May. Opposition to Meech dominated the hearings, which were marked by a significant degree of anti-Quebec feeling.[124] The final reports of both sets of hearings would not be presented until late October; the delay reflected these provinces' desire to avoid complicating the September election in Quebec. Hence, there was treading of the ratification waters through the summer and fall of 1989.

There were rumours that a side deal or "parallel accord" was being discussed, whereby the hold-out provinces would ratify Meech Lake in return for a guarantee that a second package of constitutional changes—the "add ons"—would also be passed, from aboriginal and women's rights to the authority and future of the territories.[125] But Quebec's Bourassa rejected renegotiations, and Senator Murray was categorical: "If the passage of a parallel accord is made a condition of the passage of Meech Lake, that is just not on...reopening or renegotiating Meech Lake will kill it."[126] Prime Minister Mulroney was also dubious about this approach. In a four-page letter to the premiers in February, rallying them to the Meech Lake cause, he confirmed that the federal government would not reopen discussions: "The burden of proof must lie with those who claim they could reconstruct unanimous support for an improved accord." He accused opponents of trying to isolate Quebec and exhorted Canadians to say "yes" and repay Quebec. He reiterated at the February First Ministers' Conference that Meech Lake was a "done deal." There was optimism that a nation-building mood would prevail at the next First Ministers' Conference in Prince Edward Island in September, the 125th anniversary of the start of the confederation talks in Charlottetown. In early July, though, Mulroney cancelled this meeting: "There will be little utility to a September meeting," he explained, as the Manitoba and New Brunswick task force reports would not yet have been released.[127]

Through the first half of 1989 there was "growing hostility towards the accord," as Opposition leader Turner put it.[128] Despite the fact that 69 per cent of Canadians knew little or nothing about it, it was supported by only 30 per cent of the population.[129] The Prime Minister sent his English cabinet ministers on the road to explain Meech Lake to English Canada, but there was widespread criticism that the federal government had done an inadequate job selling Meech

Lake. The lack of support was reflected within the political parties. The Saskatchewan Liberals picked a strongly anti-Meech leader, and the Ontario wing of the federal Liberal party unanimously denounced Meech Lake at its annual convention.[130] In March the NDP's national council set up a review of the party's position on Meech Lake. The council concluded that "a limited number of changes...are both necessary and desirable if a true national consensus is to be found and if constitutional change is in fact going to happen." Outgoing leader Ed Broadbent—an early and fervent supporter of Meech Lake—admitted that "some of the concerns, whether in Manitoba or elsewhere, have to be addressed in order to get Meech Lake passed." He pleaded with Mulroney to make changes or watch Meech die: "It does not do any good to pretend that Canada is just the same as it was two years ago." At its national convention in December, the party rejected a compromise resolution and voted to "[work] now for improvements and changes to the Meech Lake accord either by direct amendment or through another amendment process."[131]

The accord's growing unpopularity was reconfirmed on 20 April 1989. Clyde Wells led his Liberals to victory in an election in Newfoundland, where the accord had already been ratified. A former constitutional adviser to Trudeau, Wells believed that the accord weakened the federal government's capacity to help have-not provinces and protect Charter rights. He did not support the idea of giving Quebec special status. His election boded ill for the ratification process: "I don't want...to be difficult to get along with...but if it becomes necessary to rescind the Meech Lake resolution...it will be done." Foreshadowing the rough relationship between Wells and the federal government, Senator Murray warned him that rescinding the resolution would set a bad precedent (for other federal-provincial agreements) and Trade Minister Crosbie threatened Newfoundland with hardship if it did not cooperate. New Brunswick's McKenna welcomed Wells' election: "There is...a tremendous amount of significance in his election, in the fact that he shares a lot of our concerns with respect to Meech Lake."[132] The electoral process had now produced three provinces who opposed ratification of the Meech Lake accord.

Ratification Challenge: New Brunswick, Manitoba and Newfoundland Set Their Conditions

The 25 September 1989 re-election of the Bourassa government in Quebec set the stage for a crucial round in the ratification process. Flushed with winning 92 of 125 seats, Bourassa staked out a firm position: "For a growing number of Quebeckers the ratification of the Meech Lake Accord has become linked with the acceptance of Quebec as a distinct society by the rest of Canada, or the acceptance of Quebec, period."[133] In Quebec, rejection of Meech Lake by even one province would be interpreted as a rejection of Quebec by all of Canada, regardless of the motives of the dissenting province. Quebec's business leaders—like former Quebec cabinet minister Castonguay, head of the Laurentian Group—warned ominously that "if the Meech Lake accord is not accepted...[it] will again create an image of instability and that is negative for the economy."[134] On the other hand, with the Quebec election over, the recalcitrant provinces could become more articulate and specific in their declarations on Meech Lake, many of which had little to do with Quebec. Each province released reports or opinions immediately after the election. The extent, substance, and (conflicting) variety of these recommendations suggested that the task of ratification would be formidable—if not impossible.

Newfoundland was first off the mark. Relations between Ottawa and Newfoundland had taken on the character of guerilla warfare since Clyde Wells' election. In response to Wells' threat of rescinding Newfoundland's ratification, Ottawa had threatened to rescind various financial arrangements with the economically dependent province.[135] Wells made his position official on 20 October 1989 in an eight-page letter to the first ministers. On the eve of the November First Ministers' Conference, Wells tabled his constitutional conditions for support of Meech Lake. Newfoundland would accept the distinct society in the preamble of the constitution, but would not give Quebec any special powers and insisted on Charter supremacy over the clause. Aboriginal people and multiculturalism should also be included in the preamble as distinct and fundamental parts of Canada. An elected Senate would be assigned a special veto over any constitutional changes affecting language and culture. Opting out would be allowed only if a program was not designed to offset regional disparity.[136] These proposals—particularly those dealing with the distinct society clause—would doom the accord if pursued.

The Manitoba Task Force on Meech Lake released its report on 21 October, after travelling through the province in April and early May. It heard presentations from an incredible array and diversity of interest groups: dozens of aboriginal, Charter rights, minority language, economic, labour, multicultural, and women's groups assaulted various parts of the agreement. Of the 340 oral presentations, only 25 supported all features of the Meech Lake agreement. The Task Force concluded unanimously that it was "unable to recommend ratification of the 1982 Constitutional Accord in its present form." It maintained that "dissatisfaction with the Meech Lake Accord in Manitoba [parallels] the discontent in the hearings in other provinces...[and] provides the First Ministers with the mandate to reconsider...the Meech Lake Accord." The report made nine recommendations, six of which would require amendments to the constitutional agreement (see Inset III). Its key recommendation was the creation of a Canada clause (that specified aboriginals and multicultural communities as well as Quebec as distinct societies), with both federal and provincial responsibilities to maintain these fundamental characteristics of Canada in the context of the supremacy of the Charter of Rights. It rejected the opting-out provision of shared-cost programmes and proposed to allow Senate reform and the creation of new provinces without unanimity.[137] These recommendations mooted a more activist role for the federal government than the logic of Meech Lake suggested. The Canada clause, Charter supremacy, no opting out, and easier amending of the Senate were more or less diametrically opposed to Meech Lake. If the Manitoba government insisted on these amendments, it would alienate Quebec in particular, and Meech Lake would be dead.

The immediate reaction was predictable. Senator Murray concluded that reaching unanimity on all of the recommendations would be impossible. A Quebec official reacted as follows: "That they suggest six amendments to our five conditions shows just how popular we are in these parts." Manitoba-Quebec relations were as frosty as those between Newfoundland and Ottawa. A few days after the release of the report, Liberal leader Carstairs stormed out of a meeting with the editorial board of *Le Devoir*, after an apology was not offered for the paper's cartoon depiction of three hooded Ku Klux Klan members—presumably the Manitoba party leaders—making peace signs and holding a flaming fleur de lys.[138]

Two days after Wells' letter, and the day after the release of the Manitoba report, New Brunswick's Select Committee on the 1987 Constitutional Accord issued its report. As in Manitoba, a multitude of interest groups made representations, over ninety in all, including women's and aboriginal groups, commercial organizations and community service groups, multicultural and youth groups, linguistic associations and labour groups, and constitutional lobbies. Fourteen representatives of various governments and parties also appeared. The report concluded as follows: "We cannot share the drafters' belief in the fragility of the accord—a seamless garment that must not be altered. Rather, we see it as a constitutional cloak of great durability, once a few loose strands are sewn into place."

While the Select Committee made a number of recommendations for amendments (see Inset IV), it did *not* recommend changes to the key provisions of the Meech Lake agreement, such as the distinct society clause and the opting out provisions for shared-cost programmes. Moreover, it did not insist on changing the unanimity provision for Senate reform or for Charter supremacy. Its key

Inset III

THE MANITOBA TASK FORCE ON MEECH LAKE

The all-party Task Force included opposition leaders Carstairs and Doer, and travelled in April and May to Winkler, Island Lake, The Pas, Thomson, Brandon, Dauphin, and Winnipeg, hearing 340 presentations (there were another 40 in writing, and it also received a number of out-of-province written submissions from scholars and constitutional lawyers).

The Task Force made nine recommendations, six as amendments to the constitutional agreement and three as additions.

AMENDMENTS

1. Canada Clause

The distinct society clause "generated the most controversy and debate during the public hearings" (p. 12). Presenters wanted to see aboriginal groups and Canada's multicultural heritage treated in the same way as Quebec. The distinct society clause of the Meech Lake Accord would be expanded to include these two features, with federal and provincial responsibility to uphold these fundamental characteristics, including the reality of minority language groups.

2. Rights Protection Clause

Women's groups were concerned that Meech Lake's section 16, in not noting equality rights, was creating a hierarchy of rights (p. 21ff). Civil liberties groups and disabled groups shared this concern (p. 25). The Task Force proposed that all Charter Rights be given the same protection that aboriginal and multicultural rights were given under Meech Lake.

recommendation was for the recognition of French-speaking and English-speaking Canadians without reference to territoriality (i.e., to particular provinces), with the federal government assigned the role of both preserving and *promoting* the fundamental characteristics of Canada (to resolve differences over linguistic rights). It also recommended the affirmation of the Charter as a fundamental characteristic of Canada (to balance the distinct society clause). [139]

New Brunswick's recommendations were more conciliatory and far less demanding than those presented by the Manitoba Task Force (in Manitoba, Carstairs and Doer called New Brunswick's report "soft and mushy").[140] Whereas Manitoba recommended a "multiple" distinct society clause, Charter supremacy, dropping of opting out, and Senate reform without unanimity, New Brunswick

3. Supreme Court

It was recommended that the territories be extended the same rights as the provinces in making nominations to the Supreme Court.

4. Spending Power

The opting-out provision with compensation was "one of the most often criticized clauses during the hearings" (p. 53). There was concern that smaller, less affluent provinces like Manitoba would be hurt. The Task Force recommended that this feature of the Meech Lake agreement be dropped completely.

5. Amending Formula

The unanimity clause was universally criticized, particularly with regard to Senate reform, seen as "a betrayal of western interests." With regard to the territories, the clause was seen as "blatant disregard" (p. 59). The Task Force recommended that the seven-province, 50 per cent formula be used in each of these areas.

6. Constitutional Conferences

The majority of presenters saw this phenomenon as extending executive federalism. There was also tremendous dissatisfaction that the aboriginal issue was omitted from the list of future constitutional concerns. The Task Force recommended that the aboriginal issue be guaranteed a place on the constitutional agenda and that, once it and Senate reform had been dealt with, the provision for annual first ministers' conferences be eliminated.

The committee also recommended the creation of a Committee on Senate Reform, review of the immigration provisions in Meech Lake in five years, and the substitution of a more public constitutional process in place of the present "secretive, elitist, exclusive, hasty, unrepresentative and undemocratic" one (p. 69).

accepted the Meech Lake distinct society clause, suggested a "softer" political statement affirming the Charter, accepted opting out, and accepted the unanimity approach to Senate reform. In all cases, the New Brunswick approach was far closer to, if not identical with, Quebec's conditions, although it proposed a federal role in protecting language minorities that Quebec would find difficult to accept. These were substantial, qualitative differences that would not be easily resolved. Over and above these differences, New Brunswick and Manitoba agreed on a number of issues for amendment, including assigning federal responsibility for promoting Canada's fundamental characteristics, assigning authority to the territories in making Supreme Court and Senate nominations, dropping the unanim-

THE RISE AND FALL OF THE MEECH LAKE ACCORD

Inset IV

NEW BRUNSWICK SELECT COMMITTEE ON THE 1987 CONSTITUTIONAL ACCORD: RECOMMENDATIONS AND CONCLUSIONS

1. Constitutional Process

The report regretted "the lack of any debate or public scrutiny of the Accord before the final draft was agreed upon" and criticized "the First Ministers' side agreement not to propose or allow any change to the Accord" (p. 27).

It recommended that all governments create a Standing Committee on Constitutional Matters to consult and advise both before and after First Ministers' Constitutional Conferences (p. 29).

2. Fundamental Characteristics and Distinct Society

The committee accepted the distinct society clause, concluding that it was an interpretive clause that did not grant any new powers or derogate any existing ones (p. 38).

The committee concluded that the aboriginal and multicultural features of Canada had sufficient thrust and protection in various clauses of the constitution, which were adequately balanced with the fundamental characteristic clause. The committee did reject the territorial restrictions of this clause, which "constitutes an unnecessary and limited vision of Canada which renders the Accord to be a reconciliation of the two linguistic majorities. There is no reason to minimize the recognition of English-speaking Canadians living in Quebec or of French-speaking Canadians living outside Quebec." It therefore recommended that the fundamental characteristic clause, paragraph 2(1)(a), be amended to read:

> The recognition that the existence of French-speaking Canadians and English-speaking Canadians constitutes a fundamental characteristic of Canada (p. 34).

In a criticism of Meech Lake, the committee noted that "nothing in the Accord provided for the protection and enhancement of linguistic minorities," so assigned to Ottawa the role to "preserve and promote the fundamental characteristic of Canada" (pp. 39-41).

3. The Accord and the Charter

The committee rejected recommendations that the Charter be assigned "paramouncy," for it accepted the operational logic that section 1 of the Charter might be used on occasion (viz., "...guarantees the rights and freedoms set out in it subject only to such reasonable limits prescribed by law as can be demonstrably justified in a free and democratic society"). Instead, it suggested that the Charter be added as a fundamental characteristic of Canada (pp. 43-44).

4. Gender Equality

The committee was alive to fears that the Accord "did open the door to possible erosion of the equality provision contained in Section 28 of the Charter," despite the

THE RISE AND FALL OF THE MEECH LAKE ACCORD

accord's absence of intention to affect gender equality. The committee confirmed that section 28 "represents a *fundamental value* in our society" and recommended the extension to section 28 of the same "protection" afforded multicultural and aboriginal rights under Meech Lake section 16 (pp. 48-49).

5. Senate Appointments

The report recommended that the territories be given a role in Senate nominations (p. 51).

6. Supreme Court

The committee recommended that the territories be given a role in making nominations to the Supreme Court.

The committee accepted the idea of provinces having a role to play in the nomination process, but proposed a broader, participatory process, with Ottawa making the final decision (pp. 55-56).

7. Shared-Cost Programmes

The Committee affirmed the federal role in ensuring comparable levels of public services across the country, and was alive to concerns that the opting-out provision could result in a "checker-board" pattern of programs. It accepted the Meech Lake opting out approach, but suggested that the regional equality provisions of section 36 of the Constitution be strictly applied, to neutralize any negative effects of the opting-out provision (pp. 59-61).

8. The Amending Formula

The unanimity provision was seen to be too restrictive and "makes it unlikely that the territories can achieve provincial status," so the committee recommended that the 7/50 formula be used. On the other hand, it maintained that unanimity was an appropriate approach in matters affecting "fundamental democratic principles and institutions of Canada," so did not suggest a relaxed formula for Senate reform (pp. 62-64).

9. Constitutional Conferences

The Committee had "serious doubts about whether such conferences should be held annually or should have constitutionally fixed agenda." To this end, it recommended "deleting all references to specific agendae from planned inclusion in the Constitution." It was particularly concerned about placing the fisheries permanently on the agenda, which "could only be detrimental to the long-term stability of this industry" (p. 66).

11. New Brunswick Bilingualism

The Committee recommended that New Brunswick's bilingual principles be entrenched in the national constitution.

ity provision for the creating of new provinces, and giving aboriginal issues constitutional priority.

Ottawa reacted positively to the New Brunswick report, particularly to the province's endorsement of the distinct society clause. The differences among the recalcitrant provinces led Senator Murray to observe, "It is difficult to envision how unanimity could be constructed amongst the eleven governments if even the holdout provinces have different priorities." In Quebec, Intergovernmental Affairs Minister Rémillard concluded that "we have a problem with Manitoba. It is impossible to accept their report in its present form. But we are happy to see we can get together with New Brunswick and try to reach a consensus." Newfoundland Premier Wells sided with the Manitoba report, particularly with regard to Senate reform and the distinct society clause, but he wanted the latter dropped altogether.[141] McKenna continued to pitch the idea of a parallel accord, but Premier Bourassa was dubious and Prime Minister Mulroney was non-committal.[142]

The release of the constitutional documents of the recalcitrant provinces indicated three critical points. First, non-committed governments gave an opening to critics of Meech Lake, which they seized with a vengeance, articulating an array of vehement criticisms of the accord. Second, while there was some overlap in their recommendations, the three provinces were themselves divided on a number of key points. Third, these three provinces envisioned different roles for the various governments than those envisioned in the Meech Lake agreement: a more active federal government with more substantive powers, and a far more open constitutional process. Perhaps most important politically, Quebec continued to reject changes to Meech Lake and interpreted these provinces' actions as being anti-Quebec.

As the first ministers gathered for a conference on the economy in November, public support for Meech Lake continued to weaken, dropping to 19 per cent in October. In British Columbia, the annual convention of the Social Credit party voted overwhelmingly to ask the BC government to withdraw its support for Meech Lake.[143] A further complication was the startling election in Alberta of Independent Stan Waters to the Senate on 16 October, in the country's first Senate election. While Alberta had sanctioned the election, Ottawa had not indicated whether it would accept Waters into the Senate on Meech Lake's interim appointment arrangements. As the first ministers convened, Alberta Premier Getty threatened to withdraw support for Meech Lake unless Waters was appointed to the Senate.[144]

It had been anticipated that Meech Lake would take a back seat to economic issues at the 9–10 November 1989 First Ministers' Conference. Federal officials maintained that the groundwork for a proper constitutional conference had not been laid, as the New Brunswick and Manitoba reports and Newfoundland Premier Wells's position had been released so recently.[145] Meech Lake nonetheless dominated what was a tense, electrifying meeting.

Wells announced upon arrival that he would veto the Meech Lake accord regardless of what happened at the conference. He said that being forced to accept Quebec's terms was "not compromise, that's blackmail."[146] The conference nearly dissolved as it began. Despite entreaties to delay, Wells planned to announce plans for rescinding in his televised opening remarks. As conference participants learned this, Premier Bourassa let it be known that he would walk out of the conference—as television cameras watched. Ontario Premier Peterson then let it be known that he would not allow Quebec to be isolated, so that he too would walk out. This would have resulted in the national debacle of a collapsed first ministers' meeting. Mulroney quickly called a coffee break before Wells was to speak. Ontario's Attorney General Ian Scott then convinced Wells to delay his announcement, lest this awful possibility unfold.[147]

During the introductory session, Wells and Mulroney became involved in a heated, emotional exchange. Picking up Mulroney's claim that the constitution could not have been patriated in 1981–82 without Ontario, Wells declared:

> We most certainly would have if Ontario had been holding out and saying "we won't go along unless we get special status" (as Quebec receives from Meech Lake)...
>
> To say that failure to reject the Meech Lake accord as it is is a rejection of Quebec is a political misrepresentation...
>
> I am rejecting a Canada with a class A province, a class B province, and eight class C provinces.

Mulroney replied:

> You said "We would have proceeded without Ontario, if Ontario had demanded something we thought was unacceptable: special status." My question...is: Who is "we"? Where would you think you would have got the right to proceed without the most populous province, and impose on that province a constitution that was unacceptable and not in its interests?...It's inconceivable. It would never happen that we would ever impose a constitution on Ontario. If it is true that a constitution should never be imposed on Ontario, or Alberta, where, then, do you get the moral authority to impose a constitution on Quebec?

> ...I tell you, sir, because I was there...it would have been a lot easier to walk out [of the Meech Lake talks] and say no. I tell you, it is true.... I would have spent no less time to bring Ontario in.

Wells came right back at the Prime Minister:

> I say no province in this nation has the right to hold up the rest of the nation. No province can hold up the constitutional development of this country forever.

To which Ontario Premier Peterson responded, "You must reflect very carefully on your own logic, my friend."[148] Later that night in a television interview, Wells challenged Mulroney again: "If you think you're speaking for the Canadian people, and you're prepared to honour the wishes of the Canadian people, then call a referendum." Mulroney brushed this aside: "Referendums are not the Canadian way."[149]

The next day, the conference reached a compromise and a semblance of progress and unity. Wells promised that Newfoundland would not rescind its ratification of Meech Lake, in return for an agreement that Manitoba and New Brunswick would not approve the accord until Newfoundland had had a chance for further discussions. Senator Murray was directed to "intensify and seek to accelerate" discussions aimed at a consensus, and Prime Minister Mulroney promised to hold a first ministers' conference on Senate reform next November— if Meech Lake survived. He declared, "I think we've moved the process along somewhat." However, the three hold-out provinces were hanging tough—as was Quebec's Bourassa, who continued to insist that changes to Meech Lake would be unacceptable.[150]

There were now only seven months to the ratification deadline, and three of the eleven governments were not on side. Over the next four winter months, there were amazingly few developments in resolving the Meech Lake impasse. The ubiquitous Senator Murray continuously toured the provincial capitals in search of a consensus. The federal government's attitude towards the parallel accord strategy appeared to be softening. In New Brunswick, Murray used language similar to McKenna's: "We want to build on Meech without undoing what has already been done." But Manitoba Premier Filmon refused to meet Murray, claiming that Ottawa, Quebec, and many other provinces were showing no willingness to compromise. Nonetheless Murray continued his tour, with the apparent willingness of Premiers Buchanan and Ghiz to sign a parallel accord giving the strategy increased political momentum. NDP leader McLaughlin suggested that this would be the only way to save Meech Lake.[151] The year ended on a con-

THE RISE AND FALL OF THE MEECH LAKE ACCORD

troversial note, the New Year's Day message from Governor-General Jeanne Sauve appearing to include an endorsement of Meech Lake.[152]

Public support for Meech Lake continued to be low—in the 20-25 per cent range (although one poll showed support as low as 17 per cent).[153] This public antipathy towards the accord continued to be based on little to no knowledge of its substance—as 71 per cent of Canadians admitted. To address this situation, a number of blue-ribbon interest groups in favour of the Meech Lake agreement were formed in the new year. These included Canadians for a Unifying Constitution, comprised of a who's who of Canadian business leaders, academics, retired civil servants, and former politicians, and the Friends of Meech Lake, a non-partisan group whose spokespersons were former Progressive Conservative leader Robert Stanfield, former Ontario NDP leader and United Nations ambassador Stephen Lewis, and Senator Solange Chaput-Rolland.[154] These groups had limited success in changing public attitudes, particularly in Newfoundland, where Premier Wells's popularity remained high despite their interventions. The legislature voted in late November to support Wells in his condemnation of Meech Lake and the speech from the throne officially announced that Newfoundland would rescind its approval of the accord.[155]

In Quebec, Premier Bourassa ominously noted that "Quebec will not sit passively and watch with indifference the rest of Canada reject its political will to rejoin the Canadian federation on the basis of a particularly moderate set of demands." As public support for independence rose in Quebec—58 per cent if Meech Lake failed—Bourassa started musing about a new political or supra-national structure for Quebec and Canada along the lines of the European parliament. Quebec business began to make its presence felt; 94 per cent claimed that Meech Lake was essential or preferable for the future of the province. Claude Castonguay warned that Quebec was headed for a "divorce" from Canada if Meech Lake was not ratified: "It would not be a legal divorce, rather a separation. It would be the end of legal exchanges.... Quebeckers are fed up." For the first time since the late 1960s, the traditional St. Jean Baptiste parade would be held, in Montreal as part of a $1 million party on 24 June—the day after the Meech Lake deadline.[156] In late January British Columbia premier Vander Zalm issued a five-point plan to break the constitutional impasse, which included the proposal to classify all of the provinces as districts.[157] This plan was more or less ignored by the federal and Quebec governments.[158]

The mood surrounding Meech Lake became even more embittered as a result of a language controversy in Ontario. On 29 July 1989 the city council of Sault Ste. Marie voted 11-2 to endorse English as the city's official language. This was the most dramatic in a series of municipal declarations of unilingualism. As the country reeled in reaction, a week later Thunder Bay became the twenty-seventh council to declare unilingualism. These actions were unexpected and puzzling to most Canadians, and the intolerance behind the actions was unsettling. Politicians, language groups, and regions blamed each other for this development, which was seen to reflect in some ways an anti-Meech Lake as well as an anti-Bill 178 backlash. The federal opposition parties blamed the government for a lack of leadership in explaining Canada's language policies and the Meech Lake proposals, and called on the government to endorse a resolution reaffirming Canada's commitment to the principle of bilingualism and minority language rights. The Prime Minister insisted that a clause be added to the motion saying that bilingualism and linguistic duality reflect the intent of the Meech Lake accord. These parliamentary skirmishes and petty gamesmanship soured the national mood: politicians appeared to be incapable of transcending political partisanship in addressing prejudice and language intolerance. None of this helped the Meech Lake cause.[159]

The divisions and mood of Meech Lake were mirrored in the Liberal leadership race. Leadership hopeful Jean Chrétien attacked Meech Lake in an election manifesto in January. "I'm not for Meech in its present form.... The difficulty is that in two and a half years they have not tried one minute to find a solution. They put the gun there and said, 'You sign or else.' And I don't think it will work." The next day, Paul Martin—Chrétien's main leadership rival—officially launched his campaign, declaring himself an unconditional defender of the Meech Lake agreement. The Liberal infighting over Meech during the leadership campaign was particularly nasty.[160] The markets were also unsettled by the Meech Lake impasse, with rumours abounding of cancelled or delayed investment decisions. Ottawa encouraged the business community to actively support the accord.[161] The Prime Minister resisted the widespread calls for a first ministers' conference, and continued to sell Meech Lake as a Quebec issue, its rejection a rejection of Quebec. External Affairs Minister Joe Clark cautioned Canadians, "Critics of Meech Lake forget history. They forget the very real threat to the fabric of Canada which existed in the 1970s. They forget the War Measures Act, the bombs, the kidnappings, the soldiers in the street."[162] This was hardly likely to get the recalcitrant provinces to ratify the accord. As the mood surrounding Meech acidified, Premier Filmon warned that the operational deadline for action was rapidly approaching: unless a motion endorsing the Meech Lake accord was introduced in the Manitoba legislature by 1 April, it would be "impossible to get it through the legislature" by the 23 June deadline.[163]

Ratification Roller Coaster

With only three months to go before the 23 June ratification deadline, New Brunswick's Premier McKenna started the ten-week roller coaster ride that hurtled Meech Lake wildly towards its destiny. After close consultation with Ottawa, McKenna introduced two resolutions before the New Brunswick legislature. One was the Meech Lake constitutional accord. The other was a companion resolution, which proposed that a number of constitutional amendments be adopted *after* Meech Lake had been proclaimed. The ratification of Meech Lake was made conditional upon evidence that Parliament and the other provincial legislatures had made progress in adopting the companion resolution. The key ingredient of the resolution assigned the federal government responsibility not only for preserving the fundamental characteristics of Canada, but for *promoting* them as well (i.e., Ottawa would be responsible for defending minority language rights). How this would coincide with the distinct society clause was unclear. Other features included exclusive federal responsibility for the creation of new provinces, placing of aboriginal issues on the agenda, and a guarantee of sexual equality rights. Senate reform was notable by its absence, as was the issue of the precise role of the Charter. But McKenna made it clear that his resolution was not a seamless web and that New Brunswick would be flexible, "even at some cost to our credibility if necessary."[164]

The political strategy behind the McKenna move was clear, as evidenced by Senator Murray's reaction: "We like [McKenna's] approach," he said, "because it moves for the adoption of Meech Lake without any subtractions and proposes a number of additions to build on and improve Meech Lake." The next night, Prime Minister Mulroney made a rare, prime-time television appearance (only his second in his years as prime minister). In an emotional and sentimental speech (see Inset V), he appealed for national unity and gave quick approval to the McKenna approach (if not to its precise substance). The Prime Minister stated that he would introduce the McKenna proposal in the House of Commons and refer it to a special House of Commons committee, which would hold public hearings and make recommendations. Days later, he introduced the McKenna resolution and invited the hold-out provinces to bring proposals to the committee hearings and build on the McKenna resolution. However, he made it clear that the Meech Lake constitutional accord had to be passed unamended before a companion resolution could be adopted.[165]

While several provinces were supportive of the McKenna/Mulroney manoeuvre, some of the key ones were unimpressed. Manitoba remained opposed to a "pass Meech now, fix it later" approach, and was disappointed that the unan-

Inset V

MULRONEY'S TELEVISION SPEECH, 22 MARCH 1990

We are at a critical juncture in our history. The decisions we take in the next ninety days will profoundly affect our lives...For 123 years our will to live together has never failed us. It has prevailed whenever tested. But much of Canada's promise is yet to be redeemed.

A constitution endorsed by only nine provinces out of ten lacks the unifying vision and strength such a fundamental document must bring to the life and dreams of a nation. It is important that Quebec sign the Canadian constitution—and this we achieve with the Meech Lake accord...

I know that Meech Lake is not perfect. But it is an important instrument for good in Canada.... In the three years since the accord was endorsed by all eleven first ministers, circumstances have changed: new provincial governments have been elected and some Canadians have raised concerns during public hearings. Unfortunately, for some, Meech Lake has become a lightening rod for long-standing tensions in this country—tensions that once again are challenging our collective will to live together...

Last Friday, Premier McKenna wrote to inform me of his intention to improve on Meech Lake through a companion resolution that would add to, but not subtract from the accord, and would adress a number of concerns that had been raised. Those concerns include equality of the sexes, aboriginal rights, northern interests, minority language rights, the commitment of governments to reduce regional disparities, and public participation in a constitutional reform.

This is not a take-it-or-leave-it proposition.... I believe it is possible to extend a hand to Canadians who feel they were overlooked by the Meech Lake accord—aboriginal Canadians, northern Canadians, certain women's groups—without undermining the accord and the consensus it represents.

Meech Lake would become part of the Canadian constitution by the June 23 deadline. And a companion resolution would follow. Premier McKenna has not closed any doors on the timing of the second resolution—nor on the range of amendments it would contain.

...I have decided to introduce Premier McKenna's companion resolution to the House of Commons next week and immediately refer it to a special committee of the House.

The committee will begin public hearings at the earliest possible moment. Once the resolution has been given a full hearing, it will be brought to Parliament for a vote—with whatever suggestions for further improvements emerge from the hearings.... This is not just a constitutional problem, nor is it a debate among politicians. This is above all a question of will—the national will to be true to the legacy of tolerance and generosity of spirit on which this country was built.

THE RISE AND FALL OF THE MEECH LAKE ACCORD

imity provisions for Senate reform and the threats to Charter rights were not addressed. Premier Bourassa was brutally clear: "If it modifies [Meech] it's unacceptable." Parti québécois leader Parizeau suggested that "if Quebec accepts anything that dilutes Meech Lake, it won't be federalism on our knees, it will be federalism on all fours." The Quebec legislature passed a resolution directing the government to "officially reject...all constitutional proposals including New Brunswick's...which would constitute an amendment or modification susceptible to changing the content and scope of the Meech Lake Accord." Premier Wells characterized the approach as a "first step towards flexibility," but this did not deter him from introducing and passing a motion to rescind Newfoundland's approval of Meech Lake.[166]

Despite these reservations, there were hopeful expectations that the special committee—chaired by Jean Charest—might be able to construct a Meech-saving compromise. By the time the committee got organized, held public hearings, and wrote and released its report, it was 17 May. In the two-month interim, governments engaged in verbal warfare and public disapproval of the Meech Lake accord rose in the spring to 59 per cent. Quebec-Newfoundland relations deteriorated. Premier Bourassa reminded Wells that 51 per cent of the Newfoundland government's revenue came from the federal government, and 68 per cent of that came from Quebec and Ontario. After Newfoundland had rescinded its support of Meech Lake, Intergovernmental Affairs Minister Rémillard suggested that "Canada can very well survive without Newfoundland." Lucien Bouchard, federal environment minister, suggested that Canada might have to choose between Newfoundland and Quebec: "If Newfoundland gets isolated as a consequence of Wells's adventures with the constitution, it could be that Canada would have to make a choice about what Canada will be, a Canada without Quebec or a Canada without Newfoundland." In a talk show, Denis Pronovost, assistant deputy speaker of the House of Commons referred to Clyde Wells as "this crazy, mental case...he's not worth much. I've met him. He's a dangerous man. [Newfoundland] is a third world country."[167] (Pronovost later resigned.) Newfoundland replied in kind. Wells insisted that "I don't want this province to be doomed forever to accept what I was told by the premier of Quebec...that Ontario and Quebec paid 68 percent of the support of Newfoundland." Finance Minister Kitchen argued that "it's important to do what's right and to take bold steps and not be coward cravens always forever crying, 'The sky is falling. Quebec will separate'." He later quipped, "They got us by the short hair on Upper Churchill. We've got them in the same place on Meech Lake."[168] In Manitoba, analysts suggested that the province's hard-line stand against Meech Lake reflected its continued disgruntlement with the loss of the lucrative CF-18 contract to Quebec.[169] For Premier

THE RISE AND FALL OF THE MEECH LAKE ACCORD

Filmon, "it's Senate Reform or no deal." Premier Buchanan mused on a post-Meech Quebec separation scenario for Nova Scotia: "What are we going to do? Form our own country? That's absurd. Stay as a fractured part of Canada? A good possibility, but that's all. Or be part of the United States?"[170] There were continuing signs that the Meech Lake impasse was having negative economic effects. Power Corporation chairman Paul Desmarais claimed that Meech Lake had cost the firm two $100 million deals: "People say, 'We like you, we like the projects we talked to you about, but if you don't mind, we'll wait until after July'."[171]

The Charest Committee issued its report on 17 May in a mood of hopeful but anxious expectation. It had held televised hearings in six cities, hearing 160 witnesses, including Premiers Ghiz, Buchanan, Peterson, McKenna, and Wells and the usual incredible array of interest groups. There was tremendous irony in the fact that this committee listened to criticisms about Meech Lake and contemplated and devised amendments—a month before the ratification deadline—in a way that the joint constitutional committee had not in 1987. The fifteen-member, all-party committee's unanimous report was an attempt to "set the table" for a First Ministers' Conference. It reported that "a Companion Resolution process that formally adds to the Meech Lake Accord, without subtracting from it, has the best prospect of solving the current constitutional impasse" (the report was vague as to when the House of Commons would adopt the companion resolution). The committee accepted the 23 June 1990 deadline as a non-negotiable political reality and called on the Prime Minister to convene a First Ministers' Conference on the constitution. The report's twenty-three recommendations included suggestions for a number of amendments to the companion resolution:

- a section should be included affirming that the distinct society clause does not impair Charter rights;
- the federal government should be empowered to promote, not simply preserve, English and French;
- Senate reform should be a priority for the next round of constitutional talks; if unanimous agreement on Senate reform is not attained in three years, then an easier amending formula should be adopted, requiring less than unanimity;
- unanimity should not be required for the territories to become provinces;
- the territories should participate in Senate and Supreme Court appointments;
- separate constitutional talks should take place on aboriginal rights;
- public hearings should take place in future constitutional talks.[172]

THE RISE AND FALL OF THE MEECH LAKE ACCORD

Political reaction to the Charest report was mixed. Federal opposition leaders praised the report and called for a first ministers' conference. Mulroney was cautious, and instead telephoned all the premiers, most of whom seemed keen to have a meeting. Senator Murray was sent on a weekend tour (19-20 May) of the provincial capitals to see if the Charest report's recommendations could be the basis for a successful first ministers' conference. There were ominous rumblings from Quebec City, however. An impatient Robert Bourassa complained that "English Canada does not understand Quebec and that's why they are making unacceptable demands." While Clyde Wells felt that the Charest report was too soft on the distinct society clause, Bourassa insisted that it had gone too far: "Suggesting that the distinct society does not entail any new power...waters down something that was already quite limited.... I don't see how...I could accept a reduction of the powers we got in the Meech Lake Accord." Prime Minister Mulroney insisted that "there is nothing in the Charest report that diminishes what was achieved by Meech Lake." Nonetheless, François Gérin quit the Conservative caucus in protest over the Charest report, and Quebec's Opposition leader Parizeau claimed that the report "takes Quebeckers for nitwits." After four days of provincial shuttling, Senator Murray reported that "I can't, in good conscience, say that a First Ministers' Conference would have a chance of success."[173]

Whatever momentum the Charest report might have had was smothered by a spectacular development over the weekend. The Parti québécois was marking the 10th anniversary of the Quebec referendum at a national council meeting in Alma, Quebec, in the home riding of environment minister Lucien Bouchard. Bouchard was a long-time friend of Mulroney and ex-member of the Parti québécois, who had joined Mulroney as his Quebec lieutenant. Attending meetings in Europe when the Charest report was released, he sent a telegram of encouragement to the Parti québécois: "The memory of [former PQ premier] Levesque unites us all this weekend. For he helped Quebeckers discover their inalienable right to decide for themselves their destiny." The impact of this development was electrifying. There was sympathy for Mulroney that his friend had betrayed him, but this did not stop opposition calls for Bouchard's resignation. When Bouchard finally read the Charest report, he was livid, particularly over its recommendations on limiting the distinct society clause's impact on the Charter and the federal government's responsibility to promote minority language rights. "When I read the Charest report, I concluded that I had a big problem, an immense problem. I...thought...that the process was pretty cavalier, putting things in the report they knew I couldn't accept.... I was furious. I said to myself [Liberal leadership hopeful Jean] Chrétien had more to say in the writing of the report than I did, and I am going to have to endorse it and live with it." He quit the cabinet via another telegram: "I dissociate myself from the ambiguous Charest committee recommendations, which gut the accord of its meaning." Upon returning to Canada, he met with Mulroney and handed him his resignation letter (see Inset VI). He later publicly resigned from both the cabinet and the Conservative caucus: "This country doesn't work any more. We have to remake it. I believe that the solution is sovereignty-association. If you think this is a bluff, then I called my bluff. I quit the cabinet. Read our lips, because we mean business."[174]

The timing of Bouchard's actions could not have been worse for the Prime Minister and the ratification process. The momentum towards a constitutional conference was halted, and the Charest report was more or less assigned to the

---

Inset VI

LUCIEN BOUCHARD'S RESIGNATION LETTER
(edited version)

Mr. Prime Minister:

When I entered active politics in response to your call, all the country's heads of government had agreed to follow you on the path of national reconciliation. They had all understood that this required an act of atonement to Quebec, which had been ostracized by Pierre Elliott Trudeau's strong-armed coup.

After intense negotiations, the Meech Lake accord established Quebec's conditions to adhere to the Constitution. Everybody in Quebec thought these conditions were pretty thin. But Quebecers had a deep desire to offer their hands to their fellow citizens. They largely supported Quebec Premier Bourassa when he cut to the bare bones the cost of Canada's atonement to Quebec.

But like all Quebecers I then watched the reactions against the accord in English Canada with dismay. Instead of Quebec being pardoned, it was hauled on the carpet. Other provinces repudiated their premiers' signatures and shouted out their own demands—"the shopping list."

I have nothing against preparing for other changes to the Constitution, for example, on sexual equality and the tightening of guarantees for native people.

That's why—while insisting that the Meech Lake accord be passed as it is—I supported the creation of the parliamentary committee. I was dumfounded to learn that the report proposed a list of 23 modifications, some of which change the essential nature of the accord.

I refer, primarily, to the trivialization of the clause establishing the distinct nature of Quebec's society by the provision under the same article for the equality of the English-speaking and French-speaking communities of New Brunswick.

THE RISE AND FALL OF THE MEECH LAKE ACCORD

dustbin. In Quebec, the report was anathema; *La Presse* columnist Lysiane Gagnon wrote; "The insult is not in the recommendations...but in the process which led to it...in this new grocery list...of demands that they've hurled in our face to put us in our place. The insult is in the irresponsible stubbornness of the recalcitrant provinces to 'readmit' Quebec 'into the family' on their own conditions." Gilbert Chartrand—MP for Verdun-St.Paul—joined Bouchard in leaving the Conservatives and embracing sovereignty-association. There appeared to be an inexorable separatist drift building up in Quebec: a May Gallup poll indicated that 61 per cent of Quebeckers supported sovereignty-association. International markets sold off their Canadian holdings as the Canadian dollar fell to US$.8415.[176]

The distinct society clause is even more diluted by the proposal that it be applied jointly with the Charter.

And, in particular, I consider totally unacceptable the recommendation to attribute to Parliament and the federal government a role not only to protect linguistic duality, but a role to promote it.

The government of Quebec cannot agree to these proposals.

It appears to me that this report is written by the opponents of the Meech Lake accord. It is not surprising that they are happy with it. I can see several of them gloating, led by Mr. Jean Chrétien.

I reject this report and refuse to give it tacit approval by remaining silent.

I believe very deeply that we have to reconsider the very nature of this country.

We have to stop desperately trying to force Quebec into the same mold as the other provinces; whether you call it association, confederation or something else, this participation requires negotiations on fundamentals. We will have to talk from a position of strength.

Only a Quebec state with a clear democratic mandate to recover its full powers will dispose of the political authority to negotiate the Canadian association of tomorrow.

As the tribulations of Meech Lake show, English Canada did not take Quebec's minimal demands seriously. If you start by negotiating on your knees, you end up on your belly.

I deeply regret that the Conservative MPs of the parliamentary committee allied themselves with the Liberals and New Democrats. They paid too high a price for unanimity.

When all is said and done, honorable disagreement is better than dishonorable agreement.

In any case, nothing would be worse than a dishonorable disagreement and I am convinced that is what would happen to those who would attempt, in vain I believe, to convince Quebec to attend a booby-trapped federal-provincial conference so as to rip out some final humiliating concessions.[175]

THE RISE AND FALL OF THE MEECH LAKE ACCORD

On 23 May the Prime Minister put off an informal first ministers' dinner he had planned for 25 May. It had become apparent that the Charest report's twenty-three recommendations—at least ten of which were core issues—constituted too big an agenda for consensus building for a conference finale. Ottawa slimmed the negotiating list down to a few key items. On 24 May Mulroney announced that he was inviting the premiers to Ottawa for one-on-one talks, starting that evening and continuing through the weekend. "This is an effort...to narrow the differences. Hopefully," declared Mulroney, "this will give legitimate rise to the reasonable expectation of calling a first ministers conference that might be successful." Mulroney's four-hour meeting with Wells was the longest, and it appeared to be fruitful. Wells emerged to say he felt that the distinct society issue could be dealt with in a companion resolution, as an add on, rather than changing the Meech Lake agreement. What became clear from the meetings with Wells and Manitoba's Filmon was that Senate reform had emerged as a key—if not *the* key issue—with Manitoba and Newfoundland insisting that the unanimity principle be changed while Quebec's Bourassa insisted on retaining a Quebec veto. "Why should I compromise," asked Bourassa, "when my province said yes to Canada three times. Why should I be the one to compromise?" After these meetings it was anticipated that the Prime Minister would announce a constitutional conference. Instead, he sent Senator Murray back to Newfoundland for further talks with Clyde Wells on 29 May. There appeared to be a consensus building on the distinct society clause, but the Senate veto issue continued to loom large. Senator Murray admitted that "a first ministers' conference held today would fail." On 30 May, Premier Wells tabled his add-on list in the Newfoundland legislature.[177]

After a fortnight of intensive intergovernmental negotiations, Mulroney finally made his move. On 31 May, he announced in the House of Commons, "I am inviting First Ministers to a working dinner on Sunday evening [3 June] to find out if sufficient political will truly exists. If our discussions go well, we will continue as a First Ministers' Conference to begin the next morning." The next day the Prime Minister wrote to the premiers, outlining an agenda that included a full, formal meeting for Monday 4 June.[178]

This would be three years to the day since the signing ceremonies after the Langevin meeting. The ratification process was finally reaching its denouement. The first ministers would gather at the Museum of Civilization in Hull, Quebec, where they would eat supper and watch the sun set on the Parliament buildings, and try to make a new constitutional deal.

THE RISE AND FALL OF THE MEECH LAKE ACCORD

Ratification Circus: Ottawa, 3–9 June 1990

As the first ministers gathered in Hull, there were nineteen days remaining to the ratification deadline. For the next seven days, they closeted themselves in the longest closed session of first ministers in Canadian history. Over the week, ever larger numbers of Canadians gathered in Ottawa around the conference centre, chanting, cat-calling, singing O Canada, and generally giving a carnival-like character to the event. Up to the last day, the first ministers' discussions remained closed and secret, but rumours abounded and leaks were whispered, raising and dashing hopes with each agonizing passing hour. The week was jokingly called the "Don and Wendy show", in honour of CBC reporters Don Newman and Wendy Mesley, the only reporters first ministers seemed willing to talk to as they emerged from the conference centre for some fresh air or a clean shirt. As the week dragged on, Canadians became increasingly bewildered—if not disgusted—by the spectacle of eleven men, however well-meaning, engaged in a secret endurance test with the fate of the nation in the balance.

DAY ONE: SUNDAY, 3 JUNE 1990. As Ontario Premier Peterson arrived in Hull, he declared that "there is not any particular time pressure.... I'll stay here a month if I have to." He nearly did. The week that was began with dinner at the Museum of Civilization: arugula leaf salad, fiddleheads, roast beef, potatoes, and fruit compote, to be washed down with Pinot Noir and Inniskillin. Five hours later, the first ministers retired until the next day, having decided only to continue these informal, private talks the next morning. They met without aides, although Senator Murray joined them later in the evening. It took the entire evening for the eleven to state their positions, which, ominously, remained as tough, assertive, and inflexible in private as in public. The Prime Minister emphasized the economic consequences of the failure of Meech Lake, with the dollar battered and interest rates soaring. Quebec continued to insist that no changes be made to the accord. Manitoba's Filmon was especially forceful. No new positions were presented. There was some provincial concern and frustration that the federal government did not present formal position papers, which suggested to some that Ottawa had not produced the groundwork for an agreement.[179]

DAY TWO: MONDAY, 4 JUNE 1990. The first ministers met for three and a half hours in another informal, closed session. The premiers then met in groups until late in the evening. The federal government presented a "framework document," which proposed a four-stage plan. The Meech Lake constitutional accord would first be passed; then non-controversial add-ons would be dealt with, followed by increasingly controversial items in later stages, with the distinct society issue last. New Brunswick's McKenna was keen, but Manitoba and Newfoundland were cool, seeing it as essentially another pass-Meech-now-and-fix-it-later approach. Filmon did not like the idea of putting off the harder issues until later. Premier Wells stated, "I see no more room for optimism—as a matter of fact, I probably have less now."[180]

DAY THREE: TUESDAY, 5 JUNE 1990. The third day was a marathon private negotiation session which lasted until 9:30pm. Many topics were discussed, including a new preamble to the constitution and sexual equality rights. But Senate reform dominated the discussions. Countless formulae were presented, but a tentative agreement was apparently reached on the PEI proposal. This would see the continuation of the Meech Lake unanimity formula for a specified period, perhaps three years. If reform was still not attained, then the proportional distribution of Senate seats would be altered: western and Atlantic provinces would increase to ten Senators (PEI from five to six) while Quebec and Ontario would retain twenty-four each. Over the three years, a constitutional commission—with equal federal/provincial representation—would travel the country holding hearings on how to improve the Senate.

At the end of the day, the Prime Minister reported that "small progress" had been made. There was a sense that it was a good sign that talks were continuing.[181]

DAY FOUR: WEDNESDAY, 6 JUNE 1990. The closed, informal sessions continued in a twelve-hour session. Premier McKenna observed, "Meech Lake is the biggest roller coaster in the world." The federal government presented a new framework document that reversed the logic of the previous one. Instead of the difficult issues being put off to the last, they would be dealt with first. Premier Bourassa found the discussions "extremely constructive...very positive" and Premier Wells was happy, saying that this sort of approach could eliminate the necessity of a referendum in Newfoundland. The financial markets picked up the good vibrations and became buoyant, and the Bank of Canada rate fell by twenty basis points the next day.[182]

DAY FIVE: THURSDAY, 7 JUNE 1990. The closed-door sessions continued and, at one point in the day, it looked as if the end was in sight. A four-point agreement was shaping up. The PEI Senate plan was gaining acceptance, albeit with some lingering Quebec concern that its percentage of seats would decline under the plan. While Manitoba remained unconvinced, there was movement towards sending the idea of a Canada clause to a House of Commons committee for study. Various constitutional amendments were agreed to—dealing with sexual equality, New Brunswick's bilingual character, aboriginal participation in constitutional talks, territories nomination rights, the formula for creation of new provinces—although there was as yet no agreement on whether these amendments would take place before or after 23 June. The fourth point, dealing with the relationship between the distinct society clause and the Charter, was the key one.

On Wednesday night and Thursday morning, a crack team of constitutional experts met to work on a statement explaining this relationship. They wrote a text that the first ministers liked. The remaining issue was whether the text would be placed in the constitution (the "hard" option) or be appended to a constitutional agreement and signed by the constitutional experts (the "soft" option). The consensus seemed to be developed that the soft option was the way to go. A break was then called, to allow Premier Filmon—head of a minority government—to brief his opposition leaders, Carstairs and Doer. The latter were not at the meeting, so apparently did not have a clear sense of whether this was a matter still up for discussion or a decision that had been reached. In the event, they opted for the hard option, and Manitoba and Newfoundland returned to the first ministers' session and informed their colleagues of their position. This stunned the others. Most importantly, it shocked Premier Bourassa who, at 9:30 that night, issued a news release: "Concerning the distinct society clause, as far as Quebec is concerned, that question has been settled." Quebec would no longer take part in any discussions where the distinct society clause was under consideration.

Day Five, then, ended in disarray, apparently as a result of a misunderstanding by political leaders who were not at the meeting. The next morning, the financial markets unloaded their Canadian dollars, stocks, and bonds.[183]

DAY SIX: FRIDAY, 8 JUNE 1990. The closed sessions continued for another long, gruelling day. But early in the morning of 9 June, a tentative deal appeared to be made and a decision taken to go into a formal, open constitutional conference on Saturday.[184]

DAY SEVEN: SATURDAY, 9 JUNE 1990. The Prime Minister was determined *not* to have a First Ministers' Conference until there was enough agreement to reach a deal. All day Saturday private negotiations and discussions continued. Not until 8pm was the last draft of the agreement sent to the first ministers. Finally, late on Saturday night, the open, televised First Ministers' Conference began at nearly midnight in the Maritimes. The first ministers had come to a six-point agreement, the major features of which were as follows (see Appendix III for the full text of the agreement):

- Manitoba, Newfoundland, and New Brunswick agreed to make "every possible effort" to ratify the Meech Lake constitutional agreement by 23 June 1990; Manitoba's agreement was subject to full legislative hearings, while Newfoundland's was contingent on holding a referendum or a free vote in the legislature;

- the question of a Canada clause would be considered by a parliamentary committee;
- a legal opinion would be appended to the agreement, unsigned by the first ministers, indicating that the Charter is not "infringed or denied" by the distinct society clause;
- the federal and provincial governments would set up a commission to study how to make a "Triple E" Senate (elected, equal, and effective), and issue a report to a First Ministers' Conference to be held in British Columbia before the end of the year; if by 1995 Senate reform was not attained, then the allocation of seats in the Senate would change, with western and Atlantic representation increasing, Ontario representation decreasing, and Quebec representation staying the same;
- the territories would be assigned the authority to make nominations to the Supreme Court and the Senate;
- issues such as aboriginal rights, minority language rights, and sexual equality would be dealt with later as constitutional amendments.

During the three-hour, televised open session, each of the first ministers made a statement. Prime Minister Mulroney opened the session: "To Quebec...I would like to extend on behalf of all Canadians a heartfelt welcome back into the Canadian family." He claimed that "the idea of Canada had been vindicated" and declared the deal to be a "fair and honorable agreement." Breaking with the traditional speaking order, Premier Wells spoke second, and dampened the meeting's potential enthusiasm. He alone of the first ministers refused to endorse the agreement (see Inset VII): "I am not approving of this particular accord. I am submitting it to the Newfoundland people or the legislature.... Having recognized Quebec as a distinct society," he went on, "I say to my friends in Quebec I believe it is the responsibility of all of the citizens of Quebec to place Canada first and recognize, like all other provinces, Quebec is second." For the rest, the speeches comprised a mutual admiration meeting, with Premier Peterson lauded for his apparent deal-saving concession to give up some Ontario Senate seats to allow Quebec's proportion of the mooted post-1995 Senate to stay the same.[185]

For many of the participants, the exercise had been successful. Premier Peterson commented: "It was a great exercise in nation-building. It was a big reach for everybody. There was blood on the floor but it was common blood." For hold-out Manitoba, the deal generated mixed feelings. Premier Filmon stated that "I've put my blood, sweat and soul into this, and I say that this is the best I could bring home." In Quebec, PQ leader Parizeau was blunt: "Mr. Bourassa sold out"; but Bourassa insisted that the "text...respects Quebec's objectives totally." New

Inset VII

CLYDE WELLS' STATEMENT AT THE CLOSE OF
THE FIRST MINISTERS' MEETING

...It is unfortunate that we had to discuss these major, major matters [without the] ability to assess them on...what was right for Canada, on the basis of principles. Instead we had to think of it in terms of having to do on the basis of fear that we would cause irreparable harm to Canada...

We must never again implement this process for constitutional reform.... You get caught up in a whirling pool or vortex that you can't get out of, going round and round despite the urge that everybody has to go and tell the people of this country what we feel...

In that situation, I was faced with a grave difficulty, the most difficult decision I have ever made in my life.... I was faced with assessing issues that in my own heart and conscience and conviction I thought was the wrong thing to do. That judgment may be entirely wrong, it may be contrary to the opinion of the first ministers but it was based on a...conviction on what was right for Canada first and Newfoundland second. And I found myself constantly being pressured to do something under the fear and threat that failure to do it may do irreparable harm to the country. I don't want any responsibility for doing irreparable harm to any part of this country.

So that left us in a dilemma. In the end I had to take the responsibility to refuse to agree with what was proposed. But neither do I have the right to refuse or cause it to be refused.... I propose therefore to take the proposal back, and this is what I have committed to do and this is what my signature on the document means. And it only means that.

That I will take the document back to the cabinet and caucus in St. John's and ask them to make a decision as to whether we would seek legislative approval on the basis of a free vote in the House of Assembly or whether we would hold a referendum in the province...

...I do not share [the first ministers'] convictions, but I am only one opinion and when I see all this talent and conviction arrayed around me, I have grave doubts that my conviction is correct. I cannot but have grave doubts.

...I will not myself seek to cause the legislators or the people of Newfoundland and Labrador to reject the accord. I will leave it open to them on the basis of all the information before them.

My own personal conviction is that the Meech Lake accord is not the proper way to be generous to Quebec...and at the same time be fully faithful to the principles of federalism....

THE RISE AND FALL OF THE MEECH LAKE ACCORD

Brunswick's McKenna guaranteed passage of the agreement in the next few days. By early week, the Canadian dollar had risen by a fifth of a cent.[186]

Outside of government circles, there was general relief that an agreement had been reached. But there was substantial negative reaction. While francophone and multicultural groups were satisfied with the result, women's groups and particularly native groups were outraged. George Erasmus, national chief of the Assembly of First Nations, stated, "This is the time we had to be heard and we were sold down the river." "We're always an afterthought," commented Saul Terry, President of the Union of BC Indian Chiefs, "They leave us right out of it. The old boys' club lives on. It's a slap in the face." "We're left on the outside looking in," complained Phil Fontaine, leader of the Assembly of Manitoba chiefs, "It's unfair and the perpetuation of a double standard. Quebec has been here for 350 years, but we've been here for thousands of years."[187]

There was unanimity that this process of constitutional reform had to change. Ontario NDP leader Bob Rae described it as "nine guys beating up two guys for seven days." Feminist activist Judy Rebick observed that "the decisions are still being made by middle-class white men." The participants themselves agreed that the process had to change. Saskatchewan Premier Devine declared that "this is a terrible, terrible, unacceptable process to put not only the first ministers through, but first and foremost to put a country and people through." The Prime Minister stated that "none of wants to put the country through this wrenching process again...and none of us wants to go through it ourselves again." Premier Wells put it most dramatically: "You get caught up in a whirling pool or vortex that you can't get out of, going round and round despite the urge that everybody has to go and tell the people of this country what we feel. It is an extremely difficult and I say a totally unacceptable approach."[188]

23 June 1990 and Meech Lake's Destiny

The last twelve days of the Meech Lake ratification process had a surreal quality to them. A general euphoria was generated by the ostensibly successful conclusion of the first ministers' discussions: Canadians hyperventilated at the climax of the meetings, as the nation's existence seemed secured. Yet the ratification of the constitutional agreement remained a longshot at best. In New Brunswick, where Premier McKenna commanded all of the seats in the legislature, passage of the agreement was guaranteed. But in Newfoundland, Premier Wells had not endorsed the accord, and was soon to decide whether to submit it to a referendum or a free vote in the legislature—hardly sure bets. And in Manitoba, the agreement would have to go through an involved process of public hearings. To do this within twelve days would require bending the legislative rules, which would require virtual unanimity amongst the MLAs. It would take but one member to tie up proceedings and ensure that the 23 June deadline was not met.

In Manitoba, native groups announced that they planned to meet with NDP member of the legislature Elijah Harper, to see whether he might block the accord in the legislature. "He could make it difficult," said Phil Fontaine, leader of the Manitoba Assembly of Chiefs. In Newfoundland, Premier Wells requested that the provincial legislatures extend the 23 June ratification deadline—a request that was quickly rebuffed. This led him to choose a free vote in the legislature over his preferred referendum option, there being insufficient time for the latter. He invited the Prime Minister and premiers to come to Newfoundland and defend the accord. Despite the claim that he would not express his personal opinions, he made a severe attack on the first ministers' meeting. He declared that none of Newfoundland's substantial concerns were addressed, and maintained his view that the determining—and specious—argument was that "if you didn't accept what Quebec wanted you were breaking up Canada."[189]

In an electrifying development on 11 June, the *Globe and Mail* published comments from an interview with Prime Mulroney. He admitted that the final constitutional meeting had been delayed as part of a plan to get a constitutional deal via eleventh hour, crisis-atmosphere negotiations. "About a month ago," he said, "I called [my senior advisers].... I told them when this thing was going to take place...when we were to start meeting. It's like an election campaign...you've got to pick your dates and you work backward from that...and I said that's the day that I'm going to roll all the dice." In the weeks following the release of the Charest report, the Prime Minister had given the premiers and political leaders the rather different impression that a conference could not be called until "common ground" was found. The Prime Minister also defended the closed-room, private character of the constitutional talks. He maintained that this was all part of the Canadian tradition starting with Sir John A. Macdonald: "In Charlottetown, the boys arrived on a ship, spent a long time in places other than the library, eh?... This is the way it was done. This is the way Confederation came about. There was no public debate." Television hearings, as in 1982, involved at most "just let[ting] the boys know they were alive...no work was done there...then...right back to the barn."

These were unfortunate and cynical remarks that weakened the drive to ratification. The interview undermined what little legitimacy the constitutional process and its final agreement had retained. The participants were made to feel that they had been manipulated and Canadian citizens felt even more alienated from the political process. The "roll the dice" phrase came to haunt the Prime Minister, as he was to admit after 23 June.[190]

On 12 June Wells introduced the accord into the House of Assembly for a free vote. Newfoundland then underwent an agonizing, divisive province-wide debate. Ontario Premier Peterson and New Brunswick Premier McKenna travelled to St. John's on 20 June to defend Meech Lake in the legislature. In an impassioned speech, McKenna reminded Newfoundlanders that "what is taking place in Quebec is an extraordinary feeling of rejection. Seven million souls who almost universally feel Canada doesn't want them.... Is there anything in Meech so odious that its defeat is worth the collapse of Canada?" The next day Saskatchewan Premier Devine spoke to the Legislature, as did the Prime Minister:

> I don't know what the results of a referendum would be, but I do know that if Mr. Parizeau gets a chance, on referendum night, one thought is going to be going through your minds.... "Do you mean we could have avoided all this for Meech Lake?" If that night ever comes, I can tell you that the terms of Meech Lake are going to look very, very reasonable.

As 23 June approached, it was unclear whether the accord would be accepted or rejected by the House of Assembly.[191]

While Newfoundland appeared to be the ratification stumbling block, the Manitoba situation was more complicated. The ratification process required five days of legislative debate both before and after public hearings.[192] Given that there were but twelve days to the ratification deadline, normal legislative rules would have to be bent—if not broken. Thus, on the afternoon of 12 June 1990, Premier Filmon rose on the floor of the legislature to ask for the unanimous consent required to bend the rules and introduce the accord without the normal two days' notice.

This was not to be. Elijah Harper—an Ojibway-Cree Indian, the second of thirteen children born in a tent on an isolated reserve near Red Sucker Lake in northeastern Manitoba—quietly said no and denied Filmon the required unanimous consent. Responding to the anger and frustration expressed by native groups over decades of failures at constitutional conferences, Harper stated that "the first ministers should have dealt with aboriginal issues. It was not easy for me to make this decision. But who's going to speak for [us].... We're saying that aboriginal issues should be put on the priority list." He took this action "to symbolize that aboriginal people are not being recognized as the first people of this country and not being recognized as founders of this country." Harper was applauded by people in the public gallery.[193]

THE RISE AND FALL OF THE MEECH LAKE ACCORD

Premier Filmon rose on nine occasions to try and bend the legislative rules to speed up the adoption of the Meech Lake accord. And on all nine occasions Elijah Harper quietly said no. Working with the Assembly of Manitoba Chiefs—who had hired former deputy clerk of the Manitoba legislature Gordon Mackintosh and former dean of law at the University of Manitoba Jack London to give procedural advice—Harper used legislative rules and flaws in the government's procedures to delay introduction and debate.[194] Harper assailed the Manitoba party leaders in the legislature: "Why didn't you leave the conference when it became obvious that others weren't prepared to give us the respect we deserve?"[195] As time slipped away, Filmon recounted that he had warned Ottawa as early as January that he needed at least four weeks to pass the legislation: "Maybe they didn't believe it, but now I'm sure it's hitting home very strongly in every capital of the country." John Turner made a rare appearance in the House of Commons and castigated the Prime Minister: "Let no one put blame on Elijah Harper or on the aboriginal people of this country. The blame rests squarely on...the man, who, in his own words, chose to roll all the dice and he chose the date when to roll the dice. By delaying the first ministers conference he has gambled with the future of our country." But in Quebec City, Bourassa warned the natives of the consequences of blocking Meech Lake: "They can't think that we'll be ready to discuss constitutional reforms that interest them if they block the reparation to the injustices that Quebec suffered in 1981."[196]

As the clock ticked to 23 June, the federal government tried to convince Harper and native groups to allow the Meech Lake legislation to proceed. On 17 June Manitoba native leaders agreed to a meeting with top federal officials. The leaders would listen but not negotiate. The federal team arrived in Manitoba with a six-part federal offer, which included promises on constitutional conferences, aboriginal participation, definition of treaty rights, and a royal commission.[197] After a one-hour presentation of the federal offer, the Manitoba chiefs declined the package. This prompted Senator Murray to call on the Manitoba government to suspend its rules, cut short public hearings—about 3,500 people wanted to speak—and force a vote on the constitutional motion: "I find it incredible that one MLA can tie up a legislature in knots indefinitely...[and that] everybody who expressed an interest was given the opportunity to appear personally." Premier Filmon was adamant: "We have the most democratic process anywhere in Canada.... I have absolutely no intention of attempting to get around the rules." He blamed Mulroney for the situation: "Those who put us in this situation by rolling the dice a little too late are the ones who obviously now have to examine in their conscience...what happened to this."[198] Prime Minister Mulroney demanded that Manitoba take a vote: "The nation and the world are expected

THE RISE AND FALL OF THE MEECH LAKE ACCORD

to believe that a dilatory tactic by one member...can indefinitely paralyze a duly elected legislative assembly. This does not make sense.... There are ways that this matter can be dealt with." Other first ministers concurred. But Filmon hung tough: "They had better accept the fact that they have bungled this and bungled it badly, and they can't start pointing fingers somewhere else."[199]

The doomed legislative debate began in Manitoba, but there was insufficient time for its conclusion. Clutching a symbolic eagle feather, Elijah Harper delivered a forty-minute anti-Meech Lake speech: "What we're fighting for is democracy. We have been excluded in this country for many years." Harper maintained that Quebec would not have the moral authority to separate after the death of Meech Lake, because native people—not English Canada—would have caused its death. If Quebec refused to participate in constitutional conferences and blocked discussions of aboriginal issues, native people would be willing to hurt a little: "We are prepared to wait ten years or twenty-five years. We're not interested in short-term solutions. We are fighting for the future of our children."[200] At 12:26pm on Friday, 22 June 1990, Elijah Harper said no for the ninth time, disallowing the extension of sitting hours in the Manitoba legislature. The legislature later adjourned for the weekend without a vote having been taken on the Meech Lake resolution. "Today is a great day for Canada and for aboriginal people in this country," declared Harper. "We have won. We have said no to Meech Lake."[201]

But one last card remained to be played. The federal government had a number of fall-back options for an end-play scenario such as this. Senator Murray announced one of them: provided the Newfoundland legislature ratified the accord, the federal government would ask the Supreme Court to rule that the ratification deadline could be moved to 23 September, the date on which the second province—Saskatchewan—had ratified the accord. Quebec would then have to reintroduce and pass the accord, but this would give Manitoba three months to hold public hearings and pass the constitutional resolution. This plan infuriated political leaders in Manitoba, who had been told by Ottawa that there was no option but to invoke closure to force a vote. "This appears to be another roll of the dice," observed Filmon. In Newfoundland, an incredulous Clyde Wells watched Senator Murray on television announcing his plan. "That's the final straw," he snapped. "We're not prepared to be manipulated again." That night, as in Manitoba, the House of Assembly adjourned without a vote being taken on the Meech Lake accord.[202]

Meech Lake was dead. There were no miracle possibilities, no eleventh-hour meetings, no procedural rabbits to pull out of a hat. Meech Lake was dead.

Prime Minister Mulroney spoke to Canadians on television on 23 June 1990. In this address and in following weeks, he placed ultimate blame for the accord's failure not on native groups and Elijah Harper, but on Clyde Wells and New-foundland. He admitted that the accord had become widely unpopular, "a light-ning rod for discontent about budgets, interest rates, free trade and taxes. It attracted accusations of racism...and stimulated regional rivalries and even linguis-tic tensions...the accord came to be expected to respond to all of the preoccupa-tions of the country." In subdued tones he stated that "we must guard against two dangers. First, to despair that anything can be done and, second, to delude ourselves that nothing has happened." But he maintained that today "is not the day to launch new constitutional initiatives. It is a time to mend divisions..."

Premier Bourassa's televised address was moderate in tone but gave a firm message: "If there is one thing that we can learn from these negotiations, it's that the process of constitutional reform in Canada has been discredited.... How could you expect me to return to the constitutional table...now that the agreements have been rejected after being ratified?" In the National Assembly, he reminded English Canada that "Quebec is today and forever a distinct society, capable of ensuring its own development and destiny."

In Calgary, the anti-Meech Lake candidate—Jean Chrétien—won the Liberal leadership race. After the predictable criticisms of Mulroney's handling of the constitutional process, he told Canadians to take a break from Meech Lake and go and enjoy the summer.[203]

DISCUSSION

The Meech Lake story was one of agony and ecstasy, consensus and division, achievements and—ultimately—futility. It was conceived quietly in Quebec's set-ting of its five conditions and died a silent death in the adjourned legislatures of Manitoba and Newfoundland five years later. In between, there were the noisy and raucous "what ifs" and "becauses" of history: the marathon Meech Lake and Langevin meetings; Trudeau's "Goodbye to the Dream of One Canada" article; the New Brunswick, Manitoba, and Newfoundland elections; the Supreme Court decision on Bill 101 and Quebec's subsequent Bill 178; the Ontario language controversy; Clyde Wells and Brian Mulroney debating at the November 1989 First Ministers' Conference; the New Brunswick and Manitoba hearings and reports; Frank McKenna's companion resolution; the Charest hearings and report; Lucien Bouchard's resignation; the week-long first ministers' meeting in June 1990; Elijah Harper saying no; the Murray deadline extension plan; Wells cancelling the Newfoundland vote. Some of these events will fade in memory as time passes, and the dollar miraculously survived without incident. But Meech

Lake has taken on mythic, symbolic qualities, and now has a permanent place in Canada's political culture and memory—despite its death.

The Meech Lake episode exposed the uneasy relationship between the two broad worlds of Canadian politics: executive federalism and what might be called the "citizen's world." It also exposed the tension between competing visions of Canadian federalism and competing visions of Canadian political life.

Of all the myriad worlds of Canadian politics, the world of amending the constitution has been, perhaps, the most closed and elitist. It is the domain of executive federalism. Governments—the first ministers—have shaped and altered the constitution in Canada. Citizens and groups have watched this process, perhaps making suggestions or complaining. But they have had no power or authority, and no formal avenues of intervention in the constitutional amendment process. Not surprisingly, their impact on constitutional evolution has been negligible. For some observers, this has not been particularly unsettling. Indeed, it has been seen to be a necessity of political life. The challenge of getting eleven governments to agree on something is immense, they maintain, particularly with regard to issues and concerns over which substantial social disagreement and fragmentation exists. How could a participatory approach to constitution-making be devised when a social consensus around complex issues cannot be assumed, on matters that are technically and legally daunting? For others, this closed world reflects the nature of Canada's deferential political culture, which has encouraged Canadians to invest considerable authority in their elected (and non-elected) leaders to construct the political structures, processes, and policies that shape citizens' lives. But others see this world as smacking of a paternalistic and elitist political style inherited from an earlier, pre-democratic era.

How people viewed the Meech Lake chapter of Canada's constitutional evolution turned on two variables: one's view of how politics ought to work and whether the results appeared to be acceptable. With regard to the latter, Meech Lake was a classic example of how the symbols of politics dominate both political substance and process. In the last analysis, the Meech Lake experience remained a Quebec one. To the bitter end, most first ministers continued to characterize it as the Quebec Round, even though the other provinces stood to gain as much as Quebec and even though other issues came to swamp the constitutional agenda. In its early stages, Meech Lake's bottom line was: Quebec was finally signing the Canadian constitution. A flaw was being repaired, the wounds were being healed, a political embarrassment was being remedied, atonement was being made, the family was all together again. As to the concerns raised by natives, women, northerners, linguistic minority and multicultural groups, and others—these would have

THE RISE AND FALL OF THE MEECH LAKE ACCORD

to wait until the Quebec situation was finalized. Until Quebec signed the constitution, these issues could not be pursued. To try and improve Meech Lake risked throwing the baby out with the bathwater. In Meech Lake's latter stages, the stakes grew even larger: rejection of Meech Lake was equated with rejection of Quebec and the encouragement of Quebec separatism.

This is not to trivialize Meech Lake's potential accomplishment. Quebec *was* dealt with shabbily in 1981–82. Moreover, the absence of its signature from the constitution could hardly be allowed to become a permanent state of affairs and, besides, constitutional progress in other areas was contingent on Quebec's participation. Nor is it meant to exaggerate Quebec's constitutional gains, which were relatively modest and led to accusations of selling out by the Parti québécois and other nationalist groups. The fact was that this was but one accomplishment amongst an infinite series of potential political accomplishments and values—and it had the capacity to override the rest in the minds of many political actors and observers. These other possibilities were smothered—or seriously constrained, at the end—by the prospect of Quebec's rejoining the constitutional family.

In the spring of 1987 Quebec's signature was the hinge on which the Meech Lake deal and its acceptance swung. It cooled the antagonistic position of provinces who were vehemently opposed to the special status that might have been implied by the distinct society clause. It forced the Liberals to accept the deal—despite their litany of reservations—lest they alienate their Quebec caucus and lose support in that electorally critical province. In the process, traditional positions and principles were swallowed in order to avoid appearing to be anti-Quebec. Similarly, the normally centralist, nationally oriented federal NDP was fairly mute despite its deeply felt reservations about the accord. The Quebec angle ensured that Meech Lake became a non-partisan issue at the national level, with the result that scrutiny and debate of Meech Lake was narrowly contained. It also neutralized the substantial concerns raised by various interest groups and even first ministers. For example, early concerns in 1987 about the impact of the distinct society clause on sexual equality rights were negated by Mulroney's kiss-of-death characterization of this as a cover for anti-Quebec sentiments. And long-time Meech Lake critic Premier McKenna—and many other adversaries—finally blinked at the last moment, fearing the political consequences in Quebec if Meech died. To the extent to which participants and observers valued Quebec's signing as the highest constitutional priority, concerns about Meech Lake's other features and the process surrounding it were more or less pushed to the side. The ratification debate became asymmetrical, because opposition to Meech Lake was made to look selfish in light of the noble accomplishment of Quebec's return to the constitutional family.

THE RISE AND FALL OF THE MEECH LAKE ACCORD

Supporters of the constitutional package saw Meech Lake as a historic opportunity to complete the constitutional circle, and a tremendous accomplishment in the face of the challenges involved. After all, the 1981–2 constitutional stage had left an uncomfortable legacy: Quebec would have to be offered *something* to get it to sign, and regardless of what it signed, any deal could easily be portrayed as showing favouritism to Quebec. The construction of an all-provincial consensus required that something be offered to the other provinces as well; a political trade was devised, and they received more or less what Quebec received, as well as the promise of future constitutional talks on *their* priorities. Quebec's signature and inter-provincial consensus were accomplishments that calmed participants' and supporters' concerns that the process had been too rushed and closed. Indeed, there had been no public participation in the run-up to Meech Lake, which was tightly controlled and played out amongst bureaucratic officials. The sessions at Meech Lake and in the Langevin building were restricted to the first ministers and a few advisers. Documents, drafts, position papers were never released. And the first ministers agreed that the resulting constitutional agreement could not be amended, which emptied the ratification process of any meaning (until provincial elections changed premiers).

This was a process consciously designed to avoid a public relations problem: appearances of favouritism to Quebec. The closed process minimized public squabbles and disagreements and maximized the probability of success. The process, then, made tremendous political sense. Moreover, it was very much in equilibrium with what it was accomplishing: institutional processes are never neutral, but they substantially shape the outcome. Meech Lake was a deal by *governments* and for *governments*. The Meech Lake deal was made at first ministers' meetings, attended by first ministers alone. The substance of the 1987 agreement dealt exclusively with relationships between the two levels of governments. The Quebec government—not the Quebec people—was convinced by the other governments to sign an agreement. The other governments—not their citizens—were assigned certain powers and authority in return for supporting Quebec. Heads of government made the deal amongst themselves (even as the process unravelled in 1990, the trump issue at the closed sessions in June was Senate reform, another first ministers' issue). Then the first ministers returned to have their legislatures ratify what they had already decided—with no opportunity for changes.

This might have developed to its logical conclusion, save for another legacy of 1981–82: the three-year ratification process. This was the seam where the two broad "worlds" of Canadian politics met: the world of executive federalism, dominated by the first ministers, and what might be termed the "citizens' world," which includes political parties, elections, interest groups, and so on. The Prime Minister expressed it aptly at the end:

> I genuinely feel that the three-year waiting period had a great deal to do with it.... If you bring anything forward in this country and say you've got three years to finalize it, governments get defeated, people succeed one another, attitudes change, governments change, people change their opinions...
>
> "I thought...that within a matter of months...all provinces would have signed it.... Nobody anticipated that...a very simple, straightforward document of unity would become a catch-all for everybody else's wish list as governments changed across the country."[204]

There was an odd asymmetry in the Meech Lake story. On the one hand, the first ministers' meetings took place over days, the leaders closeted together until a deal was reached. These meetings lent themselves to the Stockholm Syndrome, the phenomenon wherein hostages become sympathetic to their hostage-takers.[205] The leaders leave the closeted meeting, their differences worn down by personal as much as policy interaction, the resulting deal nurtured by mutual empathy but understood by themselves alone. On the other hand, the ratification process was potentially three years long. Whereas the interest and logic of governments prevailed exclusively in the former, these would have to confront non-governmental pressures and realities over the extended ratification period. Indeed, governmental concerns were immediately swamped by the entry of new players and their bewildering and eclectic array of issues: women's rights, multiculturalism, native rights, the territories' future, language issues, social programmes, and so on.

The first ministers had prepared themselves for this onslaught by a simple and ruthless device: they agreed that amendments would not be allowed. It would be Meech Lake or nothing. After the Langevin constitutional conference, six governments did not allow public hearings (Alberta, British Columbia, Saskatchewan, Newfoundland, Nova Scotia, Quebec) and three others held hearings with the clear understanding that amendments would not be considered (Ontario, Newfoundland, Canada). Citizens and interest groups were given few opportunities to air their concerns and alternatives, and no opportunity for effective impact. Moreover, the Quebec issue prevailed against much of what came on to the agenda, particularly as there was no obvious way, or institutional mechanism, via which all of these other issues could be made to fit together in a constitutional consensus.

THE RISE AND FALL OF THE MEECH LAKE ACCORD

However, a simple feature of the citizens' world—elections, the antithesis of the closed first ministers' meeting—changed all of this and, perhaps, determined Meech Lake's fate. Over the three year ratification period, Canadians had five opportunities to be democratically active in this direct sense. On 13 October 1987, 16 April 1988, and 20 April 1989, Canadians in respectively, New Brunswick, Manitoba, and Newfoundland used the electoral process to vote out of office three of the governments that were party to the Meech Lake deal. The three new first ministers were openly critical of the accord. This opened up the ratification process considerably, as critics of the accord focused their energies and criticisms—with effect—on the public hearings offered by two receptive and sympathetic provinces, Manitoba and New Brunswick. The governments that remained faithful to the accord were unsuccessful in neutralizing these criticisms. On the one hand, the newly elected premiers had not attended the first ministers' meetings, so were not party to the pressures, interactions, feelings, and logic of these meetings and the resulting tightly wound constitutional agreement. They simply didn't feel the same way towards the accord that the Meech Lake participants did. On the other hand, because the constitutional process had been so secret and exclusive, the Canadian public did not really know or understand what was in the accord—as polls only too shockingly indicated. As a result, the public was not susceptible to entreaties from Meech supporters about its importance, and were more likely to be swayed by the arguments of groups speaking "citizen" as opposed to "government" language and issues. When it became clear that the hold-out provinces would not sign the accord without amendments or add ons, the federal government was forced to "re-hold" its public hearings and do what it had refused to do in 1987 and over the ensuing three years: entertain alternative views and amendments to the accord.

As Banting and Simeon maintain, constitutional processes "are important because they are not neutral. Different institutions weigh different interests differently, giving fuller expression to some and minimizing others."[206] As in 1981, the Meech Lake process saw the interests of the provincial governments predominate in the closed, exclusive first ministers' meetings at Meech Lake and the Langevin building—they outnumbered the federal government ten to one. But in the subsequent ratification process, provincial issues and concerns were smothered by citizens' and social issues. The New Brunswick, Manitoba, and Charest *public* hearings produced recommendations for amendments that reflected citizens', rather than governments', interests and goals, whereas the *private* first ministers' meetings had done the opposite.

The Meech Lake story reflects two different visions of what the constitutional process is all about. As Cairns explains,[207] Canadian politicians have felt that the constitution was theirs—a governments' constitution. On the other hand, since the constitutional exercise of 1981 and the advent of the Charter, there has developed an alternative, citizens' view of the constitution. Various social groups—particularly women, multicultural groups, and natives—actively secured a presence in the constitution, which led them to feel that the constitution was theirs. Governments have seen the constitution as primarily a regulator of governmental relations, with governments alone to be involved in its amending—the substance and domain of executive federalism. Citizens' groups see it as regulating relations between governments and citizens, with the latter having a role in its amending. The Meech Lake process dealt exclusively with governmental concerns—revamping the federal system—and did not deal with other, citizen priorities. The result was that the population was politically alienated and never supported Meech Lake.

These two worlds came together in the marathon June meeting—albeit in an incomplete way. The New Brunswick, Manitoba, and Charest hearings had generated a series of non-governmental issues to be inserted into—or added on to—the governmental concerns of the Meech Lake accord. These included multicultural, northern, aboriginal, women's, language, and other concerns. But the *format* for their discussion and inclusion remained the same: it was a first ministers' conference. Despite its marathon length—and the undoubted goodwill of the participants—most of the non-governmental, citizen concerns remained to be dealt with in the future despite the 9 June agreement.

Nowhere was this more striking or critical than in the area of aboriginal rights. There had been four first ministers' conferences on aboriginal matters between 1983 and 1987 to little effect, and native people remained outsiders to the constitutional processes that determined the character of their political existence in Canada. There was widespread public—and, obviously, native—criticism of the fact that aboriginal peoples had not been assigned a constitutional role by Meech Lake and had not been included as part of the definition of the fundamental characteristic of Canada. This was a message contained in each of the New Brunswick, Manitoba, and Charest reports, which made recommendations for substantial amendments on aboriginal matters. Nonetheless, native peoples were not formal participants in the June meeting and—sadly, but not surprisingly—gained nothing from this meeting. There was yet another promise of a separate constitutional track for discussion of aboriginal rights—but Senate reform would be the constitutional priority for potentially five years. And Canada's English-French duality was reaffirmed, the Canada clause to be sent on legislative tour where, presumably, native groups could stand in line at public hearings with other groups to plead for their inclusion as part of Canada's fundamental characteristics. In the uprising of the citizens' world against executive federalism, it was symbolically appropriate that Canada's first citizens pulled the plug on Meech Lake.

Canada's parliamentary system assigns considerable political authority to political executives, who are called to political account only every four or five years. The Meech Lake case—along with the GST story—exposed a fundamental democratic dilemma: once assigned authority, to what extent should political leaders feel constrained by public opinion in doing what they think is best for the country? The first ministers felt that Meech Lake was in Canada's best interests; a substantial number of Canadian citizens and groups felt otherwise. Do political leaders lead or follow? Should Canada's constitution be regulated and amended via governmental processes or—somehow—by the people?

This will be the last time that the constitutional amendment process takes the form that Meech Lake did. There was universal criticism of the Meech Lake process, particularly its last stages, which even first ministers criticized. The Prime Minister himself stated that "a way must be found to ensure public involvement in the constitutional amendment process."[208] The unanimity principle and the three-year ratification process will be scrutinized and, perhaps, altered or rejected.[209] And there will likely be provisions for meaningful public participation and hearings before first ministers agree on a constitutional change. There have already been developments in this regard. A number of provinces have devised independent commissions on constitutional matters, and two of them—New Brunswick and Quebec—have included both elected politicians and non-elected representatives of various social and economic groups (Quebec's commission has an "Estates General" quality to it). And Prime Minister Mulroney created the Spicer Commission in November 1990, a citizen's forum on Canada's future.[210]

What will these new constitutional processes and commissions bring? The Meech Lake story illustrated a conflict between different visions of how Canadian federalism should function and of Quebec's place in the federation. From the late 1960s to the early 1980s, Canadian federalism was dominated by Pierre Trudeau's vision of a strong central, national government, speaking and acting for all Canadians, in a range of areas from bilingualism to energy policy. Jean Chrétien and Clyde Wells were the inheritors of this vision, which rejects assigning special powers to Quebec and insists that the federal government be strong enough to assist the weaker provinces. Meech Lake reflected a different vision of Canadian federalism, one in which the provinces would play a more pronounced role in an equal relationship with the federal government. The terms of the Meech Lake constitutional agreement assigned to the provinces (really, the premiers) increased political power and authority: in national institutions

THE RISE AND FALL OF THE MEECH LAKE ACCORD

(Senate, Supreme Court), in national policy (immigration, shared-cost programmes), in supra-national institutions (first ministers' conferences on the constitution and on the economy), and in constitutional evolution (the unanimity principle).

Although Meech Lake died and Jean Chrétien may very well be the next prime minister, the reality of Canadian political life is that the provinces will play an increasingly critical role at the national level of government—or in a vastly decentralized federation. It is unlikely that Quebec's constitutional commission will produce anything as modest as a Meech Lake shopping list, and may recommend some variant of sovereignty-association for Quebec, or some sort of supranational institution along the lines of developments in Europe. The western provinces continue to articulate their interest in a decentralized federation in which they have more autonomy. Ironically, the West's support for a reformed Senate contradicts its decentralist impulse, for a reformed Senate would increase Ottawa's authority and diminish that of the premiers and the provinces. This is another example of how symbols come to dominate the substance of political life.

But this regional reality is only one amongst the multiple visions of Canada that exist at the end of the century. Canada is simultaneously experienced as a country of regions (to some, nations), provinces, sexes, cultures, language groups, natives, classes, social groups, and national spirit and goals. Meech Lake demonstrated how political leaders and the policy process must be in tune with and informed by each of these visions. The expectation is that each of these visions should be articulated within the constitution. The political trick will be to try and move on all these fronts simultaneously, as each of the worlds or visions may try to sabotage any constitutional effort if its concerns are not addressed. This is particularly the case with regard to dealing with governmental issues (e.g., the role of Quebec) and rights issues simultaneously. Canada faces the prospect of endlessly changing and tinkering with the constitution. In the real worlds of Canadian politics, the political challenge will be to simultaneously make real these myriad and conflicting constitutional visions, in order to minimize political alienation and maximize national unity.

This prospect, and the Meech Lake episode, demonstrate the incredible importance the courts and the Charter have assumed in Canadian political life. The Supreme Court's declaring unconstitutional the sign provisions of Quebec's Bill 101 was one of the critical events in the unravelling of Meech Lake. It forced the Quebec government into devising Bill 178 and using the notwithstanding clause. This in turn weakened Premier Filmon's resolve to try and ratify Meech Lake, strengthened Premier McKenna's position that Meech Lake had not assigned sufficient protection to language minorities, contributed to the Ontario language fiasco, and generally undermined support for Meech Lake in English Canada. The Meech Lake case also demonstrated that a critical issue in the future will be the determination of the relationship between the Charter and the other parts of the Canadian constitution. Whether the issue is the impact of the distinct society clause on the Charter or how the constitution's multiple visions fit together, it will be the courts that decide.

The Meech Lake story illustrated other of the many worlds of Canadian politics. For John Turner and the Liberals, Meech Lake was a bad dream. It divided the party on linguistic grounds, and placed his leadership in the shadows cast by his predecessor, Pierre Trudeau, and his eventual successor, Jean Chrétien. He weathered the storm as leader, but at great personal and political cost. The Liberals' dismal electoral showing in the 1988 federal election made Turner's Meech Lake strategy look politically costly and ineffective. Pro- and anti-Meech forces fought it out through the leadership campaign, and this division has not been resolved despite Chrétien's victory. The same can be said for the NDP, whose expensive Quebec campaign reaped no fruit but did produce alienation from its Quebec wing and a certain degree of rebellion from the western provincial parties. In the aftermath of its death, neither party has developed—or seems capable of developing—a post-Meech constitutional alternative.

For other leaders, Meech Lake cruelly exposed the trials and tribulations of political leadership. After Clyde Wells escaped the vortex and incredible tension of the marathon first ministers' meeting, he broke down in tears upon his arrival in Newfoundland. In a candid interview, Manitoba Liberal leader Carstairs admitted that she had nearly resigned in the middle of the Meech Lake fracas. Wracked by self-doubt and sleepless nights, she had begun to feel that "maybe I really was the problem."[211] For the lead players—Prime Minister Mulroney and Premier Bourassa—Meech Lake had offered similar prizes but assigned very different rewards. For a period, Meech Lake appeared to be a political triumph. Both had been politically exposed, in the sense that each had actually promised that Quebec would sign the constitution. But each would gain tremendous political advantage if Meech Lake succeeded. From their positions, Meech Lake demonstrated the power that the chief executives have in setting the agenda and controlling the political process. It also showed the potential for change and accomplishment that skillful leadership offers. For Bourassa, Meech Lake's early success reflected considerable political skill. Even as Meech Lake was threatened and unravelled, Bourassa remained in political control and was lauded for his persistence and temperate style. The appointment of the Bélanger-Campeau Commission in August 1990 was matched by an equally deft move in late January 1991, the release of a Quebec Liberal Party discussion paper on the constitution.

THE RISE AND FALL OF THE MEECH LAKE ACCORD

The paper called for a shift of powers from Ottawa to Quebec, so extensive that it amounted to de facto separation. Within Quebec, however, this was now the "federalist" position.

For Mulroney, Meech was paradise lost. If ratified, Meech Lake—together with the Free Trade Agreement—would have indelibly stamped his personal imprint on the face of Canada. His electoral position in Quebec would have been secured, and he could have presented himself as the national reconciliator. Instead, Meech Lake is dead and has become, in many quarters, a dirty word. Significant parts of his Quebec caucus—including his old friend and confidant, Lucien Bouchard—abandoned him and now sit as members of the separatist Bloc québécois (which won a federal by-election in Montreal in August). Exhausted and disappointed, Mulroney then faced a population divided, anxious, cranky, and unsure of itself but for one thing—it doesn't support him. And all of this after five years of "slow boring of hard wood," as Max Weber put it, the long, tough, thankless work of devising and selling a political plan. This is part of the hard reality of the real worlds of Canadian politics.

Discussion Questions

1   What role did legislatures play in the process leading up to the Meech Lake and Langevin meetings? Could this role have been more substantial? What role did legislatures play in the ratification process? Could this role have been more substantial?

2   Why did the opposition parties in Ottawa decide to make Meech Lake a non-partisan matter? What impact did this have? What impact did this have on the opposition parties themselves?

3   Why was Meech Lake so divisive for the Liberal party? Could Liberal leaders Turner and Chrétien have done anything different to positive effect?

4   Why were interest groups and organizations incapable of making a greater impact during the ratification process?

5   Why did the first ministers play such a predominant role? To what extent did the first ministers represent "the people" in the Meech Lake process?

6   Should the newly elected governments in Manitoba and New Brunswick have felt bound by their predecessors' agreement to ratify the accord? Should Clyde Wells

have felt bound by the ratification decision of the previous Newfoundland government?

7   What role did the first ministers' conference play in the Meech Lake process? Has it replaced Parliament as Canada's highest political authority?

8   What does this case suggest about the role of the Charter in Canadian politics in the future?

9   Discuss Cairn's distinction between a governments' constitution and a citizens' one. Where do your sympathies lie?

10   Is Canada's amending process more or less democratic than other democratic countries? To what extent—and how—should citizens be directly involved in constitutional change? Should amendments be subject to a national referendum?

Chronology

20 May 1980   — Quebec referendum

5 November 1981   — Ottawa and 9 provinces agree on constitutional package

17 April 1982   — New constitution formally signed, without Quebec

4 September 1984   — Conservatives win landslide election victory

February 1985   — Quebec Liberal party position paper *Maitriser l'avenir* sets out Quebec's 5 conditions

2 December 1985   — Liberal party wins Quebec election

9 May 1986   — Mont-Gabriel conference: Quebec declares its 5 conditions

13 June 1986   — in interview with *Le Devoir*, Liberal leader Turner supports Quebec's 5 conditions

July 1986   — Quebec "sells" its package to other provinces

10–12 August 1986   — 27th annual premiers' conference: Edmonton Declaration sets out the Quebec Round

November 1986   — Vancouver first ministers' conference: agreement to pursue constitutional settlement with Quebec

March 1987	– Quebec boycotts constitutional conference on aboriginal rights; Mulroney calls conference on constitution
mid-April 1987	– Mulroney writes premiers, outlining Ottawa's response to Quebec's proposals
30 April 1987	– meeting at Meech Lake; agreement reached
8 May 1987	– Donald Johnston resigns from Liberal shadow cabinet in protest over Meech Lake
11 May 1987	– all three party leaders endorse the constitutional accord in the House of Commons
12 May 1987	– Quebec begins hearings on the accord (only government to do so)
27 May 1987	– Trudeau slams accord in *Toronto Star* and *La Presse*
2–3 June 1987	– Langevin Block meeting: constitutional agreement reached amongst the first ministers
11 June 1987	– Senate refers accord to committee of the whole
12 June 1987	– federal government proposes a joint House of Commons/Senate committee to study the accord
16, 17 June 1987	– House of Commons, Senate endorse joint committee
18 June 1987	– Quebec begins debate on accord
23 June 1987	– Quebec National Assembly passes the accord (first province to do so)
4 August 1987	– joint committee hearings begin (to 2 September 1987)
13 August 1987	– Senate establishes a task force on the accord and the north
27 August 1987	– Trudeau appears before the joint committee
16–29 September 1987	– provincial NDP holds its own public hearings in Alberta
21 September 1987	– joint committee issues report
23 September 1987	– Saskatchewan becomes 2nd province to approve the accord (debated on 17, 21, 22, 23 September)
29 September 1987	– House of Commons begins debate (continues on 30 September, 1, 5, 6, 8, 19, 21, 22 October)

THE RISE AND FALL OF THE MEECH LAKE ACCORD

13 October 1987	— anti-accord Liberal leader McKenna wins New Brunswick election
26 October 1987	— House of Commons passes accord
24 October–2 November 1987	— Senate Task Force in Whitehorse, Yellowknife, and Iqaluit
4 November 1987	— Senate committee hearings begin (continue 18 November, 2, 9, 16 December, 27 January, 2, 3, 10, 11 February, 1, 2, 16, 23, 30, 31 March)
7 December 1987	— Alberta becomes 3rd province to approve the accord (debated on 23, 25, 30 November, 2, 3, 4, 7 December)
2 February 1988	— Ontario public hearings begin (to June; report issued 23 June)
1 March 1988	— Nova Scotia ratification debate begins (continues 3, 4, 7, 8, 10, 11 March)
1 March 1988	— Senate task force on the accord and the north issues its report
9–10 March 1988	— La federation des francophones hors Quebec speaks out against the accord
4 April 1988	— Saskatchewan language controversy
21 April 1988	— Senate amends the accord
25 April 1988	— PEI public hearings begin (continue on 27 April, 2, 5, 10 May)
26 April 1988	— Manitoba election produces minority Conservative government
13 May 1988	— PEI becomes 4th province to ratify the accord
19 May 1988	— House of Commons debates Senate amendments
25 May 1988	— Nova Scotia becomes 5th province to ratify the accord (continuation of March debate on 24, 25 May)
22 June 1988	— House of Commons passes the accord for 2nd time
29 June 1988	— Ontario becomes the 6th province to ratify the accord; British Columbia becomes the 7th province to ratify the accord
7 July 1988	— Newfoundland becomes the 8th province to ratify the accord

THE RISE AND FALL OF THE MEECH LAKE ACCORD

15 December 1988	— Supreme Court strikes down Quebec sign law
16 December 1988	— ratification debate begins in Manitoba
18 December 1988	— Quebec Bill 178 and use of notwithstanding clause
19 December 1988	— Manitoba suspends Meech Lake debate in protest over Bill 178
25 January 1989	— New Brunswick Meech Lake accord hearings begin (continue to 16 February)
5–7 April 1989	— Throne Speech debate controversy over notwithstanding clause; Mulroney says constitution is not worth the paper it is written on
6 April 1989	— Manitoba hearings begin (to 2 May 1989)
20 April 1989	— Clyde Wells elected premier of Newfoundland
5 July 1989	— Mulroney cancels September first ministers' conference
16 September 1989	— NDP council demands changes to Meech Lake
25 September 1989	— Liberals re-elected in Quebec, win 92 of 125 seats
16 October 1989	— Reform Party's Stan Waters wins Alberta Senate election
20 October 1989	— Wells stakes out his position in 8-page letter to Mulroney; Mulroney responds 3 November
23 October 1989	— Manitoba report released, proposing 6 amendments to the accord
24 October 1989	— New Brunswick report released, proposing fewer (but different) changes
27 October 1989	— BC Socreds reject Meech Lake
7 November 1989	— Wells tables his constitutional proposals on eve of first ministers' conference
9–10 November 1989	— tense first ministers' meeting; showdown between Wells and Mulroney
1 December 1989	— Filmon declines invitation to talk with Senator Murray; NDP national convention supports changes to Meech Lake or a parallel accord
31 December 1989	— Governor-General Sauve's departing speech gives veiled support to Meech Lake

THE RISE AND FALL OF THE MEECH LAKE ACCORD

16 January 1990	— Chrétien's anti-Meech Lake Liberal leadership campaign manifesto
19 January 1990	— Quebec announces resurrection of St. Jean Baptiste day parade, to be held 24 June, the day after the Meech Lake deadline
23 January 1990	— Vander Zalm plan to save Meech Lake
31 January 1990	— New Brunswick Society of Acadians gives support to Meech Lake
5 February 1990	— Thunder Bay becomes 27th local Ontario council to declare itself unilingual; House of Commons scuffle over language statement
21 March 1990	— McKenna introduces companion resolution in New Brunswick legislature: will pass Meech Lake if progress made on other amendments
22 March 1990	— In televised broadcast, Mulroney unveils plan to introduce McKenna companion resolution in House of Commons; Wells introduces legislation to rescind Newfoundland support of Meech Lake
27 March 1990	— McKenna's companion resolution introduced in House of Commons; Charest Committee established; debate begins in Newfoundland legislature on rescinding Meech Lake
6 April 1990	— Quebec legislature passes unanimous motion rejecting changes to Meech Lake; Newfoundland revokes support of Meech Lake
9 April 1990	— Charest Committee hearings begin (to 4 May)
17 May 1990	— Charest report calls for a companion resolution
18–20 May 1990	— Senator Murray tours the provinces to gauge support for Charest recommendations
19 May 1990	— François Gerin quits PC caucus over Charest report; Lucien Bouchard's telegram to Parti québécois on 10th anniversary of the Quebec referendum
22 May 1990	— Lucien Bouchard quits Cabinet over Charest report; joined by Gilbert Chartrand
23 May 1990	— Senator Murray reports to Mulroney that a first ministers' conference would not be successful

THE RISE AND FALL OF THE MEECH LAKE ACCORD

24 May 1990	— Mulroney calls premiers to Ottawa for one-on-one talks, 24–29 May 1990; Senator Murray shuttles to Newfoundland
30 May 1990	— Wells tables Meech add-on list
31 May 1990	— Mulroney invites premiers to working dinner on 3 June; Denis Pronovost resigns as assistant deputy speaker after attack on Premier Wells and Newfoundland
3 June 1990	— first ministers' working dinner in Ottawa; continues informally/privately until 9 June
9 June 1990	— Saturday night first ministers' conference, new 5-part deal
11 June 1990	— Wells rejects Newfoundland referendum in favour of free vote in legislature; Mulroney "roll the dice" interview
12 June 1990	— Manitoba ratification process begins; Elijah Harper delays proceedings for 1st of 9 occasions (13, 14, 15, 18, 19, 20, 21, 22 June)
14 June 1990	— Nova Scotia Tory P. Nowlan resigns from Tory caucus over Meech Lake; New Brunswick unanimously passes Meech Lake accord (8th province)
16 June 1990	— Manitoba chiefs vow to kill Meech Lake
18 June 1990	— federal government offers 6-point proposal to natives, which is declined by Manitoba chiefs; Murray calls on Manitoba leaders to suspend rules and force a vote
19–23 June 1990	— Liberal leadership convention in Calgary
20 June 1990	— Premiers McKenna and Peterson speak to Newfoundland legislature; Manitoba finally tables the Meech Lake motion, but Elijah Harper blocks extension of sitting hours
21 June 1990	— Prime Minister Mulroney and Premier Devine speak to Newfoundland legislature
22 June 1990	— Elijah Harper says no for 9th time; Manitoba adjourns without voting on Meech Lake motion; Murray plan to ask Supreme Court to extend deadline for Manitoba to 23 September, conditional on New-

THE RISE AND FALL OF THE MEECH LAKE ACCORD

<table>
<tbody>
<tr><td></td><td>foundland passing Meech Lake; Wells cancels vote in Newfoundland</td></tr>
<tr><td>23 June 1990</td><td>— Meech Lake constitutional accord dies</td></tr>
<tr><td>26 June 1990</td><td>— 3 PC MP's and 1 Liberal MP quit caucus in protest over Meech Lake failure</td></tr>
<tr><td>27 June 1990</td><td>— Quebec City and Sherbrooke cancel Canada Day celebrations; others follow</td></tr>
<tr><td>29 June 1990</td><td>— joint announcement by Premier Bourassa/PQ leader Parizeau of a non-partisan commission to examine Quebec's constitutional future; 6 MP's form bloc in House of Commons to fight for Quebec sovereignty (announce 25 July that they will be called the Bloc québécois)</td></tr>
<tr><td>1 July 1990</td><td>— Queen Elizabeth makes rare political statement, encouraging national unity</td></tr>
<tr><td>3 July 1990</td><td>— Liberal MP Gilles Rocheleau quits federal Liberal caucus</td></tr>
<tr><td>12 August 1990</td><td>— youth wing of Quebec Liberal Party passes a resolution in favour of sovereignty-association</td></tr>
<tr><td>14 August 1990</td><td>— Bloc québécois Gilles Duceppe elected in Laurier-Ste. Marie by-election</td></tr>
<tr><td>22 August 1990</td><td>— businessmen Campeau and Bélanger named to head Quebec constitutional commission</td></tr>
<tr><td>August 1990</td><td>— Alberta announces 10-member committee to hold hearings on Alberta's constitutional future</td></tr>
<tr><td>10 September 1990</td><td>— New Brunswick announces special 9-member commission on the constitution</td></tr>
<tr><td>1 November 1990</td><td>— Mulroney creates Citizens' Forum on Canada's Future, the Spicer Commission (to report by 30 June 1991)</td></tr>
<tr><td>6 November 1990</td><td>— Bélanger-Campeau hearings begin, continue to mid-December (report expected in March 1991)</td></tr>
<tr><td>2 December 1990</td><td>— Mulroney announces joint parliamentary committee to develop a new amending formula</td></tr>
<tr><td>29 January 1991</td><td>— Quebec Liberal party (Allaire) report released</td></tr>
</tbody>
</table>

THE RISE AND FALL OF THE MEECH LAKE ACCORD

Appendix I

AMENDING THE CONSTITUTION: A SURVEY

There are two "ideal types" of constitution. A *flexible* constitution is one that is relatively easy to change. Perhaps the best example is New Zealand, whose constitution declares (in the first article), "It shall be lawful for the Parliament of New Zealand by any Act or Acts of that Parliament to alter at any time all or any provisions of the New Zealand Constitution Act of 1852." That is, all that is required to change the New Zealand constitution is a simple act of Parliament. By contrast, a *rigid* constitution is one that is difficult to change. In order to amend the constitution of the United States, an amendment must be passed by two-thirds majorities in both the Senate and the House of Representatives and by majorities in three-quarters of the state legislatures.

In Arend Lipjhart's scheme of the twenty-one continuously existing democracies since World War II,[212] only five countries are presented as having flexible constitutions: New Zealand, Britain, Israel, Sweden, and Iceland. The vast majority of democratic countries have rigid constitutions. The amending process of these countries intentionally allows for "minority vetoes," at either the local level or in both houses of the legislature. For example, the United States' amending formula offers a veto to one-quarter of the states—the smallest of which comprise less than 5 per cent of the population. In Switzerland, both a national majority and majorities in a majority of cantons are required in a referendum for a constitutional amendment to be accepted. Exceptional majorities are often required in both upper and lower houses. For example, a two-thirds majority is required in both houses in Belgium and Germany, where one of the houses directly represents regional or linguistic interests. Both approaches are based on the principle of double or "concurrent" majorities—a national one as well as a sectoral or regional one. This is designed to ensure that constitutional changes have strong support throughout the country. Whether a nation's constitution is flexible or rigid is no predictor of how often a nation amends its constitution. There has been little constitutional change in New Zealand, whereas in the first eight German Bundestags (parliaments) seventy of the constitution's articles have been changed by thirty-four amendments.[213]

Federal systems normally also have a process of "judicial review" to resolve constitutional squabbles between the two levels of government. There are only three countries comparable to Canada, as federal, with judicial review and a minority veto: Australia, Germany, and the United States. As previously noted, the German amendment process requires that an amendment be passed by a two-thirds majority in both houses. The Bundesrat is the German Federal Council, and is composed of three to five appointed representatives of each of the Laender (provincial governments). These representatives are actually members of the Laender. So, the German "provinces" are directly involved and there is a minority veto available. The United States process comprises a system of "double majorities" in which the state governments can trigger a minority veto. Australia is the only system with a minority veto and judicial review that offers a degree of direct, popular involvement in the process of amending the constitution. A proposed constitutional amendment must be passed by an absolute majority of both houses, or—after an interval of three months—twice by either house with an absolute majority (the Australian upper house is elected). Then a constitutional referendum is held, and a further double majority is required: an overall majority of electors and a majority of electors in four of the six states.

FLEXIBLE CONSTITUTIONS

New Zealand, UK, Israel	— simple legislative change
Sweden, Iceland	— legislative change by 2 successive majority governments

RIGID CONSTITUTIONS

Germany, Belgium	— concurrent majorities — special (greater than 1/2) majorities in both upper and lower houses
US, Canada	— concurrent majorities — majorities in both the national legislatures and a special majority of the subnational governments

REFERENDUM

Italy	— after amendment passed by 2/3 majority in both houses, a referendum can be triggered by *one* of 500,000 voters, 1/5 the members in either chamber, or 5 regional councils
Austria	— optional
Japan	— mandatory
Switzerland	— mandatory referendum, requiring majority of voters nationally, and a majority of voters in a majority of cantons

THE RISE AND FALL OF THE MEECH LAKE ACCORD

Belgium, Holland, Denmark, Sweden	— disguised referendum; amendment must be passed by majorities in two successive governments

COUNTRIES MOST COMPARABLE WITH CANADA

Switzerland	— federal, with minority veto, but no judicial review and direct referendum
Austria	— federal with minority veto, but amendment can be passed by a 2/3 majority in the representative chamber, thereby bypassing the sub-national government representatives in the upper chamber
Japan, Norway	— judicial review, with minority veto, but unitary systems
Australia	— federal, with minority veto and judicial review, but also requires a referendum
US, Germany	— federal, with minority veto and judicial review, but sub-national involvement via the national upper house (directly elected in US, appointed by the sub-national government in Germany)

Appendix II

CONSTITUTION AMENDMENT 1987

Constitution Act, 1867

1.   The <u>Constitution Act, 1867</u> is amended by adding thereto, immediately after section 1 thereof, the following section:

Interpretation

"2.   (1)   The Constitution of Canada shall be interpreted in a manner consistent with

(a)   the recognition that the existence of French–speaking Canadians, centred in Quebec but also present elsewhere in Canada, and English–speaking Canadians, concentrated outside Quebec but also present in Quebec, constitutes a fundamental characteristic of Canada; and

(b)   the recognition that Quebec constitutes within Canada a distinct society.

Role of Parliament and legislatures

(2)   The role of the Parliament of Canada and the provincial legislatures to preserve the fundamental characteristic of Canada referred to in paragraph (1) (a) is affirmed.

Role of legislature and Government of Quebec

(3)   The role of the legislature and Government of Quebec to preserve and promote the distinct identity of Quebec referred to in paragraph (1) (b) is affirmed.

Rights of legislatures and governments preserved

(4)   Nothing in this section derogates from the powers, rights or privileges of Parliament or the Government of Canada, or of the legislatures or governments of the provinces, including any powers, rights or privileges relating to language."

2.   The said Act is further amended by adding thereto, immediately after section 24 thereof, the following section:

Names to be submitted

"25.   (1)   Where a vacancy occurs in the Senate, the government of the province to which the vacancy relates may, in relation to that vacancy, submit to the Queen's Privy Council for Canada the names of persons who may be summoned to the Senate.

Choice of Senators from names submitted

(2)   Until an amendment to the Constitution of Canada is made in relation to the Senate pursuant to section 41 of the <u>Constitution Act, 1982</u>, the person summoned to fill a vacancy in the Senate shall be chosen from among persons whose names have been submitted under subsection (1) by the government of the province to which the vacancy relates and must be acceptable to the Queen's Privy Council for Canada."

3.   The said Act is further amended by adding thereto, immediately after section 95 thereof, the following heading and sections:

<u>**"Agreements on Immigration and Aliens**</u>

Commitment to negotiate

95A.   The Government of Canada shall, at the request of the government of any province, negotiate with the government of that province for the purpose of concluding an agreement relating to immigration or the temporary admission of aliens into that province that is appropriate to the needs and circumstances of that province.

Agreements

95B.   (1)   Any agreement concluded between Canada and a province in relation to immigration or the temporary admission of aliens into that province has the force of law from the time it is declared to do so in accordance with subsection 95C(1) and shall from that time have effect notwithstanding class 25 of section 91 or section 95.

THE RISE AND FALL OF THE MEECH LAKE ACCORD

Limitation

(2) An agreement that has the force of law under subsection (1) shall have effect only so long and so far as it is not repugnant to any provision of an Act of the Parliament of Canada that sets national standards and objectives relating to immigration or aliens, including any provision that establishes general classes of immigrants or relates to levels of immigration for Canada or that prescribes classes of individuals who are inadmissible into Canada.

Application of Charter

(3) The <u>Canadian Charter of Rights and Freedoms</u> applies in respect of any agreement that has the force of law under subsection (1) and in respect of anything done by the Parliament or Government of Canada, or the legislature or government of a province, pursuant to any such agreement.

Proclamation relating to agreements

95C. (1) A declaration that an agreement referred to in subsection 95B(1) has the force of law may be made by proclamation issued by the Governor General under the Great Seal of Canada only where so authorized by resolutions of the Senate and House of Commons and of the legislative assembly of the province that is a party to the agreement.

Amendment of agreements

(2) An amendment to an agreement referred to in subsection 95B(1) may be made by proclamation issued by the Governor General under the Great Seal of Canada only where so authorized

(a) by resolutions of the Senate and House of Commons and of the legislative assembly of the province that is a party to the agreement; or

(b) in such other manner as is set out in the agreement.

Application of sections 46 to 48 of Con-stitution Act, 1982

95D. Sections 46 to 48 of the Constitution Act, 1982 apply, with such modifications as the circumstances require, in respect of any declaration made pursuant to subsection 95C(1), any amendment to an agreement made pursuant to subsection 95C(2) or any amendment made pursuant to section 95E.

Amendments to Sections 95A to 95D or this sec-tion

95E. An amendment to sections 95A to 95D or this section may be made in accordance with the procedure set out in subsection 38(1) of the Constitution Act, 1982, but only if the amendment is authorized by resolutions of the legislative assemblies of all the provinces that are, at the time of the amendment, parties to an agreement that has the force of law under subsection 95B(1)."

4. The said Act is further amended by adding thereto, immediately preceding section 96 thereof, the following heading:

"General"

5. The said Act is further amended by adding thereto, immediately preceding section 101 thereof, the following heading:

"Courts Established by the Parliament of Canada"

6. The said Act is further amended by adding thereto, immediately after section 101 thereof, the following heading and sections:

"Supreme Court of Canada

Supreme Court contin-ued

101A. (1) The court existing under the name of the Supreme Court of Canada is hereby continued as the general court of appeal for Canada, and as an additional court for the better administration of the laws of Canada, and shall continue to be a superior court of record.

Constitution of Court

(2)　The Supreme Court of Canada shall consist of a chief justice to be called the Chief Justice of Canada and eight other judges, who shall be appointed by the Governor General in Council by letters patent under the Great Seal.

Who may be appointed judges

101B.　(1)　Any person may be appointed a judge of the Supreme Court of Canada who, after having been admitted to the bar of any province or territory, has, for a total of at least ten years, been a judge of any courts in Canada or a member of the bar of any province or territory.

Three judges from Quebec

(2)　At least three judges of the Supreme Court of Canada shall be appointed from among persons who, after having been admitted to the bar of Quebec, have, for a total of at least ten years, been judges of any court of Quebec or of any court established by the Parliament of Canada, or members of the bar of Quebec.

Names may be submitted

101C.　(1)　Where a vacancy occurs in the Supreme Court of Canada, the government of each province may, in relation to that vacancy, submit to the Minister of Justice of Canada the names of any of the persons who have been admitted to the bar of that province and are qualified under section 101B for appointment to that court.

Appointment from names submitted

(2)　Where an appointment is made to the Supreme Court of Canada, the Governor General in Council shall, except where the Chief Justice is appointed from among members of the Court, appoint a person whose name has been submitted under subsection (1) and who is acceptable to the Queen's Privy Council for Canada.

Appointment from Quebec

    (3)   Where an appointment is made in accordance with subsection (2) of any of the three judges necessary to meet the requirement set out in subsection 101B(2), the Governor General in Council shall appoint a person whose name has been submitted by the Government of Quebec.

Appointment from other provinces

    (4)   Where an appointment is made in accordance with subsection (2) otherwise than as required under subsection (3), the Governor General in Council shall appoint a person whose name has been submitted by the government of a province other than Quebec.

Tenure, salaries, etc. of judges

101D.   Sections 99 and 100 apply in respect of the judges of the Supreme Court of Canada.

Relationship to section 101

101E. (1)   Sections 101A to 101D shall not be construed as abrogating or derogating from the powers of the Parliament of Canada to make laws under section 101 except to the extent that such laws are inconsistent with those sections.

References to the Supreme Court of Canada

    (2)   For greater certainty, section 101A shall not be construed as abrogating or derogating from the powers of the Parliament of Canada to make laws relating to the reference of questions of law or fact, or any other matters, to the Supreme Court of Canada."

7.   The said Act is further amended by adding thereto, immediately after section 106 thereof, the following section:

Shared–cost program

"106A. (1) The Government of Canada shall provide reasonable compensation to the government of a province that chooses not to participate in a national shared–cost program that is established by the Government of Canada after the coming into force of this section in an area of exclusive provincial jurisdiction,

THE RISE AND FALL OF THE MEECH LAKE ACCORD

if the province carries on a program or initiative that is compatible with the national objectives.

Legislative power not extended

(2)   Nothing in this section extends the legislative powers of the Parliament of Canada or of the legislatures of the provinces."

8.   The said Act is further amended by adding thereto the following heading and sections:

"XII — Conferences on the Economy and Other Matters

Conferences on the economy and other matters

148.   A conference composed of the Prime Minister of Canada and the first ministers of the provinces shall be convened by the Prime Minister of Canada at least once each year to discuss the state of the Canadian economy and such other matters as may be appropriate.

XIII — References

Reference includes amendments

149.   A reference to this Act shall be deemed to include a reference to any amendments thereto."

Constitution Act, 1982

9.   Sections 40 to 42 of the Constitution Act, 1982 are repealed and the following substituted therefor:

Compensation

"40.   Where an amendment is made under subsection 38(1) that transfers legislative powers from provincial legislatures to Parliament, Canada shall provide reasonable compensation to any province to which the amendment does not apply.

Amendment by unanimous consent

41.   An amendment to the Constitution of Canada in relation to the following matters may be made by proclamation issued by the Governor General under the Great Seal of Canada only where authorized by resolutions

of the Senate and House of Commons and of the legislative assembly of each province:

> (a) the office of the Queen, the Governor General and the Lieutenant Governor of a province;

> (b) the powers of the Senate and the method of selecting Senators;

> (c) the number of members by which a province is entitled to be represented in the Senate and the residence qualifications of Senators;

> (d) the right of a province to a number of members in the House of Commons not less than the number of Senators by which the province was entitled to be represented on April 17, 1982;

> (e) the principle of proportionate representation of the provinces in the House of Commons prescribed by the Constitutiion of Canada;

> (f) subject to section 43, the use of the English or the French language;

> (g) the Supreme Court of Canada;

> (h) the extension of existing provinces into the territories;

> (i) notwithstanding any other law or practice, the establishment of new provinces; and

> (j) an amendment to this Part."

10. Section 44 of the said Act is repealed and the following substituted therefor:

Amendments by Parliament

"44. Subject to section 41, Parliament may exclusively make laws amending the Constitution of Canada in relation to the executive government of Canada or the Senate and House of Commons."

11. Subsection 46(1) of the said Act is repealed and the following substituted therefor:

Initiation of
amendment
procedures

"46.(1)   The procedures for amendment under sections 38, 41 and 43 may be initiated either by the Senate or the House of Commons or by the legislative assembly of a province."

12. Subsection 47(1) of the said Act is repealed and the following substituted therefor:

Amendments
without Sen-
ate resolution

"47.(1)   An amendment to the Constitution of Canada made by proclamation under section 38, 41 or 43 may be made without a resolution of the Senate authorizing the issue of the proclamation if, within one hundred and eighty days after the adoption by the House of Commonts of a resolution authorizing its issue, the Senate has not adopted such a resolution and if, at any time after the expiration of that period, the House of Commons again adopts the resolution."

13. Part VI of the said Act is repealed and the following substituted therefor:

"Part VI

Constitutional Conferences

Constitutional
conference

50.   (1)   A constitutional conference composed of the Prime Minister of Canada and the first ministers of the provinces shall be convened by the Prime Minister of Canada at least once each year, commencing in 1988.

Agenda

(2)   The conferences convened under subsection (1) shall have included on their agenda the following matters:

(a)   Senate reform, including the role and functions of the Senate, its powers, the method of selecting Senators and representation in the Senate;

(b) roles and responsibilities in relation to fisheries; and

(c) such other matters as are agreed upon."

14. Subsection 52(2) of the said Act is amended by striking out the word "and" at the end of paragraph (b) thereof, by adding the word "and" at the end of paragraph (c) thereof and by adding thereto the following paragraph:

"(d) any other amendment to the Constitution of Canada."

15. Section 61 of the said Act is repealed and the following substituted therefor:

References

"61. A reference to the Constitution Act 1982, or a reference to the Constitution Acts 1867 to 1982, shall be deemed to include a reference to any amendments thereto."

General

Multi–cultural heritage and aboriginal peoples

16. Nothing in section 2 of the Constitution Act, 1867 affects section 25 or 27 of the Canadian Charter of Rights and Freedoms, section 35 of the Constitution Act, 1982 or class 24 of section 91 of the Constitution Act, 1867.

CITATION

Citation

17. This amendment may be cited as the Constitution Amendment, 1987.

Appendix III

THE FIRST MINISTERS' AGREEMENT, 10 JUNE 1990

1. The Meech Lake Accord

The Premiers of New Brunswick, Manitoba and Newfoundland undertake to submit the Constitution Amendment, 1987 for appropriate legislative or public consideration and to use every possible effort to achieve a decision by June 23, 1990.

2. Senate Reform

After proclamation the federal government and the provinces will constitute a commission with equal representatives for each province and an appropriate number of territorial and federal representatives to conduct hearings and to report to the First Ministers' Conference on the Senate to be held by the end of 1990 in British Columbia, on specific proposals for Senate reform that will give effect to the following objectives:

- The Senate should be elected.
- The Senate should provide for more equitable representation of the less populous provinces and territories.
- The Senate should have effective power to ensure the interests of residents of less populous provinces and territories figure more prominently in national decision-making, reflect Canadian duality and strengthen the government of Canada's capacity to govern on behalf of all citizens, while preserving the principle of the responsibility of the government to the House of Commons.

Following the proclamation of the Meech Lake Accord, the Prime Minister and all the Premiers agree to seek adoption of an amendment on comprehensive Senate reform consistent with these objectives by July 1, 1995.

The Prime Minister undertakes to report semi-annually to the House of Commons on progress achieved towards comprehensive Senate reform.

The Prime Minister and all Premiers, reaffirming the commitment made in the Edmonton Declaration and the provisions to be entrenched under the Constitution Amendment, 1987, undertook that Senate reform will be the key constitutional priority until comprehensive reform is achieved.

If by July 1, 1995 comprehensive Senate reform has not been achieved according to the objectives set out above under section 41 of the Constitution Act, 1982, as amended by the Constitution Amendment, 1987, the number of senators by which a province is entitled to be represented in the Senate will be amended so that, of the total of 104 senators, the representation of Ontario will be 18, the representation of Nova Scotia, New Brunswick, British Columbia, Alberta, Saskatchewan, Manitoba and Newfoundland will be eight senators each, and the representation of all other provinces and territories will remain unchanged.

In the case of any province whose representation declined, no new appointments would be made until that province's representation had by attrition declined to below its new maximum.

In the event of such a redistribution of Senate seats, Newfoundland would be entitled to another member of the House of Commons under section 51(a) of the Constitution Act, 1867.

3. Further Constitutional Amendments

(1) Charter-Sex Equality Rights

Add section 28 of the Canadian Charter of Rights and Freedoms to section 16 of the Constitution Amendment, 1987.

(2) Role of the Territories

In appointments to the Senate and the Supreme Court of Canada.

In discussions on items on the agenda of annual constitutional and economic conferences where, in the view of the Prime Minister, matters to be discussed directly affect them.

(3) Language Issues

Add to the agenda of constitutional conferences matters of interest to English-speaking and French-speaking minorities.

Require resolutions of the House of Commons, the Senate and Legislative Assembly of New Brunswick to amend that province's Act Recognizing the Equality of the Two Official Linguistic Communities in New Brunswick (Bill 88).

(4) Aboriginal Constitutional Issues

First ministers constitutional conferences to be held once every three years, the first to be held within one year of proclamation; representatives of aboriginal peoples and the territorial governments to be invited by the Prime Minister to participate in the discussion of matters of interest to the aboriginal peoples of Canada.

The Prime Minister may lay or cause to be laid before the Senate and the House of Commons, and the Premiers will lay or cause to be laid before their legislative assemblies, a resolution in the form appended hereto, and will seek to authorize a proclamation to be issued by the Governor-General under the Great

THE RISE AND FALL OF THE MEECH LAKE ACCORD

Seal of Canada to amend the Constitution of Canada as soon as possible after proclamation of the Constitution Amendment, 1987.

4. Agenda for Future Constitutional Discussions

(1) Creation of New Provinces in the Territories

The Prime Minister and all Premiers agreed future constitutional conferences should address options for provincehood, including the possibility that, at the request of the Yukon and Northwest Territories to become provinces, only a resolution of the House of Commons and the Senate be required.

(2) Constitutional Recognitions

The Prime Minister and the Premiers took note of repeated attempts by First Ministers over the past 20 years to draft a statement of constitutional recognitions. All such attempts were unsuccessful.

The Prime Minister and Premiers reviewed drafts submitted by the federal government and Manitoba, Saskatchewan, Ontario and British Columbia, and agreed to refer immediately the drafts to an all-party Special Committee of the House of Commons. Public hearings would begin across Canada on July 16, 1990 and a report on the substance and placement of the clause—in a manner consistent with the Constitution of Canada—would be prepared for consideration by First Ministers at their conference in 1990.

(3) Constitutional Reviews

The Prime Minister and all Premiers agreed jointly to review, at the constitutional conference required by section 49 of the Constitution Act, 1982, the entire process of amending the Constitution, including the three-year time limit under section 39(2) of that Act and the question of mandatory public hearings prior to adopting any measure related to a constitutional amendment, including revocation of a constitutional resolution.

Pursuant to section 50 of the Constitution Act 1982, as proposed in the Constitution Amendment, 1987, the Prime Minister and the Premiers also committed to a continuing review of the operation of the Constitution of Canada, including the Canadian Charter of Rights and Freedoms, with a view to making any appropriate constitutional amendments.

5. Section 2: Constitutional Amendment, 1987

The Prime Minister and Premiers took note of public discussion of the distinct society clause since its inclusion in the Meech Lake Accord. A number of distinguished constitutional authorities met to exchange views on the legal impact of the clause. The Prime Minister and the Premiers reviewed their advice and other material.

The Prime Minister, in his capacity as chairman of the conference, received from the above-noted constitutional authorities a legal opinion which is appended to the final conference communique.

6. New Brunswick Amendment

Add a clause that, in New Brunswick, the English linguistic community and the French linguistic community have equality of status and equal rights and privileges.

Affirm an additional role of the Legislature and government of New Brunswick to preserve and promote the equality of status and equal rights and privileges of the province's two official language communities.

The Prime Minister of Canada will lay or cause to be laid before the Senate and the House of Commons, and the Premier of New Brunswick will lay or cause to be laid before the legislative assembly of New Brunswick, a resolution in the form appended hereto, and will seek to authorize a proclamation to be issued by the Governor-General under the Great Seal of Canada to amend the Constitution of Canada as soon as possible after proclamation of the Constitution Amendment, 1987.

The Text of the Legal Opinion on the Distinct Society Clause

Dear Prime Minister:

In response to certain concerns which have been expressed in relation to section 1 of the proposed Constitution Amendment, 1987 (Meech Lake Accord), it is our pleasure to confirm our opinion of the following.

In our opinion, the Canadian Charter of Rights and Freedoms will be interpreted in a manner consistent with the duality-distinct society clause of the proposed Constitution Amendment, 1987 (Meech Lake accord), but the rights and freedoms guaranteed thereunder are not infringed or denied by the application of the clause and continue to be guaranteed subject only to such reasonable limits prescribed by law as can be demonstrably justified in a free and democratic society, and the duality-distinct society clause may be considered, in particular, in the application of section 1 of the Charter.

The Constitution of Canada, including sections 91 and 92 of the Constitution Act, 1867, will be interpreted in a manner consistent with the duality-distinct society clause. While nothing in that clause creates new legislative authority for

Parliament or any of the provincial legislatures or derogates from any of their legislative authority, it may be considered in determining whether a particular law fits within the legislative authority of Parliament or any of the legislatures.

Signed by,

Senator Gerald Beaudon, Peter Hogg, Jamie Cameron, Katherine Swinton, Robert Edwards, Roger Tasse

Notes

1   Constitution-making "can dramatically cast into relief some of the basic characteristics of the political system and of the power of different groups within it, in ways which are sometimes hidden in the play of day-to-day politics. Constitution-making may thus be especially revealing precisely because it is not a normal process." K. Banting and R. Simeon (eds), *Redesigning the State: The Politics of Constitutional Change in Industrial Nations* (Toronto: University of Toronto Press, 1985), 3.

2   There have been federal referenda on prohibition and conscription; Newfoundland entered Confederation via a referendum; Quebec canvassed popular attitudes to independence in a referendum in 1980.

3   In 1931 the United Kingdom transferred all legislative power to the Dominion parliaments via the Statute of Westminster. Canada was asked by the UK to devise an amending formula so that constitutional/legislative ties with the UK could be severed completely. Canada's politicians could not devise a formula, with the result that Canada's constitution could not be amended except via an act of the British parliament.

   Various conventions and practices emerged out of this arrangement. The British parliament would not amend the Canadian constitution unless asked; it would pursue any request for constitutional change made by a joint address of the Canadian parliament; it never changed the constitution if the provinces alone requested a change; it never rejected a federal request for a change if the federal government had not consulted the provinces.

4   Provincial compliance was obtained when the federal government acquired jurisdiction over unemployment insurance in 1940, gained shared jurisdiction over old-age pensions in 1960, and changed the retirement ages of judges in 1960. No provincial compliance was sought in 1946, 1952, and 1974, when representation was changed in the House of Commons.

5   In the 1960s and 1970s, the policy agenda was dominated for periods of time by extensive, exhaustive efforts to develop a workable, Canadian amending formula. The two most widely known and discussed formulae centred on a *governmental* process.

   • The *Fulton-Favreau formula* (1964) comprised two parts; if a proposed amendment would change the division of powers between the two levels of government, then unanimity of the federal government and all of the provinces was required; in areas of mutual concern, the approval of two-thirds of the provinces and the federal government was required.

- *The Victoria Charter* (1971) rejected the unanimity approach of the Fulton-Favreau formula in favour of a "national consensus" approach. A proposed constitutional amendment would have to be approved by all provinces that had (presently or at some time in the past) 25 per cent or more of the population, at least two Atlantic provinces, and at least 2 of the western provinces (with at least 50 per cent of the population).

- *The Pepin-Robarts Commission* (1976) (The Task Force on Canadian Unity) proposed an amending formula similar to that of Australia: a majority in both the House of Commons and an *elected* Senate as well as a majority of voters in each of the four regions of the country in a national referendum. Approval of the provincial governments was not part of its proposal.

In 1978 Prime Minister Trudeau made a constitutional initiative in which he offered four options: the Fulton-Favreau formula, the Victoria Charter approach, a variant of the Victoria Charter approach (including various referendum mechanisms), or a national referendum. These proposals were not pursued with any significant degree of political energy or enthusiasm.

6   While Quebec did not sign the new constitution, it did nonetheless remain legally bound to it.

7   If the issue or area being altered was not a national matter, then a dissenting province could choose to opt out and not be party to the new arrangement; unilateral action could be taken by federal or provincial governments in areas of exclusive jurisdiction.

8   Pointed out by A. Cairns, in Banting and Simeon, *Redesigning the State*, 124–26, 135–36.

9   Only New Brunswick and Ontario would likely have agreed to the Charter without section 33.

10   *Canadian Annual Review*, 1983, 71; ibid., 1984, 41; *Le Devoir*, 7 August 1984. Here and elsewhere translation from the French by the authors.

11   This is the inauguration of a new Parliament. Let it also be the beginning of a new era of reconciliation, economic renewal and social justice...a priority of my government will be to breathe a new spirit into federalism and restore the trust of all Canadians in the effectiveness of our system of government...it is obvious that the constitutional agreement is incomplete so long as Quebec is not part of an accord. *While their principal obligations are to achieve economic renewal*, my ministers will work to create the conditions that will make possible the achievement of this essential accord.

House of Commons, *Debates*, 5 November 1984, 5, 6 (emphasis added).

12   Quebec Liberal Party, *Maitriser l'avenir* (February 1985). *Le Devoir*, 6 February 1985. With regard to the veto, the Liberals were prepared to accept, as a minimum condition, a veto limited to Article 42 (viz., national institutions), conditional on the acceptance of the principle of opting out with full financial compensation for all other matters dealing with the sharing of power. With regard to spending power, the Liberals argued for two features: that something akin to the amending formulae be applicable to any proposed federal initiative involving conditional subsidies, and that "conditions" be limited to general norms of communal application and not have the effect of regulating the management of those programs.

13   K. McRoberts, *Quebec: Social Change and Political Crisis* (Toronto: McClelland and Stewart, 1988), 334ff.

14   *Le Devoir*, 5 October 1985. In August, he declared that a Quebec government would accept
       the priority of the Canadian Charter over the Quebec Charter (ibid., 20 August 1985). In
       an October interview with *Le Devoir*, he stated that "I am confident I am optimistic that a
       Liberal government will be capable of signing the constitutional accord.... I know that the
       climate could allow us to sign much more easily than in the past" (ibid., 5 October 1985).

15   The newly elected Liberal government made a quick political overture in early March 1986,
       when Intergovernmental Affairs Minister Remillard stated that he hoped constitutional talks
       could start as early as October 1986. This offer was confirmed in April, when Premier Bouras-
       sa declared that "we would like to sign an agreement before the next federal election, other-
       wise it will be constantly put off." On 9 May 1986 at a conference in Mont-Gabriel, the
       Quebec government formally declared the five conditions that had been set out in *Maitriser
       l'avenir*. *Globe and Mail*, 8 March 1986, 14 April 1986.

16   Ottawa reacted cautiously through May and June. Secretary of State Benoit Bouchard warned
       governments to "be careful about the haste in wanting to finish so quickly that we sacrifice
       almost everything.... Nothing would hurt this country more than a constitutional bidding war,
       which would plunge us into endless negotiations and delay indefinitely the repatriation of
       Quebec." In a response to a question in the House of Commons on Remillard's proposals,
       the Prime Minister was non-committal; he was playing his political cards very close to his
       chest. Not until the 4 July 1986 meeting of the Priorities and Planning Committee (a kind
       of "inner cabinet" of top ministers) did Mulroney announce that "I think it's timely" to renew
       the constitutional process. *Le Devoir*, 10 May 1986; *Globe and Mail*, 12 May 1986.

17   House of Commons, *Debates*, 20 May 1986, 13410–11.

18   *Globe and Mail*, 4 July 1986.

19   In anticipation of the 27th Annual Premiers' Conference in Edmonton in August, Bourassa
       sent an "advance team" to tour the provincial capitals to sell Quebec's five conditions. The
       provinces were wary about the veto and the distinct society clause, and the expectation of a
       breakthrough was rated as unlikely by expert observers. Before the Edmonton meeting, Prime
       Minister Mulroney wrote each of the premiers, asking that they put aside their own constitu-
       tional demands to concentrate on adapting the constitution to get Quebec to sign. At the
       conference, Bourassa wanted the premiers to place Quebec's status in Confederation on the
       agenda, but Premiers Getty, Pawley, and Devine wanted the meeting to centre on the
       economy and agricultural issues. *Globe and Mail*, 9 August 1986.

20   *Globe and Mail*, 9 August 1986. See Ontario Premier David Peterson's comments, (ibid., 8,
       30 July 1986). Nova Scotia Premier Buchanan declared that "no province should have an
       individual veto. We've got to have equality within the Constitution of Canada" (ibid., 8 July
       1986).

21   This two-stage constitutional approach was later confirmed at the First Ministers' Conference
       in Vancouver in November. *Globe and Mail*, 13 August 1986.

22   "We cannot as a country afford to fail a third time.... We should have good indications that
       Quebec, the federal government, and the other provinces will be able to come to an agree-
       ment before we begin formal negotiations." *Globe and Mail*, 13 August 1986.

23   *Le Devoir*, 13 August 1986; *Alberta Report*, 1 September 1986, 10–11.

24   By late September the Prime Minister had yet to respond formally to Quebec's five conditions,
       although Senator Murray noted that the federal government found none of them to be un-

acceptable, or else the Prime Minister would not have encouraged the provinces to discuss them. *Globe and Mail*, 22, 25 September 1986.

25 House of Commons, *Debates*, 3 October 1986, 45.

26 *Le Devoir*, 13 June 1986. See also *Globe and Mail*, 14 June 1986.

27 *Le Devoir*, 3 November 1986.

28 *Le Devoir*, 16 March 1987.

29 *Globe and Mail*, 13 March 1987.

30 House of Commons, *Debates*, 17 March 1987, 4255–56.

31 "I have no intention of tabling specific proposals today.... If you want to know more about our basic philosophy, read my Sept-Iles speech..." Ibid.

32 *Globe and Mail*, 17 April 1987; *Maclean's*, 11 May 1987, 8ff; House of Commons, *Debates*, 27 April 1987, 5235.

33 House of Commons, *Debates*, 27 April 1987, 5228–29.

34 See D. Taras, "Meech Lake and Television News" and L. Felske, "Fractured Mirror: The Importance of Region and Personalities in English Language Newspaper Coverage of Meech Lake," in R. Gibbins (ed.), *Meech Lake and Canada: Perspectives from the West* (Edmonton: Academic Publishing, 1988).

35 *Le Devoir*, 30 April 1987.

36 *Maclean's*, 11 May 1987, 9.

37 *Maclean's*, 11 May 1987, 81ff; 16 August 1987, 8ff. For an extended presentation of what allegedly happened at this meeting, see A. Cohen, "That Bastard Trudeau," *Saturday Night*, June 1990, 38–43.

38 This immigration arrangement incorporated the principles of the Cullen-Couture agreement. In February 1978, federal Immigration Minister Bud Cullen and his Quebec counterpart Jacques Couture reached a voluntary agreement to establish an inter-governmental committee to regulate immigration levels and select immigrants in accordance with the province's needs. Quebec had wanted this approach to be extended and entrenched in the constitution.

Any federal-provincial immigration agreement would have to meet continuing federal standards and objectives, such as the overall national level of immigration and the determining of the inadmissibility of potential immigrants. Provinces would be given financial compensation for undertaking certain immigration services previously carried out by the federal government.

39 The accord in the first instance proposed to entrench the Supreme Court in the constitution as well as the provision that three of its members be from the civil bar.

40 The first ministers agreed to maintain the existing formula laid out in section 38 of the constitution (i.e., Parliament plus two-thirds of the provinces, containing at least 50 per cent of the population). They also agreed to continue to allow opting out of amendments that involved the transfer of provincial jurisdiction to the federal level (with reasonable compensation to be granted).

41 *Maclean's*, 11 May 1987, 8-9; *Globe and Mail*, 1 May 1987.

42 House of Commons, *Debates*, 1 May 1987, 5628–30.

43 *Globe and Mail*, 2 May 1987.

44 Ibid., 2 May 1987; Taras, "Meech Lake and Television News".

45   *Le Devoir*, 1, 2, 4 May 1987; *La Presse*, 2 May 1987.

46   House of Commons, *Debates*, 4 May 1987, 5684, 5688; *Globe and Mail*, 5 May 1987.

47   *Globe and Mail*, 12 May 1987.

48   *Le Devoir*, 12 May 1987; *Globe and Mail*, 12 May 1987; *Montreal Gazette*, 12 May 1987.

49   House of Commons, *Debates*, 11 May 1987, 5930–33.

50   Ibid., 5933–38.

51   Ibid., 5938–42.

52   The hearings were open to the public, televised, but fairly constrained: they would last but six days, five of which were devoted to hearing experts and witnesses. Seventeen individuals and twenty groups made representations before the committee. *Le Devoir*, 8 May 1987.

53   Ibid., 13 , 14 , 15 , 20 , 22 May 1987.

54   Ibid., 9 May 1987.

55   Premier Pawley had expected the talks to fail, and had not been intimately involved in the talks preceding Meech Lake. He had felt isolated at the meeting, and had left feeling that the ingredients of the accord could be changed. *Globe and Mail*, 6 May, 2 June 1987; G. Friesen, "Manitoba and the Meech Lake Accord," in Gibbins, *Meech Lake and Canada*.

56   *Globe and Mail*, 2 June 1987.

57   The Canadian Council on Social Development, the National Anti-Poverty Association, the Canadian Daycare Advocacy Association, the National Council on Welfare, the Canadian Institute of Child Health, the Canadian Council on Children and Youth, and the National Advisory Council on the Status of Women. *Globe and Mail*, 29 May, 30 May, 1 June 1987.

58   Asked why he did this, Trudeau later stated in a CBC radio interview that "I thought there would be enough people to protest that it wouldn't happen. I saw there weren't too many, so..." *Globe and Mail*, 29 May 1987.

59   Three days later, Senator Lowell Murray replied to Trudeau in *Le Devoir* and the *Globe and Mail*. The minister responsible for federal-provincial relations retorted that it was Trudeau who had bungled the constitutional process in 1981–82 by isolating Quebec; that his fear of balkanization was "inspired by an overweening centralist bias"; and that his polemics seem more like a last hurrah. *Toronto Star*, 27 May 1987; *Globe and Mail*, 30 May 1987.

60   Several prominent Liberals like Donald Macdonald—former finance minister and head of the Royal Commission on the Economic Union—supported Trudeau's comments.

61   *Globe and Mail*, 28, 29 , 30 May, 1 , 2 June 1987; *Le Devoir*, 30 May 1987.

62   Quebec's Bourassa claimed that Trudeau's remarks betrayed a centralist vision that no longer reflected Canada's reality. Alberta's Getty declared that "Albertans have never shared Trudeau's view of Canada." British Columbia's Vander Zalm commented that "he forgets that Canada is made up of provinces." Manitoba's Pawley said that "what he demonstrated is an over-obsession with federalist authority." *Maclean's*, 8 June 1987, 11; *Globe and Mail*, 28 May 1987.

63   At one point during the all night vigil, there was a sense among the federal delegation that the deal could not hold together. In fact they were telling us out on the sidewalks somewhere around 4:00 in the morning that they thought it was just about over.... Once again at Langevin, not a single technical advisor from the provinces was allowed in that room at any point.

Every time they broke for coffee, each premier would go to consult with his experts. Then they would go back in the room. Then all the experts would suddenly get together to try and find out what the other positions were. They tried to work out a consensus among themselves so when their guys came out the next time they could kind of massage their backs like boxers, and send them back in with the right line.... There are wonderful stories of premiers...coming out and talking to their advisers and repeating texts 180 degrees from what really was on the table, mixing up clauses and numbers, not understanding the relationships. It really was very difficult...

Elly Alboim, "Inside the News Story: Meech Lake as Viewed By An Ottawa Bureau Chief," in Gibbins, *Meech Lake and Canada*, p. 243. For an account of what allegedly happened at this meeting, see A. Cohen, "That Bastard Trudeau," 43–46.

64 *Globe and Mail*, 3, 4 June 1987; *Maclean's*, 15 June 1987, 8–10, 15–16. Premier Pawley's support was apparently conditional on holding public hearings in Manitoba, which might produce recommendations for changes.

65 NDP leader Broadbent made a secret phone call to Prime Minister Mulroney before the Langevin meeting, which laid the basis for the compromise that Pawley accepted.

66 There were a number of technical changes. With respect to immigration, a new clause was added (Constitution Act, 1867, section 95B(3)). There had been some concern that the 95B(1) phrase that any immigration agreement would have "the force of law" put the Charter of Rights in jeopardy in this area. Section 95B(3) insists that the Charter applies. The Supreme Court amendment underwent a minor change. A new section was added that, by implication, ensured and extended judicial independence (Constitution Act, 1867, section 101D).

67 *Globe and Mail*, 4 June 1987.

68 The Ontario government was in a minority situation in June 1987, but would be given a majority after an election in the summer.

69 *Le Devoir*, 4, 5, 8 June 1987.

70 Bourassa's quick call for legislative debate caught the Parti québécois by surprise, and it accused the government of "undue haste." The process unfolded in thirty-five hours of debate in the legislature, with no public hearings. *Le Devoir*, 10 , 19 June 1987; *Montreal Gazette*, 25 June 1987; *Canadian Parliamentary Review*, Autumn 1987, 20, 21.

71 Opposition parties focused their criticism on the immigration proposal, which was seen as jeopardizing future population growth in the province, given the guarantees made to Quebec. There were also unsuccessful calls for public hearings. In defending the unanimity requirement for the creation of new provinces, Premier Devine mused, "I wouldn't want to bring in a new province with 50 percent of the population and three or four provinces against it.... You [the new province] would feel like an ugly sister." The constitutional motion passed 43–3 in September; the Premier was absent for the vote. *Globe and Mail*, 10 July 1987; *Le Devoir*, 8 July 1987; Saskatchewan, Legislative Assembly, *Debates*, 17, 21, 22, 23 September 1987; *Regina Leader-Post*, 18, 23, 24 September 1987; *Globe and Mail*, 23 September 1987.

72 House of Commons, *Debates*, 3 June 1987, 6674–75; *Globe and Mail*, 5 June 1987; Senate, *Debates*, 9 June 1987, 1179–85; 10 June, 1987, 1198–1206; 11 June, 1987, 1215–58; 16 June, 1987, 1233–41; *Globe and Mail*, 12, 17, 18 June 1987.

73 The committee was chaired by Conservative Senator Arthur Tremblay (a constitutional expert) and Conservative MP Chris Speyer (who would later be appointed a judge of the divisional court of Ontario). The other committee members were Senators Derek Lewis, Raymond

Perreault, Brenda Robertson, and Yvette Rousseau, and MPs Suzanne Blais-Grenier, Albert Cooper, David Daubney, Leo Duguay, Benno Friesen, Charles Hamelin, Pauline Jewett, Robert Kaplan, Lorne Nystrom, and Andre Ouellet.

74   "The joint committee will do its work and make its recommendations, but as far as I am concerned...the Meech Lake accord is an impressive document...and I have no hesitation in recommending it to the rest of the country as it was negotiated."

See House of Commons, *Debates*, 3 June 1987, 6674–75; 25 June 1987, 7611; *Globe and Mail*, 23 June 1987.

75   Senate, House of Commons, *Minutes and Proceedings of the Special Joint Committee of the Senate and House of Commons on the 1987 Constitutional Accord* 1987, 2:10, 11, 14, 17. Hereafter referred to as the *special joint committee*.

76   *Globe and Mail*, 4 , 6 , 22, 24 June, 7, 22, 29 July, 5, 10 August, 1987.

77   Of the myriad groups that made presentations, only two were supportive of the accord: the Quebec Status of Women Council and the Fédération des Femmes du Québec. The array of groups against the accord represented various reactions: multicultural groups (ranging from the Canadian Ethnocultural Council to the National Association of Japanese Canadians); women's groups (NACSW, NACWL, WLEAF, CACSW); language groups (for example, Canadian Parents for French, Société franco-Manitobaine); supporters of social programmes (including the Canadian Day Care Advocacy Association and the National Anti-Poverty Association); native groups (e.g., Assembly of First Nations, Native Council of Canada); the governments of the north; and various organizations and organized interests (Canadian Bar Association, Human Rights Institute, Fisheries Council, National Farmers Union, Canadian Labour Congress, Canada West Foundation, public-sector unions, and so on).

78   "There are unquestionable risks in the agreement," maintained Sylvia Gold. A legal brief prepared by the law firm Tory, Tory, Des Lauriers and Binnington for the Ad Hoc Committee of Women on the Constitution concluded, "You cannot say that there is no risk of harm to women's rights.... There is reason to believe that it could happen." Special joint committee, 13:24, 15:127, 129; *Globe and Mail*, 11 August 1987.

79   *Toronto Star*, 19 August 1987; House of Commons, *Debates*, 20 August 1987, 8248–49.

Later, the largest women's organization in Quebec—La fédération des femmes du Québec— stated before the committee that "we do not subscribe to the unfortunate interpretation that Quebec women could see themselves deprived of their rights to equality"; the Quebec Council on the Status of Women argued that there were no legal reasons to be concerned and that Quebec had a strong record of respect for women's rights. See *Toronto Star*, 19 August, 1 September 1987. Committee co-chair Speyer found it to be "extraordinarily ironic" that legal opinion in Toronto was more concerned about the rights of women in Quebec than Quebec women were. *Globe and Mail*, 27 August 1987.

80   *Globe and Mail*, 27 August 1987.

81   Special joint committee, 14:116–23.

82   Ibid., 13:139–46.

83   Only one of the four Liberals on the committee signed the report. The report raised four concerns for the future: public participation in constitutional change, the relation of the Charter to the ingredients of the constitution, the unanimity formula as applied to the creation of new provinces, and aboriginal issues. Special joint committee, *Report*, 137, 138, 141-42.

THE RISE AND FALL OF THE MEECH LAKE ACCORD

84   *Le Devoir*, 10 September 1987; *Globe and Mail*, 11 September 1987. House of Commons, *Debates*, 29 September 1987, 9428–32.

85   House of Commons Debates, 21 October 1987, 10240-44.

86   Eleven Liberals and two NDP members broke ranks and voted against the accord. Two Conservatives broke ranks as well, and Independent MP Tony Roman voted against. Four Conservatives abstained; two others left just before the vote was taken.

87   "I'm asking the people of New Brunswick for a mandate to go in and negotiate the best possible deal.... [Premier] Hatfield didn't go to the people of New Brunswick and tell them whether he would sign it or not before he negotiated." *Globe and Mail*, 28 September 1987.

88   *Maclean's*, 11 April 1988, 8, 10; *Globe and Mail*, 16, 18, 1988. The inclusion of the fisheries on the consitutional agenda was seen as a move towards allowing Newfoundland to control who could fish in east coast waters.

89   Prime Minister Mulroney stated, "It would be a very heavy responsibility for someone to veto [the accord] and thereby preclude the possibility of bringing Quebec into the constitution." *Toronto Star*, 23 November 1987; *Globe and Mail*, 19 March 1988. "There is nothing formal, and nothing has been decided, but people are working on a political compromise so that McKenna doesn't lose face," said a Quebec provincial official. *Le Devoir*, 23 March 1988.

90   Murray's logic was that "if after all other provinces have said yes, and New Brunswick says wait two more years...then effectively the answer is no." *Toronto Star*, 23 November 1987.

91   He responded to his being characterized as a "black sheep" by saying, "It doesn't bother me. I didn't get to be premier of the province by simply going along with the crowd." Ibid.

92   *Toronto Star*, 3 October, 25 November, 19 December 1987.

93   *Alberta Report*, 8 February 1988, 8–9; *Globe and Mail*, 22 January, 1 March 1988. There was also considerable concern that the immigration provisions of the agreement would solidify the electoral dominance of central Canada, as Manitoba and other western provinces would not be able to use immigration as a source of potentially disproportionate provincial growth.

94   *Globe and Mail*, 9, 11 March 1988; *Toronto Star*, 6 March 1988.

95   *Globe and Mail*, 28 April, 30 July, 9 September, 3 October, 24 November, 1988; *Financial Post*, 2 May 1988; *Winnipeg Free Press*, 1 May 1988.

96   The opposition Liberals and NDP staged a mini-filibuster, consuming two weeks of the legislative session. Concerns centred on gender rights, an elected Senate, multiculturalism, the weakening of national programmes through opting out, and—the most intense issue—the fisheries. The government refused to call for a select committee study and public hearings. The fiercest debate centred on the issue of placing the fisheries on the constitutional agenda. Liberal leader MacLean introduced a motion asking that jurisdictional responsibilities for fisheries not be changed without the prior agreement of all four Atlantic provinces. He claimed that Nova Scotia was the only province that had given something up as the price of getting Newfoundland Premier Peckford to sign: "Perhaps the Premier did not realize the significance at the time.... He might have been tired after that 19 hours, so he might have inadvertently thought the wording did not affect the interests of Nova Scotia." Nova Scotia, Legislative Assembly, *Debates*, 1 March 1988, 177–203; 3 March 1988, 329–64; 4 March 1988, 383–416; 7 March 1988, 439–70; 8 March 1988, 512–39; 10 March 1988, 680–97; 11 March 1988, 727–56; *Halifax Chronicle-Herald*, 2 , 5 , 21 , 24 March 1988; *Globe and Mail*, 23 March 1988.

THE RISE AND FALL OF THE MEECH LAKE ACCORD

97   Senate, *Proceedings of the Senate Task Force on the Meech Lake Constitutional Accord and on the Yukon and the Northwest Territories*, chapter 8.

98   Senate, *Debates*, 30 March 1988, 2982, 2984, 2985, 2995–97; *Calgary Herald*, 10 April 1988.

       Of the dozen or so groups and individuals that the Senate heard, only one speaker was pro-Meech Lake, former Liberal cabinet minister Jack Pickersgill. On 30 March Pierre Trudeau came before the Senate, and Lowell Murray and most Conservative senators chose to be absent.

99   *Toronto Star*, 10 March 1988. The labour movement had been rather circumspect in its immediate reaction to Meech Lake, not wanting to embarrass the NDP, which had endorsed Meech Lake enthusiastically and at an early stage.

100   The language legislation had been prompted by the Supreme Court ruling in February that all of Saskatchewan's laws since 1905 were invalid—because they had been written only in English. The Saskatchewan government faced two options. It could translate all of its laws since 1905 into French, or it could pass a law that retroactively legalized all of the legislation that had been enacted. *Globe and Mail*, 6 , 7 , 8 , 9 April 1988; *Maclean's*, 25 April 1988, 12–15.

       In early July the Alberta government passed similar legislation. The Alberta legislation (two pages long, eight sections) declared Alberta to be bilingual on the floor of the legislature and in the courts, but unilingual everywhere else. This was characterized as "Saying No to Bilingualism." *Alberta Report*, 4 July 1988, cover story.

101   *Globe and Mail*, 10 March 1988.

102   *Toronto Star*, 26 November 1987.

103   *Toronto Star*, 8 May 1988; *Globe and Mail*, 13, 14 May 1988. The convention amendments dealt with Charter pre-eminence, tougher opting out provisions, and an easier amending formula for the creation of new provinces.

104   *Globe and Mail*, 8 March 1988.

105   *Toronto Star*, 26 November 1987.

106   Edward Greenspan, Morris Manning, and Timothy Danson acted on behalf of the Canadian Coalition on the Constitution, a loose coalition of academics, lawyers, and interest groups such as the National Anti-Poverty Coalition, the Canadian Daycare Advocacy Association, the Canadian Institute for Child Health, the Canadian Mental Health Association, the Canadian Ethnocultural Association and the Women's Legal Educational and Action Fund. Their argument was that the agreement amounted to an illegal transfer of powers from the federal to the provincial governments; the distinct society clause was so vague as to be destructive; and the Charter's preeminence should be established. *Globe and Mail*, 3 May, 1 June 1988.

107   House of Commons, *Debates*, 19 May 1988, 15, 633-36; *Globe and Mail*, 20 May 1988; House of Commons, *Debates*, 14 June 1988, 16, 406–8, 16, 413–17.

108   Four Liberals voted against—Caccia, Penner, Berger, Finestone—as did the NDP's McLaughlin (McCurdy and Robinson abstained) and Conservative Nickerson.

109   Alberta, *Legislative Assembly*, 23 November 1987, 2011ff; 25 November 1987, 2046ff; 30 November 1987, 2094ff; 2 December 1987, 2161ff, 3 December 1987, 2197ff, 4 December 1987, 2227ff; *Calgary Herald*, 22 , 24 November, 3 , 8 December 1987; *Globe and Mail*, 9

December 1987; H. Palmer, "The Flaws of the Meech Lake Accord: An Alberta Perspective," in R. Gibbins, *Meech Lake and Canada.*

110 *Globe and Mail*, 14 May 1988. Only one member—a Liberal—voted against the agreement.

111 Ibid., 26 January, 18 May, 6 June 1988; *Halifax Chronicle-Herald*, 25 May 1988; *Toronto Star*, 26 May, 31 July 1988; *Maclean's*, 15 August 1988, 10–11.

112 The committee also recommended that a standing committee on the constitution be established. During the final vote, proceedings were disrupted by a group of twenty women, members of the Ad Hoc Committee of Women on the Constitution, singing, "We are gentle angry people, and we are singing, singing for our rights." *Globe and Mail*, 24 , 30 June 1988.

113 *Vancouver Sun*, 28 , 30 June 1988.

114 Two NDP members and one Liberal voted with the government, while ten Liberals voted against. *St. John's Evening Telegram*, 30 June, 8 July 1988.

115 *Globe and Mail*, 17 February 1988 (see also 29 July, 17 August 1987, 31 July 1988); 27 September 1988.

116 Ibid., 23 November 1988.

117 *Globe and Mail*, 16 , 19 December 1988.

118 *Maclean's*, 2 January 1989, 39.

119 See Lowell Murray, *Globe and Mail*, 5 January 1989.

120 Ibid., 20 December 1988.

121 Ibid., According to Turner, 21 December 1988.

122 By his silence and his inaction, the Prime Minister of Canada is an accomplice to a direct attack on the basic fundamental rights of the Quebec anglophone minority.... The Prime Minister has no intention of enforcing the Charter...he has had all the time in the world and every opportunity to delete the notwithstanding clause from the constitution...but the Prime Minister [has] not lift[ed] a finger. He never raised this issue with his counterparts during the Meech Lake negotiations.

House of Commons, *Debates*, 5 April 1989, 126-29; 6 April 1989, 153; 10 April 1989, 282-83; *Globe and Mail*, 7, 8, 12, 21 April 1989.

Quebec's Bourassa looked on with a combination of concern and bemusement. "Suppressing the notwithstanding clause would result in submitting Quebec's language laws to the Charter of Rights and Freedoms. That would mean a derogation from the province's legislative powers." Mulroney, he sensed, was touched by a "temporary bout of political fever."

Later in the year, Mulroney stated, "The exclusion of Quebec and the inclusion of the notwithstanding clause were two fundamental flaws in the 1981 constitution that should, in my judgment, have prevented it from going ahead at that time. [The Canadian constitution] is the only constitution in the industrialized world that gives provinces the right to override the Supreme Court of Canada in respect of individual rights." *Montreal Gazette*, 29 December 1989.

123 *Toronto Star*, 24, 26 January 1989; *Globe and Mail*, 27 January 1989.

124 *Globe and Mail*, 14 March, 7, 12 April 1989.

125 As New Brunswick's McKenna put it, the parallel accord "certainly permits those who do not want to see Meech Lake opened the advantage of saying that it wasn't reopened...for those

who believe there have to be changes, it gives them the advantage of saying changes have been accomplished." *Toronto Star*, 26, 29 January 1989.

126 *Globe and Mail*, 10, 29 June, 17, 19, 23, 24 August 1989; *Montreal Gazette*, 24 August 1989.

127 *Toronto Star*, 25 January, 16 February, 25 June, 1 August 1989; *Globe and Mail*, 27, 28 February, 9 May, 6 July, 31 August 1989; *Maclean's*, 13 March 1989, 14; House of Commons, *Debates*, 27 June 1989, 3688; 8 November 1989, 5712-13.

128 House of Commons, *Debates*, 5 April 1989, 129.

129 *Montreal Gazette*, 14 January, 22 June 1989. The undecided rate was high, 52 per cent in January 1989, but this fell to 40 per cent by June 1989 as those against climbed to over 30 per cent.

130 *Globe and Mail*, 3 April, 1 May 1989.

131 *Toronto Star*, 17 September 1989; *Montreal Gazette*, 20 September 1989; *Globe and Mail*, 20 September, 30 November, 2 December 1989. Changes sought included guaranteed negotiation of aboriginal rights, changing the unanimity formula for Senate reform and the creation of new provinces, and recognition of Canada's multicultural heritage.

132 *Globe and Mail*, 20, 25 April 1989; *Toronto Star*, 21 April 1989; *Montreal Gazette*, 22 April 1989.

133 *Globe and Mail*, 1 July 1989.

134 *Montreal Gazette*, 2 November 1989.

135 *Globe and Mail*, 23, 27 September 1989; *Montreal Gazette*, 26 September 1989.

136 *Toronto Star*, 21 October 1989; *Globe and Mail*, 4, 8 November 1989.
     Prime Minister Mulroney responded to Wells's letter in a return letter on 3 November: "the distinct society clause works with the Charter, not against it."

137 Manitoba Task Force on Meech Lake, *Report on the 1987 Constitutional Accord*, 21 October 1989, 72–78, 80.

138 *Globe and Mail*, 24 October 1989; *Montreal Gazette*, 24, 28 October 1989.

139 Legislative Assembly of New Brunswick, Select Committee on the 1987 Constitutional Accord, *Final Report on the 1987 Constitutional Accord*, October 1989, 18–19, 21, 24, 71–72, Appendix F.

140 *Globe and Mail*, 25 October 1989.

141 *Globe and Mail*, 25, 26 October 1989; *Toronto Star*, 28 October, 3 November 1989; *Montreal Gazette*, 25 October 1989.

142 "It's an incomplete document right now, but we can build on it," concluded McKenna. "There are as many interpretations of what a parallel accord should be as there are people speaking about it," retorted Bourassa. *Toronto Star*, 21, 31 October 1989; *Globe and Mail*, 8 November 1989.

143 *Globe and Mail*, 23 October 1989; *Montreal Gazette*, 8 November 1989; *Toronto Star*, 28 October 1989.

144 *Globe and Mail*, 9 February, 18 October, 9 November 1989.

145 *Toronto Star*, 4 October 1989; *Globe and Mail*, 9 November 1989; *Toronto Star*, 9 November 1989.

146 *Toronto Star*, 9 November 1989.

147   *Toronto Star*, 11 November 1989.

148   *Globe and Mail*, 10 November 1989.

149   Ibid.

150   *Toronto Star*, 11 November 1989; *Globe and Mail*, 11 November 1989.

151   *Globe and Mail*, 24, 25, 28 November, 1, 2 December 1989, 5, 8, 9, 10 January 1990; *Montreal Gazette*, 1 December 1989; *Toronto Star*, 6 February 1990; *Peterborough Examiner*, 17 February 1990.

152   She maintained that national unity is an illusion unless it is based on "defined foundations that promise to be durable and whose durability is not beyond the testing of the building's material and organization. Such testing cannot be undertaken unless we accept, once and for all, the inevitable compromises and unless the parties involved ratify their pact and do not let Canada drift into an unforeseeable future." *Montreal Gazette*, 31 December 1989.

153   *Montreal Gazette*, 7, 13 February, 8 March 1990; *Globe and Mail*, 12 February 1990.

154   Canadians for a Unifying Constitution included four former Trudeau cabinet ministers, Jean-Luc Pepin, Monique Begin, Francis Fox, and Eric Kierans. Friends of Meech Lake was organized by two law professors at McGill University, Wade MacLachlan and Jeremy Weber. *Toronto Star*, 6 January 1990; *Globe and Mail*, 23 January 1990; *Montreal Gazette*, 23 January 1990.

155   Wells did public battle with Friends spokespersons Jack Pickersgill and Robert Stanfield. They had attacked Wells for "expos[ing] the people of Atlantic Canada to grave additional perils for no reason of substance." Wells accused them of fear-mongering and trying to muzzle him. A party of Quebec business people was coolly received when it travelled to Newfoundland to drum up Meech support. Wells's office released figures indicating that Wells had received 3,376 Meech Lake letters in the previous year, 3,354 in favour of his stand. *Globe and Mail*, 24 November 1989; 10, 11, 17 January, 10 February, 1, 9 March 1990.

156   The Quebec Liberal party began planning what to do in the event of the failure of Meech Lake (a policy blueprint entitled "Moving with the Rhythm of Change," after several cabinet members and backbenchers openly declared sovereignty-association to be an option. *Globe and Mail*, 29, 30 November, 27 December 1989; 10, 20, 23 January, 1, 9, 21, 24, 26 February 1990; *Toronto Star*, 6, 22, 24 February 1990; *Montreal Gazette*, 23 February 1990.

157   Part one of the plan was to get an agreement to "unbundle" the Meech Lake package into two groups, with one group containing those provisions that satisfy current amending procedures (these would include the immigration provisions, the distinct society section, the opting-out provision of shared-cost programmes); most of the accord would then become law in June, as at least seven provinces containing 50 per cent of the population would have ratified the accord. This would be proclaimed by 23 June 1990. The second stage would try to broaden and clarify the distinct society clause by expanding it into a Canada clause, in which "each of the provinces and territories would be recognized as distinct." The target date for this proposal would be 23 June 1991. Third, "fundamental and comprehensive Senate reform" would be undertaken, with a target date of 23 June 1992. Fourth, the remaining elements of the Meech Lake agreement—changes to the amending formula and Supreme Court matters—requiring unanimity, would be pursued after points two and three had been passed. Finally, the first ministers committed themselves to constitutional discussions by 23 June 1993 on equality rights, property rights, minority language rights, aboriginal rights, and

other matters that may be agreed upon. See Province of British Columbia, Office of the Premier, *News Release*, 23 January 1990; *Globe and Mail*, 24 January 1990.

158 The reaction to the Vander Zalm proposal was muted. Senator Murray was cautious and noted that "we are not convinced that this [plan] is constitutionally correct." He later described it as more positive than the approaches taken by Manitoba and Newfoundland. Quebec's minister of intergovernmental affairs, Claude Remillard, described the proposal as unacceptable, as ratification of all five conditions at the same time remained Quebec's minimum demand. *Globe and Mail*, 24, 26 January, 14 February 1990.

159 *Globe and Mail*, 31 January, 2, 6, 9, 16 February 1989; *Toronto Star*, 6, 8, 9 February 1989. House of Commons, *Debates*, 5 February 1990, 7823–26.

160 *Globe and Mail*, 6 December 1989; *Toronto Star*, 17 January 1990; *Montreal Gazette*, 26 January 1990; *Globe and Mail*, 16 December 1989.

161 In December 1989, a group of Quebec business leaders warned that failure to ratify Meech Lake could lead to a flight of investment. In the new year, deputy Prime Minister Mazankowski reported that foreign investors were getting nervous about investing in Canada because of the failure of Meech Lake's acceptance. Thomas d'Aquino, President of the Business Council on National Issues (representing Canada's largest 150 corporations) declared that "one of Canada's greatest assets is its comparatively high level of political stability. If we have prolonged constitutional instability, it will be bad for the economy." *Globe and Mail*, 17, 18, 29 January 1990.

162 House of Commons, *Debates*, 9 March 1990, 9049–52; *Montreal Gazette*, 4 March 1990; *Globe and Mail*, 19 January, 3, 24, 28 February, 19 March 1990.

163 *Montreal Gazette*, 3 March 1990.

164 *Toronto Star*, 21, 22 March 1990. The New Brunswick Companion Resolution is included as Appendix D of House of Commons, *Report of the Special Committee to Study the Proposed Companion Resolution to the Meech Lake Accord*, 17 May 1990 (hereafter referred to as the Charest report).

165 *Toronto Star*, 22, 23, 28 March 1990; *Globe and Mail*, 28 March 1990.

166 *Toronto Star*, 21, 22, 23, 24 March 1990; *Globe and Mail*, 23, 24, 29 March 1990; *Montreal Gazette*, 22 March 1990.

167 *Globe and Mail*, 7 April 1990; *Montreal Gazette*, 7 April 1990; House of Commons, *Debates*, 9 April 1990, 10334–35; 10475–77; *Globe and Mail*, 1 June 1990. Included in Newfoundland's resolution was a provision that gave Ottawa the power to call for a Meech Lake referendum in Newfoundland, if New Brunswick and Manitoba adopted the accord.

168 *Montreal Gazette*, 28 March, 3 April 1990; *Toronto Star*, 21 April 1990.

169 *Globe and Mail*, 2 April 1990. For the CF-18 story, see *The Real Worlds of Canadian Politics*, 1st ed. (1989) chapt. 1.

170 *Montreal Gazette*, 27 May, 19 April 1990.

171 *Globe and Mail*, 10 May 1990.

172 The fifteen-member all-party group held hearings from 9 April to 4 May in 5 cities (Yellowknife, Whitehorse, Vancouver, Winnipeg, St. John's) and the Capital Area. It heard 160 witnesses and received 800 written submissions. The witnesses included representatives of eight governments (including Premiers Buchanan, Ghiz, Peterson, McKenna and Wells); two former premiers (Hatfield, Stanfield); constitutional experts; sixteen aboriginal groups; eleven

women's groups; twelve language groups; five northern groups; five Meech Lake interest groups; five business associations; and various labour, multicultural, handicapped, and rights' groups.

The Charest Committee affirmed most of the McKenna resolution: entrenching New Brunswick's bilingual status; assigning authority to the territories to make Senate and Supreme Court nominations; exclusive federal role in the territories' becoming provinces; no constitutional changes without public hearings; a separate process of constitutional conferences on aboriginal rights, to be held every three years, the first to be held a year after the resolution is adopted; dropping fisheries from the constitutional agenda. The report *differed* from the McKenna resolution in the two areas: the proposed Senate review of regional disparity being addressed in the context of a Senate reform; and a statement saying that the distinct society clause does not impair Charter rights rather than adding sexual equality rights to section 16.

The report addressed the question of the amending formula for Senate reform; followed Manitoba and Newfoundland's suggestion that the aboriginal peoples and Canada's multicultural heritage be recognized as part of Canada's fundamental character, and recommended territorial participation at constitutional conferences. It *rejected* Manitoba's suggestion that Meech Lake's opting-out provision be dropped, and suggested that the companion resolution give assurances that this provision would not impair the federal government's capacity to provide equal opportunities and reduce regional disparities. House of Commons, *Debates*, 17 May 1990, 11525; Charest report, 5–12.

173 House of Commons, *Debates*, 18 May 1990, 11606–9; 22 May 1990, 111654-58; *Globe and Mail*, 17, 18, 19, 21 May 1990; *Montreal Gazette*, 17, 18, 19 May 1990; *Maclean's*, 28 May 1990, 14-16.

174 *Globe and Mail*, 21, 23, 24 May 1990; *Montreal Gazette*, 22, 23 May 1990; *Maclean's*, 4 June 1990, 24–25. Charest and Paul Tellier (clerk of the PCO) had tried unsuccessfully to contact him in Paris, to brief him on the report.

175 Canadian press translation, in *Globe and Mail*, 23 May 1990.

176 *Maclean's*, 4 June 1990; *Globe and Mail*, 23 May 1990. Gagnon cited in *Globe and Mail*, 22 May 1990.

177 House of Commons, *Debates*, 23 May 1990, 11706–10; 24 May 1990, 11798-802; *Montreal Gazette*, 23 May 1990; *Globe and Mail*, 24, 25, 26, 28, 29, 30, 31 May 1990.

178 House of Commons, *Debates*, 31 May 1990, 12120–23; *Globe and Mail*, 1, 2 June 1990. The Newfoundland add-on list focused on two main points: a guarantee that the distinct society clause not "override or diminish the Charter," and the easing of the unanimity formula for Senate reform by returning to the 7/50 formula if Senate reform is not achieved by 30 June 1990.

179 *Montreal Gazette*, 4 June 1990; *Globe and Mail*, 4, 5 June 1990.

180 *Globe and Mail*, 5 June 1990; *Montreal Gazette*, 5 June 1990. The four-point plan was as follows:

- dissenting provinces to ratify Meech Lake by 23 June 1990;
- first ministers agree to a series of amendments, none of which would change Meech Lake: New Brunswick's bilingual character, a provision for public hearings on constitutional change, a shorter timetable for constitutional change, a commitment to have

aboriginal peoples represented at future constitutional talks, Senate evaluation of federal spending regarding equalization, the question of sexual equality;

- first ministers agree to Senate reform, eased process of creating provinces, and the federal "preserve and promote" clause;

- first ministers then to sort out the relation between the distinct society clause and the Charter, the rights of minorities, and the spending power.

181 *Globe and Mail*, 6 June 1990; *Montreal Gazette*, 6 June 1990.

182 *Globe and Mail*, 7 June 1990. The revised schedule would be as follows:

- remaining provinces ratify Meech Lake;

- Senate reform, the PEI plan;

- constitutional amendments *before* 23 June: aboriginal rights, territories' nomination rights, fisheries dropped from constitutional agenda, examination of federal government's equalization efforts;

- post-23 June: altered provisions for the creation of new provinces, a Canada clause, the amending formula.

183 *Globe and Mail*, 8, 9 June 1990.

184 *Globe and Mail*, 9 June 1990.

185 *Globe and Mail*, 11 June 1990; *Montreal Gazette*, 10 June 1990; *Toronto Star*, 10 June 1990; *Maclean's*, 18 June 1990.

186 *Toronto Star*, 10, 11 June 1990; *Globe and Mail*, 11 June 1990.

187 *Toronto Star*, 10, 11 June 1990; *Globe and Mail*, 11, 12 June 1990.

188 *Globe and Mail*, 9, 11 June 1990; *Toronto Star*, 10 June 1990; *Montreal Gazette*, 9 June 1990.

189 *Toronto Star*, 11 June 1990; *Montreal Gazette*, 11, 12 June 1990; *Globe and Mail*, 11, 12 June 1990.

190 *Globe and Mail*, 12, 13, 30 June 1990.

191 *Globe and Mail*, 13, 20, 22 June 1990.

192 Manitoba had organized a Meech Lake Task Force in 1989, but provincial laws required that a select committee of the legislature examine constitutional amendments. The select committee had not yet had the opportunity to hold public hearings, consider the constitutional amendments, and then report to the legislature.

193 *Globe and Mail*, 13 June 1990; *Montreal Gazette*, 13 June 1990; Pauline Comeau, "The Man Who Said No," *Canadian Forum*, July/August 1990.

194 For example, it was discovered that an addendum to the resolution setting up the process for public hearings was not properly attached to the order paper, and this required the granting of another two-day notice. As a result of another technical error, the government had neglected to establish a registration cut-off date for those wishing to speak at public hearings, who numbered in the thousands. A legal provision about French translation offered another opportunity for delay. Once legislation was finally introduced in the legislature on 20 June, three days before deadline, Harper refused the unanimous consent required to extend the hours for around-the-clock debate. See Comeau, "The Man Who Said No."

195 *Globe and Mail*, 15 June 1990; *Montreal Gazette*, 15 June 1990; Comeau, ibid.

196 *Globe and Mail*, 16 June 1990; *Montreal Gazette*, 16 June 1990; *Toronto Star*, 16 June 1990; Comeau, ibid.

197 The six part offer was:
- rapid setting of an agenda for an early first ministers' conference on aboriginal self-government;
- a commitment by Ottawa to support the full constitutional recognition of aboriginal people as part of the "fundamental characteristics of Canada";
- a promise to invite aboriginal representatives to a constitutional conference to define Canada's fundamental characteristics;
- a commitment to have native representatives participate in all constitutional conferences where matters affect them;
- establishment of joint definition of treaty rights;
- establishment of a Royal Commission on aboriginal issues.

198 House of Commons, *Debates*, 18 June 1990, 12866-70; *Globe and Mail*, 19 June 1990; *Montreal Gazette*, 19 June 1990.

199 *Globe and Mail*, 20 June 1990; *Toronto Star*, 20 June 1990; *Montreal Gazette*, 20 June 1990.

200 *Globe and Mail*, 22 June 1990.

201 Comeau, "The Man Who Said No."

202 Wells had been mooting for some time the cancellation of the Newfoundland vote. On 19 June he declared that "the simple fact is that this has been a very wrenching, emotional issue for a lot of people in Newfoundland, and if Manitoba makes it impossible for any decision to be made by 23 June, why would we keep pursuing it?" *Globe and Mail*, 20 June 1990; *Montreal Gazette*, 20 June 1990; *Toronto Star*, 20 June 1990.

203 *Globe and Mail*, 25 June 1990; *Montreal Gazette*, 23 June 1990.

204 *Globe and Mail*, 30 June, 23 May 1990.

205 *Globe and Mail*, 9 June 1990.

206 Banting and Simeon, *Redesigning the State: The Politics of Constitutional Change in Industrial Nations*, (Toronto: University of Toronto Press, 1985), 18.

207 Senate, *Debates*, 10 February 1988, 2739-42; see also A. Cairns, "Citizens (Outsiders) and Governments (Insiders) in Constitution-Making: The Case of Meech Lake," in *Canadian Public Policy*, XIV Supplement, September 1988, 121-45.

208 *Globe and Mail*, 11 June 1990. In the infamous "roll the dice" interview, though, Mulroney ridiculed the participatory approach:
> You will not be able to get me to ever cut off debate on a constitutional resolution. They can go on for as long as they want, years. I want to hear everybody. I want them recorded. I want them filmed. I want documents...and if I've missed anybody I'm going to reopen it...

209 On 2 December 1990 Mulroney announced the creation of a joint Senate-House of Commons panel to study the amending formula. *Globe and Mail*, 3 December 1990.

210 New Brunswick's Commission has nine members, four elected and five non-elected. Quebec has a thirty-six-member commission, which may doom the enterprise. Headed by two business executives, it contains twenty-two politicians (from seven political parties), seven corporate

representatives, six from unions and quasi-political groups, and one from the academic/cultural domain.

Alberta has also created a commission, but it is composed exclusively of members of the legislature, and all are Conservatives. Ontario was planning to devise a commission, before the defeat of the Peterson government in the September 1990 election.

The Spicer Commission is "an independent body of eminent Canadians who will launch a dialogue with people across the country and help create a new consensus about Canada...and our future...an initiative to promote a discussion among Canadians on the future of Confederation." It containes twelve members, none politicians, from across Canada and across walks of life. House of Commons, *Debates*, 1 November 1990, 15004, 15008.

211   I seriously thought that maybe I really was the problem and maybe if I left things would get easier.... Maybe there would be less antagonism if I resigned. I began to think: "Maybe it's me. Maybe I can't see any solution because my mind is rigid and I can't open it.... Am I being principled or stubborn."

Globe and Mail, 28 May 1990.

212   A. Lijphart, *Democracies* (New Haven: Yale University Press, 1984), 187-97.

213   K. von Beyme, *The Political System of the Federal Republic of Germany* (Aldershot: Gower Publishing, 1983), 13.

THE RISE AND FALL OF THE MEECH LAKE ACCORD

A BIG DEAL?
THE CANADA-US
FREE TRADE AGREEMENT

The Canada-US Free Trade Agreement, signed just minutes before the midnight deadline on 3 October 1987, was possibly the most contentious and complex policy initiative ever undertaken by a Canadian government. Initially about removing tariffs and other trade barriers between the two economies, the agreement quickly became the focus of a debate about the very nature of Canada. Over the two years it took to negotiate, and the additional year it took to become law, the agreement became the centre of several worlds of Canadian politics. It was debated by the provinces and the regions, and raised questions about the nature of economic development in the country as well as the provincial role in international trade negotiations. It was a catalyst for business-government relations, since Ottawa needed advice from industry experts on everything from auto parts to hog marketing. It dominated Canada's relations with the United States, and became the central focus of bilateral affairs for three years. It agitated virtually every constituency in the country, from women, pensioners, and economists to wine growers, auto workers, and poets. Finally, it became the only serious campaign issue in the 21 November 1988 federal election. Once it took effect on 1 January 1989, however, the agreement virtually evaporated from public view. Occasional public debates erupted over job losses and gains due to free trade, but the passion and engagement of the election campaign was rapidly displaced by bureaucratic management of technical detail. The public all but forgot about a policy initiative that might conceivably change Canada's economic destiny.

The 1988 federal election was one of the most dramatic in Canadian history. The Liberals under John Turner were headed for third-party status in the face of a Tory campaign that oozed unctuous blandness. Brian Mulroney, who only months ago had had the lowest popularity ratings of any Canadian government in polling history, suddenly had the support of 40 per cent of decided voters. Turner seized on the Free Trade Agreement (FTA) as his issue, charging that the Mulroney government was, through the deal, dismantling Canada's social programmes and ultimately, its sovereignty.

The strategy made desperate sense. The FTA had only been initialled by Mulroney and President Reagan on 2 January 1988. The Commons debate in the summer had been vituperative, but the Tories had used their crushing majority to ram it through. Turner and Allan MacEachan (Liberal majority Senate leader) announced in July that the Senate would not pass the deal without an election. Turner challenged Mulroney to "Let the people decide!" Although the pro-FTA and anti-FTA forces had been quiet for most of the year, Turner knew that he had the populists on his side: FTA support was concentrated in the business community, while opponents spanned the union movement, many cultural organizations, and farmers.

Turner also knew his history: Canadians had rejected versions of free trade with the United States in 1891 and 1911. In both of those elections, ironically, free trade had been championed by the Liberal Party, and in both the anti-free trade party (the Conservatives) had won. The last serious attempt to negotiate even a limited trade deal with the United States came in 1965, with the drafting of the *Agreement Concerning Automotive Products between the Government of Canada and the Government of the United States* (the Auto Pact). That also had been pushed by a Liberal government, and at the time had been quite unpopular. Since then Canadian governments had see-sawed between "industrial strategies" (assisting domestic Canadian industrial growth) and "third options" (trying to diversify trade ties to Europe). Behind all of these flawed attempts was the hard and disturbing reality of Canadian economic bondage to the United States: by 1987 over 76 per cent of Canadian exports went to the US, and about 70 per cent of our imports originated there. And behind that reality was an even more politically fundamental one: the lesson of Canadian history was that if given the clear choice of intimate ties with the United States or nationalism, Canadians would ultimately decide to preserve their culture and way of life. John Turner hoped that Brian Mulroney would stumble over this almost Newtonian law of Canadian elections.

He was wrong. On 21 November 1988, in what turned out to be the most volatile election in Canadian history, the Tories won 170 seats to the Liberals' 82 and the New Democrats' 43. The Tories had an absolute majority (the first time back-to-back majorities had been won since the 1950s, and the first consecutive Tory majorities since John A. Macdonald) with national representation, even

THE CANADA-US FREE TRADE AGREEMENT

from "anti-free trade" Ontario. The FTA would go through. The people had decided.

The free trade debate from 1985 to 1988 (and it is far from over in many respects) is a garish collage of contrasts and reversals, coiling its way through every conceivable issue of Canadian politics, entwining the opposing sides in an unwilling and ungainly duet. Traditionally the Liberals had been the party of free trade in Canada; in 1988 John Turner proclaimed his opposition to the deal as "the fight of my life." In 1983 Brian Mulroney opposed free trade with the United States; in 1985 he authorized negotiations. Ontario, the province that benefitted most from trade with the United States (especially the Auto Pact), proved to be the centre of resistance to the deal. Quebec, historically Ontario's partner in demanding tariff protection for central Canadian industry, strongly supported the deal. The deal itself, hundreds of pages and clauses long, heralded as the single most extensive trade agreement in history, was hammered out only hours before the deadline over buckets of cold chicken in a Washington office.

The politics of the FTA oozed into every pore of Canadian political life. It enflamed regionalism, touched on federal-provincial jurisdictional battles, involved the Quebec question, the place of women, the viability of culture, and the influence of the United States. It drilled directly into the nerve of Canada-United States trade policy, and since it held implications for international trade negotiations (through the General Agreement on Tariffs and Trade), Canada was the subject of discussion in Geneva, Bonn, and Tokyo. Cultural icons—Margaret Atwood, Pierre Berton, Adrienne Clarkson, Mordecai Richler, Harold Town, Morley Callaghan— weighed in for one side or another. The election campaign was marked by unprecedented "third party" (that is, non-political party) advertising for and against the deal. In the final days of the campaign, numbed Canadian voters could stare at more than half a dozen party and FTA ads in the morning paper.

The free trade story evolved in three phases. The first was the negotiations themselves, entered into in 1985 and actually conducted through 1986-87. This phase yielded a deal and a ferocious debate among the Canadian intelligentsia. Curiously, the Canadian public was never as aroused as the intellectuals were over the deal, and so the legislation to implement the FTA limped through Parliament and Congress in the dog days of August 1988. The Tory majority in the House of Commons ensured passage there, but the Liberals dominated the Senate and refused to pass the FTA legislation. The Prime Minister waited almost a month to be sure that the electorate was in the proper dozy mood to re-elect his government. The campaign drove the second phase. Antennae twitching to Turner's nationalist rhetoric, the electorate reared up and away from the Tories

THE CANADA-US FREE TRADE AGREEMENT

in a historic reversal of support. With mere days to go, the Tories engineered yet another reversal and won their majority. The subsequent implementation of the FTA is the third, somewhat anticlimactic, phase of the story. Some of the passion of 1988 carried over into 1989 in the debate over adjustment policies to deal with FTA-related job losses, but within months the entire issue seemed suffocated in the details of implementation.

In examining these three phases, this chapter develops three themes or perspectives on the real worlds of Canadian politics. The first is the political world of international and bilateral negotiations. The following section on the negotiations shows how matters of great national and international importance can be embarked upon with only fuzzy ideas and watery conviction. The second theme is the difficulty of coherently debating a deal as complex as the FTA. A review of the arguments on both sides, before and during the election, shows the weight of political symbols in questions even as apparently arcane as economic trading arrangements. Finally, the chapter throws light on how political actors—parties, interest groups, the media—manoeuvre around an issue as large and strategic as the FTA. At its height, the FTA debate was not normal politics: it was all or nothing, a gamble with the country's destiny. Ironically, for all the cataclysmic rhetoric of the election campaign, the post-election implementation of the FTA rarely made headlines. The great gamble taken, most Canadians seemed uninterested in how the dice would roll.

THE NEGOTIATIONS

Taking the Plunge: 1985

Arm in arm, President Ronald Reagan and Prime Minister Brian Mulroney crooned "When Irish Eyes Are Smiling" to the assembled audience at the gala put on for the President's visit to Quebec City on 17 March 1985, St. Patrick's Day. Dubbed the "Shamrock Summit," it was a meeting of two men united by more than traces of Irish blood. Reagan thanked God for Canada in one of his speeches, and Mulroney praised the President as personifying the "success and accomplishment of today's America."[1] They were men who obviously liked one another, who shared a vision of Canada and the United States amicably living in close and intimate relation on the North American continent. They also shared a belief, though in different measure, in the efficacy of market systems and the need to minimize, where possible and appropriate, the role of government in everyday life. In the 1984 general election, the closest thing Brian Mulroney had to a coherent foreign policy was the pledge to improve relations with the US.

Rumours had been leaked before the summit that one of its specific achievements would be a statement on trade. In the end, no one mentioned free trade or comprehensive trade, phrases sure to ring alarms in both countries, but the two leaders pledged to "halt protectionism." President Reagan went further and acceded to Mulroney's request that he go to bat for Canada against protectionist measures being considered in the American Congress. The 18 March 1985 statement appointed James Kelleher (Canada's minister for international trade) and William Brock (the US trade representative) to "chart all possible ways to reduce and eliminate existing barriers to trade."[2] They were to report in six months.

These initiatives did not originate with either Brian Mulroney or Ronald Reagan. The Liberal government of Prime Minister Pierre Trudeau, not noted for its warm relations with Reagan's America, had decided in 1983-84 to pursue some form of freer trade with the US. The Department of External Affairs reviewed the question in several discussion papers,[3] and in 1984 Gerald Regan, the Liberal minister for international trade, agreed to cooperate with William Brock on studies of the possibilities for freer trade in four areas: steel, farm equipment, urban mass transit equipment, and computer services. After the 1984 election, the Tories discovered that the Americans were no longer interested in this "sectoral approach." The rising American trade deficit had generated demands for protection, not free trade. The Tory government therefore decided to change tactics but keep the broader strategy the same: it would still try for better trade and assured export markets, but would be prepared to negotiate trade-offs *between* industries, so that losses in one might be offset by gains in another. This "comprehensive approach" was the only way to attract American interest.[4]

The Shamrock Summit had raised free trade as an issue without, however, providing any real indication of what Ottawa might do, how it might pursue negotiations, and what sorts of trade-offs it would be willing to contemplate. Thus the summer of 1985 was a season of fretting and fuming, of contradictory claims by various ministers, and of what to many seemed an ominous silence across the border. Shortly after the summit Brock was nominated for secretary of labor, and so the position of US trade representative went vacant for a time. President Reagan was preoccupied with other matters, and no one in Washington paid much attention to free trade with Canada. A US International Trade Commission report was leaked shortly after the summit, indicating that American industry would have little to fear from a deal with Canada, but the study was commissioned before the leaders had met and so had a narrow focus.[5] That left the debate to Canadians.

Despite the fact that at this point no one knew what the terms of a negotiated deal might be, the pro- and anti-free trade sides congealed rapidly and hardened that summer. Over the next two years, no matter what course the negotiations took or what was thought to be on the table, virtually no prominent spokespersons from either side ever changed their minds (Premier Bourassa of Quebec was a notable exception). Once committed to support or to oppose, people stayed committed. In some ways this made the Canadian debate over free trade predictable and tiresome, but it also gave it a hard and sometimes bitter edge.

Supporters emerged early. Premier Peter Lougheed of Alberta, who had been a proponent of free trade for some years, immediately began to urge the government to go ahead and strike a deal before the opportunity was lost. (He gauged that the US climate would be favourable for no more than six months, after which protectionist forces would carry the day.) The Canadian Chamber of Commerce, a broadly representative business lobby, presented a brief to the government in April urging negotiations on a comprehensive deal, but if that were not possible, then on a sectoral basis.[6] On 15 May, for the first time, the western premiers agreed to set aside their personal reservations and jointly proposed that Canada enter into free trade negotiations with Washington.[7] Even the NDP premier of Manitoba, Howard Pawley, agreed to send a telex to Ottawa, though he wanted safeguards such as a long and gradual implementation of any deal and government assistance to workers and industries adversely affected by it.[8] Provincial support gathered momentum, and at the August 1985 premiers' meeting in St. John's, all the provinces except Ontario asked for immediate free trade negotiations.[9] Canadian business was, with a few exceptions noted below, also in favour of negotiations.[10]

Opponents emerged early as well. Labour unions took only a few weeks to announce that free trade would be a national economic disaster. The Canadian Labour Congress (CLC) presented a brief to International Trade Minister Kelleher in May claiming that free trade with the US would cost one million Canadian jobs. Dick Martin, an executive vice-president of the CLC, said, "If we went down the road of free trade, many of the manufacturing plants now located in Canada would simply move to the United States because they could have access to both markets."[11] A month later CLC president Dennis McDermott added, "We will all be bloody Americans within the decade if this comes off."[12] Bob White, director of the Canadian Auto Workers (in 1985 it was still the Canadian branch of the United Auto Workers), echoed this sentiment by arguing that free trade would make Canadians less secure, cost jobs, and endanger sovereignty.[13]

Industrial sectors that guessed they would lose under a free trade deal also voiced criticisms early. The textile industry, located in Quebec and Ontario, has survived largely due to tariff protection against third world products, and so had reservations.[14] In August farmers represented by the Canadian Federation of Agriculture expressed their opposition to comprehensive free trade, on grounds that it would undermine Canada's system of marketing boards, supply management, and tariff protection for horticulture.[15] The Motor Vehicle Manufacturers Association and the Automotive Parts Manufacturers Association, together representing companies that account for 35 per cent of Canada-US trade, were distinctly unenthusiastic about free trade as well.[16]

The final core of early opposition to a deal was the Ontario government. Premier David Peterson, heading a Liberal minority government at the time, had good reason to be concerned. As a senior Ontario trade official told a special provincial committee commissioned in the summer to review bilateral trade, "Ontario would suffer considerably" under free trade.[17] As the country's industrial heartland, heavily dependent on the auto trade and with 90 per cent of its exports already going to the US, it was not clear how Ontario could gain through reduced tariffs. Premier Peterson took his reservations to St. John's for the premiers' meeting, but failed to convince his colleagues.

In Ottawa, the government kept its head down and tried to decide on a policy. International Trade Minister Kelleher's report on trade options to cabinet in June showed some strong support for free trade across the country, but drew back from recommending negotiations.[18] By late summer, however, it was clear that the Royal Commission on the Economic Union and Development Prospects for Canada, appointed by Pierre Trudeau in 1982, would recommend a free trade deal with the US. The Commission finally released its report on 5 September 1985. The report touched on virtually every aspect of Canadian public policy, but its centrepiece was a recommendation favouring free trade.[19] The Commission rejected the sectoral approach, and while it supported a comprehensive trade deal with the US, Donald Macdonald (chief commissioner) acknowledged that the issues were so complex, even after years of study, that this support required a "leap of faith." The report did not suggest immediate free trade without conditions, however. Any deal would have to be phased in over ten years, have protections for culture, ensure that both countries could maintain separate tax and customs regimes (with respect to third countries), cover non-tariff barriers, and have a binding dispute-resolution mechanism. It also suggested bi-national panels of arbitrators, as well as rules of origin to ensure that goods from third countries would not be diverted through either Canada or the United States, and enter the other country under low or no duty.

For the first time since the Shamrock Summit in March, there was something concrete to discuss. Prime Minister Mulroney had confused the issue all summer by talking at different times about "free trade," "freer trade," and "comprehensive trade." The Royal Commission report injected some clarity into the debate, and had dozens of volumes of research to back up its recommendations. The Tories saw their chance and took it. Four days after the report was made public, Brian Mulroney announced that the Canadian government had decided to negotiate and would inform Washington within a week.[20] That was in fact done on 26 September 1985, when Mulroney called the President and told him that Canada wanted to negotiate "the broadest possible package of mutually beneficial reductions in tariff and non-tariff barriers between our two countries."[21] The Canadian government had already made some preliminary preparations in giving External Affairs Minister Joe Clark ultimate responsibility for the talks,[22] and in appointing a permanent advisory committee headed by Walter Light, former chief of the Canadian electronics multinational Northern Telecom.[23]

These announcements were followed by several weeks of bobbing and weaving on what the negotiations would actually entail. This was in part because Canadian officials, with the exception of the Canada-US desk in External Affairs, were cool to the idea of free trade. The politicians were forcing the issue, and had to carry the bureaucrats along with them.[24] It was also in part because of the different approaches the two countries took to the talks. American spokespersons consistently urged the widest possible scope for the talks. Clayton Yeutter, the newly appointed US trade representative, remarked that "almost everything ought to be discussed" in the negotiations.[25] The US ambassador to Canada, Thomas Niles, was quoted shortly after as hoping that there could be a dispassionate discussion of such things as broadcasting, book publishing, magazines, cable television, and films.[26] The Canadian government was fuzzy about what it wanted from a deal, knowing only that it had to stand firm for all that was sacredly Canadian, from auto parts to the CBC. It had to assure Canadians that the negotiations would not compromise culture, sovereignty, or popular economic programmes, while it simultaneously assured the Americans that it was prepared to bargain in good faith. So, while Joe Clark admitted that some cultural industries, like book publishing, "might" be negotiated,[27] the Prime Minister later asserted that cultural industries were not on the bargaining table.[28] Their assurances were undermined by continued American statements that the talks would have to be wide open and include the Auto Pact, agriculture, social programmes, and subsidies.[29]

A further complication that fall was the Canada-US softwood lumber dispute. It heated up in mid-year, around Clayton Yeutter's nomination hearings as US trade representative, but extended back at least two years. Canadian lumber exports had grown steadily in the 1980s until they accounted for 31 per cent of the

American domestic market. Lumber producers in the northwest American states, under pressure, had already forced one review of Canadian pricing practices by the US Commerce Department's International Trade Administration (which found no special subsidies on Canadian lumber) in 1983. Pressure had continued on the Congress, however, to limit Canadian lumber imports. In October 1985 the US Trade Commission released a study of Canadian lumber that was widely interpreted in the US to show that Canadian stumpage fees (the fee that lumber producers pay to provincial governments for the right to cut publicly owned timber) were too low and constituted an unfair subsidy. Congress was thus in a belligerent mood, which did not bode well for an FTA. On the Canadian side, complaints about lumber imports were seen as proof that the Americans were not serious about real free trade, and would never allow Canada to compete in American markets. The lumber dispute continued to irritate Canada-US relations well into the next year.

Meanwhile, preparations on the Canadian side continued on two critical issues: who would head negotiations and what would the role of the provinces be? On 8 November the Prime Minister announced that Simon Reisman would be Canada's ambassador for the US trade talks.[30] Reisman, a private consultant, had a distinguished career as a civil servant, notably as chief negotiator in 1965 of the Canada-US Auto Pact and later as deputy minister of finance. He had *carte blanche* to pick his team from the ranks of the very best and brightest civil servants in Ottawa, and soon the Trade Negotiations Office (TNO) became the place to be in official Ottawa. The issue of provincial participation was thornier. Would the provinces only be "consulted" or would they be right there at the table with Reisman? At the First Ministers Conference in Halifax in late November, Mulroney agreed to the "principle of full provincial participation" but refused to say what that meant.[31] The provinces demanded power equal to Ottawa's, but Joe Clark claimed that the Halifax agreement applied only to the "preparatory phase" of the negotiations, that is, for the next three months. After that the Government of Canada would be in charge. The issue remained unresolved by year's end.

In all this time, since the Canadian request for trade talks, there had not been any official response from Washington. This was in part because of the congressional testiness over lumber. Finally, however, on 10 December Ronald Reagan sent a letter to two key congressional committees asking for authority to negotiate a deal with Canada. The committees had sixty working days to respond, and there was no reason to assume clear sailing, since at least one committee—the Senate Finance Committee, chaired by Robert Packwood of Oregon—had strong representation from northern lumber states.

Thus were the negotiations born. The birth was far from auspicious, however. The federal government had agonized for six months before committing itself, and even then seemed unsure what precisely would be on the table. The main lines of criticism of free trade with the US were firmly sketched out by December 1985. Their point was two-fold. Living next to the American elephant, Canadian culture had thrived only by virtue of special subsidies and special protection. The "Canadian way of life" was reflected in our choice of more costly and comprehensive social programmes. Free trade threatened to dismantle our social safety net. While the talks were broadly supported by business, especially large exporting sectors, the array of opponents was formidable: the NDP, the Liberals, most labour unions, the National Action Committee on the Status of Women, the newly formed Council of Canadians headed by Mel Hurtig, and the provinces of Ontario and Quebec (Premier Robert Bourassa defeated the *Parti québécois* in December, and expressed strong reservations about free trade). The CLC had refused to join the government's advisory committee on free trade.[32] Congressional sentiment, when it thought of Canada at all, was decidedly negative, and there were strong American lobbies (e.g., lumber, grain producers, steel, paper) that were prepared to oppose a deal with Canada. All of this had its effect on Canadian public opinion. Whereas in June 65 per cent of Canadians had favoured free trade with the US, at year's end support had dropped to 58 per cent and was strongest in the West and weakest in Ontario.[33] Free trade was shaping up as the most regionally and ideologically divisive issue in post-war Canadian history.

The Long Grind: 1986-87

In one sense, the agenda was now set: organize and negotiate. Simon Reisman met at the first opportunity in the new year with provincial trade officials,[34] and began to get his TNO together and operating. One part of this involved the industrial sector committees, with members from the private sector to advise the negotiating team. On 9 January 1986 the government announced thirty-eight appointees to the Advisory Committee, chaired by Walter Light. The Committee was to report directly to the international trade minister, but would work with Reisman to give him a sense of private-sector sentiments. Despite the boycott by the CLC, the government managed to appoint one labour representative, James McCambly, head of the 220,000-member Canadian Federation of Labour, the only labour union organization prepared to support free trade. Still to come in April was the appointment of fourteen industry committees to provide specific advice, sector by sector.

The other part of Reisman's task was to build his own team of negotiators in the TNO. Reisman was in an enviable position. In contrast to the American team, which came to be headed by a mid-level official reporting to the US trade representative, Reisman had the direct support of the Prime Minister. Moreover, he knew the Ottawa ropes, had substantial prestige within the federal bureaucracy, and was permitted to skim the cream of the mandarinate for the TNO. The TNO was the sole negotiating body, and so did not have to deal with other departments and agencies trying to protect their own mandates. Reisman even succeeded in having Sylvia Ostry, the ambassador for multilateral trade, report to him.[35] This was important, since there were several departments in the federal government that were skeptical of the trade talks. External Affairs was miffed that its key role in matters of this type had been usurped, and the Department of Regional Industrial Expansion was also unhappy because it felt that free trade might undermine regional development programmes. The TNO was to have been a lean, tight operation, but as senior people were recruited by Reisman, they brought some of their own with them, and the organization soon grew to over one hundred people.

While Reisman prepared, the government also took some action. International Trade Minister Kelleher revealed a new aggressiveness in the government's attitude to its critics: he noted that the Tories had decided early in the game to turn the other cheek, but that this had not noticeably muted the criticisms coming from labour or the Ontario government. Free trade opponents were noisy, emotional, and wrong, said Kelleher.[36] This was followed only days later by what was now becoming a routine of ritualized denials that certain things were on the bargaining table. External Affairs Minister Joe Clark told the House of Commons that agricultural marketing boards would not be up for discussion.[37] (Marketing boards set quotas in the production of things like eggs and chickens, thereby raising prices to consumers and assuring a return to producers.) As part of the new strategy to win support, the government adopted a publicity plan in early February that involved circulating thousands of copies of a glossy, one-hundred-page book on free trade, as well as sending cabinet members on speaking tours.[38] In an effort to defuse claims that an FTA would leave thousands of workers unemployed, the Prime Minister promised on open-line radio in Montreal that any deal would be accompanied by re-training programmes for unemployed workers.[39]

By March the Prime Minister had to turn his attention to the US; if the American Congress turned down the President's request to negotiate a free trade deal, the whole initiative would die. The President had requested congressional approval for a "fast track" process, whereby any deal signed between Canada and the United States would be voted upon as a whole by the Congress, not clause by clause. This was critical, since it would increase the odds of clean passage through the complex congressional system. Requests of this sort to Congress have a sixty-day limit; if the Senate and House committees did not grant the President's request to proceed on a fast track, then the whole issue would have to go before legislative committees for hearings. Reagan and Mulroney both wanted to avoid this, but the Congress was pressuring the administration for action on Canada-US trade irritants, such as lumber, before acceding to free trade talks. The sixty-day limit expired on 21 April. Mulroney visited Washington in March, and lobbied hard with congressional leaders and the President—though he avoided a joint address to Congress, on the advice that the situation was too delicate and easily inflamed.

Mulroney had no success in turning the tide, in part because trade issues had tied Washington into knots for the last year. Congressional elections were scheduled for the fall of 1986, and so American legislators were extremely sensitive to protectionist pressures coming from all quarters in the face of a mounting US trade deficit. The Reagan administration was committed to free markets and philosophically opposed to protection through higher tariffs or other measures. This put Reagan at odds with Congress. Moveover, there had been some tensions within the administration on how to handle free trade talks with Canada. The chief American negotiator, Peter Murphy, had not been appointed until mid-February. Only thirty-seven years old, facing a much more experienced Reisman, Murphy's credentials came essentially from negotiating textile agreements in Geneva.[40] Murphy did not have Reisman's latitude or his seniority: he reported to Clayton Yeutter, the US trade representative, and had to borrow staff on a temporary basis from other government departments. To complicate matters further, the US Treasury Department had less than complete trust in Murphy, and insisted that it handle banking and financial negotiations itself.[41] The Americans were united on one thing, however. If negotiations were to proceed, they would not exempt anything at the outset, be it culture or agriculture. This had been a consistent posture over the previous months. As well, any hopes that a deal would include an exemption for Canada from US countervails were discouraged.[42]

These American tensions blew up forcefully and surprisingly when, less than two weeks before the deadline, ten of the members of the Senate Finance Committee said that they would vote against opening talks with Canada.[43] The Committee members were less irritated with Canada than with the President, who had rejected calls for protectionist trade legislation. The core of the opposition came from senators representing lumber states, but the trade deal provided a convenient excuse to roast the administration for its policies. Canada began a lobbying campaign, but the key efforts would have to be made by the US administration. On 14 April several members of Reagan's cabinet met to discuss options, and Clayton Yeutter and his staff began to contact senators. The Canadian ambassador to Washington, Allan Gotlieb, dispatched his embassy officials, and several American industry associations (e.g., National Association of Manufacturers, the US Chamber of Commerce, and the National Foreign Trade Council) began to lobby in favour of a deal as well.[44] Tension increased as the administration seemed unable to change senators' minds before the crucial vote on 17 April. At the eleventh hour, the administration did succeed in having the vote postponed by a week.[45] The President contacted the senators who opposed the deal, and backed his phone calls with a letter wherein he stated that he would consult the senators during the talks, and most importantly, try to resolve the lumber dispute with Canada.[46] Reagan also made it clear that if the Senate Finance Committee voted down a deal, he would simply submit another request.[47] In a tortuous cliff-hanger, the vote was again postponed until 23 April, the last possible day for a Committee decision. In a dramatic, last-minute development, Senator Sparky Matsunaga of Hawaii switched his vote to favour talks, resulting in a 10-10 vote on 23 April. American Senate rules state that a tie is as good as a win, and so the fast-track option was approved.

The President's letter contained a "wish list" that became the negotiating instructions for Peter Murphy: (1) no special exemption for Canada under US trade remedy legislation, (2) a deal on government procurement, (3) access to Canadian service markets, (4) comparable treatment of intellectual property rights and investment, and (5) guarantees that provinces would abide by an agreement.[48] Peter Murphy later emphasized that the Americans wanted to throw everything open to discussion, including the Auto Pact, medicare, and unemployment insurance, and that any trade deal would have to contain concessions from the provinces.[49]

The Canadian side moved quickly as well, once the Senate had cleared the way for negotiations. Within several days, International Trade Minister Kelleher had named the heads of the fourteen Sectoral Advisory Groups on International Trade (SAGITs) to assist Reisman. The SAGITs gave the TNO some crucial insights into key business sectors, but also reflected the symbiotic relationship that had grown up between the free trade negotiators and Canadian business. (The SAGITs were modelled on American committees that had been established in the 1970s to advise the US government on trade matters.) Canadian labour had been against the FTA from the very beginning, and now was frozen out of the negotiations.

THE CANADA-US FREE TRADE AGREEMENT

If unions deliberately remained outside the negotiating process, the provinces wanted desperately to be part of it. Ottawa wanted to be in control of the negotiations, but at the same time needed provincial cooperation for the implementation of aspects of the deal that might affect provincial jurisdiction. In March nine of the provinces (excepting Ontario) presented a proposal to the Prime Minister. They wanted to be regularly briefed by Reisman, and have access to data and sensitive strategic plans and the right to advise on issues of provincial jurisdiction.[50] When the American Senate Finance Committee narrowly passed President Reagan's request for fast-track negotiations, Mulroney could no longer waffle on the problem of provincial participation. At a private buffet dinner in a cabinet room in the Centre Block of the House of Commons on 2 June, Mulroney and the premiers met to determine how the power would be shared. The Prime Minister agreed to consult the provinces every three months on the progress of negotiations.[51]

It was a difficult meeting for Mulroney. The premiers' support for the FTA had been shaken in previous months by Ottawa's refusal to consider the power-sharing issue, but most fundamentally by American trade actions. The lumber dispute had been boiling in the background through the Senate Committee deliberations, and the President took action in late May by slapping a 35 per cent duty on imports of Canadian shakes and shingles.[52] Almost simultaneously, the House of Representatives passed an omnibus trade bill that would define Canadian timber-pricing practices as subsidies. The US east coast fishing industry succeeded in getting tariff protection against Canadian fish, and American officials began to prepare an appeal under the GATT of provincial liquor policies.[53] Canada's currency was trading at 30 per cent below the US dollar, giving Canadian exporters an advantage in US markets. A mood of protectionism and resentment against Canada was becoming evident, just on the eve of the free trade talks. For the government's supporters, this was proof that an FTA needed to be signed immediately; for critics, it showed that Ottawa was not in control of its agenda, and that it was being softened up for concessions.

With the provinces now in line, Mulroney moved to shore up political support among the populace. Opposition to the trade talks had not changed its character or any of its arguments, but it had intensified considerably over the year and improved its organization. The Council of Canadians was formed explicitly to fight the free trade deal (many of its members were from the former Committee for an Independent Canada, formed in the 1970s to attack foreign/American ownership of the Canadian economy). A Toronto Coalition Against Free Trade was formed with membership from the United Church, the Canadian Council of Churches for Global Economic Justice, the National Action Committee for the Status

THE CANADA-US FREE TRADE AGREEMENT

of Women, the Canadian Confederation on the Arts, and several labour unions. Some prominent public figures also lent their names to this group at a 17 March rally against free trade at Massey Hall in Toronto: Pierre Berton (author), Bishop Remi de Roo (head of the Canadian Conference of Catholic Bishops), David Suzuki (broadcaster), Bob White (leader of the Canadian Auto Workers), and Bruce Cockburn (singer). The union movement kept up its opposition as well. The Auto Workers handed out kits on free trade to their fourteen thousand members in February, and the Ontario Federation of Labour launched a province-wide campaign against free trade in the same month. The CLC followed with a national campaign at the end of April. In the face of this, and polls that showed support for free trade among the general population was soft to begin with, Mulroney took to the airwaves. On 16 June, the evening before the negotiators sat down in Washington to start formal talks, Mulroney made a televised address to the nation. This was the first such address since his election in 1984. He spoke for fifteen minutes, conceding that the talks would "not be easy or without risk" but that if successful, the FTA would "provide jobs and greater prosperity for the country."[54]

The talks thus began in Washington under far less auspicious circumstances than one might have predicted even six months earlier. The US Senate had shown itself to be irascible and touchy on trade questions, and in a protectionist mood. The President had two years left in his term, and the extraordinary efforts he had expended simply to extract a tie vote from the Senate Finance Committee cast doubt on his ability to carry the FTA through Congress later. Opposition to the deal in Canada had not declined. It had grown in strength and visibility, to the point where virtually no organized sector except large and medium-sized business supported it wholeheartedly. Ontario still had strong reservations, and even the western premiers had groused about their role in the negotiations. Finally, Simon Reisman's personal style irritated almost everyone. In a curious reversal of stereotypes, Peter Murphy, the quiet, youthful, and soft-spoken American negotiator, seemed more "Canadian" than the cigar-chomping, tough-talking, touchy Reisman. As one commentator put it, Reisman was the best Canadian to negotiate with the Americans, but not the best to deal with Canadians.

The first formal negotiating session was on 17 June 1986. (Reisman and Murphy had had a preliminary meeting in Ottawa on 21 May, but that was simply to get acquainted and plan the bargaining sessions.) Once again, American officials emphasized the range of possible issues: anything could and should be brought up, from medicare to the CBC, and nothing should be exempted at the outset. Peter Murphy insisted that the Auto Pact and social programmes might be on the agenda for the talks,[55] even while the Prime Minister was defending himself in the Commons for not once having used the phrase "free trade" in his address to the nation.[56] In talking to reporters after their meetings, Murphy and Reisman gave widely different interpretations of what was on the table.

The teams met a total of seven times in 1986, discussing different issues at each meeting. Their third meeting (29-31 July) focused on agriculture and US trade protection law. The fourth (9-11 September) treated government procurement. The fifth (24-26 September) marked the end of "exploratory sessions" during which the two teams simply raised issues for discussion and review. Subsequent meetings were to involve real negotiations, but discussion went more slowly than anticipated. The sixth meeting, 12-14 November, consisted of a review of the previous five meetings and of the work undertaken by ten working groups and two fact-finding committees established in earlier talks.[57] The seventh and final meeting took place in Washington over 16-18 December.

The 1986 meetings were largely exploratory, and since they were secret, there was no indication of any progress on negotiating an FTA. There were several broad developments in the talks and around them, however, that suggested that they might eventually founder by the October 1987 deadline. First, the Americans seemed less than completely committed, serious, or sensitive about the talks. This had been shown in various ways, from the difficulties encountered in the Senate Finance Committee to the appointment of Peter Murphy, a junior official, to conduct the talks. Moreover, there had been the shakes-and-shingles episode, and threats to impose a tariff on lumber. Reisman had a larger staff, more authority, and better analytical support than Murphy, suggesting differing priorities on the two sides. Second, there were continuing disputes about what actually was on the table. The Prime Minister shied away from describing his goal as "free trade," and Reisman shifted ground several times on whether or not the talks actually included social programmes and the Auto Pact. After several months of insisting that the Auto Pact would not be open for negotiation, Reisman changed his mind in November and said if it were raised by the US, then it would be reviewed.[58]

Third, there were emerging tensions on the Canadian side between Reisman and other senior officials. Pat Carney had replaced James Kelleher as international trade minister in the summer, and proceeded to centralize political authority for the trade talks. Carney cut Reisman's direct route to the Prime Minister and had him report to her. Sylvia Ostry, Canada's ambassador to GATT, chaffed at having Reisman as her boss. Reisman, in turn, resented the fishbowl within which he had to operate. The free trade talks were irritating because the media were circling like piranhas for any slips, the provinces wanted constant consultations, and interest groups across the country were pouncing on every stray remark to show that Reisman was selling Canada down the river.[59]

THE CANADA-US FREE TRADE AGREEMENT

A fourth pessimistic factor was the softwood lumber dispute that erupted in October. A decision on Canadian pricing practices had been pending for some months, but few people expected the American government to slap a 15 per cent duty on imports of Canadian lumber. Canada's lumber exports to the US amounted to $4 billion annually, and the duty threatened to cut up to five thousand Canadian jobs and reduce imports by $500 million.[60] Pat Carney vowed to "fight this all the way," and the Prime Minister promised "strong and vigorous action." Both, however, continued to support the trade talks as a mechanism for arriving at a deal that would avoid such disputes in the future. The essence of the American case was that provincial pricing policies, particularly with respect to stumpage, were artificially low and thus constituted a subsidy for Canadian producers compared to competitors in the domestic American market. Ottawa had anticipated this decision in September, and with the provinces had offered a deal to the Americans whereby stumpage fees would increase, but by less than 15 per cent. Canada made repeated offers to raise its own domestic taxes (and thereby achieve the same effect as a duty, but keeping the increased tax revenues in Canada), but the dispute was unresolved by year's end.

Virtually none of the news was good for free trade proponents in 1986. The Economic Council of Canada released a study in October claiming that a free trade deal with the US would create 370,000 jobs in Canada, but the methodology was suspect and the conclusions were overshadowed in any case by the grim war of words over lumber.[61] Congressional elections in November brought Democratic majorities to both the House of Representatives and the Senate, promising to complicate the President's efforts to push trade liberalization policies through (the Democratic Party is traditionally more protectionist than the Republican Party). The federal Tories had reeled from trade crisis to trade crisis, the Prime Minister had failed to sell the message, and Simon Reisman appeared be getting nowhere with Murphy. With the deadline less than a year away, the odds seemed heavily stacked against a deal.

The first six months of 1987 cast further doubts over the eventual success of talks. Canada resolved the softwood lumber dispute by agreeing to tax itself in the amount of the proposed duty. Public confidence in the government's negotiating skills was eroding, and so Pat Carney launched a $12 million publicity programme in January to trumpet the benefits of an FTA with the US.[62] Further doubts were raised when Peter Murphy, contradicting the US ambassador's assurances, claimed once again that the Auto Pact was on the negotiating agenda. Simon Reisman called Murphy's remarks "mischievous,"[63] while Premier Peterson of Ontario immediately announced that the Auto Pact was untouchable, hinting that he would fight a provincial election on the issue.[64] Peterson was not the only premier to claim some ultimate right of approval over the FTA: a month later, Premier Bourassa of Quebec reminded the federal government that a "ratification formula" for the FTA should be devised that would give Quebec a veto.[65]

The Canadian free trade debate continued to obey the demarcations set the previous year. One development was an attempt to rally pro-free trade opinion in the form of the Canadian Alliance for Trade and Job Opportunities, founded by former Alberta premier Peter Lougheed and former royal commission chief Donald Macdonald. Others behind the scheme included Thomas d'Aquino (president of the Business Council on National Issues), Darcy McKeough (former treasurer of Ontario and businessman), and David Culver (chairman of the Business Council on National Issues and president of Alcan Aluminum Ltd.).[66] The group's founders demonstrated again that the core support for free trade came from Canada's business class. In contrast, the Pro-Canada Network, formed in April by the now ubiquitous Mel Hurtig, was an umbrella for over twenty-five anti-free trade groups and organizations, including the National Federation of Nurses Unions, the Canadian Teachers Federation, the National Farmers Union, the Canadian Auto Workers, the CLC, and the Association for Native Development in the Performing Arts.[67] In May the Pro-Canada Network's sister organization, the Council of Canadians, published a full-page ad proclaiming "Free Trade Isn't Free. It Costs Your Independence" and asking readers whether they would "stand on guard for Canada."[68]

The federal government responded in March with the first specific list of things Canada wanted from a deal. An FTA must have a method for dealing with trade remedy legislation such as countervails and anti-dumping provisions, must gradually reduce tariffs, and must address non-tariff barriers. Any deal would have to exempt Canadian regional development policies.[69] The announcement was coupled with a government motion in the House of Commons to support bilateral trade talks with the US. The motion, which called for talks as "part of the Government's multilateral trade policy, while protecting our political sovereignty, social programmes, agricultural marketing systems, the auto industry and our unique cultural identity,"[70] was passed 160-58 on 17 March. Both opposition parties voted against it.

The negotiations proceeded under these somewhat strained circumstances. They got off to a rough start with the dispute over whether the Auto Pact was to be included in the deal, and then sank into a murk of working groups and "fact finding" through the early winter, to resurface for public attention in April. By this point Canada's main objectives had emerged, in part because of the lumber dispute and in part because of the omnibus trade legislation that was working its way through Congress. Canada wanted "national treatment" (firms and goods from the other country would be treated the same as domestic firms and goods). Canada also wanted a binding dispute-resolution system that would protect it from American trade remedy legislation. Canada wanted protection for cultural industries. Finally, and this was something that Simeon Reisman pushed for, Canada wanted to develop a subsidies code, that is, a register of those government actions that could be considered "subsidies" to firms, and some procedure for deciding on the fair application of subsidies. On the US side, a key demand now was some exemption from or relaxation of Canadian investment laws that restricted foreign ownership.[71] As Reisman put it, these were "big rocks to move," particularly since investment had not originally been on the table, and Pat Carney had not given Reisman a mandate to negotiate the question. But the Americans could use the investment chip to bargain against Canadian demands for some sort of dispute-resolution mechanism.[72] By the end of May, the talks had reached a log-jam, with the Canadians unwilling to give anything on investment without something from the Americans on dispute settlement, and the Americans demanding wide-open talks on investment before they considered anything else.[73]

Canadian frustrations with the talks led the Prime Minister to go up a level and lobby the President directly in early June at the world economic summit in Venice.[74] The President platitudinously praised the benefits of free trade, but it was clear that while Ronald Reagan supported the general concept of an FTA with Canada, he had hardly staked his political career on a deal. Prime Minister Mulroney had. The FTA was now the centrepiece of Ottawa's economic policy, and the next election would probably be fought over it. The original idea had been to get better access, but with barely four months to go the Americans were now demanding concessions in areas that cut very close to nationalist interests: investment, finance, services, and the Auto Pact. The negotiators dealt with some of these issues in the June meeting, but were far from resolving them. What at first had seemed weaknesses in Murphy's authority now became negotiating advantages: he could constantly harp on the political difficulties he would face in Congress in selling a deal that wasn't satisfactory from an American point of view.[75]

Despite being assured of getting a deal through the House of Commons because of his majority, Mulroney had his own difficulties with the provinces. On July 7 the premiers and the Prime Minister met to hear Reisman go through a preliminary version of what the deal might include.[76] The premiers, in particular Bourassa of Quebec, Pawley of Manitoba, and Peterson of Ontario, were concerned about the short time remaining to hammer out a deal (less than ninety days) and the paucity of information.[77] The premiers emerged from their seven-hour meeting united in support of Ottawa's demand that the deal include a binding settlement mechanism, though they remained sceptical and worried about the likelihood of getting a deal before the deadline.[78] On hearing of this, American senators John Danforth (Rep., Missouri) and Lloyd Bensten (Dem., Texas), both key members of the Senate Finance Committee, said that such a dispute mechanism would never get through the Congress. The US would never give up its sovereignty to apply trade remedy legislation to some quasi-judicial administrative body.[79] Administration officials later supported this view, and so the dispute-settlement mechanism quickly emerged as a major impediment to any deal.

The talks were deteriorating. The teams met in Ottawa on 19 July for what was supposed to be three days of discussion. Murphy left after half a day. After several more short meetings, the teams decided to get together for a week-long marathon session to try to merge drafts of a deal. About twenty Canadians and fifty Americans went to a government training centre in Cornwall, Ontario, each with a draft version of an agreement about one hundred pages long. They were expecting to work hard, but virtually each of the key issues—government procurement, investment restrictions, services, transportation, subsidies, and dispute resolution—was approached differently in each of the drafts.[80] The results were disappointing: while both Reisman and Murphy claimed that they were a bit closer to a deal at the end of the week, Reisman mused that perhaps, in the end, it would require a meeting of the President and Prime Minister to resolve the outstanding issues.[81]

Eight months of negotiations had produced nothing but more clarity on where the sides disagreed. In the beginning, it seemed that the Canadian team would run circles around the smaller and less experienced American one. By August, Murphy looked cool and non-committal; Reisman had acquired the image of an irritable and frustrated bulldog, straining at the Prime Minister's leash. Moreover, a whole set of completely unanticipated issues had been placed on the table by the Americans. The Canadian team had set its sights so high, with demands for a dispute-resolution mechanism and a subsidies code, that only major concessions could even begin to attract American interest. Public support for the talks was sliding, despite millions of PR dollars spent by Ottawa, and the deadline was only six weeks away.

Crisis and Decision: September-October 1987

The Canadian government knew that the talks would collapse without some high-level interventions from the administration. That had been the rationale behind Mulroney's earlier visit to Washington and the meeting with President Reagan in Venice in June. In September the Tories decided to focus the efforts of two senior ministers, Joe Clark (External Affairs) and Michael Wilson (Finance) on the powerful Economic Policy Council, a cabinet-level committee that gave Peter Murphy his orders.[82] The Council was chaired by Secretary of the Treasury James Baker, whom Wilson would see in Washington during the meetings of the International Monetary Fund. The Americans were reluctant to politicize the negotiations, holding to their view that any deal would have to stand on its commercial merits. Nonetheless, Ambassador Gotlieb and his people began to make the rounds in Washington to line up support for the talks. Trade Minister Carney was suddenly invisible, indicating that the Prime Minister had lost confidence in her ability to shepherd the deal along. Mulroney had even taken over from Carney the chairing of the cabinet committee to which Reisman reported.

These efforts at political interventions signalled desperate pessimism on the Canadian side. The first ministers met on 14 September, and Mulroney admitted that while a deal was possible, "Canadian concerns have not been, in our judgment, appropriately addressed in some important areas."[83] Provincial scepticism had increased (though Premier Bourassa had become a strong supporter of a deal). A sign that the pressure was beginning to wear away Ottawa's resolve was the decision by cabinet to offer the Americans a compromise on investment provisions. Reisman proposed to "grandfather" current investment provisions (exempting current laws from the deal), give new American investments national treatment, and raise the threshold for government review. The Canadian team would also, for the first time, discuss the Auto Pact.[84] Despite this new brief to make some progress on key issues, the sides remained far apart on the major ones of investment (the Americans wanting free entry without restrictions) and disputes (the Canadians wanting a binding tribunal).

The "make-or-break" meeting came a few weeks later in Washington, on 21 September. So crucial was this meeting, with only two weeks to go before the deadline, that Michael Wilson and Derek Burney (the Prime Minister's principal secretary) flew to Washington to join Allan Gotlieb and James Baker, the US secretary of the treasury. This was a purely political meeting designed to take stock of the negotiations and determine what the consequences of failure would be. This intervention was to be secret, and showed again the Canadian penchant for trying to apply political muscle to the bargaining process.[85] But the political indications were that the Americans would never accept a "binding" dispute-resolution mechanism, that is, a system whereby some joint panel would make final and binding decisions about the propriety of countervails or anti-dumping actions. Something "softer" would have to be proposed if the deal was to be saved.[86]

Reisman and his team went to Washington, then, to argue a weak case. They had already made some compromise proposals on investment; they now had to deal with the auto trade, and they might have to retreat on the dispute-resolution mechanism. This gave Murphy all the room he needed. After three days of bargaining, Reisman was obviously strained and tense. At one point, on the third day, he blew up with the press, saying that it did not have "any respect for the truth."[87] The next morning Reisman stunned those same reporters by calling off the talks. His prepared statement said that he was "suspending" the talks, but in answering questions later, he was more blunt: "As far as I am concerned, it's over." Negotiations would begin again only if the Americans "were to come and belly up to the bar and do what they need to do to give us a good agreement for Canada."[88] The main impediment had been the dispute-resolution mechanism, which by now had become the key Canadian requirement for a deal. The American counter-proposal had retained the supremacy of American trade law, precisely the point that troubled the Canadian side.

As Reisman briefed the Cabinet that evening on returning from Washington, the country buzzed with speculation. Had Simon been outfoxed, and simply given up in exasperation? Had he arrived at a careful judgment that the Americans were not serious about negotiating? Had the whole thing been a charade, to capture attention in Washington, force a political confrontation, and perhaps lay the groundwork for a face-saving termination of the talks by Ottawa?

The talks were suspended on Wednesday, 23 September. The next day there were "high-level" communications to work around the suspension. There were no concrete results, but the Americans appeared to show a more conciliatory attitude. Certainly, Reisman's walk-out had captured attention at the highest levels. Secretary Baker and trade representative Yeutter briefed the President on the problems, including Canada's insistence that the deal include rules on dumping, countervails, and subsidies, as well as effective dispute-resolution machinery.[89] But time was slipping away. On Friday evening, Baker called the Prime Minister's Office to explore ways of getting back to the table. The Americans wanted to get back first, before putting anything new on the table. The Canadian response was that there was no point in going back until there was some evidence of movement on the US side.

Calls continued frantically over the weekend, and by Sunday morning a deal was struck for a meeting in Washington between Michael Wilson, Pat Carney, and Derek Burney for the Canadian side, and James Baker and Clayton Yeutter on the American side. The Canadian delegation arrived on Monday afternoon, 28 September, only one week before the deadline for the talks at midnight, 3 October. The Canadian view was that this was not a resumption of negotiations, but simply an exploration to see if negotiations should be resumed.[90] The meeting had been scheduled to last two hours, but stretched to over seven. While some progress was made on the dispute mechanism issue, more problems arose later over the question of defining subsidies.[91] Nonetheless, after a full day of cabinet meetings, Pat Carney announced on Tuesday, 29 September, that it was worth consulting further on opening up talks again.

The long-distance bills mounted as the two sides continued to talk by phone. Finally, Clayton Yeutter, alarmed at the approaching deadline, asked for face-to-face talks. On Thursday, 1 October, Wilson, Carney, and Burney flew back to Washington. Technically, these were not "trade talks," just political negotiations preliminary to any talks between Reisman and Murphy, but everyone knew that this was the level at which a deal would be made or broken. The delegation went and returned the same day without having made progress. The talks seemed finally and irrevocably finished. Then, another phone call: Washington was finally proposing to accept the principle of a bi-national panel to resolve disputes, and on Friday, 2 October, the Prime Minister and cabinet decided to gamble and re-open the talks. Mulroney met with the premiers that same day, and received their blessing to try to strike a deal.[92]

Reisman and his staff flew back to Washington for the start of a complicated and risky bargaining marathon. The political-level negotiations were still underway, with Wilson and Baker addressing the permissible political trade-offs, and passing along compromises to the teams of officials for technical drafting. At the same time, administration officials kept in touch with key Senate players to ensure that any compromises could survive congressional committees. By Saturday night, only hours from the midnight deadline, 90 per cent of the outstanding issues had been resolved, but the question of a dispute-resolution mechanism was still open. The American proposal was turned down by the cabinet, and the Canadian delegation began to pack its bags. Over fried chicken in James Baker's office, senior Canadian officials expressed sadness at having come so close and failed. Pat Carney claims that Baker studied the American proposal and the Canadian one, walked out of his office and down the hall, and told his lawyers to be creative. "That was the moment. They finally understood we were not going to sign the agreement and then they improved their offer."[93] In exchange for his concessions on the dispute mechanism, Baker won Canadian concessions on investment and financial services, and an unexpected clause on energy (see Appendix I for details). At 11:40pm, a mere twenty minutes from the deadline, the deal was initialled by both sides. The most comprehensive bilateral trade agreement in history had come in just under the wire.

THE CANADA-US FREE TRADE AGREEMENT

The next few days were ones of confused and sometimes bitter reactions. Few had seen the text of the deal, and in any case there were some inconsistencies between the American version and the Canadian one. Moreover, the agreement initialled on October 3 had no official status; it needed to be put into more precise legal language. The opposition parties, without having seen the text of the agreement, complained that it had put Canadian sovereignty on the line.[94] Representatives of the cultural industries expressed concerns about the deal, though some surprise as well that it seemed to exempt them from at least the investment provisions. Bob White of the Canadian Auto Workers said that the deal destroyed the heart of the Auto Pact, and Ontario Premier Peterson warned that it would take a lot of persuading to bring him on side. (A surprising aspect of the FTA was that it did not require provincial approval. The only section that directly affected provincial jurisdiction pertained to wine, and the FTA's provisions were not much different from the GATT's.)

The next few months were marked by both the comedic and the absurd, as though Canadians, in forcing themselves to be serious about an issue as big and risky as the FTA, had to let loose a burst of silliness to break the tension. Three days after the deal was signed, the Prime Minister intoned that it would be supplemented by a "massive" retraining programme to help dislocated workers. The next day, the Minister of Finance remarked that he saw no need for any significant readjustment programmes. Remarkably, the Canadian public remained on the whole serenely uninterested in the issue, and among those who knew anything about it at all, support had been sagging steadily.[95] Perhaps this was why the government decided to have a Commons committee hold hearings across the country on the deal and report to the House before the text of the deal itself was available. These lighter moments were marred by the rising bitterness of the emerging debate over the FTA. Bob White and his Auto Workers took out full-page ads decrying the "sale of Canada" and Simon Reisman replied by charging that FTA opponents were using Nazi "Big Lie" techniques to brainwash the Canadian public.[96] In testimony to the Commons committee, Margaret Atwood, an opponent of the deal, noted that "our national animal is the beaver, noted for its industrious habits and its cooperative spirit. In medieval bestiaries it is also noted for its habit, when frightened, of biting off its own testicles and offering them to its pursuer. I hope we are not succumbing to some form of that impulse."[97]

The final text of the agreement had still to be negotiated, and so Reisman and Murphy started meeting again in mid-October, shooting for a November deadline. Unsurprisingly, the dispute-settlement mechanism raised problems from the start, once negotiators tried to figure out whether the bi-national panel should be the only route of appeal in countervail cases.[98] The American shipping industry was lobbying for an exemption from the deal, and there were questions about the revisions to the Auto Pact. Reisman refused to be hurried, saying that he was not going to "leave any nickels on the table." The negotiations stretched through November and past the first ministers' meeting to consider the FTA. The Prime Minister and premiers therefore had to discuss the FTA without seeing the final text. Three premiers—Peterson (Ontario), Pawley (Manitoba), and Ghiz (PEI)—rejected the agreement. Brian Mulroney, arguing that the country could not be run by committee, pledged to move forward with the FTA as soon as a final text became available.

The negotiators met again on 1 December, and continued to wrangle over shipping and auto trade.[99] The next day they had a gruelling fourteen-hour meeting, but in a replay of their September talks, both negotiators emerged grimly to say that they had hit an impasse. Good will was rapidly evaporating as both sides blamed the other for holding up a final agreement. The talks broke off and were re-scheduled for the next week. Pressures mounted on the American administration to exempt shipping from the deal, since the US shipping industry feared that Canadian vessels were more competitive.[100] Finally, after two days of almost non-stop bargaining, the teams completed the final text of the FTA on 7 December. Changes were made from the original October agreement.[101] The final text excluded any reference to transportation, thus satisfying the concerns of the American shipping lobby. The bi-national panel would be the final appeal for countervail cases, but the US succeeded in having only three of the five members, rather than all of the panel, drawn from the legal profession. Canada retained preferential postal rates for Canadian publications, and won a provision that allowed shares from the privatization of a crown corporation to be restricted to Canadians. The final draft of the FTA also gave more explicit recognition to Canadian agricultural supply management boards. The FTA was initialled by President Reagan and Prime Minister Mulroney separately, quietly and without ceremony, on 2 January 1988.

Both sides then prepared to draft legislation that would enact the FTA in their respective countries. On the US side, the fast-track process meant that Congress would have to either pass or reject the agreement as a whole, without amendments. This improved considerably the prospects of passage, and while there was some congressional grumbling, the FTA encountered surprisingly little opposition. On the Canadian side, because of the Tory majority, the legislative process would also be straightforward, though much more acrimonious because of the sworn enmity of the opposition parties. John Crosbie, appointed minister of international trade in April 1988, did not soothe FTA opponents when he described them as "CBC-type snivellers, the Toronto literati, the alarm-spreaders and the encyclopedia-peddlers."[102] It was Crosbie's responsibility to introduce the enabling legislation (which he did, in May 1988) and pilot it through the House.

THE FREE TRADE ELECTION

The progress of the FTA, punctuated with dramatic reversals and interventions, had been agonizingly slow. The deal was announced in the wee hours of 4 October 1987, a legal text only became available on 7 December, and the agreement was not signed until 2 January 1988. From then, however, the legislative pace picked up on both sides of the border. On the American side there was an attempt by various anti-trade lobbyists to halt the deal, but this was ignored by the administration, and the US Senate Finance Committee began consideration of the FTA on 17 March 1988. In keeping with its low profile in the United States, the bill encountered few difficulties. The House of Representatives passed it on 9 August, the Senate passed it on 19 September, and President Reagan signed it on 28 September.

The Canadian enabling legislation had more difficulty and became the key issue in the November 1988 election campaign. Bill C-130 was introduced for first reading in the Commons on 24 May 1988. During second-reading debate the opposition parties made it clear once again that they were against the deal. John Turner, the Liberal leader, claimed that if the deal went through and he subsequently was elected prime minister, he would tear it up. The New Democratic Party was unyielding in its opposition as well. In committee, the Liberals and New Democrats proposed over fifty amendments to the bill, many of which would have changed the agreement substantially through the addition of new conditions and institutions, while others sought to clarify and entrench the exemptions for Canadian social and regulatory programmes. In an unexpected development, both opposition parties demanded amendments to ensure that there would be no inter-basin water exports from Canada to the United States, claiming that the FTA allowed them and indeed that they were part of the deal.[103] In response to this pressure, International Trade Minister John Crosbie allowed an amendment stating that "for greater certainty, nothing in this act or the agreement except article 401, applies to water." The only other major amendment to the bill in committee was the removal of the clause that had stated that Bill C-130 overrode any other federal legislation that happened to be inconsistent with it. The bill was passed on 4 August and sent back for third and final reading in the Commons.

John Turner announced an even greater complication in late July. Fearing that he might be outflanked in his opposition to the deal by the New Democrats, he announced that he had asked the Liberal majority in the Senate to block the trade bill until a general election. Turner knew that nothing he or the New Democrats could do in the House would stop the bill. Ultimately, the crushing Conservative majority would prevail and the bill would be passed. But the Liberals had a majority in the Senate, and the trade bill could not become law until it passed there too. Turner insisted that the use of unelected senators was ultimately democratic, since Canadians would thereby have a chance to vote on a momentous piece of legislation that had never been part of the 1984 Tory campaign. The New Democrats, momentarily surprised, soon announced that they did not support this manoeuvre, since it was a deliberate attempt to thwart the will of Parliament.

It was hot and muggy that summer in Ottawa. The opposition parties tried to tie up Commons debate on the bill, and so on 16 August the government introduced a time-allocation request that limited debate to less than a week.[104] Accusations sizzled on the hot griddle of nationalist rhetoric, "experts" mud-wrestled over the deal's finer points, and everyone watched the clock, waiting for the election. John Turner had demanded that the "people decide." The Tories kept cool, waiting for their polling to haul in a harvest of opinion indicators. The data showed surprising satisfaction; even Brian Mulroney, once the most unpopular prime minister in Canadian polling history, had respectable numbers. Brian Mulroney finally announced the election on 1 October, to be held on 21 November 1988.

Tory strategy was to avoid issues and keep the Prime Minister away from the press. The NDP focused on its key asset: the personal popularity of Ed Broadbent. The Liberals did not have the luxury of a popular leader: John Turner had had to fight off attacks from within his own party over the previous four years, a party that was still in debt and disorganized. Turner was attacked on open-line shows and endured bungled policy announcements. The Quebec wing of the party was in turmoil, and both premiers Bourassa and McKenna (Liberals) supported the FTA that Turner had sworn to fight. The polls showed the Liberals in third place, and on 19 October the CBC reported that there had been serious consideration in senior Liberal ranks of dumping Turner and selecting a new leader, *in the middle of the campaign*.

Then came the debates. Never in Canadian political history has a campaign turned around so quickly, on such a thin dime. Two three-hour debates were held on consecutive evenings (24 and 25 October). The French debate produced no overwhelming winner, and after the first two hours of the English debate the three leaders were still even. Then, for several minutes, the tube imploded in a white-hot exchange between Turner and Mulroney. The issue? The same one

THE CANADA-US FREE TRADE AGREEMENT

that John Turner had nailed his colours to that summer: free trade. Turner's attack was emotional and scattered, but in the close boundaries of TV he hit a nerve: Canada would lose its sovereignty with the FTA. Mulroney, who had succeeded in remaining aloof through the first part of the debate, was goaded into an equally emotional response, but his was defensive while Turner had the advantage peculiar to the medium: he was jabbing with clear and calculated precision on a single, powerful point. TV news lives for "sound bites," a segment (usually twenty seconds) that purports to represent an event, and the more dramatic the better. Turner and Mulroney had provided *the* sound bite. While Turner's performance through the evening had been mediocre, he peaked in those twenty seconds, the twenty seconds that were played over and over on news broadcasts from Victoria to St. John's. The effect had pundits slack-jawed. The conventional wisdom that debates do not change voting intentions was now laughable: the Liberals went from last to first place in three days.

A new and completely different campaign dominated the last three weeks. Mulroney emerged from his cocoon, became more partisan, sparred with hecklers and even met with them to defend the FTA. There was only one issue: free trade. The NDP tried to catch up, but John Turner and the Liberals had made it their issue, and clearly it was getting a response across the country. In retrospect, the Tory strategy was carefully calibrated to first knock Turner down, attack his credibility, and then shift attention to Liberal weaknesses. Tory cabinet ministers fanned out to defend the deal and attack the man. Finance Minister Michael Wilson called Turner a liar on national TV. John Crosbie captured headlines in a brutal shouting match with students. Turner kept hammering home his theme that free trade would undermine social programmes, lose jobs, and eventually cost the country its sovereignty, but within a week it began to sound shrill. While Mulroney's cabinet ministers broke all the normal rules of campaign propriety in questioning Turner's credibility, the Prime Minister himself tried to focus on the difference between the "experienced Tory team" and the Liberal "Rat Pack" (a reference to the small, loud group of Liberals that had captured media attention in 1984-85 with their parliamentary gutter fighting). The Tories also found a fat target in Liberal election promises: Turner refused initially to say where the billions of dollars needed to pay for them would come from, and the Conservatives hammered at this contrast between their "good management" and the disarray and fiscal profligacy of their opponents.

Still, free trade was the theme, and even if Liberal efforts were losing their focus, other groups were stoking the fires. To a degree unprecedented in modern Canadian elections, third parties (that is, non-political-party groups) advertised and agitated for and against the deal. The lead opponents were the Pro-Canada

THE CANADA-US FREE TRADE AGREEMENT

Network, with strong connections to the union movement and in particular the Canadian Auto Workers. They, along with other groups like the Canadian Union of Public Employees, ran ads and produced booklets lambasting the deal and the government. The counterattack came from the Canadian Alliance for Trade and Job Opportunities, largely a business lobby, and individual businesses or producer associations. In the last days of the campaign, the papers were choked with pro- and anti-FTA ads run by third-party groups. For example, the *Globe and Mail* of 19 November ran two ads from "cultural producers." The first read: "The Mulroney-Reagan Trade Deal is a hastily concluded agreement that was made for political reasons, and not for the welfare of our country. It will irrevocably damage the Canada that we care about." It had thirty-nine signatures, including those of Margaret Atwood, Pierre Berton, Adrienne Clarkson, Timothy Findley, Margot Kidder, and Gordon Pinsent. Five pages later, a group calling itself "Artists & Writers for Free Trade" ran the following ad: "We, the undersigned artists and writers, want the people of Canada to know that we are in favour of the Canada-United States Free Trade Agreement. There is no threat to our national identity anywhere in the Agreement. Nor is there a threat to any form of Canadian cultural expression. As artists and writers, we reject the suggestion that our ability to create depends upon the denial of economic opportunities to our fellow citizens. What we make is to be seen and read by the whole world. The spirit of protectionism is the enemy of art and thought." This ad had sixty-three signatories, including Alex Colville, Ken Danby, George Jonas, W.P. Kinsella, Mordecai Richler, and Harold Town.[105] Emmett Hall, often called the "father of Canadian medicare," emerged in the last weeks of the campaign to publicly deny that the FTA would undermine Canadian social programmes.

The polls began to turn around in the last week of the campaign. But even on election eve, few pundits were prepared to give firm predictions, and most guessed gingerly at either a Tory minority or slim majority government. The TV networks began their election coverage at 8:00pm (EST); by 8:40, computers chattering away, they all predicted a Tory majority. The magnitude of that victory was completely unanticipated: Tories 169; Liberals 83; NDP 43. Perhaps most surprisingly, the Tories were able to increase their support in Quebec (from 58 seats and 49.6 per cent of the vote in 1984, to 63 seats and 53 per cent of the vote), and hold their own in allegedly anti-free trade Ontario (46 seats and 38 per cent vs. 43 seats and 39 per cent for the Liberals).

The following day, both John Turner and Ed Broadbent conceded that democratic politics had to be respected: they had fought almost exclusively on free trade and had been beaten. The "people had decided." The deal would go through. The FTA's enabling legislation was passed on 31 December 1988, one day before the agreement was to take effect.

THE FTA: ELECTION AFTERMATH AND IMPLEMENTATION

There are few if any issues in recent Canadian history that have engendered as much fierce and fiery debate as free trade. Provincial premiers, federal politicians, artists, writers, economists, industry associations, women's organizations, churches: the list is endless. Not only was the debate extraordinarily wide ranging, it was bound up with the most central issues of any polity: sovereignty, culture, survival. The free trade debate was about more than economics: it was about the nature of the country. The debate had been so fevered that in the immediate aftermath of the election there was nothing but numbed and tired silence. Partisans reflected on their battles, their arguments, their success or defeat. For several weeks people tried to focus clearly on what the issues had been and what fresh engagements lay ahead.

One overriding question was why the pro-FTA side won. Why were anti-FTA arguments ultimately rejected? On what were the judgments about free trade, both pro and con, based? At one level, perhaps the deepest if not necessarily the most crucial, the issue was about the nature of America and Americans. Is the United States of America best symbolized by Rambo or Thoreau, by Nixon or Nader, by bombs or baseball, by its crime rates or its constitution? No country, certainly not one as vast and complex as the United States, can be conveniently encapsulated in a single image, but most people have a visceral sense of the Americans, not necessarily as purely good or purely bad, but tending to one or the other. This provided important clues to the debate. The FTA, everyone agrees, binds Canada closer to the American economy. But is the American economy healthy or sick? Is it a vibrant home of innovation, wealth, and opportunity, or a final bastion of tottering capitalism relying on racism and sweatshops? A recurring theme in anti-FTA arguments was that the agreement was a pipeline that would pollute Canadian cultural and social life with American influences.

The other cue in the debate was one's view of state and market. Those who held that free, open capitalist markets with a reasonable minimum of state intervention are the best creators of wealth were inclined to support the deal. Those who held otherwise were sceptical. To the latter group, capitalist economies only work well (i.e., provide reasonable incomes and benefits) if there is a substantial degree of state intervention. The FTA operates on the logic that removal of state intervention, in this case in the tariff fields, will ultimately benefit everyone. The pro-FTA argument was that the deal would create jobs, enhance economic efficiency, and shield Canada from American protectionism, without affecting social programmes and culture. The anti-FTA argument was that the deal would de-industrialize the economy, lose jobs, fail to protect us, and create pressures that would ultimately bury everything from medicare to CanLit. In one sense, these technical arguments were entirely the plaything of experts and elites, like ancient scholastics debating arcane matters of doctrine while the peasants laboured, oblivious, outside the abbey walls. The *political* debate among the parties and the leaders and the interest groups was less precise, but drew its inspiration from and found its footing within the more deliberate engagement of the experts. The expert debate did not determine the election, but the language of the election debate cannot be understood without a grasp of how and why the experts the disagreed. The disagreements clustered around four issues: (1) energy, (2) manufacturing and industrial development, (3) the dispute-resolution mechanism, and (4) the likely economic and social consequences. There were many other issues, of course, such as the impact on tariff reductions, agriculture, the Auto Pact, the wine industry, and services; but these four captured the public's attention.

1. Energy

The debate over the energy provisions of the FTA hinged on older ones about the National Energy Program (NEP) of 1980. Those who disliked the NEP liked the FTA because under it, nothing like that programme could happen again. Those who liked the NEP, disliked the FTA for the same reason that their opponents liked it. Simon Reisman was especially proud of the energy provisions: "The energy chapter is, in my judgment, the best chapter in the agreement."[106] An opponent of the provisions, quite naturally, argued that "the deal will make permanent policies already initiated by the Mulroney government for deregulation and continental integration of Canada's energy sector."[107] Critics pointed to the way that the energy chapter makes some traditional Canadian policies difficult if not impossible: export restrictions of some resources, two price systems to favour domestic industries, and perhaps attempts to increase resource rents and use them for development (e.g. the Alberta Heritage Savings Trust Fund). There are also several gray areas: did the measures prohibiting a government from *charging* more for energy in export markets apply to crown corporations? This is an important issue for hydroelectrical utilities.[108] FTA 904 allows restrictions of energy exports from one party to another for reasons of shortage and conservation, as long as the restriction does not reduce the other party's *proportion* of the total supply made available as measured over the last three years, does not involve the deliberate imposition of a higher export price than what prevails domestically, and does not disrupt normal channels of supply to the other party. The proportionality requirement might make it impossible, in the case of a severe shortage, for a provincial government to phase out exports entirely. This may mean permanent US access to supplies that we have traditionally assumed to be simply surplus to our needs.[109] A particularly bizarre scenario is possible wherein a provincial government might cut its exports (which it has the right to do under the FTA), thereby forcing the federal government to meet its export commitment to the United States either by reducing domestic consumption somehow, or by *importing* oil to re-ship south of the border. None of this troubled supporters of the agreement. Since energy trade is largely free as it is, the FTA provisions provide a basis for sound growth in the future, particularly for the uranium sector, which was a big winner in the deal because of the lifting of American import restrictions. In other respects, the energy chapter in the FTA "represents nothing more than an extension and clarification of Canada's existing rights and obligations under the GATT."[110]

2. Manufacturing and Industrial Development

The key provisions on manufacturing in the deal include lowered tariffs, government procurement, and revisions to the Auto Pact. For opponents, "no one really knows how many Canadian firms are poised to take advantage of lower tariffs."[111] The chapter on government procurement was criticized because with it, "the Canadian government has signed away to a North American common market its decision-making authority over a Canadian tool of economic policy. In the process, it restricts future governments from using their large volume purchases to promote a wide range of domestic goals, including regional development, local sourcing, special support of particular industries, research and development, and affirmative action."[112] The chapter on automotive trade was attacked because of the change in safeguards (from 60 per cent Canadian content rule to 50 per cent North American content) and the elimination of duty remissions and waivers. The rules of origin now mean that companies will get the benefits of the Auto Pact without having to meet the old safeguards.[113] The Auto Pact still exists, but is now restricted to present members. In essence, the Pact has been "frozen," and the stick that the Canadian government formerly could use to enhance production in this country has been whittled down somewhat so that it applies with less force than before.

Proponents of the deal saw tariff reduction as good in itself, at least in the Canadian context with its reasonably flexible economy. The government procurement provisions were not seen by proponents as preventing or limiting key policy instruments, because those provisions apply only to a specific list of government entities, a specific list of goods, and only for amounts above a given threshold. Moreover, there are exceptions for small businesses. Simon Reisman had in fact hoped for a more ambitious chapter; even so, he estimated that as much as $4 billion in US contracts was now opened to Canadian bids, while $650 million in Canadian contracts was opened to Americans.[114] Finally, on auto trade, proponents tended to focus on rising concerns in the United States in the last few years over Canada's use of waivers and remissions and its extension of Auto Pact status beyond the Big Three to overseas competitors. In their view, the Auto Pact was due for revision if not abrogation, and "the automotive clauses in the FTA are about as good as could be expected."[115]

3. The Dispute-Resolution Mechanism

The dispute-resolution mechanism was a major component of the deal, and predictably generated completely different assessments from the two sides in the debate. The critics argued that Canada did not get what it set out to get from the trade deal—exemption from US trade remedy laws. All that the deal provides is a referee system that replaces the final tier of judicial review. Canada remains subject to "process protectionism," the system in the US whereby companies can take competitors through a process that amounts to trade harassment. No such thing is available for Canadian companies.[116] On countervails and anti-dumping, the two countries have only agreed to continue negotiating, and the panels reviewing trade determinations will only have the power to decide whether those determinations conform to existing law. This led critics to suggest that in effect, Canadians will be helping Americans apply their own law against Canadian products and companies. Finally, the FTA calls for an extraordinary amount of notification and consultation that in principle will be done under the aegis of the new Trade Commission, but the deal is unclear on how much scope and budget the Commission will have to do its job.[117] As well, all this notifying and consulting might lead to a centralization of the Canadian political system by forcing the provinces to accept constant federal monitoring. The existing degree of centralization, both federal and parliamentary, in Canada will ensure quicker compliance with Commission decisions, and so the Americans will have an advantage in being able to stall because of the need to clear everything with various authorities. One observer concluded that the Commission will be in the impossible position of having extraordinarily wide responsibilities without any power to back up its decisions. The consequence will be to "push Canada's political integration in a

US-controlled North America to levels barely thought possible before the Mulroney era dawned in 1984."[118]

Simon Reisman saw the dispute-resolution mechanism differently: "In effect, we have established a watchdog to ensure that the laws are interpreted fairly and applied properly and that there is no arbitrariness in the application of those laws."[119] Donald Macdonald had hoped for an agreement on subsidies, but thought that the panel system would ensure greater fairness and would have changed the outcome of the softwood lumber case.[120] The general dispute-settlement procedure for disagreements that fall within the scope of the agreement was of "long-range significance" to him. The advantages are (1) a specific forum in the Commission for consultation and mediation; (2) a defined timetable set for stages of dispute-settlement procedure; (3) an option to retaliate with "equivalent effects" if either party is not satisfied by the Commission decision; (4) a more rapid process than GATT's; and (5) the development of a body of "jurisdprudence" on Canadian-US trade within the Commission.[121] The pro-deal commentary on the dispute-resolution mechanisms seemed to concentrate on the long-term benefits of developing formal institutional structures to deal with bilateral trade issues, while recognizing the limitations of the deal's specific provisions.

4. Economic and Social Consequences

While part of the rationale behind a trade agreement, from the Canadian point of view, was to escape the wrath of American protectionism, the other larger point was to stimulate the Canadian economy and provide the basis for increased jobs and income. Everything in the deal, from the Canadian perspective, is aimed at these goals. A major part of the domestic debate over free trade focused on what the deal's economic consequences were likely to be, and perhaps even more importantly, on the deal's political and social consequences. Critics claimed that the economic payoff would be minimal and perhaps even negative, while the political and social costs would be far too high. The deal's defenders argued that it would produce modest but real short-term economic gains, had the potential to generate larger gains in the future, and would not unduly constrain Canada's sovereignty or undermine its culture.

Ironically, the FTA's economic consequences turned out to be far less important in the election debate than its impact on Canadian social, cultural, and political life. The deal exempted cultural industries and did not appear to directly affect key social programmes such as family allowances, pensions, health care, education, unemployment insurance, or child care. The deal's critics pointed instead to four broad and insidious mechanisms whereby American values and practices would infect Canada.

The first such mechanism might be called "internal mutation"; as American goods, services, and companies begin to operate more freely in Canada, they will bring the American economic style with them, a style often characterized by critics as depending on low wages, union busting, and dangerous cost-cutting. In an unregulated private market, this will place pressures on indigenous Canadian firms to compete or die.

The second and third mechanisms depend less on the commercial than on the political responses to competition of firms on either side of the border. US firms, facing competition from Canadian companies who pay less for their employee's health benefits because of medicare, or less for their employee's pension benefits because of Old Age Security, may launch countervails claiming that these public programmes are unfair subsidies. Such actions would probably be ineffective, but they would have tremendous nuisance value, so much so that they might inhibit policy makers from launching new programmes, and slowly corrode the political will that sustains the ones that now exist. On the Canadian side, firms may feel that their tax rates or employer contributions to programmes like Unemployment Insurance (which are more generous and hence more costly in Canada than in the United States) put them at a disadvantage in competing with US firms in the American market. Canadian-based firms selling to the US will still have to meet Canadian standards in wages and benefits but will sell their products in markets where their competitors have met lower and less expensive standards. This could create pressures within the Canadian business community to either roll back or at least freeze some key Canadian social policies.

The fourth and most general mechanism of importing American values into Canada derives from the very philosophy of the FTA. In fact, this is less a mechanism than a mood, one that colours both the deal and its language, so that without even knowing it, Canadians adopt an individualistic, competitive, market-oriented—in a word, American—world view. For example, the FTA accepts the American definition of culture as "business" and talks of cultural industries.[122] Gerald Caplan, chair of a recent task force report on Canadian broadcasting and a prominent member of the New Democratic Party, put the point directly: "It's not a matter of exposing our kids to Miami Vice, it's not a matter of 5 per cent tariff changes; it's a matter of the organic change. And because of that, I think the agreement should be defeated."[123]

This perspective necessarily leads to an uncompromisingly harsh view of the agreement. One nationalist concluded that "Canada's ability to establish public goals is set into a new North American framework."[124] Another went further in forseeing that when implemented, "the free-trade agreement [will become], by virtue of its scope and regulatory importance, the new national policy for Canada. All other federal and provincial policies will have to conform to its framework and goals."[125] The FTA, in short, was the end of Canada.

Canada has evidently survived at least the first two years of the FTA's implementation. The main disputes in the free trade debate concerned the deal's future consequences for jobs, growth, culture, and social programmes. Two years is a short time, but it provides at least some preliminary answers to the questions about process and effect raised during the debate in 1988.

An immediate priority after the passage of the FTA was the establishment of its institutional machinery. The Canada-United States Trade Commission posed no difficulty, since it formally consists of two people: a Canadian and an American representative of cabinet or ministerial rank. For the first two years of the agreement the Commission consisted of John Crosbie, Canada's minister for international trade, and Ambassador Carla Hills, United States trade representative. They met twice in each of 1989 and 1990. The Commission's mandate is largely supervisory, though it has undertaken several issues itself. One has been acceleration in tariff reductions, permitted under FTA 401.5. After its second meeting in November 1989, the Commission reported that it had had requests for accelerated reductions for products amounting to approximately $6 billion in bilateral trade.[126] They were implemented on 1 April 1990, by which time the Commission had another five hundred industry petitions for further accelerations in goods such as coffins and caskets, freight car components, fishing equipment, artificial sausage casings, jewellery, toys, and games.[127] Another issue that the Commission addressed in 1989 was temporary entry of business persons under Chapter 15 of the FTA. The categories were expanded, and minimum educational requirements for some professions were amended.

Under FTA 1802 the Commission has the power to establish committees and working groups on specific issues. This provision was used almost immediately. Eight working groups were established to address technical standards in agriculture (FTA 708 stipulated that the two governments would harmonize their respective technical regulatory requirements and inspection procedures). A ninth on fish was added after the Commission's second meeting. A Chapter 19 Working Group was established to review the subsidies issue; its work will continue for at least five years. As well, committees and groups were struck to deal with the auto industry, tourism, machinery and equipment, and services.[128] In 1990 a Working Group on Rules of Origin and Other Customs Matters was established.

Chapter 18 of the FTA gives the parties the right of consultation on practices and measures that may contravene the agreement. Chapter 19 deals with anti-dumping and countervail actions, and substitutes a new, bi-national appeal system to consider whether the laws of the offending party were properly interpreted. Both chapters require the appointment of panels reporting to the Commission. In 1989-90 Chapter 18 consultations ensued over plywood standards, provincial liquor board practices on American wine and beer, wool, and cable retransmission. In 1989 a Chapter 18 panel (which may review the effect of new legislative and regulatory initiatives) struck down regulations on west coast salmon and herring. In 1990 two Chapter 18 panels were struck to deal with American restrictions on lobster imports. Chapter 19 panels were established to consider countervailing duties on Canadian pork and anti-dumping duties on Canadian red raspberries and Canadian steel rails. Chapter 19 challenges on salted codfish and induction motors were settled prior to panel hearings.

The construction of this elaborate institutional machinery went unnoticed by most Canadians in the first two years of the agreement. Partisans and opponents of the FTA had, for two years, painted the agreement in the most lurid shades: it would bring either blissful growth or disastrous decline. But even the partisans had agreed that there would be a period of "adjustment," and so public debate on the FTA in 1989 first focused on what these adjustments might be and the government policies that would address them. Though signals had been mixed in 1987-88, the federal government had always admitted that some adjustment would be necessary, and in 1988 appointed an Advisory Council on Adjustment, headed by Jean de Grandpré, chairman of the telecommunications company BCE, to recommend policy options. "Adjustment" was, of course, a euphemism for unemployment, and the central issue for the Advisory Council, as it had been in 1988 and would be through 1989, was the FTA's impact on jobs. While new jobs might be created as a result of the agreement, some old jobs that had depended on trade protection would be lost. How could companies and workers be helped?

The Council's report, entitled *Adjusting to Win*, was released on 29 March 1990. Ironically, despite its mandate to "identify specific adjustment issues or circumstances arising from the Canada-US trade agreement," the de Grandpré report grounded all its recommendations on the assumption that it was impossible to directly ascribe any job losses to the FTA.

> The potential to direct specific assistance to individuals adversely affected by the FTA was exhaustively explored. A fundamental obstacle in this regard is the problem of distinguishing between the effects of the FTA and those of the larger, global economic environment. It is virtually impossible, in the Council's view, to clearly and conclusively attribute any particular economic event—such as a plant closure—solely to the effects of the FTA. Depending on the circumstances, the same event might also be attributed to global

economic changes, to technological obsolescence, or simply to poor management, among other things. Moreover, because the FTA will have many subtle and complex economic effects, virtually any job loss—whatever its actual causes—might arguably qualify for FTA adjustment assistance. Since anyone who might qualify for such assistance would undoubtedly seek it, any agency dispensing adjustment assistance would be obliged to consider the merits of virtually every job loss occurring anywhere in Canada.[129]

The Council therefore recommended against any specific FTA adjustment programme, and instead suggested measures to promote the "swift re-integration into the workforce of all workers displaced by economic change of any kind."[130] These measures included improved education and training systems, programmes to promote better labour/management cooperation on industry-based training and adjustment programmes, tax incentives for companies establishing their own training programmes, minimum standards on advance notice for layoffs and severance pay legislation, a re-orientation of labour market programmes (e.g., unemployment insurance) away from income maintenance to employment promotion, improved R&D, and reduction of interprovincial barriers to trade and labour mobility. While the recommendations appeared to be wide ranging, they clearly assumed a market-centred and private response to economic adjustment, supplemented at best with government coordination and simplification of existing programmes.

The de Grandpré report offered little solace to the FTA's critics. Indeed, it only confirmed their view that the agreement had been forged for and by business, and that even the human misery of unemployment would now be turned to a profit under free trade. And yet the report was essentially correct in its argument that while it might be possible to guess at the aggregate effects of the agreement, it was difficult to ascribe any single plant closure to the FTA. Nevertheless, it became a favourite media sport in the first year of the agreement to try to link closures, relocations, mergers, and demands for wage concessions to the FTA. Trade unions in particular were quick to blame the FTA for most if not all negative developments. For example, when Echlin Canada Inc., a producer of airbrakes, shifted production to the US, the steelworkers union immediately said that the 100 jobs lost as a result were due to the FTA.[131] The layoff of 450 textile workers by Domil in Quebec, which the company admitted was a rationalization in order to compete more effectively in the North American market under free trade, was loudly decried by union spokespersons.[132] Kimberley-Clark made headlines in June when it announced it was purchasing materials from Mexican firms, putting 50 Canadians out of work.[133] Year-end "scorecards" by FTA opponents provided a particularly depressing catalogue of layoffs and unemployment (the

Council of Canadians did not even wait a full year: by July 1989 it claimed that in six months Canada had lost 33,000 jobs).[134] Whereas the Prime Minister in his last campaign speech of the 1988 election had promised a net increase due to the FTA of 250,000 jobs, the CLC calculated that in the first year more than 77,000 jobs had been lost through over fifty major plant closings.[135] Canada's trade surplus with the United States had declined over the year, and there had been cuts to unemployment insurance (reductions in benefits amounting to almost $3 billion), regional development programmes, transportation and mailing subsidies. Thus, not only had the FTA hurt the Canadian economy, it had already in a only a few months whittled away at Canadian social programmes.

Other analyses disagreed. The government obviously had an interest in trumpeting every shred of positive news, and it did so. It claimed that 193,000 new jobs had been created in 1989, and that while Canada's trade surplus had declined over the year, it had bounced back into the black by November (the year-end figures, however, showed an overall balance-of-payments deficit with the United States of over $4 billion).[136] Press releases and ministerial announcements were always careful never to explicitly claim the FTA as the cause of all this good news, but the implication was clear. Less partisan observers rendered more sober judgements, in keeping with early economic assessments that the FTA would have rather modest effects on job creation.[137] Analysts for the C.D. Howe Institute, for example, pointed out that even the Prime Minister's claim of a net gain over ten years of 250,000 FTA-related jobs (an estimate based on Economic Council of Canada data) represented only a 1.8 per cent increase over what would have occurred without the agreement, and was almost insignificant in comparison with the five million Canadians who change jobs each year.[138] A study conducted by economists for the International Monetary Fund claimed that while the long-run effects of the agreement were likely to be positive, they would not be very large.[139] In addition to the relatively small impact that might be expected of the agreement itself, most economists agreed by 1990 that the FTA had been implemented at the worst possible time. Interest rates in Canada increased in 1989-90, as did the value of the Canadian dollar. A high dollar, combined with an economic slowdown in both Canada and the United States, hurt Canadian exporters badly. Gordon Ritchie, former deputy trade negotiator for the FTA, claimed that the high dollar "has 20 times the impact of free trade."[140]

While the FTA's ultimate impact on jobs and prices remained murky, the deal's impact on specific trade disputes was more transparent. Three major ones dealt with under FTA panel procedures concerned fish, raspberries, and pork.[141]

The fish case was the first to be decided under the new provisions of the FTA, and its result was not encouraging. In order to protect jobs and fish stocks,

Ottawa had, up until April 1989, banned any export of unprocessed west coast fish. That ban was struck down by a GATT decision, and so the government replaced it with a new stipulation that all salmon and herring caught in Canadian waters would have to be brought to Canadian ports for inspection before export. The ostensible rationale was conservation of fish stocks, but a landing requirement for fresh fish was virtually the same as an export ban. The requirement was attacked by American fishing interests, and in October 1989 the FTA panel ruled that it violated the agreement. The ruling also upheld, however, the need for conservation of fish stocks, and recommended that it might be permissible for Canada to require that at least 80 per cent of all fish caught be brought in for inspection. It said that between 10 and 20 per cent of Canadian salmon and herring might be sold directly to American fish buyers. After the ruling, the two governments began to negotiate a compromise, the Americans claiming victory because the original Canadian scheme had been struck down, the Canadians claiming victory because the right to impose conservation schemes was upheld. In February the Canada-US Trade Commission announced a new agreement wherein Americans had access to 20 per cent of the west coast fishery, rising to 25 per cent over three years. Since this involved the export of fish that would otherwise have been processed in British Columbia, it clearly lost jobs for the west coast fishing industry. Tom Siddon, the minister of fisheries, admitted that there would be some "adjustments," particularly in the processing side of the industry, but could not estimate the number of jobs that might be lost.[142] The Prime Minister noted philosophically that "you win some, you lose some." A troubling aspect of the decision was whether Canadian fisheries officials could monitor the proportions and types of fish sold to Americans at sea. If not, then the ostensible purpose of conservation would not be achieved. As well, as the first dispute settled under the agreement, the entire process had been more acrimonious and less precise than had been envisaged by FTA proponents.

The next decision was more hopeful, at least to Canadian eyes. The raspberries case was initiated by complaints from three Canadian exporters against a decision by the US International Trade Administration to impose anti-dumping duties on their products. The FTA panel found in December 1989 that the duties had been based on faulty calculations for two of the exporters, and ordered the US Department of Commerce to revise them. As a result, one Canadian exporter's duties were reduced from 2.59 per cent to 0.11 per cent, and the other's were dropped entirely.[143]

The pork dispute had its source in a decision by the US International Trade Commission in August 1989 to levy countervailing duties on Canadian imports of fresh, chilled, and frozen pork. This decision was coupled with one by the Department of Commerce that calculated Canadian government subsidies at eight cents a kilogram of exported processed pork. Four years earlier American trade authorities had determined that Canadian pork imports did not hurt the domestic industry, and so American producers successfully lobbied Congress to change the law. They then launched a new series of complaints that resulted in the countervail. Canadian pork imports account for approximately 3 per cent of the US market. A Chapter 19 panel was struck to review the validity of the decision in terms of American countervail law and the facts of the case, and in July 1990 the governments of Canada, Quebec, and Ontario, along with the Canadian pork and meat councils, appeared before it to state their arguments. The panel released its report on 28 September 1990 and found in Canada's favour. It issued a remand order to the US International Trade Commission to reconsider its original decision.

The FTA, it must be remembered, is a long-term agreement that will take ten years to fully implement. Its ultimate impact, therefore, must properly await an analysis of the period *after* 1998. Even at this early stage, however, it is possible to come to several conclusions about the deal.

First, and perhaps most perplexingly, the "numbers" are far from clear. FTA opponents, most notably the CLC and the trade union movement, have continued to attack the deal by trying to count plant closures and job losses. Unfortunately, they have not tallied plant openings and new jobs that might be related to the FTA. FTA supporters have tended to be more circumspect in their assessments, downplaying job gains in favour of emphasizing the improvements in efficiency and competitiveness over the long term that should result from the deal. Government spokespersons have tried to play it both ways, simultaneously claiming that it is too early to tell and that aggregate economic indicators on trade surplus and job creation suggest growth and prosperity. The best mainstream economic analyses have pointed to modest benefits from the deal, benefits that in any case have been completely overshadowed by the effect of high interest rates and a high dollar.

A second conclusion is that the institutional mechanisms established by the deal appear to work reasonably well. Panels and working groups were struck within the FTA's first year and operated smoothly. But it is also clear that the dry administrative procedures envisioned in the agreement have been coloured by politics. A highly volatile issue like the west coast fishery was addressed gingerly by the bi-national panel, leaving the key negotiations to the Commission and to politicians. More technical and less explosive questions like the red raspberries question have been tackled with great precision. This is entirely consistent with the way in which the FTA itself was negotiated, however. Some issues can be left to technicians, others cannot. At best the FTA is a framework that permits more routinized negotiations in some cases, perhaps even the majority of cases. But there will always be issues of such a sensitive nature that they will have to be tackled in the old way through political horsetrading.

Third, as FTA opponents predicted, the United States has continued to be as protectionist as ever. The pork and fish cases illustrate what determined interest groups are capable of in the American lobbying system. That system contains many more pressure points than does the Canadian, so that producers can approach departments, commissions, and agencies at both levels of government to demand protection from Canadian competition. If they fail with one agency or one level, they can try others. The FTA cannot prevent this, but it does provide some new avenues of recourse to Canadian interests. In some instances, like the raspberries and pork cases, Canadians can win against capricious decisions. In others, like the west coast fish case, the deal forces accommodation to American interests. The final test of the FTA may lie in the dispute-resolution mechanisms and Canada's success in thwarting American protectionism.

Finally, the deal does not appear to have had the dire consequences that many predicted for Canadian social programmes. While unemployment insurance and some regional subsidy programmes were cut in 1989-90, initiatives of this type have been imbedded in the Tory agenda since 1984. FTA opponents have charged that these cuts were due to American pressures to conform to the deal, but have as yet produced no evidence. This is not to deny that Canadian programmes like health insurance, income support, and cultural protection have suffered in the last two years. They are likely to suffer even more in the next decade, but not because of the FTA. The constraints imposed on federal and provincial governments of any political stripe by high deficits and international competitive forces make program expansion difficult if not impossible. Indeed, insofar as governments develop new or improved "adjustment" programmes, the FTA may lead to more, not less, government spending in labour market policy.

DISCUSSION

There are, in every nation's history, events that shape an epoch or define the profile of a decade. Canada has had some of these: World War II and its conscription crisis, the Quebec 1980 referendum, the battle over the constitution. The FTA is of the same magnitude and significance, not necessarily because of the economic changes it brings in its wake, but because of the passions it aroused. The debate it engendered reached far deeper into the collective Canadian psyche than perhaps anything else in the previous twenty years. It had that magical and terrifying power of great public issues to arouse, crystallize, and intensify a myriad of feelings and beliefs about the nature of the country.

All the more surprising, then, that the government practically stumbled onto it in 1985. Brian Mulroney had rejected free trade in 1983 as an economic policy option because he thought that it would tie Canada too closely to the United States. His change of heart had something to do with the developments cited earlier: the 1983 Liberal government initiatives, the climate of protectionism in the United States, the American disinterest in sectoral trade, and the question of where Canada would go in a world dominated by trading blocs. But other factors were in play, because Canadian policy might have simply continued on the multilateral track, with ginger overtures to the Americans on specific issues. Canada's job creation record was good enough that the Prime Minister could have hoped for continued, modest growth over the first term of his government. It must be understood that Brian Mulroney was the key man behind the deal: he decided to pursue it, he put his own people (Burney and Wilson) in the field when the game got rough, and he personally chaired the cabinet committee that oversaw the negotiations. As he once put it, his neck was on the line. And yet he took the risk. Why?

No one but Brian Mulroney himself knows the answer, but there are several signs of what was in his mind those fateful days in September 1985 as he weighed his options. First, Mulroney *liked* Americans. He had been raised in a small Quebec town whose prime industry was owned by Americans. Mulroney could never see America as some evil empire, wholly different from Canada in its aspirations and destiny. This psychological orientation lay behind his commitment, made in the first days of his assumption of the leadership of the Progressive Conservatives, to improve relations with the United States. Another factor was his obsession with economic growth and jobs. His one overriding mission seemed to be to give the country prosperity, and his other initiatives were subordinated to that. The FTA was ultimately irresistible from this perspective: if a good deal could be pulled off with the Americans, then the economy would get a huge boost, one moreover that might help the regions more than the centre. A final psychological factor that might have pushed the Prime Minister over the brink of decision was his own ideological leanings. One should never make too much of the ideological commitments of politicians, but the FTA clearly appealed to Mulroney's indistinct ideas of state and society. Even at the outset of the negotiations, it was reasonable to assume that the FTA would undermine the role of the state in Canadian economic life. The FTA had sex appeal for a Tory government sceptical of the traditional instruments of interventionist state power.

While it may seem frightening that a decision as momentous as the one to embark on talks was taken largely because of these background psychological factors, it helps explain the total confusion on the Canadian side as to what we wanted. Only Simon Reisman, free trade crusader that he was, knew the game and the prize: he wanted as wide open a deal as possible. The cabinet was less sure, and the Prime Minister entirely muddled at first. No one wanted to say free trade or comprehensive trade, in part out of fear, in part from confusion about what the outcomes would be. Brian Mulroney and his cabinet were not clear-eyed, right-wing warriors, smiling with grim confidence as they waded into the enemy of "snivellers and CBC types." They had gut instincts about what they thought might come from an FTA, but they were not trying to tear down the entire edifice of Canadian social and cultural life in a bid for more trade. That is why they seemed so hopelessly evasive in the early stages of the talks: they did not want culture, social programmes, the Auto Pact, or any thing else quintessentially Canadian, on the table. On the other hand, if they could get a big advantage from a small concession on any of these, they were interested. The Tory soul was cleft in two.

The real world of the FTA negotiations was even messier than this honest confusion would imply. First, there was the problem of the provinces. Mulroney had nailed his colours to the mast of federal-provincial relations early in 1984: cooperation and compromise and sweetness and light would reign again once he assumed the chair vacated by Trudeau. The premiers, especially the western ones, had supported the FTA, but Mulroney had to walk a thin and wavering line throughout the talks. The provinces, with the exception of Ontario, seemed interested in a deal with the US, but did not want to give Ottawa *carte blanche.* Ottawa knew that it could not negotiate effectively with ten governments at its elbow, but it also knew that it could not sell a deal to the US without being able to guarantee provincial cooperation. Mulroney's initial strategy was to give assurances of cooperation and participation while refusing to specify what that meant for the talks. Once the talks were underway, he managed to wrest a commitment from the provinces to give Ottawa negotiating power in exchange for provincial ratification. Squabbles continued over the ratification formula, but Reisman quietly worked at a deal that could be implemented completely within the federal domain. The reality of the negotiating process and of federal-provincial relations had forced Ottawa to bargain for a specific kind of deal, ironically one that attenuated federal powers much more than it did provincial ones. Fearing provincial power to negate a deal, Mulroney allowed a deal that further eroded federal powers.

A second complicating factor was the talks themselves. International negotiations, depending on the issues at hand, are at best gruelling, at worst a kind of political hardball where the only rule is to try to win the best deal you can for your country. Bilateral economic talks can be especially difficult, and require preparation, determination, and willpower to see them through. Simon Reisman probably was the best man for the job: he knew the area, and he was tough. He also had some of the best minds in Ottawa behind him. But he went into the negotiations from a weak position, and in negotiations, like war, position is everything. Canada had made the first move on the FTA by asking for talks. Moreover, Canada's interest was in *avoiding* American trade measures such as the omnibus trade bill and countervails. In any negotiation, the supplicant is always in the weaker position, particularly if the point of the negotiation is to win protection from the power of the other party. Canada's weak position was reinforced in the next year when various American authorities, without coordinated intent, slapped trade remedies on Canadian imports. Canada's stakes in the talks were greater than America's, and in order to avoid throwing them away, Canada did not react vigorously to the US trade actions. Peter Murphy no doubt smiled as he read the signs. Moreover, Canada eventually set its hopes impossibly high with the demand for a binding dispute-resolution mechanism and a deal on subsidies. The realities of American politics would never permit either an exemption for Canada from American trade law, or a quasi-judicial body that would override American law.

All this came to a head when Canadian authorities fought for a deal in September 1987. Reisman gave up the talks in good faith; he had had enough, and Murphy was not budging on the dispute-resolution issue. But the politicians had gone too far now, too much had been invested in the talks. It is wrong to think that the Tories "conceded" on investment, services, finances, or the Auto Pact. The Tories had never liked the investment controls of the Foreign Investment Review Agency or the baroque interventions of the National Energy Program: giving in on these issues was easy. The Auto Pact was under pressure anyway, since it was now operating in such a way as to encourage non-North American car manufacturers to set up plants in Canada to export to the US. American authorities were going to pull the plug one way or another. Financial services were being de-regulated by Ottawa already, and so this did not represent a concession in the government's mind. Nonetheless, Michael Wilson and Derek Burney finally gave the Americans what they wanted, and got a dispute-resolution mechanism in return.

This was not the way that many Canadians saw it, of course. The Tories had not conceded much if anything from *their* agenda, but they had compromised some key policy traditions extending back to the early 1960s. These traditions had been built by Liberal governments, goaded by the NDP. The policies, in investment, tariff protection, energy, and the social realm, had been symbols of central power and national will. The social programmes had always been piecemeal and inadequate, but they had been steps along the road to what many saw as a more just and humane society. The FTA became such a potent political symbol precisely because it could be seen as a frontal attack on this tradition. Despite its safeguards, exemptions, exceptions, and escape clauses, the FTA was rooted in soil quite different from that which had nourished much of Canadian federal public policy since the mid-1960s. It still allows the same goals to be pursued as before, but it constrains that pursuit by limiting the permissible policy instruments.

The FTA, like previous attempts to forge a free trade deal with the US, became a quivering lightening rod for all the electric storms of nationalism and identity that have beset the country's history. That is one reason why the debate was never monopolized by experts and elites. Salvo after salvo was fired from both camps in the form of studies, reports, commentaries, debates, analyses, and projections, using all the sophisticated weaponry of modern public policy discourse. The government did try to sell the deal to the public, but the millions it spent on advertising were little more than glossy propaganda. The public simply did not respond. Had the election campaign been held to three weeks and the vote called for October 21 instead of November 21, the Tories might have won without making much fuss at all about free trade. John Turner's intervention, desperate and perhaps even calculated, nonetheless finally dragged the issue forcibly onto centre stage. In the arc-light glare of the election campaign, the debate moved to a different plane than the one it had occupied for the experts. It became more emotional, more a matter of symbols and vision than of sections and clauses. But like a game of three-dimensional chess, the moves on this different plane were related to strategies developed on the other. Opposing politicians girded their rhetoric with references to studies done by opposing experts. The references were often elusive and fleeting, but vital, since the FTA could not be discussed *entirely* in symbolic terms. The experts did not determine the debate, nor did they even succeed in setting its boundaries, but they did provide ammunition for the war of words about the FTA's contents and consequences.

More than experts were involved in the debate. Interest groups, as noted earlier, entered the debate and the campaign with unprecedented vigour. In this case, the only clear and consistent support for the FTA came from business, especially large business already operating in the North American market. Opposition came from unions, farmers, cultural elites, and social policy advocates. It is rare to find such a clear line (though of course there were exceptions on each side) between the business agenda and the agenda of what might loosely be

THE CANADA-US FREE TRADE AGREEMENT

called the "popular sector." The business agenda won, but not because of the exercise of business pressure on government. Voters across the country made a choice to support the party that in turn supported the FTA. But institutional factors made the victory seem more decisive than it really was. Canada's parliamentary system elects MPs on a plurality basis, so that in most cases Tories were elected with less than 50 per cent of the votes; nationally, the Conservatives had the support of only 43 per cent of voters. In so far as both the Liberals and the NDP opposed the FTA, it might be said that the majority of Canadians, in fact, *voted against free trade*. But the parliamentary system operates on the basis of seats in the Commons, not votes in the hustings. The Tories, with 169 seats, have a clear majority. Moreover, the Liberal strategy of making free trade *the* issue of the campaign backfired to a degree, since by winning a majority, the Tories could claim an undisputed mandate to implement the deal.

In some respects, the 1988 election was Canadian democracy's finest hour. There was a real issue, a real debate, and stakes so high that many voters entered polling booths on the final day, after seven weeks of intense debate, still undecided about their choice and the country's destiny. Rare is the election where voters might consider a simple pencil tick the end of a nation. Equally rare, however, is an issue that resolves itself cleanly, especially one as large and complex as the FTA. The deal was passed and went into effect on schedule, and then slowly began to dissolve from the public scene. With the exception of the de Grandpré report and occasional FTA "scorecards," the entire issue of free trade was driven to the business pages. Why?

The paradox of the FTA is that while the deal itself had the power to concentrate debate on some of the most fundamental issues of Canadian politics—the nature of the welfare state, the proper scope of markets and individualism, the foundations of Canadian culture and the heights of Canadian aspiration—the deal in practice had only the most diffuse and disparate effects. The FTA as text powerfully condensed symbols and issues over which Canadians have been divided for generations; the FTA as process was a nebulous web of committees, panels, and decisions. The mirage of the FTA in one sense was due to its establishment of a framework for trade between Canada and the United States. But actual trade issues are highly industry- if not company-specific, operating at the level of raspberries, induction motors, and technical standards—hardly the stuff of sustained public attention. Businesses in these sectors are intensely interested in trade issues, but it is as though the FTA were running on a thousand separate tracks, with advances and gains on some and losses and setbacks on others. Trade unions have tried to monitor the FTA as a whole, but their public impact has been muted because of the complexity of trade and employment flows. Over the

THE CANADA-US FREE TRADE AGREEMENT

first two years, then, the FTA gradually receded as an issue on the national agenda, and became embedded in much smaller constituencies of interest defined in terms of industrial sectors. Business still talks about the FTA, and the opportunity to accelerate tariff reductions has helped build support in business circles.

The FTA may once more erupt as a national issue if a new government insists on renegotiating the deal, or if momentum continues to build for a North American free trade agreement with Mexico. As well, bi-national panel rulings—especially if they are unfavourable—will continue to draw attention. But a "leap of faith," if taken, can only be taken once. Faith gets replaced by experience, and experience has a way of cooling passion. If Canada ever debates free trade again as it did in 1988, it will do so less fearfully, less hopefully, and more soberly. For those of more pessimistic sensibility, Canada may very well have sealed its destiny. Now, few choices remain.

Discussion Questions

1   Discuss the FTA's symbolic content. In what ways could it be seen to express Canada's best aspirations as well as its ultimate doom?

2   Review the cultural arguments against the FTA. In what different ways was the FTA expected to undermine Canadian culture?

3   Business was about the only sector of Canadian society to support the FTA consistently. Discuss the significance of this.

4   In terms of what eventually emerged in the FTA, why was it logical for the western provincial governments to support the deal and Ontario to oppose it?

5   How did the differences between the Canadian and American political systems affect the negotiations and their outcome?

6   The opposition to the FTA came from what some have called the "popular sector": trade unions, women's organizations, social action groups. What ideological assumptions would unite such a disparate sector?

7   A major part of the free trade debate was about predicting consequences. But no one, not even the experts, was terribly confident of the consequences of such a huge policy initiative. Even after implementation, the "numbers" were far from clear. Discuss the problems this poses for the making of public policy.

8   What could the "political negotiations" deal with that the "technical discussions" between Reisman and Murphy could not?

9   Review the terms of the FTA as outlined in this chapter. Would they prevent a publicly funded, nation-wide system of child care centres?

10 Discuss the analytical position taken by the de Grandpré report on measuring FTA-induced unemployment. What are the implications for assessing the FTA's consequences for culture and social programmes?

Chronology

1854	— first free trade agreement between Canada and US signed; welcomed in US as step towards annexation of Canada; helped triple Canadian exports within a decade
1866	— abrogation of reciprocity treaty (encouraged by US fishing and lumber industries; US moved to protective tariffs)
1879	— National Policy—a reaction to the ending of tariff reciprocity; tariffs ranged from 25% to 40%
1891	— Laurier Liberals campaigned on "unrestricted reciprocity with the United States" and lost federal election
1911	— free trade election, in which Liberal government of Laurier and his free trade platform were defeated
1947	— aborted US-Canada free trade agreement
1953	— idea of free trade agreement raised between Eisenhower and St-Laurent; later dropped
1965	— negotiation of Auto Pact (Canadian side led by Simon Reisman)
1982	— Macdonald Commission (Royal Commission on the Economic Union and Development Prospects for Canada) set up

January, 1985	— Council of Canadians founded by Mel Hurtig
15 February, 1985	— first ministers' meeting; PM says he will proceed with FTA idea as premiers clearly approve (particularly Lougheed)
17-18 March, 1985	— Quebec Conference ("Shamrock Summit") between Reagan and Mulroney
18 March, 1985	— Reagan and Mulroney announce that USTR Brock and MINT Kelleher are to look at "all possible ways to reduce and eliminate existing barriers to trade" and report back in 6 months
late March, 1985	— Brock given new position as secretary of labor; Yeutter provisionally appointed as new USTR (appointment to be approved by Congress)
July, 1985	— Special Committee on Economic Affairs of Government of Ontario appointed to hold hearings on free trade Committee, composed of 11 members from all parties, has 14-week schedule of hearings
Summer up to 8 August, 1985	— Special Joint Parliamentary Committee on Canada's International Relations travels to 6 cities across Canada to gather views on free trade and Strategic Defence Initiative
22 August, 1985	— premiers' conference in St. John's; FTA negotiations recommended by all premiers with exception of Ontario
5 September, 1985	— Macdonald report released; strongly in favour of free trade
9 September, 1985	— PM announces in House of Commons that he will pursue a free trade agreement with US
17 September, 1985	— reports of Canada and US officials on whether to proceed with free trade (commissioned at Shamrock Summit) given to Reagan and Mulroney
26 September, 1985	— Mulroney calls Reagan, asking for FTA talks; assures House of Commons that he told Reagan cultural industries were not to be on bargaining table
2 October, 1985	— Reagan responds favourably to Mulroney proposal but makes no mention of cultural industries being exempted from FTA discussions

8 November, 1985	— PM picks Simon Reisman to lead Canadian side of FTA negotiations
28-29 November, 1985	— Halifax first ministers' meeting; PM and premiers establish 90-day period, beginning in mid-December, to work towards common ground on (1) a joint federal/provincial data base for FTA talks, (2) outlining of objectives, (3) obstacles to objectives, and (4) definition of full provincial participation
10 December, 1985	— Reagan formally notifies Congress of the administration's intent to enter into FTA negotiations with Canada; Congress has 60 working days to either veto idea or, by remaining silent, allow the talks to proceed
7 January, 1986	— Reisman has first meeting with provincial bureaucrats (objective is to negotiate role of provinces in FTA talks)
9 January, 1986	— International Trade Advisory Committee members named
20-21 January, 1986	— International Trade Advisory Committee meets for the first time in Ottawa
3-4 February, 1986	— closed meeting of provincial trade ministers in Toronto, during which protests are made about Ottawa's failure, so far, to allow full provincial participation in FTA talks
18-20 March, 1986	— ("Shamrock Summit II") Mulroney visits Washington, DC; advised not to address Congress because of fears of protectionist backlash at FTA
11 April, 1986	— 10 out of 20 Senate Finance Committee members vow to vote against FTA talks request on April 17
17 April, 1986	— after intense lobbying, Senate Finance Committee vote postponed to April 22
18 April, 1986	— President Reagan announces he will appeal to Senate Finance Committee members opposing FTA
22 April, 1986	— Senate Finance Committee vote postponed to April 23, last possible day before "fast-track" option expires
23 April, 1986	— Senate Finance Committee passes request to begin FTA negotiations on 10-10 vote just before expiry of

	60-day period during which Congress had option to tell President to proceed or hold off until a legislative committee could hold hearings on FTA
25 April, 1986	— chairman of Sectoral Advisory Groups on International Trade (SAGITs) announced
21-22 May, 1986	— Canada-US FTA talks open with Reisman and Murphy concentrating on administrative details, described by Ottawa as "exploratory talks"
2 June, 1986	— PM meets with premiers at private dinner to discuss power-sharing arrangements in FTA talks (6 months after ninety-day deadline set in November 1985); consultations every 3 months agreed upon
16 June, 1986	— PM goes on television prime time to make speech in favour of free trade negotiations
17 June, 1986	— second session of FTA talks, continuing "issue exploration"
29-31 July, 1986	— third session of FTA talks, covering specific issues of agriculture and US trade laws
9-11 September, 1986	— fourth round of preliminary FTA talks
17 September, 1986	— PM meets with premiers in Ottawa
24-26 September, 1986	— fifth preliminary FTA talks take place in Washington; objective is to complete preliminaries in this round
4 November, 1986	— mid-term congressional elections; Democrats win Senate majority
12-14 November, 1986	— sixth FTA negotiating session in Ottawa
16-18 December, 1986	— seventh FTA negotiating session in Washington, DC
January, 1987	— working groups established
late January, 1987	— more than half of US Congress sponsors omnibus trade bill
11 March, 1987	— first ministers' conference in Ottawa—discussions over formal ratification of FTA by provinces (inconclusive); premiers agree to allow at least another 3 months of negotiations with US
16 March, 1987	— special debate in House of Commons on FTA begins; motion calls for support for bilateral trade agreement that would include protection for Auto Pact, cultural heritage, and agriculture

17 March, 1987	— motion to support free trade passes in Commons 160-58
19 March, 1987	— Alliance for Trade and Job Opportunities (pro-FTA) formed
4 April, 1987	— Pro-Canada Network formed in Ottawa
5-6 April, 1987	— Reagan/Mulroney Summit; Reagan makes speech to Parliament in support of FTA
19-21 May, 1987	— FTA talks—Ottawa
19 May, 1987	— working party on investment issues formed
25 May, 1987	— FTA talks "log-jammed" because of disagreements over investment
11 June, 1987	— Economic Summit in Venice (PM brings up FTA with President Reagan)
15-22 June, 1987	— FTA talks—Washington, DC
22 June, 1987	— first ministers' conference scheduled (postponed to early July because of blockages in FTA negotiations)
7 July, 1987	— first ministers' conference—premiers complain about lack of information available, particularly in view of short time before deadline
13-14 July, 1987	— FTA talks—Washington, DC
14-20 July, 1987	— FTA talks—Ottawa; completed in half a day instead of scheduled three days; Murphy flies to Washington, DC
20 August, 1987	— negotiating teams exchange 100-page drafts of FTA
24-28 August, 1987	— "mammoth" FTA session in Cornwall (20 Canadians and 50 Americans participating)
27 August, 1987	— premiers' conference; premiers express concern at US protectionism
10 September, 1987	— Ontario election—Peterson wins majority
10-11 September, 1987	— FTA talks—Washington, DC
10 September, 1987	— meeting of Economic Policy Council, Washington, DC
14 September, 1987	— first ministers' meeting—Peterson learns Auto Pact is on FTA table (castigated 18 September by Carney for giving press confidential details of FTA)

THE CANADA-US FREE TRADE AGREEMENT

16 September, 1987	— USTR Yeutter and Murphy meet with industry group, which offers advice to US government on FTA negotiations
19 September, 1987	— "secret" consultations involving PM, Wilson, Burney before 21 September official negotiations
21-23 September, 1987	— FTA session — Washington, DC
23 September, 1987	— Canada suspends FTA negotiations
24 September, 1987	— US/Canada telephone discussions of FTA at political level with PM involved
26 September, 1987	— US sends 2-page proposal exploring ways to restart negotiations to Burney in Prime Minister's Office
27 September, 1987	— US letter rejected because it did not meet Canadian demands
28 September, 1987	— "high-level" meeting (Wilson, Carney, Burney, Gotlieb, Campbell, James Baker, Yeutter) in Washington, DC; meeting proposed by Burney in letter to Baker (letter drafted by group including Reisman but under Burney's direction) which reiterated 5 bottom-line Canadian conditions
29 September, 1987	— Canadian government sends Washington document on definition of subsidies
30 September, 1987	— Washington reponds to document; apparently some "shifting of ground" on dispute settlement
1 October, 1987	— Wilson/Carney/Burney fly to Washington to attempt to smooth ground for restarting of discussions (2 1/2 hour meeting); "bargaining has shifted to the political level." Team returns to Ottawa in evening having made "no apparent progress"
2 October, 1987	— emergency meeting of premiers in Ottawa; no details of FTA provided. Negotiating team sent back to Washington, DC
3 October, 1987	— negotiations continue; deal struck at 11:40pm and announced 1:15am Sunday
4 October, 1987	— first version of FTA released to media
5 October, 1987	— second version (with reference to Bill C-22 removed) tabled in Parliament

THE CANADA-US FREE TRADE AGREEMENT

6 October, 1987	— PM meets with premiers to review FTA, even though full agreement not yet available
7 October, 1987	— PM announces "massive" retraining programme to help workers adjust to economic upheaval
8 October, 1987	— referring to PM's statement of October 7, Finance Minister Wilson says, "We do not expect that there will be a need for any significant programmes of adjustment"
1 November, 1987	— Commons Committee on External Affairs and International Trade begins hearings on FTA (even though final text of FTA probably not ready until end of November)
16 November, 1987	— Commons resumes sitting
23 November, 1987	— Commons committee hits the road to conduct hearings on FTA, starting with Vancouver; committee uses 35-page summary of FTA
26-27 November, 1987	— first ministers' conference on the economy—Toronto; PM says that advisory council to deal with job adjustment will be formed
30 November, 1987	— negotiations on legal wording of FTA text resume
1 December, 1987	— Murphy and Reisman continue "haggling and negotiating" over legal wording of FTA text
2 December, 1987	— trade negotiators finish 14-hour meeting; in 2-hour meeting with PM and Cabinet Executive Trade Committee afterwards, Reisman admits final legal wording of text still not completed
3 December, 1987	— House of Representatives committee writes to administration asking that shipping issues be taken out of FTA
5-6 December, 1987	— work on legal text continues through weekend
7 December, 1987	— Final text agreed
10 December, 1987	— final round of negotiations completed and final text initialled
11 December, 1987	— final text released to House of Commons at noon; explained to reporters in "controlled environment"
17 December, 1987	— first ministers' conference in Ottawa—will go through final text of FTA

THE CANADA-US FREE TRADE AGREEMENT

2 January, 1988	— FTA signed by Mulroney and Reagan independently, without great ceremony
18 February, 1988	— US administration announces schedule for congressional consideration of FTA; promises vote to be scheduled by October 8, by August 12 if possible (when Congress recesses)
17 March, 1988	— US Senate Finance Committee begins consideration of FTA
1 April, 1988	— John Crosbie appointed minister for international trade
24 May, 1988	— Bill C-130, the legislation to implement the deal, introduced to House of Commons
31 August, 1988	— Bill C-130 passed in the House of Commons; opposition MPs sing the American anthem, wave the Canadian flag, and are joined by derisive hooting from the public galleries
1 October, 1988	— PM calls the election for 21 November 1988
21 November, 1988	— election held with following results: Tories 169 seats; Liberals 83 seats; NDP 43 seats
31 December, 1988	— Canadian free trade legislation passed and signed into law, to go into effect 1 January 1989
13 March, 1989	— first meeting of the Canada-US Trade Commission
29 March, 1989	— release of the report of the Advisory Council on Adjustment, *Adjusting to Win*
16 October, 1989	— bi-national panel rules that Canadian west coast landing requirements for salmon and herring violate the FTA
30 November, 1989	— second meeting of the Canada-US Trade Commission
14 December, 1989	— bi-national panel rules in favour of Canadian companies protesting antidumping duties on Canadian red raspberries
30 December, 1989	— CLC releases estimate that 77,000 jobs have been lost due to FTA
22 February, 1990	— Canada-US agreement on west coast fishing quotas and landing requirements, in response to bi-national panel ruling of October 1989

THE CANADA-US FREE TRADE AGREEMENT

18 May, 1990	– third meeting of the Canada-US Trade Commission
28 August, 1990	– US International Trade Commission assesses countervailing duties on imports of Canadian pork. Canadian governments and meat producers immediately launch request for a bi-national panel review
28 September, 1990	– bi-national panel releases report on American pork countervails and finds in Canada's favour
11 October, 1990	– fourth meeting of the Canada-US Trade Commission
5 February, 1991	– Canada announces that it will be a "full participant" in negotiations with Mexico and the United States to establish a North American free trade zone.

Appendix I
The Free Trade Agreement:
A Summary

The agreement took various forms, each more elaborate than the last, over the period October 1987 to fall 1988. First came the Principles of Agreement, signed on 3 October 1987. The text of the FTA that was then based on these principles was 305 pages long, counting various interpretive annexes, but not counting tariff schedules. Bill C-130 took up 127 pages, contained 153 clauses, and amended 27 federal statutes. As well, there was the American version of the agreement, with American explanatory notes. Since its passage, several sections of the FTA have been slightly modified and amended (e.g., Chapter 15 on temporary entry of business persons). The following summarizes the *original* agreement.

The summary will use the following reference system when citing the FTA: articles of the agreement will be cited as "FTA 301," clauses of articles will be cited as, for example, "FTA 301.4," and annexes will be cited as "FTA Annex 301."

1. OBJECTIVES AND SCOPE

The FTA is divided into eight parts. Part 1 deals with objectives and scope; Part 2 with trade in goods (containing the key chapters on rules of origin, measures, national treatment, technical standards, agriculture, wine and distilled spirits, energy, automotive goods, and various exceptions for emergencies and under GATT rules); Part 3 deals with government procurement; Part 4 with services (including investment); Part 5 with financial services; Part 6 with institutional provisions regarding dispute resolution; Parts 7 and 8 with miscellaneous issues. Each of the parts contains chapters, and the articles within the chapters are keyed, so that, for instance, all articles in chapter 19 begin with the number 19. FTA 1901 is thus the first article in chapter 19.

The FTA must be read as a whole, since many of its chapters and provisions overlap. At the most general level, the FTA is quite straightforward. It begins by establishing a free trade area, that is, an area comprising Canada and the United States, in which there will be no tariffs on goods traded between the partners, and national treatment of both goods and companies of one country by the other. The chapters on trade in goods set out the rules pertaining to most of the key sectors, along with some exceptions. The parts dealing with government procurement, services, and financial services liberalize trade in these areas. The third pillar of the agreement is the mechanism for dealing with disputes and disagreements, and is followed by some specific provisions for special cases like cultural industries.

Chapter 1 of the FTA states as objectives of the agreement the intent to "eliminate barriers to trade in goods and services," "facilitate conditions of fair competition," "liberalize significantly conditions for investment," and "establish effective procedures for the joint administration of this Agreement"(FTA 102). A central question, of course, is the degree to which the FTA overrides other laws, or might constrain Canada's ability to make nationalistic policies. The agreement is somewhat unclear on this. For example, the preamble states that one of the guiding principles of the deal is "to reduce government-created trade distortions while preserving the Parties' flexibility to safeguard the public welfare." FTA 103, however, states that the parties to "this Agreement shall ensure that all necessary measures are taken in order to give effect to its provisions, including their observance, except as otherwise provided in this Agreement, by state, provincial and local governments." FTA 104.2 says that the provisions of the FTA prevail over other bilateral *and multilateral* agreements to which both countries are parties, unless specifically provided for otherwise by the agreement.

The heart of the agreement is in FTA 105, which states that "each Party shall, to the extent provided in this Agreement, accord national treatment with respect to investment and to trade in goods and services." National treatment means just that: no discriminatory taxes or other barriers that disproportionately disadvantage the goods or services produced by one of the parties in the other party's territory.

2. TRADE IN GOODS

Tariffs. Part 2 of the FTA opens with a chapter on rules of origin. This is crucial, since a free trade area allows the partners to maintain separate tariff regimes against third countries, and the agreement applies only to trade in goods and services produced in Canada or the United States, or both. Neither country wants to allow "transshipments," whereby goods made outside the free trade area are shipped to one of the partners, perhaps with heavy domestic duties, and then simply re-shipped to the other partner. Chapter 3 of the FTA deals with rules of origin. The basic principle is found in FTA 301, which says that goods originate if they are "wholly obtained or produced" in the territory or either territory (FTA 301.1), or if they come from outside but have been "transformed" so as to be subject to a change in tariff classification. The classification system is the International Convention on the Harmonized Commodity Description and Coding System, approved by the Customs Co-operation Council, an international body, in 1983. Goods that have merely been packaged, combined, or diluted with water or some other substance do not count (FTA 301.3), though spare parts, tools, and accessories that come with equipment/machinery will be allowed (FTA 301.4). The FTA will allow partners to produce goods in their territory but ship them through a third country as long as there is no handling apart from what is necessary purely for transportation in the third country (FTA 302). This was included to prevent goods produced in the United States from being shipped to Mexico for further processing and then re-entering the United States for export to Canada duty free. FTA Annex 301.2, subsection 4(a), clarifies the notion of origin further, by stating that a good will be considered to come from one of the parties if 50 per cent of cost of production (materials plus cost of assembly) is accounted for by either or both parties. There is a saving clause for the apparel industry, so that it can continue to import raw materials (fabric) to a certain limit and still have goods counted as originating in the parties' territory.

The crux of the section on trade in goods is the reduction of tariffs. Tariffs are reduced according to three formulae over ten years, depending on the sector's ability to compete. For some sectors (e.g., computers, whiskey and skis), tariffs were completely eliminated on 1 January, 1989. For other sectors (e.g., subway cars, explosives, and furniture) tariffs will be eliminated in equal steps over five years (20 per cent per year). All other tariffs will be eliminated in equal steps over ten years (10 per cent per year). If both countries agree, the staging can be accelerated (FTA 401.5). This provision was exercised several times in the first two years of the agreement. After the agreement came into effect, neither country could increase any of its tariffs, unless specified by the agreement itself (FTA 401.1). FTA 403 ensures that special customs user fees applied by the United States, whereby importers pay for the American customs services they require, will gradually be eliminated.

The rest of the chapter contains several articles that limit the use of the tariff for industrial policy purposes. FTA 404, with certain minor exceptions, prohibits the use of what are called "duty drawbacks," whereby a manufacturer gets back the duty it might have paid on an imported product, as long as that product is incorporated into another product that is subsequently exported. Duty drawbacks have been used by Canadian governments to encourage an export orientation by domestic manufacturers. This article goes into effect on 1 January 1994. FTA 405 prohibits the introduction of any new "customs waiver" programmes that are conditional on performance requirements, and calls for the elimination of all existing programmes (except for automotive trade) by 1 January 1998. Customs waivers of this type exempt a manufacturer from paying duty on imported items as long as that manufacturer meets certain requirements set by the government, such as minimum levels of export or minimum levels of domestic purchasing of parts. If either party to the agreement can show that such a programme adversely affects its interests, the other party must either discontinue it or make it generally available to any importer. FTA 407 disallows quantitative restrictions, as well as minimum export and minimum import price requirements. These provisions affirm GATT obligations. FTA 407 allows either party to impose import or export restrictions on goods to or from a third country, even if they flow through the territory of the other party. FTA 408 prohibits export taxes unless such taxes are applied on the same goods destined for domestic consumption. So, for example, Canada could not, as it did in the 1970s, apply an export tax on oil going to the United States, thus keeping our domestic prices lower than what we charged the Americans.

Chapter 4 of the FTA seeks to eliminate tariffs and other measures such as duty drawbacks, waivers, quotas, and export taxes that restrict trade. But the FTA recognizes that in some cases, countries will need to limit trade in goods. The agreement does this by incorporating existing GATT provisions. These provisions allow import and export control measures for such reasons as protection of public morals (e.g., prohibitions on trade in pornographic materials); human, animal, or plant life; and national treasures. These exemptions are specifically listed in Chapter 12 of the FTA, but they are governed by FTA 409, which deals with GATT allowances for impositions of export controls on items in short supply, conservation schemes, and domestic price stabilization schemes. The article says that such restrictions may not include price increases due to special levies, and that the proportion of exports must remain the same (as measured by the level in the last three years). This article is identical to FTA 904 in the energy chapter, and so pertains specifically to energy exports. The point of the article is to ensure that any quantitative restrictions in energy exports are not disruptive to the other party.

The FTA also allows exceptions to the open trade in goods for emergency purposes. These are addressed in chapter 11 of the agreement, which places restrictions on the powers of either party to limit imports. FTA 1101 allows either party to temporarily raise duties on imports if those imports have caused injury to domestic interests. Such measures may last for a maximum of three years, and in any case will not be allowed after 31 December 1998. The other party must be notified and consulted if such action is taken, and has the right to demand trade concessions in another area that cancel out the negative effects of the restrictions. If such compensation is not forthcoming, the offended party may apply countervailing tariff action with trade effects "substantially equivalent" to the action taken by the other party (FTA 1101.4). As well, global actions taken by either party to limit imports will normally exempt the other party, unless imports from that party are "substantial" (from 5 to 10 per cent of total imports).

National Treatment. Chapter 5 is only one page long, but is central to the agreement. FTA 501 says that each party "shall accord national treatment to the goods of the other party" in accordance with GATT rules, especially GATT Article III. FTA 502 extends the national treatment provision to the provinces and states.

Taken together, these articles mean that Canadian governments, both federal and provincial, cannot treat American goods any differently from the way they treat domestic goods with respect to taxation, regulations for sale, transportation, distribution, or production. American governments cannot discriminate against Canadian goods. Each country may still, of course, apply taxes and regulations as it sees fit; the difference under the FTA is that they may no longer apply them differently depending on the origin of the good. The incorporation of the GATT rules is important as well, since GATT Article III, for example, exempts government procurement programmes and subsidies paid exclusively to domestic producers.

Technical Standards. Chapter 6 deals with technical standards, other than for agriculture, food, and beverages. FTA 601.02 exempts the provinces and states from the subsequent provisions, so that they apply only to national standards. FTA 603 states that no standards are to be set up to act as barriers to trade. FTA 604 aims at compatibility of standards between the two countries, but since many technical standards are set by private bodies, such as the Canadian Standards Association, FTA 605 provides that the two countries will essentially recognize the accreditation systems operating in each of their territories with respect to testing facilities, inspection agencies, and certification bodies. FTA 609 defines "make compatible" to mean mutual recognition of differing standards as being technically identical or equivalent in practice.

Agriculture. Chapter 7 deals with agriculture. It is one of the longest and most complicated of any in the agreement, and while in many respects it leaves traditional policy structures in place, it does liberalize some sectors of Canadian-US agricultural trade. FTA 701 addresses agricultural subsidies. It affirms that the parties have as their goal, on a global basis, the eventual "elimination of all subsidies which distort agricultural trade." Neither party shall "introduce or maintain any export subsidy on any agricultural goods" in bilateral trade (FTA 701.2). The agreement defines an agricultural subsidy as one that is "conditional upon the exportation of agricultural goods" (FTA 711). While these subsidy provisions go beyond existing obligations of the parties under the GATT, export subsidies are not widely used by either country, so the bulk of "real" subsidy programmes remain unaffected by FTA 701.2.

FTA 702 is the so-called snapback provision that provides an escape clause from FTA 401 and its gradual elimination of most tariffs on agricultural products over a ten-year period. Either party is allowed to temporarily apply duties on imported fresh fruits or vegetables if the price of those imports falls below 90 per cent of the average import price for five consecutive days. The article places limits on the amount of the duty that may be levied, the products against which it may be levied, and its duration. FTA 704.1 provides for free trade in beef and veal, but FTA 704.2 allows quantitative restrictions of imports from either party if those restrictions are deemed necessary to give effect to restrictions of imports from other countries. What this means is that if Canada wished to restrict imports of Argentinian beef to protect the domestic market, it could place restrictions on US beef imports as well, if it thought such imports were frustrating its goals. FTA 705 is a provision on license requirements for imports of grains. If the level of US government support for wheat, oats, and barley becomes equal to or less than that provided in Canada, Canada will eliminate import permit requirements for these products originating in the United States.

FTA 706 establishes floors for import levels of chickens and chicken products, turkey and turkey products, eggs and egg products. This article limits Canada's practice of putting quantitative import restrictions on these products. The floor for imports of chickens and chicken products is 7.5 per cent of the previous year's chicken production in Canada; the floor for imports of turkeys and turkey products is 3.5 per cent of the current year's Canadian domestic turkey production quota; and the floor for eggs and egg products varies from 1.647 per cent for shell eggs, to 0.714 per cent for frozen, liquid, and further processed eggs, to 0.627 per cent for powdered eggs.

FTA 708 deals with technical regulations and standards for agricultural, food, beverage, and related products. It is an important article, since many restrictions on agricultural trade are buried in precisely these sorts of rules. The article states that the parties "shall seek an open border policy with respect to trade in agricultural, food, beverage and certain related goods." It then goes on to list several principles that guide the regulation of such goods. The parties will "harmonize their respective technical regulatory requirements and inspection procedures" (the FTA defines "harmonization" for the purposes of this article as "making identical"), apply quarantine restrictions on a regional rather than national basis, and establish equivalent accreditation procedures for inspection systems and inspectors. The rest of the article establishes requirements for notification and consultation, as well as working groups to implement the provisions of the article.

It is important, in the case of agriculture, to note what the FTA *does not* include. It does not directly modify Canada's system of marketing boards or stabilization programmes.

Wine, Spirits and Beer. Wine and distilled spirits qualify for a separate chapter in the agreement, because of the complicated marketing and production arrangements by which they are governed, especially in Canada. Each province controls the sale of wines and spirits, and is given the exclusive power, under the federal Importation of Intoxicating Liquors Act, to import intoxicating liquors into the province from anywhere, including other provinces. Though practices vary, all provinces have as the core of their system a government monopoly over distribution, and this allows special pricing and listing policies to favour domestic producers. On 2 February 1988 a preliminary GATT ruling was made on those practices whereby Canadian provincial liquor authorities discriminated against foreign products. Those practices were found to be in violation of the GATT rules.

Chapter 8 removes discriminatory provincial pricing and listing policies. FTA 802 stipulates that procedures for the listing of wines and spirits be "transparent" and based on normal commercial considerations. An exception is made for British Columbia estate wineries producing less than thirty thousand gallons of wine annually: they are entitled to automatic listing. FTA 803 deals with pricing policies. Prices for imported products may still be higher than for equivalent domestic products, as long as the differential reflects higher costs of marketing and distribution. Apart from that, any existing price differentials must be gradually phased out by 1 January 1995 (FTA 803.2). FTA 804 provides that there should be no discrimination in the distribution of imported and domestic products, with the exception of on-premise sales by wineries and distilleries, and private wine store outlets in British Columbia and Ontario. Quebec is also allowed to maintain its requirement that any wine sold in Quebec grocery stores be bottled in Quebec. FTA 805 removes the Canadian requirement that any bulk imports of distilled spirits had to be blended with Canadian spirits, but under FTA 806 bourbon and Canadian whiskey are protected as distinctive products of the two countries that have to be made there.

Beer and malt beverages are explicitly excluded from the provisions of the agreement. Chapter 12, which deals with exceptions, grandfathers all measures pertaining to the internal sale and distribution of these products.

Energy. Despite its prominence in debates over the FTA, chapter 9 on energy is quite short. Energy products for the purposes of the agreement include coal, oil, natural gas, electricity, and fissionable materials. The existing provisions under GATT allow various exceptions in free trade of energy products, principally for reasons having to do with conservation, shortages, and national security. Also, both Canada and the United States are signatories to the 1974 Agreement on an International Energy Programme, which calls for energy sharing among members in case of specified supply disruptions.

The principal importance of chapter 9 is that it restricts the use of some of the key policy instruments that defined federal energy (especially petroleum and natural gas) policy in the 1970s through to the National Energy Program of 1980. FTA 903 is a copy of FTA 408, and prohibits special taxes on the export of energy goods unless those taxes are also levied on energy goods destined for domestic consumption. FTA 904 copies FTA 409, and allows restrictions of energy exports from one party to another for reasons of shortage and conservation, as long as the restriction does not reduce the other party's *proportion* of the total supply made available as measured over the last three years, does not involve the deliberate imposition of a higher export price than what prevails domestically, and does not disrupt normal channels of supply to the other party. If, for example, Canada wished to reduce exports of natural gas or oil, it could do so only by reducing domestic supply as well, since the proportion of exports to the United States must remain stable.

If one of the parties feels that the other has undertaken discriminatory energy regulatory actions, that party may initiate direct consultations. FTA 906 allows existing or future incentives for oil and gas exploration, development, and related activities. FTA 907 narrows the definition of national security as a basis for export or import restrictions, and applies mostly to the United States, which has relied disproportionately on this rationale.

Automotive Products. The Auto Pact was negotiated in 1965 and came into effect in 1966. It created a system of duty-free trade between Canada and the United States in automotive parts and new automobiles, and incidentally provided a huge boost to the Ontario economy. The Auto Pact provisions that created this duty-free system differed. On the US side, a rule of origin was applied so that duties were waived as long as 50 per cent of the value of a new car was created in North America. Parts were treated as "Canadian" and therefore duty free if imported by bona fide American car manufacturers. On the Canadian side, two performance criteria were used. First, manufacturers had to produce as many cars in Canada as they sold in Canada. Second, *manufacturers had to ensure that 60 per cent of* the value of their production was Canadian in origin. If they met these performance criteria, they were allowed to import automotive parts from anywhere in the world. Originally, when the only automotive manufacturers located in Canada were the Big Three, this presented no problems, since they would import parts from the United States. Later, however, as manufacturers from other countries located in Canada, they were granted duty remissions on the same terms as those applied in the Auto Pact, so that they could receive "Auto Pact status." This was a singular advantage, as it allowed them to export products to the United States duty free. The Canadian performance criteria came to be called "safeguards," since they ensured that a fixed proportion of production would be undertaken in Canada. If a company failed to meet the criteria, duties would be slapped on its parts imports, thus raising the price of its cars and putting it at a disadvantage against its competitors.

Chapter 10 of the FTA must be seen against this backdrop and that of chapters 3 and 4, dealing with rules of origin and general tariff provisions. Chapter 3 of the FTA imposes a new 50 per cent North American value rule of origin, one that is calculated more narrowly than the old US rule. Chapter 4 stipulates that aftermarket automotive parts will carry no tariff as of 1994; production parts will have their duties reduced over ten years (though of course in practice most of these parts move duty free within the North American market). What does chapter 10 say specifically about trade in automotive goods? In effect, its one key article limits the use of duty waivers or remissions by the Canadian government. FTA 1002.1 limits duty waivers to existing qualified Canadian manufacturers (listed in FTA Annex 1002.1). Export-based duty waivers are calculated, as of 1 January 1989, by excluding exports to the territory of the other party (FTA 1002.2). They will terminate on or before 1 January 1998. Furthermore, duty remissions granted to a limited list of companies (e.g., Honda, Hyundai, and Toyota) on the basis of performance requirements will terminate no later than 1 January 1996.

In a sense, these articles may be seen as a "freezing" of the Auto Pact. Canada may still engage in remissions and duty waivers, and may do so on the basis of traditional safeguards, but it may extend these breaks only to companies that currently operate in Canada and meet the requirements. As well, since trade in North American automotive parts will be free eventually, these remissions and waivers will ultimately apply only to the import of non-North American parts, estimated to be worth about $300 million annually. Canada cannot offer this deal to new manufacturers locating here, nor can it offer breaks to companies who will use Canada as a base for exports to the United States.

Finally, FTA 1003 states that Canada will eliminate its import restrictions on used cars over a five-year period.

Exceptions. Many of the key exceptions to free trade in goods have already been cited. Chapter 11 deals with exceptions that come under the rubric of emergency actions. FTA 1101 allows temporary action against imports whose reduced tariffs under Chapter 4 substantially harm a domestic industry. Tariff reductions may be halted, and tariffs even increased to some degree, as long as the party taking action notifies and consults the other party, and the action is limited in duration. FTA 1101.4 gives a right of compensation for such actions, and where such compensation cannot be agreed upon, the right to take tariff action having equivalent tariff effects.

Chapter 12 incorporates the allowable exemptions under GATT Article XX. FTA 1203 has miscellaneous exceptions that remove logs and unprocessed fish from the terms of the FTA.

3. GOVERNMENT PROCUREMENT

Governments in modern industrial states are huge buyers of everything from paper clips to missiles. Many governments typically develop "procurement" policies, which use the purchasing power of the state for wider purposes. Governments may insist that the paper clips they buy be produced domestically, even if they pay higher prices as a consequence. The point of the procurement policy is not simply to get the cheapest item, but to stimulate domestic industry, or in other cases to protect domestic sovereignty. This is not restricted to socialist or nationalist governments: the United States, at both the federal and the state level, has a multitude of "Buy America" programmes. Canada has also favoured domestic suppliers.

This was recognized by GATT members as early as 1973, in the Tokyo Round, and the GATT has had a procurement code since 1981, though it is quite limited; it covers goods only over a specific amount, excludes most services, and does not apply to sub-national levels or to defence spending. The FTA incorporates this existing GATT code, and all its subsequent changes. The FTA obligations merely lower the threshold of bids to US$25,000 and apply only to procurements between this amount and the GATT floor of US$171,000 (FTA 1304.1). FTA 1305 and 1306 expand the procedural and information exchange obligations of the two countries with respect to government procurement. FTA 1305 stipulates that all competitors be treated equally in terms of providing information and in being able to tender and make bids. FTA 1306 says that the parties will cooperate in monitoring the implementation and enforcement of obligations under the chapter, and exchange needed information. FTA Annex 1304.3 lists the government departments and agencies of both parties that are covered by the chapter. On the Canadian side, small business is exempted, while on the US side some defence items and small and minority businesses are exempted.

In monetary terms, Simon Reisman estimated that the FTA chapter on government procurement opens up about $650 million in Canadian contracts to US bids, and $4 billion in US contracts for Canadian bids.

4. SERVICES, ENTRY, AND INVESTMENT

Services. Services trade has emerged as an issue because of recent technological developments that allow, for the first time, international competition in services that once would have been provided almost exclusively at the local level. Global service industries have developed, and the FTA breaks new ground in international trading agreements by incorporating several provisions on their treatment.

The FTA covers services in chapter 14, and lists the covered services in FTA Annex 1408 (for illustrative purposes only; the official list is based on the Standard Industrial Classification numbers applicable in each country). Transportation, day care, basic telecommunications, and government-provided services such as education, health, and social services are not covered. Management of some health and social services is covered, however, as are computer services. FTA 1402.1 ensures national treatment for service providers, and FTA 1402.2 stipulates that sub-national governments must provide treatment "no less favourable than the most favourable treatment" they provide to their own service providers. This means that even if a province or state discriminates against another province or state within its own country, it must give nationals of the other country the most favourable treatment. FTA 1402.3 lists exceptions to this, so that different treatment is allowed for "prudential, fiduciary, health and safety, or consumer protection reasons." FTA 1402.5 makes it clear that all existing discriminatory provisions are grandfathered, though future changes should not make these provisions *more* discriminatory, and of course all new provisions should be consistent with the agreement. FTA 1402.9 exempts government procurement or subsidies from the chapter. FTA 1403 encourages the mutual recognition of licensing and certification requirements for the provision of covered services by nationals of the other party. Finally, FTA 1406.1 denies the benefits of the chapter to services that can be shown to have been indirectly provided by persons in a third party.

Temporary Entry for Business Persons. Chapter 15 of the FTA seeks to simplify the temporary entry of business persons into the two countries. The chapter establishes the general principle that the parties shall provide temporary entry to business persons who otherwise qualify under applicable laws relating to public health and safety and national security. It also stipulates rights of consultation and appeal of decisions.

The system creates four categories of entrants: business visitors (e.g., those involved in research and design, marketing, sales), traders and investors, professionals, and intra-company transferees. Both countries will minimize their approval procedures, eliminating, for example, petitions and labour certification tests.

Investment. Chapter 16, which deals with investment, is one of the most contentious in the entire agreement. Canada has since the late 1950s had strong reservations about foreign, especially American, investment. Since the late 1960s it has used various policy instruments to either curtail foreign investments, review their impact and ensure that they accord with the national interest, or exclude them entirely. The FTA limits the use of some of these instruments.

FTA 1601 stipulates that the chapter applies to all investments except financial services, government procurement, and services other than those covered under chapter 14. Each party is to extend national treatment to investors from the other party with respect to new investments, takeovers, the conduct of business, and sales of enterprises (FTA 1602.1). Neither party can impose minimum-equity participation in firms by its own nationals (FTA 1602.2), or require an investor of the other party to sell its investment by reason of its nationality (FTA 1602.3). The requirement of favourable treatment applies to the sub-national governments as well (FTA 1602.4). Interestingly, the key article of the chapter, FTA 1602, includes several exemptions that apply with particular force to Canada. FTA 1602.5 allows Canada to introduce "any new measure" in respect of federal or provincial crown corporations, even if it is inconsistent with the chapter. However, once such a measure is in place, it may not be made more inconsistent with the chapter (FTA 1602.6). Other exemptions follow ones cited previously concerning differences in treatment due to "prudential, fiduciary, health and safety, or consumer protection reasons" (FTA 1602.8).

The chapter goes on to place some limits on traditional policy devices to curtail foreign investment. FTA 1603 prohibits the imposition on an investor of the other party of performance requirements such as minimum exports or domestic content. FTA 1605 prohibits nationalization or expropriation of investments by investors of the other party except for a "public purpose," "in accordance with due process of law," on a "non-discriminatory basis," and "upon payment of prompt, adequate and effective compensation at fair market value." FTA 1606 limits either party from preventing investors transferring profits, royalties, or other proceeds of their investment, unless such prevention is made in an equitable and non-discriminatory way.

Existing legislation is grandfathered, though Canada agreed to raise its threshold for the review of direct acquisitions in four steps to $150 million. The current threshold is $5 million, meaning that any investment above this amount will be reviewed by Investment Canada. Raising the threshold will remove many American investments from the review process. Canada also agreed to discontinue its review of indirect investments (investments made in Canada by American-owned subsidiaries) by 1992. By grandfathering existing provisions this way, Canadian legislation controlling investment in such sensitive areas as oil, gas, uranium mining, cultural industries, and financial (other than insurance) and transportation services is maintained.

5. FINANCIAL SERVICES

The FTA gave financial services its own small section consisting of one short chapter. The United States, under FTA 1701, undertook largely to exempt Canadian financial institutions from future changes in American law that would discriminate on the basis of national origin. Canada, on the other hand, made commitments that required several changes in existing federal legislation. First, Canada agreed to exempt Americans from foreign-ownership provisions that currently prohibit non-Canadians from owning financial institutions (FTA 1703.1). However, Americans are still restricted by the general provision of the Bank Act that no person may own more than 10 per cent of a bank. Second, United States-controlled Canadian bank subsidiaries are exempted from limitations on the total domestic assets of foreign bank subsidiaries in Canada (FTA 1703.2). Finally, Canada agreed not to use its foreign investment review powers to unduly impede the entry of American financial institutions into the domestic Canadian market (FTA 1703.3).

6. INSTITUTIONAL PROVISIONS

The FTA is shot through with requirements for notification, consultation, compensation, and further negotiation. There are large areas that are unclear, others that will invite dispute, and still others in which the agreement calls for continued review and negotiation. All of these demand some institutional mechanism to manage the agreement and deal with disputes. The FTA splits the problem of disputes/consultation/negotiation into two parts. The first deals with explicit provisions of the FTA itself. This is a matter of how to manage those terms upon which the parties were able to agree. The second deals with the thorny problem of trade remedy legislation, which the parties *were not* able to resolve. Trade remedies consist of such measures as countervailing duties and anti-dumping measures, whereby a country explicitly erects protective tariffs or other measures against what it considers to be unfair competition by importers.

Managing the FTA. Chapter 18 of the FTA establishes a Canada-United States Trade Commission to deal with "the avoidance or settlement of all disputes regarding the interpretation or application of this Agreement or whenever a party considers that an actual or purposed measure of the other party is or would be inconsistent with the obligations of this Agreement" (FTA 1801). The Commission has power in all matters except those dealing with financial services (FTA chapter 17) and trade remedy cases involving anti-dumping and countervailing duties.

The Commission not only resolves disputes but supervises the implementation of the FTA and its subsequent elaborations. It is composed of representatives of both countries, the principle representatives being the cabinet-level officer or minister primarily responsible for international trade. The FTA stipulates that the Commission is to convene at least once a year, with meeting places to alternate between the two countries. It may develop its own rules and procedures, though all its decisions must be taken by consensus. It also has the power to establish and delegate responsibilities to ad hoc or standing committees and working groups (FTA 1802).

The FTA assumes that the two countries will notify each other and consult with respect to any possible measures either is considering that might affect the agreement. So, if the United States was considering legislation that might affect Canada's interests under the agreement, it would be obligated to inform Canada as early as possible, in writing, before the measure was implemented. If this is impossible, then immediate notification after implementation is required (FTA 1803.2). Even if the United States was convinced that any measure that it was considering would not affect Canada, Canada would still have the right of consultation (FTA 1804). If these consultations do not resolve a matter within thirty days, either party may request a meeting of the Commission, and unless otherwise agreed that meeting must take place within ten days (FTA 1805.1). The Commission has thirty days to try to resolve disputes; if it cannot then it must refer the dispute to binding arbitration of a specially appointed panel. If a party fails to implement the decision of such a panel, and the parties are unable to agree to compensation or remedial action, then the other party has the right to take action that will remove "equivalent benefits" from the non-complying party (FTA 1806). What this means is that if a panel found against the United States, but the Americans refused to implement the decision, then Canada could raise a tariff or take some other action whose economic effect would cancel out the gain sought through the disputed measure.

The panels are the heart of the dispute-resolution system. They consist of five members, appointed from a roster kept by the Commission. Two are Canadian, two American, with a Commission-appointed chair. If either party fails to appoint its panelists within fifteen days, they are selected by lot from those of its citizens on the roster. If the Commission fails to appoint a chair within fifteen days, then at the request of either party, the panelists have fifteen days to appoint one. If they in turn fail, the chair will be selected by lot from the roster (FTA 1807.3). Once established, the panels may set their own procedures, as long as they ensure at least one hearing and the opportunity to submit both written and oral arguments (1807.4). Their proceedings are confidential, and unless otherwise agreed, they will base their decision on the submissions and arguments of the parties.

Within three months of the chairperson's appointment, the panel must submit a preliminary report with its findings of fact and recommendations (FTA 1807.5). Panelists may submit separate opinions. parties have fourteen days to respond to the initial report, and the panel then has another sixteen days to revise and reconsider its initial report, if necessary (FTA 1807.6). The final report of the panel is to be published, along with "any separate opinions, and any written views that either party desires to be published" (FTA 1807.7), and will go to the Commission, which normally resolves the dispute in such a way as to conform with the recommendation of the panel (FTA 1807.8). Whenever possible, the resolution of the dispute will be the *non-implementation* of the offending measure that caused the panel to convene in the first place. Alternatively, the measure could go through but the other party would have to be compensated (FTA 1807.8). If the Commission cannot reach agreement within thirty days of receiving the panel's final report, and a party considers that its interests under the agreement will be impaired, that party has the right to suspend "benefits of equivalent effect" to the other party until some satisfactory resolution can be achieved (FTA 1807.9).

Anti-dumping and Countervailing Duties. As noted earlier, much of the original impetus for the free trade negotiations, from the Canadian side at least, was the concern over rising American protectionism. This protectionism took the form of capricious application of anti-dumping and countervailing duties. The first pertains to goods that are sold at prices lower than in their domestic market. The second is conceptually different, though the effect is the same. In countervail cases, a government may decide that manufacturers of imports have been unfairly subsidized in some way by their domestic governments, giving their products an unfair advantage. A countervailing duty is a special tariff set theoretically to make up the difference of the subsidy. In the early days of the free trade negotiations, it was hoped that Canada would be able to escape such actions entirely. The best that the FTA could achieve, however, was a complicated review process that leaves intact the domestic law-making powers of both countries, but also their judicial mechanisms for dealing with anti-dumping and countervail applications. A working group was established which, over five to seven years, is to develop a new subsidies code (FTA 1906 and 1907).

Each party "reserves the right to apply its antidumping law and countervailing duty law to goods imported from the territory of the other party" (FTA 1902.1).

Each party may also modify these laws, but such modifications will apply to the other party only if it is explicitly named. The other party must be notified and consulted, and such amendments must not offend the spirit of the GATT and must be consistent with the general purposes of the FTA to liberalize trade (FTA 1902.2). But the real issue, at least for the short term, is not the laws themselves, but the decisions that are made with respect to anti-dumping and countervails, based on these laws. The FTA does not affect the powers of either party to make such determinations; all it does is substitute a quasi-judicial review process to determine whether such a decision was in accordance with the party's anti-dumping or countervailing duty law (defined as "relevant statutes, legislative history, regulations, administrative practice, and judicial precedents"). The FTA establishes special expert panels to replace the final judicial review functions of the Federal Court (Canada) and the Court of International Trade (US).

Panelists are drawn from a roster consisting of fifty people, twenty-five from each country. The parties are to consult, and propose candidates of "good character, high standing and repute" who show qualities of "objectivity, reliability, sound judgment, and general familiarity with international law" (FTA Annex 1902.2(1)). Because the panels' functions are quasijudicial, the majority of members on each panel must be lawyers. Like the arbitration panels under chapter 18, these panels have five members. Each party initially proposes two panelists and has up to four peremptory challenges to the other's panelists. In the event of disagreement or inability to appoint the first two panelists and ultimately the fifth panelist, the same type of procedures apply as in the case of arbitration panels under chapter 18, though the time limits are somewhat longer (FTA Annex 1901.2(3)). The chair of the panel will be then chosen by and from the ranks of the lawyers on the panel. All panelists are governed by a code of conduct established by the parties (FTA 1910).

Either party may request panel review of an anti-dumping or countervailing duty determination made by the other. The parties have thirty days from the publication or notification of such a determination to make their written request for a panel review (FTA 1904.4). While the parties have to design rules of procedure for the review panels, these rules will be based on prevailing judicial ones pertaining to appellate courts. The procedural rules will be designed in such a way as to ensure that final panel decisions will be submitted no later than 315 days after the request for the panel was made (FTA 1904.14).

A close reading of chapter 19 shows that it contemplates two types of panels and two types of determinations. The first is covered by FTA 1903, and pertains to the review of statutory amendments. In this case, a panel can only issue an opinion as to whether an amendment to an anti-dumping or countervailing duty statute does not conform to the GATT or the spirit of the FTA. If it does recommend modifications to the statute, the parties have to consult to seek a resolution within ninety days. If they fail, and if nothing has been done within nine months of the end of this consultation period, the offended party may take comparable legislative action, or may terminate the FTA with sixty days' notice (FTA 1903.3).

The second type of panel reviews final anti-dumping and countervailing duty determinations. These panels may uphold the determination (i.e., decide that it is consistent with the law) or remand it, and its decisions are final and binding on the parties (FTA 1904.9 and 1904.10). Remanding means that the original authority that issued the order must amend it in a way consistent with the panel's ruling. There is a time limit on this, which varies, but cannot exceed the time allowed for the authority to make its determinations in the first place.

7. OTHER PROVISIONS

Part 7 of the FTA includes miscellaneous matters, but several are of critical importance. FTA 2001 exempts the treatment of taxation from the FTA, upholding rights and obligations under the 1980 Convention between Canada and the United States of America with Respect to Taxes on Income and on Capital. FTA 2002 allows various restrictions to be applied by either party, within limits, with regard to balance-of-payments issues. There are provisions on national security, intellectual property, softwood lumber, and plywood standards. On the whole these are relatively minor aspects of the FTA, but several articles are of more direct interest.

FTA 2005 explicitly exempts cultural industries from the agreement. Cultural industries are defined as enterprises engaged in the publication, distribution, sale, and exhibition (if this applies) of books, magazines, and newspapers; film or video recordings; audio or video music recordings; printed music; and radio, television, cable broadcasting, satellite programming, and broadcast network services (FTA 2012). The exemption is not complete, however. The tariff provisions of the FTA apply (FTA 401), as does the specific provision that if Canada demands the divestiture of a business in the cultural industry because of its indirect purchase by an American firm, Canada will offer to buy the business at a fair price (FTA 1607.4). Also, FTA 2006 stipulates that Canadian cable broadcasters pay a royalty for the re-transmission of American TV programmes as of 1 January 1990. Canadian cable operators traditionally have picked up American signals for free and re-transmitted them to Canadian viewers for a fee. The general right that each of the parties has to invoke consultation and dispute-settlement procedures on any measure they deem will nullify or impair any benefit reasonably expected to flow from the agreement, does not apply to cultural industries (FTA 2011.2).

FTA 2005.2 reads: "Notwithstanding any other provision of this Agreement, a party may take measures of equivalent commercial effect in response to actions that would have been inconsistent with the Agreement but for paragraph 1." Since cultural industries are not covered by the FTA, Canada may pass laws in the field that contravene the agreement, for example, prohibiting the importation of American non-pornographic films or magazines in order to protect the domestic market. FTA 2005.2 allows the United States to completely circumvent the procedures in chapter 18 on dispute resolution, and take action as it sees fit (but not inconsistent with the FTA) to exact equivalent commercial effect. The nature of this effect is not discussed in the FTA, and it need not be in the cultural area. Canadian actions against American videos could be met with American actions against Canadian fish.

Finally, there are provisions on the establishment of "monopolies" or state enterprises. FTA 2010.1 says that nothing in the agreement "shall prevent a party from maintaining or designating a monopoly." If the establishment of a monopoly might affect the interests of persons of the other party, there are requirements of prior notification and consultation, as well as an obligation of the offending party to minimize any impairment of benefits under the agreement for the other party (FTA 2010.2). A monopoly, once established, may not discriminate in its sales against persons or goods of the other party, or use its monopoly power in other markets (through, for example, subsidiaries) to compete unfairly (FTA 2010.3).

Notes

1   *Globe and Mail*, 19 March 1985.

2   *Globe and Mail*, 19 March 1985.

3   Two in particular, both released in 1983, were important: *Canadian Trade Policy for the 1980s* and *A Review of Canadian Trade Policy*.

4   *Globe and Mail*, 21 January 1985.

5   *Globe and Mail*, 23 March 1985, B1. The report studied only thirty-five industry groups, and
     looked only at tariff barriers.

6   *Globe and Mail*, 25 April 1985.

7   *Globe and Mail*, 16 May 1985.

8   *Winnipeg Free Press*, 17 May 1985.

9   *Globe and Mail*, 23 August 1985.

10   *Globe and Mail*, 9 May 1985; 26 June 1985. Also see the submissions by business organizations
     to the Macdonald Commission, particularly the pro-free trade stance by the Canadian
     Manufacturers' Association, an organization with a long history of support for tariff barriers.

11   *Toronto Star*, 28 May 1985.

12   *Toronto Star*, 28 June 1985.

13   *Toronto Star*, 27 July 1985. Both the American and Canadian branches of the United Steel-
     workers also opposed free trade; *Globe and Mail*, 4 June 1985.

14   *Globe and Mail*, 2 May 1985; 18 July 1985.

15   *Toronto Star*, 3 August 1985.

16   *Toronto Star*, 9 August 1985.

17   *Globe and Mail*, 24 July 1985.

18   *Globe and Mail*, 26 June 1985.

19   Royal Commission on the Economic Union and Development Prospects for Canada, *Report*,
     3 vols. (Ottawa: 1985).

20   *Montreal Gazette*, 10 September 1985.

21   *Globe and Mail*, 27 September 1985.

22   *Globe and Mail*, 25 September 1985.

23   *Globe and Mail*, 18 September 1985.

24   Interview, Ottawa, August 1988.

25   *Globe and Mail*, 28 September 1985.

26   *Globe and Mail*, 30 September 1985.

27   *Globe and Mail*, 1 October 1985.

28   *Toronto Star*, 4 October 1985.

29   These remarks were made variously by William Merkin (deputy assistant US trade repre-
     sentative) on 7 October and by William Brock (US secretary of labor) on 23 October.

30   *Globe and Mail*, 9 November 1985.

31   *Globe and Mail*, 30 November 1985.

32   *Toronto Star*, 11 October 1988.

33   *Globe and Mail*, 23 December 1985. These figures are from an Environics and CROP poll
     conducted from 18 November to 11 December on 2,036 Canadians.

34   *Globe and Mail*, 8 January 1986.

35   *Globe and Mail*, 11 January 1986.

36   *Globe and Mail*, 23 January 1986.

37   *Globe and Mail*, 24 January 1986.

38   *Globe and Mail*, 6 February 1986.

39   *Globe and Mail*, 8 February 1986.

40   *Globe and Mail*, 18 February 1986.

41   *Globe and Mail*, 22 March 1986.

42   *Globe and Mail*, 28 February 1986.

43   *Globe and Mail*, 12 April 1986.

44   *Globe and Mail*, 15 April 1986.

45   *Globe and Mail*, 18 April 1986.

46   *Globe and Mail*, 22 April 1986.

47   *Globe and Mail*, 23 April 1986.

48   *Globe and Mail*, 29 April 1986.

49   *Globe and Mail*, 16 April 1986.

50   *Globe and Mail*, 5 March 1986.

51   *Globe and Mail*, 3 June 1986.

52   Canada's somewhat curious response was to slap a tariff on US books and periodicals.

53   *Globe and Mail*, 27 May 1986.

54   *Globe and Mail*, 17 June 1986.

55   *Toronto Star*, 19 June 1986.

56   *Globe and Mail*, 18 June 1986.

57   *Globe and Mail*, 12 November 1986.

58   *Globe and Mail*, 13 November 1986.

59   *Globe and Mail*, 13 September 1986.

60   *Globe and Mail*, 17 October 1986.

61   *Globe and Mail*, 20 October 1986.

62   *Globe and Mail*, 19 January 1987.

63   *Globe and Mail*, 16 January 1987.

64   *Globe and Mail*, 10 January 1987.

65   *Globe and Mail*, 20 February 1987.

66   *Globe and Mail*, 19 March 1987.

67   *Globe and Mail*, 6 April 1987.

68   *Toronto Star*, 7 May 1987.

69   *Globe and Mail*, 13 March 1987.

70   *Globe and Mail*, 18 March 1987.

71   *Globe and Mail*, 27 April 1987.

72   *Globe and Mail*, 21 May 1987. Also see story on A3.

73   *Globe and Mail*, 25 May 1987.

74   *Globe and Mail*, 10 June 1987.

75   *Globe and Mail*, 17 June 1987.

76   *Globe and Mail*, 7 July 1987.

77   *Globe and Mail*, 8 July 1987.

78   *Globe and Mail*, 9 July 1987.

79   *Globe and Mail*, 9 July 1987.

80   *Globe and Mail*, 24 August 1987.

81   *Globe and Mail*, 29 August 1987.

82   *Globe and Mail*, 10 September 1987.

83   *Globe and Mail*, 15 September 1987.

84   *Globe and Mail*, 16 September 1987.

85   *Globe and Mail*, 21 September 1987.

86   *Globe and Mail*, 23 September 1987.

87   *Globe and Mail*, 23 September 1987.

88   *Globe and Mail*, 24 September 1987.

89   *Globe and Mail*, 25 September 1987.

90   *Toronto Star*, 28 September 1987.

91   *Globe and Mail*, 30 September 1987.

92   *Globe and Mail*, 3 October 1987.

93   *Globe and Mail*, 5 October 1987.

94   *Globe and Mail*, 5 October 1987.

95   *Globe and Mail*, 28 October 1987.

96   *Toronto Star*, 31 October 1987.

97   *Toronto Star*, 5 November 1987.

98   *Globe and Mail*, 17 November 1987.

99   *Globe and Mail*, 2 December 1987.

100   *Globe and Mail*, 4 December 1987.

101   *Globe and Mail*, 8 December 1987.

102   *Globe and Mail*, 12 April 1988.

103   *Globe and Mail*, 2 August 1988.

104   *Globe and Mail*, 16 August 1988.

105   *Globe and Mail*, 19 November 1988.

106   Simon Reisman, in *Assessing the Canada-US Free Trade Agreement*, ed. Murray G. Smith and
      Frank Stone (Ottawa: IRPP, 1987), 46.

107   John Dillon, "Continental Energy Policy," in *The Free Trade Deal*, ed. Duncan Cameron
      (Toronto: James Lorimer, 1988), 104.

108   Andrew Jackson, "The Trade Deal and the Resource Sector," in *The Free Trade Deal*, 98.

109   Ibid., 101.

THE CANADA-US FREE TRADE AGREEMENT

110 Edward A. Carmichael, "Energy," in *Free Trade: The Real Story*, ed. John Crispo (Toronto: Gage, 1988), 68.

111 Duncan Cameron and Hugh Mackenzie, "Manufacturing," in *The Free Trade Deal*, 118.

112 John Calvert, "Government Procurement," in *The Free Trade Deal*, 136.

113 Hugh Mackenzie, "Free Trade and the Auto Industry," in *The Free Trade Deal*, 127.

114 Reisman, in *Assessing the Canada-US Free Trade Agreement*, 44.

115 Ronald J. Wonnacott, "Labor Market Adjustments," in *Free Trade: The Real Story*, 63.

116 Duncan Cameron, Stephen Clarkson, and Mel Watkins, "Market Access," in *The Free Trade Deal*, 52.

117 Stephen Clarkson, "The Canada-United States Trade Commission," in *The Free Trade Deal*, 29. The following articles of the FTA, for example, call for the Commission to be notified of any actions: 1102.2, 1102.3, 1402.3, 1602.8, 1803. There is a blanket provision for consultation in FTA 1804, as well as specific provisions.

118 Ibid., 45.

119 Reisman, in *Assessing the Canada-US Free Trade Agreement*, 44.

120 Donald Macdonald, in *Assessing the Canada-US Free Trade Agreement*, 26.

121 Ibid., 27-8.

122 Susan Crean, "Reading Between the Lines: Culture and the Free-Trade Agreement," in *The Free Trade Deal*, 230.

123 Gerald Caplan, in *Assessing the Canada-US Free Trade Agreement*, 260.

124 Duncan Cameron, "Introduction," *The Free Trade Deal*, vii.

125 Daniel Drache, "North American Integration," in *The Free Trade Deal*, 73.

126 Canada, Minister of International Trade, *News Release*, 30 November 1989.

127 *Globe and Mail*, 20 April 1990.

128 Canada, Minister of International Trade, *News Release*, 30 November 1989.

129 Canada, Advisory Council on Adjustment, *Adjusting to Win* (Ottawa: Minister of Supply and Services, March 1990), xvii.

130 Ibid.

131 *Toronto Star*, 14 January 1989.

132 *Toronto Star*, 24 February 1989.

133 *Globe and Mail*, 15 June 1989. At this point, concerns about relocations to the Mexican Maquiladora zone—a tax-free industrial park along the Mexican-American border—had resurfaced. Within a year the US and Mexico began to discuss a free trade agreement between their two countries, and Canada formally requested a seat at the table. Canada's participation signals the possibility of a North American Free Trade Zone. Canada's strategy was dictated by the view that if a Mexico-US agreement were forged, companies would have an incentive to relocate in the US, since it would be the only country with free access to the entire North American market.

134 *Calgary Herald*, 5 July 1989.

135 *Toronto Star*, 30 December 1989. While layoffs and plant closures had been announced almost weekly through the year, the *Star* noted that the FTA "was rarely cited by the firms involved....

Only the victims, the unions, and the political critics [were] left to connect shutdowns to direct and indirect effects of free trade."

136   Canada, Minister for International Trade, *News Release*, 19 January 1990.

137   Richard G. Harris, "Employment Effects," in *Free Trade: The Real Story*, 107.

138   *Winnipeg Free Press*, 28 February 1989.

139   *IMF Survey*, vol. 18, 15 May 1989, 147.

140   *Financial Post*, 24 March 1990.

141   As noted earlier, there were several other chapter 18 and chapter 19 panels active in the first two years, but they captured less attention than the three discussed here. Potentially the most important dealt with plywood standards. Canadian standards prevent the use of some American grades in the housing industry, which led to complaints from American manufacturers. A panel was established in 1989 to develop a harmonized standards system.

142   *Vancouver Sun*, 23 February 1990.

143   Canada, External Affairs and International Trade, *Free Trade News*, July/August 1990.

FEATHER AND GUN:

CONFRONTATION AT

OKA/KANESATAKE

It was the "Indian summer" of the century. In March 1990 Mohawk Warriors erected a barricade at Kanesatake, near Oka, Quebec, to protest the commercial development of lands they claimed were their own. The barricade was at first only a political protest, but after a police raid in July, became an armed stand-off that eventually involved thousands of Canadian troops and native protests across the country. The Mercier Bridge, a vital link to Montreal for sixty thousand daily commuters from Châteauguay, was closed by barricades manned by Warriors from the nearby Mohawk reserve of Kahnawake. Mobs gathered nightly at the bridge to burn effigies of Indians and politicians, and riots broke out as Quebec seemed to teeter on the edge of civil insurrection. The Warriors surrendered on 26 September, but not before they publicized their claims that the Mohawks were a sovereign nation. These claims were dismissed by federal and provincial politicians, but were broadly supported by native leaders across Canada. The Oka crisis, apparently a bizarre departure from "normal" politics, was in fact a faithful reflection of the evolution of Canadian–native relations over the last two centuries. Oka showed that aboriginal policy is in desperate need of attention, that beneath the seemingly tranquil surface of land claims negotiations, court cases, and the Indian Act, there seethes a deep and dangerous discontent among natives. Oka also revealed the official ambivalence and constitutional impasse that plagues existing aboriginal policy. Paradoxically, the removal of the Mohawk barricades at Kanesatake and Kahnawake in turn established new barriers to understanding between natives and other Canadians, barriers that render policy-making more difficult, even as it becomes more urgent.

Oka is a bucolic little Quebec town about twenty minutes from Montreal. In more innocent days it was known principally for its pungent cheese and one or two surprisingly good restaurants. Those days of innocence, coloured by complacency and at times a wilful ignorance, are gone forever. "Oka" is no longer a synonym for pleasant gustatory sensations; say the word anywhere in Canada—indeed, almost anywhere in the world—and images boil up of barricades and police raids, bullets and stones, razor wire, tanks, feather and gun.

The confrontation at Oka mesmerized the country for almost eight weeks between August and September 1990. The events in themselves were quite simple. At dawn on 11 July, one hundred members of the Quebec police force, the Sûreté du Quebec (SQ), raided Mohawk barricades that had been erected near the town to protect what the Indians called their sacred lands from commercial development. The SQ surged towards the barricades with a front-end loader to clear the road, but were driven back. They tried and were rebuffed again. In the confusion, a thirty-one-year-old member of the SQ, Corporal Marcel Lemay, was shot in the head and killed. Mohawks captured the front-end loader, police vehicles, guns, and radios. The next day, another group of Warriors erected a sympathy blockade at the Mercier Bridge, a vital link to Montreal for over sixty thousand daily commuters from the community of Châteauguay. At first, the provincial and federal governments refused to negotiate until the barricades came down, and the Mohawks refused to take them down until negotiations took place. All attempts to negotiate failed, and on 18 August the army moved in. Soldiers took up positions around both Mohawk communities, removing the barricades. Indian bands across the country, inspired by the Mohawks, took similar direct action to close roads and rail lines. Quebeckers, particularly Châteauguay residents who now had to drive an additional three hours each day to get to and from work in Montreal, were equally enraged. Mobs burned Indian effigies at the Mercier Bridge, and in a particularly ugly incident, threw stones at fleeing cars filled with native women and children. The UN sent observers, and Canadians heard various Mohawk spokespersons declare themselves to be members of an Indian nation with full aboriginal title to disputed lands. The last Mohawk Warriors were compelled to surrender on 26 September.

It is tempting to dismiss Oka and its associated incidents as aberrations. Canadians are a markedly unmilitary people, and the sight of soldiers and armoured vehicles confronting Indians dressed in battle fatigues and masks seemed more appropriate to Lebanon than to Canada. The apparent triviality of the initial dispute—the land in question was to be developed as an extension to the existing municipal golf course—casts the affair as some sort of bizarre departure from normal politics. Indeed, the entire episode might never have happened without the botched SQ raid and Corporal Lemay's death. But while the confrontation at Oka did have aberrant and accidental aspects, it was rooted in one of the most

FEATHER AND GUN: CONFRONTATION AT OKA/KANESATAKE

stable, if usually invisible, dimensions of Canadian politics: aboriginal claims. Because Indians[1] number less than 500,000, are scattered throughout the country and in most cases on reserves, they and their problems are often invisible to other Canadians. Those problems are legion, however: poverty, inadequate education, sickness, high infant mortality, suicide, and discrimination. For more than a hundred years, Ottawa has paternalistically controlled virtually every aspect of native life through its Department of Indian Affairs and the Indian Act. Since the 1970s native leaders have increasingly demanded that control over native life be returned to the communities themselves, primarily through the resolution of land claims that recognize aboriginal title and the establishment of native self-government. The 1982 adoption of the Charter of Rights and Freedoms, which in section 35(1) recognizes and affirms "existing aboriginal and treaty rights," further stimulated native demands for self-government, demands that received a respectful hearing and support from a special parliamentary committee in 1983. Comprehensive land claims negotiations have been underway for years (without much success to date), and first ministers' conferences on aboriginal constitutional matters were held in 1983, 1984, 1985, and 1987. Native concerns became a prominent part of the Meech Lake process as well, when Elijah Harper, an Ojibway-Cree MLA killed the accord in the Manitoba legislature. Harper became an instant hero to the accord's critics, but few of them understood that his opposition was fuelled by impatience with the glacial pace of reform and redress of native issues.

Oka resonated with these ambiguous and troubled legacies. Though there were differences within the Mohawk community over tactics and the use of violence, native leaders unanimously affirmed what they saw as the moral legitimacy of the Warrior's fight. That fight evolved from a confused dispute over a small piece of land to a larger debate about native sovereignty. The more radical Warriors and their spokespersons declared the Mohawk/native peoples of Canada to be sovereign nations in their own right. They would not recognize white man's law or the legitimacy of white man's justice. The direct support the Warriors received from the native communities of Kahnawake and Kanesatake and the moral support they received from natives across Canada were rooted in the firm, unshakable assumption that historically they had been ignored and manipulated. Violence was universally deplored, but most native leaders argued that it was the only way to break through the hard crust of indifference that has suffocated the aspirations of Canada's aboriginal peoples.

It is important therefore to see the events at Oka for what they are. In themselves, while important, they were indeed an aberration, a unique explosion of force and violence in the pursuit of political ends. But to focus exclusively on these events would be like exhaustively examining a spark cast off from an inferno. In itself, Oka has changed, perhaps forever, the trajectory of Canadian/aboriginal relations. Oka is properly understood, however, as a symptom of larger forces and a deeper malaise. This chapter will tell the story of Oka, but it will also project that story onto a larger canvas that can more clearly reveal several key motifs and themes.

The first and most vibrant of these is the issue of native land claims and aboriginal title. Colonial governments began signing treaties with aboriginals in the seventeenth century, though most of the early ones involved military alliances and not transfers of land.[2] As settlement progressed and land became an issue for Europeans, the orientation of treaty negotiations shifted. Following the defeat of the French and the Treaty of Paris, the British Crown issued the Royal Proclamation of 7 October 1763, which expressly placed the "several Nations or Tribes of Indians with whom we are connected" under the protection of the British Crown. Perhaps most importantly, the Royal Proclamation stipulated that "hunting grounds" outside of existing colonial and Hudson Bay lands that had not been expressly ceded or purchased from the Indians were reserved for them. Any transfer of title had to occur first through the Crown and then to private interests. After Confederation, as settlement proceeded westward, Ottawa signed a series of eleven treaties to facilitate transportation and acquire necessary land. These "numbered treaties" sought to extinguish native title in exchange for reserves, cash payments, and other benefits sometimes as trivial as guaranteed twine payments or suits of clothing for chiefs and headmen. The territorial scope of the numbered treaties is indicated in Map 1, which graphically demonstrates a crucial fact about contemporary aboriginal policy often misunderstood by Canadians: only 57 per cent of status Indians (those registered under the Indian Act) are *treaty* Indians. Almost half of Canada's Indians, and most of its Métis and Inuit, never signed treaties with Ottawa, and so may retain aboriginal title. The dispute over land by the Kanesatake Mohawks is part of a much larger problem involving claims such as those by the James Bay Cree (signed in 1975), the Inuvialuit (known as the COPE Agreement, for Committee for Original Peoples' Entitlement, signed in 1984), the Dene/Métis (an agreement-in-principle covering the Mackenzie Basin area that was signed in 1988 but collapsed in November 1990), the Haida (most notably over South Moresby Island), the Micmac (who in 1990 filed a claim to most of Nova Scotia), and many others. To complicate matters further, some bands within the existing treaty territories never signed agreements with Ottawa and so never ceded lands or received reserves. The most vivid example of this is the 450-member Lubicon band of northern Alberta, which because of size and remoteness was overlooked when Treaty 8 was signed in 1899.[3] In

FEATHER AND GUN: CONFRONTATION AT OKA/KANESATAKE

1989 the band barricaded roads into the territory it claimed as its own, and demanded special payments from resource companies operating there.

A second, related motif is the question of sovereignty and self-government. The land claims issue is central to the question of self-determination, since without some land base it is impossible for native communities to develop economically and retain their cultural and social distinctiveness. The resolution of land claims is only a means to an end. More fundamentally, the current consensus among native leaders is that while lands may have been ceded through the treaty process, aboriginals never relinquished their sovereign rights as distinct nations. The 1763 Royal Proclamation referred to "Indian Nations" and used language that appears to affirm their independence. A moderate version of this position guided constitutional negotiations over aboriginal self-government from 1984 to 1987: a vague presumption of native sovereignty allowed some specific

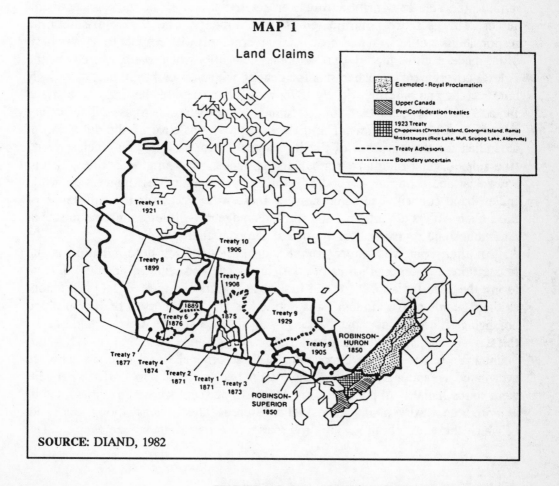

MAP 1

Land Claims

SOURCE: DIAND, 1982

FEATHER AND GUN: CONFRONTATION AT OKA/KANESATAKE

agreements on delegation of powers and responsibilities to be reached. The 1987 first ministers' conference failed, however, because there could be no agreement on the constitutional entrenchment of native self-government as a matter of principle. The more direct position on sovereignty is the one enunciated by the Mohawk Warriors at their Oka barricade: the Mohawks were a separate nation not subject to the laws of Canada except by their own agreement. Ironically, this was the same point of view expressed at the 1984 first ministers' conference on aboriginal constitutional matters by Chief Billy Two Rivers of the Kahnawake Mohawk Council: "The new constitution that has been granted to the Parliament of Canada by Great Britain will have no jurisdictional authority within our territories or over our people. Our people are citizens of our nation and do not seek citizenship within the nation of Canada."[4]

In practical terms, native self-determination has several distinct but related dimensions. Most simply but most directly as well, it requires that native communities be able to control and deliver key social and economic services themselves. This is more complicated than it appears. The fuzzy jurisdictional responsibilities of federal and provincial governments with respect to natives have often made it difficult to design workable delegations of powers. Moreover, the federal government's mechanisms for dealing with natives have been numbingly bureaucratic and paternalistic. By 1876, with the passage of the first consolidated Indian Act, it was clear that the government's approach was to assimilate natives into white, Christian society. The act's main provisions covered the definition of an Indian for the purposes of the legislation, the process of "enfranchisement" (the relinquishing of Indian status), Indian lands, governing authorities, claims, and social and economic practices in the Indian communities themselves. While Indian band councils had some powers, these were always at the sufferance of the Indian Affairs department and the Indian agent. Self-determination means at minimum some reassertion of control at the community level.

Another, somewhat more complex dimension of self-determination is the reassertion of traditional forms of aboriginal social and political practice. In legal terms, the 1876 Indian Act treated Indians as minors and the federal government as their guardian. An "Indian" was defined as any male person of Indian blood belonging to a particular band, along with his wife and legitimate children. To this day, the Department of Indian Affairs and Northern Development (DIAND) maintains a registry of the descendants of these original "legal" Indians, who are designated as "status Indians." Of the total native population in 1981, 60 per cent were status Indians, 20 per cent were Métis, 15 per cent were non-status Indians, and 5 per cent were Inuit.[5] Almost all registered/status Indians belong to a band, of which there are about six hundred scattered across Canada (see Map 2). The

FEATHER AND GUN: CONFRONTATION AT OKA/KANESATAKE

vast majority of bands are small (under six hundred persons). Ironically, status Indians in fact have very little status at all. In the past, native children were forbidden to speak their languages in reserve schools, indigenous customs such as the Potlatch were outlawed, and whole systems of government were expunged and replaced by an elected band council system mandated through the Indian Act. The Mohawks at Oka, for example, are members of the Six Nations or Iroquois Confederacy, known to themselves as the Haudenosaunee (People of the Longhouse). The Haudenosaunee have a formal 117-article constitution (memorized by elders) and an elaborate system of government involving bicameral councils of female and male representatives of major families. In 1924 the RCMP raided the Six Nations council hall near Brantford, Ontario, and confiscated all records and symbols. They were never returned, and Haudenosaunee leaders were jailed.[6] The Longhouse tradition, with its system of confederacy councils, con-

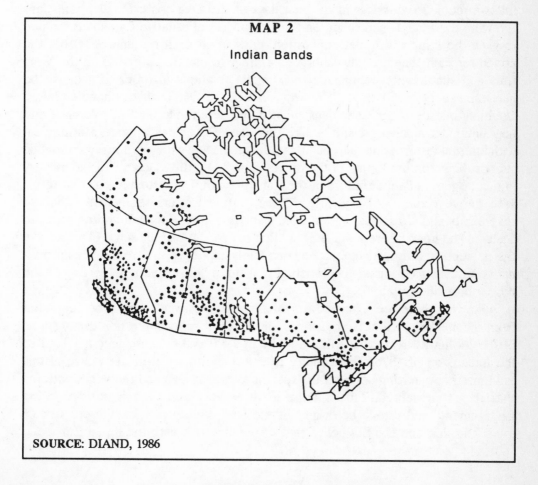

MAP 2

Indian Bands

SOURCE: DIAND, 1986

tinued but the only legally recognized government was the elected council system sanctioned by the Indian Act. The Warriors at Oka were members of one stream of a traditionalist Longhouse revival.

A third motif in the Oka affair is the way in which the federal and provincial governments handled events. The Quebec government, fresh from the Meech Lake fiasco where it had demanded the constitutional status of a "distinct society," was now confronted with radical claims of sovereignty from natives within its own borders. As we shall see, in practice the relations between Quebeckers and natives, particularly between residents of Châteauguay and Kahnawake and between residents of Oka and Kanesatake, were quite smooth. The reserve at Kahnawake enjoys a political autonomy and economic well-being not available to most reserves in Canada. Despite this, once the barricades were up and shots had been fired, Quebec, like the rest of Canada, seemed unsure how to react. The Prime Minister appeared defeated and disoriented in the wake of Meech Lake, and Ottawa seemed rudderless in the first days of the Oka crisis. Finally, politicians threw up their hands and called on the army. Most non-native Canadians seemed to view the army with quiet admiration, particularly as it became clear that the armed forces had a carefully calibrated strategy to increase pressure on the Warriors and simultaneously manage their media relations in order to achieve the maximum support and effect. The *way* in which the Oka crisis was handled raised troubling questions for Canadians: what is the acceptable limit of tolerance and negotiation in resolving disputes like this one? How does a modern army deal with internal insurrection, particularly in the media age when legitimacy and public support hinge on the "spin" of the nightly news? Did the "success" of the military in fact disguise a deeper failure of the Canadian political system to come to terms with native claims and aspirations? Can native leaders realistically demand sovereignty and virtual exemption from Canadian law? How united are natives in Canada, and how coherent are they as "first peoples"? Can the sense of grievance, the perception of injustice, ever be completely expunged, or are native and non-native Canadians doomed to perpetual tension, a "dozen nations warring in the bosom of a single state"?

Oka was therefore a microcosm of larger forces, and cannot be separated from them. The original land dispute, for example, reflects the non-treaty status of the Mohawks living there. Kanesatake in 1990 makes sense only if joined to the Indian Act of 1876. This chapter tries to capture the intricate weave of this sad tapestry by shifting between the specific events at Oka and the larger patterns that they represented. This is done in three acts. Act One is entitled "First Engagement" and treats the origins of the land dispute at Oka, the erection of the barricades, and the SQ police raid. It parallels this with the initial European

FEATHER AND GUN: CONFRONTATION AT OKA/KANESATAKE

contact and settlement through to the treaties, the Indian Act, and their evolution to the 1960s. Act Two, entitled "The New Agenda," examines the events after the arrival of the army, and how they stimulated fresh debates among natives and non-natives about the proper scope of the land claim and sovereignty. This is paralleled by the elaboration of native claims towards the idea of aboriginal title in the 1970s and the evolution of aboriginal constitutional claims through the Charter to Meech Lake. Act Three, entitled "Surrender and Defiance," describes the army manoeuvres to the denouement and surrender at Kanesatake.

ACT ONE: FIRST ENGAGEMENT

Scene 1: Oka, March to August 1990

The town of Oka (pop. 1,800) lies thirty kilometers west of Montreal on the Ottawa River, near the lovely Lac des Deux Montagnes. It depends on cheese and tourism for its livelihood, has an interesting Trappist monastery and a nine-hole golf course. It is also near the Mohawk community of Kanesatake (pop. 1,600), which, while not a legal reserve established by formal treaty, has existed as a community for over two hundred years. The Kanesatake Mohawks have, for almost all of that period, been filing land claims and protesting their treatment by Ottawa. The British Judicial Committee of the Privy Council ruled against the Mohawk claim in 1912, and Ottawa rejected it twice in 1975 and 1977. The Mohawks continued to hold to their claim, but lived alongside the non-native residents in Oka without notable friction or difficulty until city plans to increase tourism began to brew. The best type of tourist is the one who stays and spends, and so the town schemed to find ways to attract visitors for more than quick monastery tours and cheese-tastings. Golf was a sensible choice, and municipal authorities began to talk of expanding the existing nine-hole course into a more attractive eighteen-hole facility. The original course was on land that had been expropriated from private owners in 1947; the extension would take place on ninety acres owned by a resident of France, Maurice Rosseau.[7] Rosseau had purchased the land in 1967 and offered to sell two-thirds of it to Oka to expand the golf course (the other third would be developed for luxury housing). Mohawks objected because Rosseau's land was part of the parcel they claimed as their own, and moreover the golf course extension would force the relocation of a native cemetery. Sporadic but not very satisfactory negotiations had been underway for some time on two fronts: with the federal government over the larger land claim (over a year without result under federal mediator Yves Desilets) and with the Oka municipality over the expansion. The talks with the municipality finally broke down, and on 11 March a barricade appeared on a dusty and usually deserted road leading to the golf course.

The origins of the first barricade are murky. It was enough to prevent construction on the golf course extension, but had more of an air of political protest than military violence. While it had been instigated by the more radical members of the band, particularly by the Mohawk Warriors Society, Indian families and women sauntered through it, there was no inconvenience to the local Oka residents, and it soon became a fixture of town life. Developers, and in particular the town's mayor, Jean-Guy Ouellette, were losing patience, however. They wanted to start the extension, and could see no way of resolving the dispute with the Mohawks. From the town's point of view, the larger issues of land claims and historical treatment were quite irrelevant: as a matter of law, the disputed land had been owned by private interests for over a generation, and previous legal precedent had established that the Kanesatake Mohawks had never had "aboriginal title." The Indians had been attracted to the Oka region in 1717, and had no more claim on their land than Quebeckers did to the island of Montreal. The barricade stood for four months, until the town successfully sought an injunction from the Quebec Superior Court on 30 June declaring it illegal and ordering that it be removed. Quebec's minister of native affairs, John Ciaccia, wrote to Jean-Guy Ouellette on 9 July urging him to indefinitely suspend the golf course development so that negotiations could be undertaken for the removal of the barricades. Sometimes, Ciaccia said, the "law is an ass," and this case went beyond "strict legality."[8] Ouellette read the letter but then proceeded to make the biggest mistake of his life: he appealed to the SQ to enforce the injunction.

The SQ has a reputation in Quebec for heavy-handedness, and it lived up to it at Oka. No negotiation or contact with the Mohawks was undertaken. Instead, at dawn on 11 July, exactly four months after the barricade had first been erected, about one hundred SQ tactical force officers moved in to clear the area. They arrived in trucks and several police cruisers, and had a front-end loader ready to smash through the barricade and clear the road. Tear gas was fired into the enclosure, and the front-end loader inched forward to remove the barrier. Then, in a development that most Canadians believed could happen only in Beirut or Belfast, shots shattered the smoke and lifting fog, pinning the police down and killing one of them, Corporal Marcel Lemay. The SQ claimed that its orders were not to open fire because of the women and children behind the barricades; the Mohawks later claimed that they had only shot back when fired upon and that Lemay had been killed by one of his colleagues.[9] The SQ retreated briefly and negotiated with the Warriors, but then moved in once more with tear gas and about thirty vehicles. In its confused retreat, the SQ had abandoned the front-end

FEATHER AND GUN: CONFRONTATION AT OKA/KANESATAKE

loader and some cars, and the Mohawks used them to good effect to buttress the barricade. Police cars were overturned and pushed around as needed with the front-end loader. The Warriors also captured police radios, rifles, and ammunition. They then commandeered golf carts from the nearby club to manoeuvre in and around the barricade. It was a strange sight: men dressed in military fatigues, masked in ways vaguely reminiscent of PLO fighters, triumphantly waving rifles that they obviously knew how to use, whooping atop overturned police cruisers. The vision of these big, serious, and lethal men on golf carts was just incongruous enough to be frightening.

Almost immediately after this first confrontation, Mohawk Warriors at the Kahnawake reserve, across the St. Lawrence River southwest of Montreal, decided to show their support for the Oka struggle by blockading two key highways (the intersection of Highways 132 and 138) that run through their reserve to the Mercier Bridge. This action was of incalculable importance to the Oka struggle because of the prominence of the Kahnawake band and the impact of the bridge closure. The Mohawks at Kahnawake, unlike those at Kanesatake, had reserve lands of their own. With a population of six thousand, they are the largest native community in Quebec and one of the largest in Canada.[10] About half the men work in high steel construction, and so the community enjoys a more stable and lucrative economic base than most bands in the country. While alcohol and drug abuse are problems, child neglect and welfare dependency are lower than average for native communities. Kahnawake depends on DIAND for 80 per cent of its administrative funds, but most social, educational, and community services are staffed and run by band members themselves. The community at Kahnawake is predominantly Catholic, a result of successful Jesuit missionary efforts in the eighteenth century, but 10 per cent call themselves "traditionalists" and follow Longhouse practices (the Longhouse is primarily a religious, not a political, affiliation). This division is important—and prevailed in the Kanesatake community as well—because the Warrior Society is "traditionalist": it follows the way of the Longhouse and does not recognize the band council governing structure, which is an artifact of the Indian Act. Kahnawake Warriors set up the blockade at the Mercier Bridge, an action that was not initially approved by the Kahnawake band council.[11] The Kanesatake barricade was a traditionalist initiative as well, and some band council members had warned the SQ hours before their raid of the Warriors' weaponry.[12]

The closure of the Mercier Bridge was strategically important as well, however, because of its direct impact on Montreal. Some sixty thousand residents of the south shore, principally from the town of Châteauguay, near Kahnawake, use the bridge each morning and evening to commute to work. The best alternative route adds more than an hour each way, meaning that people had to wake at dawn and return sometimes well after dinner. The Oka barricade had been a visible symbol of native impatience, but it had caused no serious inconvenience to anyone except perhaps the Oka city council. It had stood for four months before the SQ moved in, and without the closure of the Mercier Bridge might have stood for another four months without impact. While there were many levels of crisis in the Oka affair, for Quebeckers the most persistent, palpable, and eventually intolerable symbol of crisis was the desolate colossus that towered over the St. Lawrence River. It made sixty thousand people angry enough that some of them vented their rage in racism and violence. Mobs gathered at the bridge nightly for the first week to burn Mohawk effigies. Later they burned effigies of politicians.

By the afternoon of 11 July, the dawn raid had turned into a political nightmare. In response to the blockade at Mercier, the SQ closed access to the reserve at Kahnawake. Members had to abandon cars and walk home on foot. Police controlling access to the highways running through the reserve wore bullet-proof vests. Within twenty-four hours of its first raid, the SQ had one thousand officers in Oka, squinting across their own barricade at perhaps one hundred (no one was sure how many) Mohawk Warriors only a few hundred metres away. One man was dead. Masked Warriors became daily icons on TV and in the press, as the media descended on Oka. Initially the Mohawk position related exclusively to its original land claim and objections to the golf course expansion into their burial grounds. A Warrior spokesman from the Akwesasne–St.Régis reserve, which straddles parts of Ontario, Quebec, and New York state, attacked the federal and provincial governments for allowing the town of Oka to "uproot, relocate and desecrate a burial ground of the Mohawk People" and demanded a peaceful solution.[13] Thomas Siddon, the federal minister of Indian affairs, made no direct comment on events, but a spokesperson for his department denied any role for Ottawa. The Prime Minister remarked from an economic summit meeting in Houston, Texas, that the situation was "serious" and pledged all "possible assistance" to provincial authorities. Ottawa could not have been more eloquent: Oka was Quebec's problem.

The problem that first day in some ways was less the barricade than the death of Corporal Lemay. The investigation of Lemay's death was turned over to the Montreal Urban Community police—a move that many suspected showed the government's lack of confidence in the SQ—but initial ballistics tests were inconclusive and the police refused to release them. Both sides had used similar semi-automatic rifles, making it difficult to guess whether Lemay had been killed by the SQ or by Mohawks. John Ciaccia was at Oka the next day, negotiating for four hours before stopping at dusk in deference to Mohawk tradition.[14] He met with the natives again the next day for seven hours, but he and Ellen Gabriel, the principal Mohawk negotiator, then announced that a resolution would be impossible without federal participation. Gabriel insisted that about twenty Mohawk "resource persons" would have to be at the bargaining table along with federal representatives if the impasse was to be broken.[15] Ciaccia's task was complicated by Gabriel's truculence—she insisted that the SQ leave Oka, that any moves against the Mercier blockade would be met by blowing up the bridge, and that any officer breaching the Mohawk "security barrier" would be taken prisoner—and by the presence of Mohawks from Kahnawake.[16] It was made no easier by the emotions and reactions that were almost immediately inflamed by the affair. Indian bands as far away as British Columbia began to set up roadblocks of their own in sympathy with the Mohawks. The SQ proceeded to lay seige to Oka. Police closed off food supplies to both Kanesatake and Kahnawake, searching cars and forbidding any but whites into Oka. Food was still getting to the reserves, and most importantly to the Mohawks in Oka, across Lac des Deux Montagnes, but when some Kahnawake residents were allowed to shop for supplies in Châteauguay, a mob of two hundred people tried to prevent them from buying anything at the supermarket.

By 15 July, after four days of negotiations, Ciaccia appeared to have made some progress. His priority was to re-open the Mercier Bridge, and towards that end he had hammered out the following package: (1) the contested land around the golf course would be recognized as Mohawk land, though how title would be transferred was unclear; (2) the SQ would gradually withdraw from Oka, and as they did the barricade would come down; (3) a religious order would monitor the process (representatives of the Roman Catholic Church observed the negotiations on the 15th); (4) Ciaccia himself would do what he could to ensure "nation-to-nation" talks between the Mohawks and Ottawa; (5) a public inquiry with native participation would review Ottawa's role in the confrontation; (6) Mohawks agreed to co-operate with police in the investigation of Corporal Lemay's death; and (7) all civil and criminal prosecutions would be referred to the World Court at the Hague.[17] This potential resolution of the crisis went nowhere for three reasons. First, it made little sense for provincial authorities to negotiate alone with Indians, since Indians are a federal responsibility. Ciaccia's commitment to encourage "nation-to-nation" talks with Ottawa illustrated the absurdity. Despite his and Gabriel's calls for federal action, and mounting demands from church groups, human rights activists, and natives across Canada, Thomas Siddon remained silent on Oka for six consecutive days. A second problem was the town council of Oka. Gilles Landreville, the acting mayor, denounced the tentative

FEATHER AND GUN: CONFRONTATION AT OKA/KANESATAKE

agreement because it had been negotiated without municipal participation. Third, it was unclear who exactly was negotiating for whom on the Warrior side. Over the seventy-eight days that the confrontation was to last, approximately 80 per cent of the residents of Kanesatake fled. Even while they remained, however, there was a split between the band council and the Warriors Society. A lawyer for the band council, Jacques Lacaille, confirmed that many of the militant Warriors who had spearheaded the Oka barricade were from the US side of the Akwesasne reserve, and had received combat training in Vietnam.[18] In May the Akwesasne reserve had had to be evacuated as rival Mohawks fought a night-time gun battle over casinos and cigarette-smuggling. Two men died in that conflict, and Canadian and American police had to occupy the reserve to restore peace. The presence of non-resident Warriors and the split in the Kanesatake community made the negotiation process murky and confused on the Mohawk side.[19] On 17 July two American human-rights lawyers (William Kunstler and Stanley Cohen) arrived in Oka at the Mohawk's request to advise them on negotiations.[20]

While the initial negotiations had held out some hope, the resulting stalemate just ignited further frustrations. The SQ had virtually severed the two native communities from the outside world. Cars were frisked at road blocks, journalists searched and monitored, and food supplies deliberately cut off. These tactics stimulated protests from Quebec and Canadian human rights groups and opposition parties. On 17 July about four hundred natives from Quebec marched on Parliament Hill demanding some federal action, and the next day, in an unprecedented meeting, 150 native chiefs from across Canada met at Kahnawake to pressure Ottawa to intervene.[21] Anger among Châteauguay residents had taken an uglier turn. For seven consecutive nights after the closing of the Mercier Bridge, crowds had gathered at the barricades and burned an Indian effigy, and taunted the SQ with obscenities and insults. On 17 July a mob of almost four thousand people surged across protective fencing and advanced on police lines, jeering that their taxes were being used to guard a closed bridge. The next night the same number gathered, but the SQ had assistance from three hundred RCMP officers with flak jackets and truncheons.[22] That same day, Thomas Siddon finally released a statement in which he described the Oka seige as "most unfortunate," and once more pledged not to inhibit Ciaccia's negotiation efforts in any way.[23] Ottawa was staying out. The Quebec government, meanwhile, also gave notice of its intentions. Premier Bourassa, for the first time since the 11 July raid on the barricades, issued a statement that hinted that Quebec authorities were prepared for a long stand-off.

Ottawa's response was glaringly inadequate, given its constitutional responsibilities in the larger Kanesatake land claim. Thomas Siddon finally called a press conference on 19 July to explain the federal government's position. "We cannot engage in negotiations at gunpoint," said the Minister, arguing that since police and the administration of justice are provincial responsibilities, it was up to the Quebec authorities to resolve the armed stand-off first before federal land negotiators would appear on the scene.[24] John Ciaccia had asked Ottawa to accede to four of the Mohawk's conditions, and Siddon indicated agreement with three of them: it would buy the disputed land near the golf course, help provide additional land for the Kanesatake Mohawks, and help improve social and economic conditions in the community. Ciaccia had also wanted Ottawa to suspend its existing, cumbersome land claims procedures in the Oka case, but Siddon was vague on this point. The Quebec minister of Native affairs, however, was firm in his view that the Mohawks' grievances, while they might not be supported in strict legal terms, had to be addressed. The delays had raised the stakes in this resolution, however. Ellen Gabriel was equally firm in demanding that food and medical supplies be allowed into Kahnawake and Kanesatake, that UN or Amnesty International observers be allowed on both sites, and that Mohawks have forty-eight hours' freedom to leave both areas.[25] Gabriel made no apologies for the barricades: Mohawks had been "invaded" and had every right to defend themselves and their territory. This, and what Ciaccia claimed were new demands unrelated to the dispute at Kanesatake and Kahnawake (e.g., immunity from criminal and civil prosecutions for Mohawks in the dispute at the Akwesasne reserve), scuttled the settlement that had seemed near only a few days earlier. "As far as I'm concerned," said Gabriel, "there's no time limit here."

In only ten days the stand-off at Oka had gone from a local/provincial affair to a national and international one. Although native leaders voiced concerns about the Mohawk Warriors' use of violence, the conflict had generated a solid consensus that justice was on the native side, that provincial authorities were responding brutally, and that Ottawa was shirking its responsibilities. The 150 chiefs who met at Kahnawake ended their sessions on 20 July by demanding a recall of Parliament to deal with this crisis in "Canada–First Nations relations." They threatened more roadblocks, as well as appeals to the international community and the UN to impose sanctions on Canada similar to those levelled against South Africa.[26] Over ten days the Mohawks at Kanesatake and Kahnawake, as well as native leaders across Canada, had begun to frame their position more directly in nationalist terms. The calls for international observers, appeals to the World Court and the UN, and demands that negotiations between Ottawa and natives take place on "native territory," posited natives as members of sovereign nations, a concession that Ottawa was hardly keen to make. Not surprisingly, Siddon rejected all these demands, saying again that the federal government could not negotiate at gunpoint. On the same day in Montreal, however, he announced that Ottawa was trying to get the municipality of Oka to sell the golf course lands that had initiated the dispute.[27] While still refusing to enter the negotiations, Siddon implied that Ottawa was preparing the conditions for successful bargaining once the barricades came down.

Government authorities seemed paralysed. Quebec politicians said that the negotiations were at a "dead end," Thomas Siddon refused to get involved, and the Prime Minister was at his Harrington Lake retreat, licking his wounds over the Meech Lake accord fiasco of June. The rhetorical heat was turned up as natives expressed their frustration at Ottawa's inaction: "Throughout history, whenever there were confrontations, it was always the Indians who had laid down their arms first. We all know what happened to them. So this time, we are saying no."[28] This profoundly historical view seeped out of virtually every comment made by every native leader: every promise broken and every battle lost, every injustice and indignity ever suffered coloured Oka. Government officials, for their part, poured some of their own frustrations into the event. On 23 July the deputy minister of DIAND, Harry Swain, confidentially briefed reporters on the Oka situation. His allegations were sufficiently serious, however, that the press attributed them to him. Calling Oka an "armed insurrection," he claimed that the Warriors were a "criminal organization" consisting of seventy-five to one hundred members who had taken control of the two native communities, threatening and intimidating traditional native community leaders in Kanesatake and Kahnawake with violence.[29] Thomas Siddon disclaimed these remarks, but John Ciaccia, in announcing on 23 July that the Quebec government was ready once more to resume negotiations, hinted that the Mohawk camp had been infiltrated by members of the radical American Indian Movement and the Akwesasne Warrior Society.[30] These claims were obviously denied by the Warriors themselves, one of whom, nicknamed Lasagna, said that the group was defending the people's land and was ready to die for it. There were some reports of disagreement within the Mohawk community over the role of the Warriors Society, but native leaders were reluctant to talk about these divisions.[31]

By the end of the second week of siege there were once more hopeful signs that a settlement might be achieved. On 26 July John Ciaccia ordered the SQ to stop its blockade of food and medical supplies to Kanesatake and Kahnawake. The blockade had been assailed by the Quebec and Canadian Human Rights Commissions, natives, and the international media. Indeed, international interest in Oka had reached the point where Ottawa was forced to dispatch an official to Geneva to explain the situation to the United Nations Working Group on Indigenous Populations (a committee of the Sub-Commission on the Prevention of

Discrimination Against Minorities).[32] Thomas Siddon, while still not engaged directly in the negotiations, met with Ciaccia in Montreal on 26 July and pressed him to resolve the stand-off as quickly as possible.[33] Ottawa then announced, after a five-hour cabinet meeting, that it had purchased twelve hectares of the twenty-two-hectare plot of land that had been part of the original golf course dispute. It paid $1.4 million (a bargain, given that conservative estimates put the cost of policing Oka and the Mercier Bridge at $1 million per day), but the remaining parcel of land was under the control of the municipal council of Oka, which was demanding $5 million in payment. The land purchase formed the basis of a new Quebec government offer to the Mohawks. Confident that the remaining parcel of disputed land would eventually be bought by Ottawa, Quebec offered to transfer it to the Mohawks, and had also secured Ottawa's committment to negotiate over the larger land claim of 675 square kilometers that had been in dispute for almost two hundred years. Ciaccia called on the Warriors to lay down their arms (in a sealed container under a tree, as demanded by the Mohawk Great Law of Peace), and promised in return to reduce the SQ contingent at both Kanesatake and Kahnawake to under twenty officers. He refused immunity from criminal and civil prosecution, but a Mohawk representative could participate in the coroner's inquest into the death of Corporal Lemay.[34]

Mohawks and Quebec government officials negotiated for thirty-one hours over the new proposal, but emerged without comment. Ironically, the two sides that they represented appeared to be equally split. On the non-native side, a group of about two thousand marchers appeared outside Oka to show solidarity with the Mohawks. Among them were representatives of the Canadian Labour Congress, the National Action Committee on the Status of Women, and the Canadian Ethnocultural Council. They were met at the town's outskirts by about one hundred Oka residents who prevented them from entering. At a town meeting on 28 July the crowd cheered Mayor Jean-Guy Ouellette when he refused to apologize for calling in the SQ on 11 July and defended the town's demand for $5 million for the remaining golf course land. Among the Mohawks, the same divisions that had riven the community in the past were at play in deciding on the government's offer. Moderates, allied for the most part with the band council, leaned towards agreement; members of the Warrior Society insisted on immunity from prosecution and dismissed the government's "purchase" of land as nonsensical, since it was in their view Indian land in the first place.[35] Joe Deom, the Mohawk negotiator at this stage, demanded written guarantees of free passage of food and medicine, spiritual leaders, and international observers (these were later promised by Ciaccia).

FEATHER AND GUN: CONFRONTATION AT OKA/KANESATAKE

The deal-making at this stage was occurring in a five-dimensional space. The first dimension was the Mohawk communities of Kanesatake and Kahnawake, with their splits between band councils, moderates, traditionalists who opposed the Warriors, and the Warriors themselves. The stakes for them were how far to push the self-government/sovereignty claim connected with immunity from prosecution for mounting the barricades, the death of Corporal Lemay, and possession of firearms; and how quickly to jump on the land settlement offer. The second dimension was Ottawa and DIAND. Federal responsibility for natives had drawn Ottawa into the dispute; indeed, it had been a partner in the larger claims process from the beginning. Ottawa wanted to avoid getting embroiled in the nastier side of the dispute over the barricades, but it was prepared to make minimal moves to purchase and transfer land and engage in land claims negotiations. The third dimension was the Assembly of First Nations and the almost six hundred bands it represents across the country. Sympathy blockades had been erected in British Columbia and throughout the western provinces, and despite concerns over Warrior methods, the confrontation at Oka had generated unprecedented levels of native solidarity and commitment. The fourth dimension was the international one. The international community, particularly Europe, is highly aware of North America's indigenous population, and native representatives were quick to exploit this by appealing to the United Nations. International media coverage of the event was largely sympathetic to the Mohawks, tarnishing Canada's reputation for racial tolerance. The fifth dimension was the community of Oka itself. It owned a part of the disputed land, and as a community had been devastated by what amounted to a military occupation over the previous three weeks.

Any situation in which this many dimensions, actors, and strategies have to be coordinated—and where coordination is not in anyone's obvious interest—can easily spin out of control. On 31 July four hundred people jammed into a local church in Oka for a town council meeting and decided that they would not agree to sell the last parcel of land to Ottawa until the barricades came down.[36] On 2 August shots were heard at Kanesatake as Warriors chased Chief George Martin from his home and the community. Martin called the Warriors outsiders: "This is not your reserve: get the hell out."[37] Warriors later claimed that five hundred Kanesatake community members had signed a petition to force Martin out of his leadership position, but the gunfire added to police and Mohawk tension at the barricades. Some Châteauguay agitators who had organized the Mercier Bridge protests threatened to escalate violence to get the provincial government's attention. Municipal leaders on the south shore, cut off by the blockade of the Mercier Bridge, also threatened unspecified "dramatic political action." The Mohawk reaction to Quebec's standing offer was to add several new conditions, the most important of which were the free passage of "necessities" in addition to food and medicine, the free passage of "advisors" other than spiritual advisors, and a commitment from the Quebec government to negotiate claims at the Akwesasne reserve.[38]

Quebec could not accept these new demands, and on the evening of 5 August Premier Bourassa issued a forty-eight-hour ultimatum for the negotiation of an agreement to bring down the barricades. "If that is impossible, at a cabinet meeting Wednesday we will have to draw conclusions and take appropriate steps."[39] Ellen Gabriel responded, "We will not be bullied by the power and arrogance of Quebec." The Mohawks sent their demands to the Prime Minister and then settled down to prepare. As the ultimatum expired, residents began to stream out of the affected communities. About half the population of Oka fled, and several dozen families left Kanesatake. The Quebec cabinet met on 8 August to make its decision: it would call on Ottawa to send in the armed forces to replace the SQ. While many Canadians, particularly in Châteauguay, expected that the army would forcibly remove the barricades, both Ottawa and armed forces spokespersons tried to downplay the significance of the move, implying that it was merely the replacement of SQ police officers with soldiers. The troops were being sent in "with a view to stabilizing the situation."[40] Premier Bourassa asserted that the Quebec government's priority "is that the role of the army be peaceful." The two governments had joined with the Mohawks in the appointment of Chief Justice Alan Gold of the Quebec Superior Court as mediator of the three outstanding conditions that had scuttled the deal John Ciaccia had tried to forge with the Warriors. There was even modest relief on the Mohawk side when the army announcement was made, since it meant the removal of the universally despised SQ and a clear acknowledgement of federal responsibility for the issue, something Thomas Siddon had tried to avoid since July.

It was a month few had ever believed possible. The Mohawk Warriors at Kanesatake and Kahnawake had together managed to bring the Quebec government to its knees. The costs of the SQ alone, at a conservative estimate, had topped $30 million. After the closing of the Mercier Bridge, the provincial government spent $1 million establishing a commuter train from the south shore to Montreal, and then in early August pledged another $12.5 million for road and bridge expansions to handle traffic. The federal government, still reeling from the collapse of the Meech Lake accord, was confronted almost immediately by a crisis directly in its jurisdiction. A weak minister and a disengaged, almost disinterested prime minister had created a vacuum in Ottawa, a lethargy that allowed the confrontation to expand from an issue over golf course development to the sovereignty of the *Kanienkehaka*, the Mohawk Nation. In Geneva, the UN Working Group on Indigenous Populations asked Canada to provide an informal explanation of its treatment of the Mohawks (particularly of the forty-eight-hour ultimatum), and international media reports tended to portray Canadian government actions unsympathetically.

Then, within a day of Justice Gold's appointment, a deal to at least negotiate an agreement was struck. On 12 August Thomas Siddon, John Ciaccia, and representatives of five Mohawk communities gathered in the pine forest at Oka where Corporal Lemay had been killed a month earlier, and signed an agreement that conceded the two key points the Quebec government had rejected only days earlier. The Mohawks were permitted access to "necessities" and "legal advisors," and the stand-off would be monitored by twenty-four representatives of the Paris-based International Federation of Human Rights. Quebec had initially opposed the first two items out of fear that military materials and advisors would leak into Kanesatake and Kahnawake, but Ottawa was distinctly uncomfortable with the third. It had wanted observers from the Quebec and Canadian Human Rights Commissions, which would have signalled that the affair was a domestic one. The reliance on international observers to the exclusion of domestic ones was an important symbolic victory for the Mohawks: it implied that they were a nation equal in status to Canada. The signing meant that the barricades could now come down, and broader negotiations on disputed lands could proceed. Ellen Gabriel pointed out that the removal of the barriers was only a prelude to the pursuit of justice. "Let this be a basis, a foundation for claiming our rights in this land."[41]

That night and the next, police at the Mercier Bridge shot tear gas at thousands of demonstrators flinging rocks, bottles, and Molotov cocktails. "We want the army," they chanted.

Scene 2: From Contact to the Indian Act

One of John Ciaccia's frustrations as he tried to negotiate with the Warriors was that the Mohawk "team" kept changing, and often consisted of members from outside Kanesatake and Kahnawake. The Mohawk response was that place did not matter, since they were all Mohawks. This minor irritant thus reflected a cultural clash over how natives are defined and identified. To understand Oka one must understand some characteristics of the Amerindian population.

Three methods are usually used to classify that population: linguistic, tribal, and cultural. Each method is less than completely satisfactory. By linguistic group, for example, there are ten recognized Amerindian language families comprising over fifty languages. One authority notes that the language families differ among themselves as much as English does from Chinese, and that within families the differences are as English is to Dutch.[42] The language families comprise Algonquian, found between the Atlantic coast and the Rockies; Iroquoian, in eastern Canada; Siouan, in the prairies and Rocky Mountain foothills; Athapaskan, across the northern parts of the western provinces, the Yukon, and the NWT; and Salishan, Tsimshian, Wakashan, Haida, Tlingit, and Kootenayan, found in British Columbia.[43] Their geographical range makes language family as a basis of native identification problematic. For example, the Blackfoot of the plains and the Micmac of the Maritimes are both in the Algonquian language family, but share no common culture.

Tribal affiliation is equally problematic, since ties between bands within tribes have not always been strong, and tribes themselves have not always acted as distinct units in relation to other groups. The preferred method of classification (and even here there are varieties) is by what is called "culture area." DIAND, for example, uses six categories, each of which includes different tribes and language families: Woodland Indians, Indians of Southeastern Ontario, Plains Indians, Indians of the Plateau, Pacific Coast Indians, and Indians of the Mackenzie and Yukon River Basins.[44] The point is that natives are simultaneously fragmented by substantial differences in language and culture, and united across territorial boundaries by similarities in language and culture. Ottawa and Quebec were perplexed by the presence of Akwesasne Mohawks in Kanesatake and Kahnawake; from the native perspective they were members of the same group. The larger issue, of course, was not who the Mohawks were, but what they wanted. They wanted land that had been in dispute for almost three hundred years, and to understand the dispute one has to think back almost three hundred years. The Mohawk negotiators certainly did.

Treaty-making between colonial powers and natives began in the seventeenth century, but at that stage had a somewhat different character from treaties as they are understood today. Initially both France and England, the principal colonial powers in North America, sought military alliances or at least neutrality from natives, and so early treaties did not mention land or its use. Britain, for example, entered into a peace and friendship treaty with Nova Scotia Indians in 1725 to secure their support during hostilities with France. While the Crown agreed to promote Indian trade and protect traditional hunting, trapping, and fishing, it did not transfer land. Nonetheless, by entering into such agreements, even if they were only of a military nature, "the government formally recognized the existence of Indian political communities and of their interest in the land, and implicitly recognized the social, economic, and political rights of Indian peoples. Treaty making was based on the principle of obtaining the consent of aboriginal groups."[45]

FEATHER AND GUN: CONFRONTATION AT OKA/KANESATAKE

The imperative for military alliances drove colonial (especially British) policy in the latter half of the eighteenth and early part of the nineteenth century, through first the Anglo–French conflict and then the Anglo–American conflict. The Indian Department, formed in 1755, was an arm of the colonial military, and while civil authority was established in 1799, military control was again asserted between 1816 and 1830.[46] With the defeat of France and the Treaty of Paris in 1763, the British Crown issued its Royal Proclamation of the same year that codified and made explicit prevailing British practice and law with respect to native lands. The Royal Proclamation is universally regarded as the "Magna Carta" of natives living in Canada, and was enshrined in the Constitution Act, 1982. Its most important passages were:

> And whereas it is just and reasonable, and essential to our interest, and the security of our Colonies, that the several Nations or Tribes of Indians with whom we are connected, and who live under our Protection, should not be molested or disturbed in the Possession of such parts of our Dominions and Territories as, not having been ceded to or purchased by Us, are reserved to them or any of them as their Hunting Grounds...

> We do further declare it to be our Royal Will and pleasure, for the present as aforesaid, to reserve under our Sovereignty, Protection and Dominion for the use of the said Indians, all the Land and Territories not included within the Limits of our Said Three New Governments, or within the Company, as also all the Lands and Territories lying to the Westward of the Sources of the Rivers which fall into the Sea from the West and North West as aforesaid;

> And we do hereby strictly forbid, on Pain of our displeasure, all our loving Subjects from making any purchase or Settlements whatever, or taking possession of any of the Lands above reserved, without our especial leave and License for that Purpose first obtained.[47]

The Royal Proclamation of 1763, it has been argued, contained four basic principles that later "became embedded in Canada's treaty system."[48] First, it recognized collective aboriginal title to land not formally surrendered to the Crown. This principle had been established in British law as early as the seventeenth century, but was complicated by the assumption that aboriginal title co-existed with British sovereignty over those lands.[49] The Proclamation's intriguing phrase was "*our* Dominions and Territories as, *not* having been ceded to or purchased by Us." The practical expression of the Crown's claim of sovereignty was that missionaries and fur-traders were allowed on Indian territory, fugitives could be apprehended there, and liquor trade was controlled. Second, before Indian lands could be settled by whites, they would have to be surrendered to the Crown, which would then transfer them to settlers. This was combined with a third principle that the Crown claimed the power to evict persons "unlawfully occupying Indian lands."[50] Finally, Indians could cede their lands only to the Crown, and only collectively through treaties, not individual sales. Aboriginal title, in other words, was collective and not individual.

The Royal Proclamation was a two-edged sword. On the one hand it established the Crown as the protector of Indian rights to land. Even after this power was transferred to the Canadian government in 1867, the Crown retained its status of protector in the eyes of natives. It has always been part of native political practice to appeal beyond Canada's borders for justice. This occurred in 1981 when natives went to London to lobby against the first version of the Canadian Charter of Rights, and again later when Mohawks travelled to the UN in Geneva to protest against events in Oka. On the other hand, the Proclamation facilitated massive transfers of land from natives to whites through a treaty process that extended to 1923 (the last year that an agreement designated as a "treaty" was signed). It also laid the foundations for a policy framework of paternalism and assimilation. The paternalism arose in part from simple racism in the guise of "humanitarianism," in part from the exigencies of administration. The racism underlying policy was exemplified in a phrase by the British colonial secretary, Lord Glenelg, in 1838, to the effect that the primary goal of Indian policy was "to protect and cherish this helpless Race...[and] raise them in the Scale of Humanity."[51] The administrative imperative could be seen in the progressively more detailed regulations emanating from the Indian Department regarding the gathering of information on tribes and bands, the monitoring of their activities and registration of their lands, and the licensing and control of interactions with white settlers and traders.[52]

After 1830 and the resolution of conflict between the United States and Britain, the imperative behind Indian policy shifted finally away from military alliances to land acquisition for settlement. The logic of the Royal Proclamation had been that all Indian lands not explicitly ceded to the Crown remained under native title; those lands *not included* in any transfers to the Crown would remain in Indian possession as reserves. It should be noted that reserves were not considered gifts or compensation for the transfer, they were simply that part of the original title not ceded to the Crown.

Enfranchisement was the vehicle for what was hoped would be the gradual assimilation of Indians into the "civilized," white community. Even Indians on reserves were seen as "noble savages" who might be induced into civilization through missionary activity and education. Those who lived in closer proximity to whites, it was hoped, would learn from example and soon relinquish their tradi-

FEATHER AND GUN: CONFRONTATION AT OKA/KANESATAKE

Inset I

BRIEF HISTORY OF THE
OKA/KANESATAKE LAND DISPUTE

Jacques Cartier sailed up the St. Lawrence in 1535, and Montréal was established a little over century later in 1642. The intervening years were peppered with wars among rival Indian tribes (principally Algonquian and Iroquois) and Europeans (French, Dutch, and English). Algonquian bands controlled most of the St. Lawrence valley, and anthropological evidence suggests that Mohawks from the Iroquois Confederacy began to move into the area by force around 1600. Complex patterns of wars and alliances erupted among Indian bands as they tried to monopolize trade with the Europeans, and the Mohawks were particularly successful in military campaigns through the first half of the seventeenth century. The Iroquois Confederacy (including the Mohawks) finally made peace with the French in 1653, but at Mohawk instigation war resumed again in 1658. The French were only able to impose peace with the Iroquois in 1666. While there had been Iroquois longhouse settlements on the island of Montréal when Cartier had landed there, they had been dispersed in the Indian wars over the next century. With the peace, Mohawk bands began to find their way back to Montréal, where Sulpician priests established a chapel and mission.

The Sulpician mission moved in 1696, and once again in 1718 to settle around Lac des Deux Montagnes after the King of France granted the Sulpician Order the seigneury and its lands (a further concession of land was made in 1735). The mission was established there to minister to Mohawks, as well as the Huron, Pawnee, and Algonquin. It was the only one of its kind granted by the French king to a religious order other than the Jesuits. After the fall of New France, the missions and rights enjoyed by Indians there were preserved, but in a 1762 decision over a dispute between the Jesuits and the Mohawks at Kahnawake, British authorities determined that the terms of the Jesuit seigneuries did not grant the full, traditional rights of "Temporal Lords" to the missions. Land under these grants had been solely for the Indians. In 1775 the Jesuit missions were dissolved and their administration vested with the Crown. The grants to the Sulpicians were different, however. They had been made by the French king to the Seminary of St. Sulpice in Paris with full seigneurial rights. In 1784 the Order of Paris transferred the lands at Oka to the Seminary of St. Sulpice in Montréal.

Indians in the Oka area lodged a claim to lands on both sides of the Ottawa River in 1822 in order to prevent white settlement of areas they argued had been traditional hunting grounds. The claim was denied. The Indians at the Sulpician mission were also concerned about their lands, and an agreement was struck to grant specific lots of mission land to Indians for cultivation and settlement. This dispute, as well as legal doubts about the original transfer of title from the Paris Order to Montréal, led to the passage of a statute of the legislature of the Province of Canada in 1841 confirming the title of the Seminary to the original land grant of 1718 at Oka. While other Indian lands and reserves were transferred to the Commission of Indian

Lands for Lower Canada in 1850, the lands owned by the Sulpicians in Oka were not. Disputes between the Sulpicians and Indians at Oka continued. Mohawks complained of unfair treatment and restricted access to agricultural land and timber resources. In 1868 the Algonquins at Oka submitted a formal petition of complaint to Ottawa, laying claim to the lands at Oka. The petition was denied.

The same year, a Methodist chapel was established at the mission, and it supported the Indians in their fight against the Catholic order. The Sulpicians ordered the Methodist chapel torn down, and in 1877 the Sulpician church mysteriously burned to the ground. The dispute was reviewed once again in 1878 by the minister of justice, who once again ruled in favour of the Sulpicians. An 1881 agreement to move Indians from Oka to a new reserve at Gibson, Ontario, was accepted by only about one-third of the Indians at Oka, some of whom subsequently returned. In 1908 the elected Mohawk chiefs at Oka went to court to claim ownership over the Seminary lands. The Dominion government paid the legal costs of both sides of the dispute. A 1910 decision of the Superior Court concluded that the 1841 statute conferred clear title to the Seminary, and that in any case the Indians at Oka could not demonstrate original occupation of the area. On appeal in 1911, the Court of King's Bench upheld the original ruling and noted that there had never been a transfer of title from the French king or the English Crown to the Mohawks. This was appealed to the Judicial Committee of the Privy Council in London, which in 1912 upheld the Sulpician title.

The Sulpicians continued to sell parts of their lands, and the Mohawks continued to petition Ottawa. Finally, in 1945 the Department of Indian Affairs bought what was left of the Sulpician lands (about 730 hectares) as well as an adjacent woodlot for Indian use, and agreed to assume the Seminary's obligations (exclusive of religious ones) to the Mohawks. The Mohawks were not consulted, however, and no formal reserve was set aside for them. In 1959 the Town of Oka succeeded in having the Québec legislature transfer a parcel of disputed land to it in order to build a nine-hole golf course. In 1975 the Mohawks of Kanesatake, Kahnawake, and Akwesasne filed a comprehensive claim with Ottawa to lands making up most of southern Québec. The Minister of Indian Affairs and Northern Development rejected the claim on the grounds that the Mohawks could not demonstrate possession of the lands since "time immemorial," and because any aboriginal title that may have existed had been extinguished by the French king in 1718 and subsequently by the British Crown. The Mohawks at Oka then submitted a specific land claim in 1977, which was ultimately rejected by the federal government in 1986 on the evidence of the 1841 statute and the Judicial Committee of the Privy Council's decision in 1912. At the same time, the government said that it was willing to negotiate a resolution to the claim. In 1989 it offered a reunification package to the band, whereby the Mohawks would have been moved to nearby federal lands. In August 1989, when the Oka town council announced its plans to expand the golf course, the government appointed Yves Desilets to negotiate a settlement. In March 1990 the newly elected band council requested a suspension of the talks in order to familiarize itself with the case. On 11 March 1990 Mohawks set up a barricade on the road leading to the development site.

FEATHER AND GUN: CONFRONTATION AT OKA/KANESATAKE

tional practices. This policy approach was exemplified in two pieces of legislation, the Act for the Gradual Civilization of the Indian Tribes (1857) and the Civilization and Enfranchisement Act (1859). Together, these major pieces of legislation (and others that accompanied them in this period) created a regime wherein it was hoped that Indians would eventually become "enfranchised" and enjoy full rights of citizenship. Male Indians over the age of 21, with the ability to read and write and with the rudiments of education as well as "good moral character," would be released from any restrictions of legal rights and would "no longer be deemed an Indian..."[53] Indians who applied for enfranchisement were granted fee simple title of up to fifty acres of reserve land and a sum of money "equal to the principal of the annuities and other yearly revenues received by the tribe."[54]

In 1860 the legislative responsibility for Indian affairs was transferred to the Province of Canada, and in 1867 was included as a federal power under section 91(24) of the British North American Act, which read simply: "Indians, and Lands reserved for the Indians." Administrative responsibility for Indians was assumed by the secretary of state for Canada in 1868 under the title of superintendent general of Indian affairs, and included control over Indian lands and property, and all Indian funds. The Enfranchisement Act of 1869 tried to further encourage Indian assimilation into white society through individualized land ownership, but was no more successful than its predecessor in 1859.

In 1870 Canada acquired Rupert's Land and the North-western Territory, shifting the focus of Indian policy towards the facilitation of western expansion and white settlements. This was done through a series of "numbered" treaties that eventually covered most of western and northern Canada. With Rupert's Land and the establishment of a new province of Manitoba in 1870, Treaties 1 and 2 were signed in 1871 covering all of Manitoba and some areas north and west of its initial boundaries. In Treaty 1 the Chippewa and Swampy Cree surrendered almost 42,000 square kilometers, while in Treaty 2 the Chippewa surrendered 89,000 square kilometers of agricultural and timber lands. Ottawa expected the Indians to adopt farming, and so instead of hunting, trapping, and fishing rights, provided farming implements and seeds. Treaty 3 was signed in 1873 and covered a strip of land around the Lake of the Woods to secure safe passage for settlers travelling between Ontario and Manitoba. In Treaty 4 (called the Qu'Appelle Treaty), the Cree and Saulteaux surrendered 194,000 square kilometers in 1874 between the South Saskatchewan River and the American border (what later became the province of Saskatchewan). The 1875 Treaty 5 (the Lake Winnipeg Treaty) secured 260,000 square kilometers from the Saulteaux and Swampy Cree. Treaties 6 and 7, signed in 1876 and 1877, transferred the mid-prairie and southern portions of Alberta from the Assiniboine, Blackfoot,

Blood, Peigan, Sarcee, and Stoney tribes. This first series of numbered treaties was intended to secure the southern portion of western Canada for settlement in the face of possible violence from Indians (the Métis rebellions and American Indian wars made this a real threat). While the details differed from treaty to treaty, the main provisions were the same. In exchange for agreeing to "extinguish" their title to certain lands, Indians received reserve lands (calculated on the basis of an allotment per family), individual annuities, schooling, and in some cases (Treaties 1 and 2) provision for buggies, animals, implements, and suits of clothing for chiefs. Treaty 3 included provisions for continued hunting, fishing, and trapping rights, as well as supplies of ammunition and twine, that were incorporated in Treaties 4, 5, 6, and 7. Treaty 6 include the benefit of a "medicine chest" (now argued by natives to mean free health coverage). Another complicating factor was that not all tribes or bands in a "treaty area" signed the treaty, and so in most cases had to be included as "adhesions" later (though some bands simply refused to sign, such as the Plains Cree with Treaty 6 in 1876). The parties to these treaties never discussed "aboriginal title," but the agreements "were generally seen as both a recognition of the existence of claims and as a mechanism for their negotiation and resolution."[55]

The signing of numbered treaties, the settlement of western Canada, and the establishment of several new provinces together demanded a new national framework for Indian policy that went beyond the numerous bits and pieces of legislation that had carried over from the pre-Confederation period. The 1876 Indian Act, which consolidated and extended previous legislation, created the structure that would govern native policy for the next one hundred years to the present day. The act's scope was almost limitless with respect to the organization of native life and government policy. Ponting and Gibbins describe the Indian Act as a "total institution" that governs the social, economic, political, and criminal activities of natives and those who interact with them.[56] For most of the twentieth century, the Indian Act was the *de facto* constitution for aboriginals living in Canada, a constitution over which they had little influence. It was a constitution, moreover, that deliberately treated them as minors and the government of Canada as their guardian.[57]

The act's major provisions addressed the definition of an Indian, enfranchisement, control and management of Indian lands, governing authority, pursuance of Indian claims, and the social and economic relations within the Indian communities themselves. The first item was conceivably the most important, because legal definitions were provided for the first time of contentious terms such as "Indian," "Band," and "Reserve." The act defined an "Indian" as a male person of Indian blood reputed to belong to a particular band, any child of such a person,

FEATHER AND GUN: CONFRONTATION AT OKA/KANESATAKE

or any woman who is or was lawfully married to such a person. Indian status could, however, be denied to illegitimate children, Indians who had continuously resided in a foreign country for more than five years (i.e., in the United States with another band of the same tribe), Indian women who married a non-Indian or non-treaty Indian, and Métis who had shared in the distribution of Métis lands or annuities. The act therefore established different categories of natives, categories that made sense only in terms of the legislation and government policy itself. A "status Indian" was someone who fit the terms of the Indian Act, and Ottawa kept (and keeps) careful registers of the names of all such persons and their descendants. A "non-status Indian" was someone who might be Indian or part Indian by birth or marriage, but was excluded by the act's other provisions. A "treaty Indian" was someone whose band had at some time signed a treaty with colonial or Canadian authorities; all treaty Indians are status Indians. A "non-treaty" Indian might be a status or a non-status Indian whose band had not entered into a treaty. As Gibbins and Ponting suggest, this "definitional exercise...fragmented the native population in Canada into legally and legislatively distinct blocs experiencing quite different rights, restrictions, and obligations."[58] Complicating matters even further, the act contained provisions from previous legislation regarding enfranchisement, whereby natives could relinquish their Indian status in favour of Canadian citizenship.[59]

The provisions regarding Indian lands or reserves continued the practice of government guardianship. Various clauses dealt with protection of reserves against trespassers, and Indian themselves were exempted from taxes, liens, mortgages, or other charges on their lands. No reserve or portion of a reserve could be sold, alienated, or leased until surrendered to the Crown. This provision was meant to "protect" Indians, but the act's "surrender provisions" were loose enough that a minority of a band could conceivably turn lands over to the government. Any proceeds from the sale or lease of Indian lands would be paid to the receiver general of Canada for credit to the Indian fund. These provisions give the flavour of the act's centralization of authority in Ottawa's hands. Almost every aspect of economic, social, and political life on a reserve was ultimately controlled by the superintendent general and Indian agents on site. While the act did provide for the election of band councils and chiefs, this was a form of local government alien to native traditions and designed to introduce non-native practices in the hope of accelerating assimilation.[60]

New Indian acts followed periodically (the present one was passed in 1951), but the 1876 Indian Act was the inspiration, the template of all subsequent Canadian government policy towards natives. Over its first fifty years the Indian Act would evolve from an instrument of control with the purpose of civilizing, to

FEATHER AND GUN: CONFRONTATION AT OKA/KANESATAKE

an instrument of control pure and simple. In its initial form, however, it reflected a more optimistic, if paternalist, approach to the "advancement" of natives. Its provisions were intended to encourage and protect, and assumed that natives would gradually see the advantages of "civilization," Christianity, and enfranchisement, and willingly give up Indian status to join white society. Two factors undermined this initial optimism, and led to legislative amendments that made the Indian Act more coercive and disciplinary, even as they slowly sapped enthusiasm and a sense of mission (however misguided) from its administration. The first factor was the Rebellion of 1885. To that point amendments to the act had been guided by Prime Minister Macdonald's civilization programme for Indians "to enfranchise the 'more acculturate' tribes of the older provinces and to 'advance' the Indians of the North-West through the establishment of 'model farms' and industrial schools to teach agricultural techniques or mechanical trades."[61] Few bands had availed themselves of these opportunities to "advance," and the Rebellion persuaded officials that more direct controls over Indian life would be needed. A series of amendments was passed shortly before the turn of the century, therefore, to markedly strengthen the powers of the superintendent general. Stricter provisions on the following were implemented between 1889 and 1906 (the year a new consolidated Indian Act was passed): prohibition of tribal dances; enforcement of trespass, timber, and liquor laws on Indian lands; power of local agents; trading with Indians; compulsory school attendance; management of band monies; and enfranchisement. One history of the act states that after 1885 the "Government had increased its influence over Indian moral behaviour, means of livelihood, land resources and capital funds, and had effected little legislation which gave Indians more control over their own affairs."[62]

The second factor was the impact of immigration and soldier resettlement after World War I. A million immigrants settled in the west between 1900 and 1918, and with them came towns, roads, trains, and agriculture. Development and settlement required land, and the Department of the Interior responded by changing its protective stance on Indian lands and reserves. A senior official noted in 1908, for example, that

> conditions, however, have changed and it is now recognized that where Indians are holding tracts of farming or timber lands beyond their possible requirements and by so doing seriously impeding the growth of settlement, and there is such demands as to ensure profitable sale, the product of which can be invested for the benefit of the Indians and relieve *pro tanto* the country of the burden of their maintenance, it is in the best interests of all concerned to encourage such sales.[63]

FEATHER AND GUN: CONFRONTATION AT OKA/KANESATAKE

In 1911 the expropriation provisions of the Indian Act were amended to permit all private companies and municipalities with the necessary authority to expropriate as much reserve land as they needed for public works. The act was also changed to allow authorities to remove Indians from reserve lands if that was perceived to be in the public interest. Together, these amendments clearly undermined the treaty rights that had been the foundation of Indian–white relations since the Royal Proclamation.[64]

A new Indian Act was passed in 1927 to consolidate previous amendments, and once again in 1951. The 1951 act was the result of parliamentary committee hearings from 1946 to 1948, which for the first time systematically canvassed the views of Indians themselves. These views were scattered and not always consistent, but did serve to clearly underscore Indian dissatisfaction with the act. Their recommendations focused on reducing and eliminating where possible the excessive and arbitrary powers of the Department and the superintendent general, and enforcing treaty obligations. The issue of violated or compromised treaties was pressing enough that the committee proposed the establishment of a claims commission to review the terms of all Indian treaties and settle any outstanding grievances. The government did not take up this suggestion, and the 1951 Indian Act differed little from its predecessors: it continued to promote the integration of Indians into Canadian society.[65]

Almost a hundred years had passed since Confederation and the first Indian Act of 1876, but little had changed. Indian policy and the Indian Act had evolved over this period with a depressing consistency of purpose: assimilation into white society, wavering commitment to treaty obligations, and smothering paternalism. The unthinking and overt racism of the Victorian period was gone by the 1950s, at least in official circles, but carried on in a perhaps more insidious institutionalized form in the Indian Act itself. Legislation and policy had been, for almost a century, disastrously contradictory. On the one hand, Indians were treated as different and special (hence the act, treaty obligations, and the government's image of itself as "trustee"). On the other, they were encouraged and often forced to assimilate, to extinguish their difference and "join white society." By the 1950s, Indians lived in a special hell, suspended between what they had been but could be no longer, and what others wished them to be.

FEATHER AND GUN: CONFRONTATION AT OKA/KANESATAKE

ACT TWO: THE NEW AGENDA

Scene 1: Army Manoeuvres

"The government priority is to find a way to peacefully dismantle the barricades so the process can continue in a calm and serene atmosphere."[66] The situation at Oka by mid-August, despite the hopeful signs of conciliation in the appointment of Justice Gold, was anything but calm and serene. The 12 August signing of an agreement to negotiate by Thomas Siddon, John Ciaccia, and masked Mohawk Warriors *behind* the barricades, near the site of Corporal Lemay's death, served only to inflame the already outraged mobs at the Mercier Bridge. The following night hundreds of them threw Molotov cocktails at police and for the first time brandished guns. Robert Lavigne, the head of the SQ, warned that the provincial police could no longer maintain order and expressed fears that armed crowds might try to shoot their way onto the bridge. The following night almost a one thousand people gathered once again to hurl fire bombs, and anything else they could lay their hands on, at police. That same evening the army began to move troops into the area. At an Ottawa news conference, General John de Chastelain announced the mobilization of four thousand soldiers from the Valcartier barracks near Quebec City, along with armed personnel carriers, earth movers, and medical and aerial support teams. Subsequently, other army spokespersons said that only about half that number of troops would be positioned near Oka and Châteauguay, but that their purpose would be to maintain peace and order, not to launch an assault on the barricades. All troop movements would be made public, and the media would be informed at every stage. This would later emerge as the army's single most effective weapon: its mastery of media and communicative strategy. Ultimately, given the huge imbalance of power between the army and the Mohawks, the real war at Oka was over hearts and minds.

As troops rumbled around Kanesatake and Kahnawake and the twenty-four international observers took up their positions at the barricades, Mohawk and government negotiators began to consider the Quebec government's original offer of 27 July: withdrawal of police in exchange for the disarmament of the Warriors, an immediate transfer of land to the Mohawks with a promise to negotiate the larger claim, and a sum of money for economic development.[67] Before they could address the substance of the offer, negotiators once more got embroiled in procedural issues. Ottawa and Quebec each appeared with three representatives[68] (the Ottawa team was there only to observe, not to negotiate), and were stunned to find fifty-four Mohawks from various segments of the community facing them across the table. The Mohawks eventually reduced their team to five, with a large number of "observers," but the confusion reflected a problem that had plagued talks over the previous weeks. While the Warriors staunchly maintained that they spoke for the entire community, in fact they represented the more radical of the two factions that claim allegiance to the Longhouse tradition. And it was still unclear whether the Warriors at this stage represented the broader band community.[69]

Despite this first stumble, the general mood by the weekend of 18 August was optimistic. The army announced that it would relieve the SQ at the barricades, and over the next few days troops slowly moved in to take up positions formerly held by the police. Natives and white residents for the first time in weeks agreed on something: the SQ had been an irritant to the Mohawks and had been perceived as ineffective by whites. Unfortunately, in Oka the army decided to move the police barricade closer to the Mohawk one in order to better observe native movements. The Warrior negotiating team immediately suspended talks for a day until the Armed Forces agreed to rescind the order. The agreement was amicable enough, and the relations between soldiers and Mohawks on the barricades cordial enough (soldiers shook hands with Warriors as they arrived at the SQ barricade), that the talks did not appear severely threatened.

When talks resumed, the Mohawk side dropped its bombshell. In addition to a transfer of the land originally in dispute (which Ottawa had now purchased for $5.2 million and had promised to turn over as soon as the barricades came down), the Warriors demanded a cessation of prosecution related to an illegal bingo parlour at Kahnawake, and a commitment to the establishment of Kanienkehaka, a unified, sovereign, Mohawk nation within three years. Kanienkehaka would consist of the six Mohawk communities of Kanesatake, Kahnawake, Akwesasne, Ohsweken, Tyendinaga, and Ganienkeh (spanning Quebec, Ontario, and New York state). In addition, the Mohawk negotiators raised the question of a separate native armed force to defend the nation, a native justice system, and reliance on the World Court in The Hague to rule on matters of native sovereignty.[70] Not surprisingly, Quebec government negotiators had a different agenda. From the beginning of the dispute, their priority had been to remove the barricades, in particular the barricade at the Mercier Bridge. Land claims and certainly sovereignty were, from the government perspective, issues that could be addressed later. For the Mohawks, however, the barricade was their only bargaining chip. Without it, they were merely a ragged band of protesters; with it, they could attract attention and extract concessions. A piqued Sam Elkas, Quebec minister of public security, complained: "They told us one thing and as you know, they are always coming back with other subjects of discussion."[71] Alex Paterson, the government's chief negotiator, confessed that after five days the talks "lacked focus."

The authorities had wanted a quick resolution to the issue and immediate dismantling of the barricades. The Mohawks had wanted to negotiate sovereignty. Five days was too long for one agenda, but only the beginning for the other. By 23 August, Ottawa and Quebec began to show signs of having lost patience with the negotiating process. On that day two armoured personnel carriers rumbled right up to the Mohawk barricade at Kanesatake. Given that an agreement on a "demilitarized zone" had been reached only a few days earlier, the army was clearly trying to increase pressure. Mohawk negotiators who were on their way to the bargaining table saw the army vehicles and immediately suspended talks. "If this isn't negotiating at the point of a gun, I don't know what the hell is," said Grand Chief Joe Norton.[72] The provocation at the barricades was accompanied by aerial surveillance of the two native communities and police checks on boats going to and from them. Prime Minister Mulroney made no apologies for these actions, noting instead that the negotiations could not go on eternally: "If our efforts are rejected, we will assume our responsibilities." Kim Campbell, the minister of justice, echoed these remarks: "It is intolerable that political goals, however legitimate, be pursued by means that employ violence and the threat of violence."[73] Provincial officials had already turned up the heat some days earlier. Premier Bourassa pointedly referred to "other options" should the negotiations prove fruitless, and on 23 August a sub-committee of his Cabinet met with Lieutenant General Kent Foster, head of the Mobile Command, to discuss bargaining and military strategies.

These were ominous signs, and the Mohawks knew it. After suspending talks for one day in protest over the army's manoeuvres, Warrior negotiators met again with government officials and spent a day dealing with what they considered to be violations of the 12 August agreement on access to food, medicine, advisors, and the role of international observers. Despite brave words that the barricade issue might at last be resolved, by this stage there was an emerging sense of inevitability about armed conflict. Nightly television broadcasts from the site reinforced the impression with vivid if sometimes bizarre footage of armed, masked Warriors pacing warily only feet away from stoical soldiers, themselves armed and poised for action. The Mohawk communities, split from the beginning over the barricades and the role of the Warriors, now expressed its dissatisfaction publicly. An extraordinary meeting of "condoled chiefs" of the Six Nations (the elders) was held at the Onandaga Reserve near Syracuse NY, on 24 August to search for a peaceful resolution of the crisis.[74] Chief Jake Thomas referred to the Warriors as fakes who hid behind the Mohawk tradition in order to protect their illegal cigarette and gambling interests. The Warrior's apparent isolation from their own community was reinforced by the resentment that south shore white residents continued to harbour against them. Vigilante groups had set up their own barricades to prevent Mohawks from using the Mercier Bridge and from even leaving Kahnawake. The twenty-four international observers had to be flown in to take up their positions by the barricades because of threats by angry Châteauguay residents brandishing metal clubs and baseball bats.[75]

The talks broke down once more on the weekend of 25 August. Quebec public opinion had reached a point where the Bourassa government was being criticized daily for its inaction in the face of terrorist blockades. On 27 August a grim Robert Bourassa announced that he had asked the army to remove the barricades. He accused the Mohawks of negotiating in bad faith, of making unacceptable demands, and warned that the government would not accept "groups of citizens who accept laws which they approve and refuse others."[76] The Prime Minister, on a visit to the United States, supported the Premier's request, arguing that in the face of the Mohawks' "bizarre" demands, the law of Canada must prevail. Those demands had included an amnesty to all natives participating in the barricades and the recognition of the Mohawks as a politically sovereign nation. George Erasmus, the grand chief of the Assembly of First Nations, saw nothing in the Mohawk demands that differed substantially from what natives across the country had been demanding: "If this is how Canada is going to respond here, then they might as well get ready to respond to our people all across the country the same way."[77] But according to Thomas Siddon, the federal Indian affairs minister, the government of Canada would never accept the "balkanization of Canada which would see first nations become independent sovereign states." Against this background of mutually exclusive views, the army began to move in one thousand troops and artillery to the area. The barricades would be removed peacefully or by force, but they would be removed. The Mohawks, after weeks of high tension, seemed almost relieved. They prepared to fight, and if necessary, to die.

The icy, almost detached professionalism of the armed forces as they began to remove the barricades did not obscure the possibility that someone might die in a confrontation. Politicians and Mohawks therefore did not give up negotiating, although only days earlier they had protested the futility of further talks. Native leaders across the country denounced the government and warned of civil disobedience if the army moved against the Mohawks. Micmac Indians mounted highway blockades in Quebec, and about three hundred people protested in downtown Vancouver, tying up traffic for several hours. It was clear that Oka was a national issue, not an isolated Quebec concern. The world was also watch-

FEATHER AND GUN: CONFRONTATION AT OKA/KANESATAKE

ing, often incredulously, as Canada's reputation of a "peaceable kingdom" seemed to teeter on the brink of civil violence. On 28 August, as Mohawk women, children, and elders tried to leave Kahnawake by car across the Mercier Bridge through a police cordon, a crowd of about five hundred pelted them with stones and bottles. Once again television brought the brutal scene into every living room in the country: police standing by as cars careened through a hail of rocks and obscenities.[78]

The next day, shock gave way to a measure of hope. Canadian soldiers and Kahnawake residents together worked to remove the two blockades that had shut down the Mercier Bridge for fifty days. Described as purely a "military agreement" that had nothing to do with the negotiations still taking place in a Montreal hotel room between officials and Warriors, the move was still seen as a sign that perhaps the issue might be resolved without violence. Mohawk spokespersons at Oka interpreted the joint effort cautiously, noting that while it signalled the possibility of an amicable resolution, the negotiations were still underway and the barricades at Kanesatake were still up. At this point the talks seemed to hinge on two key issues. One was the land claims question that had sparked the initial confrontation, though it was framed much more broadly now in terms of sovereignty and self-government. The other was the immediate mechanics of dealing with the barricades. Mohawks continued to press for concessions on civil and criminal prosecutions against natives on the barricades, and some way for native peacekeepers to be included in any investigation conducted by the SQ.[79] The talks broke down again on 30 August, amid mutual accusations of bad faith. Grand Chief Joe Norton complained to reporters that food and medical supplies were still being kept out of Kahnawake, and that he himself had been prevented from leaving the reserve to attend meetings. Premier Bourassa cancelled a scheduled meeting of the two sides, claiming that the Iroquois Confederacy had pulled out of the talks. Chief Terry Doxtator greeted the Premier's explanation skeptically, pointing out that the Confederacy was ready to meet at any time with government officials. What appeared to have happened was that one group particularly critical of the Warriors, the Onondaga of the Confederacy, had pulled out in frustration over the demand for immunity from criminal prosecution. In the murky game of musical chairs on the Mohawk side, the Onondaga had represented a more moderate position in the new negotiating team. The dispute over the talks led to a temporary halt in removing the barricades at Kahnawake, but removal resumed the next day.[80]

With the dismantling of the Kahnawake barricades and the promise of an imminent re-opening of the Mercier Bridge, the focus of action had now shifted to Kanesatake, where about three hundred residents of the reserve remained behind the barricades with the Warriors. At one level, the tension now visibly abated. The entire Oka affair, despite its initial basis in a land dispute, had been driven by the bridge closure. The nightly scenes of Châteauguay mobs throwing fire bombs and screaming obscenities at police had been the key ingredient that eventually exhausted the Quebec government's patience. Ironically, the re-opened bridge between Montreal and the Kahnawake reserve did nothing to open communications between natives and government negotiators. Indeed, with the pressure gone from Châteauguay, the army could turn its full attention to wearing down the Mohawks at Kanesatake. Armed forces jets flew low and loud over the reserve, and military helicopters buzzed the barricades with shrouded lights. Warriors told reporters that a soldier crept through the woods and stole a Mohawk flag perched on the barricade. On another occasion, soldiers approached the barricade and fired a flare into a Mohawk tent. It was a careful strategy of psychological warfare designed to puncture Mohawks' confidence.

Without warning, the army moved in against the Kanesatake barricades on Saturday morning, 1 September. Claiming to have reports of beatings, lootings and gunfire in the community, the army began at about 8:15am to take control of the barricades and roadblocks that had started the whole affair months earlier. Moving forward methodically, soldiers captured each barricade and immediately surrounded it with razor wire, after which it would be torn down by an armoured vehicle. As they moved forward they sometimes came within inches of defiant Warriors who taunted them to fight. About two dozen armed Warriors retreated to an alcohol treatment centre on the community's land, dug a trench around it, and prepared for battle. Almost one hundred men, women, and children, including some journalists, were holed up in the centre as well. The army surrounded the facility with four hundred soldiers, and the SQ began to scout the area behind the barricades with dogs. The scene was even more surreal because, while it had all the symbols and reality of armed conflict, there was no demilitarized perimeter between the two sides. Mohawks would scramble out of fox holes to jeer at the soldiers, often chest to chest; soldiers and Warriors would discuss protocols, and army patrols would come within feet of Mohawk trenches.

This uneasy and eerie cohabitation of combatants would drag on for almost another month before the Warriors finally gave up. At this stage the confrontation had been reduced entirely to a military engagement, a play of force and physical threat where negotiations, when they occurred at all, were about the terms of surrender. The previous two weeks had been a sorry cycle of hope, despair, and finally recrimination. A fairly simple dispute over a few acres of land had somehow been transformed into a demand for native sovereignty and self-determination. Mohawks, whatever their internal divisions over the role of the Warriors, linked the issues firmly in their minds. But government negotiators had by now washed their hands of Oka. As a spokesperson for Premier Bourassa noted, "We do not want to put an end to the army's task, which has been a success so far, and we see no reasons to undertake a negotiating process which up until now hasn't given any results."[81]

A negotiating process without results was exactly what natives had endured in Canada for the previous thirty years.

Scene 2: Citizenship, Aboriginal Title and Self-Government

The 1951 Indian Act, though it differed in no substantial respect from its predecessors, had marked an important departure in the aboriginal policy-making process. As noted earlier, the parliamentary committee examining revisions to the legislation had, for the first time in Canadian history, listened to formal presentations from various native organizations. It was a modest change, but one pregnant with significance. It signalled a growing disinclination among natives to simply acquiesce in Ottawa's decisions. The disinclination crystallized into determined resistance by the end of the 1960s, as the federal government tried to completely restructure the foundations of Canadian aboriginal policy in its 1969 White Paper. Natives had had only the most rudimentary political organization until the mid-1960s, and even then had developed national representative organs only under the auspices of the Department.[82] The 1969 White Paper, while universally despised by natives, was "the major catalyst to Indian political mobilization."[83] The politics of the White Paper changed the process and substance of Canadian Indian policy forever. Gibbins and Ponting describe the period as the "Indian Quiet Revolution."[84]

The 1969 White Paper was the result of almost a decade of re-examination of Indian policy. In the 1960s the national unity question and the emerging concern about poverty in Canadian society had helped focus national interest on Indians. Senior officials simultaneously determined that the Department's programs had to be revised and renewed efforts made to integrate Indians with the rest of Canadian society.[85] According to Weaver, the available information on Indians was meagre and the Department's own resources were inadequate to conduct a full-scale study in living conditions and policy options. Under pressure, the Minister of Indian Affairs appointed Harry Hawthorn to conduct "the first full-scale national survey of the conditions of Indians in Canada."[86] The survey substantiated what many in the Indian affairs area had known for years: on almost every important positive indicator of quality of life—e.g., income, health, housing—Indians were drastically below the national average. They exceeded the national average on virtually every negative indicator—e.g., proportion of population on welfare, infant mortality, life expectancy. Canadians learned, many for the first time, that natives lived in conditions more reminiscent of the third world than of North America.

The Hawthorn report[87] was mildly critical of the Department of Indian Affairs, particularly of its paternalism and rigidity in dealing with native needs. It stopped short of recommending the Department's dissolution, however. Instead, its guiding principle was that natives in Canada should be considered "citizens plus," enjoying all the privileges of Canadian citizenship but others as well, owing to their special status and special needs. The assimilationist goal that had guided government policy for a century would have to be abandoned, since it was up to natives themselves to choose. Provincial government social services, available to other citizens but usually denied to Indians on the grounds that Ottawa had responsibility for them, should be made available. Ottawa's role, in Hawthorn's eyes, was to act as a protector of Indian special status as natives strove to achieve equality in Canadian society. Provincial services would have to be extended to natives living on reserves, and the Department of Indian Affairs would have to cooperate more directly with provincial authorities.

Hawthorn's recommendations met with some sympathy in the Department, which was independently experimenting with various decentralization strategies and programs that would encourage native self-sufficiency and community development. However, this was an unsettled period in Canadian politics, with a succession of minority Liberal governments under Lester Pearson. There were five different ministers of Indian affairs between 1963 and 1968, a condition that made coherent planning and policy development impossible.[88] Nonetheless, by 1967 a decision had been taken to revise the Indian Act, though senior officials disagreed on whether a new act should encourage integration (i.e., treat natives like other citizens) or separation (i.e., the "citizens plus" approach). The context for policy renewal had become considerably more volatile, however, by this time.

> In all, the 1960s witnessed an increasing distrust of the government by both Indians and the public, particularly the media, to the point where the government, and not Indians, became the basic target of public concern.... The Indian Act was viewed as racist legislation which denied fundamental civil liberties, relegating Indians to reserves where they were ignored by society in general. There was a strong sense that Indians had been neglected for too long, but there was serious doubt that the Indian administration had the capacity to reform.[89]

The Department had successfully resisted suggestions that did not accord with its own traditions, but this changed dramatically with the coming to power of

Pierre Trudeau and a new Liberal majority government in 1968. The Prime Minister's own rationalistic style of policy-making lent strategic support to those who had pressed for a comprehensive review of Indian policy. However, Trudeau's philosophical and political position on national unity and the Quebec question explicitly rejected any "special status" for the French Canadian minority. In considering approaches to the Indian question, officials often referred to the Prime Minister's views on federalism and equality. The policy review was launched within weeks of the appointment of two ministers for Indian affairs, Jean Chrétien and Robert Andras, but followed two paths that ultimately would have little connection with each other. One was a public consultation process involving native groups and organizations, the other was a largely inter-bureaucratic process dominated by senior officials and ministers. The first, despite some dissatisfaction among natives, served to raise expectations that genuine consultation would occur. The second was the real source of policy development, and its eventual result, the 1969 White Paper, was anything but reassuring to Canadian Indians. By early 1969 the federal cabinet had decided that the key principle guiding policy would be "full non-discriminatory participation" for Indians in Canadian society.[90] This was a momentous shift, since whatever its shortcomings, Canadian Indian policy (as well as the Crown's pre-Confederation obligations) had been rooted in the view that aboriginals had a special status and warranted special treatment and protection.

The *Statement of the Government of Canada on Indian Policy* was released on 25 June 1969. It was short (only ten pages), but explosive. It began by noting that natives' legal and institutional status put them outside of Canadian society. This exclusion was the result of discriminatory public policies that made Indians a matter of special federal jurisdiction, insulated from the programs and services that other Canadians enjoyed. The White Paper affirmed the principles of equality and full participation, and proposed to end the special status that had kept natives out of the Canadian mainstream. The Indian Act was to be repealed and replaced with legislation transferring Indian lands to natives themselves (though not in the form of outright ownership). Services that had been traditionally provided through the Department of Indian Affairs as part of Ottawa's special responsibility to natives would be transferred to the provinces over five years. For a limited time, the federal government would provide special development funds to assist natives in the transition to equal status. On the highly sensitive issue of land claims and treaties, the White Paper rejected the concept of "aboriginal title" as a basis for claims, stating instead that Ottawa's obligations were restricted to its treaty promises. True to its underlying logic, the White Paper noted that even these narrowly legal obligations were anomalous and outdated in defining the relations

FEATHER AND GUN: CONFRONTATION AT OKA/KANESATAKE

of a group of citizens to their government. It suggested that they be reviewed with an eye to termination. From the perspective of Department officials and the cabinet, the White Paper was a ringing endorsement of individual liberty, equality, and choice. For natives leaders, some of whom had been flown to Ottawa to hear the announcement, the White Paper was both unexpected and incredible. The White Paper had implied that its proposals were a response to native demands and consultations; native leaders themselves categorically rejected every one of them.

Dave Courchene, president of the Manitoba Indian Brotherhood, claimed that the White Paper had made natives uncertain, fearful, bitter, and angry.[91] The policy had been conceived in isolation, without real consultation with natives, and represented a unilateral (and paternalistic) rejection of government responsibilities towards natives. Treaty rights and aboriginal title were casually dismissed. The National Indian Brotherhood was equally unequivocal: "We view this as a policy designed to divest us of our aboriginal, residual and statutory rights. If we accept this policy, and in the process lose our rights and our lands, we become willing partners in cultural genocide. This we cannot do."[92] As Weaver notes, the White Paper came as a "powerful shock to Indians."[93]

> The White Paper became the single most powerful catalyst to the Indian nationalist movement, launching it into a determined force for nativism—a reaffirmation of a unique cultural heritage and identity. Ironically, the White Paper had precipitated "new problems" because it gave Indians cause to organize against the government and reassert their separateness....[94]

A formal native response to the White Paper came in the form of *Citizens Plus*, initially drafted by the Indian Chiefs of Alberta. The title referred explicitly to the framework that had guided the Hawthorn report's analysis of the Indian problem. This document was tabled before the full cabinet during a meeting with the National Indian Brotherhood (NIB) on 4 June 1970. The NIB argued that the resolution of native problems in Canada must rest on recognition, not dissolution, of Indian status. Ottawa must accept its treaty obligations, for which Indians had paid dearly with their land, to provide education, welfare, health, and economic development services. Indian peoples, the NIB argued, "see the treaties as the basis of all their rights and status,"[95] and from the native perspective, the treaty promises were "contained in the text of the treaties, some in the negotiations, and some in the memories of our people."[96] Despite severe criticisms of the paternalism of the Department of Indian Affairs, the NIB did not recommend its abolition, at least not until treaty issues, land transfer, and forms of local government and community economic development had been decided.[97] The

FEATHER AND GUN: CONFRONTATION AT OKA/KANESATAKE

government, and Jean Chrétien particularly as Indian affairs minister, tried to defend the White Paper in the face of withering native criticism and mounting objections from non-native opinion leaders. The defence was finally abandoned, and in a rare repudiation of its own policy, the government formally announced in March 1971 that it would not implement the White Paper.

Experienced observers of Canadian Indian policy argue that the White Paper was designed to "protect the government from external criticism"[98] and from "future accusations of discrimination."[99] Its failure set the stage, however, for subsequent developments in the policy field. First, as noted earlier, it rapidly accelerated the development of native political organizations. The reaction from natives was uniformly critical, but underneath it lay a bitter sense of betrayal after the promises of participation. From the more cynical and perhaps realistic perspective of the 1990s, this reaction seems overblown. But the catch-phrases of the day—participation and the just society—were being used for the first time, and natives expected real consultations and some influence in the policy process. Second, the withdrawal of the White Paper may be seen as a watershed in the evolution of Canadian native policy because it signalled the official rejection of assimilation as a policy goal.[100] Third, the White Paper fiasco left a policy vacuum and hence an opportunity for natives to assert some control over events. They were able to do this in part because the federal government (through the Department of Secretary of State) began in 1969-70 to provide funding for native political and community organizations. Native organizations grew in number and multiplied their political strategies, targeting the government and the Department at the national as well as regional level. Other federal agencies (e.g., the Secretary of State, Treasury Board, and Auditor General) began to encroach on Indian policy. After a short period of retreat and withdrawal, the Department of Indian Affairs was restructured (into Indian Affairs and Northern Development), but suffered from high turnover rates at the ministerial and senior levels.[101]

The White Paper had adopted a consistent, if for natives an inappropriate, philosophical framework for addressing the "Indian problem." That problem had often been defined at root as one of paternalism and colonization; the solution would therefore be the recognition of natives as free individuals, equal in every respect to other Canadian citizens. The Prime Minister's response to arguments that this effectively withdrew all supports and protection for native culture and community life was that cultures that required protection to survive were doomed anyway. Natives would become like any other ethnic group in Canada, distinct and valuable, but not separate or protected. The native position on the White Paper was that Canada had in the past assumed certain undertakings through treaties and other promises, and these undertakings had to be honoured. In cases

FEATHER AND GUN: CONFRONTATION AT OKA/KANESATAKE

where there were no undertakings or treaties, natives retained aboriginal rights and titles to land, and these required negotiation. Finally, the legacy of the Indian Act and past practices had devastated native culture and society to the point where, irrespective of treaty or other obligations, Canadian governments and the Canadian people had to provide special assistance and support. In short, Indians wished to have their old treaties honoured, their traditional claims recognized, and their right to self-determination accommodated. These ideas expressed the central tendencies of native politics in Canada for the next twenty years. The aspirations were expressed in a hundred different ways by diverse organizations, at all levels of government, but were principally channelled in two main initiatives over the 1970s and 1980s: the new comprehensive claims process, and the con-stitutional recognition of aboriginal rights and self-government.

Native claims have a history as long as Confederation itself. The oldest category of comprehensive claims concerns the Indians of British Columbia, where with only a few small exceptions,[102] no treaties were ever signed with the govern-ment of Canada. Prior to joining Confederation in 1871, British Columbia had followed an Indian policy considerably less generous than the one guiding Ottawa and its dealings with Plains Indians. Whereas Ottawa tried to sign treaties and determine reserves prior to settlement, the British Columbia practice had been to unilaterally allot reserves a fraction of the size agreed to on the prairies.[103] After 1871, responsibility for BC Indians was assumed by the federal government, but Ottawa depended on transfers of land from the province to deal with native claims. Provincial and federal authorities disagreed almost immediately on the proper allotments for reserve lands. A Reserves Commission operated briefly from 1877 to 1910, but without marked success. BC Indians asserted prior aboriginal title to provincial lands, to the extent of sending delegations to the King in 1906 and again in 1909. Various administrative attempts were made over the ensuing years to work out a practical compromise on reserve lands, but BC Indians insisted on a judicial resolution of their claim based on the aboriginal title. This did not occur until the 1973 Nishga case. Though the specifics of the claims differed, Mohawks had faced similar frustrations over the Oka case, which was in open dispute in 1868 and came before the Judicial Committee of the Privy Council in 1912, which decided against the Indians. In addition to claims of this type, which hinged on a concept of prior ownership of land or basic rights inhering in aboriginal title, there were constant grievances over treaty provisions and ad-ministration of the Indian Act, particularly concerning expropriations of reserve lands. Indians were hobbled in making their case, however, because of a general prohibition under Canadian law against initiating proceedings against the

FEATHER AND GUN: CONFRONTATION AT OKA/KANESATAKE

Crown,[104] and specific provisions in the Indian Act, discontinued only in 1951, prohibiting Indians from raising money or hiring a lawyer to pursue a land claim.[105]

After 1945, in conjunction with the legislative review that led to the 1951 Indian Act, there was consideration of a "comprehensive" process that would examine all Indian claims and grievances. Comparisons at this stage were often made with the United States, which in 1945 established the Indian Claims Commission (it lasted until 1978) to deal with similar issues in that country. While the advantages of a national claims commission were widely accepted among officials, politicians, and natives, nothing came of the idea until the 1969 White Paper. Ironically, the government's desire to dissolve the Department of Indian Affairs and transform Indians into ordinary Canadian citizens as quickly as possible led it to suggest the appointment of an Indian claims commissioner. The White Paper was eventually repudiated, but not before a commissioner (Dr. Lloyd Barber) was appointed to review claims and grievances and recommend mechanisms for their adjudication and resolution. Because this initiative was connected to the White Paper, and because it promised only further study rather than immediate solutions, natives criticized it severely. But the appointment did serve to raise the claims issue to greater prominence. The White Paper itself had served to do much the same thing, since its attack on treaties and, by imputation, on aboriginal title had reinforced native perceptions that these were the bedrock of their rights in North America.

While the White Paper and the Prime Minister explicitly rejected the concept of aboriginal title as a basis of claims, from 1970 to 1976 the federal government (through the Privy Council Office, the Department of Secretary of State, DIAND, and the Indian claims commissioner) funded native organizations in their research on the historical and legal basis for aboriginal claims. The turning point occurred with the decision of the Supreme Court of Canada in January 1973 in *Calder v. The Attorney-General of British Columbia*. The Nishga Indians of British Columbia claimed aboriginal title to their traditional lands in the Nass Valley of British Columbia, which had never been signed away in a treaty.[106] They narrowly lost the case, but the Court's decision for the first time gave judicial credence to the notion of aboriginal title. Of seven judges who heard the case, three ruled that aboriginal title existed and had not been extinguished, three ruled that it existed but had been extinguished, and one (the deciding opinion) rejected the claim on technical grounds. Thus while the initial claim was denied, the court gave almost unanimous agreement to the idea of aboriginal title. According to Little Bear, the *Calder* case, combined with previous legal decisions, defined the scope and extent of aboriginal title in the following terms:

FEATHER AND GUN: CONFRONTATION AT OKA/KANESATAKE

1   Aboriginal title is a personal and usufructuary interest, recognizable in
     Canadian law.

2   Its existence can be traced either to the Royal Proclamation of 1763 or it
     can be based on possession from time immemorial.

3   Its continuing existence is at the goodwill of the Sovereign, and aboriginal
     title can be extinguished at the whim of the sovereign.

4   The Sovereign is not necessarily obligated to pay compensation for the ex-
     tinguishment of aboriginal title.[107]

Most natives oppose the third and fourth points in this interpretation, arguing
that they beg the question of how, in the absence of conquest or purchase or
other transfer, the Crown (i.e., the Canadian government) can claim sovereignty
over native lands. Another legal issue is whether, even in light of the specific
wording of some treaties, aboriginal title and aboriginal rights were indeed ever
completely extinguished.[108]

The decisions in the *Calder* case prompted Ottawa to admit in 1973 that
Indian rights might be more extensive than initially contemplated in the White
Paper. In August 1973 Jean Chrétien, then minister of DIAND, announced the
establishment of a comprehensive claims process to deal with situations "where
rights of traditional use and occupancy had not been extinguished by treaty or
superseded by law."[109] As well, there would be a more flexible approach to specific
claims and grievances against the administration and interpretation of existing
treaties. On July 1974 Ottawa established the Office of Native Claims in DIAND
to conduct research and represent the government in the comprehensive claims
process. From the native perspective, while almost any movement on the claims
front was welcome, the process still seemed like a stacked deck, since the Office
would simultaneously judge the validity of claims and negotiate for the government over those claims.

The government's policy framework for the negotiation of comprehensive
claims was reviewed in 1980-81 and clarified in a new statement entitled *In All
Fairness*. The new Conservative government after 1984 addressed the issue again,
appointing the Task Force to Review Comprehensive Claims Policy. Its final
report noted that between 1973 and 1985 Ottawa and aboriginal groups had spent
more than $100 million on negotiations, but had reached agreement on only three.
In 1985 another twenty-one claims were under or awaiting negotiation.[110] The
Task Force made several recommendations to alter the philosophy and process
surrounding comprehensive claims. In its view,

FEATHER AND GUN: CONFRONTATION AT OKA/KANESATAKE

Several factors have contributed to the difficulties in reaching agreements. One of the most significant obstacles has been the insistence of the federal government on finality and on the blanket extinguishment of all aboriginal rights. Other difficulties have resulted from the government's refusal to include political rights, decision-making power on land and resource management boards, revenue sharing from surface and subsurface resources, and offshore rights in the negotiations.[111]

The "blanket extinguishment" approach had not in fact been a feature of pre-Confederation treaties; it had only been introduced in the numbered treaties on the prairies. The Task Force argued that in a legal sense there was little difference between extinguishment and simple transfer of title, but that from the native perspective aboriginal rights "are intimately tied to culture and life-style and are integral to their self-identity." Surrender and extinguishment of these rights were perceived as "assimilation and cultural destruction" and had been a barrier to successful negotiations.[112]

The Task Force issued a series of complex recommendations intended to broaden the comprehensive claims process and render it more flexible. These recommendations flowed into a policy review that resulted in a revised framework in 1987. The new policy adopted many of the Task Force's suggestions, with provisions "for new approaches to the cession and surrender of title, self-government, wildlife and environmental management, the inclusion of offshore areas in negotiations, resource revenue-sharing and negotiating procedures."[113] Previous policy had restricted the scope of negotiations to real estate transactions, and the government's objective, as noted in the Task Force report, was to exchange land for complete extinguishment of aboriginal rights and title. In principle, the new policy broadened the scope considerably to include such matters as self-government and environmental management, and the government accepted that there might be alternatives to complete cession of aboriginal rights. The alternatives hinged on renunciation of aboriginal *land title* combined with the continuance of certain defined rights through either the reserved or non-reserved areas (e.g., hunting rights, free access). Ottawa was prepared to consider the transfer of subsurface rights through the claims process, sharing of resource revenue even in the absence of any transfer of title, as well as mechanisms for self-government. The new policy also proposed a revised negotiating process consisting of five phases. The first phase would involve preliminary negotiations where the minister "judges the likelihood of successful negotiations to be high, the settlement of claims in the area to be a priority, and where active provincial and territorial involvement may be obtained as necessary."[114] The second phase would conclude "framework agreements" to determine the "scope, progress, topics, and parameters for negotiation."[115] The third phase would result in agreements-in-principle, the fourth in "final agreements," and the fifth would involve implementation plans.

The new policy framework on comprehensive claims was thus joined to the existing provisions for dealing with specific claims or grievances arising from existing treaties and agreements. At the time of the Oka crisis, the DIAND claims procedures had not been notably successful. By spring 1990, the Department faced 578 specific claims, 205 of which were considered by authorities to be "resolved," usually because they were rejected by the government. The remainder were still under negotiation.[116] The comprehensive claims process had produced only one major agreement since being revised in 1987, with the Dene and Métis of the Northwest Territories. The final agreement affected fifteen thousand natives, and would have transferred to them 180,000 square kilometers of land, subsurface mineral rights, special hunting and fishing rights, and $500 million over twenty years. In return, natives would have renounced aboriginal title as well as specific rights contained in Treaty 8 and Treaty 11. The agreement was rejected at a 18 July 1990 ratification meeting, with particularly strong objections by southern Métis. Bill Erasmus, the Dene president, argued that the agreement would have extinguished aboriginal rights: "Our rights are entrenched with the Canadian Constitution: Supreme Court cases are beginning to define those rights and we as Dene are not prepared to give up any of those treaty or aboriginal rights."[117]

The Dene and Métis rejection of this agreement was not simply an indictment of a cumbersome negotiating process. It also reflected the growing prominence of the other great initiative of this period: the constitutional recognition of native rights and self-government. Like the comprehensive land claims process, this was stimulated by the Supreme Court 1973 *Calder* decision that appeared to affirm the existence of aboriginal rights. These rights could easily be read as the rights of sovereign or at least semi-independent peoples, and so implicitly raised the issue of accommodation within the country's larger constitutional context. The sporadic intergovernmental negotiations over the constitution from 1968 to 1974 were given a tremendous boost with the election in 1976 of the separatist Parti québécois. The Trudeau government addressed constitutional questions with renewed vigour, and after its surprise re-election in 1980 and the defeat of the Quebec referendum, was implacably committed to constitutional renovation. Aboriginal title and rights were by no means a priority for Ottawa, given its focus on the Quebec dimension, but the constitutional negotiations that ensued in 1981 provided an opening for native leaders and their organizations to press their case.

Natives were far from united in their positions on constitutional patriation or the Charter. The Inuit, the Native Council of Canada, and the National Indian Brotherhood staked out different tactical positions on these questions. The NIB, for example, opened an office in London in October 1980 to try to lobby British MPs to prevent passage of the constitutional resolution until aboriginal rights had been defined and included. On one thing, however, all natives were agreed: in any new agreement, the federal and provincial governments would have to address native constitutional rights *somehow*. White politicians were far from convinced that any priority should be placed on these native concerns, as evidenced by the "in again, out again" progress of aboriginal rights over the fall and winter of 1980–81 when the new constitution and Charter of Rights and Freedoms were being forged. The first public version of Ottawa's proposal almost failed to contain any provisions on aboriginal rights; only an eleventh-hour intervention succeeded in adding an anaemic phrase to the effect that the Charter's guarantees should not be construed as denying the existence of any other rights or freedoms that pertained to native peoples in Canada.[118] At this stage, Pierre Trudeau and Jean Chrétien, key players in the development of the ill-fated 1969 White Paper, argued that aboriginal rights could not be written into the constitution before they were defined. Under pressure from the NDP, which threatened to withdraw its parliamentary support of the government's constitutional resolution, the cabinet agreed to an amendment that "recognized and affirmed" the aboriginal and treaty rights of the aboriginal peoples of Canada.[119] At the end of January 1981 Chrétien made further concessions. The federal government agreed to include a clause in the Charter affirming *existing* aboriginal rights, made a major concession by defining Métis peoples as "aboriginals,"[120] and protected aboriginal rights from federal and provincial legislation. Though the NIB had been involved in the lobbying effort to extract these concessions, in April 1981 it reversed itself and declared them unacceptable. Calling Canada a racist state, native leaders demanded that aboriginal rights take precedence over federal and provincial laws. Ironically, the NIB's London lobbying strategy allied it with the "gang of eight" provinces who opposed the Charter and its aboriginal rights clause.[121]

"Recognition and affirmation" of aboriginal rights was code for the possible transfer of large amounts of land to native peoples. Since land and property rights fall into provincial jurisdiction, with a few major exceptions pertaining to the North, most such transfers would involve the provinces. Unsurprisingly, the amendment was opposed by premiers, particularly western premiers. And in the federal–provincial meeting of November 1981 that hammered together a compromise between the federal government and all provinces except Quebec, the amendment was dropped to gain agreement over the inclusion of the Charter.[122]

FEATHER AND GUN: CONFRONTATION AT OKA/KANESATAKE

Most native leaders were incensed but hardly surprised. Gibbins notes that had the restoration of the clause depended entirely on native political pressures, it likely would never have occurred, but native agitation was joined to and strengthened by a rearguard action by Canadian women's groups as they sought to restore the sexual equality clause (section 28), which had also been dropped in the November meeting. Women's protests were better organized and more effective than the scattered and often divided reactions of native groups, and so created an opening that might not otherwise have been exploited.[123] Aboriginal rights were thus reinstated in the Charter, though less because of astute native lobbying and receptive politicians than because of a fortuitous conjuncture of forces over which native leaders had exercised little control. Despite this, native organizations launched court cases in Britain arguing that unilateral patriation of the constitution was illegal without native consent. On appeal, the case was heard by Lord Denning in December 1981. His ruling was handed down in January 1982; the decision upheld Canada's right to patriation, but contained several *obiter dicta* sympathetic to the native cause. Ironically, there was much more attention paid to the aboriginal question in the British Commons debates on the constitution than in the Canadian ones. Ultimately, however, the constitution was patriated. The NIB declared 17 April 1982, the day the constitution was signed, a day of mourning. One native leader said that to celebrate patriation was to celebrate a "treasonous act against the Indian nations and their citizens."[124]

The key sections pertaining to aboriginal rights were contained in section 25 of the Charter of Rights and Freedoms and section 35 of the Constitution Act, 1982:

25. The guarantee in this Charter of certain rights and freedoms shall not be construed so as to abrogate or derogate from any aboriginal, treaty or other rights or freedoms that pertain to the aboriginal peoples of Canada including:

    (a) any rights or freedoms that have been recognized by the Royal Proclamation of October 7, 1763; and

    (b) any rights or freedoms that may be acquired by the aboriginal peoples of Canada by way of land claims settlement.

35. (1) The existing aboriginal and treaty rights of the aboriginal peoples of Canada are hereby recognized and affirmed.

    (2) In this Act, "aboriginal peoples of Canada" includes the Indian, Inuit and Métis peoples of Canada.

FEATHER AND GUN: CONFRONTATION AT OKA/KANESATAKE

There are several important aspects to these clauses. First, they mark the formal recognition by the Canadian state of the existence of aboriginal rights. As Gibbins has argued, section 35 "ends debate on the existence of aboriginal rights and shifts the terms of debate to the meaning and implementation of such rights."[125] Second, the Charter now recognizes, through section 25, the status of the Métis as aboriginals, and therefore the existence of Métis aboriginal rights (as yet undefined). Third, section 35 deliberately refers to "existing aboriginal rights," a phrase insisted upon by more reluctant premiers in the constitutional negotiations as a means of restricting the potential scope of claims. Gibbins has argued, however, that this strategy may have backfired, since aboriginals never directly surrendered the right to self-government through the treaty process, and thus these rights may still exist. The right to self-government is perhaps the broadest construction that could be placed on the meaning of "aboriginal rights," and so the first ministers may have unwittingly widened, not narrowed, the constitutional foundation of native sovereignty. Fourth, the inclusion of aboriginal rights in the Charter was complemented by a special provision for a first ministers' meeting, with native groups, to discuss aboriginal constitutional issues. Section 37 of the Charter called for a meeting within one year of the passage of the new constitution, and one of the items to be on the agenda was "constitutional matters that directly affect the aboriginal peoples of Canada, including the identification and definition of the rights of those peoples to be included in the Constitution of Canada..." This provision clearly implied that aboriginal constitutional issues could not be decided without the participation and conceivably the approval of native peoples themselves.

Until the Meech Lake accord began to be cobbled together (see Chapter 2), aboriginal issues remained the country's only major unresolved constitutional item, and so native organizations could no longer rely on allies to assist their cause.[126] A first ministers' conference was held as required in March 1983 and was an impressive symbolic advance for native peoples who, for the first time, were seated at the table with Canada's premiers and prime minister. The conference made several important substantive advances as well, resulting in the first set of amendments to the 1982 constitution. Section 25(b) was amended to read: "any rights or freedoms that now exist by way of land claims agreements or may be so acquired." Section 35 received several additional clauses. One included existing and future land claims agreements in the definition of treaty rights; another brought it into line with section 15 equality provisions pertaining to gender so as to guarantee aboriginal and treaty rights equally to men and women notwithstanding any other Charter provisions (e.g., section 35(1), which might be used to rationalize gender inequality on the basis of traditional native practices); and

FEATHER AND GUN: CONFRONTATION AT OKA/KANESATAKE

another stipulated that constitutional changes affecting aboriginal rights would have to be agreed to by native peoples at a specially convened first ministers' conference. Finally, section 37 was amended to stipulate that at least three more constitutional conferences on aboriginal issues would be called in 1984, 1985, and 1987. While a wide range of issues were discussed at this 1983 meeting and proposed for the subsequent ones, clearly the most important agenda item to emerge was the question of Indian self-government.

The self-government issue was given even further national prominence through the November 1983 report of the Special Committee on Indian Self-Government, or the Penner report. The report deliberately referred throughout to "Indian First Nations," a term that itself reflected the vast changes in the aboriginal policy field since 1969. Native organizations now preferred this designation, and it carried a double rhetorical edge: not only were natives "first" but they were "nations" as well. The report's key recommendation was that "the federal government establish a new relationship with Indian First Nations and that an essential element of this relationship be recognition of Indian self-government."[127] It suggested that the right to self-government be "explicitly stated and entrenched" in the constitution, thereby establishing the Indian First Nations as a "distinct order of government." The First Nations would be defined initially in terms of existing bands, who could define their membership and constitute themselves as Indian governments. A ministry of state for First Nations would be established to negotiate the full range of powers to be exercised by Indians, but at a minimum the Penner report envisaged that these powers would include "full legislative and policy-making powers on matters affecting Indian people" and full control over territory and resources with the boundaries of Indian lands.[128] Funding relationships would have to be revised towards a direct, bloc-funding model wherein Ottawa made transfers to First Nations on the assumption that they were accountable to their own people.

The Penner report was heralded as a "major and significant document"[129] and a "fundamental forward-looking paradigmatic shift."[130] Its release only months before the scheduled 1984 meeting on aboriginal constitutional issues ensured that it would help set the terms of debate and focus attention on the question of self-government. Ottawa's response to the Penner report, released just days before the March 1984 first ministers' conference, surprised native leaders by supporting the concept of self-government. On the first day of the conference Prime Minister Trudeau tabled a proposed constitutional amendment to entrench aboriginal self-government that would have left the specific meaning of the phrase to future negotiations with individual native groups. Ontario, New Brunswick, and Manitoba agreed to the proposal, but the six other provinces[131] resisted it without

FEATHER AND GUN: CONFRONTATION AT OKA/KANESATAKE

clarification of its meaning. The conference therefore broke up without agreement.

> The 1984 First Ministers' Conference on Aboriginal Constitutional Matters was a failure of colossal proportions. No agreement was reached on either a constitutional amendment respecting aboriginal self-government, or on a work plan for achieving agreement. The Conference ended in suspicion and innuendo, with many First Ministers asking what aboriginal self-government "meant," and many aboriginal leaders demanding its constitutional entrenchment.[132]

This failure was tempered somewhat by the election in 1984 of a new Conservative government under Brian Mulroney. Mulroney had promised to direct the climate and procedures of intergovernmental relations away from the "pressure tactics" and confrontation of the Trudeau years towards national reconciliation. The 1985 first ministers' conference on aboriginal issues was the initial test of this promise, and the Prime Minister seemed committed to carrying forward the previous proposals on entrenchment of aboriginal self-government. Indeed, at preliminary ministerial meetings on the issue, the Conservatives appeared even more committed to the principle of native self-government than the Trudeau Liberals had been. The idea was to first entrench the principle and then sign an accord initiating negotiations towards specific forms of self-government.[133] Native reaction to the proposal was mixed, with the Assembly of First Nations arguing that the right to self-government was inherent in aboriginal status and so had to be affirmed without condition or constraint. The Inuit and Métis emphasized the importance of land claims settlement as the concrete foundation for any abstract right to self-government, but were generally supportive of the initiative.[134] In the face of resistance from some provinces and native organizations, Ottawa redrafted its proposal and resubmitted it on the second day of the conference, but the resistance remained and so the Prime Minister postponed any decision on aboriginal issues for six weeks, abruptly adjourning the conference. In fact, the ministerial meeting did not take place for almost two months, and when it did—at a Toronto airport hotel—it too failed. Provincial governments such as Alberta, Ontario, and British Columbia announced that they would be entering negotiations with aboriginal peoples outside of the constitutional framework, and the federal government responded by announcing that it would now pursue self-government at the local, regional, territorial, and provincial level as a preliminary step towards constitutional entrenchment. The previous model had been "top-down," assuming that the right to self-government could be entrenched before its reality was defined. The failed 1985 conference saw Ottawa shift its gears towards a "bottom-up" approach that would first try to flesh out the practical meaning of self-government and only later, in the scheduled 1987 first ministers' meeting, try to entrench it.[135] As an attempt to prepare the ground for the 1987 conference, the effort failed. First ministers and native leaders from the Assembly of First Nations, the Métis National Council, and the Inuit Committee on National Issues met 26-27 March and were once again unable to bridge the gap on self-government. At this stage, native leaders insisted on what they called an "inherent right" to self-government that would be entrenched in the constitution with some forcing provisions to ensure the progress of negotiations on details and form. Four provinces refused to go this far, agreeing only to the entrenchment of a "contingent" right that would entrench only forms of self-government that had actually been negotiated. Ottawa's own proposal included conditions as well, such as "self-government within the context of Canadian Confederation," and native leaders opposed this. Five years of constitutional skirmishes had led practically nowhere. Since only three first ministers' conferences on aboriginal constitutional issues had been stipulated by section 37 of the constitution itself, the 1987 meeting was the end of the road for constitutional entrenchment for some time.

The momentum for self-government did not abate completely, however. The 1983-87 talks between natives and first ministers focused on constitutional entrenchment. This did not prohibit a bottom-up approach of negotiated agreements on a case-by-case basis, as indeed Ottawa had proposed in 1985. From the native perspective, the absence of constitutional entrenchment left them exposed and vulnerable in a bargaining process that could be more easily dominated by federal and provincial authorities. For many natives across Canada, the goal of self-government as a reality was never abandoned, though the constitutional stalemate was a source of frustration. Ottawa's conversion to a bottom-up approach in 1986 was crystallized in the "community-based self-government" (CBSG) policy, designed in part to circumvent the constraints of constitution-making as well as the limitations of the Indian Act. The policy is very careful, however, not to impose on existing or future aboriginal or treaty rights, cannot alter the federal–provincial division of power, and any community self-government arrangements must be compatible with the institutions of Canadian government, including the Charter of Rights and Freedoms.[136] The negotiating process is bureaucratic and cumbersome, with stages similar to those used in the comprehensive claims process. DIAND officials demand evidence of community support at each stage, and any framework legislation must be ratified by the cabinet and legislature as well as the involved community. The players on both sides face contradictory pressures: natives seek greater autonomy but are reluctant to completely release the government from its trust obligations to Indians; DIAND officials are prepared to negotiate greater degrees of community self-government,

FEATHER AND GUN: CONFRONTATION AT OKA/KANESATAKE

but simultaneously wish to retain enough power to meet their departmental responsibilities and be accountable to Parliament.[137] The policy has not been notably successful. As of 1990, no agreement had reached the fourth phase in the CBSG process of implementation, though about one-third of Canada's almost six hundred bands were involved in developmental work, framework negotiations, and substantive negotiations. Each agreement under the CBSG policy is different, the entire process is vastly complex and extraordinarily time-consuming, and it holds out only modest promise of self-determination and economic development.

Natives in 1990 could be excused for feeling as though they had entered a time warp. Thirty years previously each tiny band had had to wrestle on its own with the DIAND elephant to extract concessions on even the smallest matters. After almost a generation, over a period that saw the growth of national native organizations, the battle over the 1969 White Paper, the recognition of aboriginal rights and title, and the entrenchment of those rights in a new constitution, natives found themselves in virtually the same political relationship with DIAND. Something *had* changed, of course: their own sense of themselves as nations with a right to self-determination—even to sovereignty—had been sharpened with each confrontation and each defeat. By 1990, in contrast to 1960, the goals of political autonomy and self-determination had become part of the mainstream of native politics. Impatience and frustration, like feathers in a hot wind, surged upward.

ACT THREE: SURRENDER AND DEFIANCE

Scene 1: Seige

Kanesatake was now in a tourniquet, and the army began to squeeze. At dawn on 3 September fifty soldiers sped up to the Mohawk perimeter in armed carriers, leaping into ditches with rifles aimed directly at the Warriors only a few feet away, who themselves scrambled into fox holes and trenches.[138] Army commanders shouted at their men to keep calm, and forty metres away Lasagna did the same: "We have not lost. They're trying to get on your nerves. Don't let them." In the evening the army, brandishing a search warrant, raided the Longhouse at the Kahnawake reserve, turning up assorted illegal weapons such as a .50 calibre gun, a Ruger mini-14 rifle, and three AK-47 assault rifles. The Longhouse is the traditional centre of Mohawk religion and politics, but the army justified the raid as a response to native demonstrations at the Mercier Bridge and sightings of armed Mohawks wandering the reserve.

At this stage there were about twenty Warriors holed up at the treatment centre, with about another hundred Mohawk women and children in the nearby community centre. They were surrounded by four hundred soldiers. Food, water, and medicine were initially blocked from entering the centre (a violation of earlier agreements), but the army relented within twenty-four hours. The raids, the blockade of supplies, and the activities of soldiers only feet away from Warrior trenches raised tension dramatically. While a succession of native negotiators came and went from the centre, Mohawk women physically attacked and verbally abused soldiers on the line. In Kahnawake a riot left a native woman with broken ribs, allegedly because she had been struck by a soldier's rifle butt. The army moved in fourteen hundred soldiers that night.[139] The SQ circled the reserves from time to time, at one point trying to infiltrate the army line by sending in two officers disguised as journalists. The SQ had been involved in the Longhouse raid, and its role there was reviled by native leaders. Premier Bourassa and his minister of public security, Sam Elkas, refused to acknowledge this criticism, accusing natives of engaging in a propaganda war to slander the SQ.

The tension clearly was poisoning whatever was left of the negotiating process. Native leaders travelled to Ottawa to meet with Indian Affairs Minister Thomas Siddon, who on 5 September agreed vaguely to try to help reduce the stress faced by Mohawks in the treatment centre. Noting lamely that much of the discussion had been aimed at "generating a sense of trust," Siddon claimed that he had no control over the army.[140] By this point, the stand-off had completely eroded any possibility of generating trust. On 6 September the army called on the Kanesatake Warriors to put themselves in military custody until their legal cases were decided. The offer was designed to neutralize the Mohawk fear that the SQ would seek revenge on them for the death of Corporal Lemay. It was angrily refused. Terry Doxtator, the chief negotiator at this point for the Mohawks, called it totally unacceptable, while Kahnawake Mohawk Grand Chief Joe Norton labelled the army's presence in Kanesatake an occupation: "We've been stabbed in the back by the armed forces and double-crossed by everybody."[141] Premier Bourassa responded by calling the Warriors thugs and criminals.[142] Around this time a coalition of social action groups—including the National Action Committee on the Status of Women, the Canadian Labour Congress, the Canadian Peace Alliance, and Greenpeace—published an advertisement condemning the province's use of the police and army to deal with the Oka crisis.

The situation at Kanesatake had deteriorated beyond redemption. Governments were unwillingly to negotiate until arms had been laid down, and the army demanded unconditional surrender. With the Mercier Bridge finally open again, the political pressure for a negotiated resolution had evaporated. The crisis had imploded into a mini-war zone around the treatment centre, and clashes now broke out almost daily, peppered with obscenities and threats. The army tightened the noose daily, using a variety of tactics to let the Warriors know they were outnumbered and outgunned. At 3:30am on Saturday, 9 September, a three-man army patrol made its way behind the Mohawk perimeter to reconnoitre the area (the Warriors had erected a plastic sheet to thwart army search lights). They encountered a Warrior nicknamed Spud Wrench, who later claimed that he was surprised while asleep and beaten with clubs. The soldiers claimed they had been attacked. Spud Wrench required twenty-five stitches and had to be carried out of the Mohawk encampment to receive medical attention.[143] Within two days of this incident, Mohawk negotiators tabled a nine-point peace proposal to resolve the stand-off. The plan called for the Warriors to surrender their weapons, which would then be sealed and kept in a neutral place, their eventual disposal to be decided by a joint commission consisting of representatives of the federal and provincial governments, the Mohawks, and human rights agencies. The Warriors themselves would remain in military custody at their own headquarters. The army would be permitted to search those headquarters, in the presence of native observers. The plan left the Warriors open to prosecution, but the laying of charges would be subject to the findings of the joint commission. The Quebec government flatly rejected the offer. Premier Bourassa's objections focused on the apparent immunity that the Warriors were trying to achieve: "In the name of fundamental principles of democracy and of our justice system, the proposal is unacceptable to the Quebec government...there would be no question of allowing a certain group of citizens to be treated differently than other Quebec citizens."[144] This, of course, was precisely the treatment that the Mohawks wanted to establish. On the eve of the army's removal of the barricades, the Mohawk negotiators had raised the stakes dramatically by insisting on some formal recognition of the sovereignty of the Mohawk nation. This had failed, but they could still salvage an element of symbolic recognition (as well as affirm that the Warriors had not been criminals, but protectors of the community) if the authorities agreed to joint policing, investigation, and ultimately, sentencing. Mohawk law and Mohawk practice would then have the same status as white law. Bourassa's insistence that the Mohawks were to be treated as all other citizens of Quebec underscored that the natives were governed by provincial law.

The Mohawk offer had been riddled with conditions. The Quebec government at this point insisted on an unconditional surrender, something that Warriors in turn flatly rejected. The noose was then tightened again as the army cut off Mohawk phone lines on 13 September. The Mohawks suspended talks immediately, quixotically demanding "complete freedom."[145] The following day the army cut off food and other supplies to the twelve remaining journalists holed up with the Mohawks in the treatment centre (the journalists could share in the shipments of food that were sent to the Mohawks, however). The army wanted the journalists out of the centre, claiming that they posed a security risk and might be injured in a conflict. Water supplies were mysteriously cut off at the same time, and electrical power was interrupted. A few days later the army sought and received an injunction to cut off the cellular phones used by the journalists and Mohawks in the centre. The army was still demanding unconditional surrender, but made a new offer that native peacekeepers could be present at the laying down of Mohawk arms. This was also rejected by the Warriors.

The last days of the confrontation at Kanesatake were perhaps its most symbolic. They were marked by riots and raids, mistrust and belligerence, failed negotiations, and finally a disordered surrender—turmoil had been the keynote of this crisis from its beginning. On 18 September the SQ, with support from the army, went once more onto the Kahnawake reserve searching for arms (raids of this type had become routine since the barricades had come down). The soldiers arrived in helicopters and armed carriers, and tried to make a path through a mob of Mohawks blocking the road. A riot broke out, warning shots were fired, and the crowd grew bigger as reinforcements from the reserve arrived. Troops put on masks and repeatedly fired tear gas into the crowd. About one hundred Mohawks were taken to hospital for treatment, and at least a dozen soldiers were injured. The raid yielded dozens of illegal weapons, including high-powered rifles and Molotov cocktails. Morris Manning, the lawyer retained by the Mohawks (and years before by Henry Morgentaler for his Supreme Court case; see Chapter 1), was on the reserve during the raid. "This is absolutely outrageous. What we've got here is the army acting without the direction of the federal government.... This is no different from a military junta."[146] Premier Bourassa suddenly disappeared, cancelling engagements at the last minute, and put the army in charge of negotiations at Kanesatake. (He went to the US for medical treatment.) At this stage, however, the negotiations consisted purely of the army's demand for an unconditional surrender and the Mohawks' refusal to consider that demand. Indeed, the army was preparing its withdrawal, confident that the seige would be over within days. Like everything the army had done, the announcement of withdrawal had a strategic intent. When it left, the army would be replaced by the SQ, but if the Mohawks surrendered now then they could go into military rather than police custody.[147] Native negotiators saw the tactic for what it was, warning that the presence of the SQ on the reserve would only increase the chances of violence. Once again they rejected unconditional surrender as an "attempt to criminalize the sovereignty process and humiliate native people."

Options were narrowing. On 24 September there seemed some hope that a negotiated peace plan might be accepted by both sides. John Ciaccia, the Quebec

FEATHER AND GUN: CONFRONTATION AT OKA/KANESATAKE

minister of native affairs who had been disgraced when he signed his agreement with masked and armed Warriors before TV cameras in August, had been unofficially negotiating with the Iroquois Confederacy for weeks. The sticking point remained how criminal charges would be laid against the Warriors, though now the native negotiators had dropped their demand for a joint commission, demanding instead a jointly approved Crown prosecutor.[148] The provincial government, however, rejected this proposal on the same grounds that it had the others: there would be no compromising of the application of law to the Mohawks. The next day the Prime Minister unveiled a new program for dealing with native issues in Canada, one that he hoped would defuse the situation at Kanesatake. Once the Mohawks put down their arms, he said, work could begin on an invigorated agenda of land claims, economic and social conditions on reserves, and self-government. Ottawa was prepared to negotiate more than its self-imposed limit of six land claims per year, accelerate the specific claims process, and revise the Indian Act. On the question of self-government, the Prime Minister once more urged constitutional entrenchment, though he was firm that self-government did not mean national independence: "I will be very clear on this point: native self-government does not now and cannot ever mean sovereign independence. Mohawk lands are part of Canadian territory, and Canadian law must and does apply. Everyone in Canada, Warriors included, is subject to the Criminal Code of Canada."[149]

Then, on the seventy-eighth day, it ended. The army was scheduled to pull out, and the Warriors had been discussing for days whether to surrender to them or to the SQ. Some more-militant Warriors had resisted the idea of surrender to the last, but now faced a decision. Around 7pm on 26 September, the Mohawks laid down their arms and agreed to an "honourable disengagement" whereby they would leave the treatment centre one by one to be taken into military custody. But the "disengagement" degenerated into one final bout of confused violence as about thirty Warriors, twenty-two women, and children and ten journalists began to fan out from the centre *en masse* towards waiting cameras and the woods. Soldiers were caught unprepared, and were ordered to fix bayonets as Mohawks shoved their way through, some throwing punches and scuffling with troops. Six Mohawks strode through the army line and made their way to Oka; soldiers scurried after them, tackling men and women to the ground.

Loran Thompson, holding a baby in his arms, was one of the first Warriors to stride out of the treatment centre. He walked towards Oka and disappeared.

Scene 2: Postscripts of a Crisis

- Oka's 152 businesses lose between $10 million and $12 million in tourist trade between July and October 1990. The Quebec government offers 1,200 businesses in Oka and Châteauguay who suffered losses compensation of up to $300,000 apiece.
- Kanesatake divides into several factions taking different positions on where to go from here. "We've been blown apart," said Clarence Simon, a former grand chief of the band.
- Grand Chief Joe Norton of Kahnawake, travelling on an Iroquois Confederacy passport, visits the International Court of Justice in The Hague and the European Parliament in Strasbourg to describe Canada's "colonist and suppressive laws."
- Roughly three months after the Kanesatake surrender, on 8 January 1991, the RCMP pursue a vehicle along Highway 132 onto the Kahnawake reserve. Warrior Society activists and native police arrive with baseball bats, two-by-fours, and steel pipes. About fifty SQ officers arrive as back-up for the RCMP. A riot erupts and shots are fired into the air.
- On 31 January 1991, during the first day of hearings into the Oka crisis by a House of Commons committee, Justice Minister Kim Campbell calls the Warriors an "aberration" in the native community. She tells the committee that Ottawa would do nothing differently if faced again by the Oka crisis.

DISCUSSION

The confrontation at Oka/Kanesatake and Châteauguay/Kahnawake revealed a chasm of misunderstanding between natives and non-natives in Canada. For Indians, this was the real world of their politics, embellished to be sure by historical memory and myth, but grounded in the practice of generations. The Indian Act is to them no legal abstraction: it structures their lives in ways that other Canadians can barely understand. That structure, that presence in every aspect of community and individual life, is inescapable and implacable. Natives saw the Mohawk confrontation through the dark glass of their experiences, mythologies, fears, and aspirations. The barricades and army technology faded for them into a familiar scene, into old memories of other meetings of white and red: treaties sworn and treaties broken. Oka for them was less a surprise than a reliving.

For non-natives, exposed nightly to images of masked Warriors, soldiers with locked bayonets, brutal riots, and mobs, the confrontation at Oka was surreal and incomprehensible. Most Canadians know little about natives, see them hardly at all in cities and almost never on reserves. The Indian Act is meaningless, and most assume that aboriginal relations have been well structured through treaties and other agreements. Occasional news of land claims wherein a few thousand people appear to receive millions of dollars and thousands of acres of land confirms a sense that justice is being done, if perhaps not overdone. For them, Oka was not part of the real worlds of Canadian politics—it was an anomaly, a bizarre inversion that turned the peaceable kingdom into a Lebanon of the north.

Oka was only the most recent and vivid thread in a pattern of aboriginal–white relations that has been hundreds of years in the making. Until 1763, British North America was a battleground of English and French, and aboriginals were enlisted by both sides to fight the other. With the Royal Proclamation, the British Crown defined its trust relationship to aboriginals, and set in train a pattern of paternalism that was recapitulated and reinforced through the Indian Act a hundred years later. Canada inherited obligations along with the treaty legacies of both the English and French—indeed, this was at the heart of the Oka dispute: an obscure bequest of land to a religious order by a French king in the eighteenth century was the foundation for rebellion in the twentieth. These pre-Confederation legacies were leavened by Victorian assumptions about civilization, assimilation, and Christianity, mixed in the crucible of national self-interest. The result was the Indian Act of 1876, the numbered treaties, and a Department of Indian Affairs that existed virtually as a state within a state, having its own captive and docile subjects.

It is far too facile to explain away the history of native policy in Canada as the simple result of racism. That racism existed is undeniable, but policy was driven by deep contradictions. The first was the desire to make Indians into whites, to expunge their native status and "enfranchise" them, usually against their will. The second was the use of an administrative department to control virtually every aspect of a community's life. Large bureaucracies are by their nature mindlessly punctilious, and the Indian Act encouraged a level of control and paternalism that could only sap vitality from native communities and make them more, not less, dependent on Ottawa. A third was the jurisdictional division of power that made Indians Ottawa's responsibility, when many of their difficulties in the twentieth century needed to be addressed by provincial governments as well. A fourth contradiction set Ottawa's fiduciary or trust obligations towards natives against its responsibilities to foster national economic development. Given the scattered minority status of natives in Canada, it was often impossible to resist pressures to attenuate treaty rights in favour of corporate or white community interests.

FEATHER AND GUN: CONFRONTATION AT OKA/KANESATAKE

Already weak in the face of a dominant society, natives in Canada have been weakened even further by internal divisions. Aboriginals are divided into numerous linguistic and cultural groups, but also into Indians, Métis, and Inuit. Some have treaties, others do not. Some live on reserves, others in cities. They are numerically small and dispersed through a vast country. Administrative distinctions between status and non-status only compounded the problem. One of the great challenges for natives in Canada therefore has been to articulate their agenda in a way that overarches the special concerns of each segment of their various communities. In the end, any agreements will have to accommodate the diversity of the aboriginal peoples of Canada, but their political influence depends first on unity. Aboriginals have won sporadic victories on their own strengths—the defeat of the 1969 White Paper being the most prominent—but have usually had to ally themselves with larger political forces in the dominant society in order to be effective. A sobering measure of the costs of disunity is the glacial pace of land claims and community-based self-government.

One of the ironies of Oka is that the media first brought the crisis vividly to public attention and then helped to quietly blur the larger issues it reflected. For seventy-eight days Oka "visuals" were a media staple; the day after the "honourable disengagement," they virtually disappeared. This legerdemain is perfectly understandable in terms of the logic of *news*, but it signalled a perennial weakness not only of aboriginal policy but of much of contemporary Canadian politics: the problems do not disappear, even if the visuals do. Kanesatake and Kahnawake remain, as do the Warriors. During the conflict, dozens of bands across the country showed their support for the Mohawks by engaging in civil disobedience and disruption of their own. Rail lines and roads across Canada were blocked, hydro towers were toppled, and protesters stopped traffic in major cities from Vancouver to Montreal. The dispute at Oka may be over, but the bitterness of that conflict and the larger grievances that animated natives across the country have only been heightened.

What is to be done? The Prime Minister, only a day before the Mohawk surrender, promised a revitalized aboriginal agenda and accelerated attempts to settle claims and move towards constitutional reform. No other announcements followed, and soon Ottawa sunk deep into squabbles over the GST and the war in Iraq. The notion of a "revitalized agenda," however, masks much deeper problems in Canadian aboriginal policy. First, Ottawa still seems unsure what it wants. The Prime Minister spoke with rare clarity in his September statement when he affirmed that self-government should be constitutionally entrenched, but could never mean sovereignty. But in the constitutional first ministers' conferences of 1985 and 1987, the Tories were never able to convincingly demonstrate what they thought self-government in practice would mean. Another, perhaps more deeply rooted ambiguity exists over the nature of the "solution" they seek. Canadian aboriginal policy since Confederation has assumed that the ultimate goal is a final resolution of treaties and claims, a once-and-for-all settling of accounts that would finally absolve the government of its obligations. But the nature of native communities and their needs, and the unavoidable task of managing relations between native and non-native communities as both evolve together and separately, implies that there never can be a "final resolution." Finality is a mirage. The reality is the need to find frameworks that allow accommodation to native needs and independence, along with ongoing political and administrative relationships.

This problem is compounded by divisions and inconsistencies on the native side. Aboriginal organizations have lobbied hard in the last twenty years for devolution of powers ultimately towards some form of self-government, but at the same time they have insisted on being "citizens plus," on having Ottawa's historical obligations enforced and maintained. From the native perspective this makes perfect sense, but it appears like an inconsistent blend of autonomy and dependence. Moreover, it underscores the ambiguity in the meaning of "self-government." In the mid-1980s the word appeared to mean something like municipal or even provincial autonomy within the larger structure of Canadian law and political institutions. Today, and perhaps especially after Oka, for more radical elements in the native movement it seems to mean something closer to sovereignty. But it is clear that just as federal officials lack clarity over the meaning of self-government, so too do many natives. The slogan of "self-government" has become so symbolically important that neither side wishes to probe its meaning too closely. But a frank appraisal is perhaps exactly what is needed at this juncture, since it might clear the path towards a new framework for aboriginal policy. It is remarkable how much that policy has been propelled by incremental forces in the last quarter-century. The imbroglio over the 1969 White Paper, combined with the *Calder* judgment, led to a loose commitment to "comprehensive claims" that later was joined to the constitutional politics of affirming "aboriginal rights." Each forking point has occurred almost accidentally, without design or clear purpose. The accumulation of initiatives simultaneously encouraged an accumulation of contradictions and tensions. The events of Kanesatake and Kahnawake reflected those contradictions and tensions to the nation.

Ultimately, then, the confrontation at Oka was an all too real part of Canada's political world. Like the other cases in this book, it highlights some fascinating features of constitutional politics and rights, the policy-making process, and the nature of power. With respect to the constitution, the confrontation at

Oka/Kanesatake showed how wide a gulf exists between aboriginal peoples and the federal and provincial governments. This was clear years ago, in the various first ministers' conferences that tried through the 1980s to come to some agreement on the nature of aboriginal rights and self-government. The first ministers could never reach a consensus on these questions because a recognition of rights would effectively recognize the existence of a sovereign or at least semi-sovereign entity within the state. European concepts of sovereignty, especially in the British parliamentary tradition, have historically considered nation-states as sovereign within their borders. Aboriginal peoples were posing other possibilities, ones that were enormously difficult to contemplate.

First ministers' conferences are not philosophical debating clubs; they are arenas of power. The western provinces resisted recognition of aboriginal rights and self-government because they would foot the bill in land and fiscal transfers. From Ottawa's point of view, it was a dangerous to grant too much autonomy and self-government to aboriginal peoples because of the precedent this might set for nationalist opinion in Quebec. For most of his career, Prime Minister Trudeau rigorously addressed the aboriginal claims issue in the same terms that he did the Quebec question: no special status and no concessions of sovereignty. He changed his mind with the *Calder* case, but would not actively negotiate the issue of aboriginal rights for another decade. Prime Minister Mulroney was more accommodating, but as much for political reasons (the need to show that his new approach to federalism could yield results where Trudeau's had not) as out of conviction. Oka simply magnified these traditional difficulties in the context of an armed stand-off. Guns and barricades can concentrate the mind, but provincial authorities were never prepared to negotiate Mohawk sovereignty while the Mercier Bridge remained closed. For the Warriors and the factions in the native community who supported them, the traditional methods of negotiation had failed, and this was a chance, albeit a dangerous one, to achieve rights and recognition long denied.

Consideration of the Oka crisis also raises three issues related to the broader policy-making process. First, to what extent can policy trajectories be easily reversed or altered once they become embedded in the political system? One of the saddest aspects of the barricades at Kanesatake is that they were clearly the result of a century-old legacy of Indian policy. The historical sections of this chapter showed that while decisions were regularly made over this period, they were usually made within a policy framework that had been established in the nineteenth century. The aboriginal policy process over time is something like a living tree of decisions made at each forking point, leading to narrower and narrower branches. Reversing policy at its later stages becomes increasingly difficult, since those later stages—with their constellations of political forces, issues, symbols, and language—are themselves shaped and made by the earlier ones. Public policy, whether in the aboriginal field or economic or social, is too often regarded as simply technical decision-making in the here and now. New problems, it is thought, demand new solutions, but the degree to which even new solutions are residues of old decisions is rarely considered. The *Calder* case, for example, was the result of BC's refusal in the 1870s to consider native land claims. That case was a forking point for other legal decisions that contributed to constitutional recognition of aboriginal rights in 1982, a recognition that itself raised hopes among native peoples for something more substantial. Policy-making may be incremental, but not in the sense of linear steps towards some horizon. It is incremental in the sense of layers, one decision forming the ground for the next, and over time building a hard and confining shell. To start fresh, to reverse direction, is exceedingly difficult.

A related point about the policy process raised by Oka is the issue of leadership. Leadership is not simply the quality of doing something, of acting. In its political sense, and with respect to the harsh legacies in the aboriginal policy field, it means a creative capacity to deal with issues in a way that achieves resolution by somehow altering accepted views and assumptions. This is abstract, of course, but it is impossible to define leadership precisely because so much of it appears to be creative and hence unpredictable. In retrospect, however, it is clear that there was no leadership at the federal or provincial level worthy of the name. There was action, and there was resolution of a sorts, but there was no leadership. Indian Affairs Minister Tom Siddon was a cipher throughout the affair. The Prime Minister studiously avoided dealing with the crisis. Premier Bourassa and his cabinet addressed the problem in almost purely technical terms: the bridge was closed and the bridge must be opened. Moreover, they failed to acknowledge Oka's deeper roots in failed claims and broken promises. To a great extent, they were prisoners of events, and the Mohawk demands for recognition of sovereignty posed almost insurmountable obstacles to negotiation. But by August it seemed that the entire affair was being run by the military and the Warriors. The terms of debate and the way that the issues were framed had been appropriated by men in arms, not by political leaders.

Oka also brilliantly revealed a third, if often neglected point, about the policy-making process: it depends on trust and mutual respect. This may appear as trivial or platitudinous, but a consideration of what the policy process actually entails shows that it is neither. Policy-making is a process of defining public problems and developing and implementing solutions. Politics intrudes at each stage: what the problem is, how it should be defined, what values should guide the selection of solutions, and the practical aspects of putting the policy in place, may all be contested. The wider the range of actors and values, the wider the range of policy preferences and policy conflicts. The abortion case in Chapter 1 is a dramatic illustration of the conflict generated when views differ so greatly. So are Meech Lake and Oka. But an increasing number of policy fields show similar if not as drastic fissures between opposing groups and interests. In situations like this, when people differ strongly but ultimately have to work together, the only true basis of cooperation is mutual respect and some degree of trust that cooperation will yield results all can live with. What Oka showed was that the first crucial step in policy-making in a situation of almost complete antagonism is establishing trust. Without trust and respect, the process (if indeed one ever begins) can be easily shattered by suspicion and resentment. Trust and respect were never established in Oka: deals were broken on both sides, and the army deliberately reneged on agreements in order to destabilize the Warriors. Without a foundation of trust, the odds against a negotiated settlement were very high indeed.

Finally, the confrontation at Oka/Kanesatake exposed important dimensions of the exercise of power. Oka showed, in a way that goes well beyond the struggles over the Free Trade Agreement, abortion, or the GST, that politics is about power. In "normal" politics that reality is obscured somewhat by the genteel play of political parties and interest groups operating within institutions that are designed to avoid violence. The 1988 election, for example, was bitterly fought between pro- and anti-FTA forces, but at the ballot box and through arguments and persuasion. Street demonstrations are about the closest one comes to the use of force in normal politics, and while we all understand that politicians and police exercise power, our tendency is to define that power in abstract terms: legitimacy, authority, winning the last election. Oka demonstrated that power also, as Mao said, flows from the end of a gun. The SQ raid on the first barricades near Oka was an exercise of force that, while unusual, was not entirely rare. It soon went well beyond that. The Warriors rejected the legitimacy of the civil authority and took up arms. There were attempts at negotiation, but they always foundered on the basic Mohawk claim to be outside of Canadian law, and hence Canadian sovereignty. At this point, the civil authority loses its authority, and can succeed only with force.

It would be a mistake, however, to assume that the rejection of authority and use of raw military force requires the extraordinary demands of a national movement. Only kilometers away in Châteauguay, ordinary citizens of Quebec demonstrated nightly, burning effigies and engaging in violence. While it is true that most of the trouble at the Mercier Bridge was the result of small groups, there were hundreds gathered each evening. Among them were people who in the ordinary course of events are law-abiding citizens. The closure of the bridge, the inconvenience it caused, and their perception that the civil authority was weak and outflanked, together were enough to induce them to riot. Canadians do not seethe with discontent, and neither are they ready at a moment's notice to overthrow their elected governments. The events at Oka simply demonstrate that the civility we consider to be the bedrock of our political system is actually quite fragile.

Guns and riots were the most vivid manifestations of violence in the Oka affair, but among those who supported the Mohawk side there was another dimension of violence that they felt was being ignored by the majority society. Violence can be subtle and insidious, the accretion of a thousand small violations. From the native perspective, white society had for generations perpetrated violence against Indians through instruments like the Indian Act and DIAND: rules and regulations that were perfectly legal for the majority, but perfectly hellish for the minority. The rule of law, the reliance on due process, together with the other procedures of white society, were a subtle and bureaucratic use of power and force that, while not conventionally defined as violence, had precisely the same result.

Real power depends as much on political symbols as it does on force. The FTA and Meech Lake accord debates, like Oka, are quite incomprehensible unless one is prepared to acknowledge that language and symbols are important resources and vital prizes in political struggle. If the confrontation at Oka was about land, then the Warriors had won by mid-July. Ottawa had succeeded in purchasing the disputed land, and Quebec was prepared to negotiate the larger claims issue. But the Warriors were after something both more chimerical and fundamental: they wanted some symbol of recognition of their claim to sovereignty. The events over those crucial days at the end of July may have been influenced by accidents of personality, but the support the Mohawks received from natives across the country as well as from within their own community—despite disagreements on tactics—can only be explained by a consensus that this symbolic goal was important. Indeed, symbols permeated the conflict. Why did the Warriors choose to wear masks instead of traditional native war paints? The police and army knew quite well who they were, and the Warriors would frequently take off their masks in full view of troops. The masks made the Warriors look like the fighters in the *intifada*, which had received favourable media attention in the early part of the year. The Mohawks also made much of their religious symbols and practices, and thereby reinforced the idea that they were a distinct people.

FEATHER AND GUN: CONFRONTATION AT OKA/KANESATAKE

Symbols were not an exclusive Mohawk preserve: the army used them with great effect as well. Virtually every moment at Oka was chronicled before the TV cameras, and the army knew quite well that the real battle was not with the Mohawks as such, but with the media over the presentation of the army's strategies and tactics. From the outset, the army placed great emphasis on media relations, trying as best it could to put the proper spin on the news coverage it received. It also realized that its greatest asset was the discipline of its troops, which on the nightly news compared favourably with the heated obscenities hurled at those troops by enraged Mohawks. In a sense, the Mohawks had the rhetorical advantage simply because they were weaker. The army's overwhelming superiority of men and weapons could very easily have been portrayed as the brutal bullying of a beleaguered band of freedom fighters. This image never seriously threatened the armed forces, in large part because they fought the battle in psychological and symbolic terms.

The impact of symbols in the struggle cannot be separated from the importance of history and memory for the Mohawks. Politics occurs in conceptual space as well as real space, in memory as well as in real time. This is clear in some of the other cases discussed in this book, for example, the Meech Lake accord. For the Mohawks, their struggle at Kanesatake was legitimated by memories of court battles over the disputed land, broken agreements, and recollections of their culture and political practices. Their resentments were shaped by a sense of justice long denied. Nothing helps a group take a stand more than the idea that theirs is part of a long history of stands against the same oppression, the same injustice. In a sense, theirs becomes the last stand, the point at which a historical trajectory may be redirected if not reversed. This happened at Kanesatake and Kahnawake. Mohawks there were infused with anger over much more than the issues that were directly at stake; indeed, for the Kahnawake Mohawks there was no dispute as such in the first place. They were moved by memory and recollection, which together magnified the immediate dispute into something much more significant.

The tragedy of Oka lies perhaps in precisely this fact: that it was inscribed with history and will in turn inscribe the future of aboriginal politics with its own grim signature. Natives will never forget, and the next confrontation, if it comes, will resonate with new and more vivid resentments. Sadly, for non-natives, Oka may become a symbol of conquest and power, of having used force justly to suppress rebellion. The use of force was indeed measured and careful, and in terms of the larger interests of a civilized society, justified. But the history of Canadian aboriginal policy shows that it has been remarkably easy to forget the confrontations, to paper them over and hope that in time they will disappear. Indeed, in an earlier period, some hoped that the aboriginal peoples themselves would even-

FEATHER AND GUN: CONFRONTATION AT OKA/KANESATAKE

tually disappear and their problems with them. If the 1969 White Paper was an important stimulus for the development of native political organizations and lobbying, Oka is likely to have a similar catalytic effect.

Native groups across Canada, whatever their position on the use of violence (and many were opposed), supported the Mohawks in their struggle. Among Mohawks, there is fierce debate over whether the Warriors were right to use violence, and over the very nature of the Warrior Society itself. But 1990, like 1969, was a turning point. Aboriginal peoples across Canada now look on Oka as a moment when the veil of politics fell to reveal the reality of power behind. Aboriginal impatience will increase, not abate. Aboriginal resentment at the use of the army and police will increase, not abate. Aboriginal memory will now be shaped and deepened by the events at Oka. Every native child will learn to see Kanesatake and Kahnawake as moments of pride, defiance, dignity, and determination by men and women who were prepared to die for land and rights. Some of this is mythology, of course, but mythologies shield against despair. Other Canadians cannot afford to meet this deepened sense of memory and myth with the arrogant amnesia of victors.

Discussion Questions

1   What constraints does the federal government face in developing a fresh approach to aboriginal policy?

2   Would a royal commission on aboriginal issues be a useful policy initiative? If so, why; if not, why not?

3   Discuss the role of the media in the Oka confrontation.

4   What challenges does native self-government/sovereignty pose to Quebec nationalism?

5   A great deal of political energy over the last decade has gone into the constitutional entrenchment of aboriginal rights and self-government. What are the advantages and disadvantages of the constitutional process for addressing the Indian question in Canada?

6   A view frequently expressed during the stand-off was that while Mohawk violence was regrettable, it was the only way to capture white society's attention. Discuss.

7   Refer to the chapter on the Meech Lake accord and discuss why natives might have opposed the agreement.

8   Discuss possible models of self-government that might allow band control over social, economic, and community affairs without compromising Canadian sovereignty.

9   Why was international attention to the conflict so important for the Mohawks?

10   Discuss the internal divisions among Canadian aboriginals and their political implications in the evolution of policy.

Chronology

1990

11 March	— barricade erected to stop golf course extension after talks between the Town of Oka and the Kanesatake Mohawks break down
23 March	— mayors of six communities in the area send a letter to Thomas Siddon, federal minister of Indian affairs, asking him to intervene in the dispute
3 May	— approximately 400 women, children, and the elderly evacuated from the Akwesasne–St-Régis Mohawk reserve (pop. 9,500, straddling parts of Ontario, Quebec, and New York state) after violence between Warriors (who run casinos on the American side of the border) and opponents of gambling
30 June	— the Town of Oka receives an injunction against the Mohawks in order to proceed with development of the golf course
9 July	— John Ciaccia, Quebec minister of native affairs, urges Jean Ouellette, mayor of Oka, to indefinitely suspend development of golf course to allow negotiations to bring down the barricades; in his letter, Ciaccia says that the "situation goes beyond strict legality"

11 July	— SQ raid the barricades at Oka; that same morning, to show support, Kahnawake Warriors blockade the Mercier Bridge, cutting off direct transportation to Montreal for over 60,000 daily commuters, who must now drive an extra 3 hours per day
12 July	— John Ciaccia negotiates for 4 hours with Mohawks at Oka; an important issue is immunity from prosecution for Mohawks in connection with Marcel Lemay's death
13 July	— Ciaccia meets again, and issues call with Ellen Gabriel, principal Mohawk negotiator, for federal involvement
15 July	— Ciaccia emerges from late-night meeting announcing that an agreement has been reached with the Mohawks
17 July	— William Kunstler and Stanley Cohen, two well-known American human rights lawyers, arrive in Oka at Warriors' request; that evening, an estimated crowd of 4,000 storms police fences at Mercier Bridge; Indian effigies have been burned for six consecutive nights; Thomas Siddon releases his first public statement on the affair, calling it "most unfortunate" and pledging not to inhibit Ciaccia's bargaining efforts
18 July	— Premier Bourassa, in his first public statement, hints that the Quebec government is prepared for a drawn-out process
19 July	— Thomas Siddon calls press conference to announce that Ottawa will not negotiate at gunpoint; the dispute at Oka must be resolved by Quebec before federal negotiators will step in
20 July	— 150 Chiefs from across Canada end 3 days of meetings at Kahnawake, demanding a recall of Parliament and promising to take the issue to the international community; Grand Chief Joseph Norton likens Canada's treatment of natives to the white South African government's treatment of blacks; Siddon claims Ottawa is trying to persuade the municipality of Oka to sell it the disputed lands for eventual transfer to the Kanesatake Mohawks

23 July

— DIAND Deputy Minister Harry Swain tells reporters "off the record" that the stand-off at Oka is an "armed insurrection" by an "armed gang" of violent and dangerous Warriors who had intimidated the community leaders at Kanesatake; his minister, Thomas Siddon, contradicts him; John Ciaccia announces the Quebec government is ready to engage in negotiations again; conditions rejected by Mohawks

26 July

— John Ciaccia orders SQ to allow food and medical supplies to go into Kanesatake and Kahnawake

27 July

— Quebec makes a new offer based on Ottawa's purchase, for $1.4 million, of about half the disputed golf course land; the remainder is owned by the municipality of Oka, which wants $5 million for it (it paid $90,000); Quebec promises the Mohawks this land, as well as federal cooperation in resolving the larger 675 km^2 land claim

28 July

— Ottawa announces that it has offered $3 million to purchase the remaining parcel of land; Mohawk and Quebec government officials negotiate for 31 hours over provincial offer, but make no comment on progress

31 July

— Oka town meeting refuses to sell last parcel of golf course land to Ottawa until the Mohawk barriers come down

5 August

— Premier Bourassa issues ultimatum of 48 hours to reach agreement

8 August

— Quebec cabinet meets and decides to ask Ottawa to send in the army; the federal and provincial governments and Mohawks agree on the appointment of Chief Justice Alan Gold of the Quebec Superior Court as mediator on the outstanding points that had prevented Quebec and the Warriors from reaching a negotiated truce

11 August

— Canadian armed forces begin to take up positions; Lieutenant General Kent Foster, commander of the Mobile Command, says that an armed attack on the Mohawk barricades is unthinkable

12 August	— Justice Gold mediates an agreement signed by Thomas Siddon, John Ciaccia, and 5 Mohawk communities; the agreement concedes the three points Ciaccia had rejected only days earlier: (1) free access to "necessities" as well as food and medicine, (2) access to "legal" as well as spiritual advisors, and (3) appointment of observers from the Paris-based International Federation of Human Rights
13 August	— Archbishop Desmond Tutu visits a northern Ontario Ojibwa settlement and claims to see similarities between the condition of Canadian natives and South African blacks under apartheid
14 August	— General John de Chastelain announces mobilization of soldiers and equipment to the Oka and Châteauguay area
16 August	— talks between Quebec government and Mohawks begin
18 August	— army announces it will relieve the SQ on the barricades at Oka and the Mercier Bridge
20 August	— Mohawk negotiators refuse to appear for talks in protest against army intention to move its Oka barricade 400 metres closer to the Mohawk barricade; after talks with the Mohawks, army concedes the point and leaves barricade where it was
23 August	— troops move two armoured personnel carriers directly up to the Mohawk barricade at Oka, over what Warriors had called the "demilitarized zone"; aerial surveys begin and police start to search boats going to and from Kanesatake and Kahnawake; Mohawk negotiators suspend talks in protest; Prime Minister Mulroney warns that patience is wearing thin and that "appropriate measures" may have to be taken
24 August	— Six Nations Confederacy meeting at the Onandaga Reserve near Syracuse, NY; one chief at the meeting labels the Warriors "fakes" trying to protect their lucrative cigarette and gambling interests
27 August	— talks break down again; Premier Bourassa asks army to move in and remove the barricades

28 August	— about 150 Mohawks try to leave the Kahnawake reserve by the Mercier Bridge, but are met by a mob of about 500 people, some of whom pelt the Mohawk cars with stones and bottles; at least 4 light planes use a road on the Kahnawake reserve as a runway for over an hour; suspicion that a large number of Warriors escape with their weapons
29 August	— the 2 barricades blocking the Mercier Bridge are taken down cooperatively by the army and Mohawks; described as purely a "military agreement."
30 August	— talks break down once more as Quebec government pulls out, claiming that moderates are not at the negotiating table; the removal of barricades at Kahnawake is stalled for a day, but resumes after 24 hours
1 September	— the army moves in to dismantle Kanesatake barricades; they are completely removed within 2 days, and a handful of Warriors take up position at an alcohol treatment centre
3 September	— army raids Longhouse at Kahnawake and moves closer to Warrior perimeter at Kanesatake
4 September	— clashes with Mohawk women at Kanesatake and Kahnawake lead army to increase its contingent at the latter reserve to 1,400
5 September	— native leaders meet with Thomas Siddon, who agrees to do what he can to reduce "stress" among the Warriors
9 September	— army patrol goes behind Mohawk perimeter at night and has a clash with a Warrior nicknamed Spud Wrench
11 September	— Mohawk negotiators submit peace proposal; rejected outright by the Quebec government
13 September	— army cuts off phone lines to the treatment centre; Quebec government demands an unconditional surrender, which is rejected
18 September	— SQ, supported by troops, raids the Kahnawake reserve looking for weapons; riot breaks out; 100 natives and a dozen soldiers injured

20 September	— army announces it will soon be withdrawing, to be replaced by the SQ; if Mohawks surrender soon, they can go into army rather than SQ custody; Mohawks claim that the army is preventing negotiations, and release the text of a partial agreement reached secretly with John Ciaccia that involves compromises on both sides
21 September	— 73rd day of the crisis, exceeding the previous "record" for an armed stand-off between natives and whites in the United States at Wounded Knee in 1973
24 September	— hope of a peaceful settlement increases as Mohawks indicate their interest in a deal negotiated by the Iroquois Confederacy and John Ciaccia over the previous weeks; Quebec government rejects the deal; Jesse Jackson, former US presidential candidate, visits Oka
25 September	— Prime Minister Mulroney announces federal initiatives to deal with land claims, self-government, and revisions to the Indian Act
26 September	— Mohawk Warriors at Kanesatake surrender their arms, but fan out of the treatment centre *en masse*, resulting in confusion and shoving as soldiers try to apprehend them

Notes

1   The terms "natives," "aboriginals," and "Indians" will be used throughout this chapter as appropriate. Contemporary aboriginal politics involves claims by Indians, Métis, and Inuit. A term sometimes preferred by natives themselves is "First Nations."

2   England entered into a peace and friendship treaty with Nova Scotia Indians in 1725 to secure their alliance or neutrality during hostilities with France. The Crown agreed to promote Indian trade and protect hunting, fishing, and trapping rights. There was no surrender of land. See Task Force to Review Comprehensive Claims Policy, *Living Treaties: Lasting Agreements* (Ottawa: 1985), 2.

3   William J. Reeves and J. Rick Ponting, "A Decade of Change and Continuity: An Overview of Social, Political and Legal Developments involving Western Canadian Aboriginal People," *The London Journal of Canadian Studies*, 5 (1988/1990), 140.

4   Cited in J. Rick Ponting, "Introduction," in *Arduous Journey*, ed. J. Rick Ponting (Toronto: McClelland and Stewart, 1986), 233.

5   Statistics Canada, *Canada's Native People* (Ottawa: Supply and Services, 1984), 3.

6   Canada, Parliament, House of Commons, Special Committee on Indian Self-Government, *Second Report* (Ottawa: 1983), 13.

7   *Globe and Mail*, 20 July 1990.

8   As quoted in the *Globe and Mail*, 13 July 1990.

9   *Globe and Mail*, 12 July 1990.

10   This brief description of Kahnawake is drawn from J. Rick Ponting, "Institution-Building in an Indian Community: A Case Study of Kahnawake (Caughnawage)," in *Arduous Journey*, 151-78.

11   *Globe and Mail*, 12 July 1990.

12   *Globe and Mail*, 16 July 1990.

13   *Globe and Mail*, 12 July 1990. There was more than a little irony in this demand, since in May the Akwesasne reserve had been the site of a shoot-out between Warriors and non-Warriors that killed two men. The Warriors control a network of casinos on the American side as well as contraband cigarette trade worth millions of dollars. They claim that American and Canadian laws do not apply to the Mohawk Nation, but are strenuously opposed by other members of the bands.

14   *Globe and Mail*, 13 July 1990.

15   *Globe and Mail*, 14 July 1990.

16   *Globe and Mail*, 14 July 1990.

17   *Globe and Mail*, 17 July 1990.

18   *Globe and Mail*, 16 July 1990.

19   Native leaders consistently defended this by arguing that aboriginal political forms are more consensual, democratic, and fluid than non-native forms. This was pure propaganda belied by the substantial and well-documented political divisions within both the Mohawk communities and native peoples more generally.

20   *Globe and Mail*, 18 July 1990.

21   *Globe and Mail*, 17 July 1990; 18 July 1990. Original estimates were as high as 300, but eventually only 150 chiefs attended.

22   *Globe and Mail*, 19 July 1990.

23   *Globe and Mail*, 18 July 1990.

24   *Globe and Mail*, 20 July 1990.

25   *Globe and Mail*, 20 July 1990.

26   *Globe and Mail*, 21 July 1990.

27   *Globe and Mail*, 23 July 1990.

FEATHER AND GUN: CONFRONTATION AT OKA/KANESATAKE

28   Chief Strater Crowfoot of Blackfoot Indians of southern Alberta, quoted in *Globe and Mail*, 23 July 1990.

29   *Globe and Mail*, 24 July 1990.

30   *Globe and Mail*, 24 July 1990.

31   *Globe and Mail*, 25 July 1990; 27 July 1990.

32   *Globe and Mail*, 27 July 1990.

33   *Globe and Mail*, 27 July 1990.

34   *Globe and Mail*, 28 July 1990.

35   *Globe and Mail*, 30 July 1990.

36   *Globe and Mail*, 1 August 1990.

37   *Globe and Mail*, 3 August 1990.

38   *Globe and Mail*, 5 August 1990.

39   *Globe and Mail*, 6 August 1990.

40   *Globe and Mail*, 9 August 1990.

41   *Globe and Mail*, 13 August 1990.

42   R. Douglas Francis, Richard Jones, and Donald B. Smith, *Origins: Canadian History to Confederation* (Toronto: Holt, Rinehart and Winston, 1988), 8.

43   Canada, Department of Indian and Northern Affairs, *The Canadian Indian* (Ottawa: 1986), 7; and Francis, Jones, and Smith, *Origins: Canadian History to Confederation*, 8.

44   Ibid., 9-42. Note that these categories do not include the Inuit or Métis.

45   Task Force to Review Comprehensive Claims Policy, *Living Treaties: Lasting Agreements* (Ottawa: 1985), 1-2.

46   J. Rick Ponting and Roger Gibbins, *Out of Irrelevance* (Toronto: Butterworths, 1980), 4.

47   As cited in Canada, Department of Indian and Northern Affairs, *The Historical Development of the Indian Act* (Ottawa: 1978), 5-6.

48   Ponting and Gibbins, *Out of Irrelevance*, 134.

49   Canada, Department of Indian and Northern Affairs, *A Survey of the History and Claims of the Native Peoples of Northern Canada* (Ottawa: 1983), 16.

50   Ponting and Gibbins, *Out of Irrelevance*, 134.

51   As cited in Ponting and Gibbins, *Out of Irrelevance*, 59.

52   For examples, see the detailed 1774 Instructions to Governor Carleton cited in Canada, Department of Indian and Northern Affairs, *The Historical Development of the Indian Act*, 6-9.

53   Canada, Department of Indian and Northern Affairs, *The Historical Development of the Indian Act*, 27.

54   Ibid., 28.

55   Canada, Department of Indian and Northern Affairs, *A History of Native Claims Processes in Canada, 1867-1979* (Ottawa: 1980), 14.

56   Ponting and Gibbins, *Out of Irrelevance*, 8-9.

57   Canada, Department of Indian and Northern Affairs, *The Historical Development of the Indian Act*, 60. Deputy Superintendent-General Vankoughnet, in a memorandum on 22 August

1876, noted that "the legal status of the Indians of Canada is that of *minors*, with the Government as their guardians."

58   Roger Gibbins and J. Rick Ponting, "Historical Overview and Background," in *Arduous Journey*, ed. J. Rick Ponting (Toronto: McClelland and Stewart, 1986), 21.

59   Few Indians availed themselves of enfranchisement, and so later amendments to the act were made to speed up the process of assimilation. In 1880 an amendment stipulated that Indians receiving university degrees were deemed to be enfranchised, and in 1933 another amendment empowered the government to "order the enfranchisement of Indians meeting the qualifications set out in the act, even without the request of the individuals concerned." Canada, Department of Indian and Northern Affairs, *The Canadian Indian*, 61.

60   Canada, Department of Indian and Northern Affairs, *The Historical Development of the Indian Act*, 65-66. Chiefs were allowed to frame band regulations related to, among other things, public health, observance of order and decorum at Indian assemblies, the repression of intemperance and profligacy, and maintenance of roads, bridges, ditches, and fences.

61   Canada, Department of Indian and Northern Affairs, *The Historical Development of the Indian Act*, 71.

62   Ibid., 104.

63   Ibid., 107.

64   It is important not to paint this reprehensible initiative as a consensual attack by "whites" on "Indians." The amendment, although it was passed, was criticized precisely for its violation of treaty rights.

65   Gibbins and Ponting, "Historical Overview and Background," in *Arduous Journey*, 23.

66   Laurier Thibault, chief of staff for Quebec Native Affairs Minister John Ciaccia, quoted in *Globe and Mail*, 15 August 1990.

67   *Globe and Mail*, 15 August 1990.

68   The Quebec negotiators were Alex Paterson, chancellor of McGill University, Georges Beauchemin, deputy minister of native affairs, and Marie Rinfret, a Justice official. The federal observers were Bernard Roy, a lawyer and former principal secretary to the Prime Minister, and two DIAND officials. The teams met at a hotel and later in a Trappist monastery, largely because of the criticism engendered by the 12 August meeting behind the barricade. *Globe and Mail*, 17 August 1990.

69   Grand Chief Joseph Norton, the elected leader of Kahnawake, did not sign the 12 August agreement, for example.

70   *Globe and Mail*, 22 August 1990; 23 August 1990.

71   *Globe and Mail*, 23 August 1990.

72   *Globe and Mail*, 24 August 1990.

73   *Globe and Mail*, 24 August 1990.

74   *Globe and Mail*, 25 August 1990.

75   *Globe and Mail*, 27 August 1990.

76   *Globe and Mail*, 28 August 1990.

77   *Globe and Mail*, 28 August 1990.

FEATHER AND GUN: CONFRONTATION AT OKA/KANESATAKE

78   These may not have been the only Mohawks to leave the reserve. Within two weeks the Quebec minister of public security, Sam Elkas, confirmed that on the night of 28 August at least four light planes had used a road on the Kahnawake reserve as a runway, perhaps to smuggle out Warriors and their weapons.

79   *Globe and Mail*, 30 August 1990.

80   *Globe and Mail*, 31 August 1990.

81   *Globe and Mail*, 3 September 1990.

82   Sally Weaver, "Political Representivity and Indigenous Minorities in Canada and Australia," in *Indigenous Peoples and the Nation-State*, ed. Noel Dyck (St. John's, Newfoundland: Memorial University Institute of Social and Economic Research, 1985), 116. DIAND established a National Indian Advisory Board in 1966 with delegates from regional advisory councils. Frustration over the government's agenda (a new Indian Act) led native representatives to boycott the meetings the following year, which killed the Board.

83   Ibid., 123.

84   Gibbins and Ponting, "Historical Overview and Background," in *Arduous Journey*, 34-35.

85   Sally Weaver, *Making Canadian Indian Policy* (Toronto: University of Toronto Press), 15, 20.

86   Ibid., 21.

87   H.B. Hawthorn, *A Survey of the Contemporary Indians of Canada: Economic, Political, Educational Needs and Policies*, 2 vols. (Ottawa: Queen's Printer, 1966-67).

88   Weaver, *Making Canadian Indian Policy*, 23, Table 2. Weaver notes, however, that despite this turbulence at the political level, senior civil servants in the Department had enjoyed a remarkable tenure. This combination of instability at one level and longevity at the other was highly conducive to bureaucratic rigidity.

89   Ibid., 49-50.

90   Ibid., 114.

91   *Bulletin 201* (Toronto Anglican Church of Canada, 1970), 8.

92   Ibid., 28.

93   Weaver, *Making Canadian Indian Policy*, 171.

94   Ibid., 171.

95   *Citizens Plus* (Ottawa: Indian Chiefs of Alberta, 1970), 9.

96   Ibid., 8.

97   For another, more polemical response to the White Paper, see Harold Cardinal, *The Unjust Society* (Edmonton: Hurtig, 1969). Cardinal's criticisms anticipated many of those made by the NIB in June 1970.

98   Gibbins and Ponting, "Historical Overview and Background," in *Arduous Journey*, 33.

99   Weaver, *Making Canadian Indian Policy*, 197.

100   Gibbins and Ponting, "Historical Overview and Background," in *Arduous Journey*, 34.

101   Ibid., 35-38.

102   The exceptions are the adhesions to Treaty 8 of 1899 in the northeastern portion of the province.

103 Canada, Department of Indian and Northern Affairs, *A History of Native Claims Processes in Canada, 1867–1979*, 27-28.

104 Until the 1950s all citizens, not just natives, were so restricted, but natives dealt almost exclusively with the Crown on land questions, and so were more affected.

105 Task Force to Review Comprehensive Claims Policy, *Living Treaties: Lasting Agreements* (Ottawa: 1985), 10-11.

106 Leroy Little Bear, "Aboriginal Rights and the Canadian 'Grundnorm'," in *Arduous Journey*, 253. A Nishga spokesman told a royal commission on BC Indian lands in 1883, "They [the government] have never bought it from us or our forefathers. They have never fought or conquered our people and taken the land in that way, and yet they say now that they will give us so much land—our own land.... It has been ours for thousands of years."

107 Ibid., 255.

108 This issue arose with legal appeals in 1973 by the Chiefs of the Mackenzie Valley Indian bands in connection with Treaty 8 and Treaty 11. It also arises with some pre-Confederation treaties that allowed native title to some areas. See Task Force to Review Comprehensive Claims Policy, *Living Treaties: Lasting Agreements*, 3-4.

109 Canada, Department of Indian and Northern Affairs, *A History of Native Claims Processes in Canada, 1867–1979*, 222.

110 Task Force to Review Comprehensive Claims Policy, *Living Treaties: Lasting Agreements*, i. The three agreements were the James Bay and Norther Quebec Agreement (1975), the Northeastern Quebec Agreement (1978), and the Inuvialuit Final Agreement (1984).

111 Ibid., 13.

112 Ibid., 40.

113 Canada, Department of Indian and Northern Affairs, *Comprehensive Land Claims Policy* (Ottawa: 1987), 6-7.

114 Ibid., 24.

115 Ibid., 24.

116 *Globe and Mail*, 17 August 1990.

117 *Globe and Mail*, 20 July 1990.

118 Robert Sheppard and Michael Valpy, *The National Deal* (Toronto: Fleet Books, 1982), 161.

119 Ibid., 163.

120 The Métis are a mixed race, usually native and French, that as a "people" did not exist prior to European settlement of North America.

121 Sheppard and Valpy, *The National Deal*, 169.

122 Ibid., 163-64.

123 Roger Gibbins, "Canadian Indians and the Constitution: A Difficult Passage Toward an Uncertain Destination," in *Arduous Journey*, 307-308.

124 As quoted in Douglas E. Sanders, "The Indian Lobby," in *And No One Cheered*, ed. Keith Banting and Richard Simeon (Toronto: Methuen, 1983), 324.

125 Roger Gibbins, "Canadian Indians and the Constitution: A Difficult Passage Toward an Uncertain Destination," in *Arduous Journey*, 309.

126 Ibid., 312.

FEATHER AND GUN: CONFRONTATION AT OKA/KANESATAKE

127 Canada, Parliament, House of Commons, Special Committee on Indian Self-Government, *Second Report* (Ottawa: 1983), 41.

128 Ibid., 64.

129 Sally Weaver, "A Commentary on the Penner Report," *Canadian Public Policy, 10* (1984), 215.

130 Roger Gibbins and J. Rick Ponting, "The Paradoxical Nature of the Penner Report," *Canadian Public Policy, 10* (1984), 221.

131 Quebec was not at the table, having decided after its exclusion from the 1982 constitutional agreement to boycott any further first ministers' conferences. It is questionable whether, even in the face of agreement over aboriginal self-government by nine provinces and the federal government, any realistic progress might have been made without Quebec's consent.

132 David C. Hawkes, *Negotiating Aboriginal Self-Government: Developments Surrounding the 1985 First Ministers' Conference* (Kingston: Queen's University Institute of Intergovernmental Relations, 1985), 10.

133 Ibid., 13-14.

134 It is important to note that the aboriginal representatives at the first ministers' meeting did not include treaty Indians, who, in the form of the Prairie Treaty Nations Alliance, had pressed for a seat at the table but had been refused. This reflected a split in native ranks, since for the Alliance, self-government was a treaty right that should be elaborated in bilateral negotiations with Ottawa, excluding the provinces.

135 Hawkes, *Negotiating Aboriginal Self-Government* 38-40.

136 J. Rick Ponting, "An Indian Policy for Canada in the Twenty-First Century," paper presented to the All-European Canadian Studies Conference, The Hague, 1990, 7.

137 Ibid., 10.

138 *Globe and Mail*, 4 September 1990.

139 *Globe and Mail*, 5 September 1990.

140 *Globe and Mail*, 6 September 1990.

141 *Globe and Mail*, 7 September 1990.

142 By this time several of the Warriors had been identified, and some had outstanding warrants and criminal records. See *Globe and Mail*, 8 September 1990.

143 *Globe and Mail*, 10 September 1990.

144 *Globe and Mail*, 12 September 1990.

145 *Globe and Mail*, 14 September 1900.

146 *Globe and Mail*, 19 September 1990.

147 *Globe and Mail*, 21 September 1990.

148 *Globe and Mail*, 25 September 1990.

149 *Globe and Mail*, 26 September 1990.

FEATHER AND GUN: CONFRONTATION AT OKA/KANESATAKE

Game, Set and Tax:

The Advent of the GST

*In mid-December 1990 the Canadian Senate finally passed Bill C-62, the legis-
lation to establish the Goods and Sevices Tax (GST). This concluded one of the
most turbulent and upsetting episodes in recent Canadian politics. A part of the
government's 1987 tax reform package, the GST was one element of the neo-conservative rebellion against the post-war construction of the welfare state and
government management of the economy. After three years of public and
bureaucratic discussion, including failed negotiations with the provinces to create
a national sales tax, Bill C-62 was processed briskly by the House of Commons
over a three-month period. It then proceeded to the Senate, the site where the real
politics of the GST were played out for eight often zany months. The Liberal
senators defended the policies of the post-war past, but their majority was neutralized by Prime Minister Mulroney's unprecedented and controversial appointment
of eight extra senators.*

*What began as a tax matter became a metaphor for the Mulroney government's
spectacular unpopularity as well as for public dissatisfaction with all things political. And, as the unelected Senate responded to massive public discontent with the
GST and blocked the will of the elected House of Commons, the authority of
Canada's political institutions was stretched to the limit. The politics of the GST
raised uncomfortable questions about Canada's parliamentary democracy: should
an elected government be allowed to pursue even the most intensely unpopular of
policies? Should a non-elected body be the site for the articulation and play of
popular opposition? Whatever the responses to these difficult questions, the advent
of the GST left both politicians and institutions battered, bruised, and looking for
a more effective way to govern.*

Frankly," confided Prime Minister Mulroney to an elite group of Tory fundraisers
in the fall of 1989, "I need the GST like a hole in the head."[1]

A year later, the Prime Minister's colourful political judgment had become painfully close to reality. While legislating the Goods and Services Tax, the Conservative government had managed to alienate almost every political and economic constituency in Canada, from women's groups and labour unions to funeral directors and veterinarians; from municipalities and merchants to all ten provinces and much of the business community. In the wake of the divisive death of Meech Lake and the onset of a painful recession, the GST became a focus for Canadians' discontent with their politicians and political institutions. All the while, the Mulroney government continued on its sucidal mission, piggy-backing the GST to an unprecedentedly low 12 per cent approval rating in public opinion polls as well as to a bizarre political showdown in the Senate.

The Goods and Services Tax was designed to replace the Manufacturers Sales Tax (MST). Since its introduction in 1924, the MST had been universally criticized for causing a variety of economic irrationalities, from giving imports a competitive edge over Canadian products to taxing inputs, misallocating resources, and lowering output—by an estimated $9 billion in the late 1980s. The Conservative government was ideologically disposed to actually do what expert studies and previous governments had only thought about: take the political risks of reforming the tax system and replacing the MST. As part of a tax reform package designed to foster personal initiative and lessen the government's role in the economy, the government increased the importance of sales taxes—by devising the GST as a replacement for the MST—and decreased the importance of income taxes. The Conservatives also saw this as a way of increasing revenues to deal with the burgeoning government deficit. The strategy reflected the government's neo-conservative principles, and followed in the footsteps of actions taken by the Thatcher government in Britain and the Reagan administration in the United States.

The Mulroney government was first elected in 1984 with the largest electoral majority in Canadian history. This majority allowed it to pass quite handily the first half of its tax reform package, dealing with corporate and income taxes. Re-elected in 1988 with a healthy majority, it should have had no more difficulty legislating the GST than it had had attaining the first stage of tax reform. Yet it took the government more than two painful, disruptive, and expensive years to drag the legislation into law, despite the GST's policy priority on the relatively empty Conservative agenda in the late 1980s. In the process, the government lost control of the bill, lost control of the legislative agenda, and lost its own political authority and control of its destiny. The bill was finally passed, but not before the government was forced to use an arcane constitutional device to "swamp" the Senate with extra appointments to overcome Liberal senators' opposition.

The GST saga was a painful illustration of many of the real worlds of Canadian politics. It illustrated how a majority government can fundamentally alter the political agenda, establish a new set of political priorities, and give these priorities concrete legislative effect. It also demonstrated the challenges and difficulties facing even a powerful majority government when it pursues its agenda. Despite its superior strength in the House of Commons, the government faced formidable obstacles in bringing the GST into being. Some obstacles, such as the federal system, were familiar; others, such as public opinion, were not so familiar; and some, such as the Senate, were unexpected but increasingly familiar. The GST's superiority over the MST became a lost issue as the case dragged on. The government began the legislative process in charge of the political agenda, but wider political and ideological issues emerged that the government could neither manage nor control.

Perhaps the most fundamental of these issues was the Senate's role in the legislative process. Throughout most of the post-war period, the House of Commons and the Senate enjoyed a benign relationship, as Liberal majorities held sway in both houses. With the 1984 election this situation changed; and a Conservative majority in the lower house faced a Liberal majority in the upper house. The Conservatives' majority had made opposition to the bill in the House of Commons somewhat ineffective. Opponents of the bill looked elsewhere—anywhere—to block the GST. They found the Senate, where the Liberal senators took on the role of opposition to the government with unexpected and near-fatal vigour. But the Senate was an *unelected* opposition. Did it have the moral or political authority to block the GST, which had been passed by the elected House of Commons? Ironically, the government lost the political debate over "democracy." The GST's opponents pointed to the government's plummeting support in polls and portrayed the Senate as responding democratically to the will of the vast majority of Canadians. These issues smothered the substance of Bill C-62 and raised doubts about the efficacy of Canada's political institutions.

The debate over the GST was also underpinned by tension between two "visions" of the tax system. While tax matters are inherently complicated and alienating, they harbour fundamental ideological and political issues. The GST was part of the general neo-conservative strategy to shift taxes from income to sales taxes, in order to stimulate increased private economic activity and growth. Opponents of the GST characterized this shift differently, as an unjust move away from progressive taxes towards regressive taxes. The GST debate had an unusual (for Canada) class character to it, pitting business requirements against the aspirations of middle- and low-income Canadians. Despite efforts to show that this was not so, the government was unable to shake the GST's image as favouring corporations and the wealthy to the disadvantage of lower income groups. Similarly, despite claims that the GST was revenue neutral, most Canadians simply refused to believe that this was not a new tax whose revenues would be squandered by the government. The GST may have been more viscerally opposed than understood. In the real worlds of Canadian politics, symbolic issues often come to dominate substantive claims, particularly in complex policy areas like taxation.

The GST demonstrated the extent to which policies or issues cannot be treated as "technical" matters and how difficult it is to change existing legislation. The MST had been studied and analysed continuously over the previous six decades, and the case for its replacement was technically overwhelming. The Mulroney government's technical papers and studies made a convincing case for the superiority and benefits of the GST. Regardless of these studies, the government was unable to isolate the GST's technical claims from a variety of political and ideological issues. And, despite its majority in two terms of office, the reform of the tax system took it nearly six years. The longer the legislative process dragged on, the less support the GST commanded—much like the experience of the Meech Lake constitutional accord.

The world of federal-provincial relations was in the shadows in the GST case, an unusual occurrence in the world of Canadian fiscal politics. Nonetheless, the GST case illustrated how federalism constrained the Mulroney government's— and earlier governments'—attempts to alter the MST. The GST was a *retail* sales tax, an area traditionally inhabited by the provinces despite Ottawa's constitutional authority in all tax areas. In an effort to create a national, effective, and acceptable sales tax system, the federal government entered two fruitless years of negotiations with the provinces. This two-year interlude probably sealed the GST's fate, for it led the government to split off the more attractive personal and corporate tax cuts from the less appealing sales tax reform. This made it more difficult, if not impossible, for the government to "sell" and legislate the GST.

The government had no choice but to proceed despite the GST's unpopularity and the increasing political costs associated with it. The government had promised the legislation to the business community, its strongest political constituency, and it would have lost all political credibility if it had backed down. Retailers were poised to implement the tax, and its defeat would have cost them millions. The GST was one ingredient of a tax reform package that was only semi-completed, and, besides, Ottawa needed the money. In the wake of the death of the Meech Lake constitutional accord, this was a do-or-die bill for the government if it had any hope of continuing to govern. So, it gritted its death and continued the trench warfare with the GST's opponents to the bitter end.

THE ADVENT OF THE GST

Economic matters may be unfamiliar to, and not easily understood by, students of political science, despite the importance of fiscal matters in government. The chapter begins with a discussion of the fundamental features of a tax system and a review of the politics of the MST, which will provide a foundation for the discussion of the GST. The legislative process surrounding the GST will then be presented, and can be followed with the assistance of a chronology appended to the chapter.

THE TAX SYSTEM

Of all the myriad worlds of Canadian politics, none is more inherently *political* than the world of taxation. Death and taxes may be the only certainties of life—but while nature insists on death, it is governments that decide who pays taxes and how much. Governments need revenues to pay for the public services they provide, from maintaining military and police forces to providing health and educational services. Despite the inherently complex and technical nature of the world of taxes, they are matters that generate considerable political debate and require difficult decisions. For example, particular taxes can reflect one of two tendencies: *progressivity* (higher rates of tax are paid at higher income levels, in order that the rich pay a higher proportion of their income in taxes) or *regressivity* (equal tax rates across income and spending levels, with the result that the poor pay a higher portion of their income in taxes). The politics of taxation are real and compelling, and a society's particular array of taxes says much about its ideological and political character.

Indeed, at any given moment, the tax system is perceived to be in need of reform.[2] This is not simply because most people typically feel themselves to be over-taxed and others to be under-taxed. The tax system—the set of taxes including personal, corporate, and sales taxes—houses an array of public purposes and objectives. At any moment, some purposes may be in policy ascendancy while others are being ignored. In broad terms, the tax system comprises two goals: revenue generation and social objectives.[3]

In the first instance, the primary goal of a tax system is to generate and collect the revenue required by governments. Subsumed within this revenue goal are three other objectives: that the system be *simple* and comprehensible (lest it confuse people and work against revenue generation); that it be *fair* and treat similar people and situations equitably (lest a sense of unfairness lead to tax evasion and avoidance); and that the tax system be *neutral* and not interfere with the efficient functioning of the economy (lest a weakened economy provide a diminished base upon which taxes can be levied). The tax system should generate in a predictable way the required level of revenue while not interfering with the normal functioning of the economy.

The tax system might also be directed to pursuing policy goals, of which there are a limitless number. For example, the tax system can be used for macroeconomic goals, raising taxes at inflationary times and lowering them at recessionary moments, to ensure stable economic conditions. Or the tax system can be manipulated for distributional purposes, by taxing the wealthy at a higher rate and the poor at a lower rate as the basis for transferring income from the top to the lower income levels. Or it can be manipulated to encourage or discourage certain kinds of activities—for example, lowering taxes to stimulate investment in key industrial sectors or sluggish economic regions, or raising taxes to inhibit the consumption of cigarettes and alcohol. The revenue goal is relegated to a subsidiary role.

There is a tension between the two goals of the tax system. For example, redistributive tax measures might lead to increasing tax evasion and avoidance as well as diminished economic activity, if the wealthier and investment classes resent the higher taxes which they are paying; this could weaken the economy and the tax system's capacity to raise revenue. Similarly, a government that offers tax breaks and inducements to generate certain kinds of economic activity correspondingly weakens its capacity to raise revenue. And if tax regulations, inducements, and purposes proliferate to a high degree, the simplicity of the tax system might be lost and its neutrality upset, which could weaken both economic activity and, as a result, the capacity to raise tax revenue.

Indeed, this tension between the "economic" dimension of the revenue goal and the "social" dimension of the policy goals parallels the rise and fall of the post-war Keynesian/social welfare approach and its replacement by neo-conservatism. From 1945 to 1975, Canadian governments directed the tax system to macroeconomic, welfare, and sectoral/regional goals. The tax system was made more progressive, for both redistributive purposes and stabilization goals (keep employment high and inflation low). A myriad of tax measures encouraged regional economic balance and industrial and "high tech" economic development. In the process, personal income raxes rose from 10 per cent of federal government revenue in 1940 to over 40 per cent in the 1980s; in contrast, sales taxes fell from 36 per cent of federal government revenues in 1940 to 10 per cent in the 1980s. This distribution of tax revenues was very much in tune with the philosophy of the post-war supporters of Keynesianism and the welfare state. Commodity taxes are to be avoided, in their view, because they are regressive: lower income groups pay a higher proportion of their income in sales taxes than higher income groups, because each group pays the same rate of tax on its consumption. Personal income

THE ADVENT OF THE GST

taxes are favoured, because they can be geared to ability to pay: the higher the
income level, the higher the marginal tax rate. Hence, the declining importance
of sales taxes and the increasing importance of personal taxes was not a matter
of either chance or necessity: it reflected a series of deliberate policy choices that
were ideologically informed.

From the mid-1970s on, this approach and its results were decried by
monetarists and neo-conservatives. They argued that the tax system had been
corrupted by the proliferation of multiple social goals, with the result that both
the economy's capability and the tax system's revenue-generating capacity had
been undermined—leading to slower economic growth and mushrooming government deficits. Progressive taxes and an increasingly complex tax system were seen
to have encouraged tax evasion and avoidance. They claimed that sectoral and
regional inducements had led to the misallocation of resources and declining efficiency and growth—and lower tax revenues. The distribution of sources of tax
revenue was seen as a metaphor for what was wrong with economic policy. The
higher share of personal taxes reflected a greater degree of government interference in the economy. This also made the tax revenue base less certain and
predictable (as a result of tax evasion). Neo-conservatives favour sales or commodity taxes, as being more neutral, less administratively complex, a more stable
and effective revenue generator, and fairer (taxing what a person takes out of
the economy in consumption, rather than what is put into it—represented by
income). What was needed, it was maintained, was a radical simplification of the
tax system, to make it neutral and revenue oriented rather than socially oriented.
Hence, the Mulroney government's tax reform plan included the general goal of
decreasing the role of direct, personal taxes and increasing the revenue role of
commodity taxes—the GST. Defenders of the status quo (the post-war welfare
state) would in turn militate against the alleged regressivity of commodity taxes.

The tax system, then, has been an important site where ideological and political forces have played themselves out over the last decade. Apparently merely a
technical matter for accountants and tax lawyers, the debate over direct vs. indirect taxes harbours deep political and ideological questions of tremendous controversy.

THE FEDERAL SALES TAX, 1920–1984

A tremendous irony surrounded the Goods and Services Tax controversy. The
GST was designed to replace the MST, widely referred to simply as the federal
sales tax. This was a tax that had had no supporters over the previous six decades.
Everyone—literally everyone, Liberal senators included—agreed that this was a

bad tax that should be eliminated. Despised though it was, the federal sales tax was a symbol of remarkable if undesired policy durability.

Its origins[4] lie in the aftermath of World War I (which had also introduced the "temporary" personal income tax to Canada). The federal government faced the daunting fiscal combination of huge war bills, extensive servicemen's pensions, and the looming bankrupcy of some large railroad companies. In a foreshadowing of the context of the introduction of the GST seventy years later, the federal government's indebtedness was the critical conjunctural issue. This had increased sixfold in the period 1913-20; the costs of servicing of the debt and providing war pensions consumed 75 per cent of government spending in 1920. In a move designed strictly to raise revenue, the government introduced a 1 per cent multiple-stage turnover tax—a kind of value-added tax—on the "sales of all manufacturers, wholsale dealers, jobbers and importers."[5]

This tax was universally criticized on a variety of grounds. The government replaced it four years later: in 1924 Canada became the first country to adopt a single-stage manufacturers sales tax (of 6 per cent). It was to be imposed on the selling price of all goods manufactured or produced in Canada or imported into Canada, unless specifically exempted (food, manufacturing inputs, etc.; exemptions would multiply in a topsy-turvy way over the next sixty years). The tax was seriously flawed for reasons as evident in 1924 as in 1984 (see Inset I): it lacked neutrality, favoured imports and discouraged exports, pyramided taxes on top of each other, and was invisible. It was also tremendously unpopular, leading the government to announce in 1927 that it planned to drop it. The tax was decreased yearly until 1930, by which time its level was but 1 per cent and it generated little of the government's revenue (6 per cent, compared to 18 per cent in 1924). The federal sales tax was on the verge of disappearing.

However, its importance was revived by the onset of the depression, as the federal government went scurrying in search of new revenues to replenish the emptied Treasury. The tax was raised to 4 per cent in 1931 and 6 per cent in 1932, and comprised 21 per cent of government revenue by 1935. Liberal opposition leader Mackenzie King campaigned against it in the 1935 election, only to raise the tax to 8 per cent in 1936. It persisted as a major revenue source through the remainder of the depression as well as through World War II, and was maintained after the war to help pay for the deficit. By 1950 it still constituted about 14 per cent of Ottawa's revenues. With the outbreak of the Korean War, the tax was raised to 10 per cent for revenue purposes.

Despite persistent criticism and anticipation of its elimination, the MST survived its first quarter of a century as a kind of necessary revenue-raising evil. Its rate had varied according to governments' revenue needs. From this point through

Inset I

PROBLEMS WITH THE MANUFACTURERS SALES TAX[6]

If the tax system is to use a sales tax, it should generate its anticipated government revenue while being as "neutral" as possible. That is, its imposition should not affect the allocation of economic resources or lower economic output. In order to minimize distortions, a sales tax should treat all products equally, offer no exemptions, and be imposed as close as possible to the sale of the product to the final purchaser. By these criteria, "the Canadian federal sales tax is about as far away from (the) ideal tax prescription as can be imagined."[7]

Lack of Neutrality

Because the MST is applied long before the final sale at the retail level, it lacks neutrality. The proportion of value added to goods after the tax is imposed at the manufacturer's level varies widely according to the good's distribution channel and the level of mark-up it undergoes at each stage.

If manufacturers sell directly to the public or to retailers, their price is higher than the selling price of those who sell to wholesalers. Thus, the tax bases for competing manufacturers may differ, and distortions result, as a result of applying the tax at different points in the production marketing process. Thus, manufacturing companies tried to reduce their tax liability by shifting parts of their operations beyond the point where the manufacturer is taxed. This can be done by creating *separate marketing companies* to sell their products; marketing and distribution costs are then not included in the manufacturer's price to be taxed. Or, the manufacturing process itself might be contracted out; the manufacturers' price would then not include all the prior research and development costs. The tax department lost hundreds of millions of dollars a year in tax revenues, because the MST offered an incentive to reorganize production and distribution in a perverse way.

Because the MST is applied at such an early stage, the tax distorts the structure of relative prices, which is economically inefficient and leads to the loss of significant amounts of tax revenue. Moreover, there is a basic unfairness, as different firms producing similar goods end up paying higher taxes and presenting the market with higher- priced goods. For example, the MST has always given a tax advantage to *brand name goods*, which don't have advertising, warranty, or risk costs in the manufacturer's sale price—thus avoiding the tax—as the merchandiser assumes these costs. When manufacturers market their own goods, these costs are included in the tax base.

A related problem was the fact that *transportation* costs are included in the manufacturers price to be taxed. Those companies whose source of supply of inputs—say, raw or semi-finished materials—was distant would pay higher taxes on their finished products than companies whose source of supply was close. This phenomenon distorted locational decisions and, indeed, encouraged Canadian businesses to manufacture products outside of the country.

As a result of these phenomena, the effective rates of the MST varied widely, from 1 per cent to 9 per cent. A 1984 government survey of six hundred commodities showed no two products with the same rate, with rates varying even for similar products made by different manufacturers in the same industry. For example, the tax rate on cosmetic products varied from 5.15 per cent to 17.08 per cent, and for auto parts from 4.28 per cent to 13.36 per cent.

Imports Favoured

One of the most flagrant examples of the MST's lack of neutrality was its varying treatment of imported goods and domestically produced goods. The MST is applied on imported goods as they enter the country before *they incur advertising, warranty, and marketing costs*. Domestically produced manufactured products are taxed on the higher price that includes these costs. On average, by the 1980s the effective tax rate on domestically manufactured goods was about one-third higher than on competing imports. In some cases—like household furniture—the effective tax rate was over 70 per cent higher. The MST thus acted as a tax on exports, and gave an inducement to imports, which was harmful to the Canadian economy. Moreover, it encouraged Canadian companies to manufacture their products abroad, with similar results.

Pyramiding

The MST is imposed on all sorts of items distant from the final retail price. These items act as inputs as a good moves through the production and distribution stream. An article could then be multiple-taxed. Even though construction materials and building equipment were exempted from the tax—to avoid taxing manufacturing inputs—the MST caused significant tax cascading or pyramiding. About half of the $8 billion federal sales tax revenue in 1989 derived from the taxation of inputs into the production process. This would seriously weaken investment and depress economic output. The government estimated that in the 1980s tax cascading added 0.9 per cent to the cost of exports, thus consuming 10 per cent of the competitive margin of Canadian exports on world markets.

Exemptions

From the very beginning, various products were exempted from the MST. Food and health products were exempted to neutralize the tax's regressive qualities. Manufacturing equipment and construction materials were exempted or taxed at a lower rate, to avoid or minimize tax pyramiding. Over time, various sectors of the economy made their cases for exemptions, so that by the 1980s only about one-third of all consumer goods and services were being taxed. Indeed, services themselves were not being taxed. The tax had become almost random, as a result of the accumulation of exemptions, exclusions, and multiple rates. Four commodity groupings—motive fuels, motor vehicles and parts, alcohol, and tobacco—accounted for nearly 60 per cent of total MST revenues. This had two serious economic implications. First, the tax's non-neutrality distorted economic allocation, weakening economic growth. Second, as governments would come to realize, the narrow base of taxed goods became an increasingly weak generator of government revenue, requiring the MST to be raised to levels that would themselves be economically damaging.

Complexity and Invisibility

The hidden nature of the tax was a major design flaw, save for the government that collected its revenue.

The accumulation of multiple rates, exemptions, evaluations, Finance Department ad hoc decisions, business reorganization to avoid taxes, and so on made the MST one of the most complex sales tax systems and administratively difficult. As more and more sectors and firms avoided paying the MST, there was increased incentive to devise ways to avoid it, which weakened tax compliance and increased the costs of tax administration. The federal government found itself increasingly in court battles over the tax. Despite the fact that there were only seventy-five thousand tax "units" paying the MST, there were twenty-two thousand special provisions and administrative interpretations surrounding the MST.

These flaws in the MST had been apppreciated since the mid-1920s. But by the mid-1980s their economic implications loomed large. The lack of neutrality, the constraints on investment, the harm done to exports, and other economic distortions were estimated by the federal government to lower the output of the Canadian economy by $9 billion on an annual basis. And the MST had become an increasingly unreliable and administratively complicated source of tax revenue.

the 1980s, the tax was studied and examined like some sort of dinosaur fossil by Royal Commissions, task forces, bureaucratic committees, and private-sector groups. All of these reports presented similar messages—whether in 1940 or in 1984 (see Inset II). In 1940, the Rowell-Sirois Royal Commission criticized its regressive impact on low-income groups. The Carter Sales Tax Committee recommended in 1956 that the tax be moved away from the manufacturers level forward to the wholesale level (to increase the degree of tax neutrality). The Carter Royal Commission on Taxation reported in 1967 that there was no support for the manufacturers sales tax, and recommended that it be replaced by a retail tax (even more tax neutral than a wholesale tax). The Commodity Tax Review Group issued a Green Paper with the 1975 budget, and recommended that the MST be replaced with a tax imposed on the wholesale level. A follow-up Brown Report in 1977 supported a wholesale tax. In the 1981 budget, the government announced its intention to shift the federal sales tax away from the manufactuers level to the wholesale level, and this was followed by a White Paper in April 1982. A Federal Sales Tax Review Committee reported in May 1983 on the weaknesses of the proposed move of the tax to the wholesale level and—while preferring a value-added retail sales tax—recommended instead a series of incremental improvements to the existing MST. Forty-five years of studies and recommendations came to an inauspicious end in the 1984 budget, when Finance Minister Lalonde introduced a moderate set of incremental changes to the still alive and kicking manufacturers sales tax.

Inset II

STUDIES OF THE MST, 1940-1984

The *Rowell-Sirois Royal Commission on Dominion-Provincial Relations*[8] (1940) criticized the MST on three grounds. First, the Commission saw the MST as a tax on costs, raising the costs of production. Second, it saw the tax as contributing to tax cascading or pyramiding, as taxes would be levied on top of taxes at each stage of production. Third, it maintained that commodity taxes are inherently regressive. It recommended that the tax be eliminated and that the tax system be tilted towards progressivity and away from regressivity.

In the 1955 budget, the Minister of Finance appointed a three-person Sales Tax Committee to examine the tax, in response to widespread business befuddlement over the tax's complexity and the growing realization of overpayment of the sales tax.[9] The *Carter Committee report*[10] was extremely brief and incomplete. It reviewed many of the MST's flaws, including the fact that imported goods enjoyed a tax advantage over domestically manufactured goods. It suggested a number of technical reforms and recommended that the tax base be shifted forward to the wholesale level to neutralize the tax advantage given to imports.

The *Carter Royal Commision on Taxation*[11] was appointed by the Diefenbaker government in 1962 and reported in 1967. It noted that only two groups supported the MST status quo: the Canadian Wholesale Council (which feared the shift in tax to the wholesale level, which it saw as threatening the system of distribution) and the Retail Merchandisers Association of Canada (which argued that the burden of collecting the tax should not be assigned to the retailer). Most other sectors of the Canadian economy—including the Canadian Manufacturers Association—were against the tax and favoured shifting it to to retail level, to eliminate its flaws (the import preference, tax pyramiding, unfair burdens, invisibility, the fact that services were not taxed). The Commission itself saw little good in the tax, which it criticized for undermining neutrality and offending the principles of progressivity—the latter being the operational principle informing the entire report. In general, it opted for personal direct over indirect commodity taxes, but favoured the replacement of the MST with a single-stage sales tax on both goods and services at the retail level. Regressivity would be mitigated by exempting food products, fuel and electricity, medical and health expenditures, and reading materials. Cash payments were proposed to neutralize the tax's impact on low-income groups. It also recommended that the tax be synchronized with the provinces, which would collect it. If this proved administratively too difficult, or if the combined federal and provincial sales tax was too high (over 14 per cent) then it proposed that a value-added tax be considered.

The government did not address the Carter Commission's sales tax proposals until a *Green Paper on Federal Sales and Excise Taxation*[12] was issued with the 1975 budget. The Green Paper was written by the Commodity Tax Review Group of the Department of Finance. It reviewed the flaws of the MST, focusing on its lack of neutrality, the advantages given to brand-name and imported goods, and the penalties assigned to firms with high transportation costs. It suggested that many of these flaws would be substantially repaired by moving the tax to the wholesale level (what it called the retailer's purchasing price). While the group acknowledged that a move to the retail level would involve greater tax and economic benefits, the marginal differences in benefits between a wholesale and retail tax were seen to be dwarfed by the administrative complexities involved in moving the tax collection system to retailers (200,000 business units involved) and the complications imposed on retailers. The Green Paper invited public reaction to its recommendations.

The *Brown Report of the Commodity Tax Review Group*[13] reported on public reaction to its Green Paper and was presented to the House of Commons Standing Committee on Finance, Trade and Economics (which apparently never considered the report and certainly never commented on it[14]). Two hundred submissions were received from trade associations, taxpayers, consumer groups, and the academic community. There was general public agreement with the Green Paper's analysis of the MST's flaws, but there was predominantly negative reaction to its recommendation that the tax be moved to the wholesale level (only 10 per cent supported it). Most supported either a move to the retail level (the vast majority) or incremental reform of the existing tax. Despite this public reaction, and its own declaration that a tax at the retail level was the most neutral, the Finance officials again recommended the move to a wholesale tax. The reason given was that this approach offered the maximum benefits for the least amount of administrative and business disruption, and avoided the difficulties that a retail tax would generate in its having to be integrated with provincial sales taxes. The persistence of this policy preference in the face of public opposition reflected the intensified opposition to the idea of a retail tax from the Retail Council of Canada, and led to a widespread sense that the public discussion had been a farce, the report a "snow job," and the government's wholesale position a reflection of its inability to get the provincial cooperation required in a move into the retail sales tax area.[15]

In Allan MacEachen's tax reform *1981 budget*, the government announced its intention to replace the MST with a tax shifted to the wholesale level, to be imple-

THE ADVENT OF THE GST

mented in July 1982 (the issue had been addressed in the 1980 budget as well). The MST was seen to be structurally flawed, particularly in the fact that its effective rate was almost twice as high on domestically produced goods as on similar goods imported from outside Canada. The wholesale tax would be administratively simpler, less ad hoc in its application, and at a lower rate.[16]

This was followed in April 1982 by a *White Paper*[17] on the government's proposal to shift the MST to the wholesale level, which synopsized previous reports' and studies' cataloguing of the tax's flaws and outlined the benefits of the move to the wholesale level (simplicity, neutrality, fairness, lower rate). The White Paper was tabled in the House of Commons, along with draft legislation, and reactions to it were solicited by the government over the summer.

Over 125 submissions were made. The only group that favoured the move was domestic car makers. Wholesalers fought vigorously against the proposal, not wanting to inherit the increased administrative responsibilities that would come with the new tax. Retailers complained that the tax created as many problems as it solved, and doubted whether manufacturers would actually pass on the tax savings to their customers. There was considerable concern about the inflationary impact of the move.[18]

Business reaction made the government cautious. In an economic statement in October 1982 it moved to delay implementation of the wholesale tax until January 1983, a date later extended to mid-1984.

On 10 February 1983 Finance Minister Lalonde appointed a seventeen-member private sector committee of tax practitioners and business and consumer representatives to review the proposal. The *Goodman Committee*[19] received submissions from seventy-five companies and groups, hearing numerous complaints and horror stories about the proposed tax.[20] The Committee noted the flaws in the existing system, but gave the wholesale tax proposal the kiss of death by concluding that "the marginal improvements which shifting the tax to the wholesale trade level would produce do not justify the disruption it would cause in an already functioning system."(p. v) While it favoured the introduction of a value-added tax up to the retail level, jointly administered with the provinces, it concluded that this far-reaching move required further study (as well as diplomatic negotiations with the provinces). Instead, it recommended a number of modifications to the existing MST, in order to limit its structural defects.

In the *February 1984 budget*, Finance Minister Lalonde took up the Goodman Committee's recommendations. He dropped the MacEachen proposal to move the federal sales tax to the wholesale level, save in one area—motor vehicles—where imports had a $100-200 price advantage over similar domestic cars as a result of the MST. He proposed to review on a sector-by-sector basis any inequities created by the MST and make changes where appropriate to the level at which the sales tax was applied. He also noted that governments had been inhibited from moving the tax to the retail level, "given the difficulties in seeking a federal and provincial agreement on a common system."[21]

By 1984, then, the federal sales tax had survived around two dozen finance ministers, various governments, and numerous studies that had outlined its flaws and presented alternatives. While some governments made efforts to replace it, these were half-hearted and token actions. The tax rested at the 9 per cent level, 50 per cent higher than when it was introduced in 1924, and it generated 12 per cent of the federal government's revenue. How had it persisted?

First, it should be noted that despite its economic flaws, the tax is administratively attractive—indeed, this was the only feature that recommended it. Because the tax is applied on manufacturers, it is easy and cheap to collect, as the number of manufacturers is relatively small and these companies keep good books. While moving the tax forward to the wholesale or retail level increases tax neutrality, the number of firms collecting the tax increases at an alarming rate and these firms do not keep as reliable books. Thus, the costs of tax-collecting increase.[22] Indeed, the sheer mechanical complications of shifting the tax to either of these levels acted as a deterrent to reform.

Second, "many tax reforms are proposed but few are adopted."[23] While there was consensus on the fact that the MST was a bad tax, there was no consensus on how to improve it. The Carter Commission and the Goodman Report were the most compelling in proposing a value-added tax (VAT) to be imposed at the retail level: this would be the best revenue-generator while providing the least interference with economic neutrality. However, there were substantial and costly political deterrents to this action. First, the provincial governments viewed the retail area as their tax turf and, despite the fact that section 91 of the constitution gave Ottawa authority to raise money "by any mode or system of taxation," a federal move into the retail area would require immense political finesse as well as enormous courage. Federal-provincial discussions took place but were not fruitful. Second, while the move to a retail tax would essentially involve the replacement of one tax by another, it would *look like a new tax*, because the MST was invisible and the retail tax would be very visible and very unpopular (retail taxes are perhaps the most unpopular of all taxes). The provinces were not eager to be identified with a perceived tax increase that was, really, the federal government's doing. The second-best option—the move to the wholesale level—would be more palatable politically. But it would not be a tremendous improvement and would cause a new set of administrative complications. This seemed hardly worth the effort. At bottom, only the Finance Department officials wanted a shift to the wholesale level, a move that was never favoured by business.[24] Needless to say, retailers criticized the former proposal, wholesalers the latter proposal, so there was little business consensus on the direction to move. And, given that the public did not know about the tax or discern its real impact on their lives, there was neither an elite nor a mass political constituency to move in any particular direction to replace the tax. The issue was hidden away in the arcane world of tax legislation, inhabited by federal and provincial officials and tax experts.

Finally, the fact remained that the federal sales tax had continued to generate needed revenue for the government, and so was not a gift horse to be looked in the mouth. For any incoming government, better to accept the inheritance of a bad tax and loads of revenue, than to eliminate the tax and lose a substantial revenue source.

Thus, while the MST was no one's first policy choice, it survived. Although both the economy and the public would have benefitted from the reform of the MST, "the general interest is no one's interest"—or, to put it another way, the general interest could not be called upon as an effective pressure group to get the tax changed. When the Conservatives formed the government in 1984, Canada was the last remaining industrial country to retain a sales tax at the manufacturers level—sixty years after it had introduced the tax to the world.

TORY TAX REFORM

With the landslide Progressive Conservative election victory in the fall of 1984, a new political agenda was created. The Mulroney government planned to regenerate private enterprise and the marketplace through a rolling back of government involvement in social and economic life. The post-war construction of the welfare state and government management of the economy were seen to have constrained personal economic initiative, undermined economic efficiency, inhibited growth, and created a bloated public sector with an enormous deficit. Deficit reduction and economic growth, were the top objectives, and private enterprise was to be the engine pulling Canada towards these objectives. Over the next half dozen years, the government's economic and social policies would be directed to these ends: the Free Trade Agreement (FTA) with the United States; the reform of unemployment insurance (UI), and welfare and social security retrenchment; the selling of Crown corporations such as Air Canada and Petro Canada; deregulation of various sectors such as the transportation and communication industries; the tilting of economic and industrial policy away from government management to a private-sector-driven approach. Tax reform was one ingredient of this new economic agenda, and the Goods and Services Tax was one element of the tax reform package.

In all of these actions, the Conservative government was "undoing" the more interventionist Liberal policies inherited from the past, policies informed by a

THE ADVENT OF THE GST

philosophy diametrically opposite to the neo-conservatism espoused by the Mulroney government. As a result, each of these Conservative initiatives, from the FTA to the reform of UI, was bound to be politically divisive. The debate over policy matters was always raised to a matter of moral or ideological principle, giving each of the policy debates an all-or-nothing quality that left no room for compromise.[25] Tory tax reform was no exception. Indeed, the GST was one of the bloodiest battles of them all.

The tax reform process did not take place quickly or all at once. Tax reform is a complicated matter, and highly sensitive politically. The Mulroney government proceeded deliberately and with such caution that the tax reform process took two terms of office to complete. The process unfolded in two parts. First, there was what might be called the "phoney war," the period of incremental but important tax changes in the 1984-1986 budgets. The limited deficit-reducing impact of these changes, in conjunction with a series of external events—particularly tax reform in the United States—led the government to commit itself to comprehensive tax reform. The reform process unfolded between the presentation of a White Paper in 1987 and the passing of the GST legislation in late 1990. This second part itself had two stages: stage one saw changes to personal and corporate taxes (and was completed before the 1988 election) and stage two saw the reform of the sales tax and the introduction of the GST . While stage two was announced in 1987 and widely if incompletely discussed before the 1988 election, government documents on the GST were not released until 1989 and the GST legislation was not introduced until January 1990. The splitting of tax reform into two stages may have been necessary, as will be seen below. But the process would prove to strategically flawed.

Incremental Changes, 1984-86

On 8 November 1984 Finance Minister Michael Wilson presented the newly elected Conservative government's agenda for a new economic policy orientation. Promising to deliver economic renewal via diminished government involvement and increased private activity in the economy, the minister identified the deficit and the tax system as two key obstacles to economic growth and renewal. At this point he envisioned an "evolutionary basis," rather than a radical break, for changing the tax system. He noted that a "value-added tax" was being mooted as a possible replacement for the federal sales tax. But a change of this magnitude would require "careful study" and consultation with the provincial governments.[26] Foreshadowing the battle over the GST, the mere mention of the possibility of a VAT generated an avalanche of protests and opposition from small business in particular, which was fearful of increased administrative work and costs.[27] Wilson remained cautious through to the next budget: "I'm not going to drop full tax reform on the Canadian people in too short a time. It's too complex. It's something that can't be done in a hurry."[28]

The spring 1985 budget focused on reducing the deficit and encouraging the private sector. The government also started to undo the tax inheritance from the past in two critical ways:

- Wilson proposed to partially "de-index" the personal income tax, family allowances, and old age pensions, which would save the government over $6 billion a year by 1990-91; this "undid" the indexing measures introduced by John Turner in the 1973 budget to prevent taxation of lower and middle-class income at higher rates because of inflation.

- Wilson offered a lifetime capital gains tax exemption of $500,000 at a cost of $1.2 billion. This in turn undid one of the main features of the tax reform process initated by the Carter Commission in 1967-71.

For revenue purposes, the MST was increased by broadening its base (to include, for example, candy, confectionery, soft drinks, and pet food) and increasing its rate to 11 per cent (it had been increased to 10 per cent in October 1984); this would raise over $9 billion in revenue by the end of the decade. The budget also closed some tax loopholes, eliminated some tax breaks (like the Registered Home Ownership Savings Plan), and presented the idea of a minimum corporation tax (this idea was never pursued). Sales tax reform was not mentioned, and Wilson again declared that a process of "massive tax reform" was not to be introduced for fear of creating "uncertainty and instability."[29]

Wilson continued his revenue-increasing, deficit-reduction efforts in the February 1986 budget. He imposed a 3 per cent surtax on all taxpayers and increased the MST to 12 per cent while broadening its base to include snack foods. These actions would raise about $3 billion in revenue in 1990-91. At the same time, Wilson continued to encourage private-sector activity and introduced a series of substantial corporation tax cuts. A few more tax loopholes were closed, and a refundable sales tax credit was introduced for low-income earners. The minister also stepped a bit deeper into sales tax reform waters: "It is time to act on this issue, to bring our sales tax system into line with today's reality," to deal with the MST's flaws, such as the inequities it created among competing firms and the tax disadvantages it created for exporters. On this occasion, he hinted at a new approach—a business transfer tax (BTT)—which was allegedly less complex administratively than the existing federal sales tax.[30] It was widely anticipated that a White Paper on sales tax reform would be released in spring 1986, in preparation for this tax's replacing the MST in the 1987 budget.[31]

THE ADVENT OF THE GST

But the White Paper was never released. It had become abundantly clear to the government that any new sales tax would be tremendously unpopular; this would generate huge political risks in 1986 or 1987, so close to an election (which could be expected in 1988). Moreover, despite the very substantial personal tax increases involved in de-indexing personal income taxes, imposing the surcharge, and increasing the MST from 9 per cent to 12 per cent, the government was still not generating the revenue need to handle the deficit. And the inducements given to the private sector—the capital gains exemption, the corporate tax cuts—were about to pale in comparison as the Reagan tax reform blitzkrieg roared on in the United States. Indeed, the contrast between the increases in Canadian personal tax rates and the very popular Reagan personal tax cuts would be stark and politically dangerous for the government. For these reasons, something more than incremental tax changes and sales tax reform would be needed—something like a comprehensive tax reform.

The White Paper on Tax Reform, 1987

The tax reform process continued to unfold slowly and cautiously over the next year. Finance Minister Wilson crossed the Rubicon in a press interview on 18 July 1986: "I am announcing today that the government intends to proceed with a review of options for comprehensive tax reform." While no details were given as to what the final result of tax reform would be, Wilson noted that he hoped to "reverse the trend which has resulted in greater reliance on personal income taxes." This was consistent with neo-conservative principles and suggested a larger role for the sales tax. Indeed, he stated that his officials were continuing to study the idea of a BTT and would report to him in the fall (a report on the BTT was never released).[32] The commitment to sales tax reform was reiterated by Wilson in a speech in Washington, DC, in September, in which the idea of a business transfer tax was favoured over the VAT.[33]

In October 1986 Wilson released a paper that set the guidelines for tax reform. Nine principles were presented, most of them offended by the MST:
- Fairness (the MST is imposed randomly)
- Simplicity and compliance (the MST has become administratively complex, and companies work hard to avoid it)
- Balance (the MST does not raise a sufficient share of government revenue)
- Stability (the MST has become an unstable and unpredictable revenue source)

THE ADVENT OF THE GST

- International competitiveness (the MST advantages imports over exports)
- Economic growth (the MST inhibits investment and misallocates resources)[34]

Wilson maintained that the purpose of tax reform would be to make the system simpler and fairer, and one that encourages enterprise and the generation of stable revenue for the government.[35]

Despite expectations that the tax reform plan would be presented in the February 1987 budget, this budget was "a breathing space prior to the presentation of major proposals for tax reform." The budget left a policy vacuum, and there was wild speculation about what the government proposed to do. It was not until the spring—6 May 1987—that Wilson announced that his White Paper on tax reform would be released next month.[36]

The White Paper on taxation[37] was finally released on 18 June 1987. This was almost three years into the government's term of office, and a year after Wilson's announcement of the government's plans to proceed with tax reform. The White Paper was informed by the traditional view of what a tax system should do: its first sentence read, "The objective of the tax system is to raise revenue needed to pay for publicly funded programs, and to do this in a way that supports economic growth and is fair to all Canadians." (p. 1) Its objectives were tilted more to the economic side than to the social side of taxation. First, tax reform would be directed to the invigoration of economic activity, by giving more economic incentives and encouraging economic growth. Second, tax reform would be directed to providing reliable sources of revenue to the government to deal with the deficit. In short, the White Paper aimed to reconstruct the tax system away from its existing use for multiple social and economic goals, to a simpler system that encouraged economic growth and provided needed revenue for the government.

The White Paper also proposed that the government move away from the 1984-1986 'incremental process' of tax reform to a 'comprehensive' approach:

As it became increasingly clear that the Canadian tax system was not performing many of its functions as well as it should, it became clear that the process of evolutionary and incremental reform...would need to be greatly accelerated. It also became evident through this period that some of our major trading partners...were moving forward aggressively and more comprehensively with actions to reform their tax systems and, in particular, to lower their rates. In an increasingly interdependent world, it is important not to allow Canada's tax system to put our traders, businesses, investors and highly skilled individuals at a competitive disadvantage with other countries (p. 21).

THE ADVENT OF THE GST

Put crudely, what this meant was that the 1984-86 incremental tax changes were not generating sufficient extra revenue to neutralize the deficit and that, because the Americans were lowering their direct tax rates, Canada had to follow suit (for obvious political reasons as well as for the economic requirement that Canada's tax rates could not be way out of line with the Americans'). Moreover, with the Free Trade Agreement looming (see Chapter 3), the perverse tax advantages assigned to imports by the MST loomed even larger than previously. Whatever fears the government had that a comprehensive tax reform would create "instability" and "uncertainty" were neutralized by these three factors. It would allow the government to "strike a better balance between the sales, corporate and personal income taxes" (p. 21): personal income taxes would decline in importance and sales taxes would increase in importance. The tax reform package was directly in tune with the government's neo-conservative ambitions to reduce the role of government in the economy.

The White Paper proposed a two-part tax reform package, which would unfold in two separate stages (see Inset III). The first part dealt with direct taxes—personal and corporate income taxes. Reflecting developments to the south as well as the philosophy of increasing personal incentives to generate economic growth, the White Paper proposed a radical alteration to, and lowering of, personal income taxes. The top marginal (federal) rate would be a relatively low 29 per cent, starting at $55,000. On the corporate side, rates would also be cut, to 28 per cent in general (25 per cent for manufacturers and 13 per cent for small business). It was estimated that net personal taxes would decline by $2 billion over the next five years, financed to a great extent by increased corporate tax revenue (an increase in $5 billion over the period, as a result of the elimination of exemptions and loopholes). It was anticipated that reform of direct taxes would be revenue neutral—i.e., the new system would not generate any more revenues than the existing system. In other words, tax reform would not involve tax increases.

The second part of the reform package dealt with the sales tax: "The government proposes to replace the existing federal sales tax with a broad-based multi-stage sales tax that extends to the retail level. This multi-stage tax would be a form of value-added tax" (p. 59). This was essentially the proposal made by the Carter Royal Commission over two decades earlier. No details were given about this proposal. Whereas the reform of direct taxes would be "based on familiar principles [and so] can go quickly," sales tax reform "requires building an entirely new system." This reform called for a "measured approach" and would proceed only "after consultations with the provincial governments and interested Canadians necessary to ensure the smooth implementation of the multi-stage tax"

Inset III

THE 1987 WHITE PAPER ON TAX REFORM

The White Paper proposed a "comprehensive" tax reform package involving changes to all three of the major revenue sources: personal, corporate, and indirect taxes. Reflecting neo-conservative principles, it proposed to reconstruct the balance amongst these three tax sources, with personal income taxes diminishing in importance while corporate and particularly sales taxes would account for a greater share of government revenue. The rationale for this "re-mix" was that this would increase personal incentives and investment, and hence growth and employment. This would also result in a larger and more predictable revenue base for the government.

Personal Income Taxes

There were four major reforms in this tax area:
1. Personal income tax deductions and exemptions would be transformed into tax credits, generally but not uniformly at a 17 per cent rate.
2. The ten marginal tax rates (ranging from 6 per cent to 34 per cent) would be decreased to three: 17 per cent for personal income up to $27,500; 26 per cent for income between $27,500 and $55,000; and 29 per cent for income above $55,000.
3. A number of preferential tax measures would be eliminated to broaden the tax base (which would finance some of the tax cut); some deductions and tax shelters were removed, while others were to be limited more strictly; the $500,000 capital gains tax exemption was capped at $100,000; the dividend tax credit was reduced; the $1,000 interest and dividend reduction was eliminated.
4. The refundable tax credit for low-income groups was increased.

The net impact of tax cuts, changes in exemptions and deductions, broadening of the tax base, and increase in tax credits was a $2 billion personal tax cut over the next few years (rising to $2.5 billion by 1991-2) and the removal of 850,000 people from the tax rolls. However, these tax cuts amounted to far less than the personal tax increases in 1984-86, during which time over 1 million Canadians had been added to the tax rolls. While it is difficult to estimate the net effect of the 1984-6 and 1987 White Paper changes, it appears that personal taxes have increased, albeit at a slower rate than they would have, with two groups benefitting economically: the top 1 per cent of income earners and the lowest 30 per cent (as a result of the increase in tax credits). Most Canadians would still be paying higher taxes than in 1984.[38]

Corporate Taxes

Much of the reform in this area had already been carried out in 1984-86. However, the White Paper presented two general reforms:

1. The corporate tax rate was to be lowered from 38 per cent to 36 per cent in general, from 36 per cent to 30 per cent for manufacturers, and from 15 per cent to 13 per cent for small businesses.
2. The elimination and reduction of a considerable number of exemptions, including depletion allowances and capital cost allowances.

The strategy here was to "trade off" corporate tax cuts with a broadening of the tax base. The net impact of these changes was to increase corporate taxes by over $5 billion over the next five years. It was anticipated that the corporate tax share of government revenue would increase from 15.6 per cent in 1987-88 to 17.2 per cent in 1991-92. This was not an earth-shattering change, given the already low share of revenue netted by corporate taxation (for example, in 1955 the corporate tax share of total federal government revenue was over 30 per cent). This would contribute to the financing of the personal tax cut. The idea of the minimum corporate tax was quietly dropped, in anticipation that the second ingredient of the corporate tax reform would generate the equivalent result.

Sales Tax

The White Paper's proposals in this area were not as concrete as in the direct tax areas, owing to their radical nature and the requirement to enter into detailed negotiations with the provinces. The general principle advanced was for a multi-stage tax on all goods and *services* right through to the retail level. All businesses at any stage in the economic chain would charge a tax on their sales; they would then claim a tax credit for any tax paid on their purchases (the workings of the tax are given fuller illustration in Inset IV). The White Paper proposed that all goods and services be taxed to keep the rate of tax low and that low-income families be protected from the effect of the tax by a refundable sales tax credit prepaid, even if income taxes were not paid. The White Paper also proposed to lower the middle-class personal tax rate by one more percentage point and drop all personal tax surcharges once the sales tax was in place.

Total Impact

The White Paper argued that the proposed tax reforms would stimulate the economy, by offering greater economic incentives and inducements to investment and greater competitiveness for Canadian exports. The net impact would be some increase in inflation as previously untaxed services and some goods became subject to tax, but this would be neutralized to a degree by a some price reductions in goods presently taxed at a higher rate.

The White Paper maintained that the revenue effects of these proposals over the next five years would be neutral: tax revenues would not increase as a result. However, the proposals would make the tax system more stable and revenue generation more predictable, which, over the long run, would increase the government's revenue-raising capacity. The shift from personal to sales taxes would have the same effect.

THE ADVENT OF THE GST

(p. 23). A federal/provincial working group would meet over the summer in preparation for a fall federal/provincial meeting of finance ministers (p. 81). The White Paper presented three possible options: a national sales tax (which would replace both federal and provincial sales taxes), a goods and services tax, or a value-added tax (the latter two involving the federal government acting alone). The government clearly preferred the first option: "An entirely new sales tax offers an opportunity to extend the reach of tax reform beyond the federal level to achieve truly national reform" (p. 22), what Michael Wilson would describe as "a major national achievement" if attained.[39] However, "should a consensus with the provinces on a national system not be achievable, the government will replace the current federal sales tax with a federal-only multi-stage tax."[40]

As in numerous earlier reports and analyses, the White Paper posed the re-placement of the MST as a potential contributor to renewed economic growth. No longer would the MST act as a tax on inputs, misallocate resources, and give imports an advantage over exports. Thus, output and employment would increase, investment would be spurred, and Canada's trade balance would improve. Moreover, a simpler and more comprehensive tax would reduce administrative and compliance problems and make revenue generation more stable—a not in-considerable government ambition. Like reform of direct taxes, the sales tax reform would be revenue neutral. The White Paper anticipated that comprehen-sive tax reform, in conjunction with personal tax cuts and a refundable sales tax credit (to offset the impact of the sales tax on low-income groups), would generate the same amount of revenue as the existing system—albeit with a different mix.

The White Paper contained no great surprises, as its general principles had been articulated by the government over the previous three years. Moreover, the government had consulted widely with affected parties over the "incremental" period as well as in the period leading up to the release of the White Paper. As a result, despite its "radical" quality, the tax reform process unfolded relatively quietly and smoothly over the next while—at least for stage one of the reform package. The White Paper was released relatively late in the government's term—almost three years into its electoral mandate. With an election anticipated some time in late 1988 or early 1989, the government had not left itself much time to see through the tax reform process before it had to face the electorate. Hence, the two-stage process had considerable procedural logic. As sales tax reform in-volved a more complex transformation of the tax system as well as delicate and daunting negotiations with the provinces, there appeared to be little to no hope of completing the reform before the election. So, despite the tax reform being a package, the government proceeded on two parallel and staggered tracks. This uncoupling of indirect sales tax from direct tax reform had an up side and a down side. By delaying the second-stage sales tax changes until after the next election, the Mulroney government could campaign for re-election on the basis of corporate and personal income tax cuts, leaving public scrutiny of the sales tax until after the election. This was a not unpleasant prospect. But sales tax reform would later be isolated from the more attractive direct tax cuts, which would be long forgotten by the time the sales tax legislation was introduced. As a result, the sales tax reform would be scrutinized more critically and on narrower grounds than as but one ingredient of a comprehensive tax reform package.

The Stage One Reforms

Four days after the release of the White Paper, the House of Commons Standing Committee on Finance and Economic Affairs began examining the stage one White Paper proposals. Over 550 written briefs were submitted to the Committee, and 174 witnesses were heard in ten cities across Canada in September and early October. The Committee issued a report in November 1987.[41] It contained eighty-one recommendations, mostly of a technical nature, and recommended that "the Canadian income tax system be reformed along the lines proposed in the White Paper on Tax Reform" (p. 22). While the Committee's terms of reference involved studying the stage one direct tax reforms, it recommended that there *not* be a separate stage two, but that "parliament enact a law in 1988 to reform the existing sales tax system, such law to become effective as soon as possible thereafter" (p. 111). Both the Liberals and the NDP submitted dissenting reports. The Liberals declared that the proposed personal income tax structure was "blatantly unprogressive...unjust to middle-income earners [and] provides upper-income earners with all-too-generous tax reductions" (p. 154). The NDP pointed out that the White Paper proposals would assign a $90 tax break to families with incomes less than $5,000 but a tax break of $1,615 to families with incomes above $100,000 (p. 160). Both parties were critical of the proposed sales tax's regressive qualities; as the NDP argued, "the White Paper fails to significantly change the overall balance between progressive and regressive elements of the tax system, and indeed anticipates an increase in the regressive sales tax" (p. 158). The opposition parties, then, spoke the language and values that had informed the tax system being replaced by the government—the language of progressivity and a bias to personal taxes—while focusing their attacks more forcefully on the forthcoming sales tax than on the stage one reforms. In addition, both parties criticized the government for splitting stage two from stage one and thereby making it difficult if not impossible to properly evaluate the stage one proposals. It was also seen to have been politically motivated, in order to assign maximum benefits to the government before the election.

The Senate Committee on Banking, Trade and Commerce also studied the tax reform proposals. It received over 2,000 letters and 138 briefs, and held public hearings from mid-September through late November. It issued a report[42] on 1 December that was remarkably supportive of the government's proposals, given that the committee, being drawn from the Senate, was Liberal-dominated: "The Committee endorses the broad themes underlying tax reform" (p. 17). While it argued that the middle-class income tax rate was too high, and that government proposals were too hard on investors, the Committee made but twenty-nine recommendations, none of which was damning. Indeed, with respect to the proposed sales tax, it reported that "the arguments in favour of replacing the MST with some version of a multi-stage or value-added tax are very persuasive"(p. 9) and "the Committee is pleased that the Government has finally taken the initiative to replace the distortion-laden MST with a multi-stage tax"(p. 17). Like the House of Commons committee, it criticized the two-stage approach, arguing that this needlessly complicated the tax reform process. Thus, it recommended "that as soon as is practicable the Government introduce legislation to implement a broad-based multi-stage sales tax to replace the existing federal sales tax system"(p. 55).

On 16 December 1987 Finance Minister Wilson responded to the House of Commons Committee report and tabled the notice of ways and means that would enable the government to activate the stage one changes on 1 January 1988. In the process, he confirmed that tax reform would continue to unfold in two stages—despite the Committees' urging that he proceed immediately with the stage two sales tax reforms.[43] The stage one process moved quickly in the new year. The 360-page draft legislation—Bill C-139—was released in April for consultation purposes. The bill was given first reading on 30 June; second reading moved briskly during the week of 18 to 25 July. The House of Commons Standing Committee on Finance reported back quickly on 19 August, and the House of Commons considered the report during 23-25 August. Third reading was completed on 29 August. The Senate processed the legislation in ten days—a period that included the Labour Day break—and passed Bill C-139 on 9 September.

The first stage in one of the most significant attempts at tax reform in Canada was legislatively realized in only ten weeks. This reflected a number of factors. The reform of the direct tax system was in tune with the political and ideological mood of the moment: there was widespread public feeling that income taxes were too high, so that legislation to reduce taxes—no matter how unevenly—was not a matter against which the population was likely to rebel. While there undoubtedly was substantial unevenness in the benefits that stage one assigned to individuals and groups, there were no obvious losers in the process. Moreover, the important players in tax reform—high-income earners, investors, the tax and accounting world, corporations—were all supporters of stage one. The Minister and Department of Finance had undertaken wide consultations; the legislative process began after a nearly two year pre-legislative stage that conditioned public reaction to the legislation. And stage one did not create a new tax or raise taxes. So, once the legislation was introduced by Canada Day, it had no great difficulties in being passed just after Labour Day—a very brisk passage indeed, for such far-reaching legislation.

This was not, however, the fate awaiting stage two of the tax reform process.

The Stage Two Reforms: The Goods and Services Tax

Stage two was infinitely more complicated than stage one and took five times as long to see through, even though the government commanded a healthy majority both before and after the 1988 election. Part of the problem for the government was the fact that the stage two sales tax reform was processed separately from the stage one direct tax reforms. The latter stage had involved a tax cut, part of whose logic (and financing) was related to the proposed replacement of the federal sales tax by the Goods and Services Tax. But retail sales taxes are hopelessly unpopular: they are visible, and consumers are reminded of them constantly as each purchase is made. Whatever financial, logical, and psychological cushioning the GST might have received from the cut in direct taxes was long forgotten once the Conservative government proceeded with stage two after the fall 1988 election. As a result, while the Conservatives could reasonably claim that they were replacing one tax by another, the perception was that they were creating a new tax—an invisible tax was being replaced by a visible one. And governmental promises to the contrary notwithstanding, it was widely if not universally believed that the GST would increase taxes.

The process surrounding the reform of the MST—the federal sales tax—began in July 1986, when Michael Wilson announced that the government planned to replace the MST with a broad-based, multi-stage sales tax extending to the retail level. A year later the June 1987 White Paper declared the government's intention to introduce either a national sales tax, a value-added tax, or a goods and services tax—depending on negotitations with the provinces, which were to take place that summer. Regardless of the outcome of these negotiations, the MST was to be replaced. For the next two years, the stage two sales tax reform unfolded quietly and discreetly in the shadows of the stage one tax reforms, the free trade negotiations, and the 1988 election.

As noted above, committees of the House of Commons and the Senate supported replacing the MST with a tax similar to that proposed by the government. Indeed, both reports recommended that the government move immediately to introduce the improved sales tax concurrently with the direct tax reforms. This recommendation was not taken up by the federal government. It hoped to create a national sales tax system, and this required extended negotiations with the provinces (see below). The opposition in the House of Commons assaulted the tax reform in general, and the sales tax in particular, for making the tax system regressive. But the Senate Committee was more sanguine about the likely impact of the sales tax:

> The proposed low-income sales tax credits, provided they are substantial, will go a long way to alleviating the regressive nature of the multi-stage tax. Indeed, if the introduction of the sales tax is accompanied, as indicated in the White Paper, by a lowering of marginal rates for the middle-income class and by generous tax credits for low-income persons and families, the Committee is satisfied that an increased degree of sales taxation can be integrated successfully and fairly into the overall tax system.[44]

Reaction to the idea of a national sales tax was mixed. Public focus in these early days was on whether the federal tax would be imposed on food. Polls indicated that 68 per cent of Canadians were opposed to a broad-based national sales tax and 93 per cent were "very" or "somewhat" uncomfortable with a tax on groceries. On the other hand, the Canadian Chamber of Commerce, along with most business associations, supported the idea of a broad-based tax that did not exempt groceries. Sectorally affected groups like the Canadian Council of Grocery Distributors were predictably critical: the Council noted that a national sales tax of 8 per cent would increase food prices by 12.6 per cent and would force low-income families "to change their diet or eat less food." The House of Commons Finance Committee report did not comment directly on this issue (the dissenting reports did), but concluded that "there are ways of effectively addressing the one major problem of relieving the tax burden on those with low incomes."[45]

Responding to enormous pressure from the public, the Conservative caucus, and the Prime Minister's Office, Finance Minister Wilson put the issue to rest on 10 December 1988. Up to this point, Wilson had refused to reject the idea of a tax on food for two reasons. Any exemption would lower the amount of revenue generated by the tax, and a serious exemption, such as one for food, would result in an enormous loss of revenue; a higher sales rax tax rate would be needed to attain a given revenue target. Moreover, once any exemption was made, this would open the floodgates for exemptions claims by other "worthy" causes. Emerging from a meeting of provincial finance ministers, Wilson relented and declared that "a tax on groceries is not on the table. We all share a basic commitment to ensuring that the design of the tax should be consistent with the views of Canadians. This is an area where I think Canadians instinctively feel there shouldn't be a tax."[46]

The sales tax issue remained quiet through the winter and after. In February, half the members of the House of Commons Standing Committee on Finance and Economic Affairs travelled to New Zealand, where a goods and services tax had been implemented in October 1986. The committee had twenty-two meetings with the architect of the New Zealand tax—Minister of Finance Roger Douglas—and his colleagues and officials. In mid-March, the committee issued a report. New Zealand's is a thoroughly comprehensive sales tax, with virtually no exemptions (only financial services and residential rents are exempt). The report indicated that the tax was simple and had been accepted with a minimum of public discontent. The committee accounted for this remarkable achievement as follows:

- Economic conditions were so bad in New Zealand at the time, that there was a willingness to accept fundamental policy change.
- With no exemptions, and a single rate, the tax was easy to understand and comply with.
- The advent of the tax involved extensive consultations, dispersal of information, debate, and a public-information campaign; eighteen months elapsed between the White Paper on the tax and the date it took effect.
- The key issue had been the distributional one: the impact of the tax on the poor. This concern—and the associated concern about a tax on food—was assuaged by *simultaneously* introducing substantial personal tax cuts and major increases in social security benefits to guarantee immediate compensation for the impact of the new tax.[47]

This report was somewhat ominous, as the Canadian experience to this point appeared to be out of tune with that of New Zealand. First, Ottawa had already committed itself to tax-free food. Second, New Zealand's unitary system allowed a very simple retail tax, with little compliance problems; as negotiations with the provinces dragged on, it appeared that the Canadian government might have to impose a retail tax parallel to provincial ones, which would result in a complicated system sure to upset both businesses and consumers. Third, and perhaps most crucially, years would have passed between the the personal tax cuts and the introduction of the new sales tax. This weakened the government's capacity to allay concerns about the regressive distributional aspects of the sales tax.

THE ADVENT OF THE GST

Moreover, the government had yet to really explain how the tax would work, and could not do so until negotiations with the provinces were completed.

Nonetheless, these dies were cast, or about to be cast. The debate over the Free Trade Agreement took centre stage through late 1987 and most of 1988, dominating the fall federal election. In October 1988 Finance Minister Wilson made a "read my lips" President Bush-like response to a query about the proposed sales tax being a tax increase: "The bottom line is that the sales tax will not be used to raise the revenues of the government of Canada."[48] Not until April 1989 did the sales tax re-emerge on the public agenda, in a manner that complicated matters immensely: negotiations with the provinces over the sales tax had broken down.

Back in June 1987, when the White Paper was released, provincial reaction to the idea of a national sales tax had been mildly positive if not totally promising. Only Alberta—which had no retail sales tax—expressed total uninterest in participating in a federal/provincial tax. Others declared that the opportunity for tax "harmonization" was sufficient reason to consider the change to a national sales tax. As Ontario's Treasurer Robert Nixon put it, "If the federal government proposals to reform the federal sales tax result in a simpler and more progressive system...I believe the provinces should consider coordinating their sales tax structure with the federal system."[49]

In late 1986 a National Sales Tax Working Group was set up, comprised of federal and provincial officials. Its purpose was to explore the idea of a joint national sales tax, and it met regularly over the next eighteen months. According to L.R. Leonard, Ontario's representative, the "meetings were characterized by a level of good will, energy and constructive advice."[50] Early indications were that a national sales tax was attainable: in the summer of 1987 one official declared, "I think you are going to have enough support from the provinces. If you've got four or five provinces, then we're off to the races."[51] The provinces were enticed by the prospect of expanding into the as-yet untaxed area of services: this would allow them to cut their taxes and increase their revenues at the same time. In July 1987 officials meeting in PEI announced that they would present the results of their efforts on tax integration to a fall meeting of finance ministers. However, progress was slow and completion of negotiations was extended to the spring. By year's end the provinces were still taking a cautious attitude, and left the ball in Ottawa's court.[52] In the 10 February 1988 budget, Finance Minister Wilson noted that the progress of the sales tax negotiations with the provinces "so far has been good, [but] we have more work to do."[53] Negotiations dragged on through the remainder of 1988, interrupted by the FTA debates and the fall 1988 federal election. The federal side remained optimistic: "There's an increasingly shared

Inset IV

HOW THE GST WORKS

The Goods and Services Tax is a multi-stage sales tax culminating in a tax at the retail level. "Multi-stage" means that the tax is applied *at each stage* in the movement of a good or service through importing, production, distribution and final sale to the consumer. It is a kind of value-added tax, used widely around the world (forty-eight countries use it, including nineteen of the twenty-four members of the Organization for Economic Co-operation and Development—the OECD). Using a device called an input tax credit, the GST eliminates taxing inputs (tax cascading), with the tax ultimately paid by the consumer. The tax works as follows, as a tree becomes a dining room table (a 7% rate is used).

Company	Activity	Tax Charged	Credit	Net Tax
Sawmill	Lumber sold for $100	$7		$7
Woodworker	Table sold for $300	$21	$7	$14
Wholesaler	Sale to retailer, $400	$28	$21	$7
Retailer	Final sale, $600	$42	$28	$14

Total tax paid by consumer $42

A sawmill company chops down some trees, manufactures some lumber, and sells it to a woodworker for $100. The woodworker pays $107, the $100 price of the lumber plus the 7% sales tax. The net tax paid is $7, as there was no previous tax on the wood.

understanding among the federal government and the provinces on the basic architecture of an integrated national system. There are beginnings of light at the end of the tunnel."[54] Finally, in the spring of 1989, negotiations appeared to be coming to a close. As a provincial official put it, "The elected people now have to choose either to do it or not to do it, and then we'll figure out how."[55] L.R. Leonard has noted that "For all issues, either solutions were hammered out or, at the very least, a narrow range of options was agreed to: the end result was a

The woodworker then makes a table, which is sold to a wholesaler for $300. $200 in value is added—the $300 price of the table minus the $100 cost of the wood. While he or she will charge $21 tax on the sale of the table—7% of $300—the woodworker will send only $14 to the government. This is because $7 of the $21 of tax on the table *has already been sent to the government by the sawmill company*. The GST applies only to the value added at each stage—at this stage, the $200—so the net tax is $14, or 7% of $200. This is what is meant when it is said that the GST does not tax inputs, or avoids tax cascading.

The wholesaler then sells the table to a retailer for $400. The 7% GST will be imposed on this sale, yielding $28. But only $7 will be remitted by the retailer to the government. The value added is $100 (i.e. $400 minus $300), so the GST applies to the $100, or is $7. Of the $28 tax, $21 is a credit for the retailer (effectively the $14 net tax already remitted by the woodworker and the $7 net tax already remitted by the wholesaler).

The table is finally sold to a consumer for $600 plus the 7% GST, or $42. The retailer collects the $42, but remits only $14—7% on the $200 value added. The other $28 is the credit for tax paid on the purchase, comprising the $7, $14, and $7 paid at each of the previous stages. The total tax of $42 is thus paid by the consumer, who does not receive an input tax credit, so bears the full $42 impact of the 7% GST on $600. What has happened is that the tax charged at each level of production and distribution is fully refunded at subsequent stages, until the final sale is made to the consumer.

There are two categories of exceptions to this procedure. Tax-free goods—such as groceries—see no taxes charged on sales, but the seller can still claim full input tax credits. Tax-exempt goods and services—such as residential rents and daycare and medical services—have no tax charged on sales, but the seller cannot claim input tax credits.

* This example is taken from D.G. Michener (ed), *GST Impact: The Final Countdown* (Don Mills: Deloitte and Touche, 1990), 11.

straight technical report for consideration by the Treasurers and the Minister of Finance."[56]

The finance ministers met in mid-April 1989. The provinces then declared that they were pulling out of negotiations with the federal government over the implementation of a national sales tax. Why did they withdraw from negotiations when, after all, "the National Sales Tax Working Group got very close to an agreement"? According to Leonard, time had been the critical issue. Negotiations had been interrupted for three months as a result of the federal election; passing the national sales tax would have involved all the governments legislating on a complicated matter at the same time; the federal government had called for a January 1991 implementation date, so that by April 1989 Ottawa had no more time for negotiations—it was now or never.[57] All the while, of course, provincial governments had to calculate the political costs and benefits of the national sales tax: potential increased revenues (from the broadening of the provincial sales tax to include services) vs. the political fallout from acting as a tax collector for Ottawa and being identified by the voters as having increased taxes (the combined federal and provincial sales taxes would total in the 15-20 per cent range). In the end, the latter concerns loomed larger.

Thus, in the 27 April 1989 budget, Finance Minister Wilson announced that Ottawa was going to proceed with sales tax reform on its own, without the provinces. Instead of a joint federal/provincial national sales tax, Ottawa would replace the MST with its own retail tax, which would be called the Goods and Services Tax. In a paper released with the budget, Wilson reported that

> Despite the best efforts of both the federal government and the provinces, a national sales tax has proven to be beyond reach. The need to reform the provincial sales tax is simply less pressing than the urgent need to replace the federal sales tax. Perhaps after reform at the federal level is complete, the idea of an integrated national tax can be explored once again.[58]

Ottawa was doubly penalized for the failed conclusion of two years of federal-provincial negotiations. It could have proceeded on its own back in 1987 (admittedly with some difficulties), in which case the GST could have been packaged more attractively with the direct tax cuts. The attempt to create a national sales tax system had resulted in a politically costly two-year negotiating delay—for which the federal government gained nothing. Now it would have to accept the glare of public scrutiny of the tax on its own. But by this time it had no choice. It had to accept this second political burden in order to get the tax implemented by January 1991—Ottawa wanted the tax to be implemented well before the expected 1992 election. These are the hard realities of federal/provincial fiscal politics.

It was late April 1989, then, when Ottawa was first able to give any details about the new tax—three years after Wilson's July 1986 announcement that the MST would be replaced and two years after the White Paper on Tax Reform. Nonetheless, the budget's presentation was still pretty sketchy (it was only a fortnight since negotiations with the provinces had broken down): the government planned to issue a detailed technical plan in early summer (it was not released until August) with legislation planned to be introduced by the fall (it was not introduced until January 1990). Time would continue to plague stage two of tax reform. As an interim revenue-generating measure—the defict continuing to be the major focus of budgetary policy—the still-surviving MST was raised from 12 per cent to 13 per cent.

The budget paper reviewed the familiar failings of the MST:

- The MST taxes inputs, resulting in tax cascading, higher prices, and diminished export competitiveness.
- The MST is the only consumption tax in the world that benefits imports over domestic goods, the latter taxed one-third higher.
- As only one-third of goods and services are actually subject to the MST, the tax distorts prices, particularly those of services, that are not taxed.
- The MST is an unreliable source of revenue, because of numerous exemptions, multiple rates, clever tax avoidance schemes, court challenges—all of that make the tax a weak revenue producer for the government.
- The tax is hidden from consumers, and is costly and unfair.

In total, the Depart of Finance estimated that the MST constrained domestic output by about \$9 billion on an annual basis—about 1.4 per cent of domestic output.[59]

In place of the MST, the government proposed to implement a Goods and Services Tax—at a 9 per cent level. The tax would be imposed at every stage in the production and distribution cycle through to the retail level (see Inset IV). Firms would charge the 9 per cent GST on all of their sales, but would be reimbursed by the government for the taxes paid on inputs (input tax credit). This system of taxation would be far more reliable (as the tax would be easy to collect and difficult to avoid), more neutral (it would be imposed on all economic transactions), and more rational (it would remove taxes on inputs, not favour imports over exports, not distort prices or decisions). The proposed 9 per cent rate would generate sufficient revenue to

- replace the MST revenues;
- allow a further income tax cut for the middle class; and
- fund a new GST refundable tax credit to compensate low-income families for the nex tax; the credit would be refundable and paid quarterly, with the first payment made in advance of the start-up of the new tax.[60]

The goal would be to devise rates and levels to ensure that families with incomes less than \$30,000 would be better off after the GST than before it. A number of goods and services would be tax free (basic groceries, prescription drugs, medical devices) or tax exempt (residential rents; daycare; health and dental, legal aid and educational services)—the latter group would have no taxes charged on sales, but input tax credits would not be claimed, whereas the former would involve the claiming of full input tax credits.[61]

The government's presentation of the MST's faults and the economic benefits of its replacement had now begun to sound like a broken record. These were claims that had been made by the Mulroney government since 1986 (indeed, by other governments since 1926), and they had become less urgent in the repetition. The government's case had by now—five years after it was first elected and three years into the tax reform process—lost its sense of immediacy.

The immediate reaction to the government's planned GST was predictable. A majority of businesses reported that the GST would hurt them, or were unsure of its impact; 70 per cent of the population opposed the GST; the Canadian Labour Congress and the Canadian Council on Social Development complained about the regressive nature of the tax; the Canadian Federation of Independent Business feared that the GST and provincial sales taxes would in combination create an administrative nightmare; the Consumers Association of Canada saw the GST as a "cash cow" that the government would milk at ever higher rates; the spectre was raised of the need for an army of tax administrators to collect the tax; the Conference Board predicted that seventy-two thousand jobs would be lost in 1991 while real disposable income would fall by $5.5 billion and inflation would rise to 7.3 per cent; there was an increasing sense that the exemption on food was a mistake, that it would create a series of inequities (e.g., GST applied on take-out pizza, but not on frozen pizza bought at a grocery store); particular sectors such as tourism and candy-makers feared for their future (foie gras purchased in a grocery store would not be taxed, but candy would be: confectioners pressured the government to declare candy to be a food)...the litany of problems, complaints, and anxieties was seemingly endless and would continue to grow.[62] The most intense complaint at this stage related to the question of the tax's visibility. Finance Minister Wilson insisted that the government did not have the constitutional authority to force retailers to show the GST separately on their sales slips. This was a hot political issue, for a separate accounting of the GST would force retailers to make two separate sales tax calculations at the cash register, given the continuation of the separate provincial retail sales tax. Wilson insisted instead that retailers simply post a sign indicating that prices included the GST. Critics claimed that Wilson was defying his own demand that the GST undo the MST's invisibility.[63]

The GST remained a hazy and general target through the spring and summer of 1989. The government's April budget announcement was short on details of how the tax would work, and the accompanying GST paper was a rehash of old arguments and generalizations. The government promised to fill in the details in

THE ADVENT OF THE GST

a technical report on the GST in the early summer, but this was not released until 8 August, three months after the April budget. Then the fireworks exploded.

The *Goods and Services Tax Technical Paper*[64] was the first detailed outline of the proposed GST, and was informed by the two major economic issues of the time: the deficit and the FTA. The report presented "the GST['s] contribut[ion] to the deficit reduction effort" as the number one goal. This declaration appeared to fly in the face of the government's assurances that the tax would be revenue neutral and confirmed critics' worst fears that the GST involved a tax increase. The paper gave even greater emphasis to the GST's role in increasing international competitiveness, a crucial item given the opening up of the North American market by the Free Trade Agreement. Issues raised included the following:

- The report rejected exemptions as the way to protect low-income groups. Over and above the problems of narrowing and complicating the tax system, upper income groups benefit more from exemptions because they consume more; better to target a sales tax to those who need it (pp. 6-7).

- At the proposed 9 per cent rate, the GST would generate $24 billion in 1991 dollars, sufficient to replace MST revenues of $18.5 billion and fund the GST tax credit and decreases in personal income taxes—including dropping the middle tax rate from 26 per cent to 25 per cent—and other benefits amounting to $5.4 billion (pp. 9, 43-4).

- The GST would not be applied to residential rents or to the resale of existing houses (tax-exempt goods) but would be levied on the sale of new homes. A tax rebate would offset this tax increase.[65]

- Families with incomes of less than $30,000 would be better off with the combined effects of the GST and housing and income-assistance measures (pp. 13, 23-26).

- The GST would cause a one-time increase in the Consumer Price Index of 2 1/4 per cent (pp. 39-43).

- The question of GST visibility was clumsily addressed by *suggesting* that the GST be shown separately on cash register receipts; because of the technical difficulties of showing two separate sales taxes, prominently displayed signs—indicating whether or not the GST was included in the shelf price—would suffice.[66]

- Output could grow by as much as $9 billion, with $4.5 billion of this within four years of implementation; employment could rise by sixty thousand new jobs by 1992.[67]

There was nothing terribly new or startling in the technical paper, but it gave the GST shape and focus and made the tax appear considerably closer to reality. The immediate focus of reaction was the GST's alleged revenue neutrality. Both the Liberals and the NDP criticized the government for raising taxes: "On the one hand, it [the GST] is supposed to help reduce the deficit; on the other hand it is supposed to be revenue neutral," declared Audrey McLaughlin. From this point on, no one believed the government's claim that the GST would not raise new revenues. This substantially undermined the legitimacy of the GST and neutralized the government's economic claims about its merits. For most Canadians, the GST came to be seen as just another tax grab.

The language used to describe the GST heated up. Liberal leadership hopeful Paul Martin Jr. called it "immoral," NDP finance critic Nelson Riis described it as "cruel, brutal and mean," and opposition leader Turner claimed "this sales tax has got me mad." Opponents claimed that the GST would produce an administrative nightmare. The NDP's Lorne Nystrom argued that the sales tax credits would be only partially effective in protecting low-income groups from the GST, as the credits were indexed only for increases in the inflation rate above 3 per cent: "So built right into the system is a guarantee you're going to fall further and further behind each and every year." By the end of the summer, Liberal MPs had started a national campaign to collect signatures of Canadians who opposed the GST. Said Douglas Young, "There is a tax revolt brewing out there," as thousands of Canadians signed petitions against the GST."[68] Indeed, in a 21 August Gallup Poll, only 23 per cent of Canadians supported the new tax.[69]

There was, though, a hard core of business support for the GST. Robert Brown, vice-chairman of Price-Waterhouse, dclared that "the GST is the most positive development in Canadian taxation in twenty-five years." Roger Hamel, president of the Canadian Chamber of Commerce, stated that the GST is "appropriate, fair and equitable." The Canadian Manufacturers' Association was adamant: "If it [the GST] doesn't come in, there will be...an explosion in the business community. We have been promised stage two of tax reform to restore our competitive edge. If we don't get it, we will be absolutely frustrated."[70]

But other elements of the business community were opposed to the tax:

- The Canadian Restaurant and Foodservices Association—with over seven thousand members—said that Wilson "should go back to the drawing board.... Either food should be taxed or it should be exempted...[the GST] has failed to meet the test of fairness and simplicity."

- The tourist industry claimed that "visitors...are not going to be impressed with 20 per cent worth of sales taxes"; the Conference Board's Tourism Research Institute predicted a $1 billion loss for the industry by 1993.

- The Canadian Federation of Independent Business concluded that Canada will be subjected to "the worst sales tax regime in the world"; its president, John Bulloch, described the GST as "the most anti-consumer, anti-small business sales tax system in the world."[71]

Non-business groups also lined up against the GST. The National Action Committee on the Status of Women claimed that the GST was harmful to women: "We have moved away from a progressive income tax system towards a regressive tax on consumption. That always hurts women most because they are in the lower income groups."

The Canadian Labour Congress accused the government of trying to make labour the scapegoat for the increased inflation that would inevitably result from the GST. Social groups maintained that tax credits were inadequate, were not inflation-proofed, and that low-income groups would be harmed by the GST. Periodical marketers and booksellers criticized the GST as a tax on reading and literacy.[72] There was widespread concern that the GST would increase unemployment (by making machinery cheaper), would actually decrease output over the short term, would set off an inflationary wage-price spiral, and that opportunities would be seized to increase profit margins on the back of the new tax.[73]

The provincial government's reaction to the August technical paper was similarly unsupportive. Quebec finance minister Gerard Levesque described it as a "unilateral gesture incompatible with true federalism." (Quebec would on 30 August 1990 become the first province to join the federal government in adopting the GST). This view was reiterated at the 21 August premiers' meeting in Quebec City, within a communique declaring that the tax "invades traditional areas of provincial jurisdiction" (Newfoundland Treasurer Kitchen characterized it as "a violence against what has been established in Canada") and "jeopardizes the ability of the provinces to meet their constitutional responsibilities." Ontario's David Peterson said, "Scrap it, scrap it," and suggested that Michael Wilson's loss of credibility should lead him to resign; New Brunswick's Frank McKenna warned that it would create a "tax jungle" in Canada; PEI's Joe Ghiz commented that "when you've got 10 provincial premiers agreeing this is not a good tax, I think the federal government should stand up and take heed." Wilson was not fazed by this provincial assault: "All the provinces felt that it was an easy shot to take so why not take it.... They'd like the feds to take the heat..."[74] The provinces' public position was that Ottawa should cut its spending, diminish its bureaucracy, and lower interest rates rather than impose the GST, which, if necessary, should itself be lowered. They also claimed that the GST would force them to raise their own taxes, a claim that Wilson shrugged off as being "unwarranted."[75] Confronting the premiers at the November First Ministers' Conference in Ottawa, Prime Minister Mulroney rode the high road: "If we ducked the sales tax issue and avoided the tough decisions on restructuring the economy, we would be passing

Inset V

TESTIMONY BEFORE THE BLENKARN COMMITTEE*

The House of Commons Standing Committee on Finance and Economics—the Blenkarn Committee—held public hearings on the Technical Paper on the Goods and Services Tax. These hearings were held between 18 September and 26 October 1989 in cities across Canada. Over three hundred witnesses were heard from 158 groups and organizations—a listing of witnesses runs to sixteen pages. This was the most thorough public airing given to the GST. Business organizations representing the "commanding heights" comprised the only identifiable sector favouring the government's proposed GST. For the rest, testimony was either highly critical or suggested substantive alterations in the tax. There was universal agreement that the existing MST was totally flawed.

CRITICS OF THE GST

- The *Consumers Association of Canada* was opposed to the GST (and all consumption taxes) and favoured replacing lost revenue through raising income taxes. It feared that the GST would allow increased tax fraud and that a mushrooming bureaucracy would be required to collect the tax.

- The *Canadian Federation of Independent Business* claimed that "the GST violates all of the conditions for a well-constructed consumption tax. The rate is high, there are many exemptions, the tax is inordinately complex to administer, and will create many distortions throughout the economy." Of its eighty-two thousand members, 96.8 per cent opposed the tax.

- The *National Council on Welfare* argued that protection for low-income groups was inadequate because the sales tax credit was not fully indexed.

- The *Canadian Resturant and Food Services Association* claimed that prices in its domain would rise by 15% in 1991, and demanded an exemption from the GST on all food.

- The *Conference Board of Canada* predicted that the GST-induced jump in the inflation rate would result in a wage-price spiral.

- The *Canadian Labour Congress* "emphatically reject[ed] the argument that workers must accept a 'one-time' cut in real wages to contain the problem of inflation which will result from the GST." The sales tax was seen as bearing most heavily on those who cannot afford to pay. "What we need is a major shift from regressive sales taxes to progressive taxes."

- The *BC Federation of Labour* warned that unions would seek wage increases of 10-14% in 1991 to compensate for the effects of the GST.

- The *One-Voice Seniors Network* claimed that the GST would push low- and middle-income seniors into poverty. Increases in a progressive income tax system were seen as the preferable way to increase revenues.

- The *GST Task Force of the Canadian Bankers Association* estimated that the GST would increase the cost of financial services by 9%.

- The *Canadian Home Builders Association* argued that "the GST as it applies to housing will constitute a major assault on affordability," increasing the price of an average home by $3,000.

- The *Retail Council of Canada* claimed that adding a federal sales tax system would cost Canadian businesses $2 billion annually in collection and administration expenses.

- *Canada's Funeral Directors* warned that the imposition of the GST might make funerals unaffordable for many Canadians, forcing municipalities to bury more of the dead. It claimed that funerals should be considered an essential service and not be taxed.

- The *Taxpayers' Council on National Issues* declared, "The GST...is a regressive tax. I do not know why this is hard to understand, but the nature of it is regressive. And if you are looking at tax reform, how can you possibly introduce a regressive tax? That is unfathomable."

- The *Pro-Canada Network* claimed that the GST is a free-trade-induced form of taxation that is a "suffering" tax because it is regressive and is part of a package of regressive tax reforms devised to reduce government responsibility for social programs and public services. It argued for progressive tax reforms.

- The *Economic Development Committee of the Assembly of First Nations* stated that "the imposition of a goods and services tax...violates aboriginal and treaty rights."

SUPPORTERS OF THE TAX

- The *Business Council on National Issues* (representing 150 of Canada's biggest corporations) endorsed the GST "as a matter of the highest priority," but recommended that the tax be cut to 7% and the exemption on groceries be eliminated.

- The *Canadian Manufacturers' Association* stated its belief that "a GST is both appropriate and necessary," but recommended harmonization with the provinces, reduction of exemptions, and higher visibility.

- The *Canadian Exporters' Association* "support[ed] the fundamental objective of sales tax reform."

- The *Canadian Chamber of Commerce* reported, though, that it had a "mandate...to withdraw support if there are not substantial changes in the present proposal." These included harmonization of the federal and provincial tax base, a common sales tax collection system, a comprehensive tax base, increased visibility, and use of the GST revenue for replacing MST revenue and low-income protection (i.e., no further personal tax cut), with the remaining revenue to be used for deficit reduction.

---

*   House of Commons, Standing Committee on Finance and Economics, Minutes of Proceedings and Evidence, No. 31, 18 September 1989, 56-61; No. 33, 19 September, 1989, 6; No. 34, 19 September 1989, 36-7; No. 38, 21 September 1989, 31; No. 40, 26 September 1989, 35-6; No. 45, 28 September 1989, 4-5, 32; No. 59, 10 October 1989, 6,9; No. 72, 19 October 1989, 68; No. 78, 24 October 1989, 5-6; No. 80, 25 October 1989, 5. Globe and Mail, 19, 20, 21, 22, 27, 28 September, 3, 12, 14 October 1989.

the buck to our children, leaving them a legacy of hardship and debt they might never be able to overcome." But the premiers reconfirmed their opposition to the GST (despite claims by Wilson that privately they supported the GST). Their antagonism was fired by a Conference Board study (albeit its most pessimistic model), which showed that the GST would push up inflation by 3 per cent and interest rates by 2 per cent in the first year, depress economic growth by 2.7 per cent over 1991-93, kill 185,000 jobs, and reduce provincial revenues by $6.9 billion over three years. The statistical war continued when Ottawa released its own paper, showing flaws in the Conference Board study and indicating the myriad economic benefits of the GST.[76] As 1989 came to an end, Wilson announced that the provinces had agreed to discuss the co-ordination of the collection of the federal and provincial sales taxes (to save possibly $200 million), but admitted early in the new year that "as a practical matter in the immediate future [a national GST] is not possible."[77]

Assaulted from all corners, the federal government followed New Zealand's example and initiated a campaign to sell the GST to the public. This campaign plan was similar to that organized by Ottawa during the free trade campaign: GST brochures were distributed in grocery stores, newspaper and TV ads were placed, an information hotline was set up, letters were sent to constituents, speeches were delivered to local service clubs and chambers of commerce. The government budgeted $7.6 million for this campaign (for the period September to April), which placed it in even hotter political water and further weakened support for the GST. As soon as they ran, government advertisements were deemed to be "false and misleading advertising" by the opposition. Typically, a newspaper ad would begin, "On January 1, 1991, Canada's Federal Sales Tax system will change. Please save this copy. It explains the changes and the reasons for them." The opposition claimed that the ads gave the false impression that Parliament had already changed the tax: "It's an attempt to fool the people into thinking that this is it and there's no use protesting," complained the Liberals' Herb Gray. Liberal MP Don Boudria thundered, "When are we going to get some *glasnost* in Canada? When are we going to get a government that stops using taxpayers' dollars to manipulate public opinion?" The NDP's Lorne Nystrom termed the campaign "flagrant propaganda for the Conservative Party." To the government's discomfort and embarassment, House of Commons Speaker John Fraser more or less agreed. He criticized the "objectionable" GST advertisement and warned the government that it should not be repeated.[78]

While the government fumbled its efforts to market the GST—leading to the setting up of an internal task force of the government to deal with this "management problem"[79]—the technical paper on the GST had been sent for scrutiny to the House of Commons Standing Committee on Economics and Finance, where it sat for the next three months. The committee was chaired by the entertainingly loose-tongued and unabashedly pro-GST Conservative MP Don Blenkarn. He described opponents of the GST as "out to lunch" and, reacting to an anti-GST rally in Alberta, he said, "I've never seen such stupidity in all my life. I guess what we ought to do is send a bunch of grade 5 school teachers out here." (Prime Minister Mulroney defended Blenkarn, musing that "We all know the Chairman of the finance committee is known for things other than the elegance of his language.") Blenkarn claimed that one of the GST's main attractions was to make taxation more transparent; terming it the Gouging and Screwing Tax, he declared that "we may have been gouging and screwing you with the [MST]. Now you know we are gouging and screwing you."[80]

The committee was hopelessly partisan, the Liberal and NDP members wanting the tax to be dropped altogether, the Conservative members supporting the GST's principles, if not all of the details. These political divisions made the committee hearings quite rambunctious, with the chairman's behaviour only exacerbating matters. Whatever role the committee process might have had in creating consensus around—or even understanding of—the tax measure was smothered in partisanship. Political divisions resulted in the submission of dissenting reports along with the committee report in late November. The committee heard 274 sets of witnesses and received over 1,100 briefs and other representations (a sample of which can be seen in Inset V). Critics—far in the majority—ranged from seniors' and labour organizations to restauranteurs and funeral directors, each of which saw the GST as producing a calamity for its members. The minority group of supporters comprised those business organizations representing the commanding heights of Canadian capitalism: exporters, manufacturers, the large corporations. Somewhat surprisingly, the Canadian Chamber of Commerce reported that its members had mandated it to withdraw its support of the GST unless the government proceeded with some major changes, including harmonization of sales taxes with the provinces, joint collection, increased visibility, and fewer exemptions.[81] There was substantial anticipation surrounding the release of the Blenkarn committee report. Its work had been highly visible and well covered by the media. Rumours had abounded about plans to substantially revise the tax, and the committee's garrulous chairman kept dropping hints about various recommendations that would ease the burdens of the GST. Given the widespread and deep antipathy shown towards the tax, the government would have to take a critical report very seriously. As the committee process came to an end, the Liberal and NDP members walked out of the joint efforts to write the report. "There's no point in participating any longer," stated NDP finance critic Lorne Nystrom, "We have a fundamental disagreement on approach," a view echoed by Liberal members.[82]

The Blenkarn report was issued on 27 November 1989, three long and difficult months after the release of the technical paper. The report was 250 pages long and contained a remarkable eighty-six recommendations for changes; this did not include the dissenting Liberal and NDP reports.[83] The report concurred with the government view that the existing MST should be abolished and replaced with a broadly based consumption tax. It said that a national sales tax would be the ideal but, in the absence of an agreement with the provinces, the GST was viable and acceptable, as was the January 1991 implementation date. However, it recommended that the proposed rate be lowered from 9 per cent to 7 per cent. It proposed to finance the lost revenue as follows:

- dropping the proposed 1 per cent decrease in the middle-class personal tax rate;
- lowering the level of GST credits proportionate to the decrease in the GST tax burden;
- increasing taxes on alcohol and tobacco; and
- levying a 5 per cent real estate trade-up tax on the extra cost of the real estate as an individual trades up (e.g., if one were to sell one house for $200,000 and buy another for $250,000, the 5 per cent tax would be levied on the $50,000 trade-up).

The report made a number of other interesting comments and recommendations:

- It rejected proposals that provincial governments be forced to *not* impose their sales taxes on top of the GST (as this cascading behaviour was already practiced).
- Consumers should be informed in retail outlets by signs indicating whether the posted price includes the GST or not, but retailers should *not* be forced to quote a pre-tax price.
- A national sales tax collection agency should be created, to save on administrative costs.
- The GST could be both revenue neutral *and* generate revenue for deficit reduction, because of its positive impact on the rate of economic growth; the "tax dividend" should be used to lower the deficit.

A considerable number of the recommendations dealt with technical matters, particularly with regard to charities and non-profit organizations (twenty-one recommendations), business practices and expenses, and tourism. There were some curiosities, like a proposal to make provincial lotteries tax exempt. The controversial issue of only partially indexing tax credits was to be studied further, in the context of a review of the relationship between the tax and social security systems. The report endorsed the zero-rating on groceries.

The Liberals' dissenting report claimed that the GST proposal was too flawed to be patched up, as the Blenkarn group was trying to do. It argued that the tax was ill-timed at the start of a recession, and threatened to push the economy into a depression; was not revenue neutral but a "tax grab"; was an administrative nightmare for small business; was regressive and hurt low-income Canadians; was invisible, as the government had made its display "voluntary"; hurt key sectors of the economy, such as tourism, women, the service industry, home builders, reading materials, the arts; shifted the tax burden away from corporations to individuals; and involved inadequate consultation. The Liberals' alternative? Start all over again.[84]

The NDP's dissenting report echoed many of the Liberals' concerns. The NDP expressed concern that the new tax system inspired by the 1987 White Paper on tax reform was tilted in favour of upper income groups and corporations and against middle and lower income Canadians. The former were the only ones who supported the tax, while the latter groups would see their taxes forming an increasingly large share of government revenue. The NDP proposed that a royal commission be held but, in the interim, presented a detailed alternative to the GST. This included a rolling back of the MST to 7 per cent; indexing of the enhanced tax credit; increasing taxes on alcohol, cigarettes, and gasoline; a "green tax"; limitation and elimination of tax preferences for the rich; limitation of corporate tax breaks and the introduction of a minimum corporation tax; and a tax on transfers of wealth.[85]

Public reaction to the Blenkarn report was sceptical. There was widespread feeling that Ottawa had proposed a "high" 9 per cent tax in order to allow it to garner support by magnanimously dropping the tax rate to a more "acceptable" 7 per cent at an appropriate moment. Not everyone was sanguine about this prospect. As Alberta Treasurer Dick Johnson put it, "Instead of having an elephant standing on your foot, there is a horse standing on your foot. It's still painful."[86]

As expected, the government took up the Blenkarn report's major recommendation to decrease the proposed tax to 7 per cent. As a prelude to the announcement, Treasury Board President Robert de Cotret announced a $1.4 billion program of budget cuts and fee increases. There were no dramatic cuts, only a series of niggling changes: a few government jets, a parliamentary restaurant, some Parliament Hill statues, $460 million of capital area construction projects, a reduction in postal subsidies for Canadian periodicals, increased fees for national parks and immigration visas, a 3 per cent administrative fee for new student loans.[87]

Three days later, Finance Minister Wilson announced the move to a 7 per cent GST. Over and above the spending cuts, the $5 billion loss in expected revenue would be financed mainly by scrapping the plan to cut the middle-class income tax rate from 26 per cent to 25 per cent, increasing (rather than eliminating) the income tax surcharge on higher income earners from 3 per cent to 5 per cent, reducing the sales tax credit for adults from $275 to $190, and changing the tax rebate on purchases of new homes (the Blenkarn trade-up tax was rejected).[88]

Reaction to the change in the proposed tax rate was again predictable. Big business groups were happy. Tom D'Aquino, president of the Business Council on National Issues, beamed ecstatically: "a 7 per cent GST is a vastly better animal than a 9 per cent rate." Small business was less entralled by the move. John Bulloch, president of the Canadian Federation of Independent Business, declared that "a 7 per cent GST is still a bucket of bilge—just in a smaller bucket." Political cynics and realists saw the "7 per cent solution" as an interim public relations action. Renegade Tory MP David Kilgour insisted that "I haven't talked to anyone who thinks the 7% rate is anything but a holding measure to get the tax in. It's a PR gesture. The tax will go up." The credibility of this view was not shaken by the Prime Minister's reluctance to promise that the 7 per cent GST would not be raised before the next election.[89]

The stage was now set for the government to introduce the GST legislation. The public mood was by no means obliging at this point. An Angus Reid poll in late December showed that 61 per cent of Canadians disapproved of the GST, compared to 22 per cent who approved it. A Gallup poll suggested that 59 per cent of respondents would not vote for an MP who voted in favour of the tax. And an odd amalgam of individuals and groups was organizing to stop the tax. The Pro-Canada Network—a coalition of labour, farm, and women's groups— launched a national campaign against the GST similar to the effective campaign it had waged against the FTA. The Canadian Federation of Independent Business launched a campaign against the GST called "A Nightmare on Main Street." The mayors of Canada's biggest cities became active against the tax, and Toronto held a series of forums on it. Ontario unions called for a one-day general strike to protest the GST. And in Alberta, Vaun J. Gramatovisch espoused civil disobedience and refusal to pay federal taxes: "Hit 'em where it hurts. Don't yell and howl, don't whine and complain—just hit 'em so they won't get back up. Cut off the money."[90] As the government poised itself to introduce the legislation, the GST was opposed by all ten provincial governments (three of which would later fight the GST in court on constitutional grounds[91]), municipalities, hospitals, universities and colleges, the housing and tourism industries, organized labour, women's groups, lower and middle income groups, social service organizations,

THE ADVENT OF THE GST

seniors, the food industry, the news and cultural industries, and small business. Against all this, External Affairs Minister Joe Clark said that Canada should implement the proposed GST to set an example for the reform movements of Eastern Europe: "What does it say to the people who have risked their lives in Romania and in Poland and in Czechoslovakia...if we can't find the courage...to move to a reform that everybody agrees needs to be accomplished."[92] Most observers shook their heads in disbelief.

Bill C-62—the GST legislation—was given first reading in the House of Commons on 24 January 1990. This was months behind the schedule proposed in the June 1989 budget, which had anticipated an introduction of legislation in early fall. The delay was important, as the GST was to be implemented in January 1991, and the government needed to have all businesses registered well before then to have the collection system in place. It could not legally compel any business to register until the legislation was passed, nor could the refundable tax credits be issued.

Despite its bulk (Bill C-62 was as thick as a mid-sized city's phone directory) and its complexity (it is all but impossible to read) and despite NDP House Leader Riis's vow to give the government "the toughest fight that Parliament Hill has seen in a decade,"[93] the government used its majority to move the legislation briskly through the House of Commons. Second reading began on 29 January and was completed by 7 February, comprising but six sitting days in the House. Finance Minister Wilson opened second reading for the government, the only important member of the government to actively participate in the debate. He took what was the only road left open to the government at this point—the high road: "Politically, the expedient thing would have been not to proceed with the GST—the expedient thing for the government, but the wrong thing for the country." He catalogued the by-now-familiar litany of faults with the existing MST; reviewed the failed negotiations with the provinces; indicated how the government had shown flexibility in responding to criticisms and to the Blenkarn committee's recommendations by lowering the rate from 9 per cent to 7 per cent and making numerous changes; showed the GST's many economic advantages; and ended on an optimistic note:

> I believe that in the months following January 1, 1991, when the cut and thrust of partisan debate on this issue has calmed down, when the controversy has subsided, when Canadians see our economy even more vibrant and growing, they will conclude, as I have, that this is the right policy for the right reasons at the right time."[94]

Opposition leader Turner mounted a relentless assault on the GST. He claimed that it would not stay long at 7 per cent; that Canada would be the only country in the world with two sales tax systems; that the tax was not revenue neutral, simple, visible, or fair; that the government was not able to get provincial cooperation; that the tax would be inflationary; that the GST taxed literacy; that the timing was awful, at the beginning of a recession. He voiced the theme that would remain the Liberal position over the next year:

> Canadians are against this tax. Canadians are fighting this tax. They have written letters against this tax. They have asked members from all sides to present petitions against this tax. They have said no to this tax in a thousand different ways. If we had a democracy this government would be listening to the people of Canada.[95]

NDP leader Audrey McLaughlin accused the government of pandering to the corporate agenda, and declared that the GST was part of the government's sell-out to the US under free trade. The GST was unacceptable because of its regressive nature, having the greatest impact on lower income groups while shifting the tax burden away from corporations and the rich. The GST was also economically ill advised, she argued, given its inflationary impact and its effects on interest rates and economic activity. Sounding a similar note to the Liberals, she claimed that

> this tax is opposed by more Canadians than any other policy in the history of this government. It is opposed by labour unions, women's groups, farmers' associations, senior citizens' groups, and small business people. Never before has such a coalition been formed. Can this government not hear this message? The message is that this tax must go.[96]

After second reading, Bill C-62 was sent to committee, where it sat for the next seven weeks. In the interim, the chorus of GST disapproval rose to a crescendo. The National Pensioners and Senior Citizens Federation supported a three-day national protest set for early April. Tourist associations worried that the GST "will shut the door on Canada." Three hundred people braved -20^0 temperatures in Brandon to shout insults at the Prime Minister, dubbing the GST the Greatest Scam of all Time. Retailers claimed that they were going to be unfairly perceived as the "bad guys" who had to collect the tax. The Liberals contined their petition-signing efforts, reaching over 600,000 names by mid-February, many of the petititions in ministers' ridings (which forced the ministers to present the petitions in the House of Commons). The protest group IRATE (I'm Rebelling Against Tax Excess) planned to present a multi-million-name petitition to the Liberal-dominated Senate, to sway it to block the legislation. The GST was claimed to threaten day cares. Even veterinarians got involved, asking for an exemption on the grounds that family pets are important to the psychological health of their owners (psychological services were to be tax-exempt). A community day of protest was organized (7 April 1990) on which protest cards were available in shopping malls, churches, and community centres, and on 9 April employees in thousands of workplaces were able to fill in protest cards—more than two million postcards were sent to Parliament, demanding that MPs "Axe the Tax." And, in a development that harmed whatever positive glow remained to the GST, the government announced that it was recruiting a 250-member intelligence unit of the RCMP to help enforce the GST.[97]

Within the House of Commons Standing Committee on Finance and Economics, the GST was being scrutinized yet again—this time by 106 witnesses from forty groups, from the Canadian Psychoanalysts Society and the Canadian Association of Numismatic Dealers to the Professional Art Dealers Association and the Elbow Valley Cycle Club. They all had problems with the GST. The Canadian Chamber of Commerce reiterated its demand that the GST not be implemented until there were further government spending cuts, the GST was made more comprehensive (the food exemption was dropped), and the tax was harmonized with provincial systems (to make one sales tax, and one collection agency). The food and restaurant sectors continued to complain, pointing out various anomalies (should yogurt and ice cream be taxed; are muffins food; do two, four, or six doughnuts make a package a food and hence tax-exempt?).[98] Given the comprehensiveness of the GST, it was not surprising that the more it was scrutinized, the more flaws were discovered. The committee report on Bill C-62 finally emerged on 30 March, after an NDP-led filibuster from 19 March to 21 March delayed government efforts to hasten committee proceedings. The filibuster was broken rather crudely—perhaps illegally—by Chairman Blenkarn, which led the opposition to call for his resignation and soured the political mood even further. The thirty-eight-page report listed dozens and dozens of recommendations, mainly dealing with technical matters, definitions, procedures, and so on. The report was presented to the House of Commons on 29 March.[99]

The House of Commons legislative process was then completed quickly, the government invoking closure to limit debate to one day at the report stage (29 March) and one day at third reading (10 April). This was in the effort to have the bill passed and sent on to the Senate before the Easter break. Finance Minister Wilson announced that the ultimate vote on the GST would be considered a confidence vote, meaning that any Conservative who voted against Bill C-62 would be expelled from the Tory caucus. Alberta Tory MPs Alex Kindy and David

Kilgour were not deterred by this threat.[100] Third reading was an anti-climax, the government's position led by Minister of State (Finance) Gilles Loiselle and the opposition's by Liberal finance critic Douglas Young—the big players having already fired their shots. Loiselle taunted the opposition—particularly the Liberals—for not having presented an alternative to the GST.[101]

On 10 April 1990 Bill C-62 was passed by the House of Commons, less than three months after it had been introduced. However, that proved to have been the easy part. For Bill C-62 was then sent to the Liberal-dominated Senate.

The Senate Battle

Amongst the stained-glass windows, royal red carpet, and giant chandeliers in the Senate chamber, wall murals depict World War I scenes in which weary, broken troops in khaki longcoats survey a devastated landscape, twisted trees, and spent cannons. Amidst such ravages the GST entered its trench warfare phase.

As an early foreshadowing of things to come, the Senate adjourned for three weeks after giving Bill C-62 first reading on 11 April. It returned to give the legislation second reading on 3 May, but Bill C-62 was then passed over to the Senate Banking Committee, where it stayed for the next four months. The government was livid about what it considered to be unneccessary delays, but there was little that it could do, as the Liberals commanded a majority in the Senate. Revenue Minister Otto Jelinek reported that the Senate could hold up legislation for four or five months without upsetting the implementation of the GST. But if the delay extended into October or November, there could be serious problems. Lowell Murray, Tory government leader in the Senate, insisted that the bill could pass the Senate with ample hearings and receive royal assent by the end of June. But Senate Banking Committee Chairman Sidney Buckwold mused that he did not expect the Committee to complete its report until Thanksgiving: "I think the people of Canada are expecting the Senate to spend a good deal of time looking at the legislation." Liberal Senator Royce Frith commented that "We might take the better part of a year just studying the thing in committee. How long can the Tories afford to let their unpopular business hang around before they abandon it?... Some people would like us to take as long as we want on this, or forever." One of those people was NDP leader Audrey McLaughlin, who challenged the Liberal senators to defeat the legislation: "You have a majority in the Senate. You have a chance to kill the GST bill. Use your majority in the Senate. Don't miss this chance. Stop the GST."[102] This position was not without its ironic qualities, as the NDP had long been committed to abolishing the "undemocratic" upper chamber.

Whether the unelected Liberal senators would follow public opinion and block the legislation of the elected House of Commons remained uncertain through the summer. But what was certain was that they would do everything possible to drag out the legislative process to inflict maximum political embarassment on the Conservative government. Hence, the Senate Banking Committee embarked on a twelve-city cross-Canada tour in July to keep the hated GST in the public eye over the summer. Political cynics (or possibly realists) speculated that the Liberals would attempt to delay implementation until January 1992, thereby ensuring that the GST would be fresh in the public's mind during the election expected in that year—while also guaranteeing an incoming Liberal government access to the revenues generated by the GST.

As the Senate deliberated, political life continued miserably for the government. In early May it announced the winner in the GST processing centre sweepstakes: Summerside, PEI, would receive the proposed GST data processing centre and its associated jobs. These were described by the Prime Minister as "good and enduring jobs. Taxes will be around for a long time." But it was quickly noted that the expected three hundred full-time and one hundred part-time jobs were a far cry from the thirteen hundred jobs that Summerside had lost as a result of recent military spending cuts.[103] Also in early May, Consumer Affairs Minister Pierre Blais announced the creation of a $19 million watchdog agency designed to monitor prices and corporate behaviour in the wake of the GST. The action was denounced as a public relations move designed to give the public a false sense of security. Critics claimed that the agency was toothless, as it would not be given powers to roll back prices. Moreover, no one really believed that it would be possible to judge how the GST would affect particular prices. Even the government's own supporters criticized the agency: the Standing Committee on Consumer and Corporate Affairs claimed that the agency's budget was too large and, in any event, the agency's function would be effectively realized by competitive pressures in the marketplace.[104] It seemed that the government could do nothing right: even in creating jobs and protecting consumers, it was chastised.

In September the GST watchdog agency issued two million booklets containing 140 examples of the expected price effect of the implementation of the GST. For example, prices would likely go up on some previously untaxed products, such as dry cleaning (40¢ on a suit or dress), replacement of a car muffler ($1.53), dinner out, with wine ($1.76), a root canal at the dentist ($1.32), and the hydro bill ($5.61). Other prices would likely go down as the 13 per cent MST was replaced by the 7 per cent GST: a couch ($23.19 on a $1,115 item), cars ($852.41 on a $22,000 model), stoves ($1.69 on an $850 stove). For the opposition this was simply propoganda: "the government has no idea—no one has any idea—of what effect the GST will have on the economy," claimed Liberal consumer critic Russell MacLellan.[105] Indeed, Statistics Canada scrapped plans to issue a monthly report that would measure the impact of the GST on inflation: "Nobody, but nobody, can really measure month after month just exactly what the consumer price index would have been without these tax changes," claimed its chief statistician.[106] Various better business bureaus accused the government of false advertising on radio ads that claimed the GST was not a new tax.[107] And in a move guaranteed to be unpopular, the Department of Finance announced that starting 1 September, businesses would have to start collecting the GST on any contract or service that straddled 1990-91 or would be realized in 1991. Businesses were thus placed in the unhappy position of collecting a non-legislated tax on things such as club memberships and season's tickets.[108]

Out on the road, Canadians' views on the GST were canvassed by a parliamentary committee for a third time in a year. The Buckwold Committee made a rare discovery—a new supporter of the GST: civic leaders from Summerside, PEI urged that the GST be passed so that its community could start getting back on its economic feet. For the most part, the litany of complaints and problems was rehearsed once again: the government of New Brunswick claimed that it would lose $2.4 billion in revenue annually; the Canadian Real Estate Association complained about taxation on housing; Toronto compared the GST's impact on its service industry with the impact a new petroleum tax would have on Calgary; seniors saw the GST as hitting them harder than those with larger incomes; the Canadian Federation of Independent Business asked for a year's delay to get a federal/provincial plan in place; the Pro-Canada Network predicted civil disobedience if the GST was implemented; the Consumers Association of Canada characterized the GST as a nightmare for consumers, for the confusion it would create in comparing prices and for the tax cascading it was creating (many provinces would charge their retail sales taxes on top of the GST); the Canadian Medical Association claimed that doctors would lose $3,600 a year; the beer industry claimed that beer drinkers would pay an extra $226 million a year; the Royal Canadian Legion feared that the GST would be imposed on wreaths and poppies; health associations argued that condoms should be zero-rated as a medical device; the funeral industry requested tax exemption for providing a basic service. In a model of understatement, the Liberals' deputy leader in the Senate, Royce Frith, reported, "I don't think there is any great enthusiasm for passing [the GST]."[109]

Public opinion polls indicated that support for the GST was at 14 per cent—about the level of the government's plunging popularity. But Tom D'Aquino, Business Council on National Issues president, suggested to the Senate committee that while the GST was opposed, it was also misunderstood: "the vast majority of Canadians...do not know this is a replacement tax...we are debating, making decisions...on the basis of largely misinformed people who do not understand the issue." Senator Buckwold shot back, "What bothers me most is that you downgrade the great majority of Canadians who you say are misinformed, as if 150 executives of your organization are the people who know everything." Regardless of who was better informed, the Retail Council of Canada knew something with Cartesian certainty: hundreds of millions of dollars would be lost by retailers if the tax were not passed. Catalogues had been printed, staff trained, and cash registers purchased or altered on the assumption that the GST would be in place by 1 January 1991.[110]

The GST's fate appeared to rest in the hands of the unelected Liberal senators. Any discomfort they felt about blocking a piece of financial legislation by the elected House of Commons was assuaged by the incredible public abhorrence of the tax that had built up over the last year. The plummeting popularity of the Mulroney government—a process accelerated by the June 1990 Meech Lake disaster—also bolstered the Liberal senators' sense that *they*, and not the elected government, were in tune with the people's wishes. Ironically, the decline of the Meech Lake accord handed the government an unexpected political resource. The Prime Minister would now not have to chose senators from lists of candidates provided by the premiers: he could appoint his own choices. In mid-summer the Liberals' majority in the Senate declined to fifty-two members— the first time since 1946 that they did not enjoy a guaranteed majority. If Prime Minister Mulroney decided to fill the over dozen Senate vacancies with loyal Conservatives, then the eventual GST vote in the Senate would be tight (the outcome would depend on the votes of a half-dozen independent senators). As the clock ticked over the summer, the character of the GST issue changed. Whether the GST would raise exports or increase economic output was increasingly ignored. Instead, the GST posed the question, should the unelected Senate should be allowed to block the intensely disliked GST legislation passed by the elected House of Commons? "The issue here goes right to the heart of parliamentary democracy," claimed Lowell Murray. "What we have here is an attempt by the Liberal opposition to go back to a nineteenth-century Senate."[111]

In anticipation of the showdown in the Senate, Prime Minister Mulroney started naming new senators at the end of the summer: five senators on 30 August (including former trade minister Pat Carney), three more on 6 September (including former New Brunswick premier Richard Hatfield), two more on 11 September (including Nova Scotia premier John Buchanan), and yet another five senators on 23 September (including business tycoon Trevor Eyton and former Quebec provincial cabinet minister Claude Castonguay, a strong Meech Lake supporter). This avalanche of appointments—all guaranteed to support the GST in the Senate—made the Senate a full house, with fifty-two Liberals, forty-six Conservatives, and six independents. These partisan appointments were extraordinarily controversial, as the Prime Minister had made such great political capital out of the patronage issue in the 1984 televised election debate with John Turner. No appointment was more controversial, or so universally condemned, as the choice of John Buchanan, the sitting but scandal-hit Nova Scotia premier whose office was under investigation for corruption. The Prime Minister was undaunted by criticism: "We have a job to do and we will do our job. If the public disagrees with us in two years or two and a half years in the next election, they will know how to deal with us." In almost a caricature of the 1984 televised leadership debate, Mulroney later claimed that he had "had no option" but to make these appointments to ensure passage of the GST. A Guelph lawyer—T. Sher Singh— was so outraged at the Buchanan appointment that he started a court case against the appointment on the grounds that Buchanan's link to the patronage scandal in Nova Scotia made him ineligible for sitting in the Senate.[112]

The GST legislative process edged closer to a crisis when the Senate Banking Committee, the Buckwold Committee, issued its report on 24 September 1990. The Prime Minister had made some encouraging noises earlier when he stated that the government was willing to entertain any changes proposed by the Committee: "the government always looks at suggestions that come to us in a constructive and helpful way…[we] don't exclude the possibility that someone has a better idea." Surprisingly, the Buckwold Committee did not make any recommendations for changes. A 215-page report—prepared exclusively by Senator Buckwold—condemned the GST for being unfair, technically flawed, too complex, and bad for the economy at the onset of what looked increasingly like a recession. "The GST cannot be defended by simply stating that the MST is flawed. The GST must garner support on its own merit. This has not been done." The report presented four options: adopt the GST with small changes, recommend major changes (which would insure delay until after 1 January 1991), delay proceedings until after 1 January 1991, or reject the GST and call for a royal commission on taxation. The Committee voted 8-6 to recommend to the Senate that the GST be killed. "It's a very bad piece of legislation," reported Buckwold, "that Canadians by the millions have asked the Senate to reject, and we've acted accordingly."[113] This was a surprising development, as it brought the issue to an immediate decision point: a vote by the full Senate to accept the report would kill the GST instantaneously. In the first in a wearying series of procedural wrangles, the Conservative senators began delaying tactics to avoid a vote that they would have lost. This bought time for the Prime Minister to plot his next move. In the House of Commons, Prime Minister Mulroney defended his government's authority to proceed with the GST and criticized the Liberal senators and those who supported their actions:

> Whether one accepts or not the outcome of the last election, the fact remains that the Canadian voters had been made fully aware of the GST...and they chose this government and its programs.... Under our system, after it has been elected the Canadian government has the right to be heard and to implement its program once it has been accepted by the elected members...we find repugnant any attempt at undermining the moral authority of the elected House.[114]

From this point on, the GST legislation itself was no longer being debated. The terms of reference of the debate had slid over into symbolic issues: the rights of, or limits on, the unelected Senate; the political authority of an unpopular government; the authority of the government to proceed with an unpopular piece of legislation; the rights of citizens to influence the government between elections. The character of Canadian parliamentary democracy was being debated. In the aftermath of the fatiguing and divisive demise of the Meech Lake accord, this debate took place within a dispirited, cranky, alienated, and cynical population, which lashed out at all politicians, whether government members or not. The onset of a recession soured the mood even further.

The stress on Canada's political institutions was increased on 27 September, when the Prime Minister made a dramatic and desperate move. Not assured of a government majority in the Senate, Mulroney used a little-known clause in the constitution to name eight extra senators to guarantee passage of Bill C-62. Section 26 of the constitution allowed the government to name four or eight extra senators, if the Senate's actions were resulting in a legislative deadlock. In a cabinet order delivered to the Queen by Governor-General Hnatyshyn (a Conservative minister in the previous government), the government claimed that the Senate deadlock had blocked three critical pieces of government legislation for extended periods of time: Bill C-21 for ten months (changes to the unemployment insurance system), Bill C-28 for nine months (the "clawback" of social security benefits), Bill C-62 for five months. The Prime Minister declared that he had done this "only with the greatest reluctance." But it was also done with grim determination:

> Public opinion is invariably against any new tax measure.... But to run a government, looking out for the interests of the nation five, ten, twenty years from now, you cannot do so the way you run a hotline show and make fiscal policy based on the number of telephone calls you receive.... We were

elected with a mandate and we hope to have an opportunity to execute it.[115]

Liberal leader Chretien dismissed Mulroney's claims of a deadlock, noting that a vote on the GST had not yet been taken. "It's an apprehended blockage," he claimed, "I want this tax dead." NDP leader McLaughlin continued to urge the Senate to kill the tax. And both parties insisted that the Senate "swamp" be delayed until after the courts had ruled on its legality. A number of court challenges were launched (including one by the Liberal senators, in a rare if not unprecedented example of one part of Parliament taking another part to court). The challenges were based on various grounds, including the argument that Section 26 was inoperative as a political convention because it had never been used successfully; because political convention was that consultation with the Opposition take place before its use; because Ottawa had agreed to consult with provincial governments before making Senate appointments.[116] A few days later, the NDP discovered the interesting anomaly that the government had named an eleventh New Brunswick senator, and there were only ten New Brunswick MPs, a situation outlawed by section 51a of the Constitution Act, 1867. Justice Minister Kim Campbell responded that the eight extra senators were a "different kind of senator," representing *divisions*, not provinces, of Canada (a possiblility under section 26 of the constitution). Hence the eleventh New Brunswick senator represented the Atlantic provinces.[117]

Back on the Senate floor, the Conservative filibuster was quickly replaced by a Liberal one, because the Conservatives now commanded a majority as a result of the Senate swamp. But, as Liberal Senate leader MacEachen said, "The battle has just begun." Wrangling began over an obscure procedural issue and, as the bills started to ring calling a vote on the issue, the Liberals simply abandoned the Senate and let the bells ring. A vote could not be held until both party whips re-appeared, so the bells could be left ringing forever. As the days passed and the bells kept ringing, Senate business was completely halted; the government was furious. But this was precisely the tactic used by the opposition Conservatives in the House of Commons in 1983, when the bells were kept ringing for two weeks in the battle over the National Energy Program. The bells continued to ring until 2 October, at which time the Liberal senators decided to return to the Senate. They proposed to challenge the eight "stormtrooper senators" in the Senate as well as in the courts. Within the Senate, the Speaker ruled that it was not within his power to decide on questions of constitutional law, so the Conservatives jumped over another procedural hurdle. But the Liberals raised a similar matter of privilege, and proceedings bogged down again. Liberal Senator Frith opined, "If there's the will power, we can delay this thing indefinitely."[118]

THE ADVENT OF THE GST

This claim—as well as the authority of Canada's political institutions—was seriously assaulted a few days later. On 4 October the Senate was thrown into chaos when Speaker Guy Charbonneau (a Conservative appointment) ordered a vote to be taken—even though the Liberals were not present in the Senate chamber. This was an unprecedented decision, which undermined the tradition that parties be present for the vote. The event unfolded in an odd way, the Liberal senators not attending a vote on a motion to adjourn that they themselves had moved. Speaker Charbonneau sent a letter to both the Conservative and Liberal senators, saying that he was going to force a vote on the adjournment motion "in light of the failure of the mechanisms established by the political parties...to assemble within a reasonable time." The Liberals appeared at the door of the Senate, but refused to enter. The door was then closed for the vote (a tradition) and the motion was defeated 54-0.[119]

The Liberals accused the Speaker of breaking the rules and acting in a partisan way to force the vote and assist the government. In the House of Commons, Liberal Paul Martin Jr. declared that "for the first time in the history of this country a majority government in power is seeking a *coup d'etat* on its own people." "What's the importance of our losing a battle," declared senator Frith, "we've lost parliament." Liberal senators yelled "shame," "disgrace," "Hitler," and 74-year-old Senator David Stewart yelled at a Tory senator to "crawl under the table because you're a despicable little bugger." Liberal Senator Keith Davey then invited TV camera crews and reporters to enter the Senate and sit with the Liberals because, he claimed, there were no longer any rules. Journalists and camera crews wandered freely on the Senate floor, transmitting the chaotic scene to a disbelieving Canadian public. Liberal senators hopped on chairs and tables, shouted insults, and accused Prime Minister Mulroney of dictatorship. A semblance of order was restored later in the evening by the Senate's chief of security. This tumultuous activity continued for twenty-seven hours, including seven hours of desk-thumping, whistle-blowing, noise-making, reading from the Bible, and bell-ringing to prevent Senate leader Lowell Murray from starting Senate business again the following morning.[120]

This incident did great damage to the authority of the Senate and Canada's political institutions. It also demonstrated the Liberal senators' tenuous position: the Conservatives now controlled the Senate. Finally, a Thanksgiving weekend truce was arranged: the Liberals were able to buy time until 9 October, by which time the courts might have declared on the illegality of the "Senate Eight." In return, though, the Liberals agreed to move to start debate on the Senate Banking Committee report.[121] But when the Senate resumed on 9 October, the Liberal senators resumed their filibuster—leading the Conservatives to accuse them of reneging on the truce. The Liberal senators again challenged the Speaker's controversial ruling, which was characterized by Senator Stewart—a former university professor of political science—as "parliamentary rape" and "an act of tyranny". Speaker Charbonneau was a long-time friend of Brian Mulroney and had been an effective fundraiser for the Conservatives. He had been appointed to the Speaker's chair in 1984, and was known for his fierce loyalty to the Prime Minister. "Ask Guy to represent Canada at a diplomatic function," commented a Tory senator, "and he will do it with dignity. Just don't expect him to know all the rules of the Senate." The Liberal senators promised that the filibuster would continue as long as Speaker Charbonneau remained in the chair: "The time comes when the referee is making all the calls for the other team and you just won't go on to the ice if he's going to be the referee," declared Senator Frith. In a brief but sobering presentation, the aged and ill Senator David Croll chastised the government before a hushed Senate chamber:

> There comes a time when Parliament is more important than any of us.... The debate has lost its significance. Nobody's listening. It really doesn't matter...whether the bill is passed. When the country wakes up and realizes what we have done to Parliament, there will be a furor that will last for years and years. Never mind the bill.... You have rules and you live by them. [122]

From Tuesday, 9 October, to Sunday, 14 October, the twenty-four-hour-a-day filibuster went on (there is no closure in the Senate and debating rules and limits are more relaxed than in the House of Commons). Both sides arranged six- to eight-hour shifts to allow the senators to get some rest. The increasingly tired Liberal senators took to reading thousands of names from the innumerable anti-GST petititions, in an effort to kill time while blocking any Conservative effort to move on to the debate on the Buckwold report. Whenever the Speaker attempted to speak, he was drowned out by calls of "go away," "out tyrant," "resign and repent." [123] Finally, on 14 and 15 October, the six-day filibuster was interrupted by a series of adjournments, while private talks took place amongst the key players—Senator Murray for the Conservatives, Senator MacEachen for the Liberals, and Speaker Charbonneau. Through 16 and 17 October the talks continued and the Senate met only sporadically and to no effect. In the House of Commons, the Prime Minister compared the Liberal senators to armed Mohawk Warriors, vaudeville performers, and day care monitors: "All they'd need is a little bit of make-up and they'd be something out of Cirque de Soleil." [124]

On 17 October Justice McRae of the general division of Ontario Court ruled against the Liberal senators' challenge of the Senate swamp, declaring the creation of the eight extra senators to have been a legal action. Their position weakened, the Liberals then signed a deal with the Conservatives on how to proceed with Senate business. These "rules of war" would allow the government to pass within ten days the unemployment insurance, clawback, and Hibernia bills (the latter involving continued financing of the petroleum megaproject in New-foundland—a politically sensitive issue for the Liberals). While the Liberals gave no guarantees on the GST, they agreed to allow a vote on the Buckwold report on 25 October. Indefinite bell-ringing was disallowed, weekend sittings were banned (although around-the-clock sitting was allowed four days a week), and the Liberals would be allowed to introduce eight amendments at Bill C-62's third reading. Both sides claimed victory. Senator Murray sighed with relief at the sighting of "the light at the end of the tunnel," but Senator MacEachen chortled that this was but "the tunnel at the end of the light."[125]

The Senate thus finally started business, three crucial weeks after Parliament had resumed. A GST scenario was emerging in vague form. By 25 October the Conservatives could expect to pass the UIC, clawback, and Hibernia legislation, and defeat the Buckwold report. It could then be anticipated that the Liberals would stall business for a week before third reading began. With eight amendments allowed—and all senators allowed to speak to the amendments—it would take two to three weeks to to get through the anticipated ninety-six hours of debate. Moreover, there were no limits on the number of amendments the independent senators could put forward—theoretically, one senator could present an infinte series of amendments. Assuming two weeks of processing these amendments, and a week of procedural wrangling before the final vote was taken, it appeared that the government could get the legislation passed before 1 January 1991—but only by mid-December. This would have a critical effect on the collection and tax credit systems, which were supposed to be in place no later than mid-November. Only one-half of the businesses in Canada were registered to collect the tax by the end of October, the rate of registration having fallen from sixty thousand to twenty-five thousand businesses a week as the Senate struggle dragged on. Fully sixty per cent of retailers surveyed indicated that they wanted the the GST to start later than 1 January 1991, as many were simply not ready to implement it.[126]

On 25 October the Senate voted 57-51 to reject the Buckwold report, which had recommended killing the GST. Without the Senate Eight, the vote would have been 51-49 in favour of the report, and the GST would have been dead.[127] With the UIC and clawback bills passed earlier, and the Hibernia legislation passed on 29 October, the Senate's two-week truce was completed and the stage was set for the final showdown over the GST.[128]

404The Real Worlds of Canadian Politics

Back in the House of Commons, the GST war continued. Each day the opposition hectored the government to drop the tax and challenged the remarkably unpopular government's authority to act (the government's share of declared supporters was around 15 per cent in late October). The government did not need to be told about the GST's—and its—unpopularity. It had commissioned a series of public opinion surveys between September 1989 and June 1990 that showed three-quarters of Canadians were not satisfied with Ottawa's handling of the economy and over 70 per cent did not like the GST—78 per cent thinking it would lead to increased government waste.[129] Two symbolic issues emerged that focused antagonists' attacks on the GST. First, the Conference Board released a report indicating that the economy had entered a recession. The opposition assaulted the government's record of economic management and demanded that the plans for the GST be scrapped, as the tax would only deepen the recession. The GST issue then shifted further and further from the merits of the tax itself to the appropriateness of the timing of its introduction. The second symbolic issue to emerge was that of "taxing reading," an issue bursting with political and ideological resonance. The opposition criticized the government for imposing the GST on reading materials, which, it predicted, would harm the publishing industry and increase illiteracy. Responding to a query on the GST's imposition on sales of the Bible and other religious books, Mulroney stated that "of all the criticisms I have heard [this] worries me the most." He promised to review this feature of the GST once the tax was passed and its impact evaluated. Liberal leader Jean Chrétien—in his clearest statement on the tax to date—pledged to scrap the GST if he was elected in the next election: "I am opposed to the GST. I have always been opposed to it and I will always be opposed to it. It is a tax that is both regressive and discriminatory." He declared that the Liberal senators would continue to fight the tax for as long as possible.[130]

The government held its ground, saying that it was doing the right if unpopular thing. It taunted the Liberal opposition for lacking a viable alternative to the GST, accused Chrétien of waffling on the issue and claimed that Allan MacEachen was the real Liberal leader. It reminded Liberals of their past support for replacing the MST with an alternative tax: senator McEachen had tried to do so in 1981 when he was finance minister, Jean Chrétien had criticized the MST when he was finance minister, and the Senate Banking Committee had supported the government's White Paper sales tax plan in its December 1987 report (see above, pp. 371, 373).[131]

In the Senate, the wearying cycle of Liberal procedural moves and Conservative counter-attacks recommenced once the Buckwold report had been defeated and the legislative decks cleared for considering Bill C-62. After two days of filibustering and all-night delaying sessions, the Liberals agreed to let Senate business start again—in return for a day off. This would allow third reading of Bill C-62 to begin. "We're getting there," sighed Senator Murray; "This is not even the end of the beginning," insisted Senator MacEachen.[132]

On 5 November the Senate began to debate the eight Liberal amendments that the Conservatives had agreed to allow at the third-reading stage (see above); this would continue until 22 November. These amendments included proposals to exempt products from the GST, ranging from books, magazines, and utilities to transactions in the North, as well as to provide full inflation coverage for the GST tax credits. Conservative senators had to be cautious at this point, despite their majority. "I am worried about accidents," noted one Tory senator; "this is Canada and it is November. Planes can be delayed and people can miss votes." All eight amendments were defeated, but by a narrow margin, some by only two votes. During this stage of the debate, five Opposition senators wrote a letter to the Canadian branch of the Commonwealth Parliamentary Association, asking for the appointment of a neutral international observer to monitor the final phase of the debate over the GST; they were concerned that the government might break Senate rules to pass the tax.[133]

When the last of the eight Liberal amendments was defeated on 22 November, the three-week-old truce between the Liberal and Conservative senators came to an end—with predictable results. The Senate was plunged into chaos once again, as there was no agreement on how to proceed with any amendments that might be proposed by the six independent senators. Conservative Senate leader Lowell Murray quickly tried to introduce a motion to cut off further debate. The Speaker recognized Murray, and the Liberals reacted furiously. They stormed the Speaker's chair, waving rule books and hurling insults, accusing him of once again breaking procedural rules for not recognizing Reform Party Senator Stan Waters, who had been trying to introduce an amendment. They insisted that the Senate as a whole decide who should be heard in a dispute such as this. The Speaker refused to listen to the Liberals, which led to a shouting match, punctuated by screaming, insults, and the odd bit of shoving. Chaos continued through the evening, ending only as the Senate adjourned for the weekend. By Monday an agreement was reached to allow debate on the independent senators' amendments until 28 November. This set of debates took place in a relatively quiet and calm way.[134]

As the government withstood further amendment assaults in the Senate, it faced further political problems in the House of Commons and in the provinces. On 26 November the Quebec government revised its position and decided to exempt books and reading materials from the GST. The "tax on literacy" issue

THE ADVENT OF THE GST

had taken on great political and symbolic resonance in debates, and the Quebec government's action embarrassed Ottawa and further eroded the legitimacy of the tax. On 23 November the federal government introduced its supplementary estimates, indicating that an additional $2.5 billion was required, mainly, it claimed, as a result of the unexpected costs of the Gulf war. The reality was that it needed these funds to service the national debt, as well as to pay for the costs of implementing the GST. This latter included advertising, collection, and administration costs of the GST and the mailing of GST tax credits. The original estimate for GST costs was in the $260-million range (although that had not included the $110 million spent in 1989-90). The 1990-91 costs were expected to be over $365 million. NDP leader Audrey McLaughlin ridiculed the government in the House of Commons to great effect:

> What we see is an expense of $350 million for a war in the [Persian] Gulf, but we see $379 million to implement the GST. Where are the priorities of the government?... I am sure Canadians are going to wonder why it costs more to implement this so-called fair GST than it does to have a war in the gulf.[135]

The independent senators' amendments were predictably defeated by the Conservative majority in the Senate. The concluding debate on Bill C-62 finally began on the evening of Thursday, 29 November. Each senator would be allowed to speak but once, albeit with no time limit. The final debate thus crawled on. By the following Monday only five senators had spoken—and there were fifty-two Liberal senators. One of the speeches was nearly fatal: Senator Earl Hastings, who had a history of heart problems, collapsed on the Senate floor at 5:30am after three hours of talking. Ironically, one of the senators appointed in the Senate swamp was Wilbert Keon, the renowned heart surgeon, who came to Hastings' assistance. This stark event did not stop Senator Philippe Gigantes' efforts to break the Guinness Book of Records' mark for the longest parliamentary speech (forty-three hours). Outside the Senate, the government continued to be embarassed and to fumble the introduction of the tax. On 1 December, after months of government denials, the widely felt recession was acknowledged officially; the economy had declined in two consecutive quarters (the definition of a recession). The economy was manifesting the largest set of economic declines since the 1981-82 recession; it diminished by 1.6 per cent over these two quarters, and unemployment rose to the 9-10 per cent range. The government was assaulted for this "made in Canada" recession as well as for persisting in introducing the GST at a recessionary time. Days later, two embarassing reports were released. A Statistics Canada study indicated that the export benefits of the GST were only about half of what the government had anticipated, and another study indicated that the GST's impact on northern economies would be particularly damaging. And, in a move that stunned the restaurant industry, the government's campaign to market the GST produced a cartoon encouraging Canadians to avoid paying the GST by eating at home.[136]

Regardless of its ineptness and bad luck, the government held the one weapon that would put the GST issue to rest: it enjoyed a majority in the Senate. On 11 December the government finally chose to use this weapon. A letter signed by fifty-three Conservative senators asked the Speaker to bring the issue to a vote on 13 December. Suggesting that the Senate's purpose had been undermined by the Liberal filibuster, the Conservative senators contended that "the rights to speak and to delay are not absolute. The right to delay ends where the right to vote begins." Liberal leader MacEachen termed this move a "coup d'état...a real outrageous, flagrant violation of every rule of Parliament." The Conservative majority was asking the Speaker to override the Senate's rules in order to terminate debate and force a final vote on the GST. Speaker Charbonneau obliged, and announced on the evening of 12 December that the final vote on the GST would be held the next day. The Liberals howled in protest. Senator MacEachen called Speaker Charbonneau a "gangster" and his action "the most outrageous act ever committed in Parliament." The government was unperturbed by these charges, pointing to public opinion polls taken in early November that showed 70 per cent of Canadians thought the final vote on the GST should be taken.[137]

The forced vote took place the next day, 13 December 1990, eleven years to the day after another famous parliamentary vote. On 13 December 1979 Allan MacEachen engineered the fall of the short-lived minority Conservative government, headed by Joe Clark. Lowell Murray had been a member of that government. Eleven years later, Senator Murray could garner some satisfaction from engineering the forced vote on the GST, thereby sabotaging MacEachen and the Liberal efforts to delay or destroy the GST. In a vote as anti-climactic as it was inevitable, the Senate passed Bill C-62 by a vote of 55-49.[138]

The GST legislation remained cursed for a while longer. It was to receive routine royal assent the next day. Deputy Governor General Sopinka, filling in for Governor General Hnatyshyn, arrived at the Senate at 2:30pm for the formalities. He found the Liberal senators taking one last kick at the cat, arguing that the GST had been passed illegally. The Senate debate went on until after 3:00pm. Finally, the Speaker asked the Gentleman Usher of the Black Rod to go to the House of Commons to summon MPs to the Senate. There was no one there. The House of Commons had adjourned for the weekend, having failed to get the unanimous consent required to sit past 3pm. Royal assent would have to wait.[139]

On Monday, 17 December, royal assent was given; the GST was finally law. The countdown to its 1 January 1991 implementation date was overshadowed by a more distracting countdown: the looming 15 January United Nations deadline in the Gulf. The new year arrived, with Canadians travelling across the border in droves to avoid paying the GST; postal workers by the score skipping work to avoid Canadians' wrath at paying the tax on stamps; and consumers staring in confusion at their sales receipts, wondering whether they were better off or being ripped off. The GST was now part of the fabric of Canadian life. For its efforts, the Mulroney government started the new year by breaking its own record for a government's unpopularity: its 12 per cent popular support was only marginally higher than the 9 per cent attained by the fledgling Reform Party.[140]

DISCUSSION

Bill C-62's legislative experience was hardly typical of the legislative process in Canada's parliamentary, majoritarian system. The government declared its intention to alter the MST in July 1986, but the legislation was passed only by December 1990. That the process took over four years was partly due to the GST's being part of a tax reform package; altering the tax system is typically an enormously complicated, difficult, and lengthy business. But the GST case was more than long and complicated: it was bloody and bruising and, as the saying goes, there were no survivors taken. Indeed, it is difficult to say whether there were *any* political winners—the government may have won the battle, but it will likely lose the war at the next election. If every piece of legislation took this amount of time and bother, the nation's business would have halted and the Parliament buildings would have crumbled long ago.

Yet this sort of drawn-out, divisive, and bloody legislative process became increasingly typical during the Mulroney administrations—from the epic FTA debate to the Meech Lake tragi-comedy, from the bizarre case of the Bill C-22 drug patent legislation to the drawn-out legislative processes surrounding reform of UI, changing immigration policy, and the clawback legislation. In the many worlds of Canadian politics, different pieces of legislation and different contexts generate a wide variety of legislative experiences. It is critical that students of politics recognize that different processes are possible because of the different conditions and issues that inform them. There were five factors that affected the character of the GST's experience: it was part of a general tax reform, it was part of a fundamental ideological shift, public opinion was deeply against it, the Senate became active, and federal-provincial negotiations failed.

The political process surrounding the creation of the GST was destined to be drawn out and complicated. After all, the tax it was designed to replace—the MST—had survived sixty years of universal criticism, countless studies, and numerous government efforts to replace it. There were a variety of reasons why it had been impossible to change the MST, and these would apply to the introduction of the GST as well: the sheer administrative complexity of moving from a simple tax on manufacturers to a complex tax collected and accounted for at every stage in the economic process; the political challenge of transforming an invisible tax into a visible one, while claiming that it was not a new tax; the federalist challenge of moving into the provincial retail tax domain; the public relations challenge of presenting the tax as revenue neutral and beneficial to all; the strategic challenge of building a political consensus for replacing a tax that few were aware of. On top of all this, the GST was presented as part of an ambitious, comprehensive tax reform package, many of which are called, but few chosen. Pre-Mulroney tax reform attempts had been notoriously unsuccessful. The Carter Commission proposals had popular support, but the legislative results bore only the most superficial resemblance to them as a result of business antagonism and pressure. Allan MacEachen's 1981 tax reform budget died before the ink had dried. Everyone may agree that an existing tax system is unfair and in need of reform, but everyone can just as easily find fault with a proposed tax system. Typically, proposed tax reforms either favour business, in which case there is a populist reaction, or hurt business, which then sabotages the proposed reform by withdrawing its "confidence" in the government. A tax reform proposal is doomed to failure unless it can be demonstrated that the proposal involves no substantial costs and at least some benefits for all. The larger and more ambitious the proposal, the more that faults can be found and pressures mounted to oppose it. Inevitably, the status quo comes to look acceptable, or even necessary. Tax reform is as much a public relations exercise as a matter of economic debate. Complex issues must be translated into accessible issues and phrases, but this simplification can obscure the technical merits of a proposal. Rationality, whether of individuals or of groups, tends to be eclipsed by the self-interest the issue stimulates. It is no wonder, then, that tax changes generally proceed incrementally. Marketing a tax reform proposal requires enormous finesse and a certain degree of luck. In the case of the GST, there was little finesse and even less luck. The lack of agreement with the provinces and the arrival of a recession were examples of bad luck conspiring against the Conservatives. On the other hand, the GST was never thoroughly explained or its rationale honestly presented. Few

THE ADVENT OF THE GST

Canadians believed that low-income groups would be better off, so that no matter what data the government presented, the GST was perceived to be regressive. And no matter how many computer-based statistical studies were produced indicating that the GST was revenue neutral, the perception was that the GST was a tax hike. Tax reform is difficult in general, but selling a tax *increase* that is perceived to be *regressive* is politically impossible. As a result, the GST had to be imposed. This may have been courageous, but it generated an enormous and predictable political reaction.

If tax reform is a political graveyard, why did the Conservatives do what governments had avoided doing for the previous sixty years? As Minister of State (Privatization and Regulation) John McDermid put it, "No...previous government had the guts to do it. We may understand today why they did not have the guts, but they did not have the guts to do it.[141] This leads to the second factor that affected the character of the GST's legislative experience, the ideological one. The policy agenda had been re-directed with the election of the Mulroney government in 1984. Neo-conservative concerns replaced the Keynesian/welfare state approach that had directed the post-war policy agenda. Before 1984, elections typically produced governments that would at most tinker with, or incrementally adjust, the Keynesian and welfare state policies already in place. This normally resulted in fairly predictable, routine legislative processes. But the Conservatives had ambitions to "undo" the Keynesian/welfare state system, from dismantling or altering the welfare state and withdrawing from economic management to selling off Crown corporations and reforming the tax system. The introduction of the GST was thus fired by an ideological vigour that discounted the inevitable political reaction.

Incremental or routine legislative initiatives would thus not be the Conservative norm. In moving to unravel the past through major legislative initiatives, the Mulroney government confronted a substantial core of individuals and groups who continued to support the policies of the past, indeed, who saw themselves as beneficiaries of these policies. Despite two electoral victories, half or more of the electorate did not vote for the Conservatives. Hence, on each occasion that the Mulroney government acted to undo the past—whether via the FTA, alterations to UI, changes to drug patent law, or reform of taxes—there was an enormous negative public response. A kind of morality play then ensued. Each policy initiative aroused debate not simply over the specific policy, but over the neo-conservative project itself. In the case of the GST, this philosophical debate took shape in a dispute over the purpose of the tax system, with opponents accusing the government of abandoning the post-war progressive tax system in favour of regressive, pro-business taxes like the GST. Each policy debate had this

THE ADVENT OF THE GST

philosophical or normative character, with an all-or-nothing quality to it. This made compromise and consensus impossible, and a difficult and complicated legislative process inevitable. Each policy debate became a kind of mini-election.

A third and related factor complicating the GST's passage was public antagonism towards the GST. It was not simply that 70 per cent of the population did not want the GST, although this was not unimportant; 70 per cent of the population *detested* the tax and were willing to do almost anything to stop it. It is highly unusual for a piece of legislation to suffer such widespread and intense antipathy. The core constituency in favour of altering the GST had always been relatively small, and with as many issues dividing as uniting it in a desire to replace the MST. The GST may or may not have been a tax improvement in the general interest. But there were simply too many niggling problems, philosophical doubts, operational flaws, administrative irrationalities, and blatant rearings of self-interest for the government to mould the general interest into a political constituency supporting the tax. Indeed, the reverse seemed to have happened, as the GST was poorly explained and marketed and was implemented at a politically awkward recessionary time. Regardless of the number and quality of studies and documents presented extolling the GST's merits and benefits, few were convinced by the government's attempts to persuade. Exporters and large manufacturers demanded that the government stay the course. Within the bureaucracy the Department of Finance had long been an energetic and probably the most important proponent of the tax, which undoubtedly sold the tax to the government. But this was an inadequate bureaucratic-interest group alliance to legitimize the government's position. Beyond these groups, it was hard to find supporters of the tax (outside of Summerside, PEI). The pervasive quality of the antagonism gave the issue an unusual class quality, heightened by the support given the tax by big business. This class quality mirrored the ideological debate over progressive vs. regressive taxes. Opponents of the tax portrayed the GST as unfair and unjust, transferring resources from ordinary Canadians to the well off and corporations, as part of the neo-conservative agenda. This was a powerful characterization that the tax simply could not shake, and it exacerbated the GST's divisiveness. The antagonism towards the tax was fed by conjunctural circumstances as well. In particular, the fiasco surrounding the Meech Lake accord had put Canadians in a cranky mood, and this crankiness found an inviting target in the shape of the GST. And the onset of a recession in mid-1990 created economic anxieties and antagonisms. As the GST became increasingly a class issue, and as opposition grew to startling proportions, the government could do nothing but use its majority to impose the tax on an unwilling, unconvinced population. This pursuit of the tax put an almost unbearable strain on Canada's political institutions.

The fourth complicating factor was the political revitalization of the Senate. Canada has a bicameral legislative system, with an upper house, the Senate, and a lower house, the House of Commons. In operation, though, Canada has long been a unicameral system, the Senate having lost its political authority because of its non-elected character. In contrast, the seventeenth amendment in the United States created an elected Senate, and this perpetuated the Senate's legislative role in representing the American regions in a political give-and-take with the House of Representatives. Aside from a few interludes, Liberal governments have dominated Canadian politics and Liberal prime ministers have appointed the vast majority of senators. When the Mulroney government was elected, an unusual situation was created: the upper house was controlled by one party and the lower house by another. In the context of the previous two factors—neo-conservatism's attack on the welfare state and widespread public antagonism to the GST—the Senate became the site where the politics of the GST were played out. Given the Conservatives' majority in the House of Commons, opposition to the GST in the lower house was ineffective. The public then looked to other means to block the GST—and the Senate was the obvious locale. The Liberal senators, for their part, were only too happy to oblige. Over and above issues of partisanship and ego, many of the Liberal senators were themselves architects of the Keynesian/welfare state, or certainly strong supporters of it. For example, Liberal Senate leader Allan McEachen was a progressive liberal and a strong supporter of welfare policies and progressive taxation. The stalemate in the Senate reflected an ideological and policy struggle between the past and the future: between progressive liberalism and neo-conservatism, between progressive and regressive taxes. It thus became the place where alternatives to the GST could be raised, as the Conservative government had more or less presented a *fait accompli* in the House of Commons.

The Senate's revitalization obviously complicated the legislative process surrounding the GST. It extended the process by half a year, during which time the GST was kept in the public eye where antagonism could grow. It forced Prime Minister Mulroney to name a legion of Conservative supporters to the Senate, making him vulnerable to charges of blatant political patronage. It also forced him to use section 26 of the constitution in order to swamp the Senate, exposing him to the further charge of using the government's power to tamper with political institutions in order to attain its policy. And it placed the government on the political defensive in an ironical but cruel way. As the Senate stalemate dragged on, the merits or demerits of the GST were lost in the heated debate over whether the Senate had the moral right to block or indeed kill the legislation. One would have thought that the government would have the upper hand in this debate, for, after all, it was elected and the Senate was not. But in the crazy, turbulent political world of that moment, opponents of the tax were able to portray the Senate as the place where democracy was really taking place: the government had only 15 per cent popular support, over 70 per cent of the population was against the GST, and two-thirds of Canadians supported the Senate's blocking of the tax. Even in terms of the discourse over democracy generated by the GST, the government held the weak hand. It had to impose the tax in an authoritarian-looking way. (A lingering question is why the Liberal senators chose not to defeat the tax when they had the chance, for example, at second reading or at any time before the Senate swamp. This raises questions about Liberal motives.)

This last point suggests another feature of the real worlds of Canadian politics: how symbolic matters come to be the lead issues in political debate. When the Conservatives introduced the idea of a multi-stage tax to replace the MST in the 1987 White Paper on tax reform, the substantive issues surrounding the tax were solid neo-conservative issues: increasing efficiency and initiative, improving the balance of trade, renewing economic growth, getting the deficit under control. These issues had informed the countless studies and reports that had catalogued the flaws of the MST: it taxed exports and inputs, it led to a misallocation of resources, it was an unreliable revenue source, it diminished economic output substantially. These issues and flaws disappeared from political discourse as the debate unfolded, replaced by more evocative and emotionally charged ones: unfair tax on the poor, transfer of income to business and the wealthy, taxing literacy, deepening the recession. Symbolically, the GST became a lightning rod for all of the criticisms and complaints that had accumulated against the neo-conservative project and the government's economic policy. As the legislative process became a ridiculed marathon, the GST also became a metaphor for the government's ineptness, in stumbling over everything from federal-provincial relations to tax policy. And it became a prism through which Canadians perceived the ineffectiveness of their political institutions. This was an enormous weight for a tax change to carry: the nature of Canadian society, the scrutiny of neo-conservatism, the future of Canada's political institutions. These were issues that took on a life of their own, and the government could neither manage nor contain them.

Finally, the federal system conspired to give these symbolic issues an opportunity to smother the GST issue. It will be recalled that the Conservatives had announced in the February 1986 budget that the MST would be replaced by a value-added tax, and a white paper on the sales tax was anticipated later that year. For a variety of reasons, the government did not act at that moment, and the GST issue became packaged in the larger tax reform strategy. This was to proceed in two stages, the sales tax reform after the income tax reform, because the government wanted to negotiate a national sales tax system with the provinces. Previous governments that had mooted a federal sales tax had been cowed by the prospect of provincial reaction to Ottawa's intrusion on the provinces' retail tax "turf." In the heady days of 1987—early Meech Lake days, the days of national reconciliation and the reuniting of the great Canadian family—everything seemed possible, even negotiating a national sales tax system with the ten provinces. But fiscal matters are just as tough as constitutional matters. Two years after negotiations began, the sales tax talks broke down and Ottawa moved to introduce the GST on its own. The consequences were enormous. On one level, this made the task of selling the tax that much harder, because Ottawa would not have a background chorus of ten provincial governments singing the tax's praises. Not only would it be alone, it would face ten provinces that would exploit the GST for partisan purposes. This was an unfortunate but typical burden to carry in the hard world of federal-provincial relations. Far worse, though, was that Ottawa received nothing of political advantage in return for this two-year delay in introducing the sales tax. Every single observer of tax reform—from the architects of the New Zealand GST to the House and Senate committees examining the White Paper—issued the same advice: to market the GST effectively, the government should introduce it with an iron-clad guarantee that all taxpayers will be better off as a result. Without that guarantee, the immediate political reaction would be that a harmful, regressive tax was being applied, and this would weaken if not destroy public acceptance of the tax. By creating a stage two, the government lost the opportunity to give—or at least try to demonstrate—this iron-clad guarantee. While the GST was "balanced" by the changes to corporate and personal income taxes of 1987-88, these were long forgotten by the time the GST was introduced.

The government split stage two from stage one because it wanted to negotiate a national sales tax system with the provinces. It felt that it had to negotiate this arrangement because the Mulroney government—like each previous government that had considered reforming the MST—considered the provinces to be the most dangerous potential antagonist. However, the public turned out to be a far greater and more effective antagonist than the provinces, so this two-stage strategy was fundamentally ill conceived. As Douglas Hartle has put it in evaluating earlier reform efforts, "the Federal Government could not listen to the public when its ears were turned towards the provinces."[142] In the process, the Mulroney government managed to invoke the worst of all worlds: a suspicious public, no deal with the provinces, and complaints about the administrative complexity of two retail tax systems. The cruellest irony of all was that, two months after the death of the Meech Lake constitutional accord, Quebec became the first province—and to this point the only province—to join the federal government's GST plan.[143]

THE ADVENT OF THE GST

The parallel with the Meech Lake experience is arresting. As with Meech, Ottawa worried most about the provinces, while the Canadian public was the more dangerous antagonist, refusing to accept the legitimacy of the policy. And the politics of each case were played out outside of the "normal" institutional process and in an atmosphere completely antithetical to closed, sombre parliamentary and executive federalist processes. The carnival-like atmosphere of the week-long Ottawa meeting over Meech Lake in June 1990 was nearly outdone by the circus on the Senate floor later that fall, with round-the-clock politics pressing politicians and participants to exhaustion and collapse. Both cases raised profound questions about Canada's political institutions. They exposed in a raw way the extent to which "the people" are distanced from institutions like Parliament and federalism. The articulation of public opposition, and governmental counter-reaction, strained the political institutions to their limits and led political activity to unfold outside of normal processes and in unusual ways. At the same time, both Meech Lake and the GST illustrated the limits the Canadian political system places on governments' capacity to govern. In the GST case, the government ultimately had the *power* to impose the tax, but the GST and the government's actions lacked *legitimacy*. As with Meech Lake, this was because the Canadian public felt totally alienated from the political process that had produced the GST. This will be one of the great political challenges in Canada in the last moments of the twentieth century: making political institutions and processes more open and democratic while allowing governments to govern.

Why did the government persist with Bill C-62 in the face of such adversity and at such high political costs? There are two explanations. First, the government actually believed in this legislation. This was not a compromise, incremental, wishy-washy piece of legislation with no prospects of making much of an impact. Despite the move to lower the tax to seven per cent and the compromise on exempting food—another cruel example of getting nothing for something—this was a piece of legislation that the government believed would improve Canadian economic conditions. The government believed that, over and above replacing the awful MST, a shift in emphasis from income to consumption taxes would revitalize the economy and help to lower the deficit. The legislation reflected in the clearest possible terms the Conservatives' basic ideological and political predispositions. To give up on the GST would be to give up on its mission in life. Second, the government was caught between a rock and a hard place. Not only was the GST part of its ideological battle, it was a measure that it had promised to the economic community, to induce increased efficiency and economic activity. It had promised to revive the Canadian economy by reforming the tax system, cutting the deficit, and encouraging private enterprise. Its closest supporters in the business sector expected this tax, and the retail community had reorganized its life around it. It was the second stage of a half-completed tax reform package. The government really had no choice but to proceed. In the context of the political calamity surrounding the death of Meech Lake; in the absence of other important policy measures on its policy agenda; given the growing sense that Canada's political leaders were inept and its political institutions were not working—to give up on Bill C-62 was equivalent to giving up its authority to govern, indeed perhaps even its will to govern.

If the Mulroney government had not passed Bill C-62, it would have lost everything. But in its desperation to pass Bill C-62 at any cost, it lost whatever slender chance it had of re-election. Such are the hard realities of the real worlds of Canadian politics.

Discussion Questions

1 How effective was the House of Commons in representing Canadians' views on the GST?

2 What role did political parties play in the GST saga? How effective were they?

3 Were interest groups able to make an impact on the policy process surrounding Bill C-62? Why?

4 Did the 1988 election provide a mandate for the government to proceed with the GST?

5 Discuss the role of the Prime Minister in this case. How much power did he have to affect the outcome?

6 Should an appointed Senate have the right to defeat a piece of legislation passed by the elected House of Commons?

7 Does this policy example strengthen or weaken the case for an elected Senate?

8 Discuss the role of committee hearings, commissions, and reports in the GST case.

9 How important were ideological and political cultural factors in this case? What symbolic issues emerged?

10 All other things being equal, how difficult should it be for a majority government to pass a piece of legislation? Does a majority government have the right to pass any legislation, regardless of the policy's unpopularity?

Chronology

18 May 1920	— 1 per cent turnover tax introduced
January 1924	— turnover tax replaced by manufacturers sales tax of 6 per cent
1930	— fourth in series of cuts to MST brings it to 1 per cent
June 1931	— first in series of Depression increases in MST, 8 per cent by 1936
May 1940	— Rowell-Sirois report criticizes consumption taxes as being regressive
10 April 1951	— budget increases MST to 10 per cent
January 1956	— Carter Sales Tax committee recommends that MST be moved to wholesale level
1959	— MST increased to 11 per cent
February 1967	— Royal Commission on Taxation recommends that MST be replaced by a single-stage tax at retail level
1967	— MST increased to 12 per cent
June 1975	— Discussion Paper on Federal Sales and Excise Taxation (Green Paper) recommends that MST be moved to the wholesale level
June 1977	— Commodity Tax Reform Group (Brown Paper) recommends that MST be moved to wholesale level
1978	— MST decreased from 12 per cent to 9 per cent
12 November 1981	— Budget declares that MST will be moved to the wholesale level

April 1982	— White Paper released: *Proposal to Shift the Federal Sales Tax to the Wholesale Level*
October 1982	— economic statement declares delay in implementation of wholesale tax
May 1983	— Goodman Sales Tax Committee rejects tax at wholesale level in favour of one at retail level
15 February 1984	— budget declares that MST shift to wholesale level will not proceed; moderate changes to MST instead
October 1984	— MST increased to 10 per cent; first of three increases by Mulroney government (to 11 per cent on 23 May 1985 and 12 per cent on 26 February 1986)
8 November 1984	— Agenda for Economic Renewal: new Conservative economic agenda
26 February 1986	— budget speech calls for discussion of value-added tax
18 July 1986	— Wilson announces government intention to replace MST as part of tax reform
October 1986	— GST implemented in New Zealand
23 October 1986	— Guidelines for tax reform tabled
18 June 1987	— White Paper on tax reform, includes proposal for replacing MST with a value-added tax; to be pursued as stage two after stage one (personal and corporate income tax reform) is completed
16 November 1987	— House of Commons Standing Committee reports on the White Paper
1 December 1987	— Senate Banking Committee reports on White Paper
10 December 1987	— Wilson declares there will be no sales tax on groceries
16 March 1988	— House of Commons Standing Committee on Finance reports on the New Zealand GST
30 June 1988	— Bill C-139 introduced (stage one—personal and corporate income tax reforms); second reading 18-25 July; committee report 19 August; report stage 23-25 August; third reading 26-29 August; Senate 30 August-9 September

THE ADVENT OF THE GST

April 1989	— at meeting of finance ministers, announcement that federal-provincial negotiations on a national sales tax ended unsuccessfully
27 June 1989	— Wilson announces in budget that federal government will proceed with a goods and services tax without provinces; MST raised to 13.5 per cent
8 August 1989	— GST Technical Paper released
15 August 1989	— Blenkarn Finance Committee hearings begin (public hearings 18 September - 26 October)
21 August 1989	— premiers' meeting conclusion: GST is unacceptable
13 October 1989	— 207-page draft GST legislation tabled
9-10 November 1989	— premiers insist at First Ministers' Conference that GST is not acceptable
27 November 1989	— Blenkarn Committee report released
19 December 1989	— Wilson announces GST cut from 9 per cent to 7 per cent in context of $1.4 billion spending cuts
24 January 1990	— first reading of Bill C-62, GST legislation; second reading 29 January-7 February; committee hearings 12 February-29 March; report stage 29 March; third reading 10 April
7-9 April 1990	— national protest campaign against GST
10 April 1990	— Bill C-62 sent to Senate
11 April 1990	— first reading of Bill C-62 in Senate
3 May 1990	— second reading of Bill C-62 in Senate; sent to Senate Banking Committee (Buckwold Committee)
3 May 1990	— announcement that Summerside, PEI, to get GST processing centre
7 May 1990	— government announces GST watchdog agency
23 June 1990	— Meech Lake accord dies
9 July 1990	— Buckwold Committee goes on national tour
30 August 1990	— Quebec joins federal government GST plan; Mulroney starts Senate appointments—5, with 3 more on 7 September, 2 on 12 September, including Nova Scotia Premier Buchanan, and a further 5 more on 23 September

THE ADVENT OF THE GST

31 August 1990	— Senate hearings end
12 September 1990	— GST watchdog agency issues price guidelines
24 September 1990	— Buckwold Committee recommends that GST be killed; Conservative senators begin filibuster
27 September 1990	— Mulroney names the 8 "extra" senators; Liberal senators begin on-again, off-again filibuster
2 October 1990	— Liberal senators issue court challenge of the extra senators
4-5 October 1990	— Senate chaos after Speaker's ruling allowed vote without Liberals present
9-14 October 1990	— Liberal filibuster in Senate
11 October 1990	— Alberta government announces court challenge of the GST (later joined by BC and Ontario)
17 October 1990	— Liberal senators lose court challenge; Senate resumes business
18 October 1990	— agreement in Senate on rules of war
22 October 1990	— Senate passes UI bill, after a year
28 October 1990	— Liberal leader Chrétien pledges to scrap GST if elected prime minister
29 October 1990	— two-week pact comes to an end: UIC, clawback, and Hibernia legislation passed by now
30-31 October 1990	— procedural wrangling in the Senate
1 November 1990	— GST legislation moves to third reading stage in the Senate; Liberals begin a series of 8 amendments
5 November 1990	— first of 8 Liberal amendments introduced in the Senate (continues to 22 November)
16 November 1990	— 5 senators ask for international observers to ensure that GST is passed fairly
22 November 1990	— last of Liberal amendments defeated; chaos on Senate floor regarding Speaker's ruling on how to proceed with independent senators' motions
22-28 November 1990	— independent senators' amendments debated and defeated
29 November 1990	— final Senate debate begins

THE ADVENT OF THE GST

11 December 1990	— Conservative senators write Senate Speaker Charbonneau requesting that GST debate end
12 December 1990	— Senate votes to end debate on GST
13 December 1990	— Senate passes Bill C-62, the GST legislation
14 December 1990	— Liberal senators delay royal assent
17 December 1990	— Bill C-62 given royal assent
1 January 1991	— GST comes into effect

Notes

1   *Financial Post*, 7-9 October 1989.

2   See Douglas Hartle, *The Political Economy of Tax Reform: Six Case Studies* (Ottawa: Economic Council of Canada, 1985), 1.

3   Much of the following is based on Robin W. Boadway and Harry M. Kitchen, *Canadian Tax Policy*, 2nd ed. (Toronto: Canadian Tax Foundation, 1984) and, especially, Allan M. Maslove, *Tax Reform in Canada: the Process and Impact* (Ottawa: Institute for Research on Public Policy, 1989).

4   The historical material in this section has been distilled from J. Harvey Perry, *A Fiscal History of Canada* (Toronto: Canadian Tax Foundation, 1989); Malcolm Gillis, "Federal Sales Taxation," *Canadian Tax Journal*, 33 (1), 68-98; Hartle, *Political Economy of Tax Reform*; Boadway and Kitchen, *Canadian Tax Policy*; John F. Due, *The General Manufacturers Sales Tax in Canada* (Toronto: Canadian Tax Foundation, 1951).

5   House of Commons, *Budget Speech*, 1920, 27.

6   This inset is a distillation of commentaries from the following sources: Boadway and Kitchen, *Canadian Tax Policy*; Perry, *A Fiscal History of Canada*; Hartle, *Political Economy of Tax Reform*; Gillis, "Federal Sales Taxation"; and various government reports on tax reform and the GST, cited in subsequent endnotes.

7   Perry, *A Fiscal History of Canada*, 388.

8   *Report of the Royal Commission on Dominion-Provincial Relations*, May 1940, Book 1, 212-14. Book 2, 150-62.

9   See F. Lorenzen, "Some Comments on the Administration of the Manufacturers Sales Tax in Canada," *Tax Bulletin*, January/February 1952 (Toronto: Canadian Tax Foundation).

10   See John F. Due, "Report of the Sales Tax Committee: One Year in Retrospect." *Canadian Tax Journal*, January/February 1957, 88-105.

11   *Report of the Royal Commission on Taxation*, Vol. 5, *Sales Taxes and General Tax Administration*. December 1966.

12   Department of Finance, Commodity Tax Reform Group, *Discussion Paper: Federal Sales and Excise Taxation* (Ottawa: 23 June, 1975).

13   Department of Finance, *Report of the Commodity Tax Review Group* (Ottawa: June 1977).

14   *Financial Post*, 12 July 1980.

15   *Globe and Mail*, 6 May, 24, 31 August 1978; 25 September 1982; *Financial Times*, 2 January 1978.

16   Department of Finance, *The Budget in More Detail* (Ottawa: 12 November 1981), 48-9.

17   Department of Finance, *Proposal to Shift the Federal Sales Tax to the Wholesale Trade Level* (Ottawa: April 1982).

18   *Financial Times*, 18 January 1982; *Financial Post*, 20 February 1982; *Globe and Mail*, 23 October, 30 November 1982.

19   *Report of the Federal Sales Tax Review Committee* (Ottawa: May 1983). The committee was comprised of seventeen members, four from accounting and tax firms, seven from associations (like the Consumers' Asociation of Canada, the Canadian Federation of Indepedent Business, the Canadian Manufacturers Association), and the remainder from individual companies (such as Eaton's and Ford).

20   *Financial Post*, 14 May, 30 July 1983.

21   Department of Finance, *Budget Papers* (Ottawa: 15 February 1984), 9-10. The legislation for this budget had not been passed when the 1984 election was called. The new Conservative government re-introduced most of it unchanged.

22   Boadway and Kitchen, *Canadian Tax Policy*, 276-77.

23   Hartle, *Political Economy of Tax Reform*, 1.

24   In an interview given a year after he chaired the Federal Sales Tax Review Committee, its chair—Wolfe Goodman—recalled, "It can hardly be doubted that the government's principle motive in appointing the committee a year ago [1983] was to find a way of gracefully backing out of the wholesale tax proposal, which had always appealed more to Finance officials than to the business community." *Financial Post*, 23 February 1984.

25   A policy story similar to the GST is presented in the first edition of this book. See "The Long and Winding Road: The Odyssey of Bill C-22," which presents the case of the Conservative government changing the patent law regarding pharmaceutical products.

26   Department of Finance, *A New Direction for Canada: An Agenda for Economic Renewal*, (Ottawa: 8 November 1984), 66-67.

27   *Globe and Mail*, 21 February 1986.

28   *Toronto Star*, 26 January 1985.

29   Department of Finance, *Securing Economic Renewal: The Budget Speech*, (Ottawa: 23 May 1985).

30   House of Commons, *Debates*, 26 February 1986, 10985-86.

31   *Globe and Mail*, 19 July 1986.

32   See Perry, *A Fiscal History of Canada*, 322; *Globe and Mail*, 19 July 1986.

33   Perry, *A Fiscal History of Canada*, 322; *Globe and Mail*, 6 September 1986.

34   Department of Finance, *Guidelines for Tax Reform in Canada*, (Ottawa: October 1986).

35   Department of Finance, *Notes for an Address by the Honorable Michael Wilson*, (Ottawa: 23 October 1986), 4.

36   *Globe and Mail*, 7, 8, 11 May 1987.

37   Department of Finance, *The White Paper: Tax Reform 1987*, (Ottawa: 18 June 1987).

38   Maslove, *Tax Reform in Canada*.

39   M. Wilson, *Tax Reform 1987*, House of Commons, 18 June 1987, 1.

40   Department of Finance, *Tax Reform 1987: Sales Tax Reform*, (Ottawa: 18 June 1987), 54.

41   House of Commons, Standing Committee on Finance and Economic Affairs, *Report on the White Paper on Tax Reform (Stage 1)*, November 1987.

42   Senate, Standing Committee on Banking, Trade and Commerce, *Twentieth Report of the Committee*, Issue No. 48, Tax Reform in Canada, 1 December 1987.

43   House of Commons, *Debates*, 16 December 1987, 11865-69.

44   Senate, *Twentieth Report*, 16.

45   *Globe and Mail*, 25 July, 5 September, 7 October 1987.

46   *Globe and Mail*, 11 December 1987; *Toronto Star*, 11 December 1987.

47   House of Commons, Standing Committee on Finance and Economic Affairs, *Fifteenth Report*, 16 March 1988.

48   *Toronto Star*, 8 October 1988.

49   *Globe and Mail*, 20 June 1987.

50   Cited in House of Commons, Standing Committee on Finance and Economic Affairs, *Report on the Technical Paper on the Goods and Services Tax*, November 1989, 25. Hereafter referred to as the *Blenkarn Committee report*.

51   *Globe and Mail*, 17 July 1987.

52   *Toronto Star*, 18 July 1987; *Globe and Mail*, 14 November, 9 December 1987.

53   Department of Finance, *The Budget Speech 1988*, (Ottawa: 10 February 1988), 4.

54   Michael Sabia, director, Sales and Excise Division, Department of Finance, *Globe and Mail*, 29 September 1988.

55   *Financial Post*, 1-3 April 1989.

56   Cited in Blenkarn Committee report, 25.

57   *Ibid.*

58   Department of Finance, *The Goods and Services Tax*, (Ottawa: 27 April 1989), 8.

59   *Ibid.*, 4-8.

60   Department of Finance, *The Budget Speech*, (Ottawa: 27 April 1989), 13-14.

61   Department of Finance, *The Goods and Services Tax*, (Ottawa: 27 April 1989), 21-24.

62   *Financial Post*, 13-15 May, 27-29 May, 10-12 June 1989; *Globe and Mail*, 7 August 1989; *Alberta Report*, 26 June 1989.

63   *Financial Post*, 24-26 June 1990; *Globe and Mail*, 7 August 1989.

64   Department of Finance, *Goods and Services Tax Technical Paper*, (Ottawa: August 1989). It was accompanied by the more accessible *Goods and Services Tax: An Overview*, (Ottawa: August 1989).

65   For houses priced at $310,000 or less, the rebate would be 4.5 per cent; for houses priced between $310,000 and $350,000, the rebate would be 4.5 per cent on the $40,000; thereafter, a sliding scale would diminish to no rebate on houses priced above $400,000. The rebate would be given by the builder to the purchaser immediately at the time of sale.

66   Department of Finance, *Goods and Services Tax: An Overview*, 21.

67   *Ibid.*, 30.

68   *Globe and Mail*, 9, 19, 24 August, 21 October 1989; *Toronto Star*, 9 August, 24 September 1990.

69   *Globe and Mail*, 22 August 1989. A *Toronto Star* poll showed 76 per cent opposed and 18 per cent in favour (26 August 1990).

70   *Financial Post*, 5-7 August 1989; *Globe and Mail*, 9 August, 20 September 1989.

71   *Toronto Star*, 9, 12 August 1989; *Peterborough Examiner*, 15 August 1989; *Globe and Mail*, 28 August 1989; *Financial Post*, 2-4 September, 30 September, 2 October 1989.

72   *Toronto Star*, 9, 12 August 1990; *Globe and Mail*, 18 August 1989.

73   *Toronto Star*, 26 August 1989; *Financial Post*, 23-25 September 1989; *Globe and Mail*, 9 August, 6 September, 21 September 1989.

74   *Toronto Star*, 9, 22 August 1989; *Globe and Mail*, 21-24 August, 18 October 1989; *Peterborough Examiner*, 23 August 1989.

75   *Globe and Mail*, 28 August, 16 September, 18, 19 October 1989.

76   *Globe and Mail*, 9 November 1989; *Alberta Report*, 20 November 1989; Department of Finance, *Economic and Fiscal Effects of the GST*, November 1989; *Notes for an Address by the Right Honorable Brian Mulroney*, First Ministers Conference Opening Statement, Ottawa, 9, 10 November 1989, 11.

77   *Globe and Mail*, 8 December 1989; *Financial Post*, 17-19 March 1990.

78   *Peterborough Examiner*, 26 August 1989; *Financial Post*, 12-14 August 1989; *Globe and Mail*, 29 August, 26 September, 11, 28 October 1989; *Toronto Star*, 23 September 1989.

79   *Globe and Mail*, 4 October 1989.

80   *Globe and Mail*, 5-7, 14 October, 8 November 1989.

81   House of Commons, Standing Committee on Finance and Economics, *Minutes of Proceeedings and Evidence*, No. 38, 21 September 1989, 31.

82   *Globe and Mail*, 21 November 1989.

83   House of Commons, Standing Committee on Finance and Economic, *Report on the Technical Paper on the Goods and Services Tax*, November 1989.

84   *Ibid.*, *Liberal Minority Report*, November 1989.

85   *Ibid.*, *New Democrats' Minority Report on the Goods and Services Tax*.

86   *Globe and Mail*, 28 November, 12 December 1989.

87   *Globe and Mail*, 16 December 1989.

88   *Globe and Mail*, 20 December 1990.

89 *Globe and Mail*, 20, 23 December 1989; *Maclean's*, 1 January 1990, 47; *Alberta Report*, 1 January 1990, 10.

90 *Toronto Star*, 25 November 1989; *Globe and Mail*, 21 October, 4 November 1989, 16 January 1990; *Alberta Report*, 22 January 1990, 11-2. The small Saskatchewan village of Elstow declared itself to be a tax-free zone with regard to the GST, after a 98 per cent referendum vote. *Globe and Mail*, 8 June, 21 September 1990.

91 Alberta was the lead province in taking the federal government to court, British Columbia and Ontario joining the challenge later. In a complex challenge, Alberta claimed that the GST forced business to collect the sales tax from customers, something traditionally done by the provinces; that the GST taxes provincial Crown property; that the GST would be imposed on a whole range of provincial government services. *Globe and Mail*, 22 September, 12, 18 October 1990.

92 *Globe and Mail*, 11 January 1990.

93 *Toronto Star*, 25 January 1990.

94 House of Commons, *Debates*, 29 January 1990, 7559-63.

95 *Ibid.*, 7563-69.

96 *Ibid.*, 7569-74.

97 *Globe and Mail*, 2, 9, 14, 17 February 1990, 10, 28 March 1990, 25 June 1990; *Toronto Star*, 31 March, 8, 9 April 1990; *Peterborough Examiner*, 15, 17 February 1990.

98 House of Commons, Standing Committee on Finance, *Minutes of Proceedings and Evidence*, No. 95, 8 March 1990, 34; No. 101, 14 March 1990, 1-5.

99 House of Commons, Standing Committee on Finance, *Third Report to the House of Commons*, Issue No. 197, 29 March 1990.

100 *Globe and Mail*, 5, 6 April 1990; *Edmonton Journal*, 11 March 1990; *Toronto Star*, 5 April 1990.

101 House of Commons, *Debates*, 10 April 1990, 10412-54.

102 *Globe and Mail*, 13, 21 April, 1, 2, 9, 16, 17, 23 May 1990; *Alberta Report*, 6 November 1989, 13; *Toronto Star*, 2 May 1989.

103 *Globe and Mail*, 4 May 1990.

104 *Globe and Mail*, 8, 11 May, 13, 14, 19, 20 June 1990; House of Commons, Standing Committee on Consumer and Corporate Affairs and Government Operations, *Third Report: Living with the GST*, 14 June 1990.

105 *Globe and Mail*, 8 September 1990.

106 *Globe and Mail*, 9 May 1990.

107 *Globe and Mail*, 1 June 1990.

108 *Globe and Mail*, 2, 27 August 1990.

109 *Toronto Star*, 10 July 1990; *Globe and Mail*, 11, 17, 19, 21, 28 July, 30 August 1990; *Peterborough Examiner*, 29 August 1990.

110 *Toronto Star*, 25 July 1990; *Globe and Mail*, 31 August 1990; *Peterborough Examiner*, 29 August 1990.

111 *Globe and Mail*, 25 June 1990, 7, 17 August 1990, 21 September 1990.

112 *Globe and Mail*, 31 August 1990, 7, 12, 20, 24 September 1990, 6 November 1990.

113 *Globe and Mail*, 25, 26 September 1990.

114 House of Commons, *Debates*, 25 September 1990, 13294-95.

115 *Globe and Mail*, 28 September 1990; House of Commons, *Debates*, 26 September 1990, 13444.

116 *Globe and Mail*, 26-28 September 1990, 4, 5 October 1990.

117 *Globe and Mail*, 29 September 1990; *Montreal Gazette*, 30 September 1990; House of Commons, *Debates*, 28 September 1990, 13568; 1 October 1990, 13610.

118 *Globe and Mail*, 28, 29 September 1990, 2-4 October 1990.

119 *Globe and Mail*, 5 October 1990.

120 *Globe and Mail*, 5, 6 October 1990; House of Commons, *Debates*, 5 October 1990, 13860.

121 *Globe and Mail*, 6 October 1990.

122 *Globe and Mail*, 9, 10 October 1990.

123 *Globe and Mail*, 11-14 October 1990.

124 *Globe and Mail*, 15-17 October 1990; House of Commons, *Debates*, 16 October 1990, 14221.

125 *Globe and Mail*, 19 October 1990.

126 *Globe and Mail*, 19, 25, 31 October, 6 November 1990.

127 For the first time since 1933, the Speaker voted. The independent senators split evenly; Edward Lawson, Daniel Day, and Reform Party Stan Waters coming out against the GST and Douglas Everett, Hartland Molson, and former Trudeau super-bureaucrat Michael Pitfield supporting the GST.

128 *Globe and Mail*, 26, 27, 30 October 1990.

129 *Globe and Mail*, 7 November 1990.

130 House of Commons, *Debates*, 10 October 1990, 13976-79; 11 October 1990, 14037ff; 15 October 1990, 14135ff; 23 October 1990, 14578ff; *Globe and Mail*, 23, 29 October 1990.

131 *Globe and Mail*, 29 October 1990.

132 *Globe and Mail*, 1, 2 November 1990.

133 *Globe and Mail*, 7, 13, 14, 17, 21, 23 November 1990; *Maclean's*, 26 November 1990.

134 *Globe and Mail*, 23, 29 November 1990; *Maclean's*, 3 December 1990.

135 *Globe and Mail*, 24, 28 November 1990; House of Commons, *Debates*, 23 November 1990, 15654-55; 28 November 1990, 15843, 15849.

136 *Globe and Mail*, 29 November, 1, 4, 6, 7, 15 December 1990.

137 *Globe and Mail*, 11, 12, 13 December 1990.

138 *Globe and Mail*, 14 December 1990.

139 *Globe and Mail*, 15 December 1990.

140 *Globe and Mail*, 7 January, 1991; *Montreal Gazette*, 17 January, 1991.

141 House of Commons, *Debates*, 22 November 1990, 15590.

142 Hartle, *Political Economy of Tax Reform*, 229.

143 *Globe and Mail*, 31 August 1990.

INDEX